Apokalypsis

Terry Kwanghyun Eum

CreateSpace
North Charleston, SC

© 2016 Terry Kwanghyun Eum

All rights reserved. No part of this book may be reproduced or transmitted in any form or by any means, electronic or mechanical, including photocopying, recording, or by any information storage or retrieval system, without permission in writing from the publisher. For information, address CreateSpace, 7290 Investment Drive Suite B, North Charleston, South Carolina 29418.

The Book of Revelation is translated by the author, Terry Kwanghyun Eum; except as otherwise indicated, other Scripture is quoted from the New International Version of the Bible, copyright © 1984 by International Bible Society.

The NIV text may be quoted in any form (written, visual, electronic or audio), up to and inclusive of five hundred (500) verses without express written permission of the publisher, providing the verses quoted do not amount to a complete book of the Bible nor do the verses quoted account for 25 percent or more of the total text of the work in which they are quoted.

Apokalypsis
ISBN-10: 1519299559
ISBN-13: 978-1519299550

For

ἡ βασιλεία τοῦ θεοῦ

My Beloved Wife, Chelsea I. Eum

1st Son, Isaac S. Eum

2nd Son, Caleb Y. Eum

3rd Son, Enoch H. Eum

Papyrus 115, 𝔓115 (Gregory-Aland)
Fragment(13:16-14:4) of the Book of Revelation

Acknowledgement

To this day, Catholic and Protestant lectionaries have only minimal readings from the Book of Revelation, and the Greek Orthodox lectionary omits it altogether. However, I believe that it is an important book of the Bible which provides direction and sustenance for the life of the Christians and the Church.

This commentary has grown out of my teaching and sharing of the Book of Revelation with my beloved Living Grace Ministry congregants at Emmaus United Methodist Church at Stratford hills. I am thankful for the privilege of engaging biblical texts with such faithful, intelligent, and interesting people of God.

As I publish this commentary, I'd like to publically say a word of thank-you to my family – my wife Chelsea I. Eum, and our children Isaac, Caleb, and Enoch. The four of them have always given me the space I need to study and reflect and the encouragement upon which I have depended to work through the difficult times that come with ministry and writing a long-term project. It is to their love and faith that I dedicate this commentary.

In this book, "*Apokalypsis*," I will use New International Version (NIV) Bible translation as well as my raw translation (Terry's Translation, "*TT*") of each text from the biblical Greek.

Through my research of the Book of Revelation, I learned that the Greek term, "*Tereo*" (which is the Greek root of my legal name, Terry) means "*to hold,*" "*to keep,*" *to keep promise,*" "*to keep position,*" and "*to preserve.*" It is one of key terms for the Book of Revelation. As we "*Tereo*" the name of Jesus Christ, faith, we also need to testify ("*witness*") what we "*Tereo.*"

May this commentary enlighten you what our God through the Book of Revelation, "*Apokalypsis*" is trying to tell you.

Terry Kwanghyun Eum
Richmond, Virginia

Contents

Introduction	1
Authorship	4
Date	9
Genre	11
Addressees	23
Social Setting	24
The Options	34
The World-Historical View	37
Dispensationalism	39
Literary Structure	41

The Book of Revelation / "*Apokalypsis*"

Rev. 1:1-8	Prologue and Letter Opening	45
Rev. 1:9-20	John Introduces Himself and Christ	67

Writing to the Seven Churches

Rev. 2:1-7	To Ephesus	83
Rev. 2:8-11	To Smyrna	93

Rev. 2:12-17	To Pergamum	101
Rev. 2:18-29	To Thyatira	111
Rev. 3:1-6	To Sardis	121
Rev. 3:7-13	To Philadelphia	134
Rev. 3:14-22	To Laodicea	149

The Glory of God and the Lamb

Rev. 4:1-11	Heavenly Throne	159
Rev. 5:1-14	Standing Slaughtered Lamb	181

The Opening of the Seven Seals 211

Rev. 6:1-8	The Opening of the Four Seal: The Four Horsemen	213
Rev. 6:9-11	The Fifth Seal: The Cry of the Slaughtered Souls	233
Rev. 6:12-17	The Sixth Seal: The Wrath of the Lamb	244
Rev. 7:1-8	Intermission (1): The 144,000	249
Rev. 7:9-17	Intermission (2): An Innumerable Multitude	265
Rev. 8:1	Transition – The Seventh Seal: Silence in Heaven	281

The Sounding of the Seven Trumpets 285

Rev. 8:2-6	Introduction to the Trumpets	286

Rev. 8:7-13	The First Four Trumpets	299
Rev. 9:1-12	The Fifth Trumpet	311
Rev. 9:13-21	The Sixth Trumpet	330
Rev. 10:1-11	Intermission (1a): A Little Opened Scroll	342
Rev. 11:1-13	Intermission (2a): Two Witnesses	369
Rev. 11:14	Transition	400
Rev. 11:15-19	The Seventh Trumpet	401
Rev. 12:1-14:20 Visionary Flashback		409
Rev. 12:1-17	Flashback: The Dragon's War	410
Rev. 12:18-13:10	Flashback: The Beast from the Sea	446
Rev. 13:11-18	Flashback: The Beast from the Land	468
Rev. 14:1-5	Flashback: The Lamb and the 144,000	484
Rev. 14:6-13	Flashback: An Eternal Gospel	498
Rev. 14:14-20	Flashback: Harvest Time	512
Rev. 15:1-8	Prelude to the Seven Bowls	520
The Seven Bowls of God's Wrath		539
Rev. 16:1-4	The First Three Bowls	540
Rev. 16:5-7	Hymn	544
Rev. 16:8-12	The Fourth, Fifth, and Sixth Bowls	551
Rev. 16:13-16	Intermission (1b): Envisioning Final Battle	559
Rev. 16:17-21	The Seventh Bowl	568

The Whore/Rome/Babylon		573
Rev. 17:1-6a	Vision: The Whore and the Beast	576
Rev. 17:6b-18	The Vision Interpreted	589
Rev. 18:1-24	The Fall of Babylon	604
Rev. 19:1-10	The Hallelujah Chorus	632
The Final Battle and Its Aftermath		
Rev. 19:11-16	The Rider on the White Horse	649
Rev. 19:17-21	The Final Battle	663
Rev. 20:1-15	Aftermath of the Final Battle	669
Rev. 21:1-8	A New Creation	699
Rev. 21:9-27	The New Jerusalem	717
Rev. 22:1-5	The New Life of the City	739
Rev. 22:6-9	Transition	748
Rev. 22:10-21	Epilogue & Letter Closing	755

Excursuses

Excursus 1	Ephesus	86
Excursus 2	The Nicolaitans, Balaam and Jezebel	91
Excursus 3	Smyrna	95
Excursus 4	Jezebel	116

Excursus 5	The Book of Life	133
Excursus 6	The Synagogue of Satan	141
Excursus 7	The Cosmology in Revelation	166
Excursus 8	The Hymns in Revelation	178
Excursus 9	The Lion and the Lamb	207
Excursus 10	Parthians	222
Excursus 11	The Seven Archangels	290
Excursus 12	Darkening the Sun	307
Excursus 13	Watchers	318
Excursus 14	The Woman Clothed with the Sun	445
Excursus 15	The Number of the Beast 666, 616, or 665?	482
Excursus 16	Armageddon	566
Excursus 17	Gog and Magog	690
Excursus 18	Interpreting the "*Near End*"	758

Bibliography 787

Index of Ancient and Biblical References 794

Introduction

Many say that the Book of Revelation is *"dangerous," "mean,"* and *"difficult."* All of them may be correct. Even early Church Fathers did not know what to do with the Book of Revelation. Some thought that it needed to be omitted from the Bible.

The inclusion of Revelation in the Christian Bible did not happen without a struggle. From the moment of its composition, Revelation has been a controversial writing. A second-century Christian leader named Montanus rejected Revelation, Gaius, an influential presbyter of the Roman church (ca. 210) wrote a manifesto declaring that Revelation had been written by the gnostic heretic Cerinthus. About 250 the Bishop of Alexandria, Dionysius, made a careful study of the language and grammar of Revelation and concluded that it could not have been written by the same author as the Gospel of John and that it was therefore not apostolic. Thus as late as the fourth century, Eusebius classified Revelation as a *"disputed"* Christian literature. Cyril of Jerusalem (315-386) was even more negative, omitting it from the list of canonical books and forbidding its use publicly or privately.

The Protestant Reformers had different views of the Book of Revelation. Although Martin Luther included

Revelation in his Bible, he denied it functional canonical status because in his view, it was not theologically adequate. The Swiss reformer Ulrich Zwingli likewise refused to base Christian teaching on Revelation, pronouncing it *"no biblical book."* John Calvin passed over it in silence in his biblical exposition, writing commentaries on twenty-six New Testament books.

There is no Book of *"Revelations"* in the New Testament. The *"Revelation"* is singular, one document designed to be read aloud and heard all at once. The writing cannot be understood by extracting a sentence or paragraph from its context, but must be experienced as a whole. John's narrative is about the single revelation that comes through the many visions that populate his book. The Book of Revelation seems very difficult and complicated. It is true that John used some biblical images, motifs, and themes, (approximately about 200 to 1,000 Old Testament allusions in the Book of Revelation) including non biblical sources to write Revelation. He drew on ancient mythic stories found in Greece, Egypt, and other parts of the Near East. Also Revelation shares much in common with the non-biblical Jewish apocalypses, such as *1 Enoch* and *Psalms of Solomon*. On top of it all, the book uses Hebraic number code system, *"Gematria."* So it may take quite a bit to understand the message of the Book of Revelation.

John however, expected the ordinary men and women of the churches of Asia to understand the book, though they were not biblical scholars, historians, or theological experts. They did not find it necessary to have study groups to discuss its meaning. Nor did they seal up the book for later centuries, when it would be understood (22:10, and contrast Dan. 12:4, 9).

The overarching message of the "*Apokalypsis*" for the Johannine community and contemporary audience of the Book of Revelation is clear and simple: Jesus Christ is the Lord (not Caesar).

Authorship

Identifying the John behind this work is a daunting and, in the end, impossible task. We call him John because he gives himself that moniker (1:1, 4, 9; 22:8). Because apocalyptic literature was often pseudonymous, written in the name of an important figure from the past, one cannot even be certain that the author's real name was John. It is unlikely, however, that an author would have mislabeled himself when writing so openly to church communities that could easily have identified him and thereby challenged his pseudonymous claim. The name John was likely the author's real name.

Knowing which John he was is the problem. Given the authority with which he writes, one can assume that he was a John of some stature in the Asia Minor Christian community. Two such figures come immediately to my mind. As early as 155 C.E., Justin Martyr was the first to identify the most famous of these two, one of Jesus' twelve apostles, the son of Zebedee, as the book's author (Dialogue with Trypho 81.4):

> Moreover, a man among us named John, one of Christ's apostles, received a revelation and foretold that the followers of Christ would well in Jerusalem *for a thousand years*, and that afterwards the universal and, in short, *everlasting resurrection and judgment* would take place. To this our Lord himself testified when he said, *They shall*

neither marry, nor be given in marriage, but shall be equal to the angels, being sons of God, being of the resurrection. (Justin, trans. Falls, 127; emphasis original).

Wiring in the fourth century, Eusebius quotes Papias of Hierapolis who around 120 C.E. penned thoughts that Eusebius took to give authorship to a different John. This other John was also an authoritative figure in nascent Asia Minor Christian circles:

> But if anyone came who had followed the presbyters, I inquired into the words of the presbyters, what Andrew or Peter or Philip or Thomas or James or John or Matthew, or any other of the Lord's disciples, had said, and what Aristion and the presbyter John, the Lord's disciples, were saying. For I did not suppose that information from books would help me so much as the word of a living and surviving voice. (*His. Eccl.* 3.39.4)

Eusebius understood Papias to mean that the first John mentioned was one of the apostles, and thus the evangelist. The other John was an elder or presbyter. Eusebius' conclusion, on Papias' authority, was that the second, presbyter John, was the one responsible for authoring Revelation.

> It is here worth noting that he twice counts the name of John, and reckons the first John with Peter and James and Matthew and the other Apostles, clearly meaning the evangelists, but by changing his statement places the second with the others outside the number of the Apostles, putting Aristion before him and clearly calling him a presbyter. This confirms the truth of the story of those who have said that there were two of the same name in Asia, and that there are two tombs at Ephesus both still called John's. This calls for attention: for it is probable that the second (unless anyone prefer the former) saw the revelation which passes under the name John. (*Hist. Eccl.* 3.39.5-7)

No doubt Eusebius was also working from evidence he recorded in the name of Dionysius of Alexandria. Writing in the third century, Dionysius had approached the problem from a literary angle. He operated from the assumption that the apostle had written the Gospel and the three Johannine Letters. Because the literary style and expression of Revelation is so distinct from the aforementioned works, it was clear to him that the apostle could not have written Revelation.

> But I should not readily agree that he was the apostle, the son of Zebedee, the brother of James, whose are the Gospel entitled According to John and the Catholic Epistle. For I form my judgment from the character of each and from the nature of the language and from what is known as the general construction of the book, that [the John mentioned] is not the same. (*Hist. eccl.* 7.25.7-8)

Eusebius goes on to quote Dionysius as saying that John had plenty of opportunity in Revelation to identify himself as the apostle John and thereby claim apostolic authority for his work. He never did, no doubt because he was not the apostle. Dionysius subsequently muddies the waters of author recognition even further when he admits that there were so many people who named their sons out of respect for the apostle that there were a multitude of John's circulating throughout Asia Minor.

> I hold that there have been many people of the same name as John the apostle, who for the love they bore him, and because they admired and esteemed him and wished to be loved, as he was, of the Lord, were glad to take also the same name after him; just as Paul, and for that matter Peter too, is a common name among boys of believing parents. (*Hist. eccl.* 7.25.14)

The author also could not have been the famous John Mark, since he did not accompany Paul and Barnabas to Asia (Act 13:13). In the end, Dionysius came to the same conclusion that a responsible contemporary reader must: the work was written by a mostly unidentifiable man named John who was not the same John credited with authoring the Fourth Gospel.

Two things, however, can be ascertained from the work itself about the John who authored Revelation. First, he considered himself a *prophet*. He calls his work a word of prophecy (1:3; 22:7, 10, 18, 19) and in developing this work depends heavily on the efforts of Hebrew prophetic figures like Moses, Isaiah, Jeremiah, Ezekiel, and Daniel. John apparently belonged to a prophetic community that gave itself responsibility for directing the communal lives of the Asia Minor churches. It was no doubt the conflict between his own view of God's revelation in the community and that proclaimed by other, competing prophets – like those whom he nicknamed Jezebel and Balaam – that heightened the intensity of his own vision-inspired proclamations. Though the future orientation of the visions gets all of the notoriety, it is secondary to their prophetic intent. The visions service the prophecy; the prophecy is not determined by the visions. The present is also not overshadowed by the future. The references to the future are meant to influence a person's behavior in the present. Beale writes *"Therefore, the book's 'prophecy' includes divine precepts for living in the present, about which the readers must make a decision. This understanding of 'prophecy' is consistent with the OT idea, which emphasizes revealed interpretation of the present together with the future, demanding ethical response for the present audience."*

Second, as his heavy dependence on Hebrew biblical material implies, John was most likely a Palestinian Jew who had come to the conclusion that Christ was God's messianic agent charged with the task of ushering in God's reign. He writes in a kind of Semiticized Greek that suggests someone whose native language was not Greek but the Aramaic spoken by Palestinian Jews. He also appears very knowledgeable about the topography of Jerusalem, the design and cultic practice of the Jerusalem temple, even prior to its destruction in 70 C.E., and the broader landscape of Palestine itself.

Date

Dating the Book of Revelation can be as challenging a task as identifying its author. Based largely on the external evidence of Irenaeus (ca. 140-202 C.E.; *Against Heresies* 5.30.3) that John's visions were witnessed at the end of the reign of the emperor Domitian (81-96 C.E.), the book is most commonly dated at 95 C.E. Commentators rightly point to two primary internal reasons that support such a dating. First, there is the obvious assignment of the name Babylon to the city and Empire of Rome. John clearly intends a critical correspondence between the two imperial forces: the sacking and destruction of Jerusalem. Babylon's devastation occurred in 587 B.C.E. Rome ruined the city in 70 C.E. The connection between the two names and empires would not have made sense unless John wrote after 70 C.E. A second internal factor adds at least two decades (from 70 C.E.) to the probable writing time of the work's final edition. In chapter 13 and 17, John works from an apparent preoccupation with a belief current during the latter years of the first century that Nero (died 66 C.E.) would return to power and wreak vengeance upon the Roman west that had rejected him. *"The legend of Nero "redux" or "rediyivus," upon which the author-editor of Revelation seems to depend, is attested as early as A.D. 69, though a later date for the widespread currency of this legend seems required."* (Aune 1:lxix-lxx).

Roman Emperors 49 B.C.E – 138 C.E.	
Julius Caesar	49 – 44 B.C.E.
Augustus (Octavian)	31 B.C.E – 14 C.E.
Tiberius	14 – 37 C.E.
Gaius (Caligula)	37 – 41
Claudius	41 – 54
Nero	54 – 68
Galba	68 – 69
Otho	69
Vitellius	69
Vespasian	69 – 79
Titus	79 – 81
Domitian	81 – 96
Nerva	96 – 98
Trajan	98 – 117
Hadrian	117 – 138

Genre

Revelation is apocalyptic literature, and Revelation is the last book of the Christian Bible. However, John did not write it as the *"last book of the Bible."* It was written in the form of a letter to Jewish-Christian communities in Asia Minor. It has a formal greeting, and benediction. This book is about the single revelation that comes through the many visions. Revelation has some elements from the Old Testament such as Daniel, Ezekiel, Isaiah, Jeremiah, Zechariah, Torah, and also some elements from the Synoptic Gospels. *"Apokalypsis"* or the Book of Revelation is a letter or a letter format of apocalypse. It informs what Jesus will do, it warns the idolatrous people, it persuades people to repent, and it promises the rewards.

An apocalypse intends to reveal a long-anticipated truth of prophetic significance about the end time. Unfortunately, that truth defies the logic of human language. There is much more to the truth than words can convey. Poetic and sometimes cryptic imagery must therefore be used instead. John's Revelation operates in just this literary way. It intends to reveal the truth about the future, a truth that enables its hearers and readers to see the present in a new light. But that truth is so powerful, so overwhelming, that John's words cannot properly convey it. He therefore appeals to symbols and codes that must bear the weight of what language cannot. John seems to believe that a person must viscerally feel odd and frightening imagery that prevails throughout his apocalypse. The imagery is odd for a reason: it represents John's understanding of the future. Future hope, particularly in the case of the spiritually distraught and politically dispossessed, does not agree with present reality. They are contrary and combustible, so hostile to each other that the images related to each seem to ignite upon narrative contact. Whenever the future hope that is the inbreaking of God's eschatological reign and present reality that is the historical truth of the Roman Empire encounter each other in John's presentation, the results are explosive images of global war, natural catastrophe, and human death on a scale so massive as to be almost incomprehensible. It is this explosion that John wants to narrate. The truth behind the explosion (the lordship of God and Jesus Christ) is the truth that his Revelation intends to reveal. Because there are no words capable of revealing the power of that truth, he resorts to symbol.

The symbols' roots are grounded in Hebrew prophecy. John J. Collins argues that thinking on the *"end time"* goes all the way back to the eighth century B.C.E. and the prophet Amos. In his proclamation that the northern kingdom was doomed, he talked about the "day of the LORD," a day of darkness and not light. While he did not speak of it in terms of the end of the world, he did intend the end of northern Israel's history as a sovereign nation. It was an end orchestrated by God (see Amos 5:18-20; 8:2).

There were three developmental periods for apocalyptic thinking and writing in Jewish history. The first period is that of the postexilic prophets, prophets like Second Isaiah writing in the aftermath of the Babylonian exile. Isaiah 24 – 27 records prophetic oracles so striking in their vision and tone that they are often referred to as *"the apocalypse of Isaiah."* Isaiah 24:1 offers an illustrative example: *"Now the LORD is about to lay waste the earth and make it desolate, and he will twist its surface and scatter its inhabitants."* Just as revealing is 24:19-20: *"The earth is utterly broken, the earth is torn asunder, the earth is violently shaken. The earth staggers like a drunkard."* The prophet proclaims that God will swallow death (Isa. 25:7) and punish Leviathan and slay the sea dragon (Isa. 27:1). And Babylon, that great fortified city and palace of aliens (Isa. 25:2), will be laid low. These images of Isaiah are the images of John's book of Revelation as well. Isaiah even hints at the very Johannine talk of resurrection for the faithful: *"Your dead shall live, their corpses shall rise. O dwellers in the dust, awake and sing for Joy! For your dew is a radiant dew, and the earth will give birth to those long dead"* (Isa. 26:19).

Ezekiel deploys an even more vivid resurrection accounting in his chapter 37 vision of the valley of dry bones. Like John's apocalyptic account, Ezekiel also added frightening monster combat scenes. As does Rev. 20:8, Ezek. 38 and 39 depict God battling Gog, the representation of Gentile power, from the land of Magog.

Third Isaiah, chapters 56 – 66, are just as intense, so intense in fact that in 1975 Paul Hanson called these chapters *"The Dawn of Apocalyptic."* During the time when Israel was trying to rebuild the temple, during a time when the people of Israel felt utterly alienated from God and hopeless regarding their situation as a national entity, Isaiah conjured up the hope for a new heaven and a new earth: *"For I am about to create new heavens and a new earth; the former things shall not be remembered or come to mind"* (Isa. 65:17). Revelation 21:1 comes immediately to mind. This is prophetic language where the future looks radically different from the present. It is that future that the people of the present seek.

Hellenistic period, apocalyptic comes into its own. This is the time of literature written pseudonymously. Visionary authors write under the names of important figures in Israel's past so as to give authority to the message of their visions for the present. Works like *1 Enoch* flourish during this period. The Book of Daniel also derives from this time. In the first six chapters, the seer/prophet Daniel interprets two dreams for the Babylonian king. As in John's Apocalypse, Babylon is the enemy. In Daniel's case, Babylon stands in symbolically for the Seleucid kingdom and its kings like Antiochus Epiphanes. Daniel interprets the king's dream by showing that there are human kingdoms, one of them Babylon, that will perish, while God's kingdom, which is coming, will endure forever (Dan. 2:44).

Daniel's point, much the same point that John's Revelation wishes to reveal, is that God is in control of history, no matter how unlikely such a claim appears to be in a present dominated by the Seleucid Empire (Rome in John's case). Despite appearances, God's kingdom and God's people would be vindicated on God's final day. Daniel 7, one of the most influential apocalyptic passages in history, picks up on this theme with imagery that was instrumental for John's crafting of Revelation. Daniel envisions four beasts coming out of the sea, each one more fearsome than the preceding (cf. Rev. 13). But also sees thrones, and a deity, an ancient one, who passes judgment on the beasts. And then one like a *"son of man"* on the clouds of heaven appears and is given dominion and glory, and a kingdom that will never be destroyed. A battle of epic proportions erupts between God and the forces arrayed against God. The mythological enemy forces use the Gentile powers as their historical representatives. Just as God will defeat the heavenly forces on the mythological level, so God will soon enable the defeat of the earthly enemies and the vindication of God's earthly followers. The Seleucid Empire will be overthrown and the kingdom of God/reign of God will be lifted up. This is the truth that Daniel's imagery wants to convey.

There is, however, an interesting twist. Daniel does not counsel his readers to join the revolutionary activity of the Maccabees, the historical force that represented God against the Seleucid Empire. Much like John in Revelation, he understands that the role of God's people is a nonviolent one. The difference between his accounting and John's is that Daniel counsels his enduring people to wait for God to act. Passive, nonviolent waiting, though, is not the only alternative in apocalyptic literature. Daniel's choice is not the only choice. Much of the Enoch material encourages God's people to join the earthly revolution. Through the language of witness, John will also champion action. In his case, it will be action of perseverance/endurance/nonviolent resistance.

Also important for comparative purposes is the realization that Daniel is the second of two types of apocalyptic literature. One is typified by otherworldly journeys. The imagery is escapist, searching for a future hope beyond this world. Daniel, though, is a historical apocalypse. Its goal goes beyond the envisioning and expectation of an otherworldly transformation; it just as fervently anticipates a transfiguration of the human world and human history. This worldly transformative hope of this kind is very much on display in John's Revelation, too.

The final apocalyptic stage is the Roman era, John's era. Works like *4 Ezra, 2 Baruch,* and *3 Baruch* derive from this period. The Qumran *Scroll of the War of the Sons of Light against the Sons of Darkness* also stems from this period. While the *War Scroll* focuses on a final, apocalyptic battle that will reveal God's kingdom in power and victory, the *Psalms of Solomon* look to the hope of resurrection and the raising up of a Davidic Messiah. The *Sibylline Oracles*, while attempting to predict the course of history, divide history into periods that lead to a God-directed end. The *Oracles* convey the belief, developed ominously in Revelation, that Nero, the infamous persecutor of Christians, would be revived as a mythical figure that would fight against God and God's people in the time leading up to the final war (cf. Sib. Or. 4.150-157, 175-77; 5.38-47; 8.88, 193-201). That final war would reveal the truth that God is in charge of the present as well as the future (Rev. 17:11).

Even before John put the content of his visions on Patmos into writing, then, an influential worldview that might be called "*apocalyptic*" had developed. This worldview is characterized by several traits. There is supernatural revelation that is above human understanding. This disclosure clarifies the truth of the present because it can see the present from the perspective of the future. The truth is this: the people who hold power in the present are deluded about the scope of their historical control. God's goals, not theirs, will ultimately be achieved. This truth means that human affairs are in a sense already determined. Because humans do not know what that determination is, they must live as though human choices make a difference. Humans cannot see where the road of the future leads. The path, though, is already ordained. Nothing the power of the present can do to alter it. God and God's people shall be vindicated. This truth is the hope even in the midst of a horrific present.

This apocalyptic understanding is built upon a dualistic understanding of reality. There are two mutually exclusive eras: the present and the future. Humans must choose between them. The option is either/or, not both/and.

To commit to the present and the forces that run the present is to give up on God's future. To commit to the future, even if the forces in the present persecute and kill believers because of that commitment, is to be assured of eschatological relationship with God. God will defeat the forces of Satan in heaven, and God's human agent, the Messiah, the *"Son of Man,"* will defeat Satan's human representatives on earth. Divine judgment on a cosmic scale will follow. Entire nations and people will be judged. Humans will be held accountable for their decisions. Thus, what humans do and say in the present, they must do and say with an eye always toward that future. The future visions thus serve a very present prophetic end.

Apocalyptic literature, then, has an ethical motivation. It implores people to act in the present in a way that agrees with its understanding of the future. Such an expectation may mean that followers should endure the persecutions of the present, join in battles against the forces of the present, or simply wait for the future in any way they can. In every case, it means that they must choose sides. They must put themselves on God's side, as the apocalyptic writer understands God's side. They must live for God's future in the present, even if making that choice means that they will come into conflict with the leaders of the present, even if the price of that choice is present death. Ironically, with such death comes true life, a resurrected life that will follow God's judgment.

Yet there are a multitude of problems with such an apocalyptic worldview. For many theologians, its view of history is embarrassing. An apocalyptic worldview encounters difficulty with ongoing history because its imminent expectations about the future inevitably go unfulfilled. Apocalyptic dreamers are always, critics say, disappointed.

The deterministic and often pessimistic view of history also make apocalyptic distasteful to the contemporary believer who wants to believe that history is not planned out, that human behavior can effect changes in the course and direction of human living. Other critics charge that the dualistic worldview of a hoped-for future in competition with a hoped-against present encourages the rejection of the present world in favor of an illusory future that never comes. And, it should be noted, this future is a very patriarchal one, where women are either evil whores or passive madonnas, but not human agents working to inspire and impact the shape of the future.

Indeed, in her book "*Apocalypse Now and Then*," Catherin Keller argues that while a people poised on critical precipices like ecological collapse or individual destruction cannot escape the impact of an apocalyptic worldview, contemporary humans must reconfigure it. She argues for a counter-apocalyptic perspective that draws from the hopeful expectation for the future, but is not based in deterministic, either/or, patriarchal, or escapist categories. I argue that the perspective she seeks exists in a nascent way already in the New Testament apocalyptic materials. The counter-apocalyptic presence in New Testament apocalyptic is to be found in its prophetic roots. The

Hebrew prophets fervently believed that the choices humans made would influence the direction in which God would choose to move the future. The prophet Jonah is an entertaining example of just this principle. He did not want to serve God, because he knew that God would adjust the course of God's intended future if people repented of their ungodlike behavior in the present. Jonah hated the Ninevites with such passion that he desired a predetermined destruction for them instead. True to God's word, though, when the Ninevites changed their behavior, God changed the course of their future. It is on this ethical expectation – of human behavior that changes until it matches God's desires for human living – that John bases his understanding of the future. He, too, believes that repentance is offered, even for the most egregious offenders (Rev. 2:20-22). When humans choose to change their behavior, God will choose to change the course of their future. For John, then, the future is not all laid out so that some are doomed and others are not.

There are other Christian legacies of apocalyptic perspective also suggesting that, already in the first century, writers were struggling with the issues that so rightly concern Keller. Paul is fervently apocalyptic. He, too, looks for the triumph of God, but he also realizes the power of God's spiritual activity in the present. Paul never abandons the present. There is room in the present for transformation and ethical activity while humans await God's action in the future. The author of the Gospel of Mark is another writer with apocalyptic tendencies. He sees Jesus through an apocalyptic lens. Mark finds a way around the destructive either/or dualism by looking forward to God's future in a way that does not give up on the present. Mark already sees the future, represented through the boundary-breaking ministry of Jesus, operating in the present. Mark's Jesus teaches his disciples to do as he himself is doing, to represent in powerful ways the force of God's future kingdom/reign in the present.

For Christian apocalyptic writers, the key event in God's future rule has already taken place in the historical present: Jesus' death on the cross. That death is a significant in Revelation as it is in any other New Testament materials (cf. Rev. 5:9; 12:5). This event colors all of history and the expectations of the future and how believers are to live in anticipation of that future. It was key for Paul and Mark; it was key for John in his crafting of Revelation. What does this realization mean? Most important, it means that humans need not wait for God to act. God has already acted! Humans only need to find a way of responding appropriately to that past act, which has completely transfigured the future. This expectation for response means that waiting for the consummation of God's future need not be passive. John develops his expectation for active apocalyptic engagement through his witness language.

Finally, Christian apocalyptic encompasses a concern for the world, not just the individual. In his debates with Rudolf Bultmann, Ernst Kasemann recognized that – in order to prevent apocalyptic from devolving into exactly the kind of eschatological enthusiasm that threatened to wreck the church at Corinth, where believers felt themselves already saved through their existential encounter with the living Christ – the church must not lose its focus on the coming of God's *"kingdom"* as a true objective reality that would transform exterior reality as well as inner hearts. It is this objective expectation that John certainly intends. This is why, in his climactic visions of the end, he connects Christ's coming not with personal confessions of faith but with a tangible, measurable, objective city. The Christ who comes soon comes not just to the human heart but also to the world.

John presents his apocalyptic message in the literary form of a letter. His initial moves follow the conventional norms of Hellenistic correspondence. In his epistolary greeting or salutation (Rev. 1:4-6), he identifies himself as the sender. Immediately afterward, he points out seven churches of Asia Minor (present day Turkey) as the recipients (1:11). Like the apostle Paul, he adjusts the Hellenistic letter-writing formula by including an offering of grace and peace (cf. Rom. 1:7; 1 Cor. 1:3; 2 Cor. 1:2; Gal. 1:3; Phil. 1:2; 1 Thess. 1:1; Phlm. 3). John closes the work he began with an epistolary greeting by appealing appropriately to an epistolary benediction (22:21).

Addressees

The letter is addressed to *"the"* seven churches of Asia (1:11; 2:1-3:22). The seven represent all the churches, for there were more than seven churches in Asia (e.g., Colossae, near Laodicea; see Col. 4:15-16). Asia is the Roman province on the west coast of what is now Turkey. The churches were in the area in which the Pauline mission had founded new churches a generation earlier, and where a strong tradition of Pauline Christianity, centered in Ephesus, continued after his death.

Social Setting

In Roman-occupied Asia Minor in the last decade of the first century, during the reign of the Emperor Domitian, there existed a strong motivation to accommodate. In Rome's ideological infrastructure, religion and politics were quire intentionally mixed worship often mutated into politics; politics was often exercised through religion. Worship of Roman deities not only demonstrated a cultic devotion and communal piety; it also signaled loyalty to the Roman state, which was mythologically connected to and practically founded upon them. It is not surprising, then, that the mother goddess would savor the name *Roma*, or that the messianic hopes for the empire should be bound up in the person of the emperor. This blending of politics and worship was especially evident in Asia Minor, where John and his seven churches were located. There, particularly during the last decade of the first century, emperor worship flourished, "*Under the Flavians, especially Domitian, the imperial cult was strongly represented in the Roman provinces. Domitian demanded that the populace acclaim him as 'Lord and God' and participate in his worship. The majority of the cities to which the prophetic messages of Revelation are addressed were dedicated to the promotion of the emperor cult*" (Fiorenza, *Justice*, 193).

Thyatira was an illustrative case in point. The city was caught up in the throes of idol and emperor worship. Here, in fact, cultic propaganda went so far as to declare the Roman emperor to be the incarnation of Apollo and therefore a son of Zeus. This religious-political alliance heightened the risk for people who tried to opt out of the Greco-Roman cultic infrastructure; rejection of the gods implied resistance to the state. Complicating matters even further was the fact that Thyatira hosted a large number of trade guilds that had strong cultic affiliations. Especially important were industries of wool, textile, and the manufacture of purple dye (cf. Acts 16:14-15). Since the guilds had patron deities, Christian guild members would be expected to pay homage to pagan gods at official guild meetings, which were usually festive occasions often accompanied by immoral behavior. Nonparticipation would lead to economic ostracism. Socially, economically, and politically, then Christians in Thyatira had every reason to accommodate themselves to the expectations and practices of Greco-Roman religion and culture.

So did the Christians in Pergamum. Because they clearly did not believe in the reality or lordship of pagan deities, their participation at the cultic festivals and other social gatherings where elaborate meals and rituals were prepared to honor those deities was socially, economically, and politically motivated. Their complicity in artisan, trade, and funeral associations allowed for upward social and economic mobility. They passed themselves off as Roman cultic devotees in order to avail themselves of Roman resources. Unlike the believers in Smyrna, who apparently opted out of such accommodating activities and thereby found themselves impoverished and persecuted as a result, many Pergamum Christians blended in and therefore moved up socially, politically, and economically.

While John was exiled on Patmos, the prophets he named Jezebel and Balaam, and Balaam's Nicolaitan colleagues, offered some Christian counsel. They taught the people that it is permissible to eat meat that has been sacrificed to idol gods at these guild, quasi-cultic functions. For John, people who eat meat that has been sacrificed to foreign gods give credence to the reality and lordship of those gods; those people have therefore prostituted themselves to a foreign faith. Where Paul had, in his Corinthian correspondence (1 Cor. 8-10), offered the very practical advice that strong Christians could eat meat sacrificed to idols unless their behavior offended the spiritual psyche of weaker Christians for whom such activity seemed sinful, John theologically overrules the behavior outright.

Jezebel, Balaam, and the Nicolaitans, like Paul, were probably trying their best to help their fellow Christ-believers adapt their faith to the new circumstances in which they found themselves. John's very conservative, intolerant attitude disallowed any kind of compromise; Jezebel, Balaam, the Nicolaitans, and those who followed their teaching were guilty of spiritual prostitution. The backside of Christ's double-edged sword (Rev. 1:16; 2:12, 16) was therefore meant for them. Christ was coming soon; if they did not repent of their accommodating behavior, his

Pergamum coming would not be salvific, but judgmental. John's rhetorical move is a complex endeavor that recognizes the problem of accommodation, understands its practical motivation, but simultaneously argues that the evil of believing in the lordship of a human force as more powerful than the lordship of God requires such accommodation. He then showcases the role his accommodating believers unwittingly play in sustaining that evil.

The evil that John fears is so manipulative and seductive that his only parallel for it is the seductive evil of the prostituting whore. His demonization of Greco-Roman cultic, social, economic, and political expectations is one of the most regrettable side effects of his prophetic effort. But it is helpful to know what he is doing and why he is doing it. Though he clearly sees a problem with what Christians are doing in accommodating themselves to Greco-Roman life, his agenda ranges far beyond a critique of the Christians themselves. He wants the Christians to see that they are caught up in a draconian, prostituting system. The only challenge to that system resides in the will of those who refuse to participate in its many social, economic, and political benefits. Whatever it costs them, those Christians must find a way to stand up and then opt out. That, in essence, is his prophetic charge.

A final appeal to the social location of John and his Asia Minor Christians brings further clarity to his prophetic urgency. In a historical reconstruction that represents today's prevailing scholarly thinking, Loren Johns argues that there was no wholesale persecution of Christians during the time of Domitian's reign (Johns 122). In fact, applicable source material from the period suggest only sporadic mistreatment that targeted specific people who were charged with being Christ-believers, and only when they either refused to deny the allegation or would not repent of their delusion. A letter (ca. 112 C.E.) from the governor of the Asian province of Bithynia, Pliny the Younger, to the Emperor Trajan (98 – 117 C.E.) is indicative of the official thinking that was no doubt in vogue during the reign of Domitian just a few years prior.

> I have never been present at the interrogation of Christians. Therefore, I do not know how far such investigations should be pushed, and what sort of punishments are appropriate. I have also been uncertain as to whether age makes any difference, or whether the very young are dealt with in the same way as adults, whether repentance … and renunciation of Christianity is sufficient, or whether the accused are still considered criminals because they were once Christians even if they later renounced it, and whether people are to be punished simply for the name "*Christian*" even if no criminal act has been committed, or whether only crimes associated with the name are to be punished.
>
> In the meantime, I have handled those who have been denounced to me as Christians as follows: I asked them whether they were Christians. Those who responded affirmatively I have asked a second and third time, under threat of the death penalty. If they persisted … in their confession, I had them executed. For whatever it is that they are actually advocating, it seems to me that obstinacy and stubbornness must be punished in any case. Others who labor under the same delusion, but who were Roman citizens, I have designated to be sent to Rome.
>
> In the course of the investigations, as it usually happens, charges are brought against wider circles of people, and the following special cases have emerged:
>
> An unsigned placard was posted, accusing a large number of people by name. those who denied being Christians now or in the past, I thought necessary to release, since they invoked our gods according to

the formula I gave them and since they offered sacrifices of wine and incense before your image which I had brought in for this purpose along with the statues of our gods. I also had them curse Christ. It is said that real Christians cannot be forced to do any of these things.

Others charged by this accusation at first admitted that they had once been Christians, but had already renounced it; they had in fact been Christians, but had given it up, some of them three years ago, some ever earlier, some as long as twenty-five years ago. [Note that this would be in the time of Domitian]. All of these worshipped your image and the statues of the gods and cursed Christ.

The emperor responded with praise for the governor's actions.

My Secundus! You have chosen the right way with regard to the case of those who have been accused before you as Christians. Nothing exists that can be considered a universal norm for such cases. Christians should not be sought out. But if they are accused and handed over, they are to be punished, but only if they do not deny being Christians and demonstrate it by the appropriate act, i.e., the worship of our gods. Even if one is suspect because of past conduct, he or she is to be acquitted in view of repentance. (Pliny, *Ep.* 10.96-97)

Such evidence suggests that John was writing more about the "*expectation of persecution rather than the present experience of persecution*" (cf. Rev. 2:10-11; 7:13-14; 11:7-9; 12:11; 16:6; 17:6; 18:24; 19:2; 20:4-6). The problem lay with the imminent conflict he knew would erupt if his hearers and readers lived out the kind of non-accommodating Christianity that he himself professed and refused to back away from the faith when Asia Minor officials demanded that they do so.

Extensive trouble, however, had not yet arisen. This peaceable reality is the historical proof that validates

John's literary claim: the Asia Minor Christians were passing themselves off as every other emperor-worshipping, meat-sacrificed-to-pagan-gods-eating Greco-Roman. The resistance called for was an offensive maneuver as John tried to unmask the spiritual powers at work behind the churches' compromising involvement in the empire, in its commerce, and in its imperial cult. John was unyielding; there could be no compromise with any activities that gave credence to the idea that Caesar, Rome, or Rome-sponsored divinities held title to the allegiance due only God and Jesus Christ. No matter what the cost.

But if all this is correct, if there was only sporadic persecution, if John's people were not vulnerably standing out because they were finding ways comfortably to blend in and accommodate, then the seer's immediate problem was more spiritual than social and historical. The social-historical crisis would not arise unless John's people actually started living by the ethical mandate of witness that his apocalyptic prophecy demanded. And so Loren Johns concludes: *"The resolution of that spiritual crisis would ironically induce a very real and dangerous social crisis as the churches began faithfully to resist the imperial cult and to face the consequences of their allegiance to Christ"* (Johns 127).

Here is where both John's prophetic call and a consummate prophetic problem arise. If John was indeed asking his people to stand up and stand out in a world they had accepted and that had accepted them, a world into which they had covertly and successfully passed, he was essentially telling them to go out and pick a fight! No matter the consequences! He was ordering his people to self-identify, to declare that they were not non-accommodating Christians who could no longer participate in a world that had not really noticed them since they had heretofore been accommodating to it. In a classic *"Don't ask, don't tell"* (that I am a Christian) kind of environment, John was essentially ordering his Christians to be about the business of telling on themselves, with full knowledge of the repercussions such telling might bring (recall Pliny's letter). He was asking them to come screaming out of the Christian closet, knowing that it could well solicit the same consequence it had attracted to the Lamb: slaughter.

John's visions operate in support of his effort to incite his followers to self-identify and then stand behind that self-declaring, that revelation, no matter what the consequences. There are many visions; there is only one Revelation, and it is hiding in plain sight. Many claim that there is some great mystery translation and computation to break the code of Revelation. Revelation's revelation is that *"Jesus Christ is the Lord!"* It is that simple and that straightforward. Jesus Christ is the Lord of human history, the director of human destiny, the controller of human fortune. Jesus is the Savior, Redeemer, transformer, and Lord.

Why does John need so many complex, frightening visions to support such a single, clear point? John is like a great sports coach who tries to rally his team before the most important game of their season. He wants to whip up a frenzy that will lift them to physical and emotional highs where confessing a subversive allegiance to Christ before hostile forces that promote the lordship of Rome becomes not only a possibility but also an imperative.

His confessional witness ("μάρτυς") language is, then, his prophetic language. "μάρτυς" is a word of active engagement, not sacrificial passivity. A believer's witness might provoke such a hostile response that it leads to the believer's death, but always, at least in the first-century mind-set, it seems, the transformative focus was on the provocative testimony that had to be given, not a passive life that had to be extinguished. When someone in John's turn-of-the-first-century environment said "*witness*," he/she meant witness, not martyr.

John meant witnessing to their identity, self-declaring in a world that previously did not care about them because previously they had blended into it. They had allowed their world to believe that they were as Greco-Roman as everybody else. John wants them to self-declare that they believed not in the lordship of Rome, its gods, its social, political, and economic infrastructure, nor its emperor, but in the lordship of Jesus Christ, and that they would now fight to make that religious lordship of the future the governing principle of social, political, cultic, and religious practice in the present. Knowing what vicious response such a seditious claim would provoke, John nonetheless demanded that his followers make it.

John himself was their forbidding, prophetic role model. He makes it clear that his banishment to Patmos was a direct result of his witnessing to the lordship of Jesus Christ. Even knowing the dangers, he wants them to stick their necks out and partner with him in both the witness and the tribulation it will surely bring.

The Options

Christians in Asia during the nineties of the first century were under tremendous political, economic, and social pressure to go through the *"formality"* of veneration of the image of the Caesar or face the fearful consequences. What options were available to one who confessed Jesus as the Lord in around 95 C.E.? Christians in John's churches passionately discussed the possibilities before them. These may be briefly listed:

1. Quit. Some Christians chose this option. When they became Christians they had not expected it to cost them their reputation, job, freedom, or life; and so they cursed Christ and bowed before Rome. John is not easy on those who took this option.

2. Lie. A good *"situation ethics"* case can be made (and most probably was made by sincere and thoughtful people) for doing this. Their reasoning was that the Romans did not understand the Christian faith and that it was not God's will for anyone to actually die for a misunderstanding. Veneration of the Emperor was only a formality not to be taken seriously in any case. It was the lesser of two evils or what love (for children, parents, neighbors) required in this situation. Therefore Christians should go through the ceremony that showed they were loyal and grateful subjects of the Empire, but with mental reservations, keeping their real religious faith to themselves. *"True religion is a matter of the heart, not the formalities of public life."* John's word for such people is *"liars,"* and he reserves places in the lake of fire for them (Rev. 21:8).

3. Fight. Although active resistance was hardly a real possibility for Christians in John's context, it was at least a theoretical option. Only a few years before, the Zealots of Palestine had initiated a disastrous armed rebellion against the Romans under the slogan that only God can be worshiped as God. John may have been in contact with the Zealot movement during his earlier period in Palestine, but he had rejected the Zealot option of violence.

4. Change the *"law."* This too was a theoretical possibility, but hardly a real one. Government in the Roman Empire did not work by democratic process, and in any case the members of John's churches were without political and economic power. *"Working within the system"* through a lobby in Rome to change an unjust law was not a real option.

5. Adjust. Many Christians in John's churches were tempted to think as follows: *"The ideas and practices of Christianity had been developed by earlier generations, in another time and place. In the light of the modern situation, perhaps there is a good way to preserve the essential elements of Christianity and combine them with the good features of Roman culture and religion. Christian theology should be rethought in such a way that it could incorporate the ways God is revealed in other religions, including the* *emperor cult. In any case, intolerance and exclusiveness must be avoided, so that Christians should do nothing that would indicate disrespect for the religion of other people."* It is likely that many of John's readers had already adjusted to the cultural *"civil religion"* and thus did not see themselves as living in a situation of crisis as Adela Yarbro Collins has pointed out. In this case John's letter was written to them not so much to encourage or console them in their experienced crisis but to make clear to them the crisis they had not yet perceived.

6. Die. The present situation was an opportunity to bear witness to the reality and meaning of Christian faith in the one God and Jesus as the only Lord, even if it meant dying at the hands of the Romans as had Jesus himself. John affirms this as the only Christian response.

The World-Historical View

Prophecy is understood as prediction of the long-range future. To be sure, the messages to the seven churches of chapter 2 – 3 are regarded as addressed to churches of John's own time, but the visions of 4 – 22 are interpreted as predictions of all of history from John's time through many centuries to the end of the world. In practice this meant that each interpreter saw John as predicting the course of history down to his or her own time. Practitioners of this approach typically see themselves as living in the last period predicted by the Book of Revelation.

The author of the oldest extant commentary on Revelation, Victorinus of Pettau (ca. 300), understood himself to be living in the time of the sixth seal, just before the End. A certain parochialism is inherent in this view: Since it flourished in Europe, John was seen as predicting the course of European history, primarily church history, from the first century to the interpreter's own time. Various seals and trumpets are supposed to represent various events and rulers in European history, and the disasters they brought about. Following Luther, Protestant exegetes often saw the Papacy symbolized by the beast. Roman Catholics, in turn, found ways to make the name "*Martin Luther*" equal 666. Because there is no agreement among the exponents of this view, which has generated a bewildering variety of interpretations, Revelation has the reputation of being interpreted in many different ways. However, all these are variations of one interpretation.

The value of *"the world-historical view"* was that it allowed the reader to see Revelation as relevant to his or her own time, which it supposedly predicted, and it affirmed that all of history was under the sovereignty of God. The major problems, of course, are apparent: (a) The book would have meant nothing to its first readers, who would have to wait centuries before it could be properly understood; (b) it misunderstands prophecy by reducing it to prediction; (c) the variety of interpretations cancel each other out and invalidate the method. Although widely held by Protestant interpreters after the Reformation and into the twentieth century, no critical biblical scholar today advocates this view.

Dispensationalism

It is this interpretation that has become so pervasive among media *"evangelists"* and the purveyors of pop-eschatological literature. It is an insidiously dangerous interpretation of Revelation, since it often advocates the necessity of a nuclear war as part of God's plan for the eschaton *"predicted"* in the Book of Revelation. The preacher or teacher might well be aware of the historical roots and rationale for this interpretation. This is the most recent type of interpretation, its basic lineaments having been devised by a group of British and American fundamentalist ministers during the late nineteenth century's concern for the *"apostasy"* of the church. It was congealed into a doctrinal system by John Nelson Darby (J.N. Darby; also Darby is credited with originating the "*rapture*" theory) within the group of Plymouth Brethren in England, then popularized in America by Charles Ingersoll Scofield. Scofield was a St. Louis lawyer-turned-preacher without theological education who published an edition of the Bible, the Scofield Reference Bible, with his interpretative scheme embodied in the footnotes and incorporated into the outline headings of the biblical text itself. Scofield found the Correspondence Bible School in Dallas, Texas, as his own personal enterpreise, not representing any church. The Correspondence Bible

School continued after Scofield's death as Dallas Theological Seminary and has been the major center for the dissemination of this dispensational view. (Further details of dispensationalism are found in Ahlstrom, pp. 808-12. On recent militarist use of Revelation to advocate nuclear war, see Halsell).

Literary Structure

1:1-8 Prologue
1:9-3:22 A Word from the Lord
    1:9-30 Jesus Introduces Himself and Christ
    2:1-3:22 Letters to Seven Churches of Asia
        2:1-7 To Ephesus
        2:8-11: To Smyrna
        2:12-17 To Pergamum
        2:18-29 To Thyatira
        3:1-7 To Sardis
        3:7-13 To Philadelphia
        3:14-22 To Laodicea
4:1-22:9 A Series of Visions
    4:1-11:19 An Introductory Vision Cycle
        4:1-11 Heavenly Throne
        5:1-14 The Lamb
        6:1-8:1 The Opening of the Seven Seals
        8:2-11:19 The Seven Trumpets
    12:1-14:20 The Start of the Story
        12:1-7 The Dragon's War
        12:18-13:18 Resistance is futile
        14:1-20 Visions of Judgment
    15:1-22:9 A Concluding Vision Cycle
        15:1-16:21 The Seven Bowls
        17:1-19:10 Judgment of Babylon
        19:11-21:18 The Final Battle
        21:9-22:9 The New Jerusalem
22:10-21 Epilogue and Letter Closing

Two notions about the structure of the Book of Revelation, more fully developed in the relevant commentary sections, should also be introduced here. First, the series of seven visions – the seals, trumpets, and bowls – do not represent a succession of sequentially occurring events. Instead, John intends his hearers and readers to perceive them as happening simultaneously. He has in mind what a contemporary reading might call a three-ring apocalyptic circus. The judgment of God represented in each series of seven events happens only once. All three of the series happen at the same time. From one audience perspective the judgment of God appears in the symbolism of seven broken seals, from another vantage point it looks like the blowing of seven trumpets, and from a third and final angle it has all the symbolic earmarks of even bowls of wrath. John, then is intensifying, not repeating, the judgment scenario with his triple-play presentation. He wants to make certain that his hearers and readers recognize just how serious and significant God's act of judgment is.

Second, in terms of real time, John starts his book in the middle of his story. In chapters 2 and 3, he writes to churches that he believes are already under siege. He intends to encourage the members of those churches to continue resisting the lordship claims of Rome even as he implores them to self-declare their allegiance to the exclusive lordship of God and Jesus Christ. Any reader who comes to this work without sufficient awareness of its overall context would be confused as to how the churches arrives at the precarious situation John describes. How did Satan establish a throne in the affected regions (2:13)? Who is Satan? How is this mythological figure related to the imperial force that is historical Rome? How is Rome related to the regional and local authorities in Asia Minor? Why are believers threatened by them? And where is God and what is God doing in the midst of these troubling circumstances?

In terms of narrative time, John withholds a response to these questions until he inserts the chapters 12-14. In those texts, he offers the mythological explanation for the circumstance that bedevils his believers. Chapters 12-14 therefore interrupt the judgment and vindication visions with an explanatory set of visions.

Why does he not, then, begin his narrative with these visions? He does not because his primary, prophetic intent is to influence the behavior of the Christian communities that receive his Apocalypse. He therefore begins with an introduction of himself and their Lord and then moves quickly to the ethical expectations their Lord has for the churches that worship in his name. An apocalyptic letter that the author calls a word of prophecy would most logically begin with prophetic expectations for living rather than mythological combat stories steeped in symbolism. John ultimately turns to the symbolism in order to ratchet up the sense of urgency: to emphasize just how important it is that his hearers and readers abide by the prophetic-ethical expectation to witness to and for the lordship of God and the Lamb. Had he started the letter with material that emphasized the dragon and the beasts from the sea and land, surely his hearers and readers would have been so caught up in the mythological drama that they would have lost sight of ethical expectation.

Oddly enough, across the centuries, even with the mythology safely tucked inside the book's midsection, too often even Christian readers have focused on the draconian beasts, their probably contemporary identity, and the timetables for and consequences of war with them, at the regrettable expense of hearing, interpreting, and enacting the message of *"Apokalypsis"*: *"Jesus Christ is the Lord."*

Revelation

Ἀποκάλυψις

Revelation 1:1 - 8 → Prologue and Letter Opening

NIV	TT
1 [1] The revelation from Jesus Christ, which God gave him to show his servants what must soon take place. He made it known by sending his angel to his servant John, [2] who testifies to everything he saw—that is, the word of God and the testimony of Jesus Christ. [3] Blessed is the one who reads aloud the words of this prophecy, and blessed are those who hear it and take to heart what is	**1** [1] This **is**[1] a **Revelation**[2] of **Jesus Christ** [3]proclaimed, which God gave him to reveal to his servants what must happen soon; he made it known by sending his messenger to his servant John, [2] who witnessed to all that he saw: the word of God, **which is** [4]**the witness proclaimed by Jesus Christ**[5]. [3] Blessed is the one who reads and those who hear the

---

[1] Because the Greek does not have a verb, one is supplied.

[2] Ἀποκάλυψις → This means *"revelation," "discourse,"* and *"apocalypse."*

[3] Ἰησοῦ Χριστου → The genitive (*"of Jesus Christ"*) is treated here as subjective. That the revelation was something controlled by Jesus is confirmed by the following relative clause, which assumes that Jesus first received it and then passed it along.

[4] καὶ → The "καὶ" (and) is epexegetical rather than correlative; the second clause clarifies the first.

[5] →In the phrase *"witness of Jesus Christ,"* the genitive noun is subjective; when John speaks of the *"witness of,"* he means *"the witness proclaimed by."* So the revelation of Jesus as john defines it in this transmission chain is the revelation – the witness – proclaimed by Jesus Christ.

written in it, because the time is near.
 	
⁴ John, To the seven churches in the province of Asia: Grace and peace to you from him who is, and who was, and who is to come, and from the seven spirits before his throne, ⁵ and from Jesus Christ, who is the faithful witness, the firstborn from the dead, and the ruler of the kings of the earth. To him who loves us and has freed us from our sins by his blood, ⁶ and has made us to be a kingdom and priests to serve his God and Father—to him be glory and power for ever and ever! Amen. ⁷ "Look, he is coming with the clouds,"
 	
   and "every eye will see him,
even those who pierced him";
 	
   and all peoples on earth "will mourn because of him."
So shall it be! Amen. ⁸ "I am the Alpha and the
	words of the prophecy and keep what has been written in it, for the time is near.
	
	⁴ John, to the seven churches that are in Asia. Grace and peace to you from the one who is, who was, and who is coming, and from the seven spirits who are before God's throne, ⁵ and from Jesus Christ, the faithful witness, the firstborn of the dead, who is the ruler over the kings of the earth. To the one who loves us and liberated us from our sins by his blood, ⁶ and made us a reign, priests to God, who is his Father: To him be the glory and the power forever. Amen. ⁷ **Indeed**[6], he is coming with the tribes of the earth will mourn for him. Amen. ⁸ "I AM the Alpha and the Omega, the one who is, who was, and who is coming, the **Almighty**[7]," says the Lord God.

---

[6] Ἰδοὺ → This means *"you look," "you see," "behold," "indeed"* or left untranslated.

[7] παντοκράτωρ → This means *"Almighty," "All-Powerful," "Omnipotent One,"* and *"Only of God."*

| Omega," says the Lord God, "who is, and who was, and who is to come, the Almighty." | |

John's opening chapter establishes the seer's primary theme: witness. His entire work is a witness to the revelation that God has disclosed: God, working through the historical expression of Jesus as the Christ, is Lord. His hearers and readers must witness to others the truth that John reveals to them, no matter the cost.

While vv. 4-6 constitute the letter greeting proper, John's presentation of God as the one who is, who was, and who is coming at vv. 4 and 8 shows that he thought of vv. 4-8 as a unit.

- **1 – 2** John's single and graphic deployment of the term "*apokalypsis*" (revelation) conveys the word's abiding narrative importance. The revealing of Jesus conjures up the image of his crucifixion, where he was stripped naked and hung out to die. As God's intervening resurrection made clear, however, this revelation ultimately was not something someone did to Jesus; it was what Jesus revealed to everyone else. While being humiliated by hostile authorities and executed on the cross, Jesus stripped world history and human reality bare by clarifying something that was heretofore apparently obscure: his own lordship.

  Basing this part of his work on Dan. 2:28-47, where King Nebuchadnezzar realizes that God can use humans to reveal even the mysteries of the dream world, John sets up Jesus as the Messianic middleman, who takes the stripping (of world history and human reality) that God has given him and passes it on to an angel, who in turn passes it on to John. In v. 2, this chain of transmission develops a functional equivalence between the concepts *"word of God"* and *"witness of Jesus Christ,"* both of which refers back to *"revelation."* John is actually defining revelation by connecting it narratively to one clarifying object, not two. The word of God is the witness of Jesus Christ. The "καὶ" (and) that connects the two is epexegetical; that is, the second formulation clarifies and develops the first. In four key places in his text, John dramatically connects *"word"* and *"witness"* in this way: 1:2, 9; 6:9; 20:4. The intended clarification actually causes an interpretive problem. John has defined his book of prophecy as the Revelation of Jesus Christ, and has in turn defined that revelation by the formula *"word of God, which is the witness of Jesus Christ."* The formula is unclear because the defining component is itself undefined. What exactly is the witness of Jesus Christ?

In the phrase *"witness of Jesus Christ,"* the genitive noun is subjective; when John speaks of the *"witness of,"* he means *"the witness proclaimed by."* So the revelation of Jesus as John defines it in this transmission chain is the revelation – the witness – proclaimed by Jesus Christ.

In the twenty-first century, "μαρτυρίας," the Greek term for *"witness,"* means something quite different than it did for John and his hearers and readers. The confusion is contextual. When contemporary interpreters transliterate the Greek letters of "μαρτυρίας" into their corresponding Roman letters, we see and hear the word *martyr*. H. Strathmann testifies that for John and his hearers, "*The proper sphere of μαρτυς is the legal, where it denotes one who can and does speak from personal experience about actions in which he took part and which happened to him, or about persons and relations known to him*" (Strathmann, *TDNT* 4:476). Allison Trites offers corroboration: "*The idea of witness in the Apocalypse is very much a live metaphor and it to be understood in terms of Christians actually bearing witness before Roman courts of law*" (72). It is a word of provocative testimony and therefore active engagement, not sacrificial passivity. Martyr language, as John introduces (μαρτυρεω, testify, 1:2; μαρτυρία, testimony, 1:2, 9; μαρτυσ, witness, 1:5) and develops it, is language preoccupied not with dying, but declaration.

John identifies the kind of witness he encourages through key characterization. At 1:5, he identifies Jesus, by name, as the faithful witness. At 3:14, as witness, Jesus is both faithful and true. Whatever else he might appear to be to his followers (e.g., Lamb), Jesus Christ is first and foremost God's prime witness. Every other characterization must be interpreted in that light, and not the other way around. The question we are narratively driven to ask, then, is this: how are we to understand the spilling of Jesus' blood (1:5) and ultimate killing (5:9) in the light of his role as God's faithful witness? What is it about his witness that connects with and perhaps even causes his killing? The implication from the context of Asia Minor at the end of the first century is suggestive; Jesus, the prophetic witness figure, apparently testified to (proclaimed) a truth. He faithfully adhered to that testimony even under the direst of circumstances, at the cost of his own life. As Trites notes, *"From the context of the Apocalypse as a whole, it seems probable that the witness of Jesus (τὴν μαρτυρίαν Ἰησοῦ) in these passages refers primarily to Christ's passion, where he witnessed the good confession before Pontius Pilate (cf. 1 Tim. Vi 13)"* (76). What else could that confession be in the narrative of John's Revelation other than the proclamation of cosmic and human lordship that follows directly upon the rhetorical heels of Jesus' introduction as the faithful witness (1:4-8)?

According to v.1, God reveals this deadly testimony to God's servants. According to 1:4, however, the final stop for the revelation was the seven churches of Asia Minor. Did John intend that the servants would be understood as equivalent to the churches, or did he intend a separate group of servants who would then, having received the revelation from John, relay it to John's churches? A relevant passage in Amos 3:7 indicates that God does nothing without first revealing divine intent to God's servants, the prophets. John has a similar way of talking about God's servants as prophets (see 10:7; 11:3, 18; 22:16). Servant-prophets (e.g., Jezebel, 2:20-23; Balaam, 2:14) worked as interpretive links between God and God's churches. John sees himself and even God's angelic messengers as such servant-prophets (22:9; cf. 19:10). The servants, then, are prophetic colleagues to whom John reports his revelatory visions. They in turn are expected to broadcast, that is, witness the report to the churches.

Two other stages in the transmission chain also warrant individual reflection. God does not operate directly with humans, but through appropriately designated intermediaries. That presence is symbolized here by the unidentified angel. He bridges the gap between the divine and human so that God's revelation can make its necessary move.

John is another matter. He identifies himself as a link in the revelatory chain because he wants his hearers and readers to recognize his place of authority in their communal lives. John self-identifies on three other occasions: 1:4, 9; 22:8. At both 1:4 and 22:8, the self-references establish John as the writer of the text. Was he the same John identified as the son of Zebedee, one of the twelve apostles of the historical Jesus? Most likely not. Having given himself the prime literary opportunity to lay claim to such an identity and the authority that would go with it, John tellingly demurs. He claims not the authority of a Jesus apostle for his revelation, which would be powerful indeed, but that of a collegial servant-prophet working among other servant-prophets. When he challenges the prophetic work of Balaam and Jezebel in chapter 2, he does not do so on the basis of his personal relationship with the historical Jesus and the knowledge and authority he would have derived from it. Instead, he bases his argument on the truth of the prophetic revelation he has received. In fact, in his single reference to Jesus' historical apostles (21:14), he speaks of them as though they are historical figures with him he has had no direct contact. Further, the dramatic difference between the realized eschatology that predominates in the Gospel traditionally attributed to Zebedee's son and the future eschatology of the Apocalypse suggest that this John and the author of the Fourth Gospel come from dramatically different places in theology as well as time.

There are obvious structural parallels between this portion of the prologue and the epilogue (22:10-21). Though it leaves out the transmitting role played by Jesus, 22:6 explains how God sent God's angel to God's servants to "*reveal*" what must happen soon. At 22:16, John reinserts Jesus into the chain so that there is no mistaking that Jesus has conveyed the revelation to the angel. Though John uses a noun form to express imminence only here (1:1) and at the 22:6 parallel, he does express an adverbial sense of imminence throughout. The expectation of an imminent arrival of God's judgement fits the exhortative mood of the book. Since God is on the way, and right soon, one should act in the ethical manner that the book demands. These two opening verses already describe that ethic in terms of witness language. The implication is clear: the transmission of God's revelation must not stop with the servants but must carry on to the churches (1:4) and from the churches to the world.

The theme of necessity is as potent here as the theme of imminence. When John speaks of what "*must*" take place, he talks in terms of apocalyptic necessity rather than fatalistic determinism. Given the conflict that has developed between God's forces and the draconian forces of empire, which have demanded cultic and political allegiance to its lordship, both the persecution coming to those who testified exclusively to the lordship of God and Christ and God's responding judgment of the imperial forces and saving of Christ-believers are inevitable.

- **3** Beatitudes, or macarisms, are formulaic expressions initiated with the word "Μακάριος" (blessed). They exist in two forms: wisdom (e.g., Ps. 1:1 *"Happy/Blessed are those who do not follow the advice of the wicked, or take the path that sinners tread, or sit in the seat of scoffers"* and apocalyptic (e.g., Dan. 12:12-13: *"Happy/Blessed are those who persevere and attain the thousand three hundred thirty-five days. But you, go your way, and rest; you shall rise for your reward at the end of the days"*). That the beatitude form is important to John is clear from the fact that he has exactly seven of them (1:3; 14:13; 16:15; 19:9; 20:6; 22:7, 14). Operating from an Old Testament sensibility, where it represents wholeness and completion, the number *"seven"* is as theological for John as it is numerical. His first beatitude, like the six that follow, is apocalyptic, as are those that occur in Matthew's Sermon on the Mount.

    In fact, the forty-four New Testament beatitudes are most often found in the apocalyptic mode. Both modes (wisdom and apocalyptic) recognize that the person who seeks to do God's will is blessed. In that sense they have both indicative and imperative potential. As an indicative statement, the macarism describes the participant who is in right relationship with God. There are also clear indications, however, that "Μακάριος" formulations have an imperative sense. As then Dan. 12:12-13 passage demonstrates, the person who performs a particular activity is considered blessed and is subsequently rewarded. By envisioning a proleptic reward, the macarism encourages what is considered to be positive, *"salvific"* behavior.

By nature, beatitudes are comparative. In the indicative mode, secular blessings are relegated to a position inferior to the joys associated with the reign of God. In the imperative, while some behaviors are considered "Μακάριος," others are not. What is blessed behavior in 1:1-3? The blessed person is the one who witnesses to what Jesus himself testified. The person who reads this witness aloud so that others may hear it and the people who hear this witness and keep it are also those whom John considers blessed. The implicit ethic is so important that before he closes, he will pronounce the commendation again in the epilogue at 22:7: *"See, I am coming soon! Blessed is the one who keeps the words of the prophecy of this book"* (cf. Luke 11:28). John encourages his hearers and readers to realize the importance of this *"keeping"*; he promises eschatological victory to those who do (2:26-29; 3:10). (On the connection between *"hearing"* and *"keeping"* as an ethical combination in Revelation, see 22:17).

When John describes his own work as a word of prophecy, he has a particular point in mind. A prophet is a servant who witnesses to the lordship of God and

Christ, even in imperial circumstances where government representatives seek either to co-opt or to annihilate that testimony. The primary objective of prophecy, then, is not to foretell the future, but to model and thereby incite present witnessing behavior that resists imperial attempts to hijack the lordship that belongs exclusively to God and Christ. It is his prophetic exhortation to this kind of witnessing that John wants his people to hear and keep. John urges Christ-believers to witness because the time (of God's movement for judgment and salvation) is near. In the epilogue, at 22:10, John hears an angel make the same claim. Was John wrong? Given that the twenty-first century has dawned without the onset of God's new heaven and new earth, one would have to say yes. To concentrate on the error of timing, though, would be to miss John's primary theological point. To his credit, he never offers a timetable. Instead, he uses the imminent expectation to craft a sense of urgency that he hopes will foment passionate witnessing for God's exclusive lordship, even in a context where Christ-believers were sure to be persecuted for making such an outrageous claim.

- **4** As was the case with the apostle Paul, John's initial moves follow the conventional norms of Hellenistic correspondence. Like Paul, though, he does not simply take over the Hellenistic conventions of letter writing; he adapts them to his particular Christian purpose. First, he identifies himself as the sender. Immediately afterward, he points out seven churches of Asia Minor (present-day Turkey) as the recipients. Since the number "*seven*" is a symbol of completion for John, it is probable that the entire church in the region was his target audience. He makes this clear by ending each of the seven letters with a formula that identifies all the churches as the target audience. Perhaps he singled out these seven because each of them hosted a Roman law court where believers could be forced to testify about allegations that they were Christ-believers (Boring, *Revelation*, 87).

Like Paul, John further adjusts the Hellenistic letter-writing formula by including an offer of grace and peace (cf. Rom. 1:7; 1 Cor. 1:3, 2 Cor. 1:2; Gal. 1:3; Phil. 1:2; 1 Thess. 1:1; Phlm 3). He repeats the grace sentiment in the benediction at 22:21. Here, as in the benediction, he unleashes an epistolary shot across Caesar's imperial bow. Allegedly, the prosperity of Asian life was owed solely to the emperor's beneficence. According to John, however, the grace and the peace has developed from it comes from some ones else: God, the seven spirits before God's throne, and Jesus Christ. John has twisted the innocuous form of a Greco-Roman letter written for religious intent into what Pablo Richard calls "*a liturgical text that amounts to a theological and political manifesto.*"

Religious rhetoric continues its morph into political counterpropaganda when John provides a descriptive title for this God of grace (on John's skewing of the grammar to make a theological point). At vv. V and 8, he identifies God as the one who is, who was, and who is coming. In Greek speaking world such a threefold formulation was a commonplace way of celebrating a deity's eternity and immutability. *"It was said, for example, that "Zeus was, Zeus is, and Zeus will be' (Pausanias)."* Athena also laid claim to such a testimonial. Plutarch preserves an inscription from the base of one of her statues that reads, *"I am all that has been, and is, and shall be."* John hijacks the formulation for God. He then adds a direct provocation. His God was also coming to bring the reality of supernatural rule to the natural realm. By identifying God as the Alpha and the Omega, as God would do Godself in the second recitation of this threefold formula at v.8, John claims that God transcends human history and therefore controls it. Rome had already staked that claim by conquering Asia Minor and the people of God who lived in it. It is at just the point of this theological difference of opinion that religious confrontation escalates into political combat. When John records God's second self-reference at v.8, he uses the very language Moses used to describe the liberator God in the Exod. 3:14 account: *"I AM."* This direct reference reinforces the Exod. 3:14 allusion *"the one who is"* already present in the threefold formulation. The Almighty Lord of Hosts who brought down Pharaoh and set the people of God free was on the verge of unveiling a similar liberating act for the people of God in Asia. In John's historical context that necessarily meant that this Almighty One would be acting against Rome.

    This Almighty One was not acting alone. The seven spirits symbolize God's expansive power. They represent the fullness (seven) of God's force in the world through the active presence of the Holy Spirit. Beale sees a connection here with 4:5, where John describes the seven flaming torches burning before the heavenly throne. Interestingly, John also characterizes the churches in 1:12, 13, and 20 as seven lampstands. It does not take much imagination to theorize that the churches (lampstands) are powered by the force of God's Spirit (flames). But if God uses God's power (Spirit) to contest Roman control of human history, and God also uses God's power to empower the churches to whom John is writing, then it must also be the case that John's churches will form one of the principal mechanisms through which God will win the fight against Rome. This Holy Spirit, then, is very much a political Spirit.

- 5 John heightens the probability for even more controversy by the way he describes Christ. He does not use proper grammar. John's problems with Greek are legendary; many have argued that his flawed writing can be attributed to the fact that he thinks in Hebrew or Aramaic. Allen Callahan counters that he operates this way intentionally. Because *"most of the grammatical rules violated are flawlessly observed elsewhere in the work,"* he believes that John chooses to write in a Greek that is heavily influenced by Semitic principles. He does so because he wants his use of language to be a representation, a working symbol, as it were, of the social and political resistance his people must wage.

Since "*Jesus Christ*" is in the genitive case, operating as the object of the preposition "*from*," the titles that follow should also be in the genitive. Instead, John puts *"the faithful witness," "the firstborn of the dead,"* and *"the ruler over the kings of the earth"* in the nominative case. As Callahan might say, John is not making a mistake; he is making a point. He is following the same pattern he initiated in v. 4, where the threefold formula about God is in the nominative case even though its function as the object of the preposition *"from"* should have it in the genitive. There, as here, John stays with the nominative because he wants to direct attention to an allusion he is making to Ps. 89:37 (88:38 LXX), where the controlling moniker, faithful witness, also occurs in a nominative formulation. But it occurs there with a specific orientation, as does *"firstborn"* in 89:27 (88:28 LXX). The context of the two references in their Old Testament location is one of kingship, *"the unending reign of David's seed on his throne. John applies the phrase directly to the Messiah's own faithful witness, which led to establishment of his eternal kingship."* Indeed, the reference to *"firstborn"* in the psalm is directly associated not only with kingship but also with the highest kingship on the earth. That is exactly the kind of kingship John envisions for Jesus Christ here. John has skewed his grammar in order to shepherd his hearers and readers toward this very pointed connection. Now the actual content of the titles can have the force the visionary intended.

Witness is key, not only because of its lead position in the chain of three, but also because it follows up on John's opening three verses, which convey his entire work as the witness – that is, revelation – proclaimed by Jesus. The "καὶ" (and) that connects the two trailing titles is epexegetical rather than correlative. An appropriate translation would be, *"the firstborn of the dead, who is the ruler of the kings of the earth."* The entire phrase clarifies what it means for Jesus to be a faithful witness; the image of universal kingship clarifies what it means for this faithful witness to be first born of the dead. As God is ruler of all, "παντοκράτωρ" (*"Almighty"* 1:8), Jesus is ruler of the entire human realm. This is the revelation proclaimed by Jesus Christ.

In a cultural context where Rome already lays claim to ultimate kingship, it is also a revelation bound inevitably for trouble. Christ's kingship, by claiming to be the one abiding and universal kingship, necessarily resists any established rule making the same claim. In John's context, the rule would be Rome's.

What does such an interpretive perspective do? John's commendation of Jesus as the one who witnesses faithfully, even at the cost of his life, incites emulation. Christ-believers cannot be the firstborn of the dead, nor the ruler over the kings of the earth, but they can, like Antipas (Rev. 2:13) and like John himself (1:2), be faithful witnesses to the testimony that Jesus himself proclaimed: God is the Almighty One, and Jesus Christ is God's coming king. John follows up this combative description with an equally combative doxology. The first two rationales for human praise of Jesus Christ are his love and his ransoming of humans from sin because of that love. John's verbal use of the concept *"love"* ("ἀγαπάω" 1:5; 3:9; 12:11; 20:9) is so sparse that one can hardly draw conclusive thoughts about it (even the noun form occurs only at 2:4, 19). Where Christ is the subject of the love (1:5; 3:9), the result is the salvation/vindication of Christ-believers. Where believers are the subject (12:11), John highlights their love for the lordship of Christ above even their own lives. It is understood from the limited evidence John allows, it is a primary motivation for the salvation/vindication and human participation in that victory. The expected goal for all believers is that they become *"those who conquer"* (2:7, 11, 17, 26; 3:5, 12, 21). Such conquest can only be achieved if humans love life less than the lordship of God and Jesus Christ.

John goes on to describe the salvation/vindication achieved by Christ as a ransoming from sin (cf. Isa. 40:2). This is the only pairing of sin and redemption language in the *"Apokalypsis*[8]*."* One wonders if, even here, redemption is really John's primary concern. He ties the release from sins to one of his most potent images: blood. Blood in Revelation symbolizes not sacrifice and atonement but execution and, as 12:11 illustrates, conquest. The executed one ransoms as Moses ransomed Israel from Egypt in a liberating rather than atoning sense.

To be sure, John expects repentance from sin. However, his remarks to the churches in chapters 2 and

---

[8] The only other mention of sin occurs at 18:4-5, with reference to Babylon's sins, and has nothing to do with the concept of redemption.

3 indicate that he desires repentance from a particular kind of sin. He wants those who are accommodating themselves to cultic practices, social affiliations, economic buy-ins, and demonstrations of political loyalty that acknowledge, celebrate, and support the lordship of Rome to repent from such activity. Sin, then, is specifically tied to affiliation with Rome and the Roman imperial cult and its practices. By contrast, conquest behavior witnesses to – that is to say, promotes, celebrate, worships, and extends – the opposition lordship of God and Christ. John's hearers and readers are ransomed, set loose for this witnessing purpose in the same way that the people of Israel were ransomed by Moses so that they could acknowledge Yahweh's lordship. Highlighted here, then, is not atonement, but nonviolent resistance. Jesus looses (ransoms) believers from their sin (accommodation to the lordship of Rome) through a ministry of nonviolent resistance (witness to the lordship of God and his own connection with that lordship) that will become the model for their own witness, that is, ministries of resistance.

- **6** The third reason for praise extends the Exodus imagery. Christ establishes believers as a reign of priests to God (cf. Exod. 19:6), a theme that is reengaged at the end of the book (22:5). At 5:10, the establishment of this reign is the third reason for acknowledging the Lamb as worthy. Those who are redeemed by Christ's blood have been liberated for a very social purpose. Here on earth, they will be established as a reign that will serve neither Rome nor any Greco-Roman divinity, but God. Where Rome is concerned, any such reign is unauthorized. Any such unauthorized reign is by definition a counter-reign and therefore a political provocation that Rome must (cf. 1:1) necessarily challenge.

John specifies the relationship between God and Christ as that of father and son. The "καὶ" (and) that connects "*God*" and "*his Father*" is epexegetical; John means to say: God, who is his Father. John continues the close relating of God to Jesus Christ with the final refrain of the doxology. The glory and might ascribed rightfully to God (4:11; 5:13) also belong properly to Christ (cf. 5:12).

The concluding "*amen*" affirms that what has been declared in the doxology about Christ is true and valid.

- **7** The affirmation of the "*amen*" in v. 6 is immediately corroborated by the particle "'Ιδοὺ" ("*behold*) that opens v. 7, a combination of Dan. 7:13 and Zech. 12:10 that was also celebrated at Matt. 24:30 (cf. Mark 14:62). Aune points out helpfully that in the twenty-six occurrences of the particle in Revelation, there are two different, though related meanings. When used in speech (1:7, 18; 2:10, 22; 3:8, 9 [2x], 20; 5:5; 9:12; 11:14; 21:3, 5), the form affirms and validates whatever statement it precedes and should be translated "*indeed.*" When used in narrative (4:1, 2; 5:6; 6:2, 5, 8, 12; 7:9; 12:3; 14:1, 14; 15:5; 19:11), it draws attention to the material it introduces and is best translated "*look*" or "*behold.*" Here it follows up the "*amen*" of v. 6, with an antiphonal affirmation.

Indeed, this Christ, who is the appropriate subject of the 1:5b-6 doxology, will soon demonstrate his eschatological bona fides by coming with the clouds. This highly anticipated event answers the implicit question raised by the comment that the time is near (1:3). What time is near? The time of Christ's coming, his Parousia. In Dan. 7:13-14 one like a son of man, a child of humanity, comes to claim a lordship and dominion on earth that, according to Rev. 1:5, belongs to Jesus Christ. The cloud reference indicates that the royal coming is for the purpose of judgment.

With his remark that every eye will see this coming, John alludes to Zech. 12:10. In the Old Testament account, the enemy nations would mourn for ("κόψονται ἐπ' αὐτὸν" the same idiom that occurs at Rev. 1:7) the house of David, which they had pierced, and the people of God would be redeemed after repenting of their *"piercing"* of God's servant. John's additions of *"every eye"* and *"tribes of the earth"* are his way of universalizing the account. All the world will participate in the vindicating move to lordship that Christ's coming represents.

Even those who pierced Christ will witness and acknowledge his vindicating lordship (cf. 1:5; 5:9). Once again John's politics rise through his cultic claims. The Romans who pierced him, the Romans who now lay illegitimate claim to cosmic and historical lordship, are hereby forewarned that even they will come to see that true lordship resides in the hands of the very one they thought they had destroyed. At the end of the verse, John's universalism (cf. 5:9-10; 12:5; 15:3, 4;

21:3, 14, 24, 26; 22:2) pushes him beyond the Romans. Every tribe will mourn on account of this pierced, coming, reigning Christ. While tribes are first mentioned positively in Revelation (5:9; 7:9) as those ransomed by the Lamb, in the latter portions of the narrative (11:9; 13:7; 14:6), they are clearly designated as those who refuse to acknowledge God's and Christ's lordship and are therefore due judgment. If John is alluding, however, to the tribe reference in Gen. 12:3 (cf. 28:14), where blessing would accrue through God's servant to the tribes of earth, the mourning in Rev. 1:7 may be seen clearly emphasized throughout the narrative (e.g., 8:7-13; 9:20-21; 11:1, 13; 15:4; 22:11). Indeed, the Zech. 12:10 context suggests repentance, as do the contextual implications drawn from John's use of the "*tribe*" metaphor in the early part of his work. Beale is therefore right to conclude that here "*repentant Gentiles are viewed as fulfilling the Zechariah prophecy at the second coming of Christ.*" To this suggestion, John shouts "*Amen!*"

- **8** John closes his salutation by returning to the threefold designation of God that was prominent in the salutation's opening (v. 4). He also makes several notable adjustments. First, he makes the tripartite title part of a quotation from God, one of only two God quotes in the entire work (21:5-8). Second, God's quotation begins with the powerful Exod. 3:14 words of self-identifying lordship: "*I AM.*" In Isa. 41:4, 44:6 and 48:12, these words not only identify God as Lord but also connect this lordship to what is for John an equivalent identifier: "*first and last.*" John builds upon his allusion to Isaiah's claim of *"first and last"* with his third adjustment. God declares, as God does in the only other place where God speaks in the text of Revelation (21:6), that God is the *"Alpha and the Omega."* These references to the first and last letters of the Greek alphabet symbolize God's role at the one who exclusively exists at the beginning and end of all time. This title, applied in the epilogue also to Christ (22:13), implies that the one who presides at the start and close of time is rightly recognized as the Lord of everything that occurs through time. In the final adjustment, God is the "παντοκράτωρ" (*"Almighty One"*). John applies the title to God multiple times 4:8; 11:7; 15:3; 16:7, 14; 19:6, 15; 21:22.

Revelation 1:9~20 → John Introduces Himself and Christ

NIV	TT
⁹I, John, your brother and companion in the suffering and kingdom and patient endurance that are ours in Jesus, was on the island of Patmos because of the word of God and the testimony of Jesus. ¹⁰On the Lord's Day I was in the Spirit, and I heard behind me a loud voice like a trumpet, ¹¹which said: "Write on a scroll what you see and send it to the	⁹I, John, your brother and colleague in the persecution and reign and **patient endurance/non-violent resistance**⁹ in Jesus, was on the island of **Patmos**¹⁰ because of the word of God, which is **the testimony proclaimed by Jesus**¹¹. ¹⁰I was in the spirit on **the Lord's Day**¹² and I heard behind me a foreboding voice, like a trumpet,

---

⁹ ὑπομονή → This term means *"steadfastness," "constancy," "endurance," "sustaining,"* and *"perseverance."* The key Christian virtue in the Book of Revelation, this occurs seven times. But in John's context, he is not asking his followers simply to endure the persecution that comes their way; he instead is championing an active response of faith that resists.

¹⁰ → An Island of the Dodecanse, lying some 55km off the SW coast of Asia Minor. To this island John was banished from Ephesus, evidently for some months about the year 95 C.E., and here he wrote his Revelation (Rev. 1:9). The island is about 12km long, with a breadth of up to 7km, and it has been suggested that the scenery of its rugged volcanic hills and surrounding seas find their reflection in the imagery of the *"Apokalypsis."* The island now belongs to Greece.

¹¹ τὴν μαρτυρίαν Ἰησοῦ → Literally it means *"the testimony of Jesus."* This phrase has been much debated. The phrase can be understood as *"the testimony about Jesus"* or *"the testimony the Jesus offered."*

¹² τῇ κυριακῇ ἡμέρᾳ → The phrase means *"the Lord's day"* (the adjective "κυριακός"*"belonging to the Lord"* is found elsewhere in the New Testament only in 1 Cor. 11:20, referring to the Lord's supper). It is probably a reference to Sunday rather than to the Sabbath (Cf. Matt. 28:1; Acts 20:7; 1 Cor. 16:2).

seven churches: to Ephesus, Smyrna, Pergamum, Thyatira, Sardis, Philadelphia and Laodicea." ¹² I turned around to see the voice that was speaking to me. And when I turned I saw seven golden lampstands, ¹³ and among the lampstands was someone like a son of man, dressed in a robe reaching down to his feet and with a golden sash around his chest. ¹⁴ The hair on his head was white like wool, as white as snow, and his eyes were like blazing fire. ¹⁵ His feet were like bronze glowing in a furnace, and his voice was like the sound of rushing waters. ¹⁶ In his right hand he held seven stars, and coming out of his mouth was a sharp, double-edged sword. His face was like the sun shining in all its brilliance. ¹⁷ When I saw him, I fell at	¹¹ saying, "Write what you see in a **scroll**¹³ and send it to the seven churches: to Ephesus, and to Smyrna, and to Pergamum, and to Thyatira, and to Sardis, and to Philadelphia, and to Laodicea." ¹² Then I turned to see the voice that was speaking to me, and when I turned I saw seven golden lampstands, ¹³ and one like a son of man was in the midst of the lampstands, wearing a long robe and a golden sash wrapped around his chest. ¹⁴ The white hair on his head was as white wool, like snow, and his eyes were like a flame of fire, ¹⁵ and his feet were like bronze as refined in a furnace, and his voice was like the sound of many waters, ¹⁶ and he had in his right hand seven stars, and out of his mouth went a sharp, double-edged sword, and his face shone as the sun in its full force. ¹⁷ When I saw him, I fell at his feet as

---

¹³ βιβλίον→ This term means "*a small book*," "*a scroll*," "*a document*," and "*a bill of divorcement*."

his feet as though dead. Then he placed his right hand on me and said: "Do not be afraid. I am the First and the Last. [18] I am the Living One; I was dead, and now look, I am alive for ever and ever! And I hold the keys of death and Hades. [19] "Write, therefore, what you have seen, what is now and what will take place later. [20] The mystery of the seven stars that you saw in my right hand and of the seven golden lampstands is this: The seven stars are the angels of the seven churches, and the seven lampstands are the seven churches.	though dead, and he put his right hand on me, saying, "Stop being afraid; I AM the first and the last [18] and the living one. I was dead but indeed I am alive forever, and I have the keys of Death and Hades. [19] Therefore, write about what you saw, what is, and what is about to take place after this. [20] As for the mystery of the seven stars that you saw in my right hand and the seven golden lampstands: the seven stars are the angels of the seven churches, and the seven lampstands are the seven churches."

The body of Revelation begins in 1:9. While in exile on the island of Patmos, John saw the risen Lord. It happened as he was in the "*Spirit*" on the Lord's Day. Suddenly he heard behind him a loud voice like the sound of a trumpet. The voice declared that John should write down what he would see and send it to the seven churches: to Ephesus, Smyrna, Pergamum, Thyatira, Sardis, Philadelphia, and Laodicea.

- **9** For the third time in the opening nine verses, John self-identifies. It is particularly intriguing that he names himself at the start of each of the primary units of the chapter (vv. 1-3: 1; vv.4-8: v.4; vv.9-20: v.9). He authenticates the content of each section with his personal authority. Church members can trust his description of revelation and its chain of transmission because it has come to them through him. They can trust the doxological claims about Christ because it is he who praises with them. In offering what amounts to a narrative signature, he vouches for it all. Both he and Christ self-identify in the epilogue for the same authorizing reason (22:8, 16).

Though John is a community leader, he is also one with the Asia Minor Christ-believers. He has already indicated this equality by introducing himself as a servant among many other servants (1:1). John reinforces that collegial relationship with the filial metaphor. He does not use the term "ἀδελφός" (brother/sister) often, but when he does, it is at critical points that indicate a nonhierarchical relationship of witness. At 6:11, all are kin in the faith who suffer because of their witness to the lordship of God and Christ. At 12:10, those same kin-witness conquer the dragon because of that testimony. Even angels, when they are operating for God, operate not as powers over believers, but as fellow-servants in the faith (19:9-10; 22:8-9).

These brothers and sisters are colleagues in the persecution (cf. Phil. 4:14). The presence of the definite article suggests that "*the*" persecution was a well-recognized event. Scholars, though, have rightly pressed that there was no long-standing or strategically organized system of persecution during the time of Domitian's reign (81-96 C.E.), when John wrote. What kind of persecution, then, does he envision?

In a reconstruction of the social-historical situation of the "*Apokalypsis*" that represents today's prevailing scholarly thinking, Loren Johns argues that John was writing about the understanding "*expectation of persecution rather than the present experience of persecution.*" The members of the churches forestalled that persecution by accommodating themselves to the social, cultural, and religious expectations that centered around Greco-Roman pagan and imperial worship. As long as they did not witness openly for the exclusive lordship of Christ, as long as they blended into a world that did not recognize that lordship, they would be physically, socially, politically, and economically secure. It is no wonder, then, that these believers were "*probably succumbing to the temptation not only of maintaining a low profile as Christians in such contexts, but also of paying token acknowledgement to the pagan gods (whether to Caesar or the patron gods of the guilds). As also in the other churches, the motive for this was probably fear of persecution, especially economic ostracism.*" The problem therefore lay with "*the*" imminent persecution John's colleagues knew would erupt if they lived out the kind of non-accommodating Christianity that he himself professed.

If John was asking his people to stand up (i.e., witness) and thus stand out in a world they had accepted and that had accepted them, he was essentially telling them to go out and pick a fight! He was ordering them to declare that they were now non-accommodating Christ-believers who could no longer participate in a world that had not previously noticed them since they had heretofore been accommodating to it. In a classic *"Don't ask, don't tell"* (that I'm a Christ-believer) kind of environment, John was essentially ordering his followers to be about the business of telling on themselves, with full knowledge of the kind of repercussions such telling would bring. He was asking them to come screaming out of the Christian closet, knowing that it would solicit the same consequence it had attracted to the one true and faithful witness: execution (see 7:14; 13:10).

Because John firmly believed that witness would not only draw persecution but also effect conquest (12:11; cf. 2:7, 11, 17, 26; 3:5, 12, 21), it is not surprising that he would offer here the odd pairing of persecution and reign. Christ had made believers a reign of priests (1:6); they consummate that reign, inaugurated by Christ's blood, through the power of their own stubborn witness (12:11) to the lordship of this Crucified One (Mark 16:6). No wonder, then, that John climaxed his enumeration of collegial traits by pointing to their "ὑπομονή," a term often translated *"endurance,"* but in John's context has more the sense of nonviolent resistance. John is not asking his followers simply to endure the persecution that comes their way; he instead is championing an active response of faith that resists both the belief in the lordship of Rome and the hostile practices Rome wields to propagandize that belief. Though he never asks them to fight with violence, he does urge them, like Jesus and himself, to fight.

John's own location and the reason for it are signs that he practices what he preaches. Patmos is a small island that measure approximately 30 miles in circumference and sits some 37 miles west-southwest of Miletus and 75 miles west of Ephesus. Though it seems clear that the Romans did not use the island as a penal colony (there is no historical evidence that anyone was banished there), there is debate as to whether the Romans used it as a place of exile (some troublemakers were sent there). Ascertaining truth in the matter may be neither possible nor necessary. Location is not the seer's crucial point. The issue is that he had been removed from their presence because of his witnessing activities on behalf of the lordship of God and Christ. The location of his exile was not as important for his rhetorical purpose as its reality and its rationale.

He stresses that rationale at the climactic close of the verse. Whenever he uses the phrase "διὰ" with a following object in the accusative (*"because of"*), he does so to refer to the result of an action. John has been banished to Patmos as a direct result of his preaching the word of God, which is the testimony proclaimed by Jesus, that is, the revelation that God and Christ are Lord.

- **10 – 11** When John declares that he was in the spirit (cf. Ezek. 3:12), he speaks not about an ecstatic experience but a prophetic one. His primary focus is not spiritual fervor but ethical awareness. God's energizing of his human spirit enabled him to comprehend God's revolutionary message of lordship and the behavioral expectations that message raised for him and the people of the Asia Minor churches.

The ambiguous reference to the *"Lord's Day"* applies to Sunday, the first day of the week, when Jesus was raised from the dead (cf. Acts 20:7; Mark 16:2; 1 Cor. 16:2; *Did.* 14:1). Christ-believers had taken to holding their worship of God and Christ as Lord on this day, a recent custom John defiantly adhered to even while in exile.

The *"great voice"* John hears registers like a trumpet. *"Great voice"* is a literary cipher for John: it anticipates an urgent, dramatic message that generally bears the foreboding tone of impending judgment. The trumpet comparison brings to mind the theophany of Exod. 19:16, where the cloud, thunder, and lighting on Sinai were accompanied by the foreboding blast of a trumpet. Over the centuries, Israel ritualized the trumpet sound in the blowing of the shofar, a ram's born, in both battle and worship. A similar trumpet-like voice invites John to come up to heaven for a peek into the throne room at 4:1. In 1:10-12, this voice is identified as that of Christ, the one *"like a son of man."*

The voice directs John to write the visions he will see in a scroll (cf. Isa. 30:8). The command to write occurs often in the work (Rev. 1:19; 2:1, 8, 12, 18; 3:1, 7, 14; 14:13; 19:9; 21:5). While the directives in chapters 2 and 3 refer to the specific letters John was to write to each of the seven churches, the command here, like the other remaining ones, probably has in view the entire "*Apokalypsis.*"

The seven churches, already mentioned as the recipients of John's letter (1:4), are now identified by name.

- **12 – 13** The throne room décor, reminiscent of Dan. 7:9-10, is illuminating. John first notices the seven lampstands, which symbolize the seven churches (1:20). Clearly, they are crafted from the Exodus image of the stand of seven lamps made from pure gold, designed for placement in the tabernacle of the Lord (Exod. 25:31-37; 37:17-24; cf. Num. 8:1-4). The prophet Zechariah also envisioned a golden lampstand with seven lamps (Zech. 4:2). That John also had Zechariah's vision in mind is clear from the use he later makes of the two olive trees that flank the lampstand (Zech. 4:3, 14); in chapter 11, John draws directly from this vision for constructing the portrait of his two witnesses. It is unclear whether John intends to say that each of his seven stands has seven lamps, as the Exodus and Zechariah menorahs would have had, or whether each of his stands has a single lamp. Given that he is building from the prophetic images, he probably pictures each stand as a menorah, despite the fact that such a constellation would have confused the numerical point he was trying to make. One thing is clear: John deploys the number "*seven*" in order to draw an explicit connection between the spirits of God before the throne – that is, God's Holy Spirit) – and the seven churches symbolized by the seven lampstands. The lamps, meaning the churches, are fired by the power of God's Holy Spirit.

One *"like a son of man,"* a figure obviously drawn from the characterization in Dan. 7:13-14; 10:15-21, walks among the lampstands (Rev. 2:1). Two points are important about this *"son of man"*; one is relational, the other concerns identity. Though the identity of Daniel's messianic figure was uncertain (the people Israel? the archangel Michael? a human individual?), for John he is certainly the faithful witness, Jesus Christ. Like the Daniel figure, Christ comes with the clouds (1:7; Dan. 7:13) and is the true Lord (1:5-6; Dan. 7:14). The relational point is that this *"son of man"* walks among the lampstands. The symbolisms is clear; these churches, who are called to the counter-witness of Jesus' kingship and are therefore destined for persecution (1:9), are not alone. Jesus, who is both their priest and their king, is with them. His distinctive dress corresponds to his dual function. The long robe (cf. Dan. 10:5; Ezek. 9:2, 11) resembles Aaron's priestly garment (Exod. 28:4). The golden sash (for priestly implications, see Exod. 39:29) worn across the chest is the accoutrement of kings (cf. 1 Macc. 10:89).

- **14** The *"son of man's"* hair, which is as white as snow, has the texture of wool. The description reminds hearers and readers of Daniel's description of the Ancient of Days (Dan. 7:9, *1 En.* 46:1; 71:10; 106:5-6). John's intention is clear; he is indissolubly linking the identities of God and Christ. They, like their lordship, are one. The hair's texture is interesting for another reason. In the cosmopolitan Roman Empire (and no doubt in Daniel's context as well), where people with hair like wool, were well known, it is interesting that Christ is depicted this way, rather than with the straight hair commonly associated with those of European descent. The Gospels do not give any physical descriptions of Jesus; Revelation gives just this one. It is provocative, to say the least.

His eyes are like flames of fire. Operating from the Dan. 10:6 depiction of a *"son of man,"* and the Dan. 7:9-10 accounting of God's fiery presence, John uses this description to cultivate an image of judgment. That concept is reinforced when he recalls the fiery eyes at 2:18, just before he threatens with judgment Jezebel and the Thyatirans who follow her, and again at 19:12, where the rider on the dazzling horse operates as cosmic judge.

- **15** Christ's feet of burnished bronze (or copper) have the aesthetic appeal of metal refined in a furnace. The seer continues to work from the Daniel account of a messianic leader who has anything but clay feet (Dan. 10:6; cf. Ezek. 1:7). At 2:18 and 10:1, similar depictions resurrect the theme of judgment.

The powerful, trumpet-like voice (1:10) is said now to have the volume of many waters (cf. Dan. 10:6). In Ezek. 1:24, the wings of the living creatures that guard the throne produce this same sound effect, as does the movement of God's glory in Ezek. 43:2. In John's own work, at 14:2, the voice of heaven carries with the same force, as do the voices crying *"Hallelujah!"* at 19:6. In each case, the sound is connected to the moving of

God's judgment, an event that will also bring salvation to those allied with God.

- **16** The earthbound Christ (1:12) holds seven stars in his right hand. According to v.20, the seven stars are the seven patron angels of the seven churches (vv. 4, 11). Somewhere between 81 and 84 C.E., the emperor Domitian minted coins with the image of his dead, infant son standing astride the earth and playing with seven stars. Since the stars were thought to control human life, the one who controlled the stars had ultimate power. For the Romans, such power lay in imperial hands. John's counterprogramming gave the seven stars, and the fullness of cosmic power symbolized by them, to Christ. Human destiny lies with Christ, not with the power of Rome or the grip of astrological fate.

Out of his mouth issues a sharp, double-edged sword. Cutting both ways, it strikes the failures of the faithful (2:12, 16) as surely as it gouges those who would harm them (19:15, 21). The mouth location indicates that this sword is Christ's word of universal, impartial judgment (cf. Heb. 4:12). As is the case at 19:15, 21, the imagery builds from the depiction of the sharp prophetic word of judgment in Isa. 49:2 (cf. Isa. 11:4). Witness language is the cutting, prophetic word of God's lordship. That word is the weapon to be wielded against the powers that tout and enforce the lordship of Rome. The sword, then, is not a literal reference to violence, but a metaphor of nonviolent resistance.

Christ's shining face anticipates the later discussion of the judgment oriented angel whose beaming face shines like the sun (10:1). Daniel 10:6 pictured *"a son of man's"* face shining like the sun. At Matt. 17:2, Jesus' transfigured face was said to so shine. John clearly escalates eschatological matters here; Christ's entire countenance has a blinding impact.

- **17** John is so overwhelmed that he falls to his feet in a trancelike state. The seer has a penchant for going to his knees in the presence of the divine. Later, 19:10 and 22:8-9 will see him consciously falling prostrate before angelic messengers. In those future instances, he will be chided. Here, given that he is responding to Christ, the fear and awe that push him to the ground seem more narratively appropriate (cf. Matt. 28:4). Historically, his response is similar to that of the prophet Ezekiel, who fell to knees at the appearance of God's glory in the sky (Ezek. 1:28).

As at Dan. 8:18, where Daniel fell to the ground in a trance before the angel Gabriel, John finds his empowerment to rise after he is touched by the figure who induces the faint. Christ explains that he is, like God, the first and the last (1:4, 8; 2:8; 22:13). Knowing Christ's status should relieve John's fears about Roman claims to ultimate lordship and Rome's oppressive enforcement of those claims (cf. 2:10). Rome should not be feared, because Christ is the true Lord. Christ's counsel corresponds to God's advice that Jacob should not fear because the God who forms humans in the womb, and was therefore in charge of history, had chosen Israel (Isa. 44:2).

- **18** The forceful "*I AM*" declaration that concluded v. 17 runs into and initiates v. 18. John punctuates each of the three descriptors that follow the "*I AM*" with a definite article that signals a functional equality between them. The one who is *the* first and *the* last is also *the* living one. To the witless hearer and reader, the claim seems ridiculously redundant. Christ's "*aliveness*" must be understood within the context of resurrection, which John previewed at 1:5 with his claim that Christ is "firstborn of the dead" and immediately clarifies here when he quotes Christ as saying, "*I was dead, but indeed, I am alive forever.*" There are two key points: (1) though dead, he was raised, and (2) he was raised to eternal rather than historical life (on God as one with eternal life cf. 4:9, Deut. 32:40; *Sir.* 18:1).

  The consequence of Christ's resurrection goes beyond his eternal status. Christ also claims now to be uniquely empowered. Death is the force that snatches the essence of human life. Hades is the place where that essence is eternally warehoused. As such, Hades is equivalent to the abyss (cf. 9:1-2). The two forces are presented together because they operate in a grim, caging partnership in the "*Apokalypsis*" (cf. Job 38:17, which speaks of the gates of death). Through God's power, though, Christ got away. He did not escape empty-handed. He absconded with their keys and now promises to use them as the ultimate ransom tool (1:5b; 20:13). His possession of the keys represents his ability to control the process of judgment and salvation, to decide who obtains eschatological relationship with

God and who does not, an ability that parallels his holding of the key of David in 3:7.

Why is this point about Jesus holding the keys of Death and Hades particularly important for John's hearers and readers? John knows that punishment will occur if his followers do indeed witness for the lordship of God and Christ in a world hell-bent on institutionalizing the lordship of Rome. The ultimate punishment would be death (2:13), certainly a potent deterrent to the discipleship behavior John exhorts. Rome's greatest power is its ability to consign Christ-believers to death. John mitigates that power with his declaration, made in the vision by Christ himself, that Christ has the keys that will release people from death into eternal life.

- **19** Just as Isaiah was told to declare what he had seen and heard (Isa. 48:6), so John is now ordered to publish his visionary accounts. Already, at 1:11, he had been given this same order. It is now reinforced in a more comprehensive way. He is to write about *"what you saw," "what is,"* and *"what is about to take place after this."*

  "What you saw" probably pertains to the visions about Christ and his lordship that have just immediately taken place (1:12-18). The "therefore" that initiates the verse sets vv. 19-20 apart from that vision of Christ's lordship, which is now, though a recent past account, nonetheless a past account. These last two verses subsequently operate as a discussion of the consequences that develop from that lordship symbolism.

"*What is*" pertains more broadly to the threatening situation that looms over anyone who would dare to proclaim the lordship of God and Christ. As chapter 12 indicates (especially 12:17), the draconian forces of imperial lordship hunt the churches. This mythical reality comes to historical ground in chapters 2 and 3, which address the circumstances daily faced by the members of the seven Asia Minor churches.

"*What is about to take place*" pertains to the certain reprisals that will come when Christ-believers "*out themselves*" as Christ-believers by testifying demonstrably to his lordship. The "*after this*" that closes the verse, then, does not refer as much to "*this apocalyptic age*" as it does to the specific circumstances surrounding the after math of John's visions of Christ's lordship and the people's testimony to it.

- **20** This verse is self-explanatory; it refers back to material already presented and clarifies it. The seven stars are explained as the seven patron angels of the seven churches. Most likely, John is building from the traditional Jewish idea that each people or nation had an angel ruling over it as a patron or representative. To address them is a way of addressing the community as a whole (Rev. 2:1, 8, 12, 18; 3:1, 7, 14).

Revelation 2:1~7 → To Ephesus

NIV	TT
2 ¹ "To the angel of the church in Ephesus write: These are the words of him who holds the seven stars in his right hand and walks among the seven golden lampstands. ² I know your deeds, your hard work and your perseverance. I know that you cannot tolerate wicked people, that you have tested those who claim to be apostles but are not, and have found them false. ³ You have persevered and have endured hardships for my name, and have not grown weary.	2 ¹ "To the **angel**[14] of the church in **Ephesus**[15], write: Thus says the one who holds the seven stars in his right hand, the one who walks among the seven golden lampstands: ² 'I know your **works**[16], which are your **struggle**[17] and your **perseverance**[18]. Because you cannot **bear**[19] evil people, you tested the ones who call themselves apostles but are not and you found them to be liars. ³ You demonstrated perseverance; that is, you bear up for the sake of my name and have not **grown weary**[20]. ⁴ But I have against you that

---

[14] ἄγγελος → The term can mean *"messenger," "envoy," "angel," "guardian," "mediator," "servant of God,"* and also *"servant of Satan"* (Matt. 25:41).

[15] Ἔφεσος → Ephesus, a seaport in w. Asia Minor, famous for the worship of Artemis. (see Excursus 1: Ephesus)

[16] ἔργον → The term means *"work," "deed," "action," "manifestation," "practical proof," "practice," "deed," "accomplishments," "occupation,"* and *"thing."*

[17] κόπος → The term means *"difficulty," "trouble," "work," "labor,"* and *"struggle."*

[18] ὑπομονήν → The term means *"patience," "endurance," "fortitude," "steadfastness,"* and *"perseverance."*

[19] βαστάζω → The term means *"bear," carry," "pick up,"* and *"put up with."*

[20] κοπιάω → The term means *"become weary," "tired," "struggle,"* and *"work hard."*

⁴ Yet I hold this against you: You have forsaken the love you had at first. ⁵ Consider how far you have fallen! Repent and do the things you did at first. If you do not repent, I will come to you and remove your lampstand from its place. ⁶ But you have this in your favor: You hate the practices of the Nicolaitans, which I also hate. ⁷ Whoever has ears, let them hear what the Spirit says to the churches. To the one who is victorious, I will give the right to eat from the tree of life, which is in the paradise of God.	you have forsaken your first love. ⁵ Therefore, remember how far you have fallen and **repent**[21] and do your former works. If not, I will come against you and remove your lampstand from its place, unless you repent. ⁶ But this you do have: you hate the works of the **Nicolaitans**[22], which I also hate. ⁷ Whoever has ears, let them hear what the Spirit says to the churches. I will give the one who conquers permission to eat from **the tree of life**[23], which is in the paradise of God.'"

Ephesus was one of the most important cities of Asia Minor. Municipally, it housed the residence of the Roman governor. Commercially, though it now sits some six miles

---

[21] μετανόησον → This term means "*repent*," "*feel remorse*," and "*change one's mind*." All churches except Smyrna and Philadelphia are challenged to repent. Repentance is not a once-for-all act as a part of initial conversion, but is also a continuing aspect of the Christian life, which must be continually reoriented to the call of Christ.

[22] Νικολαϊτῶν → "*Nicolaitans*," "*followers of Nicolaus*," and it is an unknown sect. (see Excursus 2: The Nicolaitans, Balaam, and Jezebel)

[23] → In the symbolic story, sin had caused humanity to lose its access to the source of life in the Garden of Eden, and so death prevails over all humanity. The triumph of God's reign/Kingdom at the end of history will restore this original blessedness of creation. The Book of Revelation does not picture a return to the Garden, but the bringing forward of the Garden into the eschatological New Jerusalem. This means a forward-looking, hopefully affirmation of human history in this world rather than its ultimate negation (see 21:1-22:5)

inland, at the end of the first century it was a productive port. Religiously, it was a hotbed of pagan worship. The apostle Paul first visited the city briefly in the company of Priscilla and Aquila, whom he left there (Acts 18:19-21). Later, according to Acts 19:8-10, he operated in the city for close to three years. It was during this stay that he wrote his Letters to the Corinthian congregation. The apostle encountered difficulty because of conflicts with artisans crafting images of the Greek goddess Artemis (19:23-41). The Roman imperial cult was also influential; the divination of Julius Caesar had been established in 29 B.C.E. at the direction of his heir, Octavian: Caesar Augustus. Cities granted the privilege to build temples to patron deities were given the "νεωκόρος" or "*temple keeper*" (Acts 19:35). Ephesus received this honor four times, on one significant occasion (ca. 90 C.E.) for the right to honor Domitian, the emperor who ruled when John wrote the Book of Revelation.

- **1** As he does at the beginning of each of the letters, Christ orders John to write to the church's patron angel. The letter must begin with "*thus says....,*" a Hebrew prophetic formula that directly links Christ with Yahweh, the formulation's rightful subject. Christ next describes himself as the one holding the seven stars (Rev. 1:16, 20) and walking among the seven golden lampstands (Rev. 1:12, 13, 20).

> **Excursus 1: Ephesus**
>
> After Rome, Alexandria, and Antioch, Ephesus was the largest city in the Roman Empire (ca. 150,000) and the most important city in Asia; the political, economic, and cultural capital of the province. Ephesus was then a harbor city, but the harbor has silted up over the centuries, and the city is now six miles inland. Tourists can still visit its impressive ruins, including its magnificent theater and library. It contained numerous temples, including no less than six dedicated to Roman emperors. A large temple with a colossus to Domitian was excavated in 1960. A generation before John's time, the city had been a center of the Pauline mission (Acts 18-21; 1 Cor. 15:32; 16:8), and it was still a flourishing center of Pauline Christianity as well as for Christians of other traditions.

- **2** Works are an important concept in the Book of Revelation. John uses the term 20 times; 12 of those occurrences are crammed into chapters 2 and 3. On almost all of those occasions, works are connected to judgment (cf. Rev. 2:23; 18:6; 20:12, 13; 22:12). One's eschatological relationship with God (or lack thereof) depends on the number and caliber of one's works.

John connects and therefore identifies works with the activity of witnessing to the lordship of God and Christ. Christ develops this connection here by associating the word with two clarifying terms: "κόπος" (struggle) and "ὑπομονήν" (perseverance); The "καὶ" ("*and*," translated here "*which are*") that links the clarifying terms is epexegetical; it operates as a clarifying connective. Christ means to say: "*I know your works, which are your struggle and your perseverance/nonviolent resistance…"* The packaging suggests that struggle and perseverance, like works, refer to witnessing activity. John's later use of the terms confirms this thinking. In his only other use of *"struggle,"* he places it in a context where works and the concept of witness are integrally related (Rev. 14:13). At 1:9 and 13:10, the work of endurance/nonviolent resistance and the concept of witnessing are also linked. This same packaging occurs in the opening of Paul's First Letter to the Thessalonians (Thess. 1:3). Perhaps the grouping indicates, as scholars suggest, that John and Paul are operating from a traditional understanding about the relationship of the terms.

    Christ praises the witness work of the Ephesians because it materializes in an important way: they do not tolerate the evil ones who call themselves apostles. Having tested them (cf. 1 John 4:1), the Ephesians recognized them for the liars that they were. John does not use the term *"apostle"* often. It occurs here, at 18:20, and at 21:14. Revelation 21:14 refers to the twelve historical apostles of Jesus. Clearly, they are in view here, though John more likely intends communal leaders, like servants and prophets. The apostle, too, is an authority figure whose words are worthy of obedience, and whose lifestyle is worthy of emulation. These *"apostles"* no doubt were prophetic figures who entered the community in the same manner that false (according to Paul) apostles entered Corinth following Paul's departure and preached a different gospel than the one he had himself taught (2 Cor. 11. And 12;

especially 2 Cor. 11:13, where Paul uses the term "*false apostle*").

How would the Ephesians have tested them? The contextual stress on witnessing suggests that they evaluated communal leaders by judging whether they accommodated themselves to the lordship claims of Rome or defiantly proclaimed the lordship claims of God and Christ. Prophetic leaders like Balaam (2:14), Jezebel (2:20-23), and others who followed the ways of the Nicolaitans (2:6, 15) might claim apostolic status. Nevertheless, because they counseled accommodation with economic, social, political, and cultic activities that either implied or declared outright the legitimacy of imperial lordship, their self-assertions were a lie.

- **3** The Ephesians have demonstrated nonviolent resistance/perseverance, which is to say, they stood behind Christ's name – that is, his lordship – despite the consequences (persecution; cf. 6:9-11). Christ makes his very serious point in an almost entertaining way with two wordplays that cross over from v.2 to v.3. in v. 2, using the verb "βαστάζω" (bear, "*endure*"), he has already announced that the Ephesians do not tolerate false prophets. Appealing to the same verb, he now celebrates that the people who do not bear with evil people do bear up for Christ. The wordplay climaxes in the second half of the verse with the verb "κοπιάω" (labor, struggle) in v. 2. The Ephesians do not grow weary in their wearying struggle to testify to the lordship of God and Christ.

- **4** Despite his praise of the Ephesians, Christ is concerned, for they have abandoned their first love. The loss of love should be interpreted within the broader context of the letter's primary theme: witness to the lordship of God and Christ. Given that the only other time John uses *"love"* (2:19), he also connects it to *"works"* and therefore makes it a defining characteristic of resisting witness, one might reasonably conclude that Christ was annoyed because the church had developed some sort of *"works litmus test"* to determine which efforts of resistance, such as a love for Christ's lordship, were worthy and which were not. Faithful believers were to be celebrated because of the work of witnessing; false apostles were to be tested against it. Apparently, the Ephesians became too discerning. Preoccupation with the work of love for the lordship of Christ overwhelmed an allegiance to the first love they had once demonstrated toward each other. In the same way that a healthy cell can metastasize into a cancerous one, their commendable insight degenerated into discrimination. They segregated those who were deemed workers of appropriate righteousness from those determined to be unrighteous. Once known as a loving community, they had suddenly become a policing one. Ephesian faith had become a matter of Ephesian quality control. Assessment became more important than love.
- **5** Christ's counsel could not be clearer. Using the same command he will again issue at 3:3, he orders the Ephesians to remember what they were doing when they demonstrated their first love. Here and at 3:3,

repentance is preceded by and no doubt based upon this remembrance. Only after the Ephesians remember both the witnessing and the loving behavior that stood them in right relationship with their fellow church members, and therefore with Christ, can they turn back to it. At 2:16, the command to repent occurs without being introduced by the exhortation to remember, but there it is followed up, as are the repent commands here and 3:3, with the threat of judgment. That judgment is expressed through the imagery of the lampstands that Christ used to open his remarks in v. 1. The one who walks in the midst of the lampstands and cares for them will remove this one, this Ephesian church, from its place with the others, people whom it represent repent. Repentance is a key theme throughout Revelation (cf. 1:7; 8:7-13; 9:20-21; 11:1, 13; 15:4; 16:9, 11; 22:11); it is a response to God's forgiving love, the kind of love the Ephesians no longer demonstrate toward one another.

- **6** Christ returns to a mood of praise when he commends the Ephesians for hating the works of the Nicolaitans. Acts 6:5 references a certain Nicolaus, listed with Stephen, as one of a select group of deacons. Whether he has any relation to this group is impossible to determine. Psalm 139:21 expresses a similar sentiment of joy at the people's hatred of an evil that God hates. By definition, hated works must be the opposite of the witnessing works, which Christ favors. They are acts of accommodation to economic, social, political, and cultic practices that promote the lordship of Rome or give direct testimony to that lordship.

> **Excursus 2: The Nicolaitans, Balaam, and Jezebel**
>
> These are all groups of Christians within the churches of Asia. The identity of the Nicolaitans is unclear; neither is it known whether they are identical with those who accept the teaching of *"Balaam"* (2:14) and *"Jezebel"* (2:20). *"Balaam"* and *"Jezebel"* are not the actual names of John's opponents, but are derogatory labels taken from the Old Testament. Balaam was a pagan false prophet who misled Israel during the wilderness period after the exodus from Egypt (Num. 22-24; Deut. 23:5; Josh. 13:22; 24:5). Jezebel was the pagan wife of King Ahab, who persecuted the true prophets (1 Kgs. 16-21; 2 Kgs. 9). The Nicolaitans were probably named after an actual leader. Some Church Fathers of the second century supposed the Nicolaus of Acts 6:5 later developed teachings that were considered heretical by John, but there is no evidence for this. Even if they represented different groups, their common denominator was that in the name of *"progress"* they advocated accommodation to pagan culture, represented by participation in festivals and social occasions that included eating meat ritually sacrificed to idols. John considered such actions an unacceptable compromise with paganism. That the groups existed at all shows that even though John was a Christian prophet who claimed to speak the word of the Lord, his leadership was not uncontested.

- **7** Christ closes with a rare statement that recalls the Jesus of the Gospel tradition. The exhortation, *"Let the one who has an ear hear* [cf. Matt. 11:15; 13:9, 43; Mark 4:9, 23; Luke 8:8; 14:35] *what the Spirit says to the churches,"* repeats at the close of each of the seven letters (Rev. 2:11, 17, 29; 3:6, 13, 22; cf. 13:9). In the Synoptic Gospels, Jesus uses this phrase to encourage an appropriate response to the message he has just conveyed. In Revelation, Christ endorses the ethic of defiant witness. God's Spirit is the medium through which Christ continues to speak.

    A Statement of reward begins with another address that is used at the close of each of the letters: *"to the one who conquers"* (Rev. 2:11, 17, 26; 3:5, 12, 21). To conquer is to witness resistantly. Such conquest, however, does not mean that a believer *"wins."* Jesus, after all, was executed because of the revelation he proclaimed (Rev. 5:6, 9, 12); John is exiled on Patmos (1:9); Antipas was executed (2:13), as are many like him (6:9-11; cf. 11:7; 13:7). Conquest does, however, mean that ultimately the believer will, like Christ, through the very act of witnessing, overwhelm the bestial forces of draconian Rome (12:11; 15:2; 17:14) and obtain eschatological relationship with God. That relationship is symbolized here by the tree of life and paradise, two direct references to the Garden of Eden (Gen. 2-3; cf. Ezek. 31:8-9). John's Christ is initiating a thought here that he will fully develop at 22:2. In the Genesis account, humans were forbidden to eat from *"the tree of life"* for fear they would obtain eternal life (Gen. 3:3, 22-24). Here, eternal life is precisely the reward!

Revelation 2:8~11 → To Smyrna

NIV	TT
⁸"To the angel of the church in Smyrna write:	⁸"And to the angel of the church in **Smyrna**[24], write:
These are the words of him who is the First and the Last, who died and came to life again. ⁹ I know your afflictions and your poverty—yet you are rich! I know about the slander of those who say they are Jews and are not, but are a synagogue of Satan. ¹⁰ Do not be afraid of what you are about to suffer. I tell you, the devil will put some	Thus says the first and the last, who was dead and lived: ⁹ 'I know your **affliction**[25] and your **poverty**[26] (though you are rich), and the slander from those who call themselves Jews, but are not, but are a synagogue of **Satan**[27]. ¹⁰ Fear nothing that you are about to suffer. Indeed, the devil is about to throw some of you into prison so that

---

[24] σμύρνα → "*Smyrna*," a large city on the west coast of Asia Minor (see Excursus 3: Smyrna).

[25] θλῖψις → The term means "*affliction*," "*tribulation*," "*persecution*" and "*oppressions*." It is a word that is often used of the time of crisis and catastrophe that marks the climax of history (e.g., Matt. 24:21), and it is in such terms that Paul might have construed his sufferings (2 Cor. 1:4; 6:4; Phil. 1:17; Col. 1:24) and the suffering of his churches (Phil. 4:14; 1 Thess. 1:6; 3:3, 7).

[26] πτωχεία → The term means "*poverty*," it appears only three times in the New Testament (2 Cor. 8:2, 9; Rev. 2:9). Though riches and poverty could be used in a spiritual sense in the New Testament, as already the case in Judaism (cf. Matt. 5:3; 1 Cor. 4:8,; Eph. 3:8; Rev. 3:17), here literal poverty is meant. This is not because Christianity attracted only poor people in the first century. More likely, church members in Smyrna had suffered economic reversals because of their faith (losing jobs, confiscation of property, vandalization and boycott of their businesses)

[27] σατάν → It means "*the Adversary*," "*Satan*," and "*the enemy of God and his people*." Satan is introduced for the first time. In the vision proper, readers will learn that Satan has been thrown out of heaven and will be bound in prison (Rev. 20:7; cf. 18:2), so its presence on earth is only to be expected (Rev. 12:12; 1 Pet. 5:8). "*Satan*" and "*devil*" are used interchangeably in the Book of Revelation (cf. Rev. 12:9; 20:2).

of you in prison to test you, and you will suffer persecution for ten days. Be faithful, even to the point of death, and I will give you life as your victor's crown. ¹¹ Whoever has ears, let them hear what the Spirit says to the churches. The one who is victorious will not be hurt at all by the second death.	you might be tested, and you will have persecution for ten days. Be faithful until death, and I will give you the crown of life. ¹¹ Whoever has ears, let them hear what the Spirit is saying to the churches. The one who conquers will certainly not be harmed by **the second death**[28].

The address to the angel of the church in Smyrna comes from one who is both eternal (Rev. 1:17) and who has died and is alive (Rev. 1:18). The letter is written to a church that is undergoing *"affliction."* It is one of only two churches of whom nothing negative is said (the other is Philadelphia 3:7-13).

- **8** As he does at the beginning of each of the letters, Christ orders John to write to the church's patron angel. The letter again begins with *"thus says ...,"* a Hebrew prophetic formula that directly links Christ with Yahweh, the formulation's rightful subject. Christ next describes himself as *"the first and the last"* and as the one who was dead, but came back to life.

---

[28] τοῦ θανάτου τοῦ δευτέρου → The phrase means *"the second death."* This is one of John's apocalyptic images for the ultimate judgment of God (Rev. 20:6, 14; 21:8). Those executed for their faith by human courts will be vindicated by God's own verdict at the Last Judgment. See the similar teaching of the Matthean Jesus (Matt. 10:26-33, esp. 10:28). The Jesus of Revelation is no more severe on such issues than the Jesus of the Gospels.

> **Excursus 3: Smyrna**
>
> Smyrna was a wealthy city. Its harbor made it a strong commercial port center. Located approximately thirty-five miles to the north of Ephesus, it also sat at the end of a lucrative Asia Minor trade route. The city was also well known for its dedication to Rome and Greco-Roman cultic religion. As early as 195 B.C.E., the city built a temple dedicated to the worship of the goddess Roma, patron divinity of the Empire. In 26 C.E., the emperor Tiberius, who had already allowed the people of Smyrna to dedicate a temple in honor of the deceased Augustus, and the Roman Senate established Smyrna as a "νεωκόρος," "*temple keeper*" (Acts 19:35), for the cult of Tiberius. Despite its devotion to the imperial cult and its construction of numerous pagan temples, like that to the healing god Asclepius, the city also developed a strong Christian presence. Polycarp, the bishop of Smyrna, is a well-chronicled figure. Ignatius, bishop of Antioch, stopped in the city when he was being escorted to Rome for execution (ca. 107 C.E.). Before his death, he wrote letters of encouragement both to the church at Smyrna and to Polycarp, who would suffer a similar fate (ca. 155 C.E.).

- **9** Christ claims to know both their persecution and their poverty. Though he speaks about the two together, he does not equate them. Their persecution is not their impoverishment. At 1:9, John testifies that his persecution occurs as a direct result of his witnessing to the lordship of God and Jesus Christ. The fact that he and Christ-believers are partners in this grim reality implies that their persecution, too, is a direct result of their comparable witnessing.

Persecution is also a by-product of the hostility that erupted between the Smyrna church and its Jewish neighbors. Like its six sister cities, Smyrna was a hotbed of imperial cultic worship. Because Greco-Roman culture did not separate the sacred and secular realms, spiritual activity had dramatic political implications. Citizens were required by law to sacrifice to the emperor on various special occasions, and *"those refusing to participate were seen as politically disloyal and unpatriotic."* Apparently, Smyrna's Jewish community took advantage of this situation. Being an ancient religion with an established tradition, Judaism had achieved sufficient status to broker concessions with regard to the worship of other deities. Jews were not required to participate in the imperial and Greco-Roman cultus in ways that compromised their monotheistic beliefs. The Romans were not so accommodating to newer religions. Fortunately for Christ-believers, the Romans, before the Neronian persecutions, were either unable or did not care to distinguish between Christians and Jews. Following that transitional moment in history, however, Christians lived a much more precarious existence if the Romans were able to identify them and require from them recognition of their gods' and their emperor's divinity, and instead encountered resistance. According to *"The Martyrdom of Polycarp,"* *"[Polycarp] was told by the Roman governor that he would be executed if he did not give a public, token acknowledgement to Caesar as Lord.*

John apparently believed that in Smyrna the Jewish community did the Romans' investigative work for them. Knowing that the Christ-believers, many of whom were themselves probably Jews, would not acknowledge Caesar's lordship, synagogue members pointed them out and thereby offered them up to persecution. It is for such scandalous squealing that John labels their fellowship a synagogue of Satan. The epithet is not so much an anti-Jewish denunciation as it is a reference to an intra-Jewish conflict that leads to betrayal. (A similar contextual circumstance of intra-Jewish debate probably lies behind a corresponding situation in John 8:30-47, where people who refer to themselves as children of Abraham are rejected as such because of their rejection and condemnation of Jesus.) The witness to the lordship of Christ rankled Smyrna's synagogue community as much as it did the Romans, if for quite different reasons.

It is important to speak carefully about John's *"synagogue of Satan"* language. John lashed out against one minority community that tried to protect its religious turf by seeking approval and status from the powerful majority community and subverting the status of a similarly situated minority group. The harsh language is, however, incredibly unfortunate. Taken out of its social and historical context, it can be and has been used to incite virulent forms of anti-Judaism. When teaching or preaching from this text, or the comparable one in the Philadelphia letter (Rev. 3:7-13), the contemporary interpreter must focus on John's intent rather than his words. The seer's condemnation applies to any minority community that would sell out another for reasons of doctrinal difference or social standing. The enduring issue, then, is one of ethics, not ethnicity.

Context is also crucial for understanding John's comment about the church's poverty (cf. Rev. 3:17). Smyrna was a wealthy city. The church's impoverishment was an indication that its members did not participate in the life of the city in ways that would move some of that wealth in its or its members' direction. *"Indeed, the imperial cult permeated virtually every aspect of city and often even village life in Asia Minor, so that individuals could aspire to economic prosperity and greater social standing only by participating to some degree in the Roman cult."* Their impoverishment was an indication that they had not bought in or, one might more appropriately say, sold out.

- **10 – 11** The malevolent circumstances plaguing the church are a direct result of the satanic behavior that John describes in chapter 12 (cf. Rev. 12:17). This behavior lives itself out through the activities of the synagogue (Rev. 2:9), which John believes is, like Rome (Rev. 13), acting at Satan's behest. The resulting imprisonments will be a time of testing. John's description of this imprisonment as persecution indicates that witnessing even if such witness was compelled because of the blasphemous slander of synagogue members, triggers the hostility. The testing language also reminds John's hearers and readers of Christ's commendation of the Ephesians for testing false apostles (Rev. 2:2). Those who are castigated and those who are praised are tested on the same content: witness.

To encourage the Smyrnaeans, Christ reveals that their time of trial will be brief. The ten days, reminiscent of a short period of trial in Dan. 1:12-15, can and will be endured, even to the death. Christ surely means even to the first death. It is the second death, the one that separates humans from God forever, that the Smyrnaeans should fear. A first death that occurs because of one's faithful witnessing is not the end, but the sure beginning of eschatological relationship with God. The Lord who engaged death and through resurrection conquered it offers this people who populate a portion of the reign of priests (Rev. 1:6; 5:10; 20:6) a crown, not of kingship or valor, but of eternity (cf. Zech. 6:11, 14, where a crown is bestowed upon the high priest). At 20:6, John reiterates with direct language what he pictures here through the symbolism of the crown: these conquering priests will escape the destruction that is the second death. The Smyrnaeans were much richer than they had ever known; their impoverishment, or more correctly the witnessing behavior that led to their impoverishment, had already bought them eternal life.

Christ closes this letter as he does the others, with a call for those in the churches with an ear to listen to what the Spirit says and a promise for those who conquer. The actual content of the promise, freedom from the second death, is unique to the Smyrna congregation.

Revelation 2:12~17 → To Pergamum

NIV	TT
¹² "To the angel of the church in Pergamum write: These are the words of him who has the sharp, double-edged sword. ¹³ I know where you live—where Satan has his throne. Yet you remain true to my name. You did not renounce your faith in me, not even in the days of Antipas, my faithful witness, who was put to death in your city—where Satan lives. ¹⁴ Nevertheless, I have a few things against you: There are some among you who hold to the teaching of Balaam,	¹² "And to the angel of the church in **Pergamum**[29], write: Thus says the one who has **the sharp, double-edged word**[30]: ¹³ 'I know where you live, where the throne of Satan is. Yet you hold[31] fast to my name and you did not deny **my faith**[32] in the days of Antipas, my faithful witness, who was executed among you, where Satan lives. ¹⁴ But, I have a few things against you: you have some there who hold to the teaching of Balaam, who

---

[29] → Starting in 133 B.C.E. this city was the capital of the Roman province of Asia. It was the center of imperial worship. This is the first city in Asia to have a temple dedicated to Augustus and to Rome in 29 B.C.E

[30] τὴν ῥομφαίαν τὴν δίστομον τὴν ὀξεῖαν →The Phrase means "*The sharp double-edged sword.*" It cuts both ways; it strikes the failures of the faithful as well as the enemy.

[31] κρατέω → The term means "*arrest*," "*take hold of,*" "*grasp,*" "*seize,*" "*attain,*" "*hold,*" "*hold back,*" "*hold fast,*" "*keep,*" and "*retain.*" This term appears three times in this text. "*hold my name*" in verse 13, "*holding the teaching of Balaam*" in verse 14, and "*holding the teaching of the Nicolaitans*" in verse 15. This is one of the key terms in this text. The theme of holding the name of Christ and his faith is important and emphasized in this text.

[32] τὴν πίστιν μου → The phrase means "*the faith of me,*" so "*my faith.*" The construction is a subjective genitive. The voice refers to the faith that Jesus himself bore, not faith in Jesus (objective genitive).

| who taught Balak to entice the Israelites to sin so that they ate food sacrificed to idols and committed sexual immorality. ¹⁵ Likewise, you also have those who hold to the teaching of the Nicolaitans. ¹⁶ Repent therefore! Otherwise, I will soon come to you and will fight against them with the sword of my mouth.

¹⁷ Whoever has ears, let them hear what the Spirit says to the churches. To the one who is victorious, I will give some of the hidden manna. I will also give that person a white stone with a new name written on it, known only to the one who receives it. | taught Balak to throw a stumbling block before the people of Israel, so they would **eat meat sacrificed to idols**[33] and commit the sexual offense of prostitution[34]. ¹⁵ Thus you also have some who hold to the teaching of the Nicolaitans as well.

¹⁶ **Repent**[35] therefore; if not, I will come against you soon and wage war against them with **the sword of my mouth**[36].

¹⁷ Whoever has ears, let them hear what the Spirit is saying to the churches. To the one who conquers I will give some of the hidden manna, and I will give that one **a white stone**[37], and on |

---

[33] εἰδωλόθυτον → Only as a noun. It means *"meat offered to an idol."*

[34] πορνεῦσαι → The term means *"to prostitute," "practice prostitution,"* and *"practice sexual immorality."* In the Septuagint, particularly in Hosea chapter 1 through 3, this term was used for the activities of Israel, *"forsaking the Lord."* In 1ˢᵗ Timothy, it was used to describe sexual immorality, in 1ˢᵗ Corinthians, it described sexual intercourse with prostitutes, and elsewhere it describes *"greedy"* and *"godless."* Thus the term does not only refer to sexual sins, but as a characteristic of idolatry.

[35] μετανοέω → The term means *"to repent," "feel remorse,"* and *"change one's mind."*

[36] → The mouth location indicates that this sword is Christ's word of universal, and sharp prophetic word (*"tongue"*) of judgment. The word is the weapon against the powers and the lordship of Rome.

[37] ψῆφον λευκήν → The phrase could mean *"bright pebble,"* or *"white/shining vote."* The term "ψῆφον" means *"vote,"* and white is a positive color in the Book of Revelation. So it may mean *"favorable vote,"* or a token of membership. Also *"white stones"* were

> the stone is written a new name that no one knows except the one who receives it.'"

Though the governing Roman proconsul may have officially resided in Ephesus, the seat of Roman administration for all of Asia Minor was Pergamum. This large and vibrant city housed one of the most celebrated libraries in the ancient world, even rivaling the grandeur of the more acclaimed library in Alexandria. The worship of Greco-Roman deities flourished in the city. Pergamum boasted not only a great temple to Zeus and an entire complex dedicated to Asclepius, but also temples to divinities like Athena, Dionysus, and Demeter. There were also powerful ties to the Roman imperial cult. In 29 B.C.E., the emperor Augustus allowed the city to become the first municipality in Asia Minor to build a temple honoring the emperor's deified status.

- **12** As he does at the beginning of each of the letter, Christ orders John to write to the church's patron angel. The letter must begin with *"thus says…,"* a Hebrew prophetic formula that directly links Christ with Yahweh, the formulation's rightful subject. Christ next describe himself as the one who has *"the double-edged sword."*
- **13** Christ confides that he knows where the church members live. The verb is so important that Christ repeats it at the close of the verse. John consistently

---

used as entrance tickets to plays and banquets. I think either of these explanations could apply, *"favorable vote"* in the final judgment or a ticket to the messianic banquet.

uses it (3:10; 6:10; 8:13; 11:10; 13:8, 12, 14; 17:2, 8) to designate the inhabitants (dwellers) of the earth who have accommodated themselves to Rome's domination and the lordship claims that arise from it. Such inhabitants necessarily contest both the witness to the exclusive lordship of God and Jesus Christ and anyone testifying to such a rebellious claim. Perhaps John alludes here to Ezek. 12:2, where the prophet was warned by God that he was living in a dangerous, rebellious place. John's Christ so irrevocably connects Pergamum with such rebellion against God and he labels it the abode of Satan's throne.

There are several plausible reasons why the city may have earned such a deleterious moniker: (1) it was the seat of Roman administration for Asia Minor; (2) it hosted a great temple to Zeus; (3) it boasted a plethora of pagan temples; and (4) it reveled in its celebrity as the first Asia Minor municipality to build a temple deifying an emperor. Probably some combination of these factors led to the dubious designation. John had in mind the opposition to the lordship of God and Jesus Christ that the categories represented.

Despite their precarious location, the Pergamum Christ-believers hold ("κρατέω," 2:25; 3:11; cf. 14:12) to Christ's name and do not deny Christ's faith. A similar formulation occurs at 3:8, where Christ commends the Sardis church for keeping his word and not denying his name. Though the verb he uses there for "*keeping*" ("τηρέω") is not the same one used here, 3:11 follows up with the same verbal formulation, so as to suggest that Christ is thinking in the same thematic terms. These are the same terms of praise that Christ offers the Ephesians who bear up Christ's name. The name of Christ is a euphemism for the reputation of Christ as the true Lord, "*Christ's faith*" is not faith "*in Christ*," but the very faith that Christ himself bore, the faith in his own lordship, to which he testified and for which he died on the cross. The Pergamum Christians emulate the faith that Christ himself demonstrated. This is how they witness faithfully. The poster child for "*faithful witness*" is the executed Antipas. Except for this salutary recognition here, he is an unknown figure. Christ describes him with the same terminology that is used to describe Christ himself at 1:5. Antipas is the ultimate representative of non-violent resistance.

- **14 – 16** Just as Christ tempered his initial praise of the Ephesians with chastisement (2:4), so here, after extolling the Pergamum believers for their faithfulness, he declares that he has a few things against them. He really has one primary concern. Perhaps he speaks about it in the plural because the single concern involves two false prophetic entities: Balaam (cf. 2 Pet. 2:15; Jude 11) and the Nicolaitans. He calls up Balaam first. The fact that some believers "*hold to*" the teaching of Balaam rather than Christ's name indicates that Balaam was a prophetic leader respected (by some) in the community. Though the Pergamum believers have stood fast before external inquisition, they have not been so successful at resisting internal forces that lure them away from a proper witness to Christ's lordship.

Balaam could well have been the historical name of John's opponent at Pergamum. It is more likely, given John's penchant for symbolism, that the name was chosen for paradigmatic reasons. It has a colloquial Hebrew meaning, *"one who consumes the people,"* which partners well with John's other opponent group in the city, the Nicolaitans (cf. 2:6). Their name, in Greek this time, means *"one who conquers the laity [people]."* Even more likely, John is, as he will do with the so-called Jezebel of Thyatira, crafting a cunning scenario of guilt by association. He applies to his historical opponents the names of people who are well known as traditional enemies of God's people. The Balaam of Num. 22-24 and 31:16 was a seer sent by Balak, a king rivaling the Israelites, to curse the people of God. Overwhelmed by God's power, Balaam blessed the people instead. And yet, his story's narrative connection with Num. 25, where Israelite men became sexually involved with foreign women and therefore cultically involved with their deities, and the explicit condemnation in Num. 31:16, led tradition to charge Balaam with leading the people idolatrously astray.

Pergamum's Balaam teaches the people that it is permissible to eat meat that has been sacrificed to idol gods and to commit the sexual offense of prostitution. In reality, both offense are the same. For John, people who eat meat that has been sacrificed to foreign gods give credence to the reality and lordship of those gods; those people have therefore prostituted themselves to a foreign faith (cf. 17:2, 5, 18:3, 9). While some commentators argue that the term John employs, "εἰδωλόθυτον," refers to the meat that was sacrificed and then eaten later, after the sacrificial ceremonies had concluded. Beale contends that the term refers to the eating of the contraband meat as a part of the ceremony itself. He therefore argues that John is concerned not just about the leftover eating, but the actual participation in foreign cult (248). The narrative does not itself offer enough evidence to decide the matter. Either way, the impact of the concern is the same. John sees the eating of the meat, whether as part of the service or afterward, as worthy of the fullest measure of condemnation. Where Paul, in his Corinthian correspondence (cf. 1 Cor. 8-10), had offered the very practical advice that strong Christians could eat meat sacrificed to idols unless their behavior offended the spiritual psyche of weaker Christians for whom such activity seemed sinful, John overrules the behavior outright. He does so no doubt knowing that the members of his church in Pergamum do not believe in the reality or lordship of such deities. Their participation was exclusively social and economic. The sacrificial ceremonies and meals were as much communal as religious affairs. Artisan, trade, and other business associations aligned their groups with patron deities. Funeral associations often did the same. Participation in such groups, which allowed for upward social and economic mobility, often included the obligatory participation in such a group's cultic activities. Unlike the believers in Smyrna, who apparently opted out of such activities and thereby impoverished themselves as a result, many believers in Pergamum wanted to participate, wanted to move up socially, and therefore wanted assurance that their behavior was not problematic. Balaam provided that assurance with his teachings. Since the Nicolaitans are mentioned as operating similarly to Balaam, it is probably that they provided the same assurance. The "*thus*" which opens the Nicolaitan discussion (v. 15) intentionally refers hearers and readers back to the concern about Balaam (v. 14) as though they were in reality the same concern. Indeed, given John's close narrative association of the two, it is likely that Balaam was an identifiable leader within the Nicolaitan movement. There is little doubt that both were trying their best to help their fellow Christ-believers accommodate their faith to the new circumstances in which they found themselves. However, John's conservative, intolerant attitude disallowed any kind of compromise; Balaam and the Nicolaitans and those who followed their teaching were guilty of spiritual prostitution.

    Christ heightens the stakes by declaring that he is coming soon. For unrepentant, accommodating church members, his coming would not be salvific, but judgmental. The backside of the double-edged sword was meant for them. The language of repentance in Revelation has this consistent sense of turning back to the kind of committed faith that church members first exhibited, presumably when John was teaching in their midst. Of the twelve occurrences of "μετανοέω" (repent) in the Book of Revelation, eight occur in the letters to the seven churches (Rev. 2-3), and six of those target the infamous eating of meat sacrificed to idol gods (cf. 2:16, 21 [twice], 22; 3:3, 19).

- **17** Christ closes this letter as he does the others, with a call for those in the churches with an ear to listen to what the Spirit says and a promise for those who conquer. In Pergamum, Christ promises to give the conquerors the hidden manna and a white stone with a secret name. the hidden manna was a stroke of rhetorical brilliance; to a people starved for idol food, he offered food delivered directly from the one true Lord and God (cf. Exod. 16:31-35; Numb. 11:6-9; Deut. 8:3, 16; Ps. 78:24). According to the tradition that surrounded the destruction of Jerusalem by the Babylonians (586 B.C.E.), the prophet Jeremiah hid the ark of the covenant, which contained some of the Exodus manna, so that it would not be captured (2 Macc. 2:4-8). The ark's location was lost and was promised to remain a secret until the final age. For the Pergamum Christ-believers, this final age would no doubt appear as a messianic banquet feast (cf. Mark 14:25; Matt. 22:2-9), as opposed to an idol feast, where the served food would be (eternal) life affirming. The meal choices were clear: seek false satisfaction now or be granted true satiation upon Christ's imminent return.

The other victory symbol was a white stone. Though such stones were often used as magical amulets, given this context of entrance into the eschatological meal, it is likely that John was borrowing from the tradition of the white stone used in antiquity to acquit a person of a crime or enable a person's entrance into a coveted affair. *"Either of these explanations could apply, the former indicating that the faithful are acquitted in the final judgment, the latter symbolizing their entrance into the messianic banquet"* (Reddish 62). The new name that no one knows (cf. 19:12), except the one who receives the stone, was no doubt Christ's new name, which Christ later says he himself will write on the person of the believer (3:12). In chapter 3, too, the inscription of the name is tied to the metaphor of entrance into God's eschatological life (cf. 14:1; 22:4). In essence, John is declaring that even now Christ is engraving tickets to Christ's own messianic banquet.

Revelation 2:18~29 → To Thyatira

NIV	TT
¹⁸ "To the angel of the church in Thyatira write: These are the words of the Son of God, whose eyes are like blazing fire and whose feet are like burnished bronze. ¹⁹ I know your deeds, your love and faith, your service and perseverance, and that you are now doing more than you did at first. ²⁰ Nevertheless, I have this against you: You tolerate that woman Jezebel, who calls herself a prophet. By her teaching she misleads my servants into sexual immorality and the eating of food sacrificed to idols. ²¹ I have given her time to repent	¹⁸ "And to the angel of the church in **Thyatira**[38], write: Thus says **the Son of God**[39], the one who has eyes like a flame of fire and whose feet are like burnished bronze: ¹⁹ 'I know your works and your love and your faith and your **service**[40] and your perseverance, and your last works are greater than your first. ²⁰ But I have against you that you tolerate the woman **Jezebel**[41], who calls herself a prophetess and teaches and deceives my servants to commit the sexual offense of prostitution and to eat

---

[38] **Thyatira** → A center of industry and commerce forty-five miles southeast of Pergamum, mentioned elsewhere in the New Testament only as the city of the Christian businesswoman Lydia (Acts 16:14).

[39] ὁ υἱὸς τοῦ θεου → The phrase means *"the Son of God."* This was used only here in the Book of Revelation. The title contrasts the risen Christ with the Caesars, who also claimed to be *"sons of God."*

[40] διακονία → This term means *"service," "ministry," "feeding others," "distributing of charities," "the office of the deacon in the church,"* and *"teaching of the Word."* This term appears only here (2:19) in the entire Book of Revelation.

[41] Ἰεζάβελ → Jezebel from 1 Kgs 16:31-33 (see Excursus 4: Jezebel)

of her immorality, but she is unwilling. ²² So I will cast her on a bed of suffering, and I will make those who commit adultery with her suffer intensely, unless they repent of her ways. ²³ I will strike her children dead. Then all the churches will know that I am he who searches hearts and minds, and I will repay each of you according to your deeds.

²⁴ Now I say to the rest of you in Thyatira, to you who do not hold to her teaching and have not learned Satan's so-called deep secrets, 'I will not impose any other burden on you, ²⁵ except to hold on to what you have until I come.'

²⁶ To the one who is victorious and does my will to the end, I will give authority over the nations— ²⁷ that one 'will rule them with an iron scepter and will dash them to pieces like

meat sacrificed to idols. ²¹ And I gave her time to repent, but she does not wish to repent of her prostitution. ²² Indeed, I am throwing her into a **sickbed**[42], and I am throwing the ones who commit sexual offense with her into great distress unless they repent of her works; ²³ I will even kill her children with the plague. Then all the churches will know that **I AM**[43] the one who examines minds and hearts, and I will give to each of you according to your works.

²⁴ But I say to the rest of you in Thyatira, as many as do not hold this teaching, who do not know the (as they say) deep things of Satan: I do not throw another burden upon you. ²⁵ Only hold fast to what you have until I come.

²⁶ And, as for the one who

---

[42] κλίνη → This term means "*a small bed*," "*a small bed/couch on which a sick man is carried*," or "*a sickbed.*"
[43] ἐγώ εἰμι → The phrase means "*I AM*," the sacred name of God in Exodus 3:14.

pottery'—just as I have received authority from my Father. ²⁸ I will also give that one the morning star. ²⁹ Whoever has ears, let them hear what the Spirit says to the churches.	conquers and keeps my works until the end, I will give authority over the nations, ²⁷ and that one will shepherd them with a rod of iron as when clay pots are shattered. ²⁸ Just as I have received from my Father, so I give to him the morning star. ²⁹ Whoever has ears, let them hear what the Spirit is saying to the churches.'"

In Thyatira, cultic propaganda went so far as to declare the Roman emperor the incarnation of Apollo, and therefore a son of Zeus. This religious-political alliance heightened the risk for people who tried to opt out of the Greco-Roman cultic infrastructure; rejection of the gods implied resistance to the state. Complicating matters even further was the fact that Thyatira hosted a large number of trade guilds with strong cultic affiliations. Especially important were industries of wool, textile, and the manufacture of purple dye (cf. Acts 16:14-15)

- **18** As he does at the beginning of each of the letters, Christ orders John to write to the church's patron angel. The letter must begin with *"thus says ...,"* a Hebrew prophetic formula that directly links Christ with Yahweh, the formulation's rightful subject. At this point, Christ offers something unique, the titular designation of Christ as the Son of God. Unlike the other designations for Christ at this point in each of the letters, this title does not refer back to the description of Christ at 1:12-20. In fact, it occurs nowhere else in all of Revelation. There is a metaphorical connection to Christ as *"son"* at 12:5. Even here, however, the title Son of God is not deployed. It does, however, reinforce the presentation of Christ offered at 1:12-20 revealed him to be; he is not just an emissary for God, but God's own Son. The designation of sonship contributes to the political polarization. Emperors often proclaimed themselves as *"sons"* of the deceased and deified emperor whom they had succeeded. The point could not be missed: Christ's sonship is the true one, established in relationship to the true Lord. Having made this provocative point, Christ returns to the pattern of connecting to the character traits revealed at 1:12-20. He describes himself as the one whose eyes are like a flame of fire and whose feet are like burnished bronze.

- **19** Christ knows about the work of witness in the Thyatiran community. Their witness is exemplified by love, something the Ephesians no longer were demonstrating (see 2:4). In celebrating their faith, Christ alludes to the kind of witness that refuses to deny the name and thus the lordship of Christ (see 2:13). Such defiant witness performs a great service (a term John uses only here) in bolstering the larger mission of testimony to the lordship of God and Jesus Christ. Such work is a nonviolent resistance to claims of Roman imperial lordship. In fact, some of their more recent acts of defiant witness were the most noteworthy of all.

- **20** As he did in his comments to the churches of both Ephesus and Pergamum, Christ chastises the community after concluding his initial salutary remarks (cf. 2:4, 14). The problem is simply stated: the community tolerated the woman Jezebel.

    Jezebel's name, and the connection made between this name, fornication, and the eating of idol meat clarifies the problem. Like Balaam, who, as an apparent member of the Nicolaitans (2:15), counseled a "*gospel*" different from John's, this Jezebel operates as a prophetic leader in the church. Since the objectionable message she proclaimed was the same message proffered by Balaam and the Nicolaitans, it is probable that she, too, was a Nicolaitan. The name "*Jezebel*" was doubtless not her real name but an epithet that John attached to this rival charismatic leader for the same reason that he attached the legendary name of Balaam to his Pergamum prophetic rival. It is demagoguery by association. John undermines her counsel by discrediting her person; he associates her and her teaching with the work of the infamous person from Israel's past (cf. 1 Kgs. 16:31; 18:4, 13; 19:1-3, where she even tries to kill the prophet Elijah; 1 Kgs. 21; 2 Kgs. 9).

    The first Jezebel was immortalized as the manipulative foreign wife of the Israelite king Ahab. The queen used her influence to prop up her native Baal cult, discredit and destroy the prophets of Yahweh, and lead the people idolatrously astray. The rival woman prophet of Thyatira was correspondingly influential. Christ therefore describes her evil in exactly the same way that he described Balaam's offense. Though the sequence shifts slightly, the words themselves are the same; she approves the eating of meat sacrificed to idols, an act that causes a believer to prostitute one's faith in Christ. She assured John's charges that it was perfectly acceptable to participate fully in the imperial and pagan cult activities of one's trade guild, given that one knew the guild's patron deities to be nothing more than empty idols. Her counsel allowed Christ-believers to integrate themselves into the social, political, and economic life of the city and thereby prosper from the connections they made.

Excursus 4: Jezebel
1. The daughter of Ethbaal, priest-king of Tyre and Sidon. She was married to Ahab, to ratify an alliance between Tyre and Israel, by which Omri, Ahab's father, sought to offset the hostility of Damascus towards Israel (880 B.C.E.). Provision was made for her to continue to worship her native god Baal in Samaria, her new home (1 Kgs. 16:31-33).

She had a strong, domineering character, and was self-willed and forceful. A fanatical devotee of Melqart, the Tyrian Baal, her staff numbered 450 of his prophets and 400 prophets of the goddess Asherah, by the time Ahab was king (1 Kgs. 18:19). She clamored for her god to have at least equal rights with Yahweh, God of Israel. This brought her into conflict with the prophet Elijah. A battle between Yahweh and Baal was fought on Mt. Carmel, when Yahweh triumphed gloriously (1 Kgs. 18:17-40). Even so, this and the massacre of her prophets, instead of diminishing her zeal, augmented it.

> Her conception of an absolute monarchy was at variance with the Hebrew covenant-relationship between Yahweh, the king and the people. She took the lead in the incident of Naboth's vineyard with high-handed, unscrupulous action, affecting the whole community as well as undermining the throne of Ahab. It resulted in the prophetic revolution and the extermination of the house of Ahab. She had written letters and used her husband's seal (1 Kgs. 21:8).
>
> After Ahab's death, Jezebel continued as a power in Israel for 10 years, in her role as queen-mother, throughout the reign of Ahaziah, then during Jehoram's lifetime. When Jehoram was killed by Jehu she attired herself regally (2 Kgs. 9:30), and awaited him. She mocked Jehu, and went to her fate with courage and dignity (842 B.C.E.).
>
> It is remarkable that Yahweh was honored in the naming of her three children, Ahaziah, Jehoram and Athaliah (if indeed she was Athaliah's mother), but they may have been born before her ascendancy over Ahab became so absolute.
>
> 2. In the letter to the church at Thyatira (Rev. 2:20), *"that Jezebel of a woman"* is the designation given to a prophetess who encouraged immorality and idolatry under the cloak of religion. This could refer to an individual, or to a group within the church. It indicates that the name had become a byword for apostasy.

- **21 – 23** The theme of repentance recurs (cf. vv. 5, 16). Interesting here is the fact that God's gracious offer extends not only to the people who have been led astray but even to the person intentionally misguiding them. Jezebel, however, rebuffs God's overture. In punishment, John's Christ promises to throw her onto what is most likely a sickbed. Even her children would be struck dead. This discomforting image is metaphorical. John is no more speaking about literal children than he is speaking about the literal, historical Jezebel. Her children are the "*offspring*" of her activities, which commend accommodation to the lordship of Rome; they emulate Jezebel's idolatrous ways, live them, and subsequently teach them to others. They will therefore be struck down as she herself will be struck down. They must be struck down, lest they continue leading God's people astray.

As a result of Christ's intervention, all the churches will know that Christ is indeed the Lord who is responsible for executing eschatological judgment. The "*I AM*" establishes Christ's connection with God and thus authorizes his activity. The theme of judgment continues with the clarification that Christ examines hearts and minds as if they are open books and, on the basis of what he finds, gives to each what their works of either witness or accommodation deserve. This discerning activity also connects Christ integrally with God. In the Hebrew Scriptures, God is the one who judges hearts and minds (Prov. 24:12; Jer. 11:20; 17:10); Paul confirms this assertion at Rom. 8:27.

- **24 - 25** All Christ wanted was that his people stand fast for their faith. Jezebel apparently claimed some deeper insight into how God was operating in the world. These "*deep things*" were probably the rationales she used to endorse idol cult participation. She no doubt intended some deep knowledge from God; Christ mocks it as *"of Satan."* Many Thyatirans were drowning in this so-called deep way of thinking. Christ therefore endorses and celebrates those who recognized the truth and saw her teaching for the evil that it was. He refuses, however, to substitute his own counter-complexities of (deep) mystical thinking. Christ's only burden is a simple one (cf. Acts 15:28-29): until his imminent return, the people must hold fast to the work of resisting imperial lordship claims, a resistance symbolized here by their refusal to eat meat sacrificed to idols.

- **26 – 28** A statement of reward begins the address at the close of each letter: *"to the one who conquers."* Here, Christ promises authority over the nations. Unfortunately, that authority is already held by the Romans. If John's believers are to have it, God must, on their behalf, take it away from others. Indeed, just after God promises universal authority to the people of God at Ps. 2:8-9, God warns the kings of the earth that if they do not submit to this new reality, they will be destroyed (Ps. 2:10-11). John's spiritual vision has a potent and threatening political implication. The threat operates through the imagery of the iron rod. The symbol mimics Christ's own rule at 12:5 and 19:15 as one of shepherding. Such symbolism provides not only for the reality of the nations' judgment but also for the possibility and even hope of repentance. The warning, then, if people properly receive it, should guide them back into the proper work of witnessing to the lordship of God and Christ.

The eschatological portion of the promise resides principally in the image of the morning star. Used again at 22:16, where Christ is himself identified as the star, and appealing to Num. 24:14-20, the symbol refers to Christ's messianic status and future rule. Christ's promise that he will convey this star to the believers in Thyatira is a powerful testimony that he will give them a prized place in his messianic reign. Ironically, in the Numbers account it is none other than Balaam who declares the oracle that, according to the interpretation here, establishes Christ's eschatological status. While the present Balaam, the Nicolaitans, and Jezebel lead the people astray, the past Balaam, in spite of himself, proclaimed the word and the circumstance to which the people should hold fast: Christ, and only Jesus Christ, is Lord.

- **29** Christ closes this letter as he does the others, with a call for those in the churches with an ear to listen to what the Spirit says.

Revelation 3:1~6 → To Sardis

NIV	TT
3 ¹ "To the angel of the church in Sardis write: These are the words of him who holds the seven spirits of God and the seven stars. I know your deeds; you have a reputation of being alive, but you are dead. ² Wake up! Strengthen what remains and is about to die, for I have found your deeds unfinished in the sight of my God. ³ Remember, therefore, what you have received and heard; hold it fast, and repent. But if you do not wake up, I will come like a thief, and you will not know at what time I will come to you. ⁴ Yet you have a few people in Sardis who have	**3** ¹ "And to the angel of the church in Sardis, write: Thus says the one who has the seven spirits of God and the seven stars: 'I know your works; you have a name for being alive, but you are dead. ² **Wake up**[44] and strengthen the remaining things that are about to die, for I have not found your works complete in the sight of my God. ³ Therefore remember what you have received and heard; **hold to**[45] it, and **repent**[46]. If, therefore, you do not wake up, I will come like a thief, and you will not know at what hour I will come to you. ⁴ But you have a few people in Sardis who have not soiled their clothes; they will walk with me in **white/dazzling**[47]

---

[44] γρηγορέω → A periphrastic construction whose literal imperative sense is "*be watchful*," "*be alert*," and "*keep awake*."

[45] τηρέω → It means "*keep watch over*," "*hold*," "*reserve*," "*preserve*," "*keep promise*," and "*obey*." One of the key terms in the Book of Revelation.

[46] μετανοέω → It means "*feel remorse*," "*repent*," and literally "*change one's mind*."

[47] λευκός → The term means "*white*," "*shining*," "*bright*," "*dazzling*" and "*gleaming*."

| not soiled their clothes. They will walk with me, dressed in white, for they are worthy. ⁵ The one who is victorious will, like them, be dressed in white. I will never blot out the name of that person from the book of life, but will acknowledge that name before my Father and his angels. ⁶ Whoever has ears, let them hear what the Spirit says to the churches. | splendor, because they are worthy. ⁵ Thus the one who conquers will be clothed in dazzling clothes, and I will certainly not blot his name out of **the Book of Life**[48]; I will **acknowledge**[49] his name before my Father and before his angels.

⁶ Whoever has ears, let them hear what the Spirit says to the churches. |

Sardis was the proverbial fortified city set on a hill. Thought by its inhabitants to be impregnable, it cultivated a reputation of invulnerability. As the capital of the kingdom of Lydia, Sardis was the seat of Croesus, a king whose legendary wealth derived from two primary sources: the gold in the river running through the city and the export trade of woven textiles. Ironically, the city was also renowned because of the infamous collapses of its acclaimed defenses. In 549 B.C.E., Croesus, engaged in a conflict with Cyrus of Persia, retired to Sardis, convinced that Cyrus would not engage him there. He was mistaken. Cyrus attacked but after two weeks bogged down in his siege. The offensive prevailed through an act of stealth. Like a thief in the night, one of Cyrus' soldiers stole into

---

[48] τῆς βίβλου τῆς ζωῆς → It means "The Book of Life" or literally "the scroll of the living." (see Excursus 5: The Book of Life)

[49] ἐξομολογέω → It means *"to confess," "to profess," "to acknowledge openly and joyfully,"* and *"to give praise to."* This term appears only here in the entire Book of Revelation.

the city through an unguarded spot in the fortifications. Centuries later, in 195 B.C.E., the Seleucid King Antiochus III also claimed control of the city because of the negligence of its protectors. The moral lessons derived from this series of events (one must avoid pride, arrogance, and over-confidence and be prepared for unexpected reversals of fortune) became a *topos* for later historians and moralists.

- 1 Christ begins by reminding the faithful Sardis that he is the one who has the seven spirits and the seven stars. He is, in other words, the same Lord identified at 1:16, 20; and 2:1. As in those earlier cases, so here the stars are the angels who represent the churches. At 5:6, Christ's vision operates through the metaphorical lens of these seven spirits, who are in fact the Holy Spirit.

  Christ knows their works. Heretofore this declaration of knowledge has been a prelude to commendation for some positive aspect of a church's ministry (cf. 2:2, 9, 13, 19). Hearers and readers are therefore caught by surprise when Christ, as he does later in the message to Laodicea (3:15), goes immediately on the attack. There is a regrettable parallel between the (witness) works of the church and the history of the city that hosts it. Sardis squandered its name, its reputation of invulnerability, because its benefactors did not stay alert to the dangers around them. The members of the Sardis church, while likewise reveling in their past reputation for witness, were also frittering that reputation away. This is why John plays with the word *"name"* by using it four times in this short letter. This word-play emphasizes the problem. They have become a church in name only.

To make his contrast between living and dead, Christ does not pit one adjective (alive) against another (dead); he balances a kinetic verb ("ζάω" being alive) against a static adjective ("νεκρὸς" dead). Every time the author uses the verb "ζάω" (being alive) in relationship to a witness(cf. 1:18; 2:8; 20:4-5), he does so in a context where eternal life trumps death. The adjective "νεκρὸς" (dead) is also used primarily in a context where someone dead lives again (cf. 1:5, 17, 18; 2:8; 3:1; 11:18; 14:13; 16:3; 20:5, 12, 13). John's point becomes grammatically clear whenever the adjective and verb are used together (cf. 1:18; 2:8; 20:5). It is because of their costly witness to the lordship of Christ that believers can cheat death by springing to eternal life. In every case other than 3:1, "*dead*" gives way to "*being alive.*" Surely, this is a pattern no believer would want to see reversed. Unfortunately, that is precisely what has happened; though having a name for "*being alive,*" the Sardis believers are really "*dead.*" Because they only maintain an appearance of resistant witness, their eschatological prospects are grim.

- **2** Christ demands that the Sardis church resurrect itself from the lethargy that holds it captive. It is time for it to wake up. He then issues the mysterious injunction that the believers must strengthen the remaining things that are about to die. In recording this demand, John offers his only neuter use of the adjective "*remainder.*" In every case other than 8:13, where John uses the term, he does so to refer to a human remnant. There are therefore two options for interpreting the term. It could be that Christ wants the Sardis believers to strengthen the remaining human witnesses who are about to die because of their testimony. This interpretation would fit John's predominant use of *"remainder"* to refer to human subjects. The problem, though, is obvious. The neuter form indicates a unique intent. A second option is thus more likely. The Sardis believers must strengthen the remaining (i.e., incomplete) works that are about to die.

The final thought of the verse, *"for I have not found your works complete in the sight of my God,"* is a clarification that operates from the thought already conveyed at the end of 3:1. There, Christ describes the works (i.e., resistant witness) of the Sardis church as being alive in name only. Here, Christ restates the same thought with different language when he declares that their works are incomplete before God. They are performing acts of witness that do not fulfill the obligations of witness. In other words, they are engaged in a witness façade. While flamboyant, their effort has absolutely no transformative effect.

This interpretation fits well with the presumed historical situation of the Asia Minor churches in general and the Sardis church in particular. Like the churches mentioned in chapter 2, Sardis is infested with cultic affirmation for pagan deities and for the Roman imperial regime. The temple of Artemis, constructed by Antiochus III after refounded the city in 213 B.C.E., was the fourth largest Ionic temple known to have been constructed in the ancient world. Temple dedicated to Augusts and possibly Vespasian were also on grand display. Believers were invited to accommodate themselves to the lure of social and economic progress that was promised to those who participated cultically in these religious systems. Still, even in those churches where many were following the lead of Balaam, the Nicolaitans, and Jezebel and eating meat sacrificed to idols in order to blend themselves into the Greco-Roman social world, appropriate witnessing was also no doubt taking place. Christ does, after all (except in Sardis and Laodicea), find much to praise. Even in Sardis (v. 4, there is a faithful remnant. One should suppose, then, that even in the most reckless situations, believers were doing more than eating meat sacrificed to idols. That was the problem activity. Apparently, there were many corporate faith activities that expressed a genuine Christian commitment and therefore were not a problem for John and Christ. Christ celebrates some of these activities (e.g., 2:2, 3, 6, 9, 13, 19) and no doubt leaves others out. Such praiseworthy works were, however, incomplete. They needed to be shored up before they, too, died out.

  One might suspect, for example, that John's Sardis believers were worshiping together every Lord's Day. Yet they were not doing the other necessary work of resisting the lure of Greco-Roman cultic-social life by witnessing transformatively to the lordship of Jesus Christ. Cultic correctness, while necessary, was insufficient. Unless they upgraded their remaining work of cultic observance by adding acts of transformative resistance, it too would soon wither and die. The church's death would then be complete; it would be as dead in name as it was already in resistant witness.

This interpretation allows the more dynamic verb "*be alive*" to match up ironically with the static adjective "*dead*" at the conclusion of verse 1. They are dead as a community, but their works still have a chance to live (i.e., become complete) and perhaps in their living revitalize the community as well. Like a drowned man whose vital organs still struggle to function while they await the return of oxygen that flooded lungs cannot without help provide, they have died. And yet, for a brief moment at least, they hope for resuscitation.

- **3** Christ desires a selective memory. He wants believers to remember the life strategy they saw and heard from him, while they forget the egregious teachings of those who have said that accommodation with Greco-Roman cultic-social life is acceptable. Having recalled this more rigorous way, they must hold to, that is, keep ("τηρέω") it. The verb "τηρέω" is a primary ethical term for Revelation, and it is integrally connected to the language of witness. At 3:8, Christ celebrates those witnesses who "*hold to*" his word and thereby resist every opportunity to deny his name. Then at 3:10, he promises eschatological reward for those witnesses who keep resisting the lure of Greco-Roman cultic, social, and political success. At 12:17, the dragon fights those who resist his demands by "*holding to*" their word, and at 14:12, eschatological reward is implied for those who resist the threat of persecution and maintain their witness. At 22:9, John's mediating angel declares satisfactorily that he is in the good company of those who have kept the witness demanded by Christ in the book. Indeed, John declares in three of his seven macarisms that the blessed person is the one who "*keeps*" to the resistant witness that the book demands (1:3; 16:15; 22:7).

If the Sardis believers do not rouse themselves to the kind of resistant witness Christ has taught and modeled (cf. 1:5, 9; 2:13), he will come to them like a thief in the night. The imagery is familiar. Several other New Testament texts highlight the coming of the end time as the surreptitious movement of a night bandit (Matt. 24:42-44; Luke 12:39-40; 1 Thess. 5:2-4; 2 Pet. 3:10). Revelation, though, is the only text to identify this thief as Christ. Already, Christ promised the church at Ephesus that he would come in judgment if they did not remember and turn back (repent) to the witness that they offered at first. Given the thematic parallel with 2:5, one might imagine that the thief would do here what Christ threatened to do in Ephesus: take the lampstand, the church, and remove it from its place of relationship with God.

Thus far in the text of Revelation, Christ's judgment against the churches occurs for only one reason: not enduring, not resisting the temptation to accommodate oneself to Greco-Roman cultic, social, and economic expectations. Being awake and alert must therefore be a euphemism for resisting those expectations. This understanding is corroborated by John's only other use of "*γρηγορέω*" (wake up) in 16:15, where it is the key vocabulary in one of the seven macarisms or blessings. First, there is a familiar warning: Christ is coming like a thief in the night. Who will be blessed when that circumstance unfolds? Only those who are awake – who have not shamed themselves by throwing off their clothes. As 3:4 demonstrates, John forges a strong link between clothing and the behavior of resistant witness.

This particular coming, related as it is specifically to this church's behavior, is not the ultimate coming of the end time that is prophesied in other sections of the book. When Christ describes his coming as conditional, as based upon the behavior of believers, it is a specific revelation of punishment within history (cf. 2:5, 16). The unconditional coming, though also imminent, will occur regardless of human behavior and will bring with it the end of the historical era (1:3; 2:25; 3:11; 22:7, 10, 12, 20).

- **4** Christ defines the remnant as those who have not soiled their clothing and who thus walk with him wearing clean, white garments. Appealing to Daniel and the Synoptic Gospels, many commentators observe that "*white*" and Mark 16:5, it is worn by heavenly beings, and at Jesus' transfiguration, his clothing transforms to a white that no launderer could match (cf. Matt. 17:2; Mark 9:3; Luke 9:29). For believers, there is a connection between the color of clothing and an eschatological relationship with the divine: It was customary in the ancient church, when believers came out of the waters of baptism, to dress them in a new, white garment to indicate the beginning of a new life of purity and victory. This historical observation matches the literary implication that resides in Christ's plea that the Sardis believers remember their former work of witness and return to it (repent). As defiant witness to Christ's lordship, they once wore the color of eschatological acceptability; they have soiled that clothing, however, by accommodating themselves to the cultic and social expectations associated with Greco-Roman pagan and imperial lordship. Only a few have held on to their earlier commitment to bear witness to the lordship of God; they, and thus their garments, remain in their pristine state. They alone are worthy.

In John's religious and ethical vision, worthiness is earned through endeavor. God is worthy because God created all things (Rev. 4:11). Christ is worthy because he witnessed so aggressively to the lordship of this Creator God, and indeed to his own related lordship, that he was executed (Rev. 5:2, 4, 9, 12). The faithful and true witness (1:5; 3:14) is therefore adorned in the quintessential clothing of resistance (dipped in blood, 19:13; inscribed with the name "*King of kings*," 19:16). It makes sense, then, when John explains that believers are made worthy to wear the clothing of eschatological victory only if they too witness to that lordship. In their dazzling dress, they will stand out in a filthily clad crowd.

Dazzling is the right word. Though "λευκός" does translate literally as "*white*," its emphasis in the Book of Revelation is more on qualitative essence than on exterior pigmentation. Too often the color has been connected uncritically with ethnicity and race. Biblical affirmation of the color has therefore often been taken incorrectly as a biblical affirmation of the white race. It is clear, however, that for John the term is an ethical not an ethnic one. It is an earned salutation. One is not born "λευκός"; one becomes "λευκός." People of any ethnicity and hue can become "λευκός." All one needs to do is heed the command that Christ issues to the Sardis believers: wake up and witness relentlessly to the lordship of Christ, no matter how much it costs. That is how a believer, any believer, can "*dazzle*."

- **5 – 6** Christians already established those who conquer as people who resist accommodation to Greco-Roman cultic, social, and economic expectations. In connecting the language of conquest with the metaphor of the dazzling clothing, he thereby reestablishes it as triumph over the beastly machinations of imperial Rome (cf. 6:9-11; 7:9, 13). It makes sense, therefore, that the twenty-four elders, who were presumably model witnesses and conquerors, are so clothed at 4:4. As a negative example, the church at Laodicea is warned that it must do a better job of witnessing if its members are to earn this glorious attire (3:18).

Two specific rewards await the "*dazzlingly*" clad believer. First, Christ declares that he will not blot the name of such a person from the Book of Life. The Book of Life (cf. Exod. 32:32-33; Ps. 69:28; Isa. 4:3; Dan. 12:1-2; Phil. 4:3; Luke 10:20; Heb. 12:23; *1 Enoch* 108:3) registers those who enjoy an eternal relationship with God. Those whose names are not written in it have lost their connection with God (Rev. 17:8) and are due eschatological punishment (13:8; 20:15). On the surface it might first appear, given the ethical context in which the term arises in the Sardis letter, that believers are expected to earn their way into the book. Nothing could be further from the truth! Through improper (cultically and socially accommodating) behavior, one can cause one's name to be stricken from the ledger. One cannot, however, cause one's name to be entered there. Entries had already been made from the moment God created the world (Rev. 13:8; 17:8).

John is working out a fundamental tension that resides still in contemporary Christianity. God determines who has relationship with God. It appears that God graciously decides in favor of everyone – at least at the start. John presumes that even those in the majority at Sardis, the ones whom Christ indicts, have had their names inscribed in the Book of Life. Why else would he threaten them with a blotting out? Works, therefore, do not enable eschatological entry. Witnessing, though, do affirm entry, while inappropriate works (accommodation) negate it. This bit of literary dexterity allows grace and works to stand together in a firm, if very tense, relationship.

As a second reward, Christ declares that he will confess the name of the "*dazzling*" believer before God and God's heavenly entourage. John uses the term "ἐξομολογέω" (confess) only here. By placing it in this context, where he encourages a witnessing to (or confession of) Christ in a hostile environment, John is building upon the tradition of the historical Jesus (Luke 12:8; Matt. 10:32; *2 Clem.* 3:2) who demanded similar behavior from his followers.

> **Excursus 5: The Book of Life**
> The Book of Life in Hebrew is "סֵפֶר חַיִּים" and in Greek is "τῆς βίβλου τῆς ζωῆς."
> **1.** It is used of natural life. Ps. 69:28, where "*let them be blotted out of the Book of the Living*" means "*let them die*"; in Exodus 32:32, Moses prays to be blotted out of God's book if Israel is to be destroyed; Ps. 139:16 ("*in your book were written ... the days that were formed for me*"); Dan. 12:1, where all the righteous who "*shall be found written in the Book*" will survive the eschatological tribulation.
> **2.** In later Judaism and the New Testament it is used of the life of the age to come. Thus Isa. 4:3, where "*everyone who has been enrolled for life in Jerusalem*" refers to natural life, is re-interpreted in the Targum as speaking of "*eternal life.*" So in the New Testament, the Book of Life is the roster of believers (cf. Phil. 4:3; Rev. 3:5; 22:19). At the last judgment everyone not enrolled in the Book of Life is consigned to the fiery lake (Rev. 20:12, 15); this is the Book of life of the slaughtered Lamb (Rev. 13:8; 21:27), in which the names of the elect have been inscribed "*from the foundation of the world*" (Rev. 17:8). The same idea is expressed in Luke 10:20, "*your names are written in heaven*"; Acts 13:48, "*as many as were ordained (i.e., inscribed) to eternal life believed.*"

In verse 6, Christ closes this letter as he does the others, with a call for those in the churches with an ear to listen to what the Spirit says.

Revelation 3:7~13 → To Philadelphia

NIV	TT
⁷ "To the angel of the church in Philadelphia write: These are the words of him who is holy and true, who holds the key of David. What he opens no one can shut, and what he shuts no one can open. ⁸ I know your deeds. See, I have placed before you an open door that no one can shut. I know that you have little strength, yet you have kept my word and have not denied my name. ⁹ I will make those who are of the synagogue of Satan, who claim to be Jews though they are not, but are liars— I will make them come and	⁷ "And to the angel of the church in **Philadelphia**[50], write: Thus says the holy one, the true one, the one who has **the key of David**[51], who opens and no one will shut, who shuts and no one opens. ⁸ 'I know your works. Indeed, I have set before you an opened door, which no one can shut, because you have little power and yet kept my word and did not deny my name. ⁹ Indeed, I will make those of **the synagogue of Satan**[52] who call themselves Jews, and are not but are lying – indeed, I will make them come and grovel before your feet, and they will

---

[50] Φιλαδελφεία → Philadelphia, a city in west central Asia Minor. It means *"the city of brotherly"* – brother/sisters (*adelphos*) + love (*philos*). Modern Alashehir, twenty-eight miles southeast of Sardis, not mentioned elsewhere in the New Testament. The city honored the emperors by adding *"New Caesarea"* and *"Flavia"* to its name in gratitude for Roman help in rebuilding after the devastating earthquake of 17 C.E.

[51] τὴν κλεῖν Δαυίδ → The phrase means *"the key of David,"* which means *"the authority of the Davidic kingdom"* (Isa. 22:22). For the early church's picturing the coming kingdom of God as the renewal of David's kingship (Luke 1:28-33; 3:23; 20:41-44; Acts 13:22-23).

[52] ἧς συναγωγῆς τοῦ σατανᾶ → The phrase means *"the synagogue of Satan."* (see Excursus 6: The Synagogue of Satan)

fall down at your feet and acknowledge that I have loved you. ¹⁰ Since you have kept my command to endure patiently, I will also keep you from the hour of trial that is going to come on the whole world to test the inhabitants of the earth. ¹¹ I am coming soon. Hold on to what you have, so that no one will take your crown. ¹² The one who is victorious I will make a pillar in the temple of my God. Never again will they leave it. I will write on them the name of my God and the name of the city of my God, the new Jerusalem, which is coming down out of heaven from my God; and I will also write on them my new name. ¹³ Whoever has ears, let them hear what the Spirit says to the churches.	understand that I have loved you. ¹⁰ Because you have kept my word of perseverance, I will keep you from the hour of trial that is about to come upon the entire inhabited earth to test the inhabitants of the earth. ¹¹ I am coming soon. Hold on to what you have, so that no one may take your crown. ¹² As for the one who conquers, **I will make him a pillar in the temple of my God**[53], and he will never leave it. Moreover, I will write on him the name of my God and the name of the city of my God, the new Jerusalem, which comes down out of heaven from my God, and my new name. ¹³ Whoever has ears, let them hear what the Spirit says to the churches.

---

[53] "*I will make you a pillar in the temple of my God*" → The promise of eschatological reward is to be included in God's eschatological temple, not as a visitor, but as a part of it. Christian leaders had been called "*pillars*" (Gal. 2:9), but in the final temple all faithful Christians will share this role. But there will be no temple in the new Jerusalem (21:22)! Such conflicting imagery may point to the use of different sources or traditions by the author, but this is somewhat beside the point. Both Rev. 3:12 (temple) and Rev. 21:22 (no temple) have their own valid theological point to make and should not be superficially "*harmonized.*"

Philadelphia, the city of brotherly love, housed the only church other than Smyrna to receive exclusively positive remarks. While the Smyrna church witnessed in spite of its impoverishment (2:9), the Philadelphia community sustained its work despite the fact that it was powerless before hostile communal forces. The city's name, then, did not represent the circumstance of the believers living in it. It was derived instead from the legends of two royal figures. According to one tradition, the city was named for Attalus Philadelpus, an Attalid king who ruled from 159 to 138 B.C.E. His legendary love for his brother, who preceded him as king from 197 to 159 B.C.E., was the alleged foundation of the moniker. A competing tradition gave credit to the founding efforts of Ptolemy Philadephus (308-246 B.C.E.). Yet John was not preoccupied with the city's foundational history. He was concerned instead about the city's role in hosting a caustic feud between his followers and the synagogue community, from which they had likely emerged. The city's name was therefore bitterly ironic. In this municipality of *"brotherly love,"* two communities of kindred Jewish roots, one witnessing to Jesus Christ, the other opposing any such proclamation, found absolutely no love lost between them.

- 7 – 8 The situation in Philadelphia was uncomfortably similar to the one John's believers had experienced in Smyrna. There, too, the Christ community was enduring conflict with some portion of the city's Jewish community. In both cases, Christ uses the derogatory appellation *"synagogue of Satan"* to describe the churches' opponents. In Philadelphia, one gets the impression that members of the specified synagogue were not only betraying Christ-believers' identities: they were also teaching that those who had been expelled from the synagogue had forfeited any chance to be a part of God's eschatological community. This is why Christ describes himself to the church in the way that he does and present them with the particular message that he delivers.

Christ is, first of all, the holy and true one. Isaiah, whom Christ will quote momentarily, conspicuously identified God as the Holy One (Isa. 1:4; 5:19; 40:25), and a number of Old Testament texts affirm that God is the true one (LXX: Exod. 34:6; Num. 14:18; Isa. 65:16). Christ is so integrally identified with this God that he speaks with and for God as the holy and true eschatological judge. Revelation 6:10 is the only other place where John employs this title. There, souls who have been executed for presenting the very witness these seven letters have been advocating cry out to the holy and true Christ for an avenging judgment against their persecutors. The implication is that this Christ, who is himself also the true witness to the lordship of Christ (3:14), will execute judgment against all who defy that testimony and torment those who profess it.

Christ now strategically enters his Isaiah quotation. Appealing to the prophet's testimony at Isa. 22:22, he maintains that he (Christ) holds the key of David. In the Isaiah text, the steward Eliakim is given the key to the historical house of David and thereby the power to determine who can and who cannot enter the king's presence. Christ, however, wields his apocalyptic version of the key for the purpose of exclusively opening and closing the door to David's eternal kingdom. In the celebrated instance of Matt. 16:19; 18:18, after Jesus gives Peter custody of the heavenly keys, it is Peter who has permanent power to bind and loose authoritatively both in heaven and on earth. In the Book of Revelation, Christ retains key ownership for himself. Christ, in other words, is the keeper of the eschatological gate.

At 9:1 and 20:1, an angel is handed the key to the bottomless pit. At his discretion, he can open its door and consign the guilty to its punishing judgment. Jesus' key, by contrast, opens the lock on the promise of heaven. Perhaps it is keys to free himself from the captivity of death. He displays them before his followers so that they know he can release them from the death to which any human person or force might consign them. They can therefore witness, no matter what the punishing consequence, knowing that Christ has the wherewithal to set them free from it. Once Christ is freed, with heavenly key in hand he can open the door to heaven and usher them in. No one else has the power to shut that door and, presumably, keep them out.

This would have been an especially welcome message in Philadelphia, where the synagogue community claimed to be the only door to a relationship with God. By excommunicating the Christ-believers, the community claimed to have shut that door on them forever. The picture of Christ holding the key of David is a striking statement to the contrary. It would not have been lost on John's hearers and readers that Christ speaks about the heavenly realm in Davidic language. Surely it would not have been lost on the members of the offending synagogue community either. Christ has taken charge of the door to their eschatological future. He is ready to open it not for them but for those whom they have thrust aside.

The positive emphasis on the ethically loaded verb "τηρέω" (keep) is a clear indication that the Philadelphians maintained the primary exhortation of the book. They kept *"my word."* Given that God and Christ are indissolubly linked, Christ's word is indistinguishable from God's word. John has equated God's word with the testimony proclaimed by Jesus (1:2, 9; 6:9; 12:11; 20:4), which is the same testimony desired of Christ's followers. Christ made the connection specific for the Philadelphians when he restated that the community kept his word (3:10). Christ is celebrating here what he has been demanding all along; the Philadelphia believers have endured in their witness in spite of the arduous circumstances that have plagued them. He is also celebrating their confession of his name. Confession, too, is identified with witnessing. He makes the point negatively. By saying that they refuse to deny his name, he acknowledges their confession of it. That refusal, at least as it is expressed in relationship to Antipas and the other faithful members of the Pergamum church, is the very essence of witness (2:13; 13:6). It retains that sense in Philadelphia.

For this reason, this witness, Christ has opened the door of the eschatological future to them (cf. 4:1). *"I know your works,"* he declares. *"Indeed, I have set before you an opened door, which no one can shut, because you have little power and yet kept my word and did not deny my name."* This reading sets up the parallel causal clause in v. 10, where once again historical witness yields eschatological reward.

- **9** Christ's charge that the opponents of the Philadelphians comprise a synagogue of Satan, whose members call themselves Jews but are liars, is intentionally reminiscent of the allegation earlier leveled against the opponents of the Smyrna church (2:9). Though he uses descriptive language that is almost exactly the same, in this latter case he does not focus on the resulting persecution. Instead, he spotlights the actions he will take to vindicate the church's position as the eschatologically favored entity. In doing so, he maintains the mocking tone he established in v. 7, where he declared that he would use the Davidic key to open up the Davidic kingdom exclusively to those whom the alleged people of David persecuted. This time, he takes a vision of eschatological vindication that was supposed to operate on behalf of the synagogue and uses it deliberately against those who populate it. Isaianic prophecy (Isa. 45:14; 49:23; 60:14) declared that the people of Israel would be vindicated when God forced the Gentile nations who had persecuted them to kneel in submission before them (cf. Ps. 86:9). As it turns out, at least as far as Philadelphia was concerned, the synagogue had become the tormenting, ungodly force. God would therefore force its members down upon their knees instead. Though Christ does use the language of worship, it cannot be his intention that the synagogue members are actually made to worship the members of the Philadelphia church. Only God and Christ are worthy of worship (Rev. 4:10; 5:14; 7:11; 11:1, 16; 14:7; 15:4; 19:4, 10; 20:8). Christ is mocking them. In their humiliation, they would be forced to genuflect, to grovel at the very feet they had sent running for cover.

> **Excursus 6: The Synagogue of Satan**
> To understand such harsh words from a Christian, spoken in the name of the risen Christ, one must remember several factors:
> 1. "*Jews*" in this sentence is a positive characterization. The problem with those he speaks against is not that they are Jews, but they do not live up to their name (cf. Rom. 2:28-29).
> 2. Race is not involved. The statement is not anti-Semitic in the racial sense, but expresses a religious conflict.
> 3. Such epithets were routinely used in inter-Jewish religious conflicts, in which each party called the other "*children of the devil*," a practice adopted by Christians: in 1 John 3:4-10 "*children of the devil*" is applied by Christians to other Christians.
> 4. Such language represents the dualistic framework of thought inherent in apocalypticism.
> 5. In John's situation Jews were a substantial minority in the Roman population (a total of about 3 million Jews in the Roman Empire of about 60 million, about 5 percent of the total population = fifty Jews per thousand). Though an old and often respected community, they also had to deal

> with suspicion and prejudice, and sometimes had a precarious existence. But the Jewish community was thirty times the size of the Christian community. Estimates of the number of Christians in the Roman Empire at the end of the first century range from 50,000 to 320,000. Taking 100,000 as a rough median figure, there would have been 1.6 Christians per thousand population – a much smaller, more recent, and more suspect minority than the Jewish community. Non-Christian Jews were understandably resentful that some Jewish Christians attempted to maintain their identity with the synagogue, thus making trouble between the Jews and the Roman authorities. It is understandable that in such a situation Jews sometimes denounced Christians to the Roman authorities. Something like this had apparently happened in Smyrna and Philadelphia. John responds by charging them with being a synagogue of Satan.
>
> 6. While historical study can make such New Testament texts more understandable, it does not authorize later generations to make use of such language. No one today may refer to Jews in such terms. Modern Christians, precisely on the basis of the New Testament, can only lament that such texts have been used in Christian history to support anti-Semitism.

- **10** Christ reminds the Philadelphians of the eschatological promise he made with the metaphor of the open door in v. 8. This time he uses the language of ethics. As they have "*kept*" his word of nonviolent resistance through a singular witness that refused to acknowledge any claim to lordship by pagan deities or Roman emperors, so he will "*keep*" them. Christ is not concerned whether they will or will not maintain their hold on some facet of doctrinal content. *"Keeping"* in this context has the ethical connotation of application; the Philadelphians have applied Christ's witness to their own lives. The language of *"keeping my word"* therefore operates in tandem with the identical language offered at the end of 3:8. There the Philadelphians were celebrated for name. Here that same *"keeping my word"* is described as an enduring witness of nonviolent resistance. The two explanatory phrases are metaphorically synonymous. Resistant witness endures precisely because it maintains the confession of Christ's lordship in an environment hostile to such a claim.

The believer who lives up to this ethical standard can expect Christ's eschatological reward. He will keep them *"out of"* the hour of testing or trial that is about to come upon the entire inhabited earth to test the inhabitants of the earth. Christ is not speaking here against the entire world, but the part that is *"organized and controlled"* by the Roman Empire, the part that is determined to celebrate a lordship other than Christ's. the *"inhabitants of the earth"* are those who in their affirmation of this imperial control find themselves necessarily in opposition to Christ and his followers (cf. 2:13; 6:10; 8:13; 11:10; 13:8, 12, 14; 14:6; 17:2, 8). As a moment of judgment, the hour is aimed squarely at them. Their testing then is actually a convicting trial. It is a period of great distress and suffering that early Judaism (Dan. 12:1; *T. Mos.* 8:1; *Jub.* 23:11-21; *2 Apoc. Bar.* 27:1-15) and early Christianity (Matt. 24:15-31; Mark 13:7-20; Rev. 7:14) expected would immediately precede the eschatological victory of God. As a time of apocalyptic woe, it is also a moment of eschatological poetic justice. The tribulation that the inhabitants of the earth brought upon Christ's followers will now be brought upon them instead.

Though Christ vows to keep the Philadelphians out of the hour of testing, he does not say that he intends to spare them from it. Indeed, Jesus does not ask that God *"rapture"* believers out of the difficult moment; he instead asks God to strengthen them so that they might endure and conquer it (John 17:15). Here, as in the Gospel, persecution is something that believers will endure (Rev. 2:10). Their witness matters as much as it does because they give it in the circumstances of such duress, just as Christ himself did on the cross. That is no doubt why in the end the hour is described in terms of a testing rather than a judgment; believers, too, will have an opportunity to make the grade. They will have the opportunity to witness.

- **11** Once again Christ heightens the urgency of loyal witness by testifying that he is coming soon. While the opening and closing of the text assure its hearers and readers in a general way that the time is near (1:3; 22:10), there are several specific declarations by Christ that mimic the one made here. At 22:7, 12, and 20 he proclaims, *"I am coming soon."* And in each case the proclamation is made in the context of his role as judge. At 22:7, the one who is coming soon rules that only the one who *"keeps"* the words of the books prophecy is blessed. Speaking more provocatively at 22:12, the one who is coming soon acknowledges that he will repay everyone according to their work/witness. At 22:18-20, the one who is coming soon says that he will remove the eschatological reward of the person who adds to or takes away from the words of prophecy contained in the book. In the references to the churches at Ephesus (2:5) and Pergamum (2:16), Christ's imminent coming is also directly connected to a theme of judgment. The sure implication is that the believers in Philadelphia must prepare themselves for this impending moment lest it dawn upon them as one of judgment rather than celebration. This is why the one who is coming soon closes the verse by challenging them to *"hold on to"* what they have (cf. 2:13, 25), to maintain their witness in spite of the social and political turbulence such witness causes, so that they might not lose the crown they already wear. The connection between imminence and judgment is even more sharply drawn with the impending woe language of 11:14.

Given the context of Christ's imminent coming and the implication that if the Philadelphian believers are not prepared, that coming will be a moment of judgment rather than celebration, it is reasonable to presume that the someone who might confiscate the crown is the same Christ who would, if the circumstances warranted, blot a believer's name from the Book of Life. The crown is a symbol of eschatological life just as it was in 2:10. It is probably no accident that there, too, the wearing of the crown is connected with a successful engagement with the moment of testing. The assumption that believers already possess the crown fits with the discussion surrounding the book of Life in 3:5. While they cannot earn their way into the book, they can earn their way out of it by accommodating to the lordship of Rome (i.e., failing the test) rather than witnessing for the lordship of Christ. Here, too, there is no suggestion that one could or would need to earn the crown of life. God's bestowal of it is an apparent given. They need only fear Christ's taking it away when he returns, if they are not ready, if their witness has not been "*kept*," if their witness has not met the test.

- **12 – 13** For the conqueror, though, for the one who "*holds*" and witnesses in the harsh circumstances of testing and trial that the Philadelphians face, there will be a specific eschatological reward. Christ will make of them a permanent pillar in the heavenly temple of God. Translation difficulties arise when one considers that, later in his work, John declares that God's new Jerusalem will have no temple (21:22). Yet these two apparently opposing realities are not really in conflict with each other. At 21:22 John goes on to say that there will be a temple, but the temple will be the Lord God and the Lamb. It would therefore be appropriate there to have any translation reflect this complex reality: Christ will make the conquering witness a pillar in the heavenly temple, which is God and the Lamb. The relationship with God and the Lamb will be an intimate one (see 19:7-8; 21:2).

To be sure, commentators are correct who suggest that this image of firm placement in God's presence and care would have been particularly relevant for the Philadelphia believers given the city's history of earthquake instability. But there is a deeper relevance here that relates directly to the circumstance narrated in the *"synagogue of Satan"* phrase at vv. 8-10. The tone of irony and mocking that Christ instituted at 3:8 with the metaphor of the open door makes an encore appearance here. Catherin and Justo Gonzalez point out helpfully that no one outside the people of Israel could enter the Jerusalem temple. Whether Jew or Gentile, John's hearers and readers were no doubt thought to be exiled from the presence of God experienced in the gathering of the community and the temple privileges that went with presence from the moment the synagogue forced their leave upon them. If the earthly temple of God had still existed in Jerusalem, these Christ-believers would therefore not even have been allowed to enter it. And yet here they were, because of the very witnessing that earned them their exile, promised to be the pillars that held up God's heavenly temple and kept it secure. Kicked out of Israel by God's alleged people, they were planted firmly in God's eschatological future, and therefore God's heaven, by God's holy and true Christ.

    Christ adds to his pillar promise a vow to scratch on it the eschatological graffiti of three names: the name of My God, the name of the new Jerusalem coming out heaven, and his own new name. How appropriate that the ones who did not deny Christ's name, even in the face of opposition are in the end inscribed with Christ's name. All of the names certainly signal the intimate eschatological relationship that the Philadelphians will have with God in God's future. The Isaiah connection that has been important throughout this letter comes to a kind of climax here. In Isa. 62:2 and 65:15, the prophet declares that the people of God shall be given a new name by God. Just as important, the Isaiah passages affirm that this new name will come as a way of vindicating the people before the nations who had tormented them. Now, reversing the design one final time, Christ bestows this triple new name – and the identification as the people of God that goes with it – upon his followers as a way of vindicating them before the synagogue community that has surely thought that the Isaiah promise was meant exclusively for them. To push the point even further, Christ implies that God has been the architect of this momentous reversal of fortune. Wealthy patrons of temples often had their names inscribed on the pillars of such edifices to show their support. In the case of the heavenly temple, the columns *"will bear the inscription that will tell all that they were placed there by none other than God!"* (Gonzalez and Gonzalez 35).

In verse 13, Christ closes this letter as he does the others, with a call for those in the churches with an ear to listen to what the Spirit says.

Revelation 3:14~22 → To Laodicea

NIV	TT
¹⁴ "To the angel of the church in Laodicea write:	¹⁴ "And to the angel of the church in Laodicea, write:
These are the words of the Amen, the faithful and true witness, the ruler of God's creation. ¹⁵ I know your deeds, that you are neither cold nor hot. I wish you were either one or the other! ¹⁶ So, because you are lukewarm—neither hot nor cold—I am about to spit you out of my mouth. ¹⁷ You say, 'I am rich; I have acquired wealth and	Thus says **the Amen**[54], the faithful and true witness, the **beginning**[55] of God's creation: ¹⁵ 'I know your works; you are **neither cold nor hot**[56]. I wish you were either cold or hot. ¹⁶ So, because you are **lukewarm**[57] and neither hot nor cold, I am about to vomit you out of my mouth. ¹⁷ Because you say, "I am rich and I have become wealthy and I need

---

[54] ὁ ἀμήν → The phrase means *"the Amen."* It reflects the Hebrew text of Isa. 65:16, where *"the God of faithfulness"* is literally *"*אָמֵן*,"* אלהי*," "the God of Amen."* (i.e., *"Amen"* is understood to be a title of God 2 Cor. 1:19-20)

[55] ἀρχη → It means *"beginning," "origin," "ruler," "authority," "official," "rule," "domain,"* and *"sphere of influence."* God's creation associates Christ with the Creator (cf. John 1:1-4; 1 Cor. 8:5-6; Col. 1:15-20; Heb. 1:1-4; all reflecting the role of Wisdom in Prov. 8:22-36). However, at least in the Johannine community, the phrase would have reminded the hearers of John 1:1. Thus one prefers *"beginning"* or *"origin."*

[56] οὔτε ψυχρὸς εἶ οὔτε ζεστός → *"Neither cold nor hot."* In the ancient world, the metaphor *"cold"* did not mean *"passive"* and *"hot"* did not mean *"enthusiastic,"* but these words were rather used in the sense of *"against me"* and *"for me."* The Laodiceans attempted to be neither for nor against. Their problem was not lack of enthusiasm but wavering in the either/or choice. It is not only Revelation that insists there is no middle way. The Jesus of the Gospels likewise defines only two groups, those who are for and those who are against; those who gather with him and those who scatter (cf. Matt. 12:30).

[57] χλιαρός → The term means *"tepid,"* and *"lukewarm."* It appears only here in the entire New Testament. There is some evidence that the water supply of Laodicea, which came through an aqueduct from hot springs several miles away, delivered tepid and barely drinkable water to the city. This is one of several indications that the author knew the circumstances of each city and tailored the message to each church.

do not need a thing.' But you do not realize that you are wretched, pitiful, poor, blind and naked. ¹⁸ I counsel you to buy from me gold refined in the fire, so you can become rich; and white clothes to wear, so you can cover your shameful nakedness; and salve to put on your eyes, so you can see. ¹⁹ Those whom I love I rebuke and discipline. So be earnest and repent. ²⁰ Here I am! I stand at the door and knock. If anyone hears my voice and opens the door, I will come in and eat with that person, and they with me. ²¹ To the one who is victorious, I will give the right to sit with me on my throne, just as I was victorious and sat down with my Father on his throne. ²² Whoever has ears, let them hear what the Spirit says to the churches."	nothing," but you do not know what you are miserable and pitiful and poor and blind and naked, ¹⁸ I counsel you to buy from me gold refined by fire so that you might be wealthy, and white/dazzling garments so that you might be clothed and the shame of your nakedness might not be revealed, and slave to anoint your eyes so that you might see. ¹⁹ I **correct**[58] and discipline those whom I love; therefore, be earnest and repent. ²⁰ Indeed, I stand at the door and knock; if someone should hear my voice and open the door, I will come in to that person, and I will dine with that one that person with me. ²¹ As for the one who conquers, I will allow that one to sit with me on my throne, just as I also conquered and sat with my Father on his throne. ²² Whoever has ears, let them hear what the Spirit says to the churches."

---

[58] ἐλέγχω → It means "*bring to light*," "*expose*," "*set forth*," "*convict*," "*convince*," "*point out*," "*reprove*," "*correct*," "*discipline*," and "*punish*."

Christ is as consistently negative toward the Laodiceans as he was invariably positive toward the Philadelphians. He cannot find even a tiny remnant within the community upon whom he might render the slightest offering of praise. The better one understands the history of this city and the place of the church community within it, the better one understands and perhaps appreciates the divine hostility. Laodicea – colonized by the Seleucid King Antiochus II between 261 and 246 B.C.E., and named for his wife, Laodice – was the richest city within the region of Phrygia. It was so wealthy that after it was utterly destroyed by an earthquake in 60 C.E., the city proudly refused imperial disaster assistance and rebuilt itself completely with its own resources.

Located six miles south of Hierapolis, ten miles northwest of Colossae, and a hundred miles east of Ephesus, the city sat at a major intersection, which enabled it to operate as a hub on a lucrative trade route. Its main highway was an east-west thoroughfare that connected the port of Ephesus with the western region of Asia Minor. Its other primary passage connected Pergamum, Thyatira, Sardis, and Philadelphia to the north with cities like Colossae and Perga and the regions of Pisidia and Pamphylia to the south. The city was also well known and well endowed by its textile, banking, and medical industries. Its signature commercial items were a shiny black wool and a so-called Phrygian powder, from which a medicinal eye salve was made. The city also had a signature water problem. It had no water source of its own but had to pipe water in from the hot medicinal springs of Hierapolis.

Unfortunately, by the time it arrived there, its tepidness and mineral content made the water nauseating. People were prone to spit it from their mouth.

This wealthy Asia Minor city also had an apparently long-standing church community that interacted with nearby church communities. Five times the church is mentioned in the Letter to the Colossians (Col. 2:1; 4:13, 15, 16 [twice]). At one point (Col. 4:12-13) the letter acknowledges a certain Epaphras as a missionary whose endeavors linked him to the churches in Colossae, Laodicea, and Hierapolis and thereby connected those churches with each other.

- **14** Christ is *"the Amen."* In the Hebrew text of Isa. 65:16, *"amen"* is applied specifically to God. Its use here established an integral relationship between Christ and God. Why else was the term used? In both Judaism and the early church, *"amen"* was used as a way of signifying what was true and valid. *"Amen"* was introduced in Revelation at 1:6 and again at 1:7 as an affirmation of the testimony about Christ that had just been proclaimed. Later in the book, it is a closing hymnic response (Rev. 5:14; 7:12; 19:4): heavenly beings (angels, four creatures, and twenty-four elders) antiphonally affirm the praise of God and Christ that has just been sung. At 22:20, it occurs at the close of the entire book as an affirmation of its primary promise: Christ is coming soon. By identifying himself here as *"the Amen,"* Christ indicates that he is the affirming, closing proclamation of praise in response to all that

God has previously done in God's role as Creator. This is why the definitive self-identifier speaks specifically to Christ's role as the origin of God's creation. If the Laodiceans were familiar with the Hebrew understanding of wisdom and particularly the portrait of it in Proverbs, they would no doubt have discerned in this self-reference a connection between Christ and the power of wisdom that God used to construct the world (Prov. 3:19; 8:22-31). Moreover, if they were familiar with the Letter to the Colossians, they were already comfortable with the idea that Christ was the firstborn, the beginning of God's creation (Col. 1:15). He is also the affirmation of that creation, the antiphonal Word that God utters in response to what God has done.

Even more specifically, Christ is *"the Amen"* to all that has been said thus far to challenge the seven churches. It is as though a preacher had concluded a sermon or finished a prayer with the immodest declaration *"I am the guarantor of all that I have just proclaimed. It is I who certify its validity and its importance for your lives."* Christ *"amens"* himself because he is himself *"the Amen."* He is not just the response; he is also what makes the response truthful and faithful to God's intent. This is why he is also recognized as the true and faithful witness (cf. Jer. 42:5, where Yahweh is described as a true and faithful witness).

- **15 – 16** The faithful and true witness knows about the lackluster witness of the Laodiceans. Lukewarm, they are neither hot nor cold. The adjective *"hot"* and *"cold"* should not be taken to represent different kinds of

Christian witness, so that, for example, the cold Christian does not witness properly, whereas the hot one maintains the zeal and fire that Christ demands. Once I heard how the Presbyterians are "*cold*," when the Baptists are "*hot*." Wrong! Christ opposes the hot and the cold to the lukewarm. He wishes that they were one or the other, but not one as opposed to the other. He intends simply that, knowing definitively where they should stand, they stand there. They should surely stand where all other witnesses should stand, against any form of accommodation to Roman imperial or pagan lordship. The lukewarm believer is therefore the accommodating Laodicean believer. The hot or cold Laodicean is the one who has made a decision to identify oneself with the lordship of Christ. Christ in this text is saying, '*Declare yourselves! Be hot or cold! Be Clear! Witness for my lordship alone!*' Otherwise, Christ will respond by doing to them what the oft-nauseated Laodiceans did to the lukewarm mineral water piped in from Hierapolis; sickened, he will vomit them from his mouth. The warning sounds eerily familiar to the threat Christ issued to the Ephesians, when he promised to throw their lampstand from its place if they did not repent (Rev. 2:5).

- **17** The Laodiceans do not recognize the precarious nature of their situation. Laodicea was a wealthy, self-sufficient town, and the Laodiceans have apparently incorporated this secular perspective into their ecclesial self-understanding. They are a wealthy, self-sufficient community of faith. They are the opposite of Smyrna, which was described as materially destitute but rich in witness (Rev. 2:9). Though rich in possessions, Laodicea is poor in doing works of enduring, witnessing. Indeed, their very wealth suggests that they have been accommodating themselves to the social and economic expectations of the Greco-Roman society in which they live. By attending the festivals, trade gatherings, cultic ceremonies, and other social situations where upward financial mobility could be bought at the high price of eating meat sacrificed to idols and acknowledging in other ways imperial and pagan lordship, the Laodiceans have enriched their historical circumstance at the expense of their eschatological one. Christ piles up the adjectives so that they will not miss the point; they are wretched, pitiable, poor, blind, and naked. Biblical scholars have well recognized how Christ's last three metaphorical points operate directly from the social circumstance of the Laodicean community. This city of wealthy bankers would feel chagrined at being labeled poor. This city of medical schools that pioneered pharmaceuticals for the betterment of sight would not appreciate an insult that labeled their entire municipality blind. This city full of merchants who outfitted the Greco-Roman world in the finest textiles, particularly their famous black wool, would not be amused to hear someone call them naked. Clearly, though, at least as far as Christ is concerned, they are fooling themselves. Though they think they have it all, they actually have nothing.

- **18** After scolding them by using imagery they would uniquely appreciate, Christ now offers the Laodiceans a way forward by reconstituting and thereby revaluing that same imagery. Though he appeals to the last three adjectives of v. 17 in a different order (1, 3, 2), it is clear that he has the same metaphors in mind (wealth, clothing, and restoration of sight). He advises them first to buy gold that has been refined by fire so that they might become truly wealthy. Refined gold was a symbol of a purified life (Prov. 27:21; Mal. 3:2-3; *Pss. Sol.* 17:42-43). Perhaps, too, Christ has in mind the Smyrna church that already was rich and had obtained their wealth through the *"fire"* of persecution that came as a result of their obstinate, resistant witness. The text of Revelation offers two ways to become rich. One can become rich through the refinement of fire, as in 3:18, or one can become rich through accommodation (18:3, 15, 19). The opposing of fired wealth as a positive trait and accommodated wealth as a negative one suggests that the fire is indeed the persecution that occurs as a result of non-accommodating, resistant witness. Christ, then, is suggesting that the Laodicean believers gain their wealth in the same way that Smyrna gained it, by being hot or cold, by standing up for the lordship of Christ in a context virulently hostile to that message.

Christ ended v. 17 by advising the Laodiceans that they were naked. Now, in v. 18, that nakedness is described as their shame. They can cover their shame by clothing themselves with the white/dazzling garment of the witness-induced victory they are now offered.

The eye salve to end their blindness is yet one more phase of redundancy on the same theme. Their blindness is their *"lukewarmness,"* their accommodation to Greco-Roman lifestyle and authority. The salve is the witness that can cure it. Christ offers the opportunity for that witness now.

- **19 – 22** The Laodiceans must repent. This is why Christ has been so harsh on them in this letter. He is only harsh toward those whom he loves, and his harshness is meant not to destroy but to teach. The point of instruction here is simple: witness for the lordship of Christ!

Though the Laodiceans are not where Christ wants them to be in terms of witnessing discipleship, they do form a community of faith and apparently practice all the ritual expressions of that faith, evidently even the Lord's Supper. Because of their lukewarmness, though, they do so without Christ's approval and presence. This is why Christ likens himself to someone standing outside their door and knocking. In vv. 18-19, Christ offers them an opportunity to rectify the disastrous situation they have created for themselves. They can do that only if they pay attention to what he has said in this letter to them. That is how they will "*hear*" his voice. If they "*hear*" it and respond to it, if they become hot or cold, then and only then will Christ enter and share supper with them. Only at that point will they eat the Eucharist in his presence instead of tricking themselves into thinking that they do, just as they have tricked themselves into believing that they are rich when they are poor, perceptive when they are blind, and dressed in victorious garb when they are in truth naked.

To the person who conquers in this fashion, who witnesses in spite of the risks, Christ will issue the same reward God gave Christ as a result of his testimony. He will give them a seat on his heavenly throne. One final time in the seven messages to the churches of Asia, John's hearers and readers are invited to join ranks with those who, with attentive ears, hear and heed the words of prophetic encouragement and warning that the Spirit is addressing to all the churches.

Revelation 4:1~11 → Heavenly Throne

NIV	TT
4 ¹ After this I looked, and there before me was a door standing open in heaven. And the voice I had first heard speaking to me like a trumpet said, "Come up here, and I will show you what must take place after this." ² At once I was in the Spirit, and there before me was a throne in heaven with someone sitting on it. ³ And the one who sat there had the appearance of jasper and ruby. A rainbow that shone like an emerald encircled the throne. ⁴ Surrounding the throne were twenty-four	**4** ¹ After this I looked, and **behold**[59], a door **was opened**[60] in heaven, and the first voice, which I had heard as a **trumpet**[61] speaking with me, said: "Come up here, and I will reveal to you what must happen **after these**[62]." ² Immediately I was in the spirit, and behold there stood a throne in heaven, and one seated on the throne. ³ And the seated one was like **jasper**[63] stone and **carnelian**[64] in appearance, and around the throne was a **rainbow**[65] like **emerald**[66] in

---

[59] ἰδού → It means (you) "*see*," "*look*," and "*behold*." Sometimes it is left untranslated.

[60] ἠνεῳγμένη → It means "*was opened*," and it is a participle (perfect passive), simply commentators view it as a "*divine passive*." (Implication: it is God who opened the door, or God made the door to be opened.)

[61] σάλπιγξ → It means "*trumpet*" (the instrument itself, or the sound made by the instrument). The trumpet is linked with the eschatological moment in 1 Thess. 4:16 (cf. Matt. 24:30-31) and is the first of several links with Exod. 19:16.

[62] μετὰ ταῦτα → Literally it means "*after these*," "*with these*," "*among these*," and "*behind these*." The phrase appears in 1:19; 9:12; 4:1 and 20:3. I see it as a literary device to emphasize thematic connection.

[63] ἴασπις → It means "*jasper*," a precious stone of various colors (for some are purple, others blue, others green, and others brass).

[64] σάρδιον → It means "*carnelian*," "*sard(ius)*," a reddish precious stone.

[65] ἶρις → It means "*rainbow*." Rainbow appears only twice in the New Testament (Rev. 4:3; 10:1). In the Old Testament, rainbow meant "*covenant*," "*hope*" (Gen. 9:12-13), and "*the glory of God*" (Ezek. 1:28).

other thrones, and seated on them were twenty-four elders. They were dressed in white and had crowns of gold on their heads. ⁵ From the throne came flashes of lightning, rumblings and peals of thunder. In front of the throne, seven lamps were blazing. These are the seven spirits of God. ⁶ Also in front of the throne there was what looked like a sea of glass, clear as crystal. In the center, around the throne, were four living creatures, and they were covered with eyes, in front and in back. ⁷ The first living creature was like a lion, the second was like an ox, the third had a face like a man, the fourth was like a flying eagle. ⁸ Each of the	appearance. ⁴ And around the throne were twenty-four thrones, and twenty-four elders, clothed in white/dazzling clothes, sat on the thrones, with gold crowns on their heads. ⁵ And lightning and rumbling and thunder went out from the throne, and **seven**[67] flaming torches, which are the seven spirits of God, were burning in front of the throne. ⁶ And in front of the throne there was something like a sea of glass, like crystal. And in the midst of the throne and around the throne were four **living creatures**[68], covered with eyes in front and behind. ⁷ And the first creature was like a lion, and the second creature was like an ox, and the third creature had a face like a human, and

---

[66] σμαράγδινος → It means "*emerald.*" (cf. Exod. 28:18; 39:11, Ezek. 28:13, Rev. 4:3; 21:19)

[67] ἑπτὰ → It means "*seven.*" In the Old Testament "*seven*" becomes the number of "*completeness,*" and "*perfection*" (Gen. 2:2). In the New Testament, the number apparently serves as a symbol for "*fullness*" or "*completion.*" The large majority of the uses of "*seven*" in the New Testament (nearly two-thirds) occur in the Book of Revelation. In this apocalyptic genre, the number "*seven*" is normally infused with symbolic value. It is used to describe numerous items: lampstands (Rev. 1:12), stars (1:16), angels (1:2), spirits of God (3:1), seals (5:1), trumpets (8:2), heads of a dragon (12:3), plagues (15:1), etc.

[68] ζῷον → It means "*a living being,*" "*an animal,*" and "*a beast.*" Thus simply "*a living creature.*"

four living creatures had six wings and was covered with eyes all around, even under its wings. Day and night they never stop saying:	the fourth creature was like a flying **eagle**⁶⁹. ⁸ And the four living creatures, each of whom had six wings, were covered with eyes all around and inside, and without ceasing they sing day and night. "**Holy**⁷⁰, Holy, Holy, Lord God, **the Almighty**⁷¹, the one who was, who is, and who is coming."
"'Holy, holy, holy is the Lord God Almighty,' who was, and is, and is to come."	
⁹ Whenever the living creatures give glory, honor and thanks to him who sits on the throne and who lives for ever and ever, ¹⁰ the twenty-four elders fall down before him who sits on the throne and worship him who lives for ever and ever. They lay their crowns before the throne and say:	⁹ And whenever the living creatures give glory and honor and thanks to the one sitting on the throne, who lives forever and ever, ¹⁰ the twenty-four elders fall before the one sitting on the throne, and they worship the one who lives forever and ever, and they throw their crowns before the throne, singing: ¹¹ "You are worthy, our Lord and God, to receive glory and honor and **power**⁷², because you
¹¹ "You are worthy, our Lord and God, to receive glory and honor and power,	

---

⁶⁹ ἀετός → It means "*eagle,*" and "*vulture.*"

⁷⁰ ἅγιος → It means "*morally holy,*" "*ceremonially holy,*" "*sacred,*" "*consecrated,*" "*cultically set apart,*" and "*morally perfect.*" I simply translate it as "*Holy*" (nature of God).

⁷¹ παντοκράτωρ → It means "*the Almighty,*" "*All-Powerful,*" "*the ruler of all,*" and "*Omnipotent One.*" In the Hebrew Bible "צְבָאוֹת" is the term for "*the Almighty.*" The meanings of the Hebrew word are "*army,*" "*host,*" "*sun, moon, and stars,*" "*war,*" "*battle,*" "*soldiers,*" and "*service.*"

⁷² δύναμις → It means "*power,*" "*might,*" "*strength,*" "*force,*" and "*ability.*" Power is attributed to God (4:11). The term is used to describe the "*power of God*" (7:12; 12:10;

| for you created all things, and by your will they were created and have their being." | created all things, and by your will they existed and they were created." |

At 4:1 the scene moves from the earthly location on Patmos (1:9), where the initial vision was received, to the heavenly world. Chapters 4 and 5 portray the heavenly throne room and provide the setting for the remainder of the book. Chapters 4 and 5 were intended to be read as a unit. While chapter 4 focuses on God and chapter 5 highlights the Lamb, the grammatical presentation of the two characters is essentially the same. In chapter 4, John is allowed to see the reality of God's sovereignty. God is the creator of the universe (4:8, 11). Even if another lord appears to rule the world at present (chapters 12-13), such a rule can be only temporary.

- **1** The opening phrase, "*after this I looked, and behold ...*" is a grammatical indication that John has shifted to another topic. Though he uses the phrase in this exact way only once more (7:9), it is clearly a loosely developed, formulaic way of initiating a new narrative line of thought. Similar constructions occur at 7:1; 15:5; 18:1; and 19:1 (though the sensory emphasis there is on hearing rather than sight). The key words are the first two: "*after this.*" They occur without the rest of the formulaic expression at the end of 4:1 and at 1:19; 9:12; and 20:3. Although they certainly indicate that new information is breaking, the prepositional emphasis

---

15:8; 19:1) and the Lamb (1:16; 5:12). Later it is also used for the power given by the dragon to the beast (13:2) and the power bestowed in turn by the kings of the earth on the beast (17:3).

(*"after"*) refers back to what has come before. This does not mean that John is working chronologically, so that what is about to happen in the rest of the book occurs sequentially right after the events chronicled in chapters 1-3. John is instead emphasizing a thematic connection between the themes of chapters 1-3 and the imminent revelation about to occur. The coming disclosures are meant to be understood with the charge to the churches in mind; they clarify and intensify the need for John's hearers and readers to make the right witnessing choice. After being told to witness to the lordship of Christ in a context hostile to such a witness, it is encouraging to be shown that the witness will be vindicated and avenged.

John sees an *"opened door."* The passive construction is important; God has invited John inside the heavenly throne room. The opened door also symbolized earned access to God. In Ps. 78:23, God graciously opened the door of heaven despite the fact that the Hebrews did not maintain proper faith. John, though, first connects the language to the steadfast witness of the Philadelphians (3:8). It is because they kept the word and did not deny Christ's name, and therefore his lordship, that the heavenly door is opened to them. John, too, despite the physical cost, has been faithful to the word of God, which is the lordship of Jesus Christ (1:9). For this reason he is offered this special opening. Note, too, how the two witnesses at 11:12 are invited into heaven after the demonstration of their faithful testimony. Though the opened-door metaphor is not applied, the witnesses are solicited with the same words that great John in 4:1: "*Come up here.*" The overall ethical implication for the reader should be clear: faithful witness to Christ's lordship may well provoke hostility from human powers, but it will guarantee direct access to God.

The trumpet-like voice John first heard at 1:10 directs him to the opened door. Revelation 1:12-13 identified the source of that voice as "*the Son of Man.*" This makes sense given the Son of Man's assertion at 3:8 that he is the one who makes the opened door available to believers and believing communities. After telling John to "*come up here,*" Christ explains why he should: he will reveal to him the things that must necessarily occur after this. This promise is Christ's personal follow-up to the narration John used to open his text. At 1:1, he described his entire writing effort as the revelation proclaimed by Jesus Christ to reveal the things that must necessarily occur soon. He repeats this narration almost verbatim at 22:6. After accounting for the differences mandated by the fact that 1:1 is the introduction to the book and 22:6 is moving quickly toward its conclusion, one finds that the grammatical presentation is almost the same.

There are only two key differences between those two occurrences and Christ's use of the same language at 4:1. The infinitive construction ("*to reveal*") of 1:1 and 22:6 changes to a first-person verb ("*I will reveal*") in 4:1. That is understandable given the fact that in 4:1 Christ is speaking directly. The other change is in the timing. What was necessarily to happen "*soon*" in 1:1 and 22:6 must happen "*after this*" in 4:1. One could argue that *"after this"* is synonymous with "soon." If that were the case, however, why does John not simply repeat the phrase for which he has already demonstrated fondness in 1:1 and to which he will return in 22:6? The change in wording suggests a change in intent. The change in timing suggests a specificity that can occur because of what the hearers/readers now know that they did not know at 1:1. That can only be the information acquired in chapters 1-3. Christ wants to show John what must happen after the initial vision of his lordship (chapter 1) and the ensuing ethical mandate to witness to that lordship (chapters 2-3). In view of the fact that what will happen after all this must happen, one necessarily assumes that the events of chapters 1-3 in some way trigger everything that follows in the rest of the Book of Revelation. In other words, if believers witness to the lordship that has been revealed to John in chapter 1 in the ways he exhorts in chapters 2-3, tribulation will necessarily result. Nature will suffer alongside human beings as a result of the ferocious reprisals that will be unleashed against those who would testify against the lordship of Rome. In such a context of apocalyptic conflict, the *"necessity"* is not surprising. If Rome indeed believes in its own lordship and prosecutes that belief through conquest, empire building, and self-deification, it has no alternative but to eliminate any for within its realm that witnesses to a contrary belief. If Rome truly is lord, Rome cannot countenance the obstinate testimony that someone else is Lord. Rome must fight back. God, though, cannot allow Rome's resistance to God's own true lordship to stand. God, too, must therefore engage. Through the activities of the Christ, God will oppose the enemy, destroy him, and vindicate God's people.

> **Excursus 7: The Cosmology in Revelation**
>
> The cosmology assumed is that of the triple-decker universe with the flat earth situated between heaven above and the under-world below (which also is entered through a door or pit, to which there are keys; cf. Rev. 1:18; 9:2; 20:3). The triple-decker model of the universe is also found elsewhere in the New Testament (e.g., Phil. 2:5-11), but there are other models as well. Gnosticizing Christianity pictured the earth as the lowest level, with cosmic powers located between the earth and heaven (Eph. 2:2; 4:7-10). The more common apocalyptic view that there are seven heavens above the earth is also reflected in the New Testament (2 Cor. 12:2, where paradise is located in the *"third heaven"*). In the first century this cosmology was giving way to the *"new"* view that regarded the earth as a sphere surrounded by seven concentric *"planetary"* spheres (the sun, moon, and five planets), beyond which was the realm of the gods. John reflects one version of the older Jewish and biblical view, but his revelation is not intended to give astronomical or cosmological information. As elsewhere in the Bible, his message is expressed within the worldview he assumes to be real. The modern interpreter must distinguish between the truth of the message itself and the ancient worldview within which it is expressed. The variety encourages the reader not to take any of them literally.

- **2 – 3** Immediately after seeing the opened door, John is caught up *"in the spirit."* The phrase *"in the spirit"* occurs three other times in the Book of Revelation (1:10; 17:3; 21:10). Allusion to Old Testament prophecy is strong (cf. 1 Kgs. 22:19; Isa. 6:1-13). Of particular note, the phrase is a reflection of the prophet Ezekiel's repeat *"in the Spirit"* (cf. Ezek. 11:24). John, though, has much more than a spiritual high in mind. In the cases where he speaks about being in the spirit, he appears to be describing circumstances where he has been enabled to see things that are crucial to God's plan and God's expectation for God's people. John has not been caught up in the spirit of ecstasy, but the spirit of prophecy.

  At 1:10, the first occurrence of the phrase, using the same language that he deploys in 4:2, John declares, *"I was in the spirit"* on the Lord's Day. The result of this encounter is a command to write what he sees and send it on to the seven churches as chronicled in chapters 2-3. Moreover, 1:3 has already clarified that John writes prophetically to encourage appropriate ethical behavior; the letters of chapters 2-3 make that ethical purpose explicit. At 17:3, an angel carries him away in the spirit, not so that he can become ecstatically charged but so that he may see the whore of Babylon drunk on the blood of God's witnesses, and therefore know how egregious any act of compliance to her lordship claims must be. Finally, at 21:10, the angel's presentation of the holy city Jerusalem coming down from God is a powerful inducement for John and his hearers/readers to maintain their testimony on Christ's behalf. It is not surprising, then, that at 19:10, under the guise of an angelic interpreter, John explicitly connects that testimony to the spirit of prophecy. John's hearers and readers are expected to act *"in the spirit"* in as prophetic a manner – a witness – as John himself.

This prophetic reading reveals that the ensuing throne-room language is much more than a flaunting of the heavenly décor. For john's hearers and readers, the language should be prescriptive as it is descriptive. What they see should influence what they do. They see, first of all, a throne. John so desperately wants them to see it that he packs throne references into seven of the eleven verses that make up this chapter. Throne-room imagery is common to biblical and apocalyptic texts (1 Kgs. 22:19; Isa. 6:1-13; Ezek. 1:4-28; Dan. 7:9-14; *1 En.* 14:8-16:4; 39:1-40; 71:1-17; *T. Levi* 5:1). The Psalm texts like 103:19 establish that God has established God's throne in heaven; John follows up on that supposition by describing that throne in a manner similar to the depictions rendered in Ezek. 1:4-28 and Dan. 7:9-14. Clearly, the one sitting on the throne in v. 2 is intended to be God. The God whom John's audience sees enthroned is the God for whom they should exclusively witness.

Then, there are the special effects. The key terms – *"throne"* and *"the one sitting on it"* – are repeated, but this time in more glowing terms. The one sitting on the throne shines like a vision of illuminating jasper and carnelian; the throne itself is lit up by an emerald rainbow. (The three stones mentioned will resurface during the description of the new Jerusalem: jasper

21:11, 18-19; carnelian 21:20; emerald 21:19). The accents highlight God's glory and majesty. In heaven, the place of royal recognition is reserved only for God. In heaven, God rules. That realization should temper the fear that John's hearers and readers have about the historical rule of Rome. It should overcome the hesitancy they have about proclaiming the lordship of God and God's Christ in the Roman world. Despite the pretensions to control asserted by Rome, ultimate power belongs to God. God is therefore due ultimate and singular witness.

- **4** The heavenly council models the ethic that the throne room images: all glory is due to God. Just as the rainbow surrounds the throne and therefore illuminates it, so do the twenty-four lesser, encircling thrones. In fact, John uses the same preposition "κυκλόθεν," (surround) to describe the positioning of both the rainbow (v. 3) and the twenty-four thrones (v. 4). He will use the same word only once more, at 4:8 as an adverb, when depicting the eyes that envelop (surround) the four living creatures. A similar preposition "κύκλῳ" (around, surrounding), occurs at 4:6; 5:11 and 7:11. It describes the positioning of the four living creatures and later the angels who also attend God's throne. The suggestion here is one of concentric circles. Just beyond the perimeter of the emerald bow sit the attending chairs of God's divine congress. Just as the power of a great leader of the ancient world was magnified through the attentiveness of the lesser leaders who courted him, so the magnificence of God's throne is enhanced by its relationship to subordinate figures whose heavenly stature suggests that they nonetheless wield great power. The implication is that the subordinates' thrones are all facing God's throne. They are thereby offering, by their very posture and position, a kind of narrative, celestial salute.

Though they apparently do not comprise the ring of honor close to God's throne, the 24 elders who occupy the 24 lesser thrones are mentioned first. There is great debate and no consensus regarding their identity. A heavily subscribed position contends that the 24 represent the combined presence of the 12 tribes and the 12 apostles. In them, the wholeness of the people of faith is represented. Those who find the representation of entire tribes in single thrones too unwieldy opt for a variation of this proposal. Just as each of the seven churches is represented by an angel in chapters 2-3, so too are the tribes and the apostles represented on the heavenly throne by surrogate angels. There are numerous other hypotheses. The 24 elders alternately represent the 24 star gods of Babylonian zodiac; the 24 courses (i.e., shifts) of either the priests or Levites who served the Jerusalem temple before its destruction (1 Chr. 24:1-19); or the 24 hours of the day, and thus the fullness of time, which should be spent praising God.

In the end, John is more interested in narrating the significance of the elders than he is in identifying them. The symbolism is indeed all about wholeness. He takes the number "*twelve*" (a figure of wholeness) and doubles it. Here in this heavenly worship scene, believers find the complete and sure picture of how humanity is to orient itself in faithful repose before God.

The narrative also clarifies how these 24 earned the privilege of worshiping in such close proximity to God. Through their dress, they are revealed as complete witnesses. Their white/dazzling robes (cf. 3:4) are a reward bestowed because the 24 have witnessed to the lordship of Christ in spite of the hostile response they had expected and in turn did receive from the imperial force of Rome. At 3:4 and 7:9-13, the imagery of white/dazzling clothing is directly linked to the act of resistant, witnessing that provokes hostile Roman response. At 19:14, the believers who make up the armies of heaven are suggestively attired in white linen. And at 6:11, following the clear statement that the believers in question were slaughtered because of their testimony to the lordship of Christ (6:9), white/dazzling garments are explicitly tied to resistant witness. Witnessing – washing oneself in the blood of the Lamb – is the gory enterprise that ironically brightens one's apparel (7:9-14) and simultaneously maintains its white and dazzling appearance (3:4).

If the white/dazzling robes have any other meaning, it is that of conquest. At 3:5, Christ declares that they are the proper payment for those who conquer by witnessing faithfully in a hostile context. The crown reference (cf. 4:10) picks up this language of victorious commendation and extends it (cf. 2:8-1; 3:11). At 6:2, the description of the rider on the white horse connects the images of conquest and crown. Nowhere, though, is this linkage more dramatic than in 14:14, where the Son of Man, the ultimate conqueror, is said also to be capped with a golden crown. How impressive have been the exploits of these twenty-four? They have earned them the same headgear as the Christ! Their witness has conquered indeed. What they have done is more important to John than who they are. Humans who are encouraged to emulate their praise of God are invited through John's presentation to mimic the behavior that enabled their praise to take place where it does.

- **5** The shock and awe of the throne room theophany add to the splendor that the throne and its room decor already exude. The imagery builds from a wealth of Hebrew Bible sources where this kind of heavenly activity signals God's cosmic prominence. Key among them is the Sinai theophany at Exod. 19:18-21. There are many others, however, among them Job 36:30-32; Pss 18:7-19; 77:17-18; Ezek. 1:4, 13, 14, 24, 26-28; Dan. 7:9-10. John effectively returns to these dramatizations at 8:5, 11:19 and 16:18-21. Perhaps just as important is the recognition that the imagery has a competitive edge. Lightning and thunder were used in association with Greco-Roman deities and emperors. (The thunderbolt was closely associated with the Greek god Zeus, as it was with his Roman counterpart Jupiter, and was consequently used as a symbol suggesting the divinity of several Roman emperors including Domitian.) John's presentation presumes a more natural and longstanding association with God instead. The seven flaming torches further increase the sense of grandeur. Their presence, though, is more than a special effect, for they recall the lampstand of Zech. 4:2 and the seven flames that burn upon it. For the prophet, the stand and its lamps represented the presence and vision of God throughout all creation. Also reminding the reader of the lamps that burned before the ark of the covenant, they expand on the discussion that John introduced at 1:4. The spirits at 1:4 represented the fullness (the number "*seven*") of God's force in the world through the active presence of the Holy Spirit. The all-seeing nature of that Spirit is declared in 5:6.

- **6 – 8a** The sea of glass appears to be an allusion to the heavenly dome of crystalline ice at Ezek. 1:22. In John's mind, it threatens the access to God that the opened door represents. The sea is the site of chaos in the Bible (Job 26:12-13; Pss. 74:12-15; 89:9-10; Isa. 27:1; 51:9-11). The raging sea represents resistance to God, God's people, and the future of God's people. Before God can create and secure the world, God must first seize control of the sea. John repeats at 13:1 the belief that Daniel initiated (Dan. 7:2-3); great beasts of terrible destruction are fomented in and from the sea.

Remarkably, in the staging that John envisions, the sea appears closer than the twenty-four elders to the throne. Indeed, that portrait fits Revelation's witness theme. To gain access to God, believers must cross over the chaos of the sea. That is, they must find a way to witness to the lordship of Christ by pushing past the torrential forces that demand celebration of Rome's lordship.

God has made the crossing easier by freezing into place the sea and the hostility it represents. God has not, however, realized the goal that John's vision now exists with God. It sits in heaven, next to the throne. God harboring the sea in the throne room is like the president of the United States stashing an unstable, active, Soviet-era nuclear bomb on the credenza behind the desk of the Oval Office. Indeed, the sea is glassed over like a cosmic throw rug. It is, however, still there, waiting to break open and flood away the hopes and dreams of heaven itself. Locked down is not thrown out. When John sees the sea through the opened door, he therefore knows that the future, even God's future, is still a very dangerous place.

Back closer to the throne (it is as if John's enraptured eyes are flashing back and forth, seeing erratically, certainly not in sequence), John now glimpses what he had apparently missed before: four oddly appointed, living creatures – the cherubim. The use of the preposition "κύκλῳ" (surrounding) indicates that they represent another of the concentric circles ringing the throne. They are so close to the throne, in fact, that John also says that they are in the midst of it. This odd description most likely means that they are right up against the throne. Their placement, then, would make them the first of the attendees to God's presence. The rainbow, the seven flaming spirits, the sea, and the twenty-four elders would all apparently follow them in turn.

Clearly, these four living creatures are a composite picture drawn from the visionary recollections of Ezek. 1:5-25 and Isa. 6:1-4. (Variations of the cherubim – Gen. 3:24; Exod. 25:18; Num. 7:89; 1 Sam. 4:4; 2 Kgs.

19:15; Pss. 80:1; 99:1; Ezek. 10:1-22) While Ezekiel's creatures had four wings, John's like Isaiah's have six. The match with Isaiah, however, is not a perfect one in this regard. In Isaiah's presentation, the wings are paired together as they perform certain functions. In Revelation they apparently operate individually. The creatures are also positioned differently. Isaiah situates them above the throne; in Ezekiel, they appear to bear the throne (with the assistance of their adjoining wheels) from a position below. John sees them stationed right next to the throne. They are also described differently. In Ezekiel, each creature has four faces; however, Revelation presents four different creatures with four different faces. In Ezekiel, the creatures move but do not speak; in both Revelation and Isaiah, they introduce a worship of God that begins with a resounding cry of "*Holy, Holy, Holy.*" The echo reminds John's audience that his vision is an accurate prophetic rendering, but with a new clarity and emphasis that comes in the wake of the identity of God's Christ being revealed.

Building from the parallels with the creatures in both the Ezekiel and Isaiah accounts, John describes and thereby characterizes the cherubim he sees. As in Ezek. 1:18 and 10:12, they are filled (or "*covered*") with eyes. This description characterizes them as all-seeing. The wings suggest that they are completely mobile. Indeed, their very number symbolizes their omnipresence. They are themselves the representation of the four compass points and thus personify the entirety of the cosmos (cf. Rev. 7:1).

The creatures' omnipresence suggests that they may well be a metaphor for all of living creation, as so many commentators take them to be. Yet I argue instead that their divine character traits link them more closely to God than to humanity. It has closer association with angelic rather than human being. Maybe they represent the highest order of angels, those who stand closest to the throne of God.

Whoever they are, their function is clear: they exist to praise God (cf. 4:9; 5:8, 11, 14; 7:11; 14:3; 19:4). They are paired with the twenty-four elders as models of appropriate worship behavior. This makes them divine witnesses to the lordship of God and God's Christ. These omniscient creatures, who see everywhere and who personify the expansiveness of the cosmos, are in the perfect position to recognize true power. They are genuflecting before God, not before Caesar. They are therefore modeling and exhorting appropriate witness behavior. No matter the circumstances, whether one is lifted to the highest reaches of the heavens or crushed beneath the foot of Rome, one's primary duty is to PRAISE GOD. The one true Lord will soon intervene in human affairs and set history right (cf. 1:3; 3:11; 22:7, 10, 12, 20).

- **8b – 11** Playing the role of heavenly liturgists, the four creatures initiate a hymn that praises God's holy and glorious lordship. As did their Isaiah counterparts (Isa. 6:3), they jump-start the singing with the "*trisagion*," a threefold declaration acknowledging the holy nature of the Almighty. John transforms the "*trisagion*," (Three "*Holy*"s) however, by adding the information that was so well highlighted in chapter 1 (vv. 4, 8): the one who was, who is, and who is coming. Here, the creatures corroborate the testimony offered by John (1:4) and then declared in God's own voice (1:8). By using this formula which was often attributed to human leaders, and attaching it to the title "*Almighty*," the creatures turn their worship into an act of political counter-praise. They therefore model exactly the kind of witness John expects from his hearers and readers in Roman-occupied Asia Minor.

This worship of the creatures is affirmed antiphonally by the twenty-four elders. In John's description of the ongoing heavenly choreography, the creatures initiate an act of praise to which the elders respond. The pattern repeats forever. Having fallen before the one who sits on the throne and rules forever, they worship. In the process, they cast at God's feet the crowns for which they have expended so much effort – bearing their courageous witness – to earn. The gesture that kings used to demonstrate their fidelity to Caesar was performed by these heavenly authority figures toward God.[73] The ethical implications are clear. Given that the elders represent the faithful community of believers in its entirety, John's hearers and readers know they must emulate them. They, too, must respond to the praise of the four creatures by bowing and giving exclusive allegiance to God.

---

[73] → According to the Roman writer Tacitus, the Parthian [Armenian] King Tiridates placed his diadem before the image of Nero in order to give homage to the Roman emperor (*vision of a Just World*, 59).

The elders, however, do more than simply respond; they also expand the rationale for worship. While the creatures celebrate God's holy, almighty status, the elders attribute God's worthiness to God's role as Creator. Despite their connection with titles like *"dominus"* (Lord), *"dues"* (God), and *"despotes"* (Master), no Roman Caesar could claim the power to create cosmic and human being. He could never credibly claim to have brought into existence the world he so desperately wished to control. That prowess is God's alone. Knowing that the ultimate power lies with God, believers ought to feel empowered to resist any claim to lordship tendered by Rome.

> **Excursus 8: The Hymns in Revelation**
> Revelation is a dangerous blend of memorable music and recalcitrant rhetoric. There are nine hymnic units in the Book of Revelation, and seven are antiphonal (in western Christian liturgy sung or recited) in form. Call and response between God, angels, cherubim, executed believers, and even the inanimate heavenly altar cascade down to earth and rise back up to the heavens in worshipful celebration of God's identity and God's purpose for human- and heaven- kind.
>
> -The seven antiphonal hymns-
> **1.** *"Holy, Holy, Holy, is the Lord God Almighty, who was, and is, and is to come... You are worthy, our Lord and God, to receive glory and honor and power, for you created all things, and by your will they were created and have their being."* (cf. Rev.4:8-11)
> It all begins at 4:8-11, a celebratory declaration of God's transcendent and historical lordship that sets the

tone for the hymns that follow. It is no accident when the cherubim start, no accident when the twenty-four elders finish, by casting down their crowns before God's throne, and declaring God not only ruler but also Creator of all. They sing clearly so they can be heard forcefully: "You, Lord God, are worthy (only you)." Thus 4:8-11 makes the point for God, and 5:9-14 establishes the same point for God's messianic regent, the Lamb.

2. *"You are worthy to take the scroll and to open its seals, because you were slain and with your blood you purchased men for God from every tribe and language and people and nation... to the Lamb be praise and honor and glory and power, forever and ever."* (cf. Rev. 5:9-14)

It is not Caesar who sets the course of human life and gives it meaning; instead, the Lamb does so, by his blood. After opening the initial hymn with their deafening *"Holy, Holy, Holy,"* cherubim salute the claims made in this hymn with a resounding *"Amen."*

3. *"Salvation belongs to our God... and to the Lamb."* (cf. Rev. 7:9-12)

At 7:9-12, an innumerable soul multitude of every tongue, tribe, and nation stands before the heavenly throne and the Lamb, they cry out: *"Salvation belongs to our God ... on the throne and the Lamb."* According to Roman imperial rhetoric, every tongue, tribe, and nation owes its peace and salvation exclusively to Caesar. Salvation is imaged as a transformative, historical victory.

4. *"The kingdom of the world has become the kingdom of our Lord and of his Christ, and he will reign forever and ever... We give thanks to you, Lord God Almighty, the One who is and who was..."* (cf. Rev. 11:15-18)

The fourth antiphonal hymn clarifies what the third one

left implicit. The kingdom of the world – it has to be Rome – becomes the kingdom of God and the Lamb instead. They, not Caesar, will reign forever.

5. *"You are just in these judgments, you who are and who were, the Holy One... And I heard the altar respond: Yes, Lord God Almighty, true and just are your judgments."* (cf. Rev. 16:5-7)

It is all about justice now. In the fifth antiphonal hymnic unit, the angel of the waters sings accompaniment to the Almighty's destruction of Rome and its political and economic minions. Even the furniture (altar) is compelled to sing.

6. *"Hallelujah! Salvation and glory and power belong to our God...Hallelujah..."* (cf. Rev. 19:1-4)

7. *"Hallelujah...Hallelujah For our Lord God Almighty reigns."* (cf. Rev. 19:5-8)

The sixth (19:1-4) and seventh (19:6-8) hymnic units erupt in a hallelujah chorus of affirmation. This is the only place in the New Testament where *"Hallelujah,"* *"Praise Yahweh"* occurs (4 times here). The Almighty God, not Rome, is the ultimate historical judge, the Almighty God, not Rome, reigns Supreme.

-The other two hymns-

8. *"Now have come the salvation and the power and the kingdom of our God, and the authority of his Christ."* (cf. Rev. 12:10-12)

9. *"Great and marvelous are your deeds, Lord God Almighty."* (cf. Rev. 15:3b-4)

The other two hymnic units 12:10-12 and 15:3b-4 celebrate the same primary themes: while resisting the lordship of Rome, they worship the lordship of God and the Lamb.

Revelation 5:1~14 → Standing Slaughtered Lamb

NIV	TT
5 ¹ Then I saw in the right hand of him who sat on the throne a scroll with writing on both sides and sealed with seven seals. ² And I saw a mighty angel proclaiming in a loud voice, "Who is worthy to break the seals and open the scroll?" ³ But no one in heaven or on earth or under the earth could open the scroll or even look inside it. ⁴ I wept and wept because no one was found who was worthy to open the scroll or look inside. ⁵ Then one of the elders said to me, "Do not weep! See, the Lion of the tribe of Judah, the Root of David, has triumphed. He is able to open the scroll and	**5** ¹ Then I saw in the right hand of the one seated on the throne a **scroll**[74] written inside and on the back, sealed with seven seals. ² Then I saw a mighty angel **preaching**[75] in a great voice: "Who is worthy to open the scroll by breaking its seals?" ³ And no one was able in heaven or on the earth or under the earth to open the scroll or look into it. ⁴ And I **wept greatly,**[76] because no one was found worthy to open the scroll or look into it. ⁵ Then one of the elders said to me: "Stop weeping. Behold the lion from the tribe of Judah, the root of David, has conquered, so that he is able to open the

---

[74] βιβλίον → It means *"book,"* and *"scroll."*
[75] κηρύσσω → It means *"to proclaim," "to publish,"* and *"to preach."*
[76] ἔκλαιον πολύ → The phrase means *"I wept/cried" "greatly," "much" "many," "loudly," "severe,"* and *"strong."*

its seven seals."	scroll and its seven seals."
⁶ Then I saw a Lamb, looking as if it had been slain, standing at the center of the throne, encircled by the four living creatures and the elders. The Lamb had seven horns and seven eyes, which are the seven spirits of God sent out into all the earth. ⁷ He went and took the scroll from the right hand of him who sat on the throne. ⁸ And when he had taken it, the four living creatures and the twenty-four elders fell down before the Lamb. Each one had a harp and they were holding golden bowls full of incense, which are the prayers of God's people. ⁹ And they sang a new song, saying: "You are worthy to take the scroll and to open its seals, because you were slain,	⁶ Then I saw a Standing Slaughtered **Lamb**[77] among the throne and the four living creatures and the elders, having seven horns and seven eyes, which are the seven spirits of God sent out into all the earth. ⁷ And he went and took the scroll from the right hand of the one seated on the throne. ⁸ And when he took the scroll, the four living creatures and the twenty-four elders fell before the Lamb, each holding a harp and golden bowls filled with incense, which represent the prayers of the saints. ⁹ And they sing a new song: "You are worthy to take the scroll and open its seals, because you were slaughtered and by your blood you **purchased**[78] for God people from every tribe and tongue and people and

---

[77] ἀρνίον → It means "*Lamb*," and "*sheep*." John uses this term 28 times in the Book of Revelation as a metaphor for the Christ. This term appears elsewhere in the New Testament only once (John 21:15), and in that case it refers not to Jesus but to his followers.

[78] ἀγοράζω → It means "*buy*," and "*purchase*." Theological language may be "*ransom*."

and with your blood you purchased for God
persons from every tribe and language and people and nation.
¹⁰ You have made them to be a kingdom and priests to serve our God,
and they will reign on the earth."

¹¹ Then I looked and heard the voice of many angels, numbering thousands upon thousands, and ten thousand times ten thousand. They encircled the throne and the living creatures and the elders. ¹² In a loud voice they were saying:

"Worthy is the Lamb, who was slain,
to receive power and wealth and wisdom and strength
and honor and glory and praise!"

¹³ Then I heard every creature in heaven and on earth and under the earth and on the sea, and all that

nation. ¹⁰ And you made them, for our God, a kingdom and priests, and they will rule on the earth."

¹¹ Then I saw and I heard the sound of many angels surrounding the throne and the living creatures and the elders (and their number was myriads of myriads and thousands of thousands), ¹² singing with a great voice, "Worthy is the Lamb, who was slaughtered to receive power and wealth and wisdom and strength and honor and glory and **blessing**[79]."

¹³ Then I heard every creature in heaven and on earth and under the earth and upon the sea, and all in them, singing:

"To the one seated on the throne and to the Lamb be blessing and honor and glory and power forever."

¹⁴ And the four living creatures said, "Amen."

---

[79] εὐλογία → It means "*praise*," and "*blessing*."

is in them, saying: "To him who sits on the throne and to the Lamb be praise and honor and glory and power, for ever and ever!" ¹⁴ The four living creatures said, "Amen," and the elders fell down and worshiped.	And the elders fell down and worshiped.

The chapter division here is unfortunate, since chapters 4 and 5 compose one scene. The central theological question of chapters 4-5 as well as of the whole church is: Who is the true Lord of this world? The reader knows that God and Christ ("*Standing Slaughtered Lamb*") are Lord because the heavenly court positions and worships them as such.

- **1** *"Then I saw"* appears at 5:1 because John's vision shifts now from a general appraisal of the throne room and God, the one seated on the throne, to a more specific concern with an item located in God's right hand. Biblically speaking, the right hand is a symbol of prestige and power. (The right hand of God is a common metaphor frequently found in the Old Testament and Judaism signifying his power and authority. Exod. 15:6, 12; Pss. 18:35; 20:6; 63:8; Isa. 41:10; 48:13). In the eschatological reign, it is the coveted place to sit next to God (Matt. 22:44; Mark

12:36; Luke 20:42; Acts 2:34; Heb. 1:13). Jesus himself declares that when even his enemies see him so positioned, all will recognize him as God's messianic agent (Matt. 26:64; Mark 14:62; Luke 22:69). No wonder, then, that the disciples seek a seating at Jesus' right hand when he comes into his reign (Matt. 20:21; Mark 10:37). The image of salvation itself is positionally determined. At the moment of judgment, when the wheat is separated from the chaff or, to use another popular metaphor, the sheep is distanced from the goats, the ones favored by God (wheat, sheep) end up on the right (Matt. 25:33-34). Numerous other references demonstrate the positive symbolic value of being located on the right (see Mark 16:5; Luke 1:11; Acts 2:25, 33; 5:31; 7:55-56; Rom. 8:34; Col. 3:1; Heb. 1:3, 13; 8:1; 10:12; 12:2; 1 Pet. 3:22).

John clearly holds the right hand in high esteem. When the Son of Man secures the seven churches, he cradles their seven representative angels (stars) in his right hand (1:16, 20; 2:1). When an angel raises a hand to swear, in predictably is the right hand (10:5). When John pictures the mythological marking of the dragon showing up on a person's body at a place that represents a person's identity and life choices, he mentions the forehead and the right hand (13:16). And when the Son of Man wants to encourage John and calm him fears, he intentionally places upon the seer his right hand (1:17).

The object in God's right hand is a "βιβλίον" ("*biblion*"). John's word use is imprecise. "*Biblion*" could easily denote the flat codex-type book with cover and bound leaves that was a precursor to contemporary books. It could just as easily intend a rolled-up scroll, more commonly found in the early and middle decades of the first century. Although the codex began to be used more frequently in Christian communities toward the end of the first century, one cannot appeal to the historical context as a way of clearly determining what kind of "*book*" John has in mind. At the end of the first century, it could have been either.

The higher probability, however, is that John intends a rolled-up scroll. The metaphor he applies to the heavens just a chapter later (6:14) is suggestive. He describes the horrific vision of the sky rolled up like a "*biblion*" (cf. Isa. 34:4). There he clearly means "*scroll*." It is likely that John was operating with the same image throughout since he never feels a need to explain it differently. This interpretation gathers further corroboration from the background imagery drawn from Ezek. 2:9-10. Like Rev. 5:1, the Hebrew text speaks of a scroll written on the inside and back. Ezekiel's volume is clearly a scroll, and the LXX uses "*biblion*" to refer to it.

There remain two even more pertinent questions. How many scrolls does John include in the course of his writings? And if there are more than one, to which one is he referring here? I could understand that some argues for four scrolls.

(1) John's own scroll of prophetic visions (1:11; 22:7, 9, 10, 18, 19)

(2) The heavenly scroll of chapter 5 (5:1, 2, 3, 4, 5, 8, 9,)

(3) The little scroll of chapter 10 (10:2, 8, 9, 10)

(4) The Scroll (Book) of Life (3:5; 13:8; 17:8; 20:12, 15; 21:27)

John is clear that the scroll of chapter 5 is fully opened with the breaking of the seventh seal (8:1). Additionally, John digests the *"little scroll"* (10:9). Thus, if indeed, as I think is the case, the scroll of chapter 5 is the same scroll described in chapter 10, that scroll cannot be the Lamb's Scroll of Life, which is opened intact at 20:12. John is therefore working with three scrolls.

The second scroll is closed with seven seals (5:1). The number *"seven"* indicates a complete and total binding. The seals are themselves suggestive: In antiquity, wet clay or wax was applied to secure the closures of containers or documents. Seals were then used to make an impression in the clay or wax to identify the source of a document or object to guarantee the work's authenticity or to safeguard the document from tampering. John uses the noun *"seal"* throughout chapters 5 and 6, right up until the moment when the final scroll seal is broken at 8:1. In its only other occurrences in the Book of Revelation, 7:2 (cf. also 7:3) and 9:4, the term refers to the seal of God that ultimately marks the identity of those who have been faithful, which in John's language means that they have witnessed (i.e., have not accommodated). Those who are so sealed are marked with the name of God on their foreheads (7:3; 9:4; 14:1; 22:4). They are marked as God's authentic property. If the seven scroll seals were likewise God's seals, then they too would designate God's property.

Many scholars have tried to clarify this particular property by analyzing John's description of it. Exodus 32:15 states that the tablets bearing the Ten Commandments were written on both sides, front and back. This observation has led some to conjecture that perhaps the scroll contained either the commandments or the entire Old Testament, whose proper interpretation was only realized in and through the life of Christ. As objecting scholarship has pointed out, however, John's book, like Ezekiel's, upon which it depends, is more a metaphor of salvation and judgment than it is a clarification of the Hebrew Bible.

The closed scroll no doubt reminds John's readers of the sealed scroll in Isaiah that contained God's vision for humankind, which the people could not read (Isa. 29:11). Jeremiah speaks of a similar instrument (Jer. 32:10). Daniel writes about a scroll whose information about human destiny was so complete that God ordered it shut until the end of time, which would be preceded by days of great struggle (Dan. 12:4, 9). In John's vision, that end time, complete with days of preparatory struggle, had come. In such a time, humans might take encouragement from knowing whether humankind was destined for obliteration or restoration. That knowledge was apparently secured in the scroll. Revelation 4:1 promises that John would have access to this knowledge, that is, see all things to take place "*after these*." The scroll is the realization of that promise. "*After these*" refers to what is to happen in the remainder of John's "*book*." History's destiny is to be revealed.

- **2** After signaling the start of a new throne room scene with the *"then I saw"* construction of 5:1, John opens 5:2 in the same way. This time, though, the formula does not start a new scene but flavors the same scene with the introduction of a novel theme: worthiness.

    Initially, though, John's focus is on *"a mighty angel preaching in a great voice."* This powerful messenger bears a striking resemblance to Daniel's holy watcher sent from heaven (LXX Dan. 4:13-14, 23). Both figures evoke the symbolism of judgment. This judgment focus continues in Revelation with the appearance of mighty angels at 10:1 and 18:21. Notably, the second mighty angel is also associated with a scroll.

    John's enduring focus is on the angel's question: *"Who is worthy to open the scroll by breaking its seals?"* The hymn that begins at 5:9 supplies the answer. The continuation of the worthiness theme throughout the chapter is also an indication that John is much more preoccupied with this question than he is with any mere angel sighting. Up to this point he has seen many great sights. All of those sights, including this angelic one, take a back seat to the gradually clearing message about someone's worthiness to open the seal.

    Worthiness itself is earned through endeavor. John connected the worthiness of the remnant at Sardis to their refusal to accommodate themselves to the social, economic, political, and spiritual expectations of Greco-Roman pagan and imperial lordship. They combined their refusal to accommodate with the contrary declaration of Christ's lordship. Indeed, their very witness to that lordship was a manifestation of its reality. By testifying to it, they participated in bringing it about. In order to stop their testimony and the result it threatened, the representatives of pagan and imperial lordship could be counted upon to respond in a reactionary manner. Worthiness was thereby integrally connected with both the work of witness and the suffering such work would inevitably bring about.

- **3 – 4** John's narration assures his readers that there are no witnesses worthy enough to open the scroll. Picking up on the three-tiered mythical understanding of the universe as a heavenly upper region, an underworld region comprising the Old Testament sense of Sheol and the New Testament understanding of hell, and earth in between (cf. Exod. 20:4; Deut. 5:8), John declares that no one can be found anywhere in all the cosmos who meets the standard. For all his world power and domination, not even Caesar has attained the requisite stature. Not even Caesar, therefore, has the kind of control over human destiny that his rule pretends to exert.

  Perhaps the even greater tragedy is that the Christ-believers who have been worthy witnesses have not earned sufficient standing to accomplish this monumental task. At 1:9, John describes himself as one who has witnessed to the lordship of Christ and suffered exile as a result. Still, John cannot presume to open the book/scroll. At 2:13, he reminds his readers about Antipas, a witness so faithful that he was killed because of his testimony. Yet he, too, did not earn the right to open the scroll. At 3:4, John describes the

Sardis remnant that witnessed and suffered together as a believing community. They, too, were insufficiently worthy. Witnessing alone, even being slaughtered because of one's witnessing, is not enough.

Apparently the mighty angel wants to know if there might exist some second-level, more radical version of witnessing than has been narratively demonstrated thus far. Only such a witness would be worthy to open the book. John has offered a clue. On two separate occasions (1:5; 3:14) he went out of his way to identify Christ as the one faithful and true witness. Verse 4 adds little in the way of new information. John repeats the tragic announcement of 5:3; no one was found worthy enough to open and read the scroll. He adds only the notice of his own mournful response to this bitter news. Greatly, he wept.

- **5** The throne room attendants, however, know of a possibility that has to this point eluded John. One of the twenty-four elders tasked with heavenly worship confides to the grief-stricken seer that there is someone worthy enough to open the scroll. After telling John to cease crying, the elder describes the candidate by using two messianic descriptors that would be recognizable to John's readers as they are to him. The worthy one is first of all described as the *"lion"* out of the tribe of Judah, an image that builds upon accounts at Gen. 49:9-10; *T. Jud.* 24:5; and *4 Ezra* 12:31-32. His second attribution is the *"root of David,"* a symbol that draws its inter-textual strength from accounts like Isa. 11:1, 10; Jer. 23:5; 33:15; and Zech. 3:8; 6:12. Both images suggest great strength; the lion is a feared predator that rules whatever domain it occupies, as no doubt Israel hoped, with God's help, to do in the future. That rule would be instigated by and established through a leader of David's messianic lineage, someone from the great king's roots, who would have David's close relationship with God.

Clearly this messianic figure is a powerful force. To describe the results of his work, John uses the verb "*conquered.*" This messiah conquered. It is on the basis of that conquest that he has acquired sufficient worthiness to break the seals and open the scroll. John writes awkwardly at this point, following up his indicative verb, "*conquered,*" with an infinitive "*to open.*" The narrative context suggests that the infinitive initiates a result clause. John intends to say that the lion out of the tribe of Judah, the root of David, has conquered; as a result, he is worthy to open the scroll.

The understanding that John intends a result clause comes from the connections he has drawn between the terms "*witness,*" "*conquer,*" and "*worthy.*" For John, a faithful witness conquers by testifying the lordship of Jesus Christ. The seer makes this clear in chapters 2 and 3, where he exhorts the seven churches to live by a witness code demanding that they not accommodate themselves to the expectations of pagan and imperial lordship. John describes witnesses who are successful resisters as conquerors. As a result of their conquest, witnesses are worthy of an eschatological relationship with God (15:2; 21:7). He makes the case of each of the seven churches at 2:7 (Ephesus), 2:11 (Smyrna), 2:17 (Pergamum), 2:26 (Thyatira), 3:5 (Sardis), 3:12

(Philadelphia), and 3:21 (Laodicea). Still, a believer does not witness in order to gain an eschatological relationship. That relationship is a by-product of the witnessing act. The goal of witnessing is the declaration of the lordship of Christ in an environment hostile to such testimony. There are many possible responses to that testimony. Opposing powers will persecute and punish the witnesses. God, however, will count their witness, even if it results in the ultimate punishment of death, as a conquest worthy of eschatological relationship.

Nowhere is this connection between witnessing and conquering made more explicitly than at 12:11, where John declares that those who conquer do so by the blood of the Lamb and the word of their witness. By conquering in this way, John's believers mimic the actions of the Lamb, who himself is the faithful and true witness (1:5; 3:14) who conquers (17:14). Because worthiness is an attribute earned by the work of witness, the connection between worthiness and conquest is also narratively secured. The conquering witness is a worthy witness. The conquering believer who testifies to the lordship of Christ is worthy of an eschatological relationship with God. The conquering lion from the tribe of Judah, the root of David, is apparently exceptional. He already has an eschatological relationship with God; he is God's messianic emissary. His conquering testimony makes him worthy of something else: he can open the scroll sealed with the seven seals.

- **6** The "Καὶ εἶδον" (then I saw) of 5:6 introduces yet another novel element to the ongoing throne-room scene centered on the scroll in God's right hand. Having introduced the character who is worthy enough to open the scroll, John now identifies both his person and the conquering witness that gave him such lofty eschatological stature.

  The *"lion from the tribe of Judah,"* the *"root of David,"* is awkwardly positioned. John claims that he is *"in the midst"* of the throne and the four cherubim and *"in the midst"* of the twenty-four elders. John used this awkward phrasing *"in the midst"* before when he described the location of the cherubim as *"in the midst of the throne and surrounding the throne"* (Rev. 4:6-8). He meant that they are right next to the throne, so close to it in fact that they are the most intimately located attendees to God's presence. He means the same thing here; the one who is *"worthy"* stands so close to both the throne and the four cherubim that he is right next to them. The problem with this stated location is that John also locates him *"in the midst"* of the twenty-four elders. When we appeal to John's chapter 4 narration about the location of the attendees to God's heavenly presence, we find that their positions fall away from the throne in the following order: the cherubim, the rainbow, the seven flaming spirits, the sea, and the twenty-four elders. But if these elders represent the outer ring of the throne room attendees and the cherubim the innermost right, the messianic figure John sees cannot be in the midst of both groups at the same time. John's language therefore suggests movement. The one who is worthy is, in effect, "*working*" the throne room. He is on the move, next to God, as one might expect God's eschatological representation would be, and yet also in the midst of the representative believers, who witness to God's lordship. What appears to be impossible physically, John established kinetically by his awkward phrasing. In his envisioning, the one who is worthy to open the scroll is with God and with those who witness to God because he is moving between them.

Matters become stranger still. The scene appears to shift character focus. Without warning, John distances himself from the lion and focuses on what, in terms of strength anyway, is its polar opposite: a Lamb, standing as slaughtered. This is a striking turn of events. Why does John set the reader up to expect a text about a messianic, conquering lion, and then, after dramatic notice of a topical shift ("*then I saw*"), cut immediately to a scene whose protagonist is a slaughtered Lamb? Is he using the latter figure to subvert the former?

John will use the term "*Lamb*" ("ἀρνίον") some twenty-eight times in the Book of Revelation as a metaphor for the Christ. Though the word appears to be a diminutive Greek form, most commentators agree that by the end of the first century, when John was most likely writing, it had lost any diminutive sense and was synonymous with the word "*sheep*" ("πρόβατον"). The term "*ἀρνίον*" appears elsewhere in the New Testament only once (John 21:15), and in that case it refers not to Jesus but to his followers. In the only four New Testament texts where "*Lamb*" does refer to Jesus (John

1:29, 36; Acts 8:32; 1 Pet. 1:19), a different Greek word "ἀμνός" is deployed.

At least on the surface, the inter-textual history of the term appears to be more significant than the nomenclature in ascertaining why John so radically shifts his focus. John could have had in mind any of four possible "*lamb*" figures from Jewish history when he envisioned this messianic Lamb: (1) the "*tamid*" lamb (Exod. 29:38-42), sacrificed at the Jerusalem temple in the mornings and evenings; (2) the Passover lamb, symbolizing God's deliverance of the people from Egyptian bondage; (3) the sinless lamb of Isa. 53 (cf. Isa. 53:2, 7, 9), whose sacrifice has atoning significance; and (4) the conquering lamb of the Book of *1 Enoch* 89-90. John probably draws elements from each of these figures in creating his own portrait of the slaughtered Lamb. Reddish argues that this "*standing slaughtered Lamb*" becomes a victorious figure who conquers by self-sacrifice, who willingly gives up his life to become the faithful and true witness. John wants his hearers and readers to recognize that Christ's conquest comes by way of his sacrificial, atoning death on the cross. I offer an alternative explanation. I recognize the same variables of witness, conquest, and slaughter. The Lamb does not conquer by self-sacrifice and thereby become the faithful and true atoning witness. The Lamb already is the faithful and true witness who selflessly sacrifices concern for his own well-being in order to carry out his testimony to his God's and his own lordship in a hostile Greco-Roman, Palestinian world.

The research of Loren Johns is instructive. Johns focuses exclusively on what he calls the rhetorical force of the Lamb symbolism in the Apocalypse. After an exhaustive survey of lamb imagery in early Judaism, he reaches the conclusion that *"there is no evidence at this point to establish the existence of anything like a recognizable redeemer-lamb figure in [its] apocalyptic traditions."* John therefore would not have expected his apocalyptically oriented readers to connect his Lamb's suffering and slaughter to their own redemption. A survey of the Hebrew Bible affords no better warrant. In a study that offers the most relevance for our particular concern about the redemptive efficacy of the Lamb's slaughter, Johns explicitly rules out an agenda of transformative suffering. After comparing texts that associate lambs with atonement for sin to the Lamb language in Revelation, he concludes that *"the terminology used in the Revelation does not fit well with the lambs of the sacrificial system."* In fact, he points out appropriately that John does not even restrict slaughter language to the Lamb (cf. 6:4, 9; 13:3; 18:24). His conclusion: *"In none of these other cases is the 'slaughter' considered expiatory, reducing the possibility that the rhetorical force of the 'slaughter' of the Lamb in 5:6 is primarily expiatory."* Johns then broadens his conclusion even further. Given that only two verses (1:5-6) have even any remote expiatory themes connected to them, and given that they occur well outside the central section of the conflict visions (chapters 4-19), he argues that *"there is little in*

Revelation to support this understanding of Jesus' death as Atonement."

We can, however, support and understand his death as an act of witness. Well before John characterizes Jesus as the Lamb, he identifies him, by name, as the faithful witness (1:5). At 3:14, still before any mention of the Lamb, comes linguistic reinforcement: as witness, Jesus is both faithful and true. There is no need for interpretation; John has made his point clearly. Whatever else he might appear to be to his followers, Jesus Christ is first and foremost God's prime witness.

Except for the anomaly of 1 John 3:12, *"slaughter"* ("σφάζω") is found in the New Testament exclusively in the Revelation. Though the more sacrificially oriented term "θύω" is prevalent elsewhere in the New Testament (cf. Mark 14:12; Luke 22:7; Acts 14:13, 18; 1 Cor. 5:7), it does not occur in the Book of Revelation at all.

While the *"tamid"* lamb was apparently killed as it was standing, the symbolism need not be reduced to that literal historical meaning. Here I should explain that pagan and Jewish methods of slaughtering were similar, and that all or most males would know how to do it. The animal's throat was cut, or the carotid arteries were opened, ordinarily while it was standing. This is my personal take on the description. Normally, when the animal gets slaughtered, it collapses. However, Jesus Christ, the *"Standing Slaughtered Lamb"* is still standing. The power of the world, Greco-Roman imperial force, execution, crucifixion, or (as some churches would say) Jewish authorities, our sins, Jesus' opponents, or Satan, etc, nothing could slaughter/kill/collapse the Lamb completely. The Lamb has the final say, he is still standing, still witnessing the lordship of God and himself.

The Lamb is still standing, even though slaughtered. Though he carries with him forever the marks of his destruction (*"the Crucified One"* Mark 16:6), he remains victoriously alive. Executed because of his witness, he maintains the living. His posture is itself a sign of resurrected defiance – a powerful, hopeful message for a people who fear that their own witness may provoke a hostile government to persecute them (6:11). Even if they should fall in death, they, like the Lamb, will still stand as defiant, victorious witnesses.

What does this language do? Ethically speaking, it encourage the kind of behavior highlighted by its showcased character, the Lamb. The saints are described as those who follow the Lamb wherever he goes (14:1-5). This obviously means that they imitate the Lamb by acting as he has acted. This is why it is so important to be clear about one's interpretation of the slaughter/execution language. Did Christ conquer through his suffering and slaughter? Or did Christ conquer in spite of suffering and being executed? If indeed the Lamb conquers by being slaughtered, then an emphasis on discipleship calls for believers, too, to suffer on their own way toward eschatological relationship with God. If, however, the Lamb conquers by a provocative witness that might indeed provoke a hostile response from the powers threatened by that testimony, then the summons to discipleship would have believers engage in their own acts of non-accommodating witness despite any suffering that might result.

In describing the Lamb, John showcases his strength. He possesses seven horns. The horn is a symbol of power in key pieces of Jewish literature (Deut. 33:17; 1 Kgs. 22:11; 2 Chr. 18:10; Pss. 22:21; 89:17; Ezek. 34:21; Dan. 7:8, 20, 24; 8:3, 6, 8, 20; Zech. 1:18-21; *1 En.* 90:6-12, 37) It is also a metaphor for great power in John's narrative (Rev. 9:13; 12:3; 13:1, 11; 17:3, 7, 12, 16). Like the beast in Dan. 7, the great red dragon and the beasts who operate in its employ sport ten horns fashioned to foment shock and awe. The Lamb, though, is unimpressed. While he carries three fewer horns in number, his power over the dragon and its beasts is incalculable. The number "*seven*" symbolizes wholeness, fullness, and completion. While the dragon has more horns, the Lamb has more power, His power is Complete.

So is his vision. The Lamb's seven eyes represent complete, perfected perception in the same way that the seven horns represent complete power. As spirits, they also symbolize a consummate relationship with God. Prior to 5:6, whenever John used the plural term "*spirits*" (1:4; 3:1; 4:5), he was referring to the seven spirits of God. He was figuratively speaking about God's Holy Spirit. The reference is dependent upon Zech. 4:2, 10, where seven mysterious lamps are revealed as the seven eyes of the Lord, whose perceptive powers range throughout all the earth and whose identity is associated with Yahweh's omnipotent Spirit.

- **7** Though the ensuing action is described sparingly, much happens in this next narrated moment. The Lamb approaches *"the one seated on the throne"* (cf. Dan. 7:9-10). In Dan. 7:13, when the one like a Son of Man approaches God's throne, dominion, glory, and kingship are bestowed upon him. Something very similar is happening in John's vision. After the Lamb arrives at the throne, he removes the scroll from God's right hand. God allows the withdrawal because the Lamb is worthy.
- **8** The Lamb's special status is confirmed by the behavior of the cherubim and the twenty-four elders. Tasked with the eternal worship of God (Chapter 4), they now fall to their knees and shower their praise upon the Lamb. Twice, after John falls to his knees before them in worship, angels chastise him and redirect his praise toward its proper object: God (19:10; 22:8-9). The Lamb is as proper an object for worship as God.

In their praise of the Lamb, the cherubim and elders come equipped with two special props: harps and golden bowls filled with incense. The harps (particularly in the hands of the twenty-four elders) remind John's hearers and readers of the Levites, who like the priests worked in twenty-four orders or shifts in the Jerusalem temple. One of the Levitical tasks was the presentation of music. They were commissioned to *"prophesy in giving thanks and praising the Lord's"* by *"singing"* to the accompaniment of *"lyres, harps, and cymbals"* (1 Chr. 25:6-31).

More important to the overall meaning of the scene are the golden bowls, whose incense represents the prayers of the saints. Saints – literally *"holy ones"* – is simply John's euphemism for the people of God, more particularly to God's and the Lamb's lordship. Incense had a special place in the rituals of the Jerusalem temple. Each morning and evening, at the sacrifices that signaled the opening and close of daily worship, incense was burned on the small golden altar that stood inside of the sanctuary, near the door to the holy of holies. Psalm 141:2 not only recognizes incense as a key component in the liturgy of worship, but also connects incense metaphorically with prayer.

While John does not specify the content of those prayers, the location of the text is suggestive. The prayers would seem to be less an offering and more a challenge to God to begin the process of vindicating God's people. In the only other significant text where the term *"prayer"* and *"incense"* occur together in the Book of Revelation (8:3-4), they are also metaphorically linked. There the prayers of the people rise with incense to the heavens. As a result of that rising, the angels sound their seven trumpets and thereby initiate God's judgment upon those who have persecuted the saints. Revelation 5:8 is just as provocatively positioned. It precedes the Lamb's opening of the seven seals, which also brings about catastrophic acts of judgment that vindicate the lordship of God and the Lamb and, perhaps just as importantly, those who witness to that lordship. Seen in this way, the metaphorical prayers in 5:8 may well anticipate the under-the-altar calls for vindication from those who had been executed because of their witness to God (6:9-11).

- **9 – 10** The cherubim and elders certainly seem to think that the prayers in 5:8 are calls for God to act in judgment and vindication. They follow up those prayers with a new hymn of praise. In the Old Testament, a *"new song"* is always an expression of praise for God's victory over the enemy (cf. Pss. 33:3; 40:3; 96:1; 98:1; 144:9; Isa. 42:10).

The song is also contextually new because the object of praise has shifted. The singers who glorified God in chapter 4 sing the praises of the Lamb in chapter 5. Subsequent new songs follow the narrative pattern established here. They demonstrate a shift of either focus or content from the songs that occurred before them. The new hymn at 14:3 is sung not by the cherubim and elders but by the 144,000, and its mysterious lyrics can only be learned by the 144,000. Those who conquer the beast sing the final new hymn at 15:3. This hymn is the *"Song of Moses"* and the *"Song of Lamb."* Its very learnable lyrics are then played out in the ensuing text. The one thing that each of these new hymns has in common with the others is something they also hold in common with the hymns of the Old Testament: they anticipate God's impending judgment against those who have persecuted God's witnesses, and they celebrate God's vindication of those witnesses, who have been persecuted.

This particular new song at 5:9-10 also addresses the central concern of the chapter's first 5 verses. Who is worthy to open the scroll that contains God's historical design for judgment and vindication? The narrative answered the question at 5:5 by showcasing the *"lion of Judah," "the root of David."* In then has inexplicably shifted focus in the next major scene (5:6-10) by switching attention to the Lamb. The move would have been disorienting for a first-time reader, who would not have been sure why John was suddenly talking about the Lamb when he had led them to expect further discussion of the *"lion."* Only in v. 9 does it become clear that the Lamb and the lion are the same character. The language of worthiness that belonged to the lion also belongs to the Lamb. Only one was worthy. The lion and the Lamb must therefore be the same entity.

The lion/Lamb is worthy. After making that clear, v. 9 uses a causal formulation to explain exactly how the Lamb earned the worthiness for which he is so acclaimed. There are three reasons. First, the Lamb is worthy because he was slaughtered, executed. This surely confuses the identity issues even further. The lion, which usually conquers by might, earns its heavenly credentials in this apocalyptic case by being slaughtered.

Second, the Lamb is declared worthy because he used the blood of his execution to ransom/purchase people. John explains that those who are ransomed/purchased are from every ethnicity, tongue, people, and nation. No group is left out.

The economic nature of the language is equally clear. This metaphoric language most probably refers to the ransom of prisoners of war who were deported to the countries of the victors and could be ransomed by a purchasing agent from their own home country. The image also alludes to the exodus tradition. As the blood of the paschal lamb signified the liberation of Israel from the bondage of Egypt, so has the death of Christ made possible the liberation of Christians from their universal bondage.

At 3:18, Christ instructs the Laodiceans to buy into the relationship with God by purchasing gold, white robes, and salve from him. In the ethical context of chapters 2 and 3, the items for purchase are metaphors for the kind of non-accommodating witness that will lead to eschatological relationship with God. Witness and purchase have a natural, narrative relationship for John. That relationship continues in a negative way at 13:17, where one can only buy and sell in the Roman economy by accepting the mark of the beast (also 18:11). Just as one buys into a relationship with God by the risky act of non-accommodating witness, so one buys into a relationship with the beast by acts of compliant, self-protecting accommodation.

Purchase for John, then, is more political than it is expiatory. Only 1:5 connects Christ's liberating activity to the theme of ransoming humans from sin. In every other significant text that mentions blood in a manner that relates to the eschatological relationship believers hope to have with God, blood draws its most potent meaning from the metaphor of witness. At

19:11-13, the Lamb, who is the faithful and true witness (cf. 1:5; 3:14), exemplifies in his person the strategic connection between his identity as a living testimony to the word of God and the blood that was shed on account of that identity. At 6:10-12, slaughtered believers cry out for vengeance upon their blood, spilled because of their witness. Read through the clarifying lens of 3:2-4, the text of 7:9-14 instructs that clothes washed in the blood of the Lamb are the due of those who have witnessed to the lordship of Christ. The link becomes clear in 12:11: believers conquer by the blood of the Lamb and the word of their witness. The Lamb's blood and the believer's witness are indissolubly linked. It is by appealing to both – one as received gift, the other as engaged act – that believers find themselves in the purchase of an eschatological relationship with God. Blood and purchase are indeed linked in Revelation, but they are linked through the theme of witness, not that of expiation.

Like the faithful believers in Daniel (7:18, 22, 27) and those who followed Moses (Exod. 19:6), John's Christ-believers would also find themselves to be a reign of priests (cf. Rev. 1:6). This is the third reason why the Lamb is found worthy. By his powerful witness, and the sacrifice he makes in proclaiming that witness, he establishes God's believers as a reign of priests on earth. Revelation 20:4-6 clarifies the believer's role. Believers who refuse to accommodate to the expectations of Rome, the satanic beast, are executed because of that witness. These martyrs become the reign of priests (cf. 22:5). While John does not make the connection causal so that their witness causes their rule, he does make the connection explicit. Witnessing and reigning go together for believers just as they went together for the Lamb. It was the Lamb's witness that purchased the reality of that rule; it is the believers' witness to the lordship of the Lamb that apparently will procure – that is to say, enable – their connection with and participation in that rule.

The rule itself is an oppositional one. It personifies the very life and language of resistant witness that brought it into being in the first place. Insofar as John utilizes sociopolitical language in 5:9-10, he transforms the anthropological understanding of redemption expressed in the traditional baptismal formula of 1:5-6 into a sociopolitical one. Just as the exodus of Israel resulted in the election of Israel as a special nation and kingdom for Yahweh, so does the redemption of the Lamb's followers who were elected from the nations constitute a new alternative kingdom or empire whose members are priests.

> **Excursus 9: The Lion and the Lamb**
> John's witnessing Lamb is hardly a vulnerable figure. He is a conquering lion (5:5), armed with the fullness of God's power symbolized by the seven horns (5:6), who deposes the dragon Satan (12:10), and having taken up the sword of God's word, rides out to meet Satan's forces on the field of apocalyptic battle (2:16; 19:11-16). In the visionary world that John inhabits, the Lamb's victory depends on his power. And yet, even in victory, the Lamb carries in his person the visage of slaughter. How is one to hold these

> opposite dramatizations of vulnerability and conquest together in a believable narrative tension?
>
> I believe that this emphasis on the necessity of power is the reason John finds it necessary, before he introduces Christ as the Standing Slaughtered Lamb, to announce him as a mighty lion (5:5). There is every narrative indication that John thinks the two titles belong together. In the end, neither subverts the other. The lion reveals a Lamb; the Lamb remains a lion. The slaughtered Lamb is how the lion manifests itself in the world.
>
> Being Slaughtered was not the goal for John's hearers. The goal was an active ministry of resistance that would witness to the singular lordship of Jesus Christ. Ironically, just as Jesus' death led to his empowered life, the slaughtering would help lead to the transformative goal of eternal life in a new heaven and new earth where that lordship was on full display (12:10-12). This is how the power of the Lamb works. For those who are slaughtered because they stand up for Christ and therefore cause themselves to stand out to Rome and its Asia Minor vassals, defeat is conjured to victory, death is conjured to life.

- 11 – 12 John introduces the second hymn to the Lamb with his fourth use of the scene-shifting narrative formula *"then I saw."* Before identifying the poetic shift in emphasis, he sets up the hymn with a narrative prelude. He sees a throng of angels crowding the throne room. There are so many present that they cannot be numbered (cf. Dan. 7:10). They are readying themselves to respond antiphonally to the psalm previously sung by the cherubim and elders.

The angels open their song by echoing the thought of the cherubim and elders: the slaughtered Lamb is worthy. Then the angels shift the focus. In their song, they to not explain why the Lamb is worthy. Instead, they emphasize what the Lamb is worthy to receive. It is just here, though, that there is a great deal of similarity in the two worship refrains. Before the cherubim and elders explain why the Lamb is worthy, they too declare what the Lamb is worthy to receive. In their thinking, the Lamb is worthy to receive and open the scroll. Using the same verb of reception, then angels now observe the Lamb's worthiness to take power, wealth, wisdom, might, honor, glory, and blessing. The parallel formulations suggest that there is a relationship between the scroll and power, wealth, and wisdom, and so forth. With knowledge and control of history (i.e., the opened scroll) comes massive power. Because Caesar has been shown to be incapable of opening the scroll, he can no longer justifiably lay claim to such power. Only the Standing Slaughtered Lamb is worthy to take the scroll and open it. Therefore, only the Lamb is worthy of the formidable rights that go along with that capability (cf. Dan 7:14).

- **13 – 14** A cascading praise effect erupts, like dominoes falling, where the singing of one group ignites the responsive singing of another. Once the heavenly chorus finishes its choral response to the song of the cherubim and elders, the voices of every creature in creation rise up in yet another antiphonal reply. John appeals again to the three-tiered mythical construct of the cosmos to make certain that his hearers and readers understand the universal range of his vision. He hears voices from every realm of the created order, and he hears them singing a song of praise both to God on the throne and to the Standing Slaughtered Lamb. They are both due the blessing and honor and glory and power mentioned in 5:12. And they are due them forever. The hymn of 4:11 has explained the reason why the cherubim and elders believed God was worthy of such accolades: God is worthy because God created all things. In the hymn of 5:9-10 the cherubim and elders explained the three reasons why the Lamb is worthy. Creation is now apparently affirming those declarations with a responsive chord of acclamation. Fittingly, the cherubim and elders finish both worship scenes by sealing those affirmations with a confirmation of their own. The cherubim cry out "*Amen*" while the elders acknowledge the truth of the hymns by falling before the throne in worship.

The Opening of the Seven Seals

John is the master of a three-ring narrative circus. The seven seals (6:1-8:1), the seven trumpets (8:2-11:18), and the seven bowls (16:1-21) stage the same preparatory build-up to the Last Judgment. They do so, however, from different perspectives (see pg 785). Hearers and readers watch three different versions of the end time unfold simultaneously at three different places on the narrative set. That explains why the scenes, while loosely similar, differ in detail. Like any good rhetorician, John hammers home his single message by rearticulating it in a variety of ways. The message is simple: God will execute a cosmic verdict that will judge those who have set themselves up as lord and save those who have witnessed to the alternative lordship of the Standing Slaughtered Lamb.

When the world appears to be spinning wildly, madly, and violently out of control, even then God is firmly in charge. While it is difficult to reconcile the New Testament image of a kind, benevolent God with the chaos and destruction associated with the seals, trumpets, and bowls, there is a kind of inter-testamental continuity in John's presentation. The Old Testament God is most violent and destructive when acting as cosmic and historical judge. In Revelation, the violent executors of God's judgment are based on Zechariah's presentation of patrolling, colored horses (Zech. 1:7-17; 6:1-8) who operate by divine decree. The four forces of sword, famine, wild animals, and pestilence in Ezekiel likewise prefigure John's presentation (Rev. 6:8; Ezek. 14:12-23). Because God is consistently just, John trusts that God must act decisively, even harshly.

Revelation 6:1~8 → The Opening of the Four Seals: The Four Horsemen

NIV	TT
6 ¹ I watched as the Lamb opened the first of the seven seals. Then I heard one of the four living creatures say in a voice like thunder, "Come!" ² I looked, and there before me was a white horse! Its rider held a bow, and he was given a crown, and he rode out as a conqueror bent on conquest. ³ When the Lamb opened the second seal, I heard the second living creature say, "Come!" ⁴ Then another horse came out, a fiery red one. Its rider was given power to take peace from the earth and to make people kill each other. To him was given a large sword. ⁵ When the Lamb opened	**6** ¹ Then I saw when the Lamb opened the first of the seven seals, and I heard one of the four living creatures say, as with a voice of thunder: "**Come**[80]!" ² And I looked, and behold a white horse, and its rider had a bow, and a crown was given to him, and he went out conquering in order to conquer even more. ³ When he opened the second seal, I heard the second living creature: "Come!" ⁴ And another horse, **fiery red**[81], went out; its rider was allowed to take peace from the earth so that humans might slaughter one another. A great **sword**[82] was given to him. ⁵ When he opened the third seal, I heard the third living creature say: "Come!" And I looked, and

---

[80] ἔρχου → It is an imperative. It means *"come," "appear,"* and *"come before the public."*
[81] πυρρός → It means *"red (as fire)"* In the Book of Revelation, it only appears in 6:4 and 12:3.
[82] μάχαιρα → It means *"a large knife," " a large sword," "a curved sword,"* and *"a straight sword."*

the third seal, I heard the third living creature say, "Come!" I looked, and there before me was a black horse! Its rider was holding a pair of scales in his hand. ⁶ Then I heard what sounded like a voice among the four living creatures, saying, "Two pounds of wheat for a day's wages, and six pounds of barley for a day's wages, and do not damage the oil and the wine!" ⁷ When the Lamb opened the fourth seal, I heard the voice of the fourth living creature say, "Come!" ⁸ I looked, and there before me was a pale horse! Its rider was named Death, and Hades was following close behind him. They were given power over a fourth of the earth to kill by sword, famine and plague, and by the wild beasts of the earth.	behold there was a black horse. Its rider held a balance scale in his hand. ⁶ And I heard something like a voice in the midst of the four living creatures say: "A liter of wheat for a denarius and three liters of barley for a denarius, but **do not harm the oil and the wine!**[83]" ⁷ When he opened the fourth seal, I heard the voice of the fourth living creature say: "Come!" ⁸ And I looked, and behold a **pale greenish-gray**[84] horse. The name of its rider was Death, and Hades followed with him. They were given authority over a quarter of the earth to kill with sword, famine, and plague, and by the wild beasts of the earth.

When the Lamb opens each of the seals, horrifying events occur on earth. Those who interpret Revelation as

---

[83] → In 91-92 C.E. the emperor Domitian decreed that half the vines and olive tress in the empire should be cut down, apparently to encourage the raising of grain crops. This decree, which apparently was never carried out, caused great consternation in Asia Minor, where oil and wine were crucial elements of the economy.

[84] χλωρός → It means "*yellowish green*," "*light green*," "*grayish green*," and "*pale*."

predicting the long-range future have attempted to identify these with historical catastrophes, either those already past (various wars, earthquakes, and plagues) or those that are about to happen in the interpreter's own time. The pattern of seven seals is constructed of 4 + 3 (so also the seven trumpets; 8:2-9:21; 11:15-18). The first unit comprises the vision of the four horsemen, John reconfiguration of the imagery of Zech. 1:7-11 and 6:1-8.

- **1** The sequence of *"Then I saw"* and *"I heard"* signals John's turn to a new visionary scene that sets up an apocalyptic theology of opening. *"Opening"* language, even when neither God nor the Lamb is its subject (3:20; 9:2; 12:16; 13:6), is always salvation and/or judgment language. At 3:7-8, the Son of Man has the keys of David. This clear image of salvation/judgment is bolstered by the subsequent declaration that what the Son opens no one can shut, and what he shuts, no one can open. At 3:20, Christ begs the Laodiceans to open their door so that he may enter and bring salvation with him. At 4:1, a door apparently opened by God represents the portal into the heavenly throne room and the eschatological relationship with God connected to it. At 9:2, the angel opens the shaft of the abyss in preparation for the acts of judgment that follow the blowing of the fifth trumpet. At 12:16, the earth opens its mouth to save the woman clothed with the sun. At 13:6, the beast opens its mouth to offer the blasphemies that justify its judgment. The other occurrences of the verb in Revelation, following the opening of the seventh and final seal in 8:1, are all presented as divine passives. The implication is that either God or the Lamb is the subject of the saving and/or judging behavior. At 10:2 and 10:8, the *"opened"* little scroll recalls Ezekiel's bitter scroll of judgment (Ezek. 2:10). At 11:19 and 15:5, the *"opened"* heavenly temple and tent of meeting respectively bring to mind an image of salvation. Then 19:11 chronicles the *"opened"* heaven, which reveals the faithful and true Word of God. This Word rides into the narrative armed with the power of salvation for those who witness for God and with the assurance of judgment for those who do not. Finally, 20:12 registers the presence of *"opened"* books of the dead (judgment) sitting alongside an *"opened"* Book of Life (salvation).

The opened seals likewise symbolize judgment and salvation. Eschatological woes (i.e., acts of judgment) are unleashed each time the Lamb breaks a seal. These woes will be as destructive and judgmental for those who oppose God as they will ultimately be salvific for those who witness faithfully for God. Key to this interpretation is the understanding of the Son of Man's earlier promise that he will keep the Philadelphians who conquer from the coming trials (3:10). The vow does not mean that believers will be *"raptured"* out of the trials. The tribulation that accompanies the breaking of each seal is something that believers, too, will endure (2:10). Their faithfulness will matter as much as it does because they will perform it in the circumstance of such duress, just as Christ himself did on the cross. That is no doubt why, in the end, the hour is described as a testing rather than a judgment; believers, too, will have a chance to make the grade. They will have the opportunity to witness. Seen in this light, the eschatological moments of destruction and disturbance that follow the "*opening*" of each seal will likewise be God-initiated and God-directed opportunities for believers to demonstrate the mettle of their faith and the witness that continues from it. Believers may live through these times and be strengthened by them. By contrast, those who persecute the believers will be judged by and crushed beneath them.

It is therefore appropriate that when one of the cherubim acknowledges the opening of the first seal, his response registers as thunder. In John's moving, vision picture, thunder is the background music that precedes and therefore prefigures cataclysmic, transformative action. After the first peals of narrative thunder (4:5), John introduces his hearers and readers to the seven flaming spirits before the throne of God, the sea of glass, and the flanking cherubim who launch the first of the book's magnificent antiphonal hymns. At 8:5, thunder explodes as the first of seven angels prepares to blow the first of the seven trumpets. Then, at 10:3-4, seven thunders erupt as the heavenly voice speaks and John prepares a bitter prophecy of apocalyptic judgement. Thunder heralds the opening of the heavenly temple (11:19), the cries of the 144,000 (14:2), the horrors of the seventh bowl (16:18), and the hallelujah of the heavenly chorus (19:6) when the marriage of the Lamb and his bride occurs just before the binding of the satanic dragon. The thunder that carries the voice of the cherub here at 6:1, therefore, intends much more than aesthetic effect. Something awe-full is about to "*come*."

- **2** With a lengthened introductory formula, "and I looked, and behold," which he will deploy several more times (6:5, 8; 14:1, 14; 19:11), John warns his hearers and readers that something new is about to occur. Attention shifts from the cherub who thunders the "*Come!*" command to the horse and rider who obey. The description of the rider and the consequence of his actions are oddly familiar. In the chapters that preceded this one, John characterized Christ-witnesses as conquerors in white clothing. Now he turns both the color and the conquest on their head by attributing them to this first rider on a white horse, who comes fiercely armed with a bow so that he may conquer.

The Messianic Rider of 19:11 also rides a white horse. In fact, John's description of the two matches verbatim: "*and behold a white horse, and the one seated upon it.*" The rider in 19:11 is an instrument of God's judgment. The rider in 6:2 appears to symbolize the same reality. There are, however, significant problems with equating the two riders. In 19:11 the rider is the Lamb. Here in chapter 6, the Lamb is tasked with breaking open the seals, not riding out on horseback. In addition, the Lamb specifically targets Satan and his bestial allies, while the horseman's wrath in 6:2 is globally and cosmically indiscriminate. In this way, the horseman functions as part of a "*woe package*" with the three who succeed him in vv. 3-8. Each horseman breeds the one that follows: Nevertheless, a logical pattern repeatable throughout the age is discernible: conquest (the fist rider), together with civil unrest (especially for persecuted Christians, the second rider), leads to famine (the third rider) and death (the fourth rider). Finally, the riders in 6:2 and 19:11 are also outfitted differently. In 6:2 the horseman sports a bow for his weapon and wears a crown, while in 19:11 the figure wields a sharp, double-edged sword from his mouth and is bedecked in diadems. The rider in 19:11 deploys as his arsenal a spoken word, but the rider in 6:2 fires lethal arrows.

There is a more logical explanation for John's matching descriptions of these two riders. Because the rider in 6:2 is the first, his appearance indicates that the initial opposition to God will be one of confusing mimicry. By setting himself on a white horse and laying claim to the Lord's language of conquest, this satanic emissary tries to wreak havoc in God's own image. In this way, the first horseman would be the prelude to the many false christs who would eventually appear in Christ's name and image. Even so, he and the ones who follow him do not act independently of God's design. One of John's primary theological tasks is assuring his readers that, no matter how chaotic and destructive world affairs appear to be, God as just judge is in control. That reasoning leads to the rather uncomfortable conclusion that God's control extends even to the work of the four devastating horsemen. They act within God's direct sphere of influence. Indeed, it is God's elite cherubim who ignite their activity with the thundering *"Come!"* commands. John believes that when the horsemen go to work, they have been put to the job by God.

The first rider is the first case in point. His crown, the symbol of his authoritative victory, was given to him. The divine passive assumes God's agency. Rider also wielded a bow. Some, especially many Koreans who believe in the teachings of *"Shincheonji, Church of Jesus, the Temple of the Tabernacle of the Testimony"* commonly known as *"Shincheonji("신천지")"* have a wild interpretation of this *"white horsemen,"* and their doctrines are based on interpretations of the Book of Revelation. *"White horsemen"* are not Mangi Lee or anything like that.

According to classical historians, as fearsome as Rome was as a military power, its legendary legions never mastered the use of the bow. Archers from the ranks of client kingdoms were employed as auxiliary troops. The bow was, however, a primary weapon of several of Rome's principal enemies. In fact, it stood as a metaphor for what the kingdom Rome feared the most: Parthia (see Excursus 10: Parthians). Just in case the bow by itself was an insufficient prompt for any Roman reader, John has placed the archer prominently on a white horse. The Parthians were renowned not only for their archery skills but, even more impressively, for their ability to fire their bows accurately while mounted on galloping, white horses. The Parthian cavalry had engaged and defeated the Romans on several memorable occasions. The thought of them running roughshod across the human landscape at God's command would certainly have stirred a loathing fear in the spirit of every Roman. And that is precisely the seer's point. John is writing as much now for the Romans as he is writing to his own believing community. He wants Rome to fear this inaugural equestrian moment as the first act in God's judgment against it.

The intersection of the white color with crown and conquest instructs hearers and readers on the motivation for judgment. With the opening of the fifth seal, Christ-witnesses, described via the symbolism of white, crown, and conquest, will cry out for God's justice and judgment. The trappings of their identity (white, crown, conquer) also characterize the force that is already answering their call on God's behalf. The chaotic situation erupting in their world is therefore the working out of God's justice. Because of their plight, God has unleashed the scourge that is the first horseman. The Son of Man (seated, white, crown) who relates so poignantly to the conquering witnesses (white, crown), bears an eerie resemblance to the first horseman (seated, white/dazzling, crown). Sickle at the ready in 14:14, the Son is clearly the messianic agent of God's fierce judgment. Chapter 6 not only chronicles that judgment (vv. 16-17) but also, in the scene depicted in vv. 6:9-11, presents the rationale for it. The Son of Man may not be the first rider, but he is in charge of the circumstance that sets him loose. In the process, he gives to the rider just enough of his characteristic bearing and dress so that all who see the rider will realize that he advances under the authority of the Lamb.

The problem with this scenario is that the faithful witnesses are as plagued by the actions of the rider as are those who persecute them. John apparently believes that in these times of trial, believers will have the opportunity to demonstrate their faithfulness under duress. Because they are not *"raptured"* out of the moment but forced like everyone else to endure it, they have the unique opportunity to demonstrate their ability to witness for God in the midst of tragic circumstances, just as Jesus Christ witnessed for God from the cross. Appealing to John's dependence upon Ezek. 14:21, Beale makes a similar point: *"The purpose of the trials is to punish the majority of the nation because of its sin and simultaneously to purify the righteous remnant by testing their faith"* (cf. Ezek. 14:14, 16, 18, 20, 22-23).

Excursus 10: Parthians

Parthia, a district SE of the Caspian Sea, was part of the Persian empire conquered by Alexander the Great. In the middle of the 3rd century B.C.E., Arsaces led the Parthians in revolt against their Seleucid (Macedonian) rulers, and his successors eventually extended their empire from the Euphrates to the Indus. Their exclusive use of cavalry-bowmen made them a formidable enemy, as the Romans discovered to their cost. In the 1st century C.E., the Parthians changed their capital from Ecbatana to Ctesiphon and sought to revive the Iranian elements of their civilization at the expense of the Greek.

The Parthians were governed by a land-owning

> aristocracy, and controlled the lucrative trade with the Far East. Their own religion was Iranian Mazdaism, but they were generally tolerant of other people's religions.
>
> Parthia was one of the districts in which the deported Israelites had been settled, and according to Josephus their descendants continued to speak an Aramaic dialect and to worship the true God, sending tribute to the Temple at Jerusalem. Consequently the Parthians in Jerusalem on the Day of Pentecost (Acts 2:9) may have been only Israelites from the district ("*language*" in v. 8 could equally well be "*dialect*"), but there may have been Parthian proselytes with them.

- **3 – 4** Though the second cherub is now the principal actor, v. 3 repeats the narrative content of v. 2a. the color of the second mount is flaming red, the shade of slaughter. The only other time John uses this color is in his description of the fiery red ("πυρρός"), satanic dragon (12:3; scarlet red – "κόκκινος"- is used at 17:3, 4; 18:12, 16). The implication is that even the destructive force of the devil is harnessed under God's control. Like the first rider, this one enters the cosmic and historical fray only after it is summoned forth by cherubic command. When he acts to depose the Pax Romana and install anarchy in its place, he does so with a sword bestowed by God. John taught any Romans among his readers by using their own imperial imagery against them. A Historian Gonzalez states, "*What this second rider carries is the heavy sword that was used for swinging and cutting rather than for stabbing. It* *was also a symbol of imperial authority – in particular, the emperor's authority to decree the death penalty, which was called 'the right of the sword' and which could also be exercised by provincial governors."* John sees God snatching Rome's symbol of power, handing it over to the red rider, and allowing him to use it to stir up a bloodbath.

There is nothing redemptive about the slaughter that ensues. The term *"slaughter"* indicates horrific carnage. John uses it to refer either to the crucifixion of the Lamb (5:6, 9, 12; 13:3) or to the executions of his followers (6:9; 18:24). Here it refers to global slaughter. Later, John declares that those who kill with the sword shall likewise themselves be killed by the sword (13:10). The second rider uses his weapon to set that tragic circumstance into motion. The Romans, who used the sword to create their self-interested peace, now find the sword being used to cut them down and shred their serenity to bits. The irony is eschatologically delicious. They not only receive the justice they deserve; their own symbolic tool of pitiless oppression is used to deliver it.

- **5** Familiar language abounds. Once again, the Lamb initiates the action by breaking open a seal. And once again, John declares that he heard a cherub pronounce the command *"Come!"* once again, John appeals to the visual formula, *"and I looked, and behold"* that announces a shift in the setting of the scene. He sees a black horse. He will refer to this color once more in his narrative, when he confides that the sun turns as black as sackcloth (6:12). The connection between sackcloth and judgment is explicit throughout the Bible (1 Kgs. 20:31-32; 21:27; 2 Kgs. 19:1-2; 1 Chr. 21:16; Isa. 3:24; 37:1-2; Jer. 4:8; 6:26; 48:37; 49:3; Amos 8:10; Jonah 3:5-8; Matt. 11:21; Luke 10:13). The link with black and, by extension, sackcloth therefore implies that the third seal's opening will ignite the fury of divine judgment. The nature of that judgment is symbolized by the balance scales that the rider holds in his hand.

In biblical literature, particularly the Book of Daniel, which often serves as a direct background to John's thinking and writing, scales also have an integral connection with the theme of divine judgment (Prov. 16:11; Isa. 40:12; Dan. 5:27). Ancient balance scales consisted of a crossbeam suspended by a hook or cord with a pan suspended from each end of the crossbeam. Weights placed in one pan were used to determine the weight of commodities placed in the other pan. John is not so much interested in how the scale works as in what its presence represents. In the ancient world food was distributed by rationed amounts (using scales) when it became scarce see the metaphorical use of scales indicating famine in Lev. 26:26; 2 Kgs. 7:1; Ezek. 4:10, 16. Famine has followed naturally upon conquest and slaughter. Famine is the third seal's form of judgment.

- **6** If there was any doubt about God's association with the scales and the famine they represent, John erases it with his claim to have heard a voice from within the midst of the four creatures. Given the close proximity of the cherubim to the throne, the voice must belong to God. God issues instructions on the use of the scales:

to weigh the value of the scarce food that remains. There is an immediate problem for which the text never accounts. Scales measure weight, yet the values John records are in volume. The seer rides roughshod over such details in his attempt to reach his primary point.

The primary point is that famine has caused the price of the remaining food to soar. The going rates became "χοῖνιξ" *of wheat for a denarius and three* "χοίνικες" *of barley for a denarius."* The term *"liter"* is used as an equivalent to the Greek dry measure called a "χοῖνιξ," roughly equal to a day's ration of wheat for one person. The three *"liters"* of barley were equivalent to a day's rations for a person's horse or mule. Though barley was less attractive than wheat as the main ingredient for a meal, three *"liters"* of it could also serve as a small family's daily food ration. The denarius, according to Matt. 20:2, was the expected daily wage. If John's accounting is correct, a person's entire daily wage was committed solely to food.

While staple foods were being destroyed, there was a cruel and mostly inexplicable culinary twist. The marauding rider on the black horse was ordered not to harm the olive oil and the wine. The singular number of the verb *"harm"* indicates that God is speaking directly and only to the rider; its aorist tense specifies that the rider had not yet touched the oil and wine and was therefore being ordered not even to start. Why did God demand the protection of the oil and wine when wheat and barley rations had taken such a hit?

This calls to mind the edict of Domitian following the great famine of 92 C.E. Wealthy Roman landowners had determined that if they devoted their lands to oil and wine rather than grain, they could build greater profits. The end result, particularly during a food shortage, was devastating. While oil and wine continued to flow in abundant quantities, wheat and barley became frighteningly scarce. To ameliorate the effects of this catastrophe and ameliorate the possibility of future ones, Domitian ordered that all the vineyards, particularly those in Asia Minor, be cut back by half. In this case, the voice of God would speak with this recent imperial action in mind.

A connection with Domitian's edict would be an interesting one indeed, particularly since this would tie John's symbolic narrative to an actual historical event. There would also be interesting literary implications. Domitian's edict was apparently rescinded only after the aristocracy bitterly complained. Since John does not mention that historical detail, it could well have been his narrative intent to demonstrate that the victorious opposition to the imperial command came from God. While the emperor demanded that half the vineyards be chopped down, God commanded that they not be touched. That would mean that at the singular moment when God's desire for judgment actually matched the goal of one of Caesar's edict, God changed course. The end result would have been a human emperor humiliated by a heavenly countermand of his orders. God would have vetoed Caesar's order at the one time when accommodating to Caesar's order would have furthered God's stated plan of judgment, as that plan was embodied in the work of the first, second, and third riders. This illogical, almost fanatical opposition to Roman intentions would certainly fit the overall presentation of a narrative that begs its hearers and readers not to accommodate to Roman expectations for daily social and cultic life under any circumstances.

The problem with this explanation, however, is that the narrative itself never connects God's command to the imperial edict. It is difficult and risky to attempt such a speculative connection between historical events and John's eschatological work unless one can find a specific literary link to that event. None exists.

This brings us another possible explanation: John has an ironic point to make by demonstrating a divine intent to spare luxuries like oil and wine while destroying staples like wheat and barley. Dr. Reddish says *"The oil and wine symbolize the luxury and extravagant lifestyle of the wealthy. John envisions the final days as a time when the poor are starving while the rich are unaffected by the shortages."* Pablo Richard agrees: *"Only the wealthy enjoy the economic prosperity for which the empire is known, just as only they enjoy the Pax Romana."*

Here, too, there are problems. In the ancient world, one would be hard-pressed tag olive oil and wine as luxuries; they were as common a part of everyday meals as grains. Whether one could find enough sustenance from them alone to sustain life in the midst of a famine is, however, another question. On the other hand, one might metaphorically associate oil and wine with parties and feasts (cf. Matt. 25:1-13; Luke 7:33-34; John 2:1-10; Eph. 5:18; 1 Tim. 3:8). It is possible that John's message here is an ironic one that fits with his overall theme of witness and non-accommodation? In chapters 2-3, he showed particular concern that his hearers and readers not accommodate themselves to Greco-Roman social and cultic expectations by eating meat sacrificed to idols at celebratory social gatherings. If indeed wine and oil carry the same symbolic association with such gatherings and John is still pressing his point of non-accommodation, which I believe he does throughout the Book of Revelation, then it may well be that he offers God's order to leave the oil and wine in place as ironic sarcasm. Caught in the midst of a famine where they can find neither wheat nor barley, people still have before them the option of an accommodating participation in the cultic rituals that celebrate pagan and imperial lordship. They will have enough oil and wine to carouse but not enough food to survive. They can party themselves to an accommodating, starving death. Perhaps this is the judgment the third horseman brings. He renders to the idolatrous, accommodating, famished world exactly what it wants: oil and wine.

- **7 – 8** Though the fourth cherub is now the principal actor, v. 7 repeats the narrative content of vv. 2a, 3, and 5a. The familiar formula *"and I looked, and behold"* announces yet another scene shift. The fourth horseman will be the worst yet. John describes the color of the animal he rides as "χλωρός." Chlorophyll is the green coloration in leaves. It is also, according to

New Testament narratives, the coloration of the green grass (Mark 6:39; Rev. 8:7; 9:4). In the larger Greco-Roman world, it connotes a *"pale green"* or *"pale greenish gray,"* the color associated with sickness, death, and dying. The association is a fitting one since, by the time this horseman is through, one-quarter of the world's population will be dead.

It is not surprising, then, that this rider's name is *"Death."* There is a logistical problem on having Hades follow along with Death even though only one horse is mentioned. John, though, is not concerned with such details. He means to connect the personification of death with the equally fearful personification of Hades so that his readers may be assured that the peril now confronting them in the narrative is total. Death is the force that snatches up the essence of human life. Hades is the underworld place where that essence is eternally enslaved. The two form a partnership of grim reaping, which is why John often pictures them working together (1:18; 6:8; 20:13-14).

Should the marauding presence of Death and Hades also be attributed to the execution of God's judgment plan? Yes. At 1:18, John declares that the resurrected Son of Man holds the keys of Death and Hades. Since he holds the keys, he must be the one who has unlocked the gates that have set them loose. For those who might flinch at the prospect of God wielding death as a weapon against the enemies of God's people or even against the believers who have accommodated themselves to the cultic and social practices of those enemies, there are instructive texts like 18:8 and 2:23.

At 18:8, God brings death to the whore of Babylon as a judgment against her, and according to 2:23, God will consign Jezebel's children to death as a judgment against them.

Equally persuasive is the presence of the divine passive of the verb *"to give"* (ἐδόθη), which also accompanied the actions of the riders on the white (7:2) and red (6:4) horses. The fourth rider's power, too, has apparently been furnished by God.

The judgment theme gains further credibility when readers recognize the prophetic background against which John is writing. The closest parallel to 6:8 is Ezek. 14:21, which recounts the same four harbingers of death (sword, famine, pestilence, and wild animals) in almost the same order. Though no wild animals are mentioned in Ezek. 5:12, one-third of the population will be wiped out by sword, pestilence, and death. Jeremiah 14:12 is equally striking. An angry God will consume the people by sword, famine, and pestilence (cf. Jer. 15:2; 21:7). The destruction caused by wild animals is likewise recurring cases in God's judgment. God intends that these catastrophes take place as punishment for a particular offense. Beale states that *"Most of these references mention idolatry as the cause of judgment, which enforces the suggestion ... that idolatry was part of the reason for the afflictions on unbelievers in Rev. 6:2-8."* It is probable that this judgment was also intended against those in John's congregations who had accommodated themselves to the idolatrous behavior of the unbelievers around them in an attempt to benefit from the social and economic opportunities such an association would bring.

Revelation 6:9~11 → The Fifth Seal: The Cry of the Slaughtered Souls

NIV	TT
⁹ When he opened the fifth seal, I saw under the altar the souls of those who had been slain because of the word of God and the testimony they had maintained. ¹⁰ They called out in a loud voice, "How long, Sovereign Lord, holy and true, until you judge the inhabitants of the earth and avenge our blood?" ¹¹ Then each of them was given a white robe, and they were told to wait a little longer, until the full number of their fellow servants, their	⁹ When he opened the fifth seal, I saw under the altar the **souls**[85] of those who had been slaughtered because of the word of God and the **witness**[86] they had given. ¹⁰ And they cried out with a loud voice, saying: "**Master**[87], Holy and True, **how long**[88] will it be before you judge and **avenge**[89] our blood on the inhabitants of the earth?" ¹¹[90] Then they were each given a white robe and told to rest a little longer, until the work of their fellow servants, who

[85] ψυχή → It means *"life," "soul," "breath of life," "life-principle," "self,"* and *"earthly life."* It is often impossible to draw hard and fast lines between the meanings of this many-sided word.

[86] μαρτυρία → It means *"testimony," "witness," "record,"* and *"report."*

[87] δεσπότης → It means *"master," "lord,"* and *"owner."*

[88] → Except for John's own words, this is the first human word recorded in the Book of Revelation. It reflects the language of the Psalms used in worship that call out for God to act, to remedy the injustice in the world (Pss. 6:3-4; 13:1-2; 35:17; 74:9-10; 79:5; 80:4; 89:6).

[89] ἐκδικέω → It means *"to vindicate one's right," "do one justice," "to protect," "to defend," "to punish,"* and *"to avenge."*

[90] Verse 11 in Greek → καὶ ἐδόθη αὐτοῖς ἑκάστῳ στολὴ λευκὴ καὶ ἐρρέθη αὐτοῖς ἵνα ἀναπαύσονται ἔτι χρόνον μικρόν, ἕως πληρωθῶσιν καὶ οἱ σύνδουλοι αὐτῶν καὶ οἱ ἀδελφοὶ αὐτῶν οἱ μέλλοντες ἀποκτέννεσθαι ὡς καὶ αὐτοί. (no *"number."*)

brothers and sisters, were killed just as they had been.	are their brothers and sisters, who were about to be killed as they themselves had been, would be **complete**[91].

With the opening of the fifth seal, the focus narrows and intensifies, characteristic of the pattern. Verses 9-11 provide narrative motivation for God's judgment. In both 6:9 and 20:4a, the souls of those who have not accommodated themselves to the social and cultic benefits of Greco-Roman society find themselves executed because of their witness to the word of God.

The Christ-believers in John's communities who are trying to decide how they must respond to the pressures of the Roman emperor cult recognize their own anxious cry in the "*How long?*" reverberating through the heavenly scene. They are encouraged to persevere in their own witness, even to the point of death (2:10), when they see the victorious martyrs in heaven receive their white robes and when they hear the announcement that they must hold out only "*a little longer*" (6:11).

- **9** John refers to the resurrected remains of non-accommodating witnesses as "*souls*" for the first time here. The term "*soul*," as John uses it, can only be fully understood when read in light of the semantic domains in which the seer places it. In one set of texts it operates in a limited way as a reference to living, animate creatures (8:9; 16:3; 18:3). According to the other set of texts, the soul is the force that animates

---

[91] πληρόω → It means "*to make full,*" "*to fill up,*" "*fulfill,*" "*finish,*" "*bring to an end,*" and "*complete.*"

them (12:11; 18:14; 20:4). Particularly at 6:9 and again at 20:4, that animating force lives on after the human being it once occupied meets and earthly death.

These particular souls have made their way to heaven in a most noteworthy fashion. The human beings whom they once animated were executed on earth because of their non-accommodating commitment to the word of God, the witness to the lordship of Christ. The language of execution/slaughter connects these souls to the Lamb, whom John also has described as slaughtered/executed. In his introduction of the Lamb, John clarifies that the execution is not an act of redemption but the result of the Lamb's witnessing to a truth that resisted the claims of Roman rule and lordship. Those who follow the Lamb by testifying to the witness that he himself bore will meet a similar fate (1:9; 2:13).

In heaven, the souls who have met this fate are crammed into the crawl space beneath the heavenly altar of sacrifice. Two altars are presented in the Book of Revelation. The heavenly altars were understood to be the cosmic prototypes for their earthly counterparts in the Jerusalem temple. The Jerusalem temple had two distinct altars. The outer one, located in the court of the priests, was the sacrificial altar of burnt offering. The inner altar, also known as the golden altar of incense, was located just in front of the curtain that marked off the holy of holies from the rest of the sanctuary. It is the sacrificial altar that is imaged here and against 11:1; 14:18 and 16:7. The explicit mention of incense or being golden indicates that the references in 8:3, 5 and

9:13 are to the altar of incense. It is from the cramped space beneath the altar of sacrifice that the souls cry out for God's justice. Their presence under the altar is an indication to some scholars that John has in mind sacrificial, martyr imagery. These scholars refer to Lev. 4:7, where the blood of a sacrificial bull is poured out at the base of the altar. Since the life or soul was thought to be in the blood, John was symbolically representing the souls as the blood of the altar poured out. In this case, these slaughtered souls sacrificed themselves so that their bloody deaths would provoke God's final intervention into human history.

I instead argue for the primacy of another aspect of the altar's meaning potential: justice and judgment. It is, in fact, the imagery of justice and judgment that has been the unifying theme throughout the first eight verses of the chapter. John extends it here with his focus on the altar. Just as the heavenly throne is a symbol of God's rule, "*altar*" characterizes God's judgment. John does not picture a sacrificial slaying on the altar; the slaying, presumably with all the accompanying bleeding, takes place on earth. John images the altar to picture what will now happen as a result of the slaughtering. In other words, the altar does not represent killing; it personifies the divine response to it. At 16:7 the altar is so focused on this objective that it miraculously comes alive and voices the opinion that all God's judgments are true and just. Even though it is apparently a reference to the altar of incense, 8:3 offers helpful corroboration. In that altar reference, though the prayers of the saints are understandably offered without any mention of blood or suffering, the connection to the coming judgment is clear. Indeed, all of John's representations of the heavenly temple's two altars fit this symbolic mod (8:3, 5; 9:13; 14:18; 16:7); they point to divine recompense, not saintly suffering. By connecting both pieces of furniture to the common theme of judgment, he has given *"altar"* a uniform narrative characterization. Even the slaughtered souls are convinced of this connection. Apparently certain that God will act, their question concerns only the timing of the event. They are asking when, not if. The altar symbolism assures them that transformative, liberating justice is coming. This is why John locates them there; he wants his readers to be focused more on God's justice than on their own sacrifice.

- **10** The souls' passionate *"How long?"* no doubt reminds John's hearers and readers of similar prophetic calls for divine engagement (e.g., Zech. 1:12; Ps. 79:5). In those cases, however, a contrite people asked how long God would keep punishing them.

The souls address God as their "δεσπότης" (master, lord), a Greek translation of the two Latin terms for emperor, a point that would certainly not have gone unnoticed (cf. Acts 4:24). In hijacking this designation for God, they were rhetorically slapping Caesar in the face. Even in lament, they witnessed.

In describing their "δεσπότης"as holy and true, the souls voiced their faith that God would engage Rome and judge it. The adjectives are echoes of the self-descriptors used by the Son of Man in his opening address to the Philadelphians (3:7). Though the adjectives acted as substantives (nouns) in that case, the essence of their relationship to Christ and God is the same. There the Son of Man, as the holy and true one, holds the key of David and, like a judge beyond whom there is no appeal, has the power to close what no one can shut and open what no one can open. He would make the enemies of God's witnesses bow before their feet even as he prepared the coming trial that would judge the inhabitants of the earth. The slaughtered souls echo this appeal to the holy and true one for judgment against the inhabitants of the earth. In so doing, they also echo the cries of Old Testament figures who seemed assured that God would avenge the blood of God's people (Deut. 32:43; 2 Kgs. 9:7; Ps. 79:10). The specific term for avenge ("ἐκδικέω") appears only one other time in the Book of Revelation, at 19:2, which provides a direct narrative answer to the petition made by the resurrected souls (6:10). God justly obliterates "*the great whore of Babylon*" for spilling the blood of God's people. The other key term, "*judge*" ("κρίνω"), appears more often but operates similarly. God's judgment will bring destruction to the great city that has persecuted and killed God's witnesses (11:18; 16:5; 18:8, 20; 19:2, 11). Revelation 20:12-13 implies that this judgment, even when destructive, is just; every person will receive proper due for one's deeds.

This clarification does not dissuade contemporary commentators from rightly flinching at John's depiction of the harshness of God's punishment. Many contend that God's hyper-violent judgment in Revelation is "*un-Christian*," certainly not "*Christ-like*." Other scholars point out that the violence God displays in the book should be understood as a necessary evil since it operates in the realm of public justice rather than private vengeance. "*Justice must not only be done; it must be seen to be done*" (Caird 85). God was caught up in a war of lethal cosmic force. Rome, the power representing Satan, had no compunction about acting with extreme violence. John apparently believed that, if cosmic and historical justice were to be served, God would need to respond in kind. This expectation of violence to bring about justice is a theological premise with an impressive Old Testament pedigree. Though pointing most specifically to the imprecatory psalms (Pss. 7, 35, 55, 58, 59, 69, 79, 83, 109, 137, 139), Aune observes that there are large swaths of Old Testament and other Jewish materials that indicate God's need and right to respond appropriately to human violence.

- **11** The same God who gave destructive power of judgment to the four horsemen rewards the souls of the executed witnesses with white clothing. The white/dazzling robes mark the souls as defiant witnesses who actively engaged in testimony to the lordship of Christ. As J. P. Heil points out, their dress ties them to other key characterizations in the text. The multitude standing before the Lamb and the heavenly throne in 7:9 are similarly dressed. So, interestingly enough, are the figures of 7:13-14. These figures, presumably the same as the slaughtered souls of 6:9-11, achieved their high laundry marks only after washing their robes in the blood of the Lamb. According to 12:10-12, this high-powered plasma detergent is the cleansing force that enables God and God's people to wipe out the stain of Rome's oppressive, satanic power. The white robe is thus the symbolization of this conquering witness.

In other words, the white robe, metaphorically speaking, is not a noun; it is an action verb. The robe signifies the paradoxical washing in the blood as bringing about the transformative justice that God's people have been seeking. They have therefore not just been "*given*" white robes; they have earned them by washing, that is to say, acting in the way of the Lord that incites Rome and its agent to spill their blood. Surely this active witness is what John had in mind when he declared that the remnant at Sardis have earned their white dress because of their ongoing and victorious witness (3:4-5). Who, finally, are the ones whom John considers blessed and worthy of the liberating salvation that God will bring? Who else but those who act, who "*wash*" their robes. According to John, the only mechanism that makes this "*washing*" possible is the courageous act of witnessing to the very truth that Rome has deployed all its power to contest.

In John's narrative, there is dissonance between the social body (the expectation of emperor worship) and the witness body or "*soul*" (which symbolizes resistance to that expectation). The Roman system promotes a celebration of the physical body and physical life lived in accommodation to Roman religious and political interest. Revelation, though, symbolizes a rejection of that holding on to the physical body. It is not the body but the redressed and eternal soul that is key. This spiritual body is certainly in extreme dissonance with the Roman social one. By definition, it is therefore resistant, and actively so. A believer must make an active choice, given the social context of Asia Minor at the end of the first century, to be one type of body or the other. John dramatizes his preference with the description of slaughtered souls clothed in white robes. He has essentially reconfigured the dress of execution into the clothing of defiance and change. He takes even the worst, this slaughter, and linguistically connects it as closely to Christ's resurrection as to his death. The slaughtered Lamb, every hearer and reader will remember, was still standing. So too are the believers who take the wardrobe of Christ's slaughter upon themselves. Though huddled beneath the heavenly altar, they are well dressed and, figuratively speaking at least, still standing. Suddenly what some might view as a martyr's attire has become the fine, white linen of active, subversive, and transformative witness. These dead souls, all dressed up, are a soul force.

    The answer that the heavenly voice speaks to this soul force is one that on the surface appears to cause a problem for the thesis I am suggesting. After all, the respondent directs that the pleading souls should wait just a short time until the appropriate number of their brothers had, like them, been killed. Actually, the Greek says no such thing. Although the NRSV, NIV and many other translations report that a sufficient "*number*" of witnesses first had to be slaughtered before God would move, John himself actually says nothing about numbers. He simply writes that first the brothers and sisters must be fulfilled. Admittedly, this odd response is ambiguous. It is not surprising that translators and interpreters have sought clarification from the historical context. Commentators observe that apocalyptic texts like *1 Enoch* 47:4 and *4 Ezra* 4:35-37 expect a certain quota of slaughtered righteous to be filled before God will act.

John's idea of a martyr is that of a witness, left out any talk of a "*number*" at all. John's concentration is focused on the term "*fulfill*" ("πληρόω"). Gerhard Delling explains that "fulfill," particularly when associated with the term "*time*" ("χρονοσ"), has a temporal sense of completion. In other words, it means to finish, to execute a commanded action. That broader use of the term fits quite nicely with the way John uses the term in 3:2, the only other time he deploys it. There, it is works that are fulfilled. The Lord is angry because the works of the believers have not been "*accomplished*" in the Lord's sight. All this would suggest that when John uses the verb "*fulfill*" in 6:11, particularly in connection with rest and time, he is speaking about the works of the surviving colleagues of the slaughtered souls. The spotlight falls on that ongoing work of defiant, provocative witness, which must still be accomplished, in whatever manner it is to be done. Doing that work is the way believers operate in synergy with God to bring about the liberating transformation of history.

Corroboration comes from John's closing remark about the brothers and sisters who would be killed just as the souls under the altar had been. We already know that these souls were executed because of their witness; John is clarifying here that their brothers and sisters will be executed, slaughtered for the same reason. Nonetheless, they evidently are to keep witnessing until their work, too, is complete.

Revelation 6:12~17 → The Sixth Seal: The Wrath of the Lamb

NIV	TT
¹² I watched as he opened the sixth seal. There was a great earthquake. The sun turned black like sackcloth made of goat hair, the whole moon turned blood red, ¹³ and the stars in the sky fell to earth, as figs drop from a fig tree when shaken by a strong wind. ¹⁴ The heavens receded like a scroll being rolled up, and every mountain and island was removed from its place. ¹⁵ Then the kings of the earth, the princes, the generals, the rich, the mighty, and everyone else, both slave and free, hid in caves and among the rocks of the mountains. ¹⁶ They called to the mountains and the rocks, "Fall on us and	¹² Then I looked when he opened the sixth seal, and a great **earthquake**⁹² occurred, and the sun became as black as sackcloth made of hair, and the **whole**⁹³ moon became as blood, ¹³ and the stars of heaven fell to the earth as a fig tree shaken by fierce wind drops its unripe figs, ¹⁴ and the sky was vanished like a rolled-up scroll, and every mountain and island was shaken from its place. ¹⁵ And the kings of the earth and the important people and the generals and the wealthy and the powerful and every slave and free person hid themselves in the caves and in the mountain rocks, ¹⁶ and they said to the mountains and to the rocks: "Fall on us

---

⁹² σεισμός → It means "*earthquake*," and "*shaking of a storm*." John is not predicting earthquakes of the distant future. Asia Minor was prone to earthquakes; twelve cities had been leveled in 17 C.E., and there had been many since. In the biblical world, earthquakes were not thought of as natural disasters, but the effect and sign of God's presence: the advent of God causes the earth to shake (e.g., Judg. 5:4; Ps. 18:6-7; Isa. 6:4).

⁹³ ὅλος → It means "*whole*," "*entire*," "*throughout*," and "*complete*."

hide us from the face of him who sits on the throne and from the wrath of the Lamb! ¹⁷ For the great day of their wrath has come, and who can withstand it?"	and hide us from the presence of the one seated on the throne and from the wrath of the Lamb, ¹⁷ because the great day of their wrath has come, and who is able to withstand it?"

    The eschatological events that follow the opening of the sixth seal are a direct narrative response to the souls of the slaughtered in 6:9-11. Verses 12-17 are the end frame of an intercalation. With the help of vv.1-8, they bracket the appeal for justice and judgment (vv.9-11) around which the whole of chapter 6 pivots.

- **12** The Lamb's opening of the sixth seal is followed immediately by a great earthquake. In biblical tradition, earthquakes are often expected to occur in the end time as one effect of the presence or coming of God (Joel 2:10; 3:16; Isa. 24:18-23; 29:6; Mic. 1:4; Nah. 1:5). Earthquakes were also integrally related to the theme of judgment (Jer. 10:22; Ezek. 38:19). At 8:5, an earthquake is part of the theophany that introduces the acts of judgment accompanying the blowing of the seven trumpets. All this takes place, just as the earthquake of 6:12 follows the appeal in vv. 9-11, after the prayers of the people rise up before God with the smoke of incense (8:3-4). One gets the sense that at 8:5, too, the judgment is a direct result of a prayerful appeal for intervention. Similarly earthquakes are associated with God's acts of judgment in 11:13, 19; 16:18.

    In the second phase of this initial act of eschatological travail, the sun becomes as black as sackcloth. The strong connection between God's acts of judgment and the color *"black"* were previewed with the presentation of the rider on the black horse at 6:5 (cf. Isa. 50:3). The addition of sackcloth heightens the emphasis of judgment. At 11:3 the two witnesses are said to be outfitted with sackcloth before they enact prophetic judgment on God's behalf.

Finally, there is an accompanying bloody moon. The presence of this odd celestial combination in Acts 2:20 suggests that a blackened sun and bloody moon may well have been understood as traditional precursors to the coming of the Lord's Day.

- **13 – 14** With the stars falling out of the heavens like winter fruit shaken from a fig tree by a great wind, John is building from traditional Old Testament imagery. In Isa. 34:4 the heavens rot away like fruit withering on a fig tree just as God is about to render judgment. In Isa. 13:10; Ezek. 32:7 and Joel 2:10, the stars darken as a prelude to God's coming judgment. No doubt this is also the image the Gospel of Mark builds upon when he records Jesus' claim that the Son of Man's return in judgment would also be prefaced by falling stars and darkened heavens (Mark 13:24-25; Matt. 24:29; Luke 21:26). John uses this imagery to great effect not only here but also repeatedly in his text. The connection between falling stars, tribulation, and coming judgment is reiterated narratively at Rev. 8:10-12; 9:1 and 12:4.

    The influence of Isa. 34:4 extends from the image of a rotting heaven in Rev. 6:13 to the rolling up of the heavens like a scroll. John also wants to make it clear that everything is happening by God's command. Each of the three primary verbs in the verse parses out in the passive voice ("ἀπεχωρίσθη" was vanished, "ἑλισσόμενον" being rolled up, "ἐκινήθησαν" were moved/shaken). These divine passives presume God to be the controlling agent. At Heb. 1:12, as well, God's judgment beings with a divine rolling up of the cosmos.

- **15 – 17** Having seen the signs of God's coming judgment, the great ones and those who serve them (cf. Rev. 19:18) appropriately run for cover. In the Old Testament, the major reason for fleeing from the presence of God is to avoid judgment (Gen. 19:17; Ps. 68:1; Hos. 5:3; Zech. 14:5). In Mark 13:14 (cf. Matt. 24:15-16; Luke 21:20-21), Jesus advises that once the signs of the end began occurring, people should act in just such a manner. The lengthy enumeration of the fleeing powerful people and the slaves and free ones connected with them reads like a laundry list of people who would either run the political and economic infrastructure of the Greco-Roman world or accommodate themselves to it. Like the disobedient people chronicled in Isa. 2:10, 19, 21 and Jer. 4:29, they have become refugees who seek asylum from God's justice under the cover of nature. During times of invasion or siege, residents of cities and towns would often flee to the mountainous regions to hide from their enemies (Judg. 6:2; 1 Sam. 13:16; 14:11; Job 30:6; Ezek. 33:27; Jer. 13:4-6; 49:30; Jos. *Ant.* 6.99, 116; 12.272-75, 421; 14.429; *J.W.* 1.307; 6.370). They exist as a direct narrative contrast to the executed witnesses of 6:9-11.

In v. 16, John finally reveals his belief that everything that is happening in chapter 6 occurs as a result of God's judgment. Appealing directly to Hos. 10:8 (cf. Luke 23:30), he recounts that the refugees beg the mountains and rocks to shelter them from the face of God and from the wrath of the Lamb. The Lamb, too, executes judgment. Here, as elsewhere in the Book of Revelation (11:18; 14:10; 16:19; 19:15), divine wrath occurs as a just recompense for evil that has been perpetrated against God and God's people.

The refugees now declare what John's text has already revealed: the breaking of the sixth seal has inaugurated *"the Great Day of the Lord"* (v.17). It falls like a Great Day of Wrath upon those who have resisted Christ's lordship and have persecuted those who witnessed to that lordship. Once again, John builds from Hebraic tradition. Joel 2:11; Nah. 1:6; Zeph. 1:14-15; and Mal. 3:2 all record God's final day as one filled with so sever a judging, eschatological wrath that no one is able to withstand it.

Revelation 7:1~8 → Intermission (1): The 144,000

NIV	TT
7 ¹ After this I saw four angels standing at the four corners of the earth, holding back the four winds of the earth to prevent any wind from blowing on the land or on the sea or on any tree. ² Then I saw another angel coming up from the east, having the seal of the living God. He called out in a loud voice to the four angels who had been given power to harm the land and the sea: ³ "Do not harm the land or the sea or the trees until we put a seal on the foreheads of the servants of our God." ⁴ Then I heard the number of those who were sealed: 144,000 from all the tribes of Israel. ⁵ From the tribe of Judah 12,000 were sealed, from	**7** ¹ After this, I saw four angels standing at the four corners of the earth, restraining the four winds of the earth so that no wind could blow on the earth nor on the sea nor on any tree. ² Then I saw another angel, who had the seal of the living God, ascending from the rising of the sun, and he cried out with a great voice to the four angels who were given power to **damage**^{94} the earth and the sea, ³ saying: "Do not damage the earth or the sea or the trees until we have marked the **servants**^{95} of our God with a seal on their forehead." ⁴ And I heard the number of those who were sealed, 144,000, sealed out of every

---

[94] ἀδικέω → It means "*do wrong*," "*injure*," "*harm*," "*damage*," and "*spoil*."

[95] δοῦλος → It means "*slave*." John uses the term to describe himself and other who are obedient to God (1:1; 2:20; 19:2, 5; 22:3), just as Paul does (Rom. 1:1; Phil. 1:1; Titus 1:1). John's use of the term in Revelation is often linked with the prophetic ministry (Rev. 10:7; 11:18).

the tribe of Reuben 12,000, from the tribe of Gad 12,000, ⁶ from the tribe of Asher 12,000, from the tribe of Naphtali 12,000, from the tribe of Manasseh 12,000, ⁷ from the tribe of Simeon 12,000, from the tribe of Levi 12,000, from the tribe of Issachar 12,000, ⁸ from the tribe of Zebulun 12,000, from the tribe of Joseph 12,000, from the tribe of Benjamin 12,000.	tribe of the sons of Israel: ⁵ from the tribe of Judah twelve thousand sealed, from the tribe of Reuben twelve thousand, from the tribe of Gad twelve thousand, ⁶ from the tribe of Asher twelve thousand, from the tribe of Naphtali twelve thousand, from the tribe of Manasseh twelve thousand, ⁷ from the tribe of Simeon twelve thousand, from the tribe of Levi twelve thousand, from the tribe of Issachar twelve thousand, ⁸ from the tribe of Zebulun twelve thousand, from the tribe of Joseph twelve thousand, from the tribe of Benjamin twelve thousand sealed.

This chapter picks up the sealing theme of chapters 5 and 6, but uses it in a different way. There the opening of the seals means the beginning of the judgment of God, the wrath of the Lamb, but here there is hope for those who are sealed with God's name and have washed their robes in the blood of the Lamb.

- **1** The words "*after this, I saw*" indicate that John is working in a new subject area. John is not saying that the events in 7:1-3 take place at a later time than the events recorded in chapter 6. The preposition "*after*" has a narrative rather than a chronological sense. While

John's vision in 7:1-8 explores a new topic, the material contained in the topic relates directly to the earlier visions. It is only *"after"* John has shared the visions of chapter 6 that he can emphasize the importance of being exempted from the horror they represent.

God works via angelic proxy. Four angels have been stationed at the four compass points of a mythically conceived flat earth (cf. Isa. 11:12; Ezek. 7:2); the entire world is under their regulatory purview. Their charge is to hold back the four winds that blow out across the entire earth (cf. Dan. 7:2). This blowing is a euphemism for angelic action that will damage the entire global landscape.

Given the destructive potential of these four winds, many commentators identify them with the four horsemen of 6:1-8. It is intriguing that the four horsemen of Zech. 6:1-8, upon whom John's horsemen are obviously based, are also characterized as the four winds (Zech. 6:5). We will perhaps never be able to determine whether John is also recasting his horses in this way. What is clear is that he envisions widespread desolation in both accounts, and in both accounts the executors of that desolation operate as God's agents.

Repeatedly, in 6:1-8, the seer claimed that the horsemen's destructive power was given to them by God. He makes the same claim about the winds at 7:2 (cf. Jer. 49:36; Dan. 7:2). The association of the four winds with God is heightened by the fact that angels control them. To this point, angels have played an exclusive role as God's divine agents and messengers (Rev. 1:1, 20; 2:1, 8, 12, 18; 3:1, 5, 7, 14; 5:2, 11). The association continues through John's use of the verb "*to damage*" (ἀδικέω), which is strongly tied to the theme of judgment (cf. 2:11; 6:6). Particularly at 9:4, destructive locusts operate by God's direction. The connection to God's authority seems clear when the locusts are ordered not to harm those who have the seal of God, just as in 7:1-3 the winds are prevented from harming those who have been so sealed. The association between God and the winds climaxes in 7:2, when John explains that the power to wield the destructive winds was not something the angels acquired on their own; it was given to them by God.

The point John made in chapter 6 is therefore made anew, via different imagery, here in chapter 7: despite how chaotic many things look, God is in control. Even the desolation of the apocalyptic woes is a part of God's creative final plan. Like the fury of birth pangs, they presage the hope for new and sustained life in God's coming kingdom.

- **2** John opens the second verse by appealing to yet another familiar narrative device: "*Then I saw*." As he did frequently throughout chapters 5 and 6, he uses the term there to indicate a shift in staging within the same scene. While keeping his hearers and readers focused on the four angels and the winds they hold at bay, John now introduces a fifth and strategically critical angelic messenger. This angel's message, though, is for neither John nor his followers. He addresses his four colleagues.

The imposing fifth angel ascends from the place of the sun's rising, the east (cf. 16:12; 21:13). It is not inconsequential that in Isa. 41:25, the Lord God stirs up one who will come from the rising of the sun to trample on rulers in much the same way rulers and their patrons are trampled at Rev. 6:12-17. This fifth angel, then, is the executor of God's judgment. John reinforces the judgment theme when he characterizes this angel as speaking in a *"great voice."* John is less interested in volume than he is in tone. In earlier texts, the great voice is a cipher for urgent, dramatic messages. John was told by a great voice to write his visions (1:10). Great voices celebrated in song the worthiness of the Lamb (5:2, 12; 7:10). The remaining *"great voice"* citations share another common theme; they all convey the tone of judgment. After the souls under the altar cry out in a great voice to God for a just judgment against those who shed their blood (6:10), one great voice after another confirms the judgment to come (8:13; 10:3; 11:12; 12:10; 14:7, 9, 15, 18; 16:1, 17; 19:1, 17). In fact, judgment imagery is so consistently related to the *"great voice,"* some translates as *"foreboding voice."*

The fifth angel's gear is even more interesting than his origin and tone. He carries a key piece of eschatological equipment: *"the seal of the living God,"* which is to say, eternal God. Unlike the seven seals mentioned in chapter 5, six of which were opened in chapter 6, this seal is most likely a type of signet device for embossing an imprint upon the seals that acted as binders for the apocalyptic scroll. Worn either as a cylinder hung on a cord around the neck or as a seal mounted like a stone on a ring, the device would have been immediately recognizable in either Jewish political or Greco-Roman magical circles. By possessing God's seal, the angel acts with God's authority.

- **3** The fifth angel orders other four not to damage the earth, sea, or trees that have been positioned squarely in their sights since v.1. Critical, though, is the nature of the command; it is a stay of the action, not an end to it. The destruction is to be abated until we have sealed the servants of our God upon their forehead.

The first-person plural pronouns are curious. The fifth angel appears to be acting alone. Could it be that he expects God and the Lamb to join him in the sealing process? But if that is the case, why did God surrender control of the signet device and apparently delegate the task? In fact, God has delegated the task. The fifth angel refers instead to his four colleagues. The angels whose actions will unleash the judgment and the angel whose orders control the timing and scope of that judgment are working in concert.

If the sealing is anything like the sealing that takes place in the story of Ezek. 9:4-8, upon which 7:1-3 is surely based, then its function is to afford divine protection. (This concept of sealing is well known in apocalyptic circles; cf. *4 Ezra* 2:38, 40; 6:5). In Ezekiel's account, God commissioned six executioners to slaughter the idolatrous inhabitants of Jerusalem. At just the moment when the reader expected the bloodbath to begin, however, there was an intermission. Before commencing the kill, God ordered that all those who grieved the abominable behavior be branded with a mark upon their foreheads. When an executioner saw the mark, he was to pass by the people who bore it, leaving them unharmed. Precisely the same scenario plays itself out here. God's fierce and final judgment awaits the Lamb's breaking of the seventh seal. At just the moment when the reader expects God to act, the fifth of God's agents calls time out so that certain believers can be branded with a protective mark on the forehead. A similar branding took place in the Genesis account where the mark God placed upon Cain acted as a seal of protection from future harm (Gen. 4:15). One might argue similarly that the Hebrews in Exod. 12 sealed themselves with the mark of lambs' blood on their doorposts. That "*seal*" protected them from the destructive force of God's death angel, who eventually killed all of Egypt's first born males. Other commentators note the similarity to *Pss. Sol.* 15.6, 9, where the righteous are marked so that they may be saved. Beale writes, "*In both Ezekiel and Pss. Sol, faithful Israelites are protected from the temporal harm of the plagues. The destruction of the plagues affects only those who are unfaithful and openly demonstrates their unbelieving identity.*" Indeed, later in John's own story, the locusts, who are also obviously executing a portion of God's judgment, are specifically ordered to harm only those who do not sport God's protective seal on their foreheads (Rev. 9:4).

The seal identifies the branded people as God's possessions; John describes them as God's slaves/servants. Historically, the combination of the notions of sealing or tattooing with the term, "*slaves/servants*" indicates that this metaphor is derived from the Eastern practice of tattooing secular and religious slaves. However, incorporation into the body of Christ by baptism (1 Cor. 12:13) was sometimes pictured in Pauline churches as the seal which stamped the new Christian as belonging to God (2 Cor. 1:22; Eph. 1:13; 4:30). Later, when this select group of God's slaves/servants is again mentioned, John explains that the branding is God's own name (Rev. 14:1-5). To mark someone with one's name is clearly to mark them as one's possession.

The seal, then, secured the possession, that is, protected it. The scroll of chapter 5 was sealed and thereby protected from being opened by anyone but the worthy Lamb. God's people, or at least a select portion of them, will be similarly sealed and thereby protected against the onslaught that will come with the setting loose of the four destructive winds. Here, then, is the answer to the critical question asked at 6:17: who will be able to stand? Only those who are sealed, which is to say, are secured, protected, by God's angels.

- **4** At this point John's vision turns abruptly into an audition. He stops seeing and begins hearing. No doubt there is a certain amount of practicality involved in this shift; the witnessing of 144,000 individuals being sealed would have taken an inordinate amount of time. Narratively, the act transpires so quickly that it does not even require any descriptive space. The sealing takes place offstage, in the literary gap between vv. 3 and 4. A report summarizing the action is then released.

The report is brief. The angels have sealed 144,000 of God's servants, 12,000 from each of Israel's twelve tribes. Brevity, though, does not mean simplicity. The short report raises a long list of important narrative and theological questions. Why does God choose only 144,000 when there are surely many more faithful servants across time? Who are the 144,000? Does the fact that they are taken from the tribes of Israel mean that they are Jews? Are they to be understood as the multitude standing before the heavenly throne in 7:9-17? What is their role in God's grand strategy of eschatological judgment and salvation?

The 144,000 are the human wing of God's cosmic army. To be sure, God has heavenly armies (Rev. 9:16; 19:14); this human force on earth is tasked with the assignment of reconnoitering and then campaigning for – witnessing to – the lordship of God and the Lamb. That testimony is the weapon they wage in the victorious battle against the satanic belief that Rome and its Caesar are lord (12:11).

Grammatical and thematic hints offer clues to the identity of the 144,000. (1) The phrase "*out of every tribe of the sons of Israel*" is controlled by the genitive introduced by the preposition "*out of.*" John understands each grouping of 12,000 to be part of a larger number that would make up an entire tribe. The collective 144,000, then, is the remnant of a much larger company of God's people. (2) John's handling of the 144,000 and the innumerable multitude of 7:9-17 indicates that they are two different groups. The clearest distinction is that the 144,000 are specifically numbered while the multitude is not. At this point in the narrative, the 144,000 also operate on earth prior to the period of the end-time eschatological woes. By contrast, the innumerable multitude is located in heaven. In addition, they have already gone through the "*great tribulation*" for which the 144,000 are bracing. (3) The 144,000 in 7:4-8 are to be identified with the 144,000 in 14:1-5. Besides the fact that both groups comprise the same number of people, there are several reasons for equating them. The members of both groups are marked on their foreheads. In 7:1-8, the marking is God's seal, and 14:1-5 then explains the content of that seal as the names of God and the Lamb. In both cases, moreover, the symbolism of a remnant community abounds. While 7:4-8 speaks of 12,000 out of the larger number of each tribe, 14:4 speaks of the firstfruits of what will ultimately be an abundant harvest. The 144,000 of 7:4-8 are secured with the mark of God for the coming eschatological conflict, and the 144,000 of 14:1-5 then prepare themselves for eschatological combat in the ancient way of the holy war. They maintain themselves as virgins who do not engage in sex in order that they will be pure as they follow the Lamb wherever he goes. According to 19:11-15, he goes out to war. Finally, the remnants in 7:4-8 and 14:1-5 occupy the same historical moment. In 7:4-8 the sealing from the coming wrath indicates a time prior to the judgment and the eschatological woes that go along with it. Similarly, the fact that the remnant in 14:1-5 symbolizes the firstfruits of those to be redeemed suggests that the redemptive process has only just now gotten under way. They, too, stand in anticipation of God's judgment day.

Who, though, are these 144,000? Are they Jewish? Jehovah's Witnesses believe that exactly 144,000 faithful men and women from Pentecost of 33 C.E. until the present day will be resurrected to heaven as immortal spirit beings to eternity with Jehovah. They believe that these people are *"anointed"* by God to become part of the spiritual *"Israel of God."* The Christian-based church founded by Reverend Sun Myung Moon, *"Unification Church"* believes the 144,000 represents the total number of saints whom Christ must find *"who can restore through indemnity the missions of all the past saints who, despite their best efforts to do God's Will, fell prey to Satan when they failed in their responsibilities. He must find these people during his lifetime and lay the foundation of victory over Satan's world"* according to the *"Exposition of the Divine Principle(원리강론)"* (pg 144). Obviously, I disagree with them.

John does refer to them with the term that Jews of the period used to identify themselves: *"Israel."* There is also the obvious appeal to the twelve tribes, and then the awkward listing of those tribes in vv. 5-8. In this scenario, the 144,000 would comprise the Jewish component of God's followers, while the innumerable multitude of 7:9-17 would comprise the Gentile portion. There is, however, a problem with this reading. The144,000 of 7:4-8 are the same as the 144,000 of 14:1-5. That latter group, whose members are marked with the name of the Lamb on their foreheads, is clearly Christian. The 144,000 of 7:4-8 must therefore also be Christian.

Could it be that John took an earlier Jewish source about Jewish martyrs and turned it into a text about Christian martyrs? Unlikely. The sealing offers protection against the very tribulations that create martyrs. If 7:4-8 ever was a Jewish source about a Jewish remnant, John has certainly revised it so that its protagonists have become Christians who most decidedly do not suffer martyrdom.

This does not mean, however, that John intends to exclude Jews from the company of this sealed remnant community. The number "*144,000*" is clearly not to be taken literally: it symbolizes wholeness. John has taken a figure representative of completion, the number "*12*," multiplied it by itself and then extended the total in a millenarian way: 12 x 12 x 1000 = 144,000. In its representation of the "*whole*" or "*complete*" remnant people, the double use of 12 signifies both the 12 tribes of Israel and the 12 apostles of the Lamb. John will later confirm this inclusive reading of the two twelves in his description of the new Jerusalem (21:12-14). The city has a great wall with 12 gates. On each gate is inscribed the name of one of the 12 tribes. The great wall also has 12 foundations, on each of which is inscribed the name of one of the 12 apostles. The number "*144,000*" symbolizes the same Jew/Gentile inclusiveness implied in the description of the new Jerusalem's great wall.

John has in mind a remnant group of Christians from both Jewish and Gentile backgrounds; what does he believe is their role in this eschatological scenario? Why are they set apart and protected from the coming eschatological woes? They are set apart as the human regiment of God's apocalyptic army. Military imagery is present throughout the narrative depiction in 7:4-8. The listing of groups of 12,000 implies a census with military objectives in mind. The census is a specific form of list that occurs with some frequency in the Old Testament, where it is used for the purpose of taxation (Exod. 30:11-16; 2 Kgs. 15:19-20), for labor conscription (2 Chr. 2:17-18; cf. 1 Kgs. 5:13-18), for determining the cultic duties and social structure of members of the tribe of Levi (Num. 3:14-4:49), for determining Israelite descent (Ezra 2; Neh. 7), but most commonly as a means for determining military strength (Num. 1:2-46; 2 Sam 24:1-9; 1 Chr. 21:1-6; 1 Chr. 27:1-24). Once again, the identification of the groups in 7:4-8 and 14:1-5 is illustrative. The holy war imagery of soldiers keeping themselves sexually pure before battle reinforces a military identification and purpose for the 144,000.

When John describes this army as composed from *"the sons of Israel,"* he is speaking symbolically. At the close of the first century when he writes, the twelve tribes no longer exist. His mythical rendering of Israel's past encourages a similarly mythical or, one might say, eschatological expectation for Israel's future. Judaism knew that the original unity of twelve tribes had been disrupted by the Assyrian deportation (2 Kgs.

17; Jer. 16:10-15; Ezek. 47:13-48:29; *Bar.* 4-5; *2 Bar.* 63; 67; *Test. Mos.* 2:3-9) and had never been restored, but at the eschaton God would reassemble the full complement of all Israel (*Ps. Sol.* 17:28-31, 40; *1QM* 2; *T. Sanh.* 13:10; *2 Esdr.* 13:40-47; *2 Bar.* 78-87; Matt. 19:28; Luke 22:30). In this case, Israel would refer not to ethnic Jews, but to all those who exhibit the primary Israelite character trait of belief in the lordship of God and now God's Lamb, Jesus Christ. "*Israel*" would thus signify the Christian church, the theological understanding of the church as the continuation of Israel, which was a widespread view in early Christianity (e.g., Matt. 10:5-6; Luke 1:68-79; 2:29-32; John 1:47; 5:43-47; 11:52; Acts 2:14-21; 26:14-23; James 1:1). In this way, John can envision an eschatologically restored Israel composed of both Jews and Gentiles. The presentation of the 144,000 as the restored remnant of Israel's twelve tribes is, then, John's way of eschatologically imaging, the faith communities, the universal church, the Church of Jesus Christ.

- **5 – 8** When John informs his hearers and readers that 12,000 people are chosen from each tribe to be sealed, four points deserve notice. First, even though John is apparently working from Old Testament tribal listings, he offers his own unique list by beginning not with Reuben (whose name tended to head most Old Testament lists) but with Judah (see Gen. 49; Num. 1:16-54; Deut. 33; Judg. 5). While some earlier lists presented the tribes in geographical order from south to north and thus started with Judah (Num. 34:19-28; Josh.

21:4-7; 1 Chr. 12:23-37), John no doubt chooses to list Judah first because he believes that Judah is the originating tribe of the Lamb (5:5). John emphasizes the tribe's placement by attaching the term *"sealed"* to Judah's 12,000. Even though he always implies such a sealing, he refrains from using the key term again until he comes to the final listing: the announcement of Benjamin's 12,000 at the close of the census. The term, then, not only highlights the selection of Judah but also serves to bracket the census material off from the rest of the material in the chapter.

A second oddity in the presentation is the inclusion of the names Manasseh and Joseph in the same listing. In most traditional lists, Manasseh and Ephraim were generally mentioned together, but not Joseph, since the former two were sons of Joseph. A probable explanation for this apparent anomaly comes from a third observation: Dan is absent. Dan was apparently replaced by Manasseh because Dan was thought to have been connected with egregious activities like idolatry (Judg. 18; 1 Kgs. 12:25-33). John insisted that his readers and hearers maintain their fidelity to the lordship of God and the Lamb. He persisted with this demand even though his followers lived in an environment that rewarded accommodation and punished faithful witness. It is therefore not surprising that he would omit the names of tribes associated in Jewish tradition with idolatry, the very essence of accommodation. Given Manasseh's presence, John may well have written *"Joseph"* when he intended to write *"Ephraim."* In any case, it is Joseph's tribal lineage that is intended. Fourth, Levi's inclusion is odd. Because the tribe was not given a portion of land and its members were exempt from military service, the name Levi was generally omitted from such listings (Num. 1:49; 2:33; Deut. 10:8-9; 18:1-5; Josh 13:14, 33). Interestingly enough, however, Levi was included in the accounts of 1QM 1.2; 2.2, where the tribes were gathered together in anticipation of an eschatological war. Since John has put his census of the tribes in just such an eschatological setting, it is, in the end, unremarkable that Levi is included.

Revelation 7:9~17 → Intermission (2): An Innumerable Multitude

NIV	TT
⁹ After this I looked, and there before me was a great multitude that no one could count, from every nation, tribe, people and language, standing before the throne and before the Lamb. They were wearing white robes and were holding palm branches in their hands. ¹⁰ And they cried out in a loud voice: "Salvation belongs to our God, who sits on the throne, and to the Lamb." ¹¹ All the angels were standing around the throne and around the elders and the four living creatures. They fell down on their faces before the throne and worshiped God, ¹² saying: "Amen! Praise and glory and wisdom and thanks and	⁹ After this I looked, and behold a great multitude that no one was able to count, from all nations and tribes and people and tongues, standing before the throne and before the Lamb, dressed in white robes and with palm branches in their hands, ¹⁰ and they cried out in a great voice, saying: "**Salvation**[96] belongs to our God who is seated on the throne and to the Lamb!" ¹¹ And all the angels stood around the throne and around the elders and the four living creatures, and they fell on their faces before the throne and worshiped God, ¹² saying: "Amen! Blessing and glory and wisdom and thanksgiving and honor and power and might belong to our God forever and ever! Amen!" ¹³ Then one of the elders answered, saying to

---

[96] σωτηρία → It means "*salvation*," "*deliverance*," and "*preservation*."

honor and power and strength be to our God for ever and ever. Amen!"

¹³ Then one of the elders asked me, "These in white robes—who are they, and where did they come from?"

¹⁴ I answered, "Sir, you know." And he said, "These are they who have come out of the great tribulation; they have washed their robes and made them white in the blood of the Lamb. ¹⁵ Therefore, "they are before the throne of God and serve him day and night in his temple; and he who sits on the throne will shelter them with his presence.
¹⁶ 'Never again will they hunger; never again will they thirst. The sun will not beat down on them,' nor any scorching heat. ¹⁷ For the Lamb at the center of the throne will be their shepherd;
'he will lead them to springs

me, "Who are these who are clothed in white robes, and where did they come from?" ¹⁴ I said to him, "**Sir**[97], you know." Then he said to me, "These are the ones who came out of the great tribulation; they washed their robes and made them white in the blood of the Lamb. ¹⁵ For this reason they are before the throne of God and worship him day and night in his temple, and the one seated on the throne will shelter them. ¹⁶ They will hunger no more, and thirst no more; the sun will not strike them, nor any scorching heat. ¹⁷ Because the Lamb in the center of the throne will be their shepherd, and he will guide them to springs of the water of life, and God will wipe away every tear from their eyes."

---

[97] κύριος → It means "*owner*," "*master*," "*sir*," and "*Lord*."

| of living water.' 'And God will wipe away every tear from their eyes.'" | |

John's vision never portrays the actual martyrdom of Christians. The preceding scene pictures the sealing of faithful Christians in advance of the great ordeal. 7:1-8 presents the universal church, the faith community on earth, sealed and drawn up in battle formation before the coming struggle, 7:9-17 presents the church, after the battle, triumphant in heaven.

- **9** Once again, John opens a new subject area with the introductory phrase *"after this I looked, and behold."* As has been the case with his past uses of this phrase, the preposition *"after"* is not a chronological marker. He does not mean to say that the events chronicled in vv.9-17 occur immediately after the events described in vv. 1-8. He instead means to say that after having seen the vision of the sealing of the 144,000, he saw another vision that dealt with a different though related topic. Having conveyed the sealing scene that took place prior to God's intervening acts of judgment and justice, he now feels obliged to relate the vision that relays the ultimate fate of all believers, both those who were sealed and those who were not. In order to do so, he must jump forward rather than backward in time. In fact, he vaults so far forward that he finds himself looking beyond the very end of time. The vision assures his hearers and readers who are presently suffering – and have therefore most assuredly not been sealed – that all who are knocked down because of their witness for the lordship of the Lamb will stand eternally tall in heaven. This futuristic, spiritual vision ends up having a real-time social and political discipleship effect: it encourages the members of the seven churches to resist relationship with Rome.

The object of John's sight was a vast crowd ("ὄχλος πολύς"), a legion of people so great that no one could possibly have counted it. At this point hearers and readers could not be blamed for remembering God's great promise to Abraham. The pledge that the patriarch's seed would one day grow as innumerable as the sands of the sea and the stars of the heavens (Gen. 13:16; 15:5; 22:17; 26:4; 28:14; 32:12; Heb. 11:12) has been accomplished in two significant ways. The first is the count; as God had promised, the numbers are titanic. The second is the vast crowd's universal nature; they represent every nation, tribe, people, and tongue. This means that Jews, Abraham's literal descendants, and Gentiles, who have been metaphorically grafted onto Israel's family tree through the gift of the Christ Lamb (cf. Rom. 11:13-26; Gal. 3:7, 29; 6:16), stand together in their worship, praise, and identification as the people of God. According to this second vision in chapter 7, Abraham's light has indeed drawn all the nations, or at least representatives from each of them, to the worship and into the glory of God.

John notices two important things about the constituents of the great crowd. First, each one of them is dressed in white. By now, John has so vigorously stressed the connection between white clothing and conquering witness to the lordship of Christ that it would be impossible for any hearer or reader to miss it here (3:2-5, 18; 4:4; 6:11). The fact that they are so dressed is an indication that they have been faithful witnesses and that their witness has contributed to the destruction of satanic rule as well as the liberation of those enslaved to it. Earlier, John declares that the Lamb is worthy because he redeemed/purchased every tribe, tongue, people and nation (5:9). Though John orders the elements differently in 7:9, he clearly has the same inclusive believing congregation in mind. The members of the multitude earned their white robes through their non-accommodating, conquering witness. Their reward is the eschatological relationship with God and the Lamb that John now envisions.

The second thing John notices is that the constituents of the great crowd hold palm branches in their hands. Though the term does occur in the Gospel of John, when the crowd greets Jesus' entry into Jerusalem with the acclamation, *"Hosanna! Blessed is the one who comes in the name of the Lord – the King of Israel"* (John 12:13), this is the only time it appears in Revelation. In *1 Macc.* 13:51 and *2 Macc.* 10:7, palm branches were used to celebrate great feasts like the victorious purification of the temple. Indeed, the Greek pronunciation of the plural form (*"palm branches" phonikes*) reminded hearers of the victory (*nike*) for God that they sought. Given the eschatological context of praise for the victorious God and Lamb, it is clear that the John who authored Revelation also intended the palm branches to be a symbol for adulation. The great crowd celebrates the conquest of satanic Rome.

The presence of the universal crowd standing worshipfully before the throne also encourages a complementary explanation. Zechariah 14 chronicles the vision of the nations trekking into the new Jerusalem for an eschatological Feast of Booths. Given the connection of the palm branches and this festival (Lev. 23:40, 43; Neh. 8:14-18; *2 Macc.* 10:6-7), not to mention John's vision of an innumerable international horde, it may be that he also wants to evoke the thinking simultaneously of conquest and festival images since the author of 2 Maccabees, too, brings those images triumphantly together (*2 Macc.* 10:6-7).

- **10** In v. 10, the assembled multitude belts out a hymn of praise to God and to the Lamb. They, like the angel at 7:2, make their declaration in a great voice. John's characters are still broadcasting the judgment that will occur at the last day. Here, though, the seer emphasizes the reverse side of the end-time coinage. At the very moment that those who persecuted the Lamb's witnesses are being brutally judged, the witnesses will be saved. The direct connection between the salvation of believers and the judgment of those who persecute them is explicitly declared by great voices at 12:10 and 19:1-2. Both groups earn the end of which they come. Death and destruction will greet the satanic, oppressive forces of Rome; white robes of conquest, on the other hand, will adorn the souls of the resurrected witnesses.

It is not coincidental, then, that the only times John uses the word "*salvation*" (σωτηρία), he narrates its proclamation through a great heavenly voice in the context of God's apocalyptic judgment (7:10; 12:10; 19:1-2). These three salvation texts form a sort of narrative progression: 7:10 makes the opening declaration that salvation belongs to God and to the Lamb; 12:10 then develops the thought by explaining exactly how God and the Lamb brought about the circumstance of salvation. They obliterated (i.e., Judged) the one who had tormented believers and had enlisted Rome's institutional assistance in the effort. Finally, 19:1-2 clarifies the rationale: God has toppled satanic Rome as an act of ultimate judgment.

The connection with Rome is important. It makes the attribution of salvation to God and the Lamb as political as it is spiritual. To be sure, the picture of a robed throng in heaven encourages John's hearers and readers to think of a heavenly, spiritual reward for their active, non-accommodating, rebellious witness. But the contemporaneous understanding of salvation as an imperially guaranteed commodity also reminds John's hearers and readers that a competition for global affection is being waged. Both God/the Lamb and Rome claim to be the sole providers of *"salvation"*: the peace and security of a life freed from oppression and harm. When John makes that claim exclusively for God, as he does here at 7:10, he is not only making a positive statement about God and the Lamb; he is also making a pejorative one about Rome. He is claiming that Rome cannot live up to its own hype. It does not hold the power of salvation that it alleges. John wants his hearers and readers to recognize Rome for the false pretender that it is. So educated, they will be less likely to accommodate to Roman social and religious practices in hopes of gaining the social, religious, and economic security that Rome claims to offer. They will seek such security, such salvation, from God and the Lamb instead. John's message of salvation is therefore every bit as political as it is spiritual. Though it is a vision about the end time, it maintains an ethical message commending politically active, non-accommodating behavior in the present moment of the churches in Asia Minor. Despite the persecution that promises to follow upon rebellious witnessing to the lordship of the Christ Lamb, believers should stay the course, knowing that what Rome offers as salvation and punishment is transitory. God's judgment and salvation are eternal. It is God's judgment that believers should therefore avoid, God's salvation that they should seek.

- **11** The angels who encircle the throne and the elders and the cherubim prepare for antiphonal affirmation by falling on their faces before the throne in a classic pose of worship. The scene is reminiscent of the one at 5:11-12, where countless angels respond antiphonally to the song of the cherubim and twenty-four elders. Here, surrounded by the cherubim and twenty-four elders, they react to a heavenly and apparently redeemed multitude. The earlier praise scene (5:11-12) has cycled back upon itself. The key thought remains the same: salvation, and therefore praise, belongs to God and the Lamb.
- **12** "*Amen*" to that, exclaim the responding angels. This affirmation brackets the angelic worship refrain.

"*Amen*" signifies what is true and valid. When used as a personal referent, it typically applies to God. At 3:14, it applies to Christ, who appears as the living validation of the lofty claims made about God's blessings and glory. Here, operating as the opening and closing angelic commentary, it affirms the validity of the interior statement's claims about God. Seven key attributes, six of which were earlier mentioned in relation to the Lamb at 5:12, are noted. Blessing and glory and wisdom and thanksgiving and honor and power and might belong eternally to God. Why? Because, as the context implies, God has brought about a just and fair conclusion to history, where the evil are judged and the faithful are saved. How can John's hearers and readers be sure? They have the angels' "*Amen*" word on it.

- **13** John apparently looks puzzled. That would explain why one of the twenty-four elders answers even though John has not asked a question. Helping John frame his thoughts, the elder offers a rhetorical question to which he, but evidently not John, knows the answer. "*Who,*" the elder asks, "*are these dressed in white robes, and where did they come from?*" The elder knows that who (they are) and why (they are here) are John's main concerns.

- **14** Like the prophet Ezekiel, who tells God, "*Lord, you know,*" after God asks whether the dry bones before him can again live (Ezek. 37:3), John turns the question back to the elder. In this case, though, the moniker "κύριος"(sir/lord) is a title of respect rather than divinity. Still he presumes that the elder's heavenly status gives him access to information that John does not have.

John is not disappointed. The verbal tenses the elder deploys in his answer are as important as the content those verbs convey. This horde of people whom John sees beyond the end of time are those who went through the great tribulation that was described at 6:1-8, 12-17 and 7:1-3, and that was anticipated in the letters to the seven churches. They were unsealed and therefore unprotected. The 144,000, too, will go through the great tribulation. They, however, will navigate it unscathed. John poetically explains the very different circumstance of the innumerable multitude by declaring that they washed their robes and made them white in the blood of the Lamb. Though the participle "οἱ ἐρχόμενοι" (lit., *"the ones who are coming"*), which explains their movement through the tribulation, is in the present tense, it must, because of its clausal relationship to the aorist main verbs *"washed"* and *"made white/dazzling,"* be translated with a past sense. It present form refers not as much as a sense of time as it does to its structural relationship with the main verbs. Their movement through the tribulation was contemporary or *"coincident"* with the washing and making white. Like the washing and making white, both the tribulation in question and the movement through it have been long over.

When the elder says that these are the people who went through the great tribulation and in so doing washed their robes and made them white in the blood of the Lamb, the two uses of "καὶ" (and) employed to link the three primary clauses should be treated epexegetically.[98] That is to say, they not only connect the clauses but also identify the material in the trailing clause as a clarification of the information revealed in the preceding clause. One should therefore translate: *"These are the ones who went through the great tribulation, which is to say, they washed their robes; that is, they made them white in the blood of the Lamb."* Though they deploy different symbolism, each of the three clauses says essentially the same thing. They are narratively equivalent.

An identification of the key phrase "τῆς θλίψεως τῆς μεγάλης" (the great tribulation) is critical to understanding the meaning of 7:14. The combination of the article and the adjective *"great"* suggests that this is not just any tribulation but the great time of distress that would accompany the ushering in of God's Day of Judgment and Salvation (Dan. 12:1-4). Early Christian writers tended to view historical afflictions as a preamble to that apocalyptic moment. The synoptic Gospel declarations (Matt. 24; Mark 13; Luke 21) attributed of Jesus indicates that the response of hostile Roman and Jewish leaders to acts of faithful discipleship comprised the Great Tribulation's opening act. The connection Jesus made between acts of discipleship and present tribulation is critical for John. He use of the term "θλῖψις" (tribulation, affliction) at

---

[98] *"These are the ones who went through the great tribulation." "They washed their robes." "They made them white in the blood of the Lamb."*

1:9; 2:9, 10 betrays his belief that the struggles of his hearers and readers indicate that the great struggle of the end time is already under way. It is equally intriguing that, like Jesus in the synoptic accounts, he connects the believers' affliction to their discipleship behavior. John uses the language of witness to bring discipleship behavior to narrative life. Their witness triggers the affliction that sets the stage for the even greater tribulation to come. This is the warning John tried to deliver in his letters to the seven churches in chapters 2 and 3, as he exhorted emphasizes the point through the language of slaughter (6:9). It is precisely because of their determination to reject accommodation to Roman lordship and the economic, political, and religious benefits associated with it, and their effort to proclaim the alternative lordship of the Lamb – that is, their witness – that his people suffer as they do.

Witness, then, not martyrdom, is John's focus with his tribulation language. The Daniel text upon which he is surely building also emphasizes faithful witnessing more than self-sacrificial martyrdom. In Daniel's tribulation, the eschatological opponent persecutes the saints because of their covenant loyal to God (Dan. 11:30-39, 44; 12:10). The tribulation, whether in its early, historical or its final, apocalyptic stage, is to be connected not with martyrdom, but with witness and the sacrifices (martyrdom included) that go along with it. In John's narrative world, then, *"washing"* and *"making white"* are, like *"conquering,"* euphemisms for witness (see the comments on 3:4-5).

Even John's pointed reference to the blood of Christ is not a reference to martyrdom. John's later narrative language will not allow for such a reading. At 12:11 he does not tie Jesus' blood to the imagery of human self-sacrifice but to the language of conquest and Christian witness. Both Jesus' blood and Christian witness are necessary for realizing the conquest of satanic Rome. Jesus' blood, which is significantly attached to the witness he bore, is the component given exclusively by God. The part that believers can control is their own witness. That is why the ethical exhortations of chapters 2 and 3 are targeted toward the endeavor of witnessing. John does not want his believers to think, however, that their witness is alone sufficient for the task. Only when they work in concert with God's own work will their effort have the victorious result that they seek. That witnessing effort, euphemistically pictured as a washing and making white, takes place in concert with, and therefore in direct relation to – one might even say, as John does, in – the blood of the Lamb by testifying to the lordship of that Slaughtered Lamb. It is witness, not dying, that is ethically preeminent.

- **15** Having explained who the crowd is, the elder now clarifies why they have been awarded such lofty status. It is because of their witness. Revelation 22:14 confirms that those who wash their robes will procure an eternal eschatological relationship with God.

The eternal nature of the eschatological relationship is celebrated in two principal images. The first is that of perpetual worship. At the Jerusalem temple, worship began with the initial morning sacrifice ("*tamid*") and ended with the closing sacrifice at the end of the day. Not so in the heavenly realm. There would be neither a beginning nor an ending in the cycle of worship. The faithful would have the perpetual opportunity to stand in God's temple and celebrate God's lordship, God's rule, and the reign/kingdom of God.

The presence of the temple appears at first sight to be problematic. After all, this scene takes place in heaven in the future following God's Day of Judgment and Salvation. Later, however, John will declare that no temple exists in the new Jerusalem, because the Lord God and the Lamb are themselves now the temple. What appears at first to be a contradiction is in reality complementary. Far from disputing the affirmation of 7:15, the vision of the new Jerusalem in 21:22 essentially agrees with it. From the very beginning of his work, John has maintained that there would be some type of temple in God's future kingdom (3:12). Both 7:15 and 21:22 understand that God and the Lamb will themselves be that presence. As Beale argues, "*Rev. 7:15 does not portray a literal 'temple' in which the saints serve God. Rather, as the second part of the verse reveals, the temple now consists in the presence of the lamb and of 'the one sitting on the throne, who tabernacles over his people.'*"

When John asserts that God will dwell with the people and so shelter them the accent is once again on perpetuity. John's shift to the future-tense verb is intended to convey that the future already envisioned will itself be further extended, into forever. In this forever, God will dwell with God's people. Clearly building from Ezek. 37:26-28, John reclaims the Festival of Booths imagery that he implied with his mention of palm branches in 7:9. God will "*tabernacle* ("σκηνόω")" with the people (21:3) even as the people tabernacle in tents to celebrate God's lordship and rule. Forever.

- **16 – 17** In what many call the longest allusion to an Old Testament passage in the Book of Revelation, John draws upon the vision in Isa. 49:10 to assure his hearers and readers that those who faithfully witness, who resist accommodating themselves to Roman lordship and the benefits that go with it, will never again, even in the extended future that progresses beyond the end of time itself, experience hunger or thirst, or the heat of wandering and separation that their forebears once experienced in the post-exodus wilderness and the post Babylonian exile.

John's hearers and readers can be assured of this promise because the Lamb himself will shepherd the people (v. 17). The vision of a lamb operating as a shepherd is not as paradoxical as it first appears. It is the Lamb whose witness and execution helped to establish the people's eschatological relationship with God. In delivering that witness, in enduring and rising beyond the accompanying execution, the Lamb has shown them the way of witness that leads to God. In that sense, even as Slaughtered Lamb, he has been their shepherd, their guide once again to well-known Old Testament images (Ps. 23:1-2; Isa. 25:8; 49:10; Jer. 31:16; Ezek. 34:23), John declares that those who witness shall never again know want or distress. They shall know only the joy and praise that come in two important ways that will be dramatically developed in the eschatological visions of chapter 21: springs of the water of life or living water (21:6), and the wiping away of every tear (21:4).

Revelation 8:1 → Transition - The Seventh Seal: Silence in Heaven

NIV	TT
8 ¹ When he opened the seventh seal, there was silence in heaven for about half an hour.	**8** ¹ When he opened the seventh seal, there was **silence**⁹⁹ in heaven for half an hour.

After the intensifying crescendo of the opening of the first six seals and the sealing of God's people, the reader expects the final end. Instead, as the seventh seal is opened, there is a deafening prolonged silence. In some apocalyptic traditions the cosmos returns to its primeval silence just before the end. In Zeph. 1:7 and Zech. 2:13 silence is the prelude to the divine epiphany. Silence was also a ritual prelude to prayer, both among the Greeks and in the Jerusalem temple, just preceding the incense offering. John may also include the silence here for a literary and dramatic purpose.

- **1** Verse 1 is the natural conclusion to the visionary recounting of the first six seals (cf. 6:1-17). After the narrative interlude of chapter 7, where the seer flashed back to the past that preceded the seals episode (7:1-8) and then envisioned the future that would occur after it (7:8-17), John's hearers and readers are now ready to witness the final judgment that would accompany the Lamb's opening of the seventh seal. John uses the language of *"opening"* as a verbal metaphor for the

---

⁹⁹ σιγὴ → It means *"silence"* (cf. Acts. 21:40; Rev. 8:1).

eschatological opportunity humans have to perform the kind of witness that would lead to salvation. In this case, the opening (of that opportunity) is associated with the time unit of a half hour. The half hour is a metaphor, not a literal measurement. It is a momentary break, a respite in the horror of judgment that immediately followed the opening of each of the past six seals. Humankind has been given this brief time-out for a reason. Though they now live on the proverbial edge of time, they have a final opportunity to operate in ways that will either invite salvation (witness) or demand judgment (accommodation).

John amplifies the judgment theme with the declaration of silence. Though the seer only uses the word "σιγή" (silence) here, in both Old Testament and Jewish contexts the term conjured images of divine judgment. Though the term "σιγή" Rarely appears in the LXX, the theme of silence, particularly as related to manuscript texts, is prevalent and related to the theme of judgment (Pss. 31:17-18; 115:17; *4 Ezra* 7:30; Isa. 47:5; Ezek. 27:32; Amos 8:2-3; Lam. 2:10-11; 1 Sam. 2:9-10; Hab. 2:20; Zech. 2:13). 1QpHAB 13.1-4 interprets the silence of Hab. 2:20 as the Day of Judgment when God will destroy all those among the nations who serve idols. John enhances and broadens this emphasis with his specification of the time unit as one-half of an hour. Each of his later uses of the concept *"half"* occurs in a context that highlights either the judgment/destruction of those who have persecuted

God's people (11:9, 11) or the salvation of those whose witness endures (12:14).[100]

The relationship between the moment of silence and the breaking of the seventh seal is reminiscent of the silence that preceded God's creation of heaven and earth. In this case, following the cataclysms of the final judgment, God will create a new heaven and a new earth. As at the beginning (cf. *4 Ezra* 6:39; *2 Bar.* 3:7), so here at the end (*4 Ezra* 7:26-44), the creative moment is set up by quite.

Some commentators counter that this claim would be more compelling if the silence in 8:1 were actually followed by the creation of a new heaven and new earth instead of eschatological woe. A key point bears consideration. John is playing with narrative time, employing the techniques of flashback and anticipation. It only appears as if the moment of new creation does not follow directly upon the period of silence narrated at 8:1. The pleas of 8:3-5, together with the trumpet woes that follow, are not new (chronologically later) events but a dramatic retelling of the petition in 6:9-11 and the seals judgment, for which it forms the centerpiece. The position of 6:9-11 was described through the lens of the sacrificial altar; in 8:3-5 John again appeals to incense altar imagery. When the narration of the trumpets recapitulates the breaking of the seals, John's hearers and readers find reassurance

---

[100] → There is also thematic development of the image of "*half*" with the designation "*one thousand, two hundred sixty days,*" which represents one-half of a seven-year period. This transitory period also symbolizes a period of short duration and occurs in contexts of either explicit judgment (11:3) or salvation (12:6). For a direct connection between the theme of judgment and "*half*," see *Wis.* 18:14-16.

that God has indeed heard the cries of the faithful and has intervened. In other words, the narration that follows 8:1 recapitulates the events that have already happened (the seals episodes) from a different eschatological perspective (trumpets). Time itself has not moved chronologically forward. Just as John separated the movement from the opening of the sixth seal (6:12-17) to the opening of the seventh (8:1) with the flashback of 7:1-8 and the flash forward of 7:9-17, he separates the creative silence that follows the opening of the seventh seal from the eschatological creation that begins at 21:1. The next chronological step (after John finishes relating God's intervening acts of judgment) will be the creation of the new heaven and the new earth. The silence of 8:1 is therefore properly positioned (in real time) just before that moment. Only because of John's method of narrating his visions does the silence seem to be separated from the new creation. That separation is a literary fiction that gives John more narrative "*time*" to make his point. As far as eschatological real time is concerned, 8:1 moves chronologically right to 21:1. Everything in between is either a recapitulation of events already narrated or an anticipation of events yet to be narrated.

The Sounding of the Seven Trumpets

The acts of judgment that accompany the blowing of the trumpets by the seven archangels structurally and thematically parallel those associated with the Standing Slaughtered Lamb's breaking of the seven seals.

This section, with its vivid and alarming description of the agents of destruction, epitomizes Revelation's links with Old Testament prophets like Nahum and Zephaniah. There is another sequence of seven, this time of trumpet blasts. Once more it is interrupted in 9:13 (cf. Rev. 6:12), with the final trumpet blast occurring at 11:15. The trumpets herald the longest sequence of catastrophes to befall the earth.

In John's narrative chronology, then, the breaking of the seals and the blasting of the trumpets occur simultaneously. They are the same set of events, encountered from different perspectives. (see *"The Opening of the Seven Seals"* chap. 6)

Revelation 8:2~6 → Introduction to the Trumpets

NIV	TT
² And I saw the seven angels who stand before God, and seven trumpets were given to them. ³ Another angel, who had a golden censer, came and stood at the altar. He was given much incense to offer, with the prayers of all God's people, on the golden altar in front of the throne. ⁴ The smoke of the incense, together with the prayers of God's people, went up before God from the angel's hand. ⁵ Then the angel took the censer, filled it with fire from the altar, and hurled it on the earth; and there came peals of thunder, rumblings, flashes of lightning and an earthquake. ⁶ Then the seven angels who had the seven trumpets prepared to sound them.	² And I saw the seven angels who stand before God, and they were given seven **trumpets**[101]. ³ And another angel with a golden censer came and stood at the **altar**[102]; he was given a great quantity of incense to offer with the prayers of all the saints on the golden alter before the throne. ⁴ And the smoke of the incense went up with the prayers of the saints before God, from the hand of the angel. ⁵ Then the angel took the censer and filled it with some fire from the altar and threw it on the earth; and there were thunders and rumblings and flashes of lightning and an earthquake. ⁶ And the seven angels who had the seven trumpets prepared to blow them.

---

[101] σάλπιγξ → It means a *"trumpet"* (noun).

[102] θυσιαστήριον → It means *"altar"* – the altar for slaying or burnt offerings, or any other altar.

Before proceeding with his visions of disaster, John sets the whole in the context of heavenly worship. The Book of Revelation was composed to be read aloud in a worship service of prayer and praise. The struggling church on earth knows that it prays; during the hard times, it may wonder what happens to its prayers. John's Revelation lets the worshipping church see its prayer from the heavenward side.

- **2** The formula "*and I saw*" distinguished 8:2 from the material that precedes it. The hearers and readers remain a spectator in the seer's three-ring apocalyptic circus. Having shifted perspective, one no longer sees God acting in the first ring through the metaphor of a Lamb breaking seals. In this second ring, God's preliminary acts of judgment operate through the image of seven angels blowing seven trumpets.

  The angels are a subset of the larger group of angels whom John sees standing with the elders and cherubim at 7:11. The definite article ("*the*" seven angels) implies that his audience is already familiar with them. John has, after all, mentioned a grouping of seven angels before: the seven guardians of John's seven churches (1:16, 20; 2:1, 8, 12, 18; 3:1, 7, 14); and the seven spirits located before God's throne (1:4; 4:5). Three observations support the view that the earlier angels/spirits are introduced as the seven angels in 8:2 as though the reader has met them before. Second, he has heretofore only mentioned such a grouping in regard to the seven angels/spirits from chapters 1-4. Third, the seven spirits and seven angels are both located before the throne. John returns to them later at 15:1 and 16:1 when he re-imagines the breaking of the seals for the second time as the pouring out of God's bowls of wrath upon the earth. These archangels, then, initiate the action in both the second and the third of the three apocalyptic rings. The fact that they are doing so simultaneously is not a problem given the fact that John is describing a single event with symbolic and poetic license. The normal constraints of time and place do not apply.

These seven are the archangels mentioned in the Jewish literature of the time (*Tob.* 12:15; *1 En.* 20:1-7; 40; 54:6; 71:8-9; 81:5; 90:21-22; *T. Levi* 3:5; 8:2; *Jub.* 1:27, 29; 2:1-2, 18; 15:27; 31:14)[103]. John mentions only one of them by name. At 12:7 he credits Michael with ousting the dragon from heaven. If Michael's function and capability are any indication, these angels represent the awesome power of God to punish and thereby judge wrongdoing. It is no wonder, then, that John connects them so integrally to the eschatological judgment of the trumpets and bowls.

The seven archangels wield seven trumpets. Most often associated with the advance of an army in battle (Josh. 6:5), the trumpet was also used as a signal of warning (Ezek. 33:3-6; Joel 2:1), as accompaniment to religious ritual (Lev. 23:24; 25:9; Joel 2:15; cf. the blowing of the shofar as signal to open and close the daily temple worship), as part of theophany scene

---

[103] → The archangels are identified as *"Uriel," "Raphael," "Raguel," "Michael," "Saraqa'el," "Gabriel,"* and *"Remiel."* (see Excursus 11: The Seven Archangels)

(Exod. 19:16), and as an image of eschatological judgment (Zeph. 1:16). Perhaps the most celebrated account of the trumpet call in connection with the warfare, story, seven priests were assigned seven trumpets and ordered to blow them successively for seven consecutive days. On the seventh day, at the seventh trumpet blast, the walls of Jericho fell. The parallel to John's vision of the seven trumpets is difficult to miss. Similarly, in the Qumran War Scroll seven Levites carry seven ram's horns into the eschatological conflict (1QM 7.14). Given this background, it is no wonder that both Jewish and New Testament writers associated the sounding of the trumpet with the engagement of God's final eschatological battle (Zeph. 1:14-16; Zech. 9:14; *Apoc. Abr.* 31:1; *4 Ezra* 6:23; *Gk. Apoc. Ezra* 4:36; Matt. 24:31; 1 Cor. 15:52; 1 Thess. 4:16; *Did.* 16:6).

John picks up on this eschatological emphasis and highlights it. The noun form for trumpet "σάλπιγξ" at 8:2 and 8:6 brackets a text where God responds to the prayers of the people by pouring an avenging and judging wrath upon the earth. This word reappears at 8:13, where the blasts of trumpets are connected to three dire eschatological woes; and at 9:14, where the sixth angel's trumpet unleashes a punishing force that kills one-third of all humankind. Interestingly enough, this image of the trumpet sound is balanced with the earlier instances where a trumpet blast issues from the Son of Man or the throne of God and is both revelatory and salvific (1:10; 4:1). The verbal form ("σαλπίζω") has the same emphasis. Throughout the trumpet scenes (8:6, 7, 8, 10, 12, 13; 9:1, 13; 10:7; 11:15), this verb is applied both to God's preliminary acts of judgment and to the final act of judgment at the last day. Revelation 11:15 is illustrative. Its larger context (11:15-18) also includes an image of salvation that is as potent as the theme of judgment most often associated with the sound.

This dual focus on judgment and salvation makes sense because God is the figure who directs the trumpet blasts and orchestrates the events that respond to them. John demonstrates God's control here in the same way that he demonstrated God's control over the judgment events that took place after the Standing Slaughtered Lamb's breaking of each of the seals; he deploys the divine passive construction "ἐδόθησαν" ("*it was given*"). The trumpets, and thus the acts of judgment and salvation that follow their blowing, belong not to the angels but to God. God controls them, distributes them, and no doubt directs when and to what effect they are to be blown. Depending on how one has responded to God through either witness or accommodation, the sounding of God's trumpets will signal either the dawn of salvation of the coming of judgment.

Excursus 11: The Seven Archangels

The earliest reference to a system of "*seven archangels*" as a group appears to be in *1 Enoch* which is not part of the Jewish Canon but is prevalent in the Judaic tradition. While this book today is non-canonical in most Christian Churches, it was explicitly quoted in the New Testament (Jude 1:14-15) and by many of the early Church Fathers. The Ethiopian Orthodox Church to this day regards the Book of Enoch to be canonical.

1. **Uriel** – "אוּרִיאֵל" which means "*God is my light.*" Uriel is an archangel of Rabbinic Judaism, Anglican Communion, Eastern Orthodoxy, Folk Catholicism, and Oriental Orthodoxy.
2. **Raphael** – "רָפָאֵל" which means "*It is God who heals*," "*God heals*," or "*God please heal.*" Raphael is an archangel of Judaism, Christianity and Islam.
3. **Raguel** – His names are written differently, "*Raguil, Rauil, Rufael, Raquel, Reuel, Akrasiel.*" It means "*Friend of God*," and he is an angel mainly of the Judaic traditions.
4. **Michael** – "מִיכָאֵל" which means "*Who is like God?*" Micahel is an archangel in Judaism, Christianity, Roman Catholics, the Eastern Orthodox, and Islam.
5. **Saraqa'el** – "זהריאל" which means "*command of God*," or "*God's command.*" Other possible versions of his name are "*Suriel, Suriyel, Seriel, Sauriel, Surya, Saraqael, Sarakiel, Suruel, Surufel, Sourial.*" He is an angel, mainly from Judaic tradition and Coptic Orthodox Church.
6. **Gabriel** – "גַּבְרִיאֵל" which means "*God is my strength.*" Gabriel is an angel who typically serves as a messenger sent from God to certain people. He is an angel in Judaism, Roman Catholic, Christianity, and Easter and Oriental Orthodox Churches. Gabriel is an archangel in Islam and in the Book of Enoch.

> 7. **Remiel** – "רעמיאל" which means "*Thunder of God.*" Remiel is a fallen "*Watcher*" in the Book of Enoch. (see Excursus 13: Watchers)

- **3** Verses 3-5 are so different from the rest of the chapter that many commentators believe they were inserted here either by John or by some later editor. They certainly disrupt the otherwise smooth narrative flow of trumpet distribution and trumpet playing. Once the trumpets have been given to the seven angels, hearers and readers are ready for the sound of the horns and the preliminary acts of God's judgment that will accompany them. Instead, there is a lengthy diversion, as another angel at the altar offers incense mixed with the prayers of the saints. If indeed this is a late textual insertion, John, (or the final editor who added it) apparently recognized the problem. Diverted attention would have to be re-engaged; v. 6 would therefore be needed to remind the hearers and readers of the situation left hanging at the end of v. 2.

    Since I am more interested in a literary/narrative reading than one preoccupied with questions of source and redaction, I prefer to engage the material as we have it before us.

    Verse 3 introduces yet another angel, an eighth one. He has a priestly assignment. Golden censer in hand, he comes before the golden altar of incense (Exod. 30:1-10), which John locates before the heavenly throne.

    The seer is operating from the layout of the Jerusalem temple. There, after moving through the court of the priests where the altar of sacrifice resided, on the way to the holy of holies, a priest encountered the golden altar of incense. During his approach, the priest ascended the twelve steps from the court of the priests and entered a vestibule whose large opening was flanked by columns. A double doorway covered in gold opened into the "*Hechal*," or main chamber. Inside the "*Hechal*" were a showbread table; a golden, seven-branched menorah; and a small, golden incense altar. Incense was burned twice daily, during the morning and evening "*tamid*" sacrifices. Moreover, when the high priest entered the Holy of Holies once a year on the Day of Atonement, he bore with him a censer of incense.

There were several ways to offer incense in ancient Israel. first, while there is no clear evidence that it was sprinkled on animal sacrifices, it could be burned with grain offerings (Lev. 2:1, 15; 6:15). Second, instead of being placed on an altar, it could be offered in a long-handled censer (Lev. 10:1; Num. 16:6). Censers were either an upright vessel or a long-handled, ladle-like vessel; the fire was placed into the censer in the form of live coals secured from the sacrificial altar in the court of the priests. Third, a special recipe was used for incense offered twice a day in connection with the daily sacrifices (Exod. 30:34-38). After live coals were taken from the sacrificial altar and spread on the incense altar, the incense would be added. A fourth and special case involved the use of incense in the Holy of Holies on the Day of Atonement (Lev. 16:11-14).

John appears to envision some form of the third type. The angel pours the incense onto the altar, where the hot coals are already in place. The smoke of the incense then rises up as it no doubt once had during the morning and evening sacrifices in the Jerusalem temple. The altar imagery is important because of its symbolic implications for John. The term appears only once (Rev. 6:9) before he makes certain to include it in each of the scenes that chronicle God's preliminary acts of judgment: the seals (6:9); the trumpets (8:3-5; 9:13); and the bowls (16:7). This careful positioning of the term is one more reason for understanding the narratives of the seals, trumpets, and bowls as three distinct different viewings of the same eschatological events.

Equally important is the thematic significance that John attributes to the altar imagery. "*Altar*" symbolizes God's eschatological judgment. That is evident in the seals, trumpets, and bowls texts, given the preoccupation those texts have with God's judgment. John's other uses of the term are equally oriented to the judgment theme. The occurrence at 11:1 takes place during the interlude between the sixth and seventh trumpet blasts. There God instructs that the temple be measured so that it will not be harmed when the punishing hostilities begin. Later an angel comes out from the altar armed with a sickle, ready for the winnowing of the eschatological harvest (14:18). To be sure, in these passages John jumps between the sacrificial and incense altars, often without informing his hearers and readers which one he has in mind. perhaps that kind of specificity was not important to him. His main goal, after all, was not to identify a particular altar but to clarify what *"altar"* in its essence meant: God's judgment.

The connection with the altar in 6:9-11 is particularly interesting. Because this is an altar of sacrifice, it would be easy for a hearer or reader to interpret the imagery in chapter 6, and by way of association also in 8:3-5, through the notion of atonement. In that case, the incense would be seen as a sacrifice to God, in the way that the *"martyrdom"* of believers was often understood sacrificially. Incense, however, rarely carried the sense of atonement (only in Num. 16:46-47; *T. Levi.* 3:5-6). It certainly has no such sense for John. His mention of the altar identifies it with prayer (5:8). John develops that thematic connection here at 8:3-5. While he is careful to keep prayers and incense as distinct entities that both rise up from the incense altar, he relates all three elements (prayer, incense, and altar) to God's avenging, judging activity. The motivation for divine action thus rests with the content of the prayers that accompany the incense, much as it earlier rested with the prayerful cries of the slaughtered souls (6:9-11). As a consequence of those prayers, the altar's fire is thrown down in judgment against the earth. Here at 8:3-5, then, with the angel in the role of priest, the human prayers that rise up with the divine-priestly incense are not offerings of sacrifice or pleas for redemption but appeals for God's intervention. God answers with fire and the acts that accompany the sounding of the trumpets, just as God answered earlier with the acts of judgment that accompanied the breaking of the seals.

God is in control. God gives the angel the combustible materials that spark the people to cry out in intercessory prayer and trigger the judgment. God thus scripts the situation that ends up providing the motivation for God's own action.

The angel packages the incense with the prayers of the saints, that is, people of God. John uses a dative construction ("ταῖς προσευχαῖς"), which is repeated at 8:4, to show relationship between the incense and the prayers. Some ambiguity exists because the construction can be translated in multiple ways. As a dative of respect or reference, the phrase can mean that the angel was given the incense in order to give or offer it as a symbol of the prayers. That might have been the intent at 5:8, where the incense and prayer are identical, but it is clearly not the case here, where John strives to keep them separate. As a temporal dative, it could mean that the incense was offered at the same time as the prayers. That is obvious; an aspect of this category surely is in play. As a dative of association, the incense would simply be rendered with the prayers but have no real connection to them. The strong relationship between the two, however, argues against such a reading. As a dative of advantage, the incense would be given as a supplement to make the prayers more acceptable to God. In this case, the prayers would be somewhat like a burnt offering whose often rank smell needed to be "*adjusted*" so that it would be considered suitable for the Deity. Given that these prayers are not only pleas but also direct challenges for God to intervene, one could understand that they would need to be presented in the best possible light (cf.: *"For a blameless man was quick to act as their champion; he brought forward the shield of his ministry, prayer and propitiation by incense."* Wis. 18:21). They are, in effect, acts of worship, and worship operates by ritual prescriptions that allow the presentations to God to be acceptable in God's sight. The incense performs that ritual, liturgical function here.

- **4** When the incense hits the hot embers on the altar, it flashes into smoke that rises up with the prayers. Because this scene (like the corresponding one at 6:9) is taking place in heaven, the smoke and the prayers do not have far to travel before they reach their intended audience.

  Smoke, even when connected with God's glory, bears an unmistakable aura of wrath and judgment. Here the angel is about to pour out the fire that has produced this smoke as punishment against the earth. In every subsequent use of smoke (9:2, 3, 17, 18; 14:11; 15:8; 18:9, 18; 19:3), John makes its relationship to God's judgment clear. There is probably no more poignant a vision in Revelation than the smoke of Babylon's burning climbing into the sky (18:9, 18; 19:3).

- **5** Having sent the smoke and prayers on their way, the eighth angel captures some of the fire from the altar by scooping up some burning coals into his censer (cf. Lev. 16:12). He subsequently throws live fire onto the earth. There can be no clearer image of divine wrath (cf. Gen. 19:24; 2 Kgs. 1:10, 12, 14; Job 1:16; Ps. 11:6; 2 Thess. 1:8). Then, as if to confirm God's eschatological role in the affair, signature signs of theophany close out the scene.

In the Old Testament, thunder, rumblings, flashes of lightning, and earthquake not only indicate God's presence, but also confirm God's judgment against God's enemies and God's salvation on behalf of God's people (e.g., Exod. 19:16-18; Ps. 77:18-19; Isa. 29:6). John narrates theophanies with the same intent. There are four key passages in Revelation: 4:5; 8:5; 11:19 and 16:18. Not only is 4:5 the first occurrence; it also is the only one of the four that omits mention of an earthquake, probably because the finality of judgment associated with the simultaneous occurrence of all four events is not yet on display. The lightning flashes, rumblings, and thunders are tasked with introducing God's majesty, not God's judgment. John attaches the final three theophany scenes to presentations of God's judgment. Revelation 8:3-5, then, not only explains why judgment takes place but also shows how that judgment plays out: fire.[104]

---

[104] → As opposed to flood waters in Noah's account: Gen. 6-8.

Revelation 8:7~13 → The First Four Trumpets

NIV	TT
⁷ The first angel sounded his trumpet, and there came hail and fire mixed with blood, and it was hurled down on the earth. A third of the earth was burned up, a third of the trees were burned up, and all the green grass was burned up. ⁸ The second angel sounded his trumpet, and something like a huge mountain, all ablaze, was thrown into the sea. A third of the sea turned into blood, ⁹ a third of the living creatures in the sea died, and a third of the ships were destroyed. ¹⁰ The third angel sounded his trumpet, and a great star, blazing like a torch, fell from the sky on a third of the rivers and on the	⁷ The first **angel**[105] blew his trumpet, and there came hail and fire, mixed with blood, and the mixture was thrown to the earth; and a third of the earth was burned up, and a third of the trees were burned up, and all the green grass was burned up. ⁸ The second angel blew his trumpet, and something like a great mountain burning with fire was thrown into the sea, and a third of the sea became blood, ⁹ and a third of the living creatures in the sea died, and a third of the boats were destroyed. ¹⁰ The third angel blew his trumpet, and a great star, burning like a lamp, fell from heaven, and it fell on a third of the rivers and on the springs of water. ¹¹ The name of the star is **Apsinth**[106], and a third of the

---

[105] → Though the external evidence supports the omission of the word "*angel*," John so obviously intends to say "*angel*" here that a clear translation is obligated to supply it. (Simply speaking, there is no word, "*angel*" in the manuscripts of this text.)

[106] Αψινθος → It is the name of a star, means "*wormwood*."

springs of water—¹¹ the name of the star is Wormwood. A third of the waters turned bitter, and many people died from the waters that had become bitter. ¹² The fourth angel sounded his trumpet, and a third of the sun was struck, a third of the moon, and a third of the stars, so that a third of them turned dark. A third of the day was without light, and also a third of the night. ¹³ As I watched, I heard an eagle that was flying in midair call out in a loud voice: "Woe! Woe! Woe to the inhabitants of the earth, because of the trumpet blasts about to be sounded by the other three angels!"	waters became **wormwood**[107], and many people died from the waters because they were made bitter. ¹² The fourth angel blew his trumpet, and a third of the sun was struck and a third of the moon and a third of the stars, so that a third of them were darkened and a third of the day would not appear and likewise the night. ¹³ Then I looked, and I heard an **eagle**[108] flying in midheaven, crying with a great voice: "**Woe**[109], woe, woe to the inhabitants of the earth because of the remaining trumpet blasts of the three angels who are about to blow!"

    The seven-stage judgment John sees is the same pattern of judgment he narrated at 6:1-8:1 (seals) and the same one he will revisit at 16:1-20 (bowls). He conveys that wrath

---

[107] Αψινθος → It means "*wormwood,*" the star's name and "*wormwood*" are the same Greek word.
[108] ἀετός → It means "*eagle,*" or "*vulture.*" Many later manuscripts substituted "*angel*" for "*eagle.*" In 14:6, an angel does fly in midheaven with an eschatological message. However, in a narrative where an altar can speak (16:7), then surely an eagle can too.
[109] οὐαί → It means "*woe,*" "*alas!*" (e.g., 1 Cor. 9:16; Mark 14:21; Jude 11; Matt. 11:21)

here through familiar exodus imagery. Though the Book of Exodus remembers 10 plagues (Exod. 7:8-12:36), in two separate accounts in the psalms there are seven (Ps. 78:43-51) and eight (Ps. 105:27-36). The Psalms accounts follow the Yahwistic version of the plagues, as opposed to the Priestly account's enumeration of ten. John works from the Yahwistic perspective.

Exodus implies liberation. Liberation as a theme is appropriate to John's overall ethical intent. John asks the people to remain faithful, to refuse accommodation, no matter the threats or promises. God will respond. Boesak states, *"Each plague is God's challenge to the power of the Caesar. Each trumpet blast is a ringing command from the Liberator God: 'Let my people go!'"*

As in the case of the exodus plagues, even during the chaos and destruction, God is firmly in control. John narrates this point with a long train of divine passives. Hail and fire was mixed with blood. That mixture was thrown onto the earth. One-third of the earth was burned. One-third of the trees were burned. All the green grass was burned. A great, burning mountain was thrown into the sea. A third of the ships were destroyed. One-third of the waters was made bitter. A third of the sun, moon, and stars were struck so that their light was darkened. God is not only acting but acting more intensely from this trumpet perspective. Where John had first envisioned targets destroyed in quarters (6:8), from his trumpet angel he sees decimation by the thirds.

Many scholars seem convinced that the destructive judgment unleashed by God's angelic representatives with the blasts of their trumpets is an act of punishment, not a call to repentance. Clearly the plagues associated with the trumpets were punishing events. However, John's entire visionary effort has operated under the ethical premise that those who hear and read will respond by either witnessing or at least curtailing their accommodations to the lordship of Roman imperial rule and religions. For those who are presently accommodating, the ethical expectation would certainly be one of repentance. John's account of the devastating acts of judgment would not only report the coming desecration but also, since they are coming desecrations, spur those who take the visions seriously to use what little intervening time they have to change their ways. That certainly seems to be the spirit behind John's exhortations in the letters to the seven churches in chapters 2 and 3. It also seems to be John's expectation in 9:20-21 (cf. 16:8-9), where he laments the fact that many did not repent, thereby implying that some did. And while scholars do correctly observe that the Egyptian plagues upon which the trumpet plagues seem to be based were intended not to garner Pharaoh's repentance but to harden his heart further, it is clear that many later Jewish writers understood the plagues as inducements to repentance (Amos 4:10; Josephus, *Ant.* 2.14.1; Philo, *Mos.* 1.95).

- 7 The plague of hail and fire, mixed with blood, that accompanies that sounding of the first angel's trumpet is based on the exodus plague where hail rains down upon the Egyptians (Exod. 9:22-26). It is also based loosely on the account at Ezek. 38:22, where an avenging God threatens an outpouring of hail, fire, pestilence, and blood (cf. Joel 2:3, 30; *Sir.* 39:29). John will use hail as a symbol of God's judging wrath twice more at strategic points in the text (11:19; 16:21). The emphasis on judgment is heightened by the fact that the hail is mixed with fire and blood. At 16:6, John is as clear as he possibly can be that blood is God's way of responding directly to the shedding of the saints' blood. Rome wants blood: God will rain it down until its people drown in it.

Perhaps an even more fearsome judgment image is that of raining fire: it burns up one-third of the earth, one-third of the trees, and all the green grass. It is unclear why the dire destroys grass completely, while burning only one-third of the trees and the earth.[110] The discrepancy probably demonstrates God's freedom to act as God pleases. Once again, the seer builds from Old Testament imagery, principally the account of Ezek. 5:2, 12, where three different judgments are meted out, each punishing one-third of the people (cf. Zech. 13:9; *Wis.* 16:22).

- **8 – 9** There is thematic consistency with the punishment that ensues at the blast of the second trumpet; it, too, wipes out its target by thirds, and it mobilizes the weapons of fire and blood. Divine

---

[110] → The argument that all the grass is destroyed since it grows back more readily than the earth and the tree is not convincing since John expects that these preliminary acts of judgment are leading to a final and complete judgment. There will not be an "*old*" earth upon which the grass might grow back.

passive constructions – a burning mountain was thrown and ships were destroyed – credit the action to God.

Verse 8 is a virtual doublet of v. 10, where a burning star rockets out of heaven and burns one-third of the rivers and springs as a complement to the one-third salt water destroyed in v. 8. A similar parallel exists with 16:3, where the second angel's bowl of divine wrath is poured out. The object of the bowl's fury is also the sea. In keeping with the escalation of intensity from one end time viewing to the next (seals to trumpets to bowls), in the case of the second bowl all of the sea turns to blood and all of the sea's creatures are killed. The destruction maintains John's exodus connection. At Exod. 7:17-21, operating by God's command, Moses orders Aaron to stretch out his staff and hand over (i.e., against) the waters of Egypt. When he does, the great river of Egypt turns to blood and all of its fish are killed. In revelation, sea vessels are added to the casualty count. One could argue that because in John's vision only one-third of the fish and one-third of the ships were destroyed, the magnitude of the punishment was greater in Egypt, where the waters and fish were destroyed completely. Such an argument would miss the more important point that in Revelation all the seas on earth, not just those in a single country, were targeted.

The method of destruction was the hurling of a great burning mountain into the sea. Although one cannot with certainty connect Revelation's symbolic imagery to any historical event, there are suggestive possibilities. Surely the narration of burning mountains catapulted into the sea would have conjured the searing memory or eruption of Mount Vesuvius (August 24th, 79 C.E.). *"Debris from Vesuvius fell into the bay, making it impossible to land boats, though no streams of lava were emitted from the crater"* (Pliny, *Ep.* 6.16.11). According to the Roman historian Dio, trumpets were heard blaring just before the disaster took place (*Dio* 66.23.1).

- **10 – 11** When the third angel blows his trumpet, a flaming star explodes out of heaven (cf. 9:1), and lands on one-third of the rivers and all the springs, destroying them. Obviously, John is working symbolically here; it would be impossible for a single star literally to land simultaneously on one-third of all the rivers and all the springs on earth. His point, though, is not literal. He wants to convey God's complicity. The home of the star, a term John uses euphemistically to refer to angels (1:20; 9:1; 22:16), is heaven. God has launched it as another instrument of punishing judgment (cf. the burning mountain in 9:8-9).[111] The parallel with the inanimate mountain in vv.8-9 suggests that the burning star, too, is an inanimate missile.

While there is no parallel this time to one of the exodus plagues, there is a strong thematic connection with the pouring out of the third bowl of wrath (16:4). While one-third of the rivers and springs of water are destroyed in chapter 8, the dramatically heightened

---

[111] → One could argue that the dragon also coaxes fire out of the heavens at 13:13. The interesting point there is that the dragon does this in order to mimic God. It is precisely the awareness that God can send fire from heaven that makes the mimicry work.

intensity of the bowl episode in chapter 16 pictures the rivers and springs completely decimated.

John personalizes the destruction by giving the offending star a name that he uses only here: "*Aspinth.*" The more colloquial term would be "*wormwood.*" Wormwood is the popular name of several related plants. The wormwood mentioned several places in the Bible (Deut. 29:18 KJV; Prov. 5:4; Jer. 9:15; 23:15; Lam. 3:15, 19; Amos 5:7) is probably a small shrub with hairy, gray leaves that was known for its extremely bitter taste. The herb was so caustic that physicians used it medicinally to root worms from a person's intestines. John uses the plant's reputation for bitterness to great narrative effect. The impact on the waters is so ruinous that the seer likens it to a poisoning, even though wormwood was not technically a toxin.

According to Jer. 9:15 and 23:15, wormwood was also an appropriate punishment for the crime of idolatry. Punishing the impurity of seeking after false gods with an agent that made drinking water impure is thus an act of divine poetic justice that would most certainly have intrigued John. After all, he was preoccupied with those who accommodated themselves to the attractions and threats of Rome. One of the most visible methods of such idolatrous – that is, "*impure*" – accommodation was the eating of meat sacrificed to idols (cf. Rev. 2-3). The angelic "*poisoning*" of the waters is a deliciously ironic way of punishing a people who have so poisoned their faith.

- **12** The destruction by thirds now expands to the cosmos. When the fourth angel blows his trumpet,

John witnesses the darkening of one-third of the sun, moon, stars, and therefore the extinguishing of one-third of the day and night time light they provide. The preponderance of divine passives (*"was struck," "was darkened"*) once again indicates that everything is happening according to God's design. This is the darkness of judgment (cf. Isa. 13:10; Joel 3:15; Amos 5:20; 8:9; Matt. 24:29; Mark 13:24-25). It parallels the plague God visited upon Egypt (Exod. 10:21). Perhaps John also has in mind Amos 8:9, where God punishes the evil of the people by darkening the sun. The most striking connections, though, are found in John's own text. During his accounting of the end-time judgment that occurs with the breaking of the sixth seal (6:12), John describes the darkness through the metaphor of the sun blackened like sackcloth and the moon covered in blood. At 16:8-9, the angel with the fourth bowl pours its contents on the sun, no doubt darkening it. The sun responds by punishing the people with a vicious, searing heat.

Excursus 12: Darkening the Sun

Many people viewed this event of *"darkening the sun"* in the Book of Revelation as an *"eclipse"* (an astronomical event that occurs when astronomical object is temporarily obscured, either by passing into the shadow of another body or by having another body pass between it and the viewer). The term eclipse is most often used to describe either a solar eclipse, when the Moon's shadow crosses the Earth's surface, or a lunar eclipse, when the Moon moves into the Earth's shadow.

Christian ministers like John Hagee and Mark Biltz who promote a series of apocalyptic beliefs. Around 2008, Biltz began predicting that the Second Coming of Jesus would occur in the fall of 2015 with the seven years of the great tribulation beginning in the fall of 2008. He said he had "*discovered*" an astronomical pattern that predicted the next tetrad would coincide with the end times. When the prediction failed, he pulled the article from his website. Not only Christian ministers act like fools, a "*Messianic Rabbi and pastor*," Jonathan Cahn, the author of the bestselling novel "*The Harbinger*," cited Revelation 8 and Isaiah 9 to warn America and predict the last day, September 13th 2015. He said, "*The coming Shemitah will end September 2015. Its final climatic day, Elul 29, the Day of Remission, will fall on Sunday, September 13, 2015.*" Obviously, this one failed as well. Cahn went on to claim that his prophecy would be proved correct as long as "*something bad*" happens anytime between September 2015 and September 2016: "*That's the period.*" (Really? "*Something Bad*"?) And Michael E. Pfeil, the author of "*Rapture of the Church: Bound for Heaven, but…*" is working on the chronology of the end time. It seems like they never get it.

In the Bible/biblical narratives, when the darkness occurs, or the sun gets dark, normally it means the coming of God's divine judgment in the narrative, or a description of the end time in the biblical narrative. In the case of Book of Revelation chapter 8, it is not an eclipse, or some sort of a sign to predict the end time, nothing like that. This is the darkness of judgment in the narrative (cf. Isa. 13:10; Joel 3:15; Amos 5:20; 8:9; Matt. 24:29; Mark 13:24-25).

- **13** John's appeal to the short formula *"then I looked"* once again signals a shift to a different scene within the same narrative act (cf. 5:1; 8:2). For a moment he suspends his recital of the actions taken by the trumpeting angels, as he anticipates the even more fearsome events that will attend the blowing of the final three trumpets. These will be true eschatological woes.

  John sees and hears an eagle flying in midheaven. The term for eagle "ἀετός" is also used for vulture (e.g., Luke 17:37). Either way, the image is particularly disturbing, reinforcing the theme of judgment. The eagle is a bird of prey; its hovering above the inhabitants of the earth would imply that their destruction is imminent. The vulture feeds on carrion; its presence affirms the deathly destruction that is, through the work of the first four angels, already under way. The image of judgment is amplified through an appeal to two of the eagle's characteristics. First, it cries out in a foreboding voice (cf. 7:2). Second, its flight path confines it to midheaven. For John, midheaven is a divine dais from which the word of God's judgment and salvation are intoned (14:6; 19:17).

  Many commentators have noted John's use of onomatopoeia when describing the content of the eagle's cry. The words, when sounded out, bear the essence of a bird of prey's call: "οὐαὶ οὐαὶ οὐαί." Each woe will find itself attached to one of the final three trumpet blasts. While the first two woes are given explicit content (9:12; 11:14), the third and final one is not. It was probably John's intent that it be linked with the third and final trumpet blast (cf. 12:12), which, like the seventh seal, was not fully laid out.

Revelation 9:1~12 → The Fifth Trumpet

NIV	TT
9 ¹ The fifth angel sounded his trumpet, and I saw a star that had fallen from the sky to the earth. The star was given the key to the shaft of the Abyss. ² When he opened the Abyss, smoke rose from it like the smoke from a gigantic furnace. The sun and sky were darkened by the smoke from the Abyss. ³ And out of the smoke locusts came down on the earth and were given power like that of scorpions of the earth. ⁴ They were told not to harm the grass of the earth or any plant or tree, but only those people who did not have the seal of God on their foreheads. ⁵ They were not allowed to kill them but only to torture them for five months. And	**9** ¹ Then the fifth angel blew his trumpet, and I saw a star that had fallen from **heaven**[112] to the earth, and he was given the key to the shaft of the **Abyss**[113]. ² He opened the shaft of the Abyss, and smoke rose from the shaft like smoke from a great furnace, and the sun and the air **were darkened**[114] by the smoke from the shaft. ³ Then from the smoke came locusts on the earth, and they were given authority as the **scorpions**[115] have authority over the earth. ⁴ But they were ordered not to harm the grass of the earth nor any green plant nor any tree, but only the people who did not have the seal of God on their foreheads. ⁵ They were not

---

[112] οὐρανός → The term means "*heaven*" (Matt. 5:16, 18; Mark 1:10; 13:31; Acts 7:55), "*sky*" (Matt. 11:23; Luke 4:25; Rev. 16:21), and sometimes it is synonymous with God (Matt. 3:2; 21:25; Luke 15:18, 21).

[113] ἄβυσσος → It means "*unfathomable depth*," "*underworld*," and "*abyss*." Technically it means "*without depth*."

[114] ἐσκοτώθη → It means "*be darkened*," or "*become darkened*." It is a divine passive voice. Thus the implication is that God darkened the sun and the air.

[115] σκορπίος → It means "*scorpion*."

the agony they suffered was like that of the sting of a scorpion when it strikes. ⁶ During those days people will seek death but will not find it; they will long to die, but death will elude them.

⁷ The locusts looked like horses prepared for battle. On their heads they wore something like crowns of gold, and their faces resembled human faces. ⁸ Their hair was like women's hair, and their teeth were like lions' teeth. ⁹ They had breastplates like breastplates of iron, and the sound of their wings was like the thundering of many horses and chariots rushing into battle. ¹⁰ They had tails with stingers, like scorpions, and in their tails they had power to torment people for five months. ¹¹ They had as king over them the angel of the Abyss, whose name in Hebrew is Abaddon and in Greek is Apollyon (that is,

allowed to kill them, but to torture them for five months, and their torture was like the torture of a scorpion when it stings a person. ⁶ And in those days people will seek death, but they will not find it; they will long to die but death will flee from them. ⁷ And the appearance of the locusts was like horses prepared for battle. And on their heads were what appeared to be crowns of gold, and their faces were like human faces, ⁸ and they had hair like women's hair, and their teeth were like lions' teeth. ⁹ They had scales like iron breastplates, and noise of their wings was like the noise of many chariots with horses rushing into battle. ¹⁰ And they have tails like scorpions, and stingers, and in their tails is their power to harm humans for five months. ¹¹ They have over them as king the angel of the Abyss; his name in Hebrew is **Abaddon**[116], and in Greek he has the

---

[116] Ἀβαδδών → In Hebrew, it is "אֲבַדּוֹן." The term means *"destruction," "ruin," "the place of destruction," "the name of the angel-prince of the infernal regions," "the minister of death,"* and *"the realm of the dead."*

Destroyer).	name Apollyon.
¹² The first woe is past; two other woes are yet to come.	¹² The first woe has passed; behold, two woes are still to come **after these things**[117].

This vision does not literally correspond to any event in John's past, present, or future. With a montage of images from legend, mythology and tradition, he bombards his hearers and readers' imaginations with yet another evocative image of eschatological calamity.

- **1 – 2** When John opens with the verb "ἐσάλπισεν" (blew the trumpet) he immediately invokes the theme of God's judgment (8:6, 7, 8, 10, 12, 13; 9:1, 13; 10:7; 11:15). The trailing "καὶ εἶδον" (and I saw) introduces a new dramatic scene in the continuously unfolding act. John is still caught up in the vision of the seven trumpets, but now he sees a shift in both target and intensity. Human beings rather than inanimate objects of nature are being singled out for destruction, and an angel rather than a natural event has been dispatched to carry the catastrophe out.

  This angel/star, unlike the astral object of 8:10-11, is a living entity who can take possession of a key and use it to open the door to the great Abyss. John has used stars as metaphors for angels before. At 1:16, the Son of Man holds seven stars in his right hand. On two important occasions John likens the Son of Man himself to the bright morning star (2:28; 22:16). In building

---

[117] μετὰ ταῦτα → The phrase literally means "*after these things.*" Generally it begins sentences in the Book of Revelation (see the comment on 4:1).

this metaphorical connection, John operates from Jewish interpretive links between stars and angels (cf. Judg. 5:20; Job 38:7; Dan. 8:10; *Sib. Or.* 5.158-61).

Particularly significant are the connections between fallen stars and disgraced deposed angels[118] (Rev. 12:7-9, 13; cf. Isa. 14:12; *1 En.* 86:3; 88:3). The fallen angels' identification means that this angel is not the same one mentioned at 20:1. Though both hold the key to the Abyss, the second angel, who is not introduced as "*fallen,*" locks Satan in the pit. The "*fallen*" angel of 9:1 uses the key to open the pit and release its demonic forces. In fact, the naming in 9:11 suggests that this angel is the dragon whom John later identifies as Satan. Tradition records that Jesus saw Satan fall like lightning (like a star?) from heaven (Luke 10:18). As a result, Jesus' followers were able to walk safely across snakes and scorpions (Luke 10:19). It is probably not a coincidence that the witnesses who were sealed with God's mark upon their foreheads (Rev. 7:4) found themselves protected from the terror unleashed by the demon locusts that operated specifically with the authority of scorpions.

John does not see the angel fall. Apparently, though, he does see when God gives him the key to the shaft of the great Abyss (another divine passive: "*it was*

---

[118] → The concept of fallen angels goes back to the story about the angelic beings who came to earth and caused humans to sin (Gen. 6:1-4). The "*Book of Watchers*" in the Book of *1 Enoch* is a commentary on the tradition that developed from this brief text: "*Watchers*" is the name used in this work as well as in other Jewish writings for the disobedient angels who came down to earth, took wives from among the earthly women, and taught them practices and ideas that corrupted the earth. As a result of the angels' disobedience, God imprisoned them in a place full of fire that "*had a cleft reaching to the Abyss.*" (*1 Enoch* 21:7).

given"). Technically, "ἄβυσσος" means "*without* (ἄ)" "*depth* (βυθος)." Following the mythical understanding of a three-tiered universe (see the comment on 5:3), the Abyss was the under-worldly/hellish region below both heaven and earth. John introduces it here at 9:1-2 and quickly mentions it again in v. 11. The fact that on both occasions the angel is the authority figure of the Abyss is strong evidence that John is referring to the same angel.

    The Abyss is a place filled with fearsome, fiendish forces. At 11:7, a great beast emerges from the Abyss, makes war on God's great witnesses, and kills them; then the beast upon whom the great whore (Babylon/Rome) rides rises from the Abyss (17:8). The prelude to the final judgment will find the dragon, Satan, locked in the Abyss for a thousand years, only to be let loose when that millennium has ended (20:1, 3). John's portrait is in keeping with wider Jewish understanding: The "*Abyss*" is synonymous with the concept of Hades (Job 38:16; Ezek. 31:15; Jonah 2:6) and is the realm of suffering (Ps. 71:20) and death (Exod. 15:5; Isa. 51:10; 63:13; *Wis.* 10:19). 24:21-22 says that God will punish angels and evil kings, and they will be gathered together as prisoners in the pit, and will be confined in prison and after many days will be punished. The Abyss is a bad place. The eschatological version of a maximum security prison, it is home to the worst cosmic offenders. Knowing this, God still gives this fallen angel the key.

The image of a key is important for John. Here, and again at 20:1, the Abyss is locked behind a closed door. In both cases, a character uses a key to open the door and swing it open. In both instances, too, destruction immediately ensues. God is the ultimate keeper of this key. At 1:18, God's Son of Man introduces himself as the one who controls the keys to death and Hades, forces that are narratively synonymous for John with the place he calls the Abyss. The implication is that the Son of Man, who was exiled to the Abyss by way of the crucifixion, had laid claim to the key and used it to open the door and set himself free. According to 3:7, the Son of Man also possesses the key of David, a key that symbolizes the Son's ability to open the eschatological realm of salvation, understood as a heavenly, Davidic reign. The Son of Man's control of these two keys indicates that he secures both salvation (key of David) and judgment (keys of death and Hades). At 9:1 and 20:1, God entrusts to other divine emissaries the key that opens the door to judgment. While the angel in good standing at 20:1 recognizes that he is operating in concert with God's judgment/salvation plan, the angel in 9:1 does not. Not realizing that his effort to set his forces free is actually part of God's salvation plan, he eagerly unlocks the door and throws open the shaft of the Abyss.

It is God who decides if satanic forces are to be given the ability – the key – to open their realm and gain access to earth and the humans who inhabit it. It is God who decides when that access comes and how long it will last. It is God who decides the purpose of the destruction that access enables. In John's handling, God purposes to intervene on behalf of those who cry out for justice (6:9-11; 8:3-5), and God will use the very force of evil itself to obliterate the humans (i.e., the Romans and all who accommodate to their claims of imperial lordship) who operate under evil's employ. Here is the irony: evil will be unleashed, but evil will be made to act as God's judgment tool. The demonic, bestial forces that rise up from the bottomless pit will target and destroy the very humans who do evil's satanic, beastly bidding. While both God's witnesses and those who persecute them will die in the cataclysms that ensue, only the persecutors and those who accommodate them will die forever.

When the door finally opens, dense smoke pours out. The seer appeals to Exod. 19:18, where the people at the foot of Mount Sinai see smoke go up from the mountain when the Lord descends upon it in fire. Interestingly enough, all of this occurs at the sounding of trumpets. John likens the smoke he sees to the thick exhaust from a raging furnace. It is as though evil and those who perpetrate it are combustible agents whose perpetual blaze powers the infamy thriving inside the bottomless pit. It is the smoke of this villainous burning that rushes out when the door opens. Like the door itself, though, smoke moves under God's control. When John uses the term, he envisions God's judgment. Smoke is unmistakably linked with the prayers of the saints who request God's intervention (8:3-5). Surely John's account would have prompted his hearers and readers to recall the story of Abraham gazing out at the rising smoke of Sodom and Gomorrah's ruin (Gen. 19:28).

The smoke pollutes the air. As was the case in the Book of Joel, its darkening of the sun is an explicit indication of God's judgment (Joel 2:10, 31; 3:15). John makes the case by putting the key verb in the divine passive voice. When he says that the sun and the air are darkened, he means that God has darkened them. Throughout his narrative, John appeals to the sun as a glorious force (1:16; 7:16; 10:1; 12:1; 21:23; 22:5), but he also connects it to God's judgment (6:12; 8:12; 16:8; 19:17). In two other instances besides 9:2, that judgment is imaged as a darkening (6:12; 8:12).

> ### Excursus 13: Watchers
>
> The fallen stars/fallen angels/Watchers "עִיר" are not well described in the Christian Bible. The Book of Genesis 6:4 states *"For if God did not spare angels when they sinned, but casting them into hell handed them over to chains of darkness, to be kept for judgment..."* The brief note in Gen. 6:4 about *"the Nephilim"* does not include any account of the subsequent imprisonment of *"the sons of God."* Later Jewish tradition does.
>
> While pieces of this story surface in numerous Jewish texts, it is in *1 Enoch* that the fullest form of the story is encountered. Given the composite character of *1 Enoch* and the generally inconsistent pattern of apocalyptic texts, it is no surprise that there is no perfect uniformity in the many references in *1 Enoch* to the fallen angels of Gen. 6. However, the basic story is given in the so-called *"Book of the Watchers"* and remains consistent throughout *1 Enoch*. The angels

desire the beautiful daughters of humans (*1 En.* 6). Two hundred angels bind themselves with an oath and take human wives for themselves (*1 En.* 6-7). They teach dangerous arts that produce violence and evil on earth (*1 En.* 8-9). God decides to destroy the earth (*1 En.* 10). (The link between the activity of the Nephilim and the flood is not explicit in the Book of Genesis, but it is constant in these later accounts.) The angels are bound and thrown into a dark place, where they await final punishment (*1 En.* 10).

Throughout *1 Enoch* a variety of details are added to this core narrative. In *1 Enoch* 54, Enoch sees a valley burning with fire, where "*iron fetters of immense weight*" are being forged for "*the armies of Azael*" (on these chains or bonds, see *1 En.* 13:1-2; 14:5; 56:1-2; 88:1). This binding in chains is echoed in Jude 6 and 2 Pet. 2:4. The pervasiveness of this image is highlighted by Josephus, who connected the Jewish traditions of the fallen angels to the ancient Greek myth of Titans, who were giants that rebelled against Chronos and were bound in chains in Tartarus (*Ant.* 1.73). The announcement of doom to the fallen angels, which is accomplished by Jesus in 1 Pet. 3:19, is carried out in *1 Enoch* by Enoch himself (*1 En.* 12:4-6; 13:1-3; 15:1-16:3). This tradition of an announcement of doom is complicated in *1 Enoch* by a request made to Enoch by the fallen angels that he pray on their behalf. The watchers send Enoch to announce punishment on the angels (*1 En.* 12:4). When he does this, the angels beg him to write for them "*a memorial prayer*" that will be a "*prayer of forgiveness*" (*1 En.* 13:4). Enoch writes down this prayer, but then sees in a vision that these prayers will not be heard, that judgment has been pronounced, and that the angels will be imprisoned "*inside the earth*" forever (*1 En.* 14:3-6). The place of

> the angels' imprisonment seems quite fluid, even if the core image is that of *"inside the earth."* In *1 Enoch* 10:12, God binds the angels *"underneath the rocks of the ground until the day of their judgment."* In *1 Enoch* 21, their imprisonment is in *"an empty place,"* where Enoch sees *"neither a heaven above nor an earth beneath, but a chaotic and terrible place."* In *1 Enoch* 67, it is a burning valley in the west (*1 En.* 67:4), where ironically rivers of water are the means of punishment (*1 En.* 67:7). However, outside of *1 Enoch*, the primary location seems to be the second heaven (*2 En.* 7:1-3). Throughout *1 Enoch* and other Jewish texts, this core story is developed on the one hand, reinforces the likelihood that 1 Peter, 2 Peter, and Jude can assume their readers' knowledge of the core story of the fallen angels; but on the other hand, this diversity makes reconstruction of the precise details of the story assumed in each impossible reconstruct.
>
> In any case, the story of God's victory over the rebellious angels, along with their subsequent imprisonment and forthcoming punishment, as narrated in the vision and journeys of Enoch, was portrayed in these early Christian texts as instructive for the Christian story.

- **3 – 5** Before the smoke can clear, another source of darkness emerges: locusts. Locusts are different from grasshoppers; they swarm and migrate in large numbers, usually plundering any and all vegetation in their path. This apocalyptic horde arrives with the smoke and, like it, shrouds the earth in darkness.

    As in Joel 2:1, 15, a trumpet calls the locusts forth. The prophet Joel reflects on the plague where locusts darkened the land of Egypt (Exod. 10:5, 15). John's reference to the exodus account by way of the allusion to Joel is yet another association of the end-time judgment with the plagues against Egypt. The manner of the locusts' attack is different, though. In Exodus, the locusts devoured the vegetation and so caused a famine. Here, at the blowing of the fifth angel's trumpet, they are specifically ordered not to touch the vegetation. (It seems there is a contradiction with the notice in 8:7 that all of the green grass was burned up. However, the emphasis here is that the trumpet woe is directed against rebellious humanity and not nature.) Instead, they are to attack humans. Having gone from voracious to vicious, they are more like the locusts of *Wis.* 16:9, which, along with a legion of flies, inflicted bites from which there is no healing.

Because of their affiliation with the Abyss, the locusts also have an unmistakably demonic nature (cf. Rev. 9:11). Even so, they operate according to God's plan. They are given by God the authority of scorpions[119] on the earth. They operate very much like the locusts of *Wis.* 16:9 and *Sir.* 39:30, whose bites are instruments of God's judgment.

The similarity of John's locusts to scorpions suggests that their power is related to a sting rather than a bite. Their job is to inflict pain upon every human who has not been marked with the seal of God upon their forehead (see the comment on 7:3). Since the trumpets and bowls are recapitulations of the judgment

---

[119] → For other texts that picture scorpions as instruments of punishment, see 1 Kgs. 12:11, 14; 2 Chr. 10:11, 14.

acts associated with the seals, but from a different eschatological perspective, it makes sense that the device that provided the 144,000 protection from the seal judgments would also provide protection from the acts of judgment associated with the trumpets and bowls.

Good news for the sealed saints is ambiguous news for the rest of them. The saints at 7:9-17 were not sealed and therefore were not protected from the ravages that accompanied God's preliminary acts of judgment. This means that there will be many saints who will also be tormented by the scorpion stings of the demon locusts. As 3:10 explains, the Son of Man will keep them, enable them to endure, but will not *"rapture"* them from the circumstances that surround the coming of the end.

John clarifies that the demon locusts are given the authority by God not to kill humans, but to torture them for five months. Does God operate this way? John's hearers and readers would know that the answer is yes. According to Job 2:6, God gave Satan the authority to torment and torture Job, but not to kill him.

John's, and Job's, theological presentation is troubling. In depicting the simultaneous beliefs that evil exists in the world and that nothing exists outside of God's control, John finds himself locked into the uneasy presentation of a God who is an accomplice to a practice as hellish as torture in order to obtain a heavenly design.

Why five months of torture? Some commentators argue that five months is the typical life cycle of a locust, and thus the time of torment agrees naturally with the actual time that locusts would have lived and swarmed. Since John is rarely this literal, there is little reason to believe that he would have been so literal here. More likely the time is just a round number[120] that indicates a specified and limited time for the work of the locusts. Believers could therefore know that an end would come and that it would come relatively soon. According to Mark 13:19-20, if God does not cut short the calamities associated with the acts of judgment that prefaced the end time, no one will be able to endure it. Because of the faithful, who are apparently, as in John's account, caught up in the maelstroms, God does indeed cut the time short.

- **6** John's opening line in v. 6, *"in those days,"* is a euphemism for the period when the preliminary acts of judgment that lead up to the final judgment are taking place (Joel 2:29; 3:1). This is precisely the time that is presented from three different eschatological perspectives by the seals, trumpets, and bowls.

John means to say, then, that during this preliminary judgment period, the torment will be so horrific that humans will prefer death to life. Job 3:21 and Jer. 8:3 present Old Testament examples[121] where, because of the horrible circumstances associated with living, death becomes preferable to life (cf. Rev. 6:12-17). At 1:18,

---

[120] → Several biblical texts in which "5" appears as a round, limited number: Lev. 26:8; Jdt. 7:30; 8:9, 15; Matt. 14:17-19; Mark 6:38-41; Luke 9:13-16; 12:6, 52; Acts 20:6; 24:1; 1 Cor. 14:19.

[121] → several texts where severe suffering causes a desire for death in place of a life of torment (1 Kgs. 19:1-4; Job 3:1-26; 6:8-9; 7:15-16; Jer. 8:3; 20:14-18; Jonah 4:3, 8; Luke 23:27-30).

John pictured the Son of Man holding the key to Death and Hades. Even death lies within his control. Here though, knowing that death is the only escape from the pain and torment being inflicted by the demon locusts, the Son of Man either actively locks Death away from the suffering people's grasp or passively allows Death to scurry uselessly away. The judgment associated with the scourge of the demon locusts must be endured.

For John, death is a state of being like life. Indeed, death allows a measure of control that life does not. One cannot choose to live. One simply finds oneself alive. One can, however, choose to die, especially in a circumstance where life becomes torturously unbearable. Even then, though, people may be more likely to choose death if they believe that death does not end all sensibility, but only alters the state and place of being.

A study of noun "θάνατον" (death) and the verb "ἀποθνησκω" (to die) reveals that John understands "*death*" to have two distinct layers. First, death ends earthly existence. We might call this Type A death. This is clearly the kind of death John alludes to in 9:6. It is the type of death associated with the preliminary acts of judgment that follow the opening of the first six seals, the sounding of the first six trumpets, and the pouring out of the first six bowls. Type A death brings a merciful end to the preliminary judgment acts of God. It is Type A death to which John refers at 2:23, when the Son of Man warns that he will strike the children of Jezebel dead. It is Type A death that the fourth apocalyptic horseman brings at 6:8. Babylon's death at 18:8 is Type A death.

John's hearers and readers know that Type A death is not final because the narrative presents multiple occasions where the seer implies that there is life beyond it. When John talks about the death wound of the beast, he refers to the Type A death, from which even the beast can resurrect into a new life (13:3, 12). Similarly, the death mentioned at 20:13 is one that allows its captives new life. At 2:10, the Son of Man voices a paradox: *"Be faithful until death, and I will give you the crown of life."* Apparently one not only lives beyond Type A death but can also receive gifts in that new life, rewards for honorable behavior in the old life. The presumption is that the new life, connected as it is to the metaphor of the crown, is better than the old one. John offers a corroborating portrait in 12:11. A voice from heaven honors living witnesses who did not cling to life even in the face of death. Indeed, the souls whose cry to God sets into motion the acts of preliminary judgment (6:9-11) have endured Type A death because of their faithful witness. They now enjoy the reward of eschatological life in relationship with God. So do the witnesses mentioned at 14:13. One of the benefits for those who enjoy that relationship will be the complete cessation of Type A death (21:4).

Just as there are two lives in John's cosmology, so too are there two deaths. According to 2:11, those who have been faithful witnesses in their first life will not endure a second death. This second death, which we may call Type B death, is for John a permanent cessation of existence. It is the death that follows a guilty verdict at the final judgment. Type B death, then, is the death one should fear. Revelation 20:13 indicates that at God's final judgment a decision will be made as to whether those who have died a Type A death will be given life in eschatological relationship with God or given Type B death. God makes this ruling on the basis of how a person has lived one's first life. Given the ethical program of John's narrative, it is a life lived in witness to the lordship of God and the Standing Slaughtered Lamb that will earn eschatological relationship with God (cf. 14:13). A life lived either in witness to Roman imperial and pagan lordship or in accommodation to those who did advance such idolatrous claims would merit Type B death. It is Type B death to which John refers in 20:6, 14; 21:8.

At 9:6, though, the people who seek escape from the torture of the demon locusts surely long not for a permanent cessation of existence but for the transient reprieve of Type A death. This death is so transitory that it is preferable to earthly struggle and torment. Just as those who witness to the lordship of Jesus Christ should not fear this death, so those who are caught up in the fury of the scorpion-like locusts, believers and nonbelievers alike, do not fear it. Instead, in such a circumstance as this, they try their best to embrace it.

- **7 – 10** unable to summon any other common reference point, John characterizes the locusts as horses arrayed for battle. His hearers and readers may well have been aware of the Old Testament comparisons between the two creatures in Jer. 51:27 and Job 39:19-20. In the Job text, it is God who claims to have empowered the horse to leap like a locust. God, in other words, just as John imagines here, is in control of this bizarre mammal-insect crossbreeding. But it is Joel to whom John is indebted here the most. The prophet warns of a marauding army whose numbers are so massive that they extend like a blackness across the horizons (Joel 2:2). At Joel 2:4 he likens the foot soldiers to warhorses prepared for a charge.

John continues with a loathsome description that becomes more appalling every time he adds a new descriptor. These demonic forces wear golden crowns. Beneath the crowns, warhorse-locusts sport human faces framed by women's hair. The odd reference to female hair is an indication that their hair was long and possibly unkempt. According to legend, the dreaded Parthian warriors wore their hair long. John may well be trying to kindle the paranoia associated with Rome's famed adversaries in his description, just as he tried to do when speaking earlier about the threat of the first horseman (Rev. 6:2).

Weird turns to fearsome when John depicts the warhorse-locusts with the teeth of lions in their mouths. The invading army that Joel describes also deploys lion-like teeth (Joel 1:6). Protecting their bodies are breastplates or scales of iron. When they move their wings, the noise they make is that of the army Joel foresaw, the sound of innumerable horse chariots rumbling ominously into battle (Joel 2:4-5).

- **11** John's hearers and readers know that this is an army of demons, not mutant insects, because they are organized under the rule of a king. According to Prov. 30:27, locusts in nature have no monarch, but John immediately identifies their king as *"the"* angel of the Abyss. The fact that *"angel"* is modified by the definite article suggests that John believed his hearers and readers would be familiar with him. That familiarity follows from the description of the angel as a fallen star in 9:1-2. Luke 10:18 describes Satan in just this way.

John's name for the demon locust ruler also indicates a connection with Satan. The Hebrew form of the name is "אֲבַדּוֹן"Abaddon: destruction. The term surfaces in several significant Old Testament passages (Job 26:6; 28:22; 31:12; Ps. 88:11; Prov. 15:11; 27:20). John follows the lead of these Old Testament authors in building a relationship between the realm of death, which is Sheol, and the name *"Abaddon."* In other words, Abaddon is a literary personification of the loss and destruction that are integral to death. In the narrative world of Revelation, the power most closely allied with death is Satan (Rev. 12).

The Greek form of the angel's name is Apollyon ("Ἀπολλύων," destroyer). The name is a play on the Greek verb "Ἀπολλύμαι" (to destroy). It may also be a play on the name of the pagan god Apollo. Interestingly enough, the locust was one of Apollo's symbols. Domitian, likely the Roman emperor during the time of John's writing, had a particular fondness for Apollo and liked to suggest that he was himself an incarnation of that deity. If indeed Domitian through this identification was expressing an implicit divine foundation for his imperial lordship, then John's attribution of satanic implications to the name makes perfect narrative sense. John wrote to exhort his readers to embrace a life of witness to the lordship of God and the Lamb. He charged that accommodation to any competing claims of lordship amounted to the kind of perverse and satanic (Rev. 2:13) idolatry that he linked with the names Balaam (2:14) and Jezebel (2:20-21). As the patron god of emperor worship, Apollo – and Domitian, as his alleged human incarnation – would, like Balaam and Jezebel, have been responsible for destroying the hope of eschatological relationship with God for anyone who accommodated to the social, political, religious, and economic expectations of imperial lordship.

- **12** The preliminary act of judgment associated with the blowing of the fifth trumpet comes to an end with the identification of Satan as the destructive king of the locusts whom God uses to exact judgment in 9:1-11. The terror and torture of the demon locusts was the first woe. Though it has ended, there is no eschatological relief in sight. John confides that *"after these things"* two more woes are yet to come.

Revelation 9:13~21 → The Sixth Trumpet

NIV	TT
¹³ The sixth angel sounded his trumpet, and I heard a voice coming from the four horns of the golden altar that is before God. ¹⁴ It said to the sixth angel who had the trumpet, "Release the four angels who are bound at the great river Euphrates." ¹⁵ And the four angels who had been kept ready for this very hour and day and month and year were released to kill a third of mankind. ¹⁶ The number of the mounted troops was twice ten thousand times ten thousand. I heard their number. ¹⁷ The horses and riders I saw in my vision looked	¹³ Then the sixth angel blew his trumpet, and I heard **one**[122] voice from the four horns of the golden altar before God, ¹⁴ saying to the sixth angel who had the trumpet: "Release the four angels who have **been bound**[123] at the great river Euphrates." ¹⁵ Then the four angels who had **been prepared**[124] for the hour and the day and the month and the year were released to kill a third of humankind. ¹⁶ And the number of the soldiers of cavalry was **double myriad myriads**[125]; I heard their number. ¹⁷ And this was how I saw the horses and their riders in my vision: they had breastplates

---

[122] μίαν → It means *"one," "single,"* and *"a certain."* The numeral *"one"* can acts as an indefinite article.

[123] δεδεμένους → It is a participle perfect passive (divine passive). It means *"have been bound," "have been arrested," "have been imprisoned,"* and *"have been tied."*

[124] ἡτοιμασμένοι → It is a participle perfect passive (divine passive). It means *"have been prepared"* and *"have been kept in readiness."*

[125] δισμυριάδες μυριάδων → The phrase means *"double myriad myriads."* Myriad can mean *"a very large number," "not exactly defined number,"* or biblically *"ten thousand."* (cf. Act. 19:19; 21:20; Luke 12:1; Heb. 12:22; Jude 14).

like this: Their breastplates were fiery red, dark blue, and yellow as sulfur. The heads of the horses resembled the heads of lions, and out of their mouths came fire, smoke and sulfur. ¹⁸ A third of mankind was killed by the three plagues of fire, smoke and sulfur that came out of their mouths. ¹⁹ The power of the horses was in their mouths and in their tails; for their tails were like snakes, having heads with which they inflict injury.

²⁰ The rest of mankind who were not killed by these plagues still did not repent of the work of their hands; they did not stop worshiping demons, and idols of gold, silver, bronze, stone and wood—idols that cannot see or hear or walk. ²¹ Nor did they repent of their murders, their magic arts, their sexual immorality or their thefts.

that were fiery red and **sapphire blue**[126] and sulfur yellow. The heads of the horses were like the heads of lions, and out of their mouths spewed fire and smoke and sulfur. ¹⁸ A third of humankind was killed by these three plagues, by the fire and the smoke and the sulfur that spewed from their mouths. ¹⁹ For the authority of the horses is in their mouths and in their tails, for their tails, which are like snakes, have heads, and with them they inflict harm. ²⁰ The rest of the works of their hands, so that they did not stop worshiping the demons or the idols made of gold and silver and bronze and stone and wood, which can neither see nor hear nor walk. ²¹ And they did not repent of their murders nor their sorceries nor their idolatry nor their thefts.

In an *inclusio* that frames all the plagues within the context of God's response to the prayers of the saints, 9:13

---

[126] ὑακίνθινος → The term translated here as *"sapphire."* In antiquity, "ὑακίνθινος" could denote one of several varieties of flowers or a precious stone; either the jacinth, a yellow-red stone that is a form of zircon, or the sapphire, a dark blue stone.

points back to the scene in 8:2-5. As in the first seal, 6:1-2, John uses the almost paranoid Roman fear of the Parthian threat on the eastern boundary of the empire as the raw material for his vision of the final devastation before the End.

- **13** When v. 13 opens with the sounding of the sixth angel's trumpet, the change in trumpets is matched by a change in sensory perception. John hears a voice coming from the horns of the golden altar before God.[127] The description "*golden*" suggests that John is thinking about the altar of incense in the Jerusalem temple. It was upon the heavenly version of this altar that the prayers of the saints were mixed with incense (8:3-5). Those prayers, which most likely contained the same kind of petition as the cries of the "*Slaughtered Souls*" beneath the heavenly sacrificial altar (6:9-11), motivated the acts of judgment associated with the trumpet blowing. It is only natural that John would recapture the emphasis of those altars in the context where one-third of humankind is killed, thereby reminding his hearers and readers why he believed God was acting so ruthlessly.

    In this new altar scene, the speaker and the speech are quite different from the previous ones. The voice here comes from the altar that is before God; therefore, it is unlikely that God is the one speaking. And since John, who quite freely draws upon the talents of angels

---

[127] → For instructions regarding the golden altar of incense, complete with horns, see Exod. 30:1-10; 40:5. Exodus 27:2 speaks of altar horns positioned on the four corners of the sacrificial altar. For further mention of altar horns see Exod. 37:25-26; 38:2; Ps. 118:27; Ezek. 43:15.

when he so desires, does not position an angel in the narration, it is also unlikely that an angel is speaking. It is more likely that John hears the altar, through its horns, speak up for itself. Later it is clear that in his worldview, altars have the ability to speak their inanimate minds (16:7).

- **14 – 15** The altar orders the sixth angel to participate in the judgment that his trumpet playing ignites. He must release the four angels who have been bound by the great river Euphrates. There are two significant points here. The first is that the action takes place only upon orders from God. As God was in control during the events surrounding the demon locusts in 9:1-12, so God controls the timing and shape of these events. The second point concerns the modification of *"four angels"* with the definite article (*"the"*). John's use of the article suggests that his hearers and readers would be familiar with these divine emissaries. It is unlikely, though, that these are the same four angels who held back the four winds from the four corners of the earth (7:1-3). Unlike the previous angels, these have been *"bound."* John's use of yet another divine passive construction indicates that God has restrained them. The binding suggests that they, like the four winds of 7:1-3, are a destructive force that if not properly directed would not act in accordance with God's intent. It appears, then, *"the bound angels"* at the edge of John's world is another allusion to the mythical pattern of fallen angels discussed in 9:1-12. The four angels at 7:1-3, by contrast, were related positively to God and appeared willing to do God's bidding. They were also dispersed among the four corners of the earth, while the present four angels are positioned together at the Euphrates River.

The involvement of the Euphrates River is important. Later, the angel of the six bowl will release the contents of his bowl upon the Euphrates River and dry it up (16:12). Marauding kings from the east will use the resulting riverbed to come across and wreak devastation.

John's hearers and readers would have sensed the dread associated with the symbolic Euphrates even without a premonition of the sixth-bowl angel's exploits. For the Jewish people, the Euphrates River had always marked the outer geographical boundaries of their existence (Gen. 15:18; Deut. 1:7; Josh. 1:4). The people who lived beyond this boundary were unknown and feared. The prophets declared that God would use them to punish the people of Israel whenever they refused to repent from their sins. No doubt the presence of fallen angels standing at this river rekindled thoughts of those disturbing prophecies (cf. Isa. 5:26-29; 7:20; 8:7-8; 14:29-31; Jer. 1:14-15; 4:6-13; 6:1, 22; 10:22; 13:20; 25:9, 26; 46-47; 50:41-42; Ezek. 26:7-11; 38:6, 15; 39:2; Joel 2:1-11, 20-25; Amos 7:1 LXX; As. T. Mos. 3:1).

In the first century C.E., the river played a more international role. The Euphrates marked the literal and metaphorical boundary between the Roman and Parthian Empires (see the discussion of the Parthians at

6:2).¹²⁸ Given the history of conflict between Rome and Parthia, Parthia's ability to defeat Roman legions in key combat situations, and the unsettling legend that the disgraced emperor Nero would one day resurrect and lead a Parthian army to destroy Rome, it is easy to understand how John's hint that a hostile force massed at the river, incited by fallen angels, would have fomented fear in the minds of his hearers and readers.

The seer's use of yet another divine passive construction "ἡτοιμασμένοι" (having been prepared) indicates God's involvement in the work of these fallen ones. The same God who bound them at the Euphrates now orders them released "ἐλύθησαν" (they were released). Though it is the sixth trumpet angel who performs the physical loosing, God is responsible.

This means that God is also responsible for the killings the four fallen angels subsequently commit. John clarifies the point when he follows up the notice of their release with a relative clause that defines the purpose of that release. The four are released (by God) in order to do what they have been prepared (by God) to do: kill a third of humankind. Good news? One certainly has to search for it. No doubt John wanted his hearers and readers to discern positive value in the belief that, despite what sounded like global massacre, the world had not spun out of control. God remained in charge.

---

¹²⁸ → *1 En.* 56:5-8; *2 Bar.* 6, both depict the Parthian threat from beyond the Euphrates as an updating of the Old Testament tradition. According to those texts, the invasion was to be triggered by angels.

John's hearers and readers would have to trust, as John apparently himself trusted, that God had a plan that would make the high cost of this judgment sound not only reasonable but also preferable to whatever other options of living were available at their eschatological moment. Such trust was possible only because of the perspective on death that John counseled his readers to take. Yes, one-third of humankind would die. That death, though, was a justifiable to God through the vehicles of the sacrificial and incense altars (9:13). That death, also, need neither be feared nor considered final. It was Type A death (see the discussion of Type A death at 9:6).

Beyond Type A death was complete and certain opportunity for revival. It did not signal an end to being but an introduction to another kind of being, where humans would have yet another opportunity to make account of themselves before the divine. It must be stressed that John is not speaking about the final judgment, but about the preliminary acts of judgment that lead up to it. It must only be because he understands God's involvement to be with the Type A death naturally associated with these preliminary acts of judgment that he can relay such involvement without so much as a theological flinch.

- **16 – 19** Throughout the next four verses, John explains how the massive killing introduced in v. 15 will take place. John reveals what he has heard about the Euphrates River force that the four now unbound angels are poised to unleash. He reports their numbers as a double (two times) myriad of myriads. The term "*myriad*" symbolizes, as it does at 5:11, a number so immense that it is incalculable. Many commentators equate the term with the number "*10,000.*" For this reason the NRSV, NIV, apparently using the calculation 2 times 10,000 times 10,000, arrives at a figure 200 million (200,000,000). As a time when armies numbering 50,000 or 100,000 would have been considered invincible, the appearance of an army 200 million strong would have had a staggering effect.

Though John is unable to count and perhaps even see the entire battle force because of its massive size, he apparently is able to make out the way its troops are dressed. Perhaps because he is so overwhelmed, the seer's grammar is a little confusing at this point. He sees horses and riders on the horses (Literally "*Them that sat on them*"). It is unclear, though, whether only the horses or both the horses and the riders are equipped with breastplates. Because the horses and not the riders appear to be the instruments of imminent killing, one is right to wonder whether John is preoccupied with them and is describing their breastplates. However, the noun "ἵππους" (horses) stands farther from the participle "*having breastplates*" than does the substantival participle "καθημένους" (riders). Following the description of the breastplates, John resumes explicit depiction of the horses by writing "*the heads of the horses.*" This placement suggests that the breastplate phrase belong with either the riders or both the riders and the horses.

Like the locusts of the fifth trumpet, these killing-machine horses are mutant instruments of divine destruction. They have the heads of lions.[129] This image of lions in their human faces (9:8). With the horses, though, John focuses not on the teeth but on the exhaust that surges from their mouths. The chemicals plagues of fire (red), smoke (sapphire blue), and sulfur/brimstone (yellow). These are the elements that cause such massive human casualties. Fire and sulfur are complementary agents of judgment to which John will return later in his work (14:10; 19:20; 20:10; 21:8). Biblically, the three elements appear together in Gen. 19:24-28 as the forces of God's judgment against Sodom and Gomorrah. It is this theme of justifiable judgment that John wants to stress.

Although the mouths of these fire, smoke, and sulfur vomiting horses are ominously toxic, their tails wreak an equal amount of havoc. Their tails are serpent-like appendages that have lethal mouths. Apparently many humans who survive the plagues of fire, smoke, and sulfur as the massive army advances will be bitten to death by the rearguard action of the horses' tails as they pass. Once again, the imagery is precisely calculated to instill maximum panic. The Parthians were renowned archers on horseback. Not only did they shoot their arrows as they advanced toward their enemy, but as the archers were past, they

---

[129] → Many commentators argue that the creature was based on the legendary Chimaera: The Chimaera is consistently described as having the head of a lion, the tail of a dragon or serpent, and the body of a goat and belching fire ([Homer] *Iliad* 6.181-82; [Hesiod] *Theog.* 319-24).

turned around backwards on their horses and fired a volley of arrows from the rear.

- **20 – 21** Despite the ravages they have witnessed as a result of the plagues, the two-thirds of humans who survive refuse to repent from the works of their hands. The emphasis on repentance is suggestive. The seer's mention of repentance gives a clue to his understanding of God's motivations. From the very start of his narrative, John has made the case that the primary focus for writing has been ethical. He has exhorted the members of the seven Asia Minor churches to witness to the lordship of Jesus Christ. For those who are afraid of the consequences such witnessing will bring, he encourages resistance. For those who have so feared the loss of status, privilege, economic success, political stature, or even life that they have accommodated themselves to the expectations of Roman imperial and pagan lordship, he exhorts repentance. It is no accident that the verb *"repent"* occurs most often (and prior to 9:20 only) in chapters 2 and 3 (2:5, 16, 21, 22; 3:3, 19). Indeed, as much as John detests Jezebel for misleading the people, he maintains that there is hope for repentance even for her (2:21).

"Works of their hands" is a suggestive phrase. Employing a "ἵνα" clause as a result clause this time, John declares that their lack of repentance – their refusal to recognize God's lordship – results in their continuing to attribute divine lordship to demons and the *"works of their hands"* instead. Clearly, John is referring to idols, which are traditionally represented in Jewish literature by works of gold, silver, bronze, stone,

and wood (cf. Deut. 32:17; Pss. 115:4-7; 135:15-17; Isa. 2:8, 20; 17:8; 44:9-20; Jer. 10:1-16; Dan. 5:4, 23; *Wis.* 13:10-19). Demons were often associated with these gods and the works that portrayed them (e.g., Deut. 32:17; 1 Cor. 10:19-20). Those objects were just that, objects of human creative activity. They had no power, no capability, no life separate from that which fallible humans gave them. They were therefore incapable of directing the very human lives on which they were themselves dependent for existence.

Entities that could not shape their own destinies could not be expected to shape the destinies of others. Surely those who believed in such creations of their own hands must have realized, when the acts of judgment accompanying the seven trumpets began, that those creations were incapable of stopping the acts or even lessening their intensity. That recognition alone should have caused people to repent of placing trust in works of their own hands. Still, though, they refused. Even when humans did finally admit that God was the author of the judgment acts associated with the seals, trumpets, and bowls (16:9, 11), those who resisted God's lordship steadfastly persisted in their refusal to honor God.

Instead, they fall into a pattern of social disruption and evil that is a direct result of their idolatry, which is itself a result of their failure to repent. The four offenses John now mentions are prominently associated in other biblical texts with the sin of idolatry (2 Kgs. 9:22; Isa. 47:9-10; 48:5; Jer. 7:5-11; Hos. 3:1-4:2; Mic.

5:12-6:8; Nah. 1:14; 3:1-4; *Wis.* 12:3-6; Acts 15:20; Rom. 1:24-31; Gal. 5:19-21; Eph. 5:5; Col. 3:5).

Revelation 9:13-21 is a troubling text. Yet the combination of the liberation theme, which reverberates throughout this chapter, with the repentance theme that concludes the section infuses the text with a hint of good news.[130] It is good news that God hears those who have lifted their cries (6:9-11) and their prayers (8:3-5) upon the altars of sacrifice and incense (9:13). It is good news that God's judgment, as massively destructive as it is, even during the final preliminary stage of the sixth trumpet, intends no to destroy but to reprove. Even at the approach of the end of time, there is still time to turn back to God and find the life that is eschatological relationship with God and the Standing Slaughtered Lamb.

---

[130] → Other commentators sense good news in this text of judgment. Richard writes "*The aim of this judgment of God in history, or the realization of the Exodus in the bosom of the Roman empire, is the conversion of the oppressors and idolaters and the liberation of the holy ones. Repeating the Exodus, God attempts to rein in the Roman empire's rush to destroy the world and itself. Hence the Exodus is the good news of God's judgment.*" Fiorenze comments, "*The concluding verse 9:20-21 indicate, however, that John writes this grotesque and brutal vision not for cruelty's sake but rather the sake of exhortation to repentance.*"

Revelation 10:1~11 → Intermission (1a): A Little Opened Scroll.

NIV	TT
10 ¹ Then I saw another mighty angel coming down from heaven. He was robed in a cloud, with a rainbow above his head; his face was like the sun, and his legs were like fiery pillars. ² He was holding a little scroll, which lay open in his hand. He planted his right foot on the sea and his left foot on the land, ³ and he gave a loud shout like the roar of a lion. When he shouted, the voices of the seven thunders spoke. ⁴ And when the seven thunders spoke, I was about to write; but I heard a voice from heaven say, "Seal up what the seven thunders have said and do not write it	**10** ¹ And I saw another **mighty**[131] angel coming down from heaven, wrapped in a **cloud,**[132] with a **rainbow**[133] over his head, and his face was like the sun, and his feet like columns of fire. ² He held in his hand a little opened **scroll**[134]. He placed his right foot on the sea and his left on the land. ³ Then he cried out with a loud voice, like a lion roaring. And when he cried out, the seven thunders sounded their own voices. ⁴ When the seven thunders spoke, I was about to write, but I heard a voice from heaven saying: "**Seal up**[135] what the seven thunders said; do

---

[131] ἰσχυρός → It means *"strong," "mighty," "strong either in body or in mind,"* and *"powerful."*

[132] νεφέλη → It means *"a cloud."* The term was used to describe the *"cloud"* which led the Israelites in the wilderness.

[133] ἶρις → It means *"rainbow," "Halo,"* and *"radiance."* (only appears in Rev. 4:3; 10:1)

[134] βιβλαρίδιον → It means *"little book,"* and *"little scroll."*

[135] σφραγίζω → It means *"seal," "seal up," "keep something secret," "mark," "to identity," "attest," "certify,"* and *"acknowledge"* (cf. Rev. 7:3, 4, 5, 8; 10:4; 20:3; 22:10).

down." ⁵ Then the angel I had seen standing on the sea and on the land raised his right hand to heaven. ⁶ And he swore by him who lives for ever and ever, who created the heavens and all that is in them, the earth and all that is in it, and the sea and all that is in it, and said, "There will be no more delay! ⁷ But in the days when the seventh angel is about to sound his trumpet, the mystery of God will be accomplished, just as he announced to his servants the prophets." ⁸ Then the voice that I had heard from heaven spoke to me once more: "Go, take the scroll that lies open in the hand of the angel who is standing on the sea and on the land."	not write it down." ⁵ Then the angel whom I saw standing on the sea and on the land raised his right hand to heaven, ⁶ and he swore by the one who lives forever, who **created**¹³⁶ heaven and everything in it, and the earth and everything in it, and the sea and everything in it: "There will be no more **time**,¹³⁷ ⁷ but in the days when the seventh angel is to sound his trumpet, then the mystery of God will be completed, as he announced to his servants, the prophets. ⁸ Then the voice that I had heard from heaven spoke with me again, and said: "Go, take the **scroll**¹³⁸ which lies opened in the hand of the angel who stands on the sea and on the land." ⁹ Then I went to the

---

¹³⁶ κτίζω → It means "*create*," "*form*," "*shape*," "*make habitable*," "*to make a place*," "*to found a colony*," "*to found a city*," and "*of God creating the worlds*." In Hebrew, it is "ברא."
¹³⁷ χρόνος → The term means "*time*," "*season*," and "*delay*."
¹³⁸ βιβλίον → It means "*scroll*," and "*book*."

⁹ So I went to the angel and asked him to give me the little scroll. He said to me, "Take it and eat it. It will turn your stomach sour, but 'in your mouth it will be as sweet as honey.'" ¹⁰ I took the little scroll from the angel's hand and ate it. It tasted as sweet as honey in my mouth, but when I had eaten it, my stomach turned sour. ¹¹ Then I was told, "You must prophesy again about many peoples, nations, languages and kings."	angel and told him to give me the **little scroll**.[139] And he said to me, "Take it and eat it; it will be bitter to your stomach, but in your mouth it will be as sweet as honey." ¹⁰ So I took the little scroll from the hand of the angel and I ate it, and it was sweet as honey in my mouth, but when I ate it, it turned my stomach bitter. ¹¹ And they said to me: "You must again **prophesy against**[140] people and nations and tongues and many kings."

An interlude now separates the first six trumpet blasts from the seventh and final one. Because the trumpets vision parallels the seals vision, it is no surprise that there is also a parallel between their intermission scenes. Corresponding to the two-part seals interlude (7:1-8, 9-17) is a two-part trumpets interlude (10:1-11; 11:1-14).

- **1** After using the phrase *"and I saw"* to introduce this section as a new scene within the ongoing trumpet narrative (see the comment on 5:1), John shifts his spatial focus. To this point he has envisioned all the critical activity from what appears to be a heavenly perch. Having been invited up to the heavenly throne

---

[139] βιβλαρίδιον → It means *"little book,"* and *"little scroll."*

[140] προφητεῦσαι ἐπὶ → The phrase means *"prophesy against."* The phrase appears in the LXX only twice in Jeremiah, twice in Amos, and twenty-one times in Ezekiel.

room (4:1-2), he sees everything that happens from that lofty perspective. By the time he opens his chapter 10 narration, however, this traveler in the spirit has apparently been grounded. When he catches his glimpse of the mighty angel, his vantage point is from below. Looking up, he sees the angel coming down (καταβαίνω).

John's use of the verb "καταβαίνω" is instructive. His first and last applications narrate the descent of the new Jerusalem as a kind of eschatological reward, a temporal realization of eternal salvation (3:12; 21:2, 10). Yet John makes clear, right from the start, that a person's citizenship in this eschatological city is conditioned upon one's exercise of the appropriate witnessing behavior (3:12). Those who refused to witness and instead chose a path of accommodation to Roman legal, economic, political, and cultic expectations should instead expect that this city's gates would afford them no entry. The implication of judgment becomes explicit in John's other usages of the descent motif. At 16:21; 18:1; and 20:1, 9, God's judgment rains down. In three of those four occurrences, judgment is mediated by an angelic presence. John's use of the descent metaphor throughout the narrative suggests that he intends something specific when he records the *"coming down"* of another mighty angel (10:1). While he does not specifically mention the complementary themes of judgment and salvation, their presence must surely be felt.

That presence, particularly judgment, becomes more explicit as John fixes attention on the mighty angel. The characterization is surely drawn from Dan. 12:5-9. In the Hebrew text, during a time of great eschatological angst, Daniel sees two angelic figures by a stream. The two angels stand on the opposing banks. One of them asks a question of a man clothed in linen, who is introduced in Dan. 10:5 with traits that for John must have identified him as the one like the Son of Man.[141] One of the angels asks the man how long it will be until the end of the envisioned wonders. The man raises his right and left hands to heaven and swears by the one who lives forever that it will be a time, two times, and a half a time – apparently three and a half years – until God accomplishes God's purposes. When Daniel asks for clarification, he is sent away with the instruction that the words he has heard are to remain sealed and therefore secret.

Though in Daniel's case there were two great angels, John envisions only one. This one angel plays the role of Daniel's two angels as well as the one clothed in linen. He answers John's questions and provides the overall instruction the seer craves. But first he represents the image of God's power to effect the end time and the judgment that comes with it.

John quickly builds that representation in several ways. First, he uses the suggestive adjectives "ἄλλος" (another) and "ἰσχυρός" (mighty). Prior to 10:1, he has

---

[141] → On a face like lightning (1:16); on eyes like flaming torches (1:14); on arms and legs like burnished bronze (1:15); on his sound as the roar of a multitude (1:15).

spoken of *"another angel"* only twice (7:2; 8:3). Both of those occasions were saturated with the theme of judgment. At 7:2 another angel ascends from the east and orchestrates the sealing of the 144,000 from the great damage that will accompany God's preliminary acts of judgment. Then at 8:3, another angel stands at the heavenly incense altar and throws down the fire of God's judgment upon the earth. Anyone hearing and reading carefully would, at the precise moment of encountering *"another"* angel at 10:1, feel an appropriate sense of foreboding. It is a sense of dread that John maintains. With similar phrasing *"I saw another angel,"* 14:6 kicks off a series of presentations in which *"another"* angel six times operates in a manner that delivers some measure of God's judgment (14:6, 8, 9, 15, 17, 18). That judgment activity reaches a climax when, for the seventh time, at 18:1-2, *"another"* angel *"comes down"* from heaven and seals Babylon's fate.

The angel in 10:1 is also *"mighty."*[142] The seer reports only two other sightings of a mighty angel (5:2; 18:21). By chapter 18 the narrative atmosphere is think with judgment and doom. John attributes this punishing outcome to the fact that the city (*"Babylon"*) and its associates have so viciously persecuted those who witnessed to the lordship of God and the Standing Slaughtered Lamb (18:24). Perhaps even more

---

[142] → Some commentators suggested that John's *"mighty"* angel is Gabriel. The *"mighty"* angel has a great many of the characteristics of Gabriel in Dan. 8:15-17; 10:2-9; 12:5-13. An extra-biblical comparison would be to the Colossus of Rhodes, a famous bronze representation of the sun god Helios.

provocative is the fact that the first appearance of a mighty angel (5:2) occurs in direct connection with the scroll that John saw sitting in the right hand of the one who sat on the heavenly throne, that is, God (5:1). Surely the mention of another mighty angel in 10:1 would remind John's hearers and readers of the seven-sealed scroll that was subsequently opened in 6:1-8:1. Can it be coincidence that the scroll held by the mighty angel in chapter 10 has already been opened? Clearly, John is not talking about the same angel; this one is surely *"another mighty angel."*

The chapter 5 scroll is so significant that only the Standing Slaughtered Lamb can handle it. Similarly, only a very special divine figure can handle the scroll in chapter 10. This is no ordinary angel. John clothes his characterization with regal traits. He appears in the divine dress of a cloud. In Exod. 16:10 and 1 Kgs. 8:10, clouds are a metaphor for the presence of God. A halo-like rainbow (ἶρις) hovers over his head. John uses "ἶρις" one other time, to describe the glowing form that fills the air around the heavenly throne (4:3). His face shines like the sun. The only other time John uses the brilliance of the sun to describe someone's face, he refers to the Son of Man (1:16). Finally, though the text uses the term for feet, since John envisions them as columns of fire, he clearly intends to speak of the mighty angel's legs. Once again the imagery recalls the presentation of the Son of Man in chapter 1. His eyes are like flames of fire (1:14), and his feet have the appearance of bronze burnished in a fiery furnace

(1:15). Exodus 13:21 speaks of God leading the people of Egypt out of bondage via a pillar of fire by day and a pillar of cloud by night (cf. Dan. 10:6; Ezek. 1:27). The specific implication here is thus assurance of liberation and salvation for those who witness to this God, even as the wider language connects with judgment.

- **2** The little scroll lies opened in the hand of the mighty angel. Since 10:5 pictures him raising his right hand to heaven, he must be holding it in his left. After John has given such prominence to the scroll the Standing Slaughtered Lamb unsealed in 6:1-8:1, one could not fault John's hearers and readers for wondering if the two scrolls of chapters 5 and 10 are the same. The Lamb opened the first scroll (chapter 5) to an escalating series of judgment events; the second scroll (chapter 10) is already opened and surrounded on both narrative sides by escalating acts of judgment.

The adjective "ἠνεῳγμένον" (opened) is helpful identifier. The Greek participle occurs in the perfect tense, implying a past action that has enduring narrative effect. Such a description hints at a connection between the scroll of 5:1-8:1 and the one that appears in 10:2. Opened in the past (in the course of 6:1-8:1?), the scroll now plays a significant role in the ongoing prosecution of God's judgment (10:8-10) that began with the breaking of the first of the seven seals.

The participle's voice is passive. From chapter 6 forward, John has relied heavily on passive constructions to indicate the agency of either God or the Lamb in acts of both judgment and salvation. It would be unremarkable here, then, if John used the passive construction to indicate that either God or the Standing Slaughtered Lamb opened this scroll. This consideration is bolstered by the fact that John explicitly identifies the Lamb as the one who opens the scroll in 5:1-8:1. It seems appropriate, therefore, to presume that the scroll in 10:2 must also have been opened by the Lamb.

Yet another observation speaks to the possibility of a close link between the two scrolls. If the seals and trumpets episodes are indeed John's recounting of the same set of events from different eschatological angels, it would be logical to expect that John's hearers and readers are also encountering the same scroll.

There is also a potent intertextual reason for considering a strong relationship between the two scrolls. Both are foregrounded against Ezek. 2:9-10. Like the Ezekiel scroll, the one in 5:1-8:1 was written on the inside and back. Apparently, the Ezekiel scroll, like the one in 10:2, had already been opened; Ezekiel could make out words of lamentation and woe. Ezekiel was eventually commanded to ingest that scroll, just as John is commanded to eat the scroll in 10:9.

There is a major problem with the theory that John speaks of a single scroll: he uses different terminology for them. He calls the first scroll a "βιβλίον," the second he labels a "βιβλαρίδιον." The latter is translated *"little scroll"* since it is a diminutive for "βιβλίον," the term for scroll. On its own, this significant observation would seem to doom any presumption that the two scrolls are one and the same.

However, there are significant caveats to the observation. First, "βιβλίον" is itself a diminutive form. By the time John writes, it no longer requires the adjective "*little*" because it is a so-called "*faded diminutive*." That is to say, it was used so often in general speech that it came to be accepted as a stand-alone noun in its own right, not a diminutive descriptor of another noun. Second, John seems unsure that any significant linguistic difference exists between the two diminutive forms. While he does introduce the scroll with the form "βιβλαρίδιον" (10:2), and follows up with the same noun form in vv. 9 and 10, at the critical point when the scroll takes narrative center stage, he describes it as a "βιβλίον" (v. 8). The usage in vv. 2 and 8 suggests that John treats the two words as though they are synonymous. As many commentators point out, in this regard John would not be unlike the "*Vision of Hermas*" (2.1.4; 2.8.1-2), which treats "βιβλαρίδιον" and "βιβλίον" as though they are synonyms. There is every reason to believe that John envisioned one and not two different scrolls (see 5:1).

John's focus on the scroll does not last very long. He can probably introduce it so briefly and with such little discussion without fear of either distracting or losing his audience because his hearers and readers are already familiar with it. Its mention recalls its prior appearance and its association with the theme of judgment. He can therefore move quickly to what principally occupies him: the behavior of the mighty angel. Echoing Dan. 12:5, where two angels occupy opposite banks of a stream, John envisions this one great figure straddling all of earthly creation, with his right foot on the sea and his left on the land. Biblically speaking, the phrase, *"sea and earth"* alone generally designates the totality of God's creation (Job 11:9; Ps. 146:6; Prov. 8:29; Isa. 42:10; Jonah 1:9). The implication is that the angel has control over both sea and land.

- **3** The mighty angel roars like a lion with a loud voice that portends judgment. The metaphor intends an image of sovereign, destructive power. In the animal world, the history of Hebrew Scripture (Jer. 25:30; Hos. 11:10; Joel 3:16; Amos 1:2; 3:8), and John's narrative, the lion is a force to be feared. The first of the four awesome cherubim is described in lion-like terms. The Lamb of God is introduced first as *"the lion of Judah,"* a force thought to bring destruction upon the foes of Israel even as he delivered salvation for Israel's people. Even more significantly, two trumpet blasts correlate lion-like characteristics with divine judgment (9:8, 17).

  Seven thunders voice antiphonal affirmation of the mighty angel's foreboding roar. John is working here from Hebrew scriptural references. His introduction of thunders with the article is an indication that he believes his hearers and readers are well acquainted with the imagery. At Ps. 29:3 the glory of God's voice thunders for all to hear. At 1 Sam. 7:10, this thundering is the mighty voice of God that confounds and then routs the Philistines (cf. 1 Sam. 2:10; 2 Sam. 22:14; Job 37:2-5; Ps. 18:13; Isa. 29:6). For John, too, the thunders are a part of a theophany package that illustrates God's majesty. Thunders occur first in his narrative at 4:5, with the lightning and rumbling that emanate from the throne. In the ensuing three theophany presentations, where thunders, rumblings, and lightnings are joined by earthquake (8:5; 11:19; 16:18) and hail (11:19), there is also an unmistakable emphasis on the theme of divine judgment.

Even when the other theophany elements do not accompany thunder, it operates as a metaphor for the movement of God's justice. After the Standing Slaughtered Lamb breaks the first of the seven seals, the first of the four cherubim calls out "*Come!*" in a thunderous voice (6:1). The wave of vicious judgment that follows is unmistakable. Thunderous voices also sound in 14:2 and 19:6. In both of these cases, though, God's justice begins with an emphasis on salvation. At 14:2, hearers and readers are reminded that the 144,000 have been sealed from the acts of judgment that preface the final judgment. Thundering multitudes later praise God for the salvation that comes in the metaphor of marriage to the Lamb (19:6). In each of those occasions of celebration, though, judgment is not far off. God's punishment of those who oppress God's witnesses and accommodate to social, political, economic, and cultic expectations is quickly reasserted (14:6; 19:11).

Thunder is thus a thematic metaphor for the glorious execution of God's justice in both judgment and salvation. The number "*seven*" indicates that John is picturing that justice in its most complete and potent form¹⁴³. The thunders, then, signal total affirmation of judgment/salvation that the loud voice of the mighty angel implies. If one takes into account the Old Testament echoes, this thundering affirmation may well be God's own voice.

- **4** John's hearers and readers are not surprised when he informs them that he is ready to write down the judgment message that he heard the seven thunders convey. After all, throughout the narrative he has been commanded to transcribe his visions (1:11, 19; 2:1, 8, 12, 18; 3:1, 7, 14). The many previous orders to write make this subsequent command to abort the writing effort all the more intriguing – especially since the order comes directly from heaven.¹⁴⁴ Given the overall narrative intent to reveal God's designs for ultimate justice, why in this particular case would a heavenly agent suddenly require John to halt his revelatory efforts?

While it is impossible, given John's lack of specificity, to determine the answer to that important question, there are related matters that can be clarified. First, since John was specifically ordered to relay his visions in the writings of this book, his hearers and readers know that the message of the thunders does not include the content of John's overall narrative. Indeed, using the same verb that is so puzzling here, an angel specifically warns John at 22:10 not to seal up the

---

[143] → In Jewish tradition God's voice of thunder at Sinai (Exod. 19:16-19) is referred to as *"seven voices"* or *"sounds."*

[144] → cf. 2 Cor. 12:2-4, where Paul speaks of a person who was not to write the things he had seen when caught up into paradise.

words of this book. John's visions must be conveyed; the thunders' message must not be. Second, since the scroll of 10:2 is a virtual *"open book,"* whose content will later be internalized and then presumably proclaimed (vv. 8-11), its message also cannot be the same message as that which John hears from the seven thunders. If this scroll is the scroll of 5:1-8:1, which contains the shape, plan, and destiny of human history (see the comment on 5:1), then the seven thunders are not speaking exclusively about that plan. Through his visionary writing, John is already in the process of laying bare the direction and meaning of that plan.

At the very least, the similarity between John's recounting of the *"seal"* command and the order given to Daniel that he seal up the vision given to him at Dan. 8:26 (cf. 8:19) is instructive. Daniel's classified vision is about the happenings that will take place at the very end of time. Given John's overall focus on the end time, it takes no leap of the imagination to conclude that the thunders, too, are speaking about final events. The context here suggests that the arrival of those final events is imminent.

- **5 – 6** Verse 5 refocuses attention on the mighty angel first introduced in v. 1. John reminds his hearers and readers that the angel is a colossus; while his right foot occupies the land, his left covers and therefore controls the sea. With his left hand apparently clutching the little scroll (v. 2), he raises his right hand to heaven in what v. 6 shows to be an oath-swearing gesture.

The lifting of one's hand toward heaven as an oath-swearing gesture had a long history in Israelite tradition.

Deuteronomy 32:40, in the context of judgment against those who have persecuted God's people and mocked God's lordship (Deut. 32:35-39), records such an instance.[145] More to the point, though, is the relationship with Dan. 12:7. There is a divine figure dressed in linen lifted both hands to heaven and swore by the one who lives forever that it would be a time, two times, and a half (i.e., three and one-half) before God would accomplish all tings.

The parallel with the mighty angel in Rev. 10:5 is intentional. He, too, swears on the one who lives forever, already identified by John as the one seated on the heavenly throne: God (4:9). He secures this identification by drawing upon other unforgettable characteristics that are exclusive to God. The one whom the angel swears created heaven and every divine thing in it. This part of the oath is reminiscent of Gen. 14:19, where King Melchizedek of Salem blesses Abram by the God who made heaven and earth. Abram responds to the king of Sodom by swearing upon this same God, who has made heaven and earth (Gen. 14:22). Obviously, the emphasis upon the earth echoes in the second phase of the mighty angel's declaration. His oath operates with the Creator of the earth and all the things in it in mind. He also declares this God to be the Creator of the sea and all within it. Numerous biblical texts corroborate this testimony about God's authorship of heaven, earth, and sea (Exod. 20:11; Neh.

---

[145] → The context of Deut. 32:40 does imply the swearing of an oath, and the LXX translators read the circumstance as one of oath bearing since it narrates not only a swearing but also one using the right hand.

9:6; Ps. 146:6; Acts 4:24). That the angel swears upon so mighty a God assures the validity of his forthcoming statement. Indeed, his very posture helps build the credibility that his name-dropping intends. The one who swears upon the God who created heaven, earth, and sea has descended at God's apparent direction from heaven and now stands simultaneously upon the earth and sea as he delivers his oath. He represents the very reality upon which he swears; there can be no greater assurance of his credibility and the viability of his oath than that.

It is the content of his oath that is critical. In Dan. 12 the figure dressed in linen declared that God's final accomplishment (i.e., judgment) would take place in three and one-half times. Three and a half, half of the complete number of seven, also used by John (Rev. 11:2, 3, 9, 11; 12:6, 14), is a euphemism for a temporary, short duration of time. John makes that point here by transcribing the angel's message as there will be no more time.

The phrasing is odd, to be sure. The NRSV and NIV translate the angel's words as *"There will be no more delay."* "Χρόνος," the key term in the text, can be translated *"delay"* as well as the more customary *"time."* At this stage of the text, the translations are practically synonymous. After the sounding of the sixth trumpet, with the expectation of the seventh trumpet's imminent sounding, John has brought his hearers and readers to a critical turning point. The first six trumpet calls beckoned preliminary acts of judgment in response to the cries (6:9-11), or prayers (8:3-5), of the persecuted witnesses. The seventh trumpet, like the seventh seal and the seventh bowl, will bring the preliminaries to an end by ushering in God's final act of judgment. The mighty angel, scroll in hand, swears now that this end point has finally come. Time itself has come to completion. By definition, then, there can be no more delay before the arrival of God's final judgment act.

This interpretation makes sense if the little scroll in question is the same scroll that in chapter 5 contained the plan of human history.[146] With the scroll now open, the angel can plainly see when the end will be, and he can apparently see that it is now. He can swear confidently on the God who lives forever and who created all things because he has this God's scroll. He can see the timeline of history and where he and the rest of creation are on it. They are at the point where time will be no longer because it has reached the objective God has set for it. While *"There will be no more delay"* therefore is an accurate representation of what the angel has to say, the translation *"There will be no more time"* is more eloquent and appropriate. In this visionary scenario, it is time itself that has run out.

In every other case where "χρόνος" is used in the Book of Revelation, there is a little time left. Only a little time remains, but it is there. There is time to repent (2:21), time to rest (6:11), and time to rule (20:3). The first two occurrences seem natural because, narratively speaking, they occur prior to the declaration

---

[146] → Some views the scroll in chapter 5 containing either all of God's eschatological plans or specifically the events of 6:1-8:5, and others view the *"little scroll"* of 10:2 containing the events described in 11:1-13.

in 10:6 that there will be no longer be time. The last, though, since it occurs at the end of the narrative, appears out of place. Although the angel declares in chapter 10 that there will be no more time, Satan is loosed for yet a little more time in chapter 20. How can Satan have more time at 20:3 when the angel swears here that there will be no more time?

Clarification lies with an understanding of John's unorthodox presentation. He is not presenting events chronologically. He is jumping back and forth in real time as he renders his narrative presentation. One can sense this time-displacement phenomenon when considering John's presentation of the seven seals, trumpets, and bowls. Though they represent the same end-time events, viewed from different eschatological perspectives, John's narrative presentation implies that they occur in chronological order: first seals, then trumpets, and finally bowls. His apparent narrative progression forward in time actually represents a double reconsideration of the same set of moments in time that describe God's preliminary acts of judgment.

In like manner, the events narrated at 20:3 take place, in real time, before the declaration by the angel in chapter 10, even though in the narrative itself those events occur well after the angel's declaration. If both 10:6 and 20:3 are true, John has given us a glimpse of the end of time at 10:6, while still intending to explain the progression of events in time, such as what has happened in 20:3, that has led up to this end. He continues in the narration in order to remind his hearers and readers about events that have occurred prior to this almost-final moment. The release of Satan at 20:3 is one such prior event.

Recognition of John's calculated time displacement has an important bearing on the way hearers and readers approach the remainder of his narrative. One can never be sure that just because events follow one another narratively, they are also envisioned by John to occur that way chronologically. John is intentionally presenting his visions out of chronological place. In order to maximize dramatic effect, he pictures the end moment (e.g., 10:6) before he narrates the events (e.g., 20:3) that have led up to and shaped it.

- **7** John opens v. 7 by describing the days of the final trumpet blast. With the realization that time's purpose has been achieved, the mystery that God conveyed as good news to the prophets will be brought to its point of completion. What is that mystery? Traditionally, one would try to answer that question by initiating a query of the Old Testament prophetic records. Was there a common promissory thread that ran through all of the Hebrew prophetic writings? This is a difficult question to answer in John's terms, since the Hebrew prophets tended to seek realization of God's promises for freedom, land, the establishment of a vast people, and a return to the land following exile within history. John clearly anticipates the actualization of God's ultimate promise at the end of history. When he talks about the promise to the prophets, he therefore must be speaking metaphorically. He is not speaking about a literal promise per se. He is instead focused on the idea that God will be as faithful to God's promises regarding judgment and salvation as God was faithful to the promises God proclaimed to the prophets.

John suggests a starting point for deciphering the mystery that God revealed as good news to the prophets: his narration of the seventh trumpet's inauguration of God's reign at 11:15-19. The key verse is 11:18. John speaks specifically about the time of judgment that registers as salvation for God's servants, the prophets. He then goes on to add the saints and all who fear God's name – that is, those who testify to the lordship of God and the Standing Slaughtered Lamb – to the list of those who are saved. The clarification of any mystery at the end seems to revolve, then, not around a promise of freedom, land, life, or nationhood within history, but the promise of life in eschatological relationship with God. More particularly, it involves an identification of the categories of people who will be saved. John reminds his hearers and readers of the categories to which they must belong if they would hope for an eschatological relationship with God: servants, prophets.

John has based the critical phrase "*his servants, the prophets*" (10:7 and 11:18) on actual prophetic statements. The phrase is highlighted in Jer. 7:25-26, where it is noted that God sent the prophets in order to urge righteous and ethical behavior from the people of Israel. Moreover, like John (Rev. 10:3), Amos speaks of the heavenly message issuing forth in the sound of a lion roaring (3:8). Even more significantly, Amos speaks of that roar in the context of the Lord's message to his servants, the prophets (Amos 3:7). As with the

Jeremiah text, the focus is on the ethical behavior God expected form the people. Because they failed time and time again to demonstrate it, they were subject to judgment. Zechariah maintains this focus on the ethical behavior that God's servants, the prophets, expected from the people (Zech. 1:6). In his case, however, there was a glimmer of salvation. The prophetic word had a positive impact: the people repented. God therefore promised to punish the nations that had persecuted them and to bring them victory. This emphasis on the expectation of ethical behavior as a response to God's call for righteous living is present on almost every occasion when the phrase *"his servants, the prophets"* occurs in the prophetic literatures (cf. 2 Kgs. 9:7; 17:13, 23; 21:10; 24:2; *2 Ezra* 9:11; Jer. 25:4; 26:5; 29:19; 35:15; 44:4; Ezek. 38:17; Dan. 9:6, 10).

The most telling case comes from Daniel, who speaks of God's servants, the prophets, in a context explicitly concerned with the failure of the people to heed God's prophetic call for righteous and ethical behavior (Dan. 9:6, 10). As a result, between judgment or salvation and God's expectation for righteous and ethical behavior (witnessing) provides a natural bridge to these Hebrew prophetic themes. It must be this emphasis upon the expectation of righteous, ethical behavior, and God's reward of salvation for those who meet the expectation and judgment against those who do not, that John as in mind when he calls upon God's proclamations to God's servants, the prophets.

- **8** The scroll is the same one mentioned at 10:2. John refers to it with the definite article because his readers are already familiar with it. He also describes the 10:2 and 10:8 scrolls in almost duplicate fashion in vv. 2 and 8. As in v. 2, the scroll in v. 8 has already been opened, and it rests in the hand of the angel who stands with one foot on the sea and the other on the earth.

John's redundant and therefore emphatic effort to link the scroll of v. 8 with the *"little scroll"* of v. 2 and vv. 9-10 is all the more interesting since he does not use the diminutive form "βιβλαρίδιον" in v. 8. Apparently, for John the terms, while distinct, are interchangeable here and refer to one and the same scroll. It is, moreover, the same scroll introduced at 5:1 and opened by the Standing Slaughtered Lamb over the course of 6:1-8:1. The scroll's content therefore presents God's plan and purpose of eschatological justice for human history.

John's attention is refocused on the scroll by a voice from heaven. His use of "πάλιν" (again) indicates that this voice is the same heavenly voice that denied him permission to write down what the seven thunders had said. This time the order is an affirming one.

- **9 – 10** When John asks for the scroll, he is told, in what sounds like Eucharistic language, to take and eat it (cf. Matt. 26:26). It is at this point that allusions to Ezek. 2:8-3:3 become unmistakable. At his prophetic commissioning, Ezekiel is given a scroll written on both front and back and told to eat it. The description of the scroll clearly calls to mind the scroll introduced by John in Rev. 5:1. Ezekiel explains the content of his scroll as words of lamentation and woe. Those who do not live up to God's expectations for righteous and ethical behavior will be sorely judged. This description fits precisely the Rev. 10 scroll as well. Chapter 10 consistently emphasizes God's coming justice as a word of judgment.

Ezekiel is ordered to eat the scroll, thereby internalizing its words of lamentation and woe, and then to go and prophetically deliver it. He does eat it and finds that despite its harsh message, it is sweet as honey in his mouth. The metaphor *"sweet as honey"* is occasionally used of the commands of God in the Old Testament (Pss. 19:10; 119:100-103) and is a metaphor used for agreeable speech (Prov. 16:24). The parallels with Rev. 10:9-10 are striking. After telling John to take the scroll and eat it, thereby internalizing its content, the angel explains that it will embitter his stomach even though it will be like honey in his mouth.

Verse 10 repeats the content of v. 9 by narrating John's actual consumption of the scroll. Working backward, though, John speaks about how bitter the scroll made his stomach feel, despite its sweet taste in his mouth. Though he revels in the knowledge that he is interacting so closely with God's word of justice for human history, his stomach apparently turns when he realizes how much destructive and devastating judgment that justice will necessarily bring.

- **11** John is now recommissioned to the task of prophecy (cf. 1:3). Since he has been operating prophetically throughout the course of his work, the command intends that he recommit himself to the effort. That recommitment is necessary because the effort will become even more difficult. His judgment oracle becomes universal, and if chapter 11 is any guide, his witnessing and the witnessing of those who heed his call will provoke vicious resistance.

The clarification that it is necessary for John to "*prophesy*" again is instructive. The mandate begins oddly. Up until this point, John's primary conversation partner has been the mysterious voice from heaven (10:4). Given that voice occurs in the singular, it appears that the speaker is a single person or entity. Yet v. 11 opens with the narration that "*they spoke to me.*" Commentators have offered several somewhat plausible options as to why the narration shifts to the plural. It could be that the mighty angel and the heavenly voice, both interlocutors with John during the course of chapter 10, take this unsolicited opportunity to speak to John in unison. Other commentators suggest the even more unexpected possibility that the mighty angel and the "*angel who had been showing*" (cf. 22:8-9), who has guided John throughout, take this opportunity to speak together. There is, unfortunately, no warrant in the text to expect such a joint appearance. Finally, several commentators take the grammatical route in the quest for clarity. They "*understand the plural pronoun to be an example of the plural of indefinite statement,*" which according to R. H. Charles is "*an idiom sometimes found in Hebrew, and frequent in Biblical Aramaic*" (Reddish, Charles, Aune).

There is another option that develops from the narration of the text itself. Even though they apparently represent the singular presence of God's voice and direction, the thunders operate as a plural entity. More simply and naturally, John may intend that the same thunders issued God's directive to seal up what he has heard (to, in effect, stop what he was doing) and are now re-engaging him in his more appropriate task. His job is not to reveal the end-time mystery, at least not yet. His job is to prophesy about God's coming judgment against those who, out of loyalty to Roman lordship, have persecuted witnesses to the lordship of God and the Lamb.

No doubt, they have in mind the same kind of prophetic mandate issued to prophets like Ezekiel (Ezek. 25:2) and Jeremiah (Jer. 25:30). In both of those illustrative cases, the prophet was ordered to prophesy against the enemies of God and God's people. Though John is working thematically from Ezekiel in this Rev. 10, it is the Jeremiah text that is especially illuminating here. Jeremiah was given the specific mandate to speak as a voice of judgment against the nations (Jer. 1:10). Then, in a passage that more closely parallels Rev. 10:11, Jeremiah is commanded to prophesy against the inhabitants of the earth and to declare that the Lord will vent anger from on high with the fury and violence of a mighty roar (Jer. 25:30).[147] John's hearers and readers would no doubt recall the lion's roar in Rev. 10:3. Even more significant is Jeremiah's listing of the kings, starting at 25:18, against whom the prophet is specifically commissioned at this point to prophesy. Before it closes, John's universal charge (people,

---

[147] Note that it is the Hebrew, not the LXX, that operates with the verb form for "*roar.*"

nations, languages), also mentions the category of monarchs. John will be particularly concerned about the obstinacy of the kings as his narrative progresses (cf. Rev. 16:12, 14; 17:1-2, 12, 18; 18:3, 9; 19:18-19).

Up to this point in his narrative prophecy, John has twice mentioned similar groupings of nations, tribes, languages, and people (5:9; 7:9; Dan. 3:4). On both occasions, the groupings are mentioned positively. The Lamb sheds his blood in order to redeem them. The effort of redemption, however, morphs into a prophecy for judgment when the nations, tribes, languages, and people fail to live righteously and ethically as a result of the Lamb's redemptive effort. In this heavenly address to John, "*they*" make certain that the kings of the earth also realize that they, too, are included in this message of judgment.

On every subsequent occasion – until the consummation of God's reign as represented in the final chapters of the book – when people, tribes, languages, and nations are either specifically or euphemistically mentioned, the prophet speaks in negative terms (11:8, 18; 13:7; 14:6, 8; 17:15; 18:3, 23; 19:15). Although the kings are not explicitly named in those passages as they are in 10:11, John continues to make clear that the judgment language is truly universal. Moreover, he does include a separate flurry of specific prophecies against the kings. It is for all these contextual and intertextual reasons that translators who render the ambiguous preposition "ἐπὶ" (against) are translating correctly. John's order, as with Jeremiah and Ezekiel, is to "προφητεῦσαι ἐπὶ" (prophesy against) them.

Revelation 11:1~13 → Intermission (2a):

Two Witnesses

NIV	TT
11 ¹ I was given a reed like a measuring rod and was told, "Go and measure the temple of God and the altar, with its worshipers. ² But exclude the outer court; do not measure it, because it has been given to the Gentiles. They will trample on the holy city for 42 months. ³ And I will appoint my two witnesses, and they will prophesy for 1,260 days, clothed in sackcloth." ⁴ They are "the two olive trees" and the two lampstands, and "they stand before the Lord of the earth." ⁵ If anyone tries to harm them, fire comes from their mouths and devours their enemies. This is how anyone who wants to harm them must die. ⁶ They have power to shut up the heavens so that it will not	**11** ¹ I was given a measuring reed, like a rod, and I was told: "Arise and measure the **temple**[148] of God and the altar and those who worship there. ² But exclude the courtyard outside the temple; do not measure it, because it has been given over to the nations, and they will trample the holy city for forty-two months. ³ And I will appoint my two witnesses, and they will prophesy for 1,260 days, wearing sackcloth. ⁴ These are the two olive trees and the two lampstands that stand before the Lord of the earth. ⁵ And if anyone wishes to harm them, fire streams from their mouths and devours their enemies; and if anyone wishes to harm them, he must be killed

---

[148] ναός → It means "*temple*," "*sanctuary*," "*Holy of holies*," and "*shrine*."

rain during the time they are prophesying; and they have power to turn the waters into blood and to strike the earth with every kind of plague as often as they want. ⁷ Now when they have finished their testimony, the beast that comes up from the Abyss will attack them, and overpower and kill them. ⁸ Their bodies will lie in the public square of the great city—which is figuratively called Sodom and Egypt—where also their Lord was crucified. ⁹ For three and a half days some from every people, tribe, language and nation will gaze on their bodies and refuse them burial. ¹⁰ The inhabitants of the earth will gloat over them and will celebrate by sending each other gifts, because these two prophets had tormented those who	in this way. ⁶ They have the **authority**[149] to shut the sky, so that no rain would fall during the days of their prophecy, and they have authority over the waters to turn them into blood and to strike the earth with every plague whenever they wish. ⁷ When they have completed their **testimony**,[150] the beast that rises from the Abyss will wage war with them and he will conquer them and he will kill them. ⁸ And their corpses will lie in the street of the great city, which is prophetically called Sodom and Egypt, where also their Lord was crucified. ⁹ And members of the people and tribes and tongues and nations will see their corpses for three and a half days, and they will not allow their corpses to be placed in a tomb. ¹⁰ And the inhabitants of the earth will rejoice over them and celebrate and exchange gifts with one another, because these two

---

[149] ἐξουσία → It means *"freedom of choice," "right to act," "ability," "might," "power," "authority," "absolute power," "ruling power," "official power," "jurisdiction,"* and *"domain."*

[150] μαρτυρία → It means *"testimony," "witness,"* and *"record."*

live on the earth. ¹¹ But after the three and a half days the breath of life from God entered them, and they stood on their feet, and terror struck those who saw them. ¹² Then they heard a loud voice from heaven saying to them, "Come up here." And they went up to heaven in a cloud, while their enemies looked on. ¹³ At that very hour there was a severe earthquake and a tenth of the city collapsed. Seven thousand people were killed in the earthquake, and the survivors were terrified and gave glory to the God of heaven.	prophets had tormented the inhabitants of the earth. ¹¹ But after the three and a half days, the spirit of life from God entered them, and they stood on their feet, and **great fear overwhelmed those who saw them**[151]. ¹² Then they heard a loud voice from heaven say to them: "Come up here!" And they ascended into heaven in the cloud, and their enemies saw them. ¹³ In that hour there was a great earthquake and a tenth of the city fell; seven thousand people were killed in the earthquake, and the rest became terrified and **they gave glory to the God**[152] **of heaven.**

In this vision ("*the 2ⁿᵈ intermission*") the temple is measured, part of it is assigned to the nations who will trample on it, and God's two witnesses are persecuted,

---

[151] → The phrase "*great fear overwhelmed them*" is a Semitic expression for a collective response of awe, either because the Israelites or Jews seem invincible (Exod. 15:16; Deut. 11:25; Esth. 8:17; 9:2; *1 Macc.* 3:25; 7:18; *2 Macc.* 12:22) or as a reaction to a display of supernatural power (*2 Macc.* 3:24; Luke 1:12, 65; Acts 5:5; 19:17).

[152] ἔδωκαν δόξαν τῷ θεῷ → The Phrase means "*they gave glory to God.*" This is somewhat surprising, however, since it is the only instance in Revelation of people turning to the true God as a result of a punitive miracle. Yet there is strong evidence that "*Giving glory to God*" is an idiom for conversion. The conversion of Nebuchadnezzar is described as giving God glory (cf. Dan. 4:34; *1 Esd* 9:8; Acts 13:48; Herm. *Sim.* 6.3.6; 8.6.3).

killed, and vindicated. This section is dense with allusions from the Old Testament and earlier apocalyptic traditions.

- **1** When John opens the chapter with yet another formulaic appeal to the divine passive construction "ἐδόθη" ("*it was given*"), he means to say that God provides the tool that makes his prophetic activity possible. God operates by proxy. The singular participle "λέγων" (saying) refers most likely to the "*they*" who spoke for God at 10:11. The indefinite plural "*they*" represents there and here and singular voice of God. This continuity of speaker makes sense given that God's expectations for John's prophecy, narrated at the close of chapter 10, are enabled by God as chapter 11 opens. With that continued contextual emphasis from chapter 10, John's hearers and readers should also presume that an intermediary, not God, places the measuring reed in John's hands. God spoke through the thunders and acted through the mighty angel in chapter 10. The reader is meant to presume the same mediating activity here. In 21:15-16, the only other place in the Book of Revelation where the term "*reed*" occurs, an angel who has been charged to measure the holy city is specifically outfitted with a reed to accomplish the task (cf. Ezek. 40:5). In both Ezekiel (40-48) and Zechariah (2:1-5), there are similar angelic measurements of the city of Jerusalem. Particularly in Zechariah, the act symbolizes God's protection (Zech. 2:5).

John indicates his broader theological understanding of the measuring reed by pairing with "ῥάβδος" (rod). At 2:27 he affirms that all who conquer because of their witnessing will be rewarded with an iron rod, which they will use to rule the nations in the same way that a shepherd watched over, guides, protects and disciplines his flock. The same construction occurs at 12:5. There, the woman clothed with the sun gives birth to a child, who will shepherd the nations with an iron rod. The child is clearly Jesus Christ. In his letters to the churches (chapters 2-3), it was clear that Christ shepherds his flock in a caring but disciplinary way. It is not coincidental that at both 2:27 and 12:5, the shepherding rule is over the nations. Notably, John's prophecy at 10:11, the same prophecy that he now enacts in 11:1-2, is against the nations. This nuance suggests a shepherding, watchful, though disciplinary role for his prophecy even where the disobedient nations are concerned. The final occurrence of the term *"rod"* offers confirmation (19:15). The Standing Slaughtered Lamb, having struck down the nations, will shepherd them with a rod of iron. The terminology suggests that the judgment is reconstructive, not punitive.

Like the witnesses in the churches who conquer (2:27) and Christ (12:5; 19:15), John is to prophesy in a way that will shepherd with discipline. Although his measurement will protect, it will also chasten in the same way that Christ's letters promised both protection and judgment. The measurement here, then, is not simply a reward, but another complex stage in John's exhortation to his hearers and readers. They are set apart not so that they can exult in their saved, meaning safe, status but so that they, like John himself, can be directed toward more witnessing (and therefore conquering) behavior. Even the nations are not given up for lost. They, too, are being shepherded – toward repentance.

The object of measurement is the "ναός," the inner temple sanctuary, and two components, the altar and those who worship. The inner temple sanctuary most likely referred to the court of women, the court of the Israelites, the court of the priests, and the highest point, the holy of holies into which only the high priest entered once a year to sacrifice on behalf of the sins of the people. Despite the fact that on every other occasion when he mentions "ναός," John is referring to heavenly sanctuary, one gathers the sense that he is speaking here of the earthly one (3:12, 7:15; 11:19; 14:15, 17; 15:5, 6, 8; 16:1, 17; 21:22). First, he puts himself, a historical being, in direct proximity to it. In his heavenly citations, he relate the infrastructure to resurrected witnesses, angels, or a heavenly voice. Second, in 11:2, the nations will trample the outer part of the temple will apparently also target the inner sanctuary. Only John's protecting measurement will keep them at bay. The earthbound nations would not have destructive access to the heavenly temple. Third, at 11:19, John clearly puts the heavenly sanctuary in opposition to this one.

John similarly considers the sacrificial alter (or the room in the court of the priests that housed it) that stood in the sanctuary of the Herodian temple, not its heavenly counterpart. Although all his other altar references depict heavenly attendees (resurrected souls, 6:9; angels 8:3, 5; 9:13; 14:18; 16:7), he puts himself in direct historical relationship to this one. Likewise, though the nations target it, they cannot get at it.

Since John envisions the earthly sanctuary and sacrificial altar, when he speaks of worshipers he has in mind human celebrants. In this narrative setting, these can only be the faithful believers in his seven churches. John's prophetic activity will measure, that is to say, shepherd and protect them.

John writes well after the Roman destruction of the Jerusalem temple, and yet there is every narrative indication that he has in mind here the historical sanctuary. How can he measure what has already been destroyed? The prophecy only works on an imaginative level. John can resurrect the temple by figuratively re-creating it (over and over? Note the present tense imperative "*arise*") in the imaginations of his hearers and readers. Then he can populate it with them as its worshipers. In John's visionary imagination, the sanctuary can become the figurative representation of the people of God. In chapters 2 and 3, he raised that representation through the myth of seven churches that stood for the entire church, that is, the whole people of God. He remakes that figurative move with new casting here.

- **2** A contrast is drawn with the figurative outer court. For those familiar with the Herodian temple, this image would most likely bring the court of Gentiles to mind. Because it is not measured, and therefore it is not protected, it is trampled. What does this mean for the people who occupy it? The outer court is, after all, still part of the temple. Believers come to all parts of the temple to worship God. One must conclude, then, that the outer court is also populated by believers.[153] But which believers would be left unprotected?

The easiest answer would be that those in the sanctuary are believers of Jewish origin, while those in the outer precincts are Gentile believers. John, however, makes no such ethnic-religious distinctions anywhere else in the narrative. For him, relationship with God is based on witness, not ethnicity. A better solution can be found in John's narration. The only distinction among believers that John has thus far made (other than between those who do and those who do not witness) occurs at 7:1-8 (cf. 14:1-5) and 7:9-17.

The inner sanctuary and the worshipers who populate it correspond to the invulnerable believers of 7:1-8 and 14:1-5. This company is comprised of both Jewish and Gentile believers; those in 7:9-17 are also of both Jewish and Gentile pedigree. These believers in 7:9-17 correspond to the unmeasured and therefore unprotected outer courtyard. It is clear from the narration that they, like the souls of 6:9-11, were trampled and slaughtered. Indeed, the souls in 6:9-11 are probably a subset of this larger group in 7:9-17. The correspondence with John's language of measured

---

[153] → Three possible identifications for what the outer courtyard represents: (1) Christians for whom the time of suffering is redemptive; (2) the church in its engagement with the world; (3) the unbelieving world that will feel the full effect of God's punishment and eschatological woes. I press for something more like option number 2.

and unmeasured here at 11:1-2 works because, while the believers of 7:1-8 are protected from both the physical and spiritual savageries that engulf John's apocalyptic visions, the believers of 7:9-17 are not. Though they are not spared the horror, they are no less faithful believers. Because they are engaged with the world, in the world, they share in the fate of the nations, as does John who suffers in exile, even though they suffer for different reasons. They suffer because of their witness. The persecution imposed by the nations elicits the divine anger that erupts as both cosmic and natural disaster. Though the believers are not responsible for this disaster, neither are they *"raptured"* out of it. Theirs is a double portion of distress. They are persecuted by the nations who trample them; because they live in the world of those nations, they must also endure the retribution the unjust nations deserve. This is why John figuratively describes them as the temple's unmeasured outer courtyard. They remain part of the community of faith, just as the outer courtyard remains part of the temple. They will not, however, be protected. Like Jesus just after his baptism (Mark 1:12), they are cast directly (ἐκβάλλω) into harm's way.

 Why? Their struggle provides an even greater opportunity for witness; they witness to the nations even though the struggles they experience are a direct result of the hostility and injustice those nations impose against their witness. Here John uses the matter of theodicy as a teaching tool. Non-believers who see the suffering of the faithful (the unprotected outer courtyard), and who wonder if their God can truly be God, will nonetheless see these believers maintaining their witness to the lordship of that God. After all, God really is in control. Through yet another strategic use of the divine passive formulation "ἐδόθη" (it was given), John makes his case. The nations have the power to trample the outer courtyard only because God gives it to them. This knowledge is power. Knowledgeable believers, though physically vulnerable, witness through the horror. Their faith is not based on the historical circumstance of a troubled present, but on trust in the secure future that God promises.

That future will not suffer a long delay. The trampling will last only forty-two months. One-half of seven years indicates a time of transience, not long duration (see the comments on 10:5-6; cf. Dan. 7:25; 12:7). The fact that John raises the same half-of – seven metaphor for transience when describing the tribulation endured by the people of faith in 12:6, 14 reinforces the contention that here, too, the seer has in mind a temporary tribulation. The people of faith will endure; the destructive force of the nations, powered by Rome, will not.

- **3** Grammatically, John introduces this new section by stating declaratively what he has only alluded to passively before: God is in charge. At 11:1 he made his case with a passive formulation of the verb *"to give"* (ἐδόθη); he makes it here by appealing to a future formulation of the same verb. The future form "δώσω" (I will give) indicates that the two witnesses (like John himself 11:1) are given their task as a result of divine prerogative. It does not matter whether God is speaking directly or speaking through a proxy.

Thematically, John only uses the verb *"to prophesy"* twice in the entire narrative (10:11; 11:3). He saves it specifically for this context. The witnesses' charge to prophesy is the very same task issued to John in 10:11. As prophets, they are charged to mimic John's witness to the lordship of Christ. That witness marks out the boundaries of their belief, identifying them as part of the Lamb's community. Their identification leaves them vulnerable, like the unprotected outer courtyard of the temple.

John further establishes in vv. 6-7 the synonymous relationship he implies here between witness and prophecy. The prophecy of v. 6 finds content in the witnessing to the lordship of Christ in v. 7. Likewise, the two witnesses of v. 3 are identified as prophets (v. 10). The prophetic role of these two witnesses is, like John's own prophetic role, defined by their testimony to the lordship of Christ. In John's narrative world, one prophesies by testifying. The parallel statements at 19:10 and 22:9 are illustrative. In both cases, John is chastised for bowing down to worship an angelic figure instead of God or the Standing Slaughtered Lamb. In the first case, the divine figure tells John that he must not do that because the divine figure is a fellow servant of John and of John's brothers and sisters who bear witness to Jesus. In the latter case, the divine figure tells John the same thing. This time, however, instead of pointing redundantly to John's brothers and sisters, the witnesses, he identifies them as prophets. He means the same brothers and sisters. As witnesses, they are prophets. As prophets, they testify. Since such testimony in a context so resistant to it will inevitably lead to persecution, it is perhaps encouraging to know that one need only endure that persecution for a temporary period of 1,260 days, the same length of time the believers symbolized by the outer courtyard will be persecuted (11:2, 3; 12:6, 14; 13:5).

In symbolizing both his own prophetic work and the prophetic witness of the church, John has made the odd choice of narrating two witnesses. Commentators have connected the two with a range of prophetic figures. To be sure, the priestly and Davidic lay messiahs of Zech. 3-4 and 6:9-14 are in the back of his mind. yet in view of John's declaration that the two witnesses can redeploy plagues associated with Moses and Elijah (Rev. 11:6), those two prophets are obviously also important for his presentation. Other commentators offer Elijah and Jeremiah, Peter and Paul, Jesus and John the Baptist, the Old Testament and the New Testament, and so forth. Though he is certainly working from a Moses and Elijah connection, John is also thinking broadly. According to Luke 10:1, when Jesus sends his disciples out to witness to his gospel message, he dispatches them in teams of two. Luke 10:19 clarifies that Jesus' teams are as protected from harm as John's two witnesses initially are here. John 8:17 is equally illustrative. Jesus there appeals to the Jewish tradition that required two corroborating witnesses before any testimony was to be considered valid (Num. 35:30; Deut. 19:15). The number two is from the Old Testament law requiring at least two witnesses as a just basis for judging an offense against the law (Num. 35:30; Deut. 17:6; 19:5). The legal principle is continued in the New Testament on the basis of Deut. 19:15 (cf. Matt. 18:16; Luke 10:1-24, where there are thirty-five groups of two witnesses each; John 8:17; 2 Cor. 13:1; 1 Tim. 5:19; Heb. 10:28). Therefore, the emphasis is on a just or valid legal witness. The number of witnesses in Rev. 11 thus validates the testimony of their prophetic activity: Jesus Christ is the Lord.

The negative response to that testimony heightens the connection between the work of these two witnesses and the prophetic work of the now-exiled John. When they prophesy/testify, two results occur: protection and destruction. They are protected (measured) by God so that they can finish their prophecy (11:7). Only then is their destruction allowed. In other words, they play both the measured and unmeasured roles from 11:1-2 at different stages in their prophetic witnessing tour. The narrative point?

The sackcloth hints at the two witnesses' prophetic intent. John has already used sackcloth to symbolize God's judgment (6:5, 12). Here, too, judgment is an important theme. The plagues directed by the two witnesses (vv. 5-6) and the retribution exacted by God for their deaths (v. 13) are acts of judgment. So are the events of woe that accompany the blowing of the seventh trumpet (vv. 15-19). In this immediate context, then, their prophecy, cloaked as it is in the attire of sackcloth, is a word of judgment. Bauckham points out that there is also a hint of the theme of repentance. In the Hebrew tradition, the wearing of sackcloth could signify repentance. The Old Testament refers to sackcloth primarily with a view to mourning over judgment, though sometimes repentance is also in mind; 27 of about 42 Old Testament occurrences refer only to mourning, and an additional 13 refer to mourning together with repentance. In Matt. 11:21 and Luke 10:13, sackcloth ties in directly with repentant mourning. It seems to do so in the narrative context in Revelation as well. Through the use of the shepherding *"rod"* imagery, John describes his own work as that of harsh but correcting rebuke. The witnesses' work acts much like an extension of that figurative iron rod. Their prophetic testimony is by its very nature as much as invitation to belief as it is a condemnation of the opposing belief in the lordship of Rome. Their prophetic activity, then, like a shepherd's firmly applied staff, not only strikes a blow of judgment against reckless wandering (toward belief in and loyalty to the lordship of Rome) but also simultaneously provokes redirection.

- **4** John narrates the close connection between these two witnesses and Christ by describing them as standing before the Lord of the earth (cf. Zech. 4:14). In introducing them, he applies definite articles. These are the two olive trees and the two lampstands. He clearly expects familiarity from his readers as he builds from the narrative scenario of Zech. 4, particularly vv. 2-3 and 11-14. There, two anointed ones stand before the

Lord of the whole earth as two olive trees positioned at the left and right of a golden lampstand. If the lampstand represents the destroyed Solomonic temple (cf. Zech. 1:16), then the two olive trees represent the priestly (Joshua) and Davidic (Zerubbable) messianic hopefuls (cf. Zech. 3:8) who would guide the temple's postexilic reconstruction and, further, the apocalyptic restoration of the entire people. It is fascinating that God initiates this restoration by appointing an angel to measure and thus protect Jerusalem from hostile, satanic intent (Zech. 2-3), just as in Rev. 11:1-2 John measures and thereby protects.

John keeps the metaphors but mixes them. First, there is no need to identify the temple as a lampstand since no temple will exist (21:22). Second, he alternately envisions the anointed two as either olive trees or lampstands. Their functions are also different. They are no longer messianic figures who will usher in God's reign; the Lamb plays that role in the "*Apokalypsis*." They operate instead as exemplary witnesses who, like John, model the prophetic practice that John desperately exhorts from his church(es).

- **5** The work of these witnesses is so important that God will take extreme measures to ensure its execution. The use of fire as the witnesses' weapon is instructive. John uses fire as a metaphor for God's Spirit (4:5; cf. 2 Kgs. 1:10). Their weapon, in other words, is of God. More often, though, fire is described as a part of the heavenly armament that God deploys as a weapon of judgment (Rev. 1:14; 2:18; 3:18; 8:5-8; 9:17-18; 14:10, 18; 16:8; 18.8; 19:12, 20; 20:9-10, 14-15; 21:8; 2 Sam. 22:9; Ps.

97:3; Jer. 5:14; *4 Ezra* 13:25-38). Even when John associates fire with the dragon (13:13) or forces of evil (17:16), the connection is meant to showcase their desperate attempt to mimic God's power. At a climactic moment, fire comes down from heaven to destroy the satanic forces trying to overthrow God's people (20:9), just as here fire issues from the mouths of the two witnesses to defeat the same surreptitious agenda. It is no accident that the fire, like their testimony, comes from the orifice of speech. Their testimony is the ultimate weapon; it not only declares Christ's lordship but obliterates those who oppose it and, in so doing, establishes it (cf. 12:11). In this way, too, the witnesses, and through them the church, are like Christ. God's power operates as a testimony so forceful that is issues from Christ's mouth as a judging, obliterating sword (1:16; 2:16; 19:15, 21). Whether John uses the metaphor of sword or fire, his poetic appeal to the mouth and the testimony that issues from it to envision, establish, and protect the apocalyptic community suggests that he believes the witness (i.e., the church) are most in sync with the victorious and transformative power of God when they proclaim the lordship of Christ. The church can best protect itself from the persecutions inflicted against it not by hiding from or accommodating to the satanic forces that claim to control the world, but by directly engaging those forces with the opposing testimony that Jesus Christ is the Lord. The offense of that witness is the church's best defense.

In the second half of the verse, John affirms his position by redundantly declaring that anyone who wishes to harm the two witnesses before they conclude their objective must die. In this world of apocalyptic mortal combat, either God's forces (the witnesses, i.e., the church/the faith community of the Lamb) or Satan's forces (Rome) will win. Since there is no conceivable compromise, there can also be no peace. Because for these witnesses identity and work are synonymous, they must witness. The only way to stop them is to destroy them. To prevent that destruction from happening, the opposition must itself be destroyed.

- **6** The plagues connect the two witnesses with Moses and Elijah. The only nuance is that the powers of both Moses and Elijah are attributed to both the two witnesses equally, and not divided among them. They are identical prophetic twins. Notably, they also represent the very two prophetic figures who were expected to usher in the eschatological age. Early Christianity had to come to terms with the Jewish view that the eschatological times could not dawn until Moses and/or Elijah had returned, and did so in a variety of ways (Mark 9:2-13; Luke 1:15-17; 4:25-26; 7:11-17). By linking Moses and Elijah with the church through the metaphor of the two witnesses, John implies yet again that through its witness the church helps to usher in God's coming reign (cf. 12:11).

Like Elijah, who shut the sky for three years (1 Kgs. 17-18), the two witnesses have the power to bring drought for a particular period, in this case the time of their prophecy. Like Moses, they have the ability to turn water into blood and strike the earth with plague. John's description yields several key points. First, his description of their work as prophecy highlights yet again the fact that John holds witness and prophecy to be synonymous (cf. 11:7). A prophet is one who witnesses to the lordship of Jesus Christ. Second, the connection between prophecy and the phenomena of drought, blood, and plague is an explicit indication that the witness to Christ's lordship brings judgment upon those who testify to the lordship of Rome. Picking up on broader biblical allusions to drought (Deut. 11:16-17; Luke 4:25; Jas. 5:17), water transformed into blood (Exod. 7:17-25), and plague (1 Sam. 4:8), John narrates blood (Rev. 6:12; 8:7, 8; 16:3-4) and plague (9:18, 20; 15:1, 6, 8; 16:9, 21; 18:4, 8; 21:9; 22:18) as judgment imagery. Third, because the work of these two witnesses is a work of prophecy that follows and emulates John's own prophetic endeavors (11:1-2), one might reasonably understand the drought, blood, and plagues to be an extension of the shepherding rod of iron that intended both the disciplining and the redirection of the human flock. Indeed, biblical drought allusions also entertain a theme of repentance. Though the promise of drought at Deut. 11:16-17 is a judgment warning, it is also a threat whose ultimate goal is to turn the people back to God. Moreover, when the Epistle of James addresses drought, the climactic stress falls upon the theme of repentance (5:17, 19-20). So also, Exod. 7 contains the commonsense expectation that even Pharaoh himself, having seen the Nile bloodied, would have to concur with the testimony that God is the Lord.

Like Moses and Elijah, then, the two witnesses (i.e., the church) use their prophecy as a weapon (rod) that will simultaneously judge and redirect, even if the primary weighting is toward judgment.

- 7 Bad times are coming, but not until the two witnesses complete their work. Indeed, John's description of their prophecy as "μαρτυρία" (testimony/witness) is a hint that the bad times will ultimately be overturned. To be sure, "μαρτυρία" is inextricably linked with disaster. At 1:9, Christ is slaughtered (cf. 5:6) and John is exiled because of it. At 6:9, resurrected souls are slaughtered because of it. Though the murder of the two witnesses occurs after they finish their testimony, the causal link between that testimony and their murder is just as clear. This is the last time, however, that John uses witness in such a disquieting way. In its very next use "μαρτυρία" is a conquest tool (12:11), and 20:4 offers climactic affirmation. There, the same "μαρτυρία" that brought destruction also ensures a victorious reign with Christ. John's point is one of encouragement. Though witnessing may well bring immediate persecution, it will, as vv. 11-13 make clear, yield an ultimate, eschatological victory. The appeal, therefore, is to keep witnessing despite the temporary cost.

Even this short-term bestial conquest – as opposed to the bestial persecution that is ongoing even as he speaks – will not be allowed to occur until the work of witness is complete. John is narrating the interlude between the sixth and seventh trumpets. The apocalyptic end point has not yet arrived. Having done their victorious work, having helped to usher in God's victory (12:11), the witnesses will see the beast resurface just before the final victory. John describes this resurfacing as a bestial rising up (ἀναβαίνω) from the Abyss. The rising, completion, and fire imagery connect this verse with the apocalyptic combat imagery in chapter 20. There it is only after the victorious reign of God is finished that the dragon is given its due (20:7). At 20:9, John portrays the vindictive movement of the bestial, satanic force as a conquest-minded rising up (ἀναβαίνω). How are these forces stopped in chapter 20? Fire. A historical weapon blazing as an unrelenting testimony out of the mouth of the two witnesses in 11:5 transforms into the ultimate eschatological weapon when deployed from heaven in 20:9. The point is reaffirmed: what the witnesses (i.e., the church) do historically is mimicked and supported by God eschatologically. Ultimate victory, even during this premonition of current defeat, is assured.

The language of the Abyss taints the beast with an evil, draconian sensibility (see 9:1, 2, 11; 20:1, 3). At 17:8, John reaffirms this destructive rising (ἀναβαίνω), but immediately consoles his hearers and readers with his suspicion that any such rising will be short lived; the beast rises to its destruction. Just as helpful is the close identification between the dragon and the beast that John draws at 17:8. While he is clearly speaking about the beast, the language he uses – *"it was and is not and is to come"* – is the kind of language he reserves for God (1:4, 8). In his apocalyptic war of images, John typically pits God language against dragon language since, mythologically speaking at least, these are the two supernatural and therefore best-batched combatants. His use of imagery may seem more appropriate to the dragon, for his narration of the beast suggests a close identity between the two. There is also a similarity in mission: the beast suggests a close identity between the two. There is also a similarity in mission: the beast's work is authorized by the dragon (13:4). Like the dragon, the beast is consigned to and must arise from the Abyss (20:1, 3). For John's narrative purpose, then, the dragon and the beast are functionally synonymous. Thus, when at 20:7 John narrates yet another resurfacing as the escape of the dragon from the pit and the unleashing of its fury against the church, he is reimaging the rising of the beast in chapter 11.

Beast is an apocalyptic cipher for the historical Rome. Using the same vocabulary that is so important in 11:7, John declares in 13:7 that the beast who comes from across the sea (Rev. 13:7; Dan. 7:3) was allowed to make war against believers and conquer them (cf. Dan. 7:21). At Rev. 17:14 this same beast (note the ten horns: 13:1; 17:3, 7, 12, 16; seven heads: 13:1; 17:7, 9; and link to waters/sea: 13:1; 17:15) even has the audacity to make war directly against the Lamb. The linguistic correspondence is so close that it can hardly be unintentional. Rome, the city of seven hills (17:9) that comes from across the sea, becomes the historical symbol for the mythical Abyss as it makes war against – that is, persecutes – the believing Asia Minor churches for testifying to the lordship of Jesus Christ.

The *"war"* is Rome's reaction to and programming against the testimony to Christ's lordship that John exhorts from his churches. Rome demands worship of its lordship instead (20:4). With the military and police power of the imperial state behind it, bestial Rome will win the lordship campaign, at least in the short term (vv. 7-10; cf. Dan. 7:21).

One final note about the identity of the beast: Thought *"beast"* has not appeared before as a mythical figure in the Book of Revelation, John's use of the article (*"the beast"*) suggests that his readers are narratively familiar with it. At 13:1, however, he does not employ the article. The depiction in chapter 13 suggests that readers have not yet been introduced to the beast when, in fact, that introduction occurs already in 11:7. This apparent discrepancy is resolved when one understands how John has designed the actual visionary presentation. Chapters 12 and 13 are part of a narrative flashback that sets the scene and motivation for everything that occurs prior to the opening of the book. In other words, although chapters 12 and 13 follow chapter 11 in the narrative, they actually precede chapter 11 in the story that John's visions are relating. Chapter 13, then, is in a real sense the introduction of the beast. In chapter 11, using the metaphor of the two witnesses, John links the hostility of that beast to the witnessing of the church and explains why the beast's apparent success is in reality the prelude to God's ultimate victory. This is why the conflict between the two witnesses and the beast is envisioned as the moment immediately before the climactic blowing of the seventh and final trumpet.

- **8** Having been conquered and killed, the corpses of the two witnesses (i.e., the executed believers of the testifying church) lie in the street of the great city. It is strange that John literally speaks of a single corpse (πτῶμα) when he is referring to two dead witnesses. The confusion most likely results because the two witnesses act symbolically for the one church. It is the witnessing church's suffering and destruction that he really has in mind. Because John refers to the resting place of the corpse with a definite article, he probably believes that his hearers and readers knew precisely which street was *"the street"* in question. The ultimate scorn for the two witnesses can be inferred from the fact that no one came forward to bury them.[154]

Because John often refers to Rome as the great city (Rev. 16:19; 17:18; 18:10, 16, 18, 19, 21) and to Jerusalem as the beloved or holy city (11:2; 20:9; 21:2, 10, 14-16, 18-19, 21, 23; 22:14, 19), initially there is some question as to which *"great"* city he envisions. Here, the great city is Jerusalem, as John indicates when he identifies it as the city where the Lord of the two witnesses was crucified. The identification reinforces the relationship that John elsewhere establishes between the suffering of Christ and the suffering of believers by describing both their ordeals

---

[154] → Non-burial was an indignity in the biblical world (i.e., 1 Sam. 17:44, 46; 2 Kgs. 9:10; Ps. 79:1-5; Isa. 14:19-20; Jer. 8:1-2; 9:22; 16:4-6; 22:19; *Tob.* 2:3-8; *Pss. Sol.* 2.30-31; *Sib. Or.* 3.634-46; *Jub.* 23.23; *Josephus J.W.* 3.376-78, 380-84; 4.314-18; 5.33; *Philo, Joseph* 25).

as a slaughtering (5:6, 9, 12; 6:9; 13:8; 18:24). Now both the Lord and the church (i.e., the two witnesses) suffer and die in the same great city. Perhaps John's literary bridge was Ps. 79:2-3, which identifies Jerusalem as the city where the servants of God were killed and their corpses lay unburied on the streets. John's references to Sodom and Egypt are also instructive. Egypt maintained a traditional image as a place of resistance to God. Though the seer refers to Sodom only here, he probably has in mind Old Testament texts where a disobedient Jerusalem is mentioned in municipal relationship to that prototypically evil city (Isa. 1:9-10; Jer. 23:14; Ezek. 16:2, 46, 49).

John wishes to make the point that not even in the holy city (cf. 11:1-2) will someone stand up for those who have courageously borne witness that Christ is the Lord. This tragic turn of narrative events mirrors the historical concern John conveys in his letters to the seven churches. He worries that believers have so accommodated themselves to the styles and expectations of Greco-Roman life that they not only are afraid to witness, but even refuse to offer assistance or comfort to those who do.

- **9** Through the metaphor of three and a half days (cf. 11:2-3), John implies that the time of disgrace for the witnesses will be brief. He reinforces the intensity of the disgrace with his reminder that their corpses (this time, at least in the second half of the verse, he remembers that there are two witnesses) lie in the streets unburied. He then adds a subtle nuance. The believers in the city, at least some of them, apparently want to give the corpses a proper burial. The narration now clarifies that members of the people, tribes, tongues, and nations will not allow proper burial. The people, tribes, tongues, and nations are the very ones against whom John was directed to prophesy in the re-commissioning that ended chapter 10 (10:11) and opened chapter 11 (11:1-2). They are hostile to the work of prophetic witness. Some believers may want to assist either in the witnessing or in the care of those who do so, but fear of this opposition has paralyzed them.

- **10 – 11** John reconfirms the opposition as the inhabitants of the earth. This is a term he consistently applies to those who reject the testimony to Christ's lordship and persecute people who maintain it (6:10; 8:13; 11:10; 13:8, 12, 14; 17:2, 8). It is therefore used here as a synonym for the hostile people, tribes, tongues, and nations of v. 9.

    Restoration begins with resurrection. In this case, John does not want to rely upon a divine passive to imply God's control; he chooses an active verb instead *"entered"* to describe the entrance of God's spirit/breath of life into the dead witnesses to revive them. God's action has sanctioned their testimony even as it has rejuvenated them; God and Christ are indeed Lord.

    God and Christ control even the experience of death. For their followers, its duration will not be long. The two witnesses are down for only three and a half days before they are raised to an eternal eschatological relationship with God (v. 12; on three and a half as a number symbolic of transience, see 11:2-3; 12:6, 14; 13:5).

They were raised by a spirit of life that came from God. It is notable that John does not give "*spirit*" a definite article here. When he intends to speak of the Spirit(s) of God, he consistently employs the article (1:4; 2:7, 11, 17, 29; 3:1, 6, 13, 22; 4:5; 5:6; 14:13; 22:17). To be sure, there are prominent instances where John alludes to the Spirit of God without using the article (1:10; 4:2; 17:3; 21:10). In each of these cases, however, he speaks more about a human condition – being "*in the spirit*" – than about the divine person. It is likely that in 11:11, too, he is speaking less directly about the person of God's Spirit than about a particular quality, the empowering force of that Spirit. The language is metaphorical; it denotes the breath of God that would be very much like the breath that animates human life in the Genesis accounts (Gen. 1:30; 2:7; 6:17; 7:15, 22) and resurrects life in Ezekiel (Ezek. 37:5, 10). Oddly, the bestial forces also deploy a breath of life. At Rev. 13:15 the beast from the land breathes into the image of the beast from the sea so that it can come to life. John is suggesting that the Roman and local officials in Asia Minor (the beast from the land) breathe life into the worship of the imperial cult. In this way, the beast from the land mimics the power of God so as to animate those to whom it wishes to peddle its interests and proclaim its name.

Like the once-dry bones of Ezek. 37, the spirit-raised witnesses stand on their feet. "*Standing*" for John has theological implications. It is a metaphor for resistance. Though they were knocked down even to death, the witnesses remain defiant about the lordship of Christ.

"*Fear*" is the final important component of the verse. The fear refers back to the people, tribes, tongues, and nations (v. 9), who are then described as the inhabitants of the earth (v. 10), and who celebrate the deaths of the two witnesses for three and a half days. In Old Testament accounts fear falls upon the enemies of God's people when God moves to vindicate the people (Exod. 15:16; Ps. 105:38). This is the kind of fear that does not lead to faith but simply springs from acute alarm. In this case, the fear arises as a result of (1) the resurrection of the two witnesses, (2) the knowledge that their God is the agent of this resurrection and will avenge the death that made it necessary, and (3) realization that the defiant message of Christ's lordship was resurrected with them.

- **12** The fear generated in v. 11 is compounded when the enemies of God's people witness their elevation on "*the cloud*" into heaven. In the Book of Revelation, cloud conveyance is reserved for Christ (1:7), a mighty angel (10:1), and the Son of Man (14:14-16).[155] The presence of the definite article here indicates that this is the same cloud John saw draped around the mighty angel at 10:1. The mechanism that brought the angel down now carries the witnesses up. The visual corroborates

---

[155] → See also 2 Kgs. 2:11; Dan. 7:13; Matt. 24:30; 26:64; Mark 13:26; 14:62; Luke 21:27; 24:51; Acts 1:9; 1 Thess. 4:17.

John's claim of vindication. The loud sounds the tone of judgment. Cosmic justice is about to be enacted.

Prior to the commencement of judgment, the loud voice gives the two witnesses the same command (*"Come up here"*) that was given in the singular to John when he was invited to enter the heavenly throne room (4:1). In fact, the only two places where the verb "ἀναβαίνω" (Come up) is used in the imperative in the Book of Revelation are 4:1 and 11:12. In 4:1 it was apparently Christ's own voice that summoned John; it was identified as a voice like a trumpet (cf. 1:10-13). Christ invited John into God's eschatological presence. Is John implying that Christ also personally inviting the two witnesses, and through them, the faithful, witnessing church? To be sure. As for John, so for the church: while faithful witness to Christ's lordship will provoke hostility from bestial human powers, it will guarantee direct access to God. Indeed, Christ himself will call you up! That is motivation.

- **13** An implicit summons to repentance resurfaces in the final act of divine judgment against the great city and the inhabitants of the earth who populate it. When John uses the language of *"hour,"* he intends the imminent arrival of God's judgment (3:3, 10; 9:15; 14:7, 15; 18:10, 17, 19). Of particular note are 14:7 and 14:12, where a voice speaks in a loud voice, as one does also in 11:12, about the coming of God's judgment. In the three occurrences of the term in chapter 18, one hour is all the time necessary for the destruction of the great city of Babylon.

This particular moment of judgment, which anticipates the consummate moment of judgment that will come with the imminent blowing of the seventh trumpet (11:15-19), begins with an earthquakes signal both the presence of God and the reality of judgment, which often attends that presence. In making this connection between the quake and judgment, John follows in the theological footsteps of Ezekiel (38:19-23). It is especially interesting that John has crafted the scenario so that in both seals and trumpets episodes, the initial earthquakes at the penultimate stage of judgment (i.e., the sixth seal, 6:12; the sixth trumpet, 11:13) act as a premonition of the fuller slate of theophanic events that will occur with another earthquake at the seventh and ultimate stage of judgment (8:5; 11:19). Richard is right to point out that in seeing the metaphorical connection to judgment, we should also not miss the social and political connotations that bind earthquake and witness language together: "*As in all apocalyptic literature, the cosmic earthquake is mythical and symbolic in nature. It represents the disturbance and historical subversion brought about by the testimony of the martyrs and prophets.... The martyrs bring about true social, political, spiritual, and ecclesiological earthquakes at the heart of empires*" (Richard 92).

This penultimate stage of judgment also includes the destruction of a tenth of the city of Jerusalem. This physical decimation results in the killing of seven thousand people. The number "*seven*" surely figures rhetorically as a symbol of completion. The repetition of the verb "ἀποκτείνω" (to kill) is intentional. The beast has killed the two witnesses, who represent the whole church (v. 7). Now a complementary number of names souls who live in loyalty to that beast and its declaration of lordship will be killed in judgment for that earlier homicide.

John seems more interest, though, in those who are not killed. They respond in fear. John has already established that fear need not have anything to do with repentance. In v. 11, the human associates of the beast are terrified when they witness the resurrection of the two witnesses. But this fear has no positive value; it is merely terror. Something happens, however, in the intervening moments. The beast's associates observe both the elevation of the two witnesses on the cloud into heaven (v. 12) and the theophany and destruction that follow (v. 13a). It is not coincidental that fear is accompanied this time by glorification not of the beast but of the God who resides in heaven. There is every indication that for John this glorification amounts to repentance.

No doubt John is aware that there are times in the tradition when fear of God's presence can produce something more positive than awe, such as repentance or faith (cf. Gen. 15:12). Indeed, the formulation *"give glory to God"* has a traditional association with repentance and conversion. With obvious literary links to chapter 11, Rev. 14:6-7 narrates an angel flying through midheaven with the obvious intent of eliciting repentance. Here, at the critical judgment hour, the same opportunity for repentance opens up for the members of every nation and tribe and language and people.

John has hinted at the possibility of repentance throughout chapter 11 (see the comments on 11:1, 3, 6). More broadly, he has declared all along, in the critical ethical chapters containing the letters to the seven churches (2:1-3:22) and at other key narrative moments, that God expects repentance not only from the faithful (2:5; 3:3, 19), but also from notable recalcitrants like Jezebel (2:21; see the comment on 9:20-21; cf. 14:6-7; 16:9, 11). Unfortunately, sometimes it takes an earthquake, massive destruction, and unimaginable death to bring it about. When repentance does occur, however, it brings fulfillment to the prophetic charge of 10:11. Prophetic witness brings not only judgment but also repentance. That is the good news.

Revelation 11:14 → Transition

NIV	TT
¹⁴ The second woe has passed; the third woe is coming soon.	¹⁴ The second woe has happened; behold, the third woe is coming **soon**[156].

This verse functions as a transitional verse. It is like Rev. 8:1, after completing the narratives of 6th trumpet, and two intermissions, v.14 introduces the coming of the third woe.

- **14** Revelation 8:13 initiated the woe sequence. Verse 14 is a transitional verse, completing the narration of the second woe and inaugurating the story line of the third. The first woe was associated with the blowing of the fifth trumpet (9:1-12). The second woe is associated with the blowing of the sixth trumpet (9:13-21). Though it is never actually narrated, the third woe appears to accompany the blowing the seventh and final trumpet (11:15-19). The language of woe highlights the emphasis on judgment that has been significant throughout the trumpet narration.

---

[156] ταχύς → It means *"quick,"* *"without delay,"* and *"soon."*

Revelation 11:15~19 → The Seventh Trumpet

NIV	TT

¹⁵ The seventh angel sounded his trumpet, and there were loud voices in heaven, which said:
 	
"The kingdom of the world has become
   the kingdom of our Lord and of his Messiah,
   and he will reign for ever and ever."
 	
¹⁶ And the twenty-four elders, who were seated on their thrones before God, fell on their faces and worshiped God, ¹⁷ saying:
 	
"We give thanks to you, Lord God Almighty,
   the One who is and who was,
because you have taken
	¹⁵ And the seventh angel blew his trumpet; there were loud voices from heaven, saying:
	
	"The kingdom of the world has become the kingdom of our Lord and of his Messiah, and he will rule forever and ever."
	
	¹⁶ And the twenty-four elders who are seated before God on their thrones fell on their faces and worshiped God, ¹⁷ saying:
	
	"We **give you thanks**[157], Lord God **Almighty**[158], who are and who were, **because**[159] you have taken great power and begun to **rule**[160].

---

[157] εὐχαριστέω → It means *"give thanks," "render thanks,"* or *"return thanks."*
[158] παντοκράτωρ → It means *"the Almighty," "All Powerful," "Omnipotent One,"* and *"Only of God."*
[159] ὅτι → The term means *"that" "so that," "because,"* and *"since."*
[160] βασιλεύω → It means *"be king," "to rule," "to rule over," "rule of something,"* and *"bocomo king."*

your great power
    and have begun to reign.
¹⁸ The nations were angry,
    and your wrath has come.
The time has come for
judging the dead,
    and for rewarding your
servants the prophets
and your people who revere
your name,
    both great and small—
and for destroying those
who destroy the earth."
 	
¹⁹ Then God's temple in
heaven was opened, and
within his temple was seen
the ark of his covenant.
And there came flashes of
lightning, rumblings, peals
of thunder, an earthquake
and a severe hailstorm.
	¹⁸ The nations raged, but
	your **wrath**[161] has come, and
	the time for the dead to be
	judged, and to give the
	reward to your servants, the
	prophets, and to the saints
	and those who fear your
	name, the small and the
	great, and to destroy those
	who destroy the earth."
	
	¹⁹ And the temple of God
	which is in heaven was
	opened and the ark of his
	covenant was seen in his
	temple, and there were
	flashes of lightning and
	rumblings and peals of
	thunder and an earthquake
	and great hail.

It appears that although v. 14 announces the coming of the third woe, the woe itself never appears. Verses 15-19 instead contain for the most part an antiphonal hymn of praise. For this reason, some commentators argue that the third woe should actually be found elsewhere in the Book of Revelation, perhaps in chapters 15 and 16, which recount the catastrophes associated with the pouring out of the seven bowls. Because I see the bowls as a recapitulation of the seals and trumpets in another guise, I maintain that chapters 15 and 16 reprise rather than

---

[161] ὀργή → It means "*anger*," "*wrath*," "*indignation*," "*Judgment*," and "*punishment*."

conclude the judgment themes contained in the trumpet scenes. Chapters 12 and 13 follow chapter 11 in the narrative sequence, yet they actually represent flashbacks, recounting circumstances that took place before the events narrated in the seven trumpets. Therefore, they also cannot be the narration of the seventh trumpet and final woe. The final woe is located instead right here, in vv. 15-19. The celebration contained in the antiphonal hymn of praise is merely the flip side of the judgment. Since vv. 15-19 represent the final movement in God's eschatological act of judgment (as did the narration of the seventh seal), praise is an appropriate response.

- **15** When the seventh angel sounds his trumpet, a chorus of *"loud voices"* breaks out in heaven. If the presence of a single loud voice was an omen of judgment (see 7:2; 11:12), the increased volume from multiple loud voices must quantitatively heighten the perceived impact of the imminent reckoning.

  If it has not been clear before, John clarifies it now: the seventh trumpet blast inaugurates the reign of God and Christ. Connected as it is with the loud voices and the language of woe, it is a rule built upon the premise and expectation of judgment/justice. The lordship to which the witnesses testified has become reality. The prophecy of Dan. 7:14 that all people, nations, and languages would serve God comes to fruition now, as the remnant of people, tribes, tongues, and nations, having glorified God and repented (Rev. 11:13), will endure forever (cf. Ps. 10:16; Dan. 2:44). If the scenario that plays itself out in chapter 11 is to be taken seriously, even those who were among the ones in chapter 11 is to be taken seriously, even those who were among the ones mocking the two witnesses (i.e., the church) have an opportunity to participate in this rule.

- **16 - 17** The antiphonal response to the declaration by the loud voices that the reign of God has arrived comes from the twenty-four elders on their twenty-four thrones (see 4:4). Repeating an earlier act of bow/worship, they fall on their knees and worship in response to the good news they hear (cf. 7:11). Falling to one's knees is a formulaic posture of worship for both John (1:17; 4:10; 19:10; 22:8) and the elders (5:8, 14; 19:4).

John identifies the hymn as one of thanksgiving (v. 17). Here, for the only time in his work, he deploys the verb "εὐχαριστέω" (to give thanks).[162] The elders declare the reason for their praise with a litany of key theological titles that have been used before in anticipation of God's rule but now signal its triumph. The Lord God is first of all "ὁ παντοκράτωρ" *"the Almighty"* (cf. LXX: 2 Sam. 7:8; Amos 3:13; 4:13). In the two occurrences prior to this one (Rev. 1:8; 4:8), *"Almighty"* was also packaged with the descriptive title *"the one who is and who was and who is to come."* In 4:8, the packaging occurs, as it does here, in a hymnic context. In both the previous and the ensuing uses of the title, John offers a reason why it is an appropriate designation for God. Status as almighty is connected

---

[162] → John uses the noun form "εὐχαριστία" (thanks) at 4:9 and 7:12.

with God's role as creator (4:8), ruler (1:8; 19:6; 21:22), and judge (15:3; 16:7, 14; 19:15).

The Almighty One is not bound by time but transcends it; this is highlighted through the designation *"the one who is and who was"* (here, *"[you] who are and who were"*). Heretofore, the title has always had a threefold formulation, *"the one who is and who was and who is to coming."* John even applies a similar formulation to the beast; it portrays the beast's pitiful, failing attempt to mimic God's transcendence of time (17:8). Though negative, even that threefold formulation has a concluding future promotion: *"about to rise."* John drops the future sensibility here and in subsequent citations that relate to God (16:5), however, because it is no longer applicable. According to the praise song of 11:15, the God who was (recognized as ruler of all) now is (recognized as Lord of all). The revelation has been realized. John, therefore, appropriately changes the titular designation. In place of the phrase *"who is to come/who is coming,"* he adds an entire clause, *"because you have taken great power and begun to rule."* In other hymns, too, John uses comparable clauses to explain why praise for God is appropriate (4:11; 5:9; 12:10). The perfect-tense verb formulation, *"you have taken,"* signals both the accomplishment and the expected long-term endurance of the powerful reign God has accomplished. The aorist verb for rule operates with the controlling perfect *"you have taken"* in an ingressive grammatical sense (*"have begun to reign"*) that agrees with the narrative assessment of v. 15: the rule is under way, but it is only just under way. It has just begun. In this sense, 11:17 has close affinity with 19:6. In that hymn, too, the worship song, employing a similar "ὅτι" (because) clause, declares that the Almighty has begun to rule and is therefore worthy of praise.

- **18** The twenty-four elders are the only ones to respond positively to the news of God's inaugurated reign. The nations also respond, not with praise but with rage. The allusion to Ps. 99:1 (98:1 LXX) could hardly be clearer. In the psalm, using an aorist formulation of "βασιλεύω" (to rule) similar to the one used in Rev. 11:17, the writer declares that the people rage in retaliation. There is a similar pattern in Exod. 15:14; although the verb *"rule"* is not used, the context indicates that God's rule, through the defeat of Pharaoh's army, elicits rage among the nations.

God's response to the nations' rage is divine wrath. Every time John uses the term *"wrath"* in his work, it harbors this thematic sense of judgment (6:16-17; 14:10; 16:19; 19:15). John sees it as an appropriate instance of *lex talionis*: the punishment fits the crime.

The connection between God's wrath and judgment is made evident in the first of the three stanzas that follow the declaration that the wrath has come. Each of them is controlled by an infinitive that operates from the primary verb "ἦλθεν" (came). When God's wrath came, it spawned a new season: a time to be judged, to give reward, and to destroy. The judgment of the dead refers to those who have died the first, physical, mortal death, but who await a ruling regarding the second death (cf. Dan. 12:2). All human beings are mortal and therefore all will experience the first death. Even the two witnesses experienced it (Rev. 11:7). While that death may be punishing, it is ultimately not a judgment. The judgment refers to those who have lived in such isolation from God and the expectations God has for the living that they will be consigned to the second death, which will wipe away any possibility for eschatological relationship with God (cf. 2:11; 20:6, 12-14; 21:8).

The flip side of the judgment is life – not long, physical, mortal life, but eschatological life lived in relationship with God. This *"second"* life is the proper reward for the servants, the prophets, who have faithfully testified to the lordship of God and Christ. The synonymy between prophets and witnesses (see the comments on 11:3, 6-7, 10) suggests that John has in mind the two witnesses who were emblematic of the believing church. It is for them that judgment time is the time of eschatological relationship with God.

- **19** There is one more antiphonal response: God's. Using a divine passive construction, John indicates that God opened the temple sanctuary. In contrast to the earthly sanctuary mentioned earlier in the chapter (vv. 1-2), John with a clarifying attributive clause specifies that this is the sanctuary located in heaven. At 15:5, when he again narrates the opening of the heavenly temple, John sees seven angels with seven bowls filled with the wrath of God. When the heavenly temple opens, one thinks not of invitation but judgment.

Again, there is a flip side of judgment. In the second key movement of the verse, John sees the lost ark of the covenant. The mentioning of the ark confirms that John's visual object is the temple sanctuary, and in this case, even more specifically, the most sacred part of the sanctuary. According to 1 Kings, the ark was remanded to the holy of holies on Solomon's orders (1 Kgs. 8:1, 6; Heb. 9:1-40). According to *2 Macc.* 2:4-8, however, the ark was led out of the temple by Jeremiah and hidden. A likely possibility is that the ark was destroyed or taken as a spoil of war by the Babylonians when they captured Jerusalem and the temple in 587B.C.E. Though absent from the Herodian earthly sanctuary at its destruction in 70 C.E., therefore, its mythical counterpart apparently remained in place in the parallel heavenly universe. Traditionally, this wooden chest or box, overlaid with gold, housed the tablets of the Decalogue. Additionally, it served as a representation of both God's throne and God's presence. John's sighting of it at the moment of the inauguration of God's reign suggests that the promise of the ark is now to be realized: God's presence will reside in the midst of God's people (cf. Rev. 21:22). In other words, the ark is a metaphor for eschatological relationship with God: salvation.

The final movement of the verse chronicles the unleashing of a series of theophanies. The theophany package climaxes the theme of judgment that has been on prominent display throughout the chapter (see 4:5; 8:5; 10:3; 16:18).

12:1 – 14:20 Visionary Flashback

Why does Rome claim a lordship that belongs exclusively to God? Why cannot Rome recognize the true lordship of Jesus Christ? Why does Rome with such unmitigated violence resist those who witness to Christ's lordship? Why are the witnesses not protected by God? What set of circumstances has brought history to this point of apocalyptic conflict? As the attention of John's hearers and readers flickers between the perspectives of the seals and the trumpets, before he allows his narrative to flash over to the bowls, he pauses so he can answer those critical questions. He inserts the visions of 12:1 to 14:20. John takes the time to do what he should perhaps have done at the very beginning: provide the narrative rationale for the movement of his visionary plot.

Revelation 12:1~17 → Flashback: The Dragon's War

NIV	TT
12 ¹ A great sign appeared in heaven: a woman clothed with the sun, with the moon under her feet and a crown of twelve stars on her head. ² She was pregnant and cried out in pain as she was about to give birth. ³ Then another sign appeared in heaven: an enormous red dragon with seven heads and ten horns and seven crowns on its heads. ⁴ Its tail swept a third of the stars out of the sky and flung them to the earth. The dragon stood in front of the woman who was about to give birth, so that it might devour her child the moment he was born. ⁵ She gave birth to a son, a male child, who	**12** ¹ Then a great sign appeared in heaven: a **woman**¹⁶³ clothed with the sun; the moon was under her feet, and a crown of twelve stars was on her head. ² She was pregnant, and **cried out**¹⁶⁴ in labor, in the **agony**¹⁶⁵ of **childbirth**¹⁶⁶. ³ Then another sign appeared in heaven: behold, a great red dragon with seven heads and ten horns, and seven diadems on its heads. ⁴ Its tail swept down a third of the stars of heaven and threw them to the earth. Then the dragon stood before the woman who was about to give birth, so that it might devour her child when she gave birth. ⁵ And she bore a son, a male child, who **will**¹⁶⁷ **shepherd**¹⁶⁸ all the

---

¹⁶³ γυνή → It means *"woman," "wife," "a woman of any age, whether a virgin, or married, or a widow,"* or *"any adult female."*
¹⁶⁴ κράζω → It means *"cry out," "scream," "call,"* and *"call out."*
¹⁶⁵ ὠδίνω → It means *"suffer birth pangs,"* or *"bear amid throes."*
¹⁶⁶ τίκτω → It means *"bear," "give birth,"* or *"symbolically bring forth."*
¹⁶⁷ μέλλω → It means *"be about to," "be on the point of," "be destined," "must," "intend," "future," "to come,"* and *"delay."*

"will rule all the nations with an iron scepter." And her child was snatched up to God and to his throne. ⁶ The woman fled into the wilderness to a place prepared for her by God, where she might be taken care of for 1,260 days.

⁷ Then war broke out in heaven. Michael and his angels fought against the dragon, and the dragon and his angels fought back. ⁸ But he was not strong enough, and they lost their place in heaven. ⁹ The great dragon was hurled down— that ancient serpent called the devil, or Satan, who leads the whole world

nations with an **iron**[169] **rod**[170]. But her child **was snatched away**[171] to God and to God's throne. ⁶ And the woman fled into the **wilderness**[172], where she has a place **prepared**[173] by God, so that there she might be nourished for 1,260 days.

⁷ And war broke out in heaven. **Michael**[174] and his angels had to fight with the dragon. The dragon and his angels fought back, ⁸ but they were defeated, and there was no longer a place for them in heaven. ⁹ Then the great dragon was thrown down; the ancient serpent, who is called devil and Satan, who **deceives**[175] the whole world,

---

[168] ποιμαίνω → It means "*herd*," "*tend*," "*lead to pasture*," "*tend sheep*," "*guide*," "*rule*," "*care for*," and "*look after*."

[169] σιδηρᾷ → It means "*made of iron*," and "*siderite*" (a mineral popularly known as lodestone).

[170] ῥάβδος → It means "*rod*," "*staff*," and "*stick*."

[171] ἡρπάσθη → It means "*was stolen*," "*was carried off*," "*was dragged away*," "*was snatched away*," and "*was caught up*." It is a divine passive.

[172] ἔρημος → It means "*abandoned*," "*empty*," "*desolate*," "*lonely*," "*deserted*," "*desert*," and "*wilderness*." The verb appears only three times in the entire Book of Revelation (12:6, 14; 17:3).

[173] ἡτοιμασμένον → It means "*was put in readiness*," "*was kept in readiness*," "*was prepared*," and "*was made preparation*."

[174] Μιχαὴλ → The name means "*Who is like God?*" Michael is an archangel who is supposed to be the guardian angel of the Israelites.

[175] πλανάω → It means "*lead astray*," "*cause to wander*," "*mislead*," and "*deceive*."

astray. He was hurled to the earth, and his angels with him.

¹⁰ Then I heard a loud voice in heaven say:

"Now have come the salvation and the power and the kingdom of our God, and the authority of his Messiah. For the accuser of our brothers and sisters, who accuses them before our God day and night, has been hurled down. ¹¹ They triumphed over him by the blood of the Lamb and by the word of their testimony; they did not love their lives so much as to shrink from death. ¹² Therefore rejoice, you heavens and you who dwell in them! But woe to the earth and the sea, because the devil has gone down to you! He is filled with fury, because he knows that his time is short."

¹³ When the dragon saw that he had been hurled to the earth, he pursued the woman who had given

was thrown down to the earth, and his angels were thrown down with it.

¹⁰ Then I heard a loud voice in heaven, saying: "Now have come the salvation and the power and the kingdom of our God, and the authority of God's Messiah, because the accuser of our brothers and sisters was thrown down, who accuse, them night and day before our God. ¹¹ And they conquered him through the blood of the Lamb and through the word of their testimony, because they did not love their life even to the point of death. ¹² Therefore rejoice, you heavens and those who dwell in them. But woe to the earth and the sea, because the devil has come down to you with great wrath, for he knows that he has little time."

¹³ And when the dragon saw that he had been thrown down to the earth, he pursued the woman who had given birth to the male child. ¹⁴ But the woman was given the two wings of the great eagle, so

birth to the male child. ¹⁴ The woman was given the two wings of a great eagle, so that she might fly to the place prepared for her in the wilderness, where she would be taken care of for a time, times and half a time, out of the serpent's reach. ¹⁵ Then from his mouth the serpent spewed water like a river, to overtake the woman and sweep her away with the torrent. ¹⁶ But the earth helped the woman by opening its mouth and swallowing the river that the dragon had spewed out of his mouth. ¹⁷ Then the dragon was enraged at the woman and went off to wage war against the rest of her offspring—those who keep God's commands and hold fast their testimony about Jesus.	that she could fly to her place in the wilderness where she is being nourished for a time, and times, and half a time away from the presence of the serpent. ¹⁵ Then the serpent spewed water like a river from its mouth behind the woman, so that he might sweep her away with a flood. ¹⁶ But the earth helped the woman; the earth opened its mouth and devoured the river that the dragon spewed from his mouth. ¹⁷ And the dragon was angry with the woman and went off to make war with the rest of her **seed**[176], those who keep the commandments of God and **hold to**[177] the witness of Jesus.

Within chapter 12, John also tells the story in a non-sequential manner so that his hearers and readers can recognize the chapter's meaning from its structure. Five

---

[176] σπέρμα → It means "*seed*," "*survivors*," "*descendants*," "*children*," "*posterity*," and "*nature*."
[177] τηρέω → It means "*keep watch over*," "*guard*," "*keep*," "*hold*," "*reserve*," "*observe*," "*pay attention to*," and "*preserve*."

primary plot movements form two outer frames around a core central message. (1) Verses 1-6 introduce a celestial woman and a dragon as competing signs in the sky and then detail both the dragon's attempt to destroy the progeny of the woman and God's rescue of the woman and her son. This confrontation in heaven is balanced at the end of the chapter by a confrontation on earth. (2) Verses 13-17 represent the conflict between the woman and the dragon, the woman's rescue, and the dragon's futile attempt to destroy her progeny. (3) The first inner frame (vv. 7-9) details the result of the war: the dragon's defeat in heaven. (4) A matching inner frame (v. 12) presents the result of the war in terms of heavenly joy and earthly woe. Inside the frames is (5) a liturgical hymn of praise (vv. 10-11) that clarifies exactly how the dragon was brought down. The force of the chapter lies here, with the twin weapons of the Lamb's blood and the believer's witness. John's narration encourages thanksgiving for the blood and continuation of the witness.

- **1** Revelation 12:1-14:20 is held together by the bracketing phrase "σημεῖον ἐν τῷ οὐρανῳ" (sign/portent in heaven). In his only three uses of this terminology (12:1, 3;15:1), John introduces the interlude of chapters 12-14 and then closes it off with the presentation of the seven bowls. He reinforces his structural intentions by linking the signs together with the adjective "ἄλλο" (another). The second (12:3) and third (15:1) signs are distinctly related to the first (12:1). The second sign introduces the antagonist who will oppose the protagonist showcased in the first sign. The third sign signals the end of their narrated conflict.

In 12:1, 3, as in 11:19, John conveys his vision with an awkward aorist passive construction "ὤφθη" (was seen). Since the visions are his alone, he clearly means to say, "*I saw*." The ark of the covenant in the heavenly sanctuary and now the appearances of the cosmic woman and the dragon in the sky are so significant, though, that they and not he must be highlighted. He speaks this way because he wants attention to be focused on those objects, not on himself.

Who is the cosmic woman? Some connect her with figures in Israel's or the church's past or future: Eve, the mother whose seed would bruise the head of the dragon/serpent (Gen. 3:1-6); Mary; the mother of Jesus; or the heavenly Jerusalem as bride of the Lamb (19:7-8; 21:9-10). Others suppose a pagan or astrological connection: a queen of heaven like the Egyptian Isis,[178] or the constellation Virgo. Still others hypothesize a corporate representation of God's people: Israel, who escapes the dragon/Pharaoh into the wilderness on wings of eagles (Exod. 19:4; Ps. 74:12-15); or Zion, the mother of the persecuted people of God (Isa. 66:7-9; *4 Ezra* 13:32-38). It is unlikely that John has in mind an individual woman, historical or otherwise. Mary, the mother of Jesus, did not give birth to the entire people of God as this woman will (Rev. 12:17). Eve gives

---

[178] → Isis ("Ισισ") is a goddess from the polytheistic pantheon of Egypt. She was first worshipped in Ancient Egyptian religion, and later her worship spread throughout the Roman Empire and the greater Greco-Roman world. (Not the "*Islamic State of Iraq and Syria*")

birth to all humans, not specifically the believing community. Though the *"sign"* language clearly intends to guide hearers and readers to look to the heavens in the way that they seek out constellations, John cannot have had Virgo exclusively in mind since she is the sixth sign of the zodiac and this woman (12:1) is connected integrally with the number *"twelve."* It is even more unlikely that John, who cannot tolerate having people eat food sacrificed to foreign gods (chapters 2-3), would compose the progenitor of the believing people from the sole image of a pagan deity. It is much more likely that he has combined a great many themes from historical and mythical woman/mother images in Israel's and the church's past, present, and future and fashioned them thematically into a representation of the church's corporate existence.

We can gain a better sense of what John intends by his *"woman"* representation when we look at the way he puts it to narrative use. He deploys the word (γυνή) *"woman"* nineteen times. He is preoccupied with several primary roles for women in first-century society: wife (19:7), mother (12:4, 13, 17), and sexual threat (Jezebel's false teachings conveyed through symbolism of fornication, 2:20; sexual intimacy that defiles holy warriors, 14:4; harlotry or Rome, 17:3, 4, 6-7, 9, 18). A more comprehensive study reveals that John has oriented his use of "γυνή" around competing images. Most notable, though the images do not come into play directly in chapter 12, is the thematic opposition between the wife and the harlot. This woman is as directly associated with her children (12:17) as the harlot later is with Rome (17:18). The most intriguing opposition is the one between the competing signs of the woman in 12:1 and the dragon in v. 3. To be sure, war breaks out in heaven between Michael and the dragon (v. 7), but that later conflict is based upon the enmity that already exists between the dragon and the woman. God's intentions, as they operate through the characterization of the woman, are already being opposed by the dragon, according to vv. 1, 3. If it is not an outright hot war, it is certainly a hypertense cold one.

The important question is why John does not see God fighting directly. Instead, Michael (v. 7) and subsequently the Lamb and *"they"* (v. 11) are pressed into service. John's point is a simple one: for all of the dragon's great strength, it is never, even narratively, on a par with God. God does not need to engage the battle directly because God's representatives are sufficient for the task; they handle the eschatological *"light work."* Though the woman is not God, she is, like Michael and the Lamb (symbolized in chapter 12 as the woman's son), a representation of God's intention in and for humankind. The Lamb represents God's saving power, which can defeat the dragon by bringing the people into eschatological relationship with God. Michael represents God's capacity directly to thwart the dragon's ability to deceive and unmercifully accuse God's people (vv. 7-10). The woman, on the other hand, represents God's procreative capability. The dragon desires to eliminate God's capacity to birth a son who will shepherd all the other children who will follow him (v. 17).

The woman's attire reveals much about her identity. She is, first of all, clothed with the sun. Clothing in the Book of Revelation is more than mere outer wear; its type and color illustrate important qualities or character traits of the person wearing it. Sackcloth indicates mourning and judgment. A purple and scarlet dress symbolizes Rome's harlotry and opposition to God (17:4; 18:16). Christ's bloody robe indicates the slaughter he and his followers have endured for their witness (19:13). Yet John then declares that the followers' robes are white (19:14); this is precisely because they have washed them in the Lamb's blood (7:14). The white robe takes on a quality of particular significance; it signals a successfully established eschatological relationship with God. The mighty angel of 10:1 is robed in a white cloud. White robes are worn by those who witness victoriously to the lordship of Christ (3:5, 18; 4:4; 7:9, 13). The bride's (i.e., the church's) intimate relationship with the Lamb is indicated partially through her white attire (19:18). Even more white would be the brightness of the sun. Though John uses *"sun"* most often in reference to the physical star around which the earth orbits (even if he did not himself understand it in this way), in two other places besides 12:1 he connects the quality of the sun's color or shining with a character who populates his prophecy. At 1:16, the Son of Man has a face that shines like the sun. The face of the mighty angel clothed in a cloud at 10:1 shines similarly. In both those cases, their sunshine indicates that they are representatives of God. According to the psalmist, it is God who is apparently so adorned (Ps. 104:1-2). This woman's relationship with God and her identity as a representative for God are highlighted by the fact that she, too, is cloaked with the sun. All of her shines like the sun! Clearly, she must represent something extremely important about how God expresses God's self in the life of God's people. I have already argued and will maintain subsequently that she represents God's procreative ability to birth a people of faith.

The "*moon under her feet*" signals elevated status; as a cosmic being she stands far above the human followers who trace their faith existence through her. But it is the "στέφανος" (crown) of stars on her head that best complements the sun-cloak that robes her. Like the white robe, the crown is an accoutrement awarded the believer who conquers by witnessing faithfully to the lordship of Christ (2:10-11; 3:11-12). The twenty-four heavenly elders whose perpetual worship is highlighted in the hymnic sections are outfitted with crowns (4:4, 10), as is the one like the Son of Man himself (14:14). Interestingly, the Son of Man also holds a symbolically complete 7 stars in his hand (1:16, 20; 2:1; 3:1). This woman's crown possesses stars in another symbolically complete number: 12. Though the number of the stars no doubt operates from the cosmological understanding that there were 12 stars of the zodiac, John integrates its use into his narrative as a number representing completeness in terms of rapport with God (7:5-8; 21:12, 14, 16, 21;

22:2). Beale argues that the number represents both the 12 tribes (7:4-8) and the 12 apostles, who formed the leadership of the nascent church. This interpretation gains strength from the fact that earlier in his prophecy John equates stars with angels, who in turn represent churches (1:16, 20). The 12 stars, then, represent the completeness of the church that finds its foundation and indeed its genesis in this woman.

- **2** The woman is so intimately involved with God that she turns out to be pregnant with God's Lamb/Messiah (v. 5). Reverberations from Hebrew prophecy emphasize the point. Isaiah 7:14 LXX speaks of the "σημεῖον" (sign) of a pregnant young woman who will give birth to a son (Rev. 12:5). The close linguistic parallels indicate John's dependence on that Isaianic prophecy as he introduces the celestial woman and her eschatological role. Interestingly, at Isa. 26:15 God is seen as the one who propagates the believing community. That procreation is metaphorically portrayed two verses later as the people giving birth during a very difficult labor. In describing the hard labor of the celestial woman in Rev. 12:2, John picks up on the same Greek vocabulary used in Isa. 26:17 LXX: "ὠδίνω" (to suffer birth pangs); "τίκτω" (to give birth); and "κράζω" (to cry out). In Isa. 27 God's forces fight victoriously against a great red satanic serpent. At Isa. 66:7 LXX, the prophet declares, again using the same vocabulary that John stresses in Rev. 12:2, that Zion gives birth first to a messianic son and then to a multitude of children (also *4 Ezra* 9:38-10:57). The prophet Micah writing in childbirth but being promised, as is the woman in Rev. 12:2-6, rescue by God (Micah LXX: 4:9-10; 5:3; cf. Rev. 12:6, 14).

These Old Testament texts and Rev. 12 emphasize the same key themes. Faced with hostile opposition, God's ability to create a people of faith, symbolized in the agonizing labor process of the celestial woman/Zion, will prevail. The woman in extreme labor pain, then, is both the Israelite and apostolic (the 12 stars of v. 1) people of faith (who in turn represent God's procreative capability), who groan before their persecutors (cf. 6:9-11) as they await the birth of the Messiah, who will shepherd them toward a place in God's victorious reign.

- **3 The Parallelism** John intends between the woman and the dragon is drawn through his introduction of the dragon as another heavenly sign. Using the same aorist-passive construction *"was seen,"* John demonstrates that he regards this sign as a natural countersign to the woman. The woman represents the power of God to birth and build up the believing community; the dragon represents the power to destroy that community at any point from its inception onward.

In his first use of the term "δράκων" (dragon), John introduces the character without a definite article. Every subsequent reference is to *"the"* dragon (see 12:4, 7, 9, 13, 16, 17; 13:2, 4; 16:13; 20:2; in 13:11 the term *"dragon"* is used adverbially *"was speaking like a dragon.")*". The dragon is a metaphor for historical powers, like Egypt, that assailed God's people.[179] I have already noted in the commentary on 12:2 that Isaiah follows up his account of God's people being birthed through an agonizing labor (Isa. 26:15, 17) with an account of God slaying the sea dragon Leviathan (Isa. 27:1). Ezekiel 29:3, using the same description of a great dragon, identifies the prosecuting force explicitly with Egypt. Other Old Testament texts reinforce God's successful rescue of the people from Egypt with the metaphor of a dragon defeated in the sea (Ps. 74:13-14; Ezek. 32:2-3). Rome, for John, has become the new Egypt and therefore the contemporary incarnation of the dragon. Rome will pursue the people just as Pharaoh once did. The ultimate promise of chapter 12 is that God will defeat the dragon's Roman manifestation as surely as God defeat its Egyptian one. The new exodus will be from Rome.

John's description of the dragon reinforces its hostile nature. It is red, a color that symbolizes destruction. In its only other appearance, it stains the horse whose representation is slaughter (6:4). The dragon is the shade of slaughter. That is a powerful realization in a narrative context where the protagonist is a slaughtered (i.e., executed) Lamb.

In a display of fierce power, the dragon also sports seven heads and ten horns. Upon each head is a diadem. This description connects the dragon immediately with

---

[179] → Dragon is another Old Testament word for the evil sea monster that symbolizes evil kingdoms that oppress Israel. Jeremiah had compared Nebuchadnezzar to a dragon which had gulped Jerusalem down whole (Jer. 51); Ezekiel had pictured Pharaoh as "*the great dragon*" lying in the midst of his streams Ezek. 29.

the beast who will soon emerge from the sea (13:1-10; 17:3, 7, 9, 12, 16), who flaunts seven heads and ten horns but places its ten diadems on its horns. Because John will identify the beast from the sea as a metaphor for Rome in chapter 13, the dragon is best understood as the satanic force behind the imperial power. This fits with John's portrayal of the dragon as a metaphor for the evil that has animated historical powers like Egypt.

Rome is not the only character whose attributes resemble those of the dragon. The Lamb was also outfitted with horns (5:6). Horns represent power. Daniel's fourth beast, too, had ten horns (Dan. 7:7). Daniel went on to describe its horns as powerful and disruptive earthly kingdoms (7:20, 24). The dragon's pretense to historical power is also represented by the diadems that adorn each of its heads and symbolize a claim of kingship that opposes any lordship claims of the Lamb. By similarly outfitting these principal combatants, John compares and contrasts their relative strengths. Quantitatively, the dragon has more horns (10). Qualitatively, since the Lamb has the perfectly complete number of seven horns, it has more power. John knows, though, that those who look with eyes of logic will fear allying themselves with the woman and her son (the Lamb) against the dragon and its minion from the sea. On first view the Lamb, because he has fewer horns and is in fact a lamb, does not look the part of one who could successfully engage a great red dragon with 7 heads, 7 diadems, and 10 horns. Faith that sees beyond the evidence of sight is required.

- **4** Part of the celestial woman's magnificence is the crown of twelve stars that she wears on her head. The dragon is unimpressed. It has the power to sweep a third of the stars from the sky with a flick of its tail. The arrogant, powerful beast of Dan. 8:10 had the same capability.

  Having described the dragon, John sets out to convey its hostile intent. It takes up a position before the celestial woman so that it can devour her child as soon as it is born. One would think that since the woman is in a vulnerable position, the dragon's logical move would be to eliminate her. By terminating the woman, the dragon will terminate her even more dangerous baby. But the dragon waits. Is this because it cannot murder the woman since she, too, is a mythical figure, a metaphor for God's procreative capability that gives birth to a tangible, historical thing that can be slaughtered?
- **5** Fulfilling an Isaianic vision (Isa. 7:14; 66:7), the celestial woman gives birth to a messianic son. The son's identity and role, as well as his relationship to the woman's other children (Rev. 12:17), can be determined through consideration of the verse's key vocabulary. "ποιμαίνω" (shepherd), "ῥάβδος" (rod), and "σιδηρᾷ" (made of iron) operate as a narrative package in 2:27; 12:5; 19:15. The son will shepherd not just believers but also all the nations with an iron rod. The implication is that he will institute a rule of discipline that will turn people in the proper direction, toward faith in the lordship of God and God's Christ.

The imagery refers back to the language in Ps. 2:9 about the leadership of the Messiah. Revelation 19:15 clarifies that the one who shepherds with an iron rod is none other than Jesus Christ. There the connection is unmistakable with the rider on the white horse. At 7:17, John's only independent use of "ποιμαίνω" (tend sheep), he specifically identifies the Lamb as the one who shepherds toward springs of living water.

At 2:27 this shepherding ability also relates to believers who conquer, that is to say, who successfully witness to and for the lordship of Christ. Their testimony appears to be the rod of discipline that corrects and turns. It is not surprising that the image of shepherding is used of both the Lamb/Son and those who witness to him. John has already linked them by a similar language of witness and slaughter. What the Lamb does, the people are called to do as well.

The verb "μέλλω" (is about to) suggests that the leadership of the son will soon take place. No doubt that leadership is part of the apocalyptic moment when God's reign occurs. But John's hearers and readers know that the seventh trumpet has already sounded (11:15-19). The reign has already begun; the presence of the verb "μέλλω" here, then, is either wrong or further evidence that chapter 12 is a flashback to what occurs before the opening of the seals and the blowing of the trumpets.

Having described the child, John also indicates why he would be a threat to the dragon. He would shepherd the people toward a belief in God's power and rule and therefore away from allegiance to the dragon. Because the conjunction "καὶ" (and, but, also) that introduces the second half of the verse details God's action against the dragon's intent, it should be read adversatively. The dragon is poised to devour the child, but the child is snatched up to God and God's throne. The aorist-passive construction "ἡρπάσθη" (he was snatched by force) is another of John's divine passives that should be read with God as the active agent. God snatches the child to God's self and God's throne. This is precisely the location where the Lamb/Son is found in Rev. 5:6-7, 13; 7:9-10, 17; 22:1. Once again, via flashback, chapter 12 provides the background and rationale for earlier character placement. It is only after we read this passage that we know how the Son/Lamb arraived at the throne in chapter 5. We are also in a better position to understand the connection between his location at the throne and his shepherding of the people (7:17).

The violence implied in the verb "*to snatch by force*" gives John's hearers and readers a clue to the seer's point of reference. History and myth merge in John's effort to clarify the human eschatological situation. One might wonder why John presents the child's birth and then moves right to his ascension to the throne of God without even mentioning his death. Such a query misses the power of myth. The birth is the death. The child is begotten on the cross. The cross is also the mechanism of his leadership, his shepherding of the people. The dragon seeks to destroy him. And like the two witnesses of chapter 11, he is killed. He is crucified. And yet, as was the case for the two witnesses, this death turns out to be the road through which he finds his way to God. Death becomes the means to the child's glory and the people's future. Do not be afraid of dying for the witness of God, therefore. This is the mythic exhortation. In dying, you rise to a place of power with God (6:9-11). That is the historical truth the myth wants its hearers and readers to comprehend.

- **6** Although John will later clarify that it is God who facilitates the woman's escape from the dragon after the birth and ascension of her son (12:14), here John only notes her flight into the wilderness. John uses "ἔρημος" (wilderness) only three times (12:6, 14; 17:3). At 17:3, he describes it as a refuge where he is carried away in the spirit to view the destruction of Babylon. John is working from traditional images. Uppermost in his mind no doubt is the account of Israel's exodus from Egypt into the wilderness, where the people were nurtured and disciplined by God (Exod. 16:32; Deut. 2:7, 15-16; 29:5; 32:10; Josh. 24:7; Neh. 9:19, 21; Pss. 78:15, 19; 136:16; Isa. 40:3; Jer. 31:2; Ezek. 34:25; Hos. 13:5). There are also thematic connections. Moses flees to the wilderness to escape Pharaoh (Exod. 2:15). At 1 Kgs. 17:1-7, Elijah is nurtured and protected by God in what clearly appears to be a wilderness setting. Matthew records Joseph's flight with Jesus to escape the threat of Herod the Great (Matt. 2:13-15; cf. Hos. 11:1). God has once again prepared the wilderness as a place of refuge and nurture for the people, who are symbolized here by the woman through whom they are given existence. Notice how the symbols are allowed to shift in reference in the slippery, dreamlike world of myth. The woman who has up to this point represented the genesis of the people now takes on the identity of the people. In this new guise she is apparently vulnerable to the dragon in a way that she was not before.

The duration of the woman's stay in the wilderness is obviously symbolic. The 1,260 days s the same temporary period of time that marked the outer temple's trampling and immediately afterward the duration of the two witnesses' traumatic preaching tour. It is also the same period that the dragon was allowed earthly authority (Rev. 13:5). The time of the woman's hiding corresponds, therefore, to the time when the dragon will seek out and persecute the people of God (12:17) because of their witness (cf. Dan. 7:25; 12:7). Since the figure represents exactly half of seven years, John in each case means to suggest that it is a temporary period. The time of victory and vindication, by contrast, will be eternal.

The tie-in to the end of chapter 10 and the work of the two witnesses in chapter 11 can be seen through John's odd appeal to the third-person plural presentation of the verb "*nurture*." Who is the "*they*" who will care for the woman? One would have expected a singular reference to God, who is obviously the active agent behind the passive formulation "*a place was prepared.*" "*They*" most likely recalls the "*they*" of 10:11, the plural representation of God's singular intent (see the comment on 10:11). The key is that God intends to shelter the woman – that is, the church – from the devastation the dragon is plotting.

- 7 When war breaks out, it begins in heaven between the dragon and those who represent God. The comments on 12:1 show what John has clarified through his positioning of the dragon against the woman, rather than against God. The same conclusion reached there applies here: John does not put God and the dragon in opposition; instead, the dragon's character is balanced against Michael. Michael represents God's combat capability in the same way that the woman represents God's procreative potential. God far surpasses the dragon and therefore need not engage him directly. God's subordinates can do the job. And so, in this case, God delegates the task of battling the dragon to the archangel Michael.

Michael is another mythical figure. In Revelation his name occurs only here. In his one other appearance in the New Testament (Jude 9), he disputes with Satan over the body of Moses. Most likely, John is working more closely from the presentation of Michael in the book of Daniel, where he is a princely defender of the faithful people (Dan. 10:13, 21). (Also *1 Enoch* 54:6, Michael helps cast the fallen angels into the fire on judgment day.) He fulfills that protective role here by battling the dragon and its angels.

The language of war (πόλεμος) clarifies what is happening. John deploys the term in chapters 11-13 three key times. Once the two witnesses have finished their testimony, John explains that the beast from the Abyss will make war with them and kill them (11:7).

The description of the beast suggests that this is the same enemy who will be described in chapter 13 as Rome, the beast from the sea. Indeed, John reaffirms that this beast is allowed to make war on the saints and conquer them (13:7). At 12:17 John summarizes these events as the earthly war against the church that develops because the heavenly war is going go badly for the dragon and his angelic minions. The war is the (Roman) persecution that the people must endure on account of their witness to the lordship of Christ. If the dragon cannot rule in heaven, he is determined to destroy God's people on earth.

A more comprehensive look at the war language, along with the presentation of the woman and the successful snatching of her son in 12:1-6, suggests a parallel mythological/historical timeline. At stage one, the celestial woman is prepared to give birth. She represents God's procreative power to deliver a faith community through a firstborn son who will then shepherd the woman's other children, his figurative brothers and sisters. It is no doubt at this mythological point that John would place the historical ministry of Jesus. Stage two finds the dragon plotting to stop this communal hope by destroying the son who is so crucial to it. Stage three brings the snatching of the son, which is contemporaneous with the heavenly war that erupts between Michael and the dragon. The dragon makes the first move with the cross. It is this historical attack on Jesus' life that triggers Michael's mythical response. This scenario helps explain why the messianic son is not fighting for God in heaven along with Michael. his fight is the historical one. His charge is to engage the dragon on earth, and he does so on the cross (12:11). At the very moment that Jesus is dying historically on the cross, Michael and his angels are fighting mythically with the dragon in heaven. The snatching of Jesus to the throne – that is, the resurrection – is the historical cipher for the event of Michael's expelling the dragon from heaven. As Jesus rises into the mythical realm of heaven, the dragon is thrown down into the historical one. Stage four finds the dragon now fuming in history and taking his anger out on the people of God. Here is where John positions the 1,260 days or 42 months of persecution, the transitory time when the bestial forces of dragon (described in Rev. 13) will persecute God's people because of their witness to the lordship of Christ. In the language of myth, John describes it as the time of the woman's nurture in the wilderness (12:16), which happens historically at the same times as the dragon's bestial pursuit of her other, earthbound children (12:17). It is the time in and for which John sees himself now writing.

- **8** With the dragon's defeat comes the recognition that there is no longer a place for him and his supporting angels in heaven. Just as there was a place of nurtured prepared (ἡτοιμασμένον) for God's procreative potential (12:6), so has one of punishment been prepared (ἡτοιμασμένον) for the dragon and its bestial supporters (20:10-11).
- **9** The verse 9 highlights two points about the dragon, reaffirming that the dragon has been cast out of heaven

and detailing the dragon's identity. John deploys the aorist passive of "βάλλω" (to throw or cast) no less than three times in this single verse. The passive indicates God's agency. The repetition ensures that the point is heard: God, through representation both angelic (Michael, v. 7) and historical (the son and the witnesses, v. 11), is ultimately responsible for removing the dragon from his heavenly perch.

Before celebrating his defeat, John wants to make sure that his hearers and readers know clearly who the dragon is. It is the ancient serpent. John used the definite article because he assumes his hearers and readers will recognize this figure from their traditions. The ancient serpent was the deceiver of the entire world. His deception of Adam and Eve in the Garden of Eden led to the separation of the entire world from its intended relationship with God (Gen. 3). As punishment for deception, God promised perpetual enmity between the seed (σπέρμα) of the woman and the seed (σπέρμα) of the serpent. This explains why, when John chooses to describe the hostility between the dragon and the woman's children (12:17), he surprisingly refers to her children with the same term (σπέρμα) that is primarily used to designate a male's offspring. The battle between the church and the dragon is the eschatological result of the primordial conflict initiated by the serpent's deception.

Both narratively and historically, John's image of the serpent as deceiver connects the dragon to the bestial forces of Rome and those who accommodate themselves to it[180]. In Asia Minor serpents were often used in the pagan cults of Ascelpius, Dionysus, Sabazius, Cybele, and Zeus to symbolize divinity. These associations cannot be easily dismissed as irrelevant, for in the image of the snake John appears to have selected precisely the most pervasive image of pagan divinity in the area of his churches and he cannot have been unaware of the fact. The serpent symbol of pagan divinity therefore adds significant local dimensions to the Dragon. John will develop this local flavor when he aligns the serpent with the beast from the land in chapter 13.

Traditionally, the ancient serpent had been associated with the devil, who is also called Satan. John now makes the connection explicit. Satan is the ultimate deceiver of humankind. Just as he has operated in Israel's past (e.g., 1 Chr. 21:1), so now he operates deceptively in the life of the Asia Minor churches.

- **10** John introduces this hymn by declaring that he heard a loud, heavenly voice. The *"loud voice"* consistently introduces the theme of judgment (5:2; 7:2; 8:13; 10:3; 11:12-13, 15; 14:7, 9, 15, 18; 16:1, 17; 19:1, 17), which certainly fits the preceding narration of Satan being exiled from heaven.

The reason for praise is twofold: Satan has been conquered, and the reign of God has come. The reign, as the antiphonal hymn of 11:15-18 has already

---

[180] → Subjects of the verb "πλανάω" (lead astray, mislead, deceive) in Revelation include Jezebel (2:20), the devil (12:9; 20:3, 8, 10), the beast from the land (13:14), also called the false prophet (19:20), and Rome (18:23).

affirmed is "ἄρτι" (now). Each new stanza of this new hymn adds clarifying detail about the reality of that reign. Salvation (eschatological relationship with God) and power (realized as the defeat of the dragon) act as synonyms for the reign of God. Those synonyms are themselves placed in parallel relationship to the authority of the Christ, the messianic son whose eschatological role has been narrated in 12:1-6 and will be further clarified in v. 11. That authority, that lordship, is now in effect. It is for this reason that John so strenuously exhorts the believers in his letters to the seven churches to witness courageously to that lordship (chapters 2-3).

If chapter 12 is indeed a flashback that sets up the scenario of everything that happens from chapter 1 onward, John has offered an interesting salvific proposition. The Book of Revelation is preoccupied with the idea that persecution will occur as a direct result of believers' testimony to the lordship of Christ. John himself, a prisoner on Patmos, is living out this reality. *"Now"* is a time when believers will be persecuted for witnessing to the lordship (i.e., the sovereign authority) of Christ. But *"now"* is also the time of God's reign and the time of Christ's earthly lordship (i.e., authority). Apparently, then, the time of persecution overlaps with the time of God's reign. In the only other place where John uses the adverb "ἄρτι" (now), that possibility seems certain (14:13). Surely the dead who die in the Lord are blessed from now on because *"now"* is the turning point where the reign of

God pivots into human history. John's hearers and readers are apparently living at that critical juncture. Perhaps this is because in heaven, as the narration of the dragon's expulsion from heaven shows (vv. 7-9), the victory is already won. John reaffirms that point here. It is precisely because Satan has been cast down that the salvation/power/reign/authority of Christ can now be celebrated. What remains is a mopping up of the huge pocket of satanic resistance that the dragon has now initiated on earth (v. 17). Persecution is part of that pocket. Soon, however, that pocket of resistance, too, will be overthrown. The present ("*now*") accomplishment of God's reign in the mythic imagination (i.e., in the world as only faith can see it) is the guarantee of its future historical realization. It is this guarantee that 12:10 now celebrates.

In reaffirming the cause for celebration, John adds a piece of the dragon's character portrait that he omitted from the description in v. 9. The dragon is also the one who accuses our brothers and sisters day and night before God. The term "*accuser*" is a literal translation of the Hebrew – (שָׂטָן) Satan. Clearly, this is a pre-expulsion role of Satan. In heaven, Satan had the divinely approved appointment of divine prosecutor who brought charges against human beings before God (Job 1:9-11; 2:4-5; Zech. 3:1). In both the New Testament and rabbinic writings, Satan retained this judicial role and was often opposed by Michael, who would act as counsel for the human defense (*Jub.* 1.20; 17.15-16; 18.9-12; 48.15-18; *1 En.* 40:7; *T. Levi* 5.6; *T. Dan.* 6.1-6; 1 Pet. 5:8; Jude 9; 1 Tim. 3:6; *b. Ber.* 46a; *b.*

Yom. 20a). Caird points out that as long as there are human sinners to accuse, Satan's presence in heaven is necessary and must be tolerated, for God recognizes the need for justice. The problem with Satan as accuser is evidently similar to the problem John perceived with the church in Ephesus (Rev. 2:1-11). In his narrow, one-sided devotion to the law (he accuses day and night), he misunderstands and misrepresents God. Although the mercy of God is as real as God's justice, the mercy is not only ignored but also fought against. The prosecutor therefore finds himself at odds with God to the point of war (v. 7). It is for this reason that the perpetual struggle between Satan and Michael is as much a courtroom war as it is a battlefield one.

Satan's prosecutor ambitions targets those who might be described as God's faithful people. John calls them *"our brothers and sisters."* This terminology associates the defendants with John, who describes himself as a brother at 1:9, and with the other *"brothers and sisters"* who testify to the lordship of Christ (19:19; 22:9). They are all persecuted because of their witness (6:9). In making his case, John deploys both *"brothers and sisters"* and the personal pronoun *"them"* as objects of the prosecutor's accusations. Narratively speaking, the two terms operate as synonyms. While this observation at first appears meaningless, in 12:11 it takes on monumental force.

- **11** The *"brothers and sisters"* of v. 10 resurface immediately as referents for the personal pronoun *"they,"* which comprises the primary subject for the verb "νικάω" (conquer). John could make his point with a simple third-person construction of the verb; however, he choose to emphasize the subject by redundantly deploying the third-person plural pronoun. John pleaded with the hearers and readers in each of his seven churches to testify to the lordship of Christ and thereby conquer the satanic delusion that Rome is lord of human history (2:7, 11, 17, 26; 3:5, 12, 21). Eschatological conquest, he promised, would come through historical witness. In the "*now*" of God's reign, the aorist construction of "νικάω" (they conquered) indicates that the promise has been fulfilled. The only other place where John deploys an aorist, non-subjunctive use of "νικάω" is 5:5. That verse describes the completed conquest of the Lamb, which 12:5, drawing from the language of myth, explains as having taken place on the cross. Verse 11 adds the new dimension that this conquest has happened in large part because "*they*," the perpetually accused and persecuted brothers and sisters (v. 10), have conquered.

John expresses the instrumental nature of the conquest through his use of the preposition "διὰ" (because of) followed by the actual conquering instruments in the accusative case. "*They*" conquer the dragon with two primary weapons: the blood of the Lamb and the word of their witness to the lordship of the Standing Slaughtered Lamb.

With the Lamb's blood, they use the dragon's greatest weapon against him, just as Christ himself once did. In Rev. 5, John describes how the lion of Judah conquers by becoming a slaughtered lamb (cf. 5:5, 6, 9).

Here in Rev. 12 John recounts the conquest mythologically through the symbolism of the child being "*snatched*" to the heavenly throne. The dragon's attempt to kill the child – crucifixion – instead leads to inaugurating the child's reign (resurrection). The child/Lamb conquers by turning the dragon's ultimate weapon, death, against him. It is a mythological picture of nonviolent resistance and revolution inspired by the historical narration of the cross. The Lamb has drawn up a new combat strategy and has used it to surprise and defeat, that is, Standing Slaughtered Lamb. John's "*brothers and sisters*" have followed up by metaphorically throwing that blood victory in the dragon's face. Their testimony about the blood conquest restages and reenergizes the conquest every time they witness to it. It is for this reason that John exhorts them so strenuously to witness in his seven letters (chapters 2-3).

Will they pay a heavy price for "*throwing the blood of the Lamb*" in the face of the dragon? Indeed, they will. They will suffer persecution and perhaps even death. John has already reminded his hearers and readers, though, that their blood mingles with and is transformed by the blood of the Lamb (7:13-14). The faithful brothers and sisters (i.e., "*they*" in heaven), dressed in the white garments of victory, earned their distinction precisely because they paid that heavy price. Through them, too, God used the dragon's ultimate weapon against it; God used the death it imposed to give them the eschatological life with God, the salvation, they had always sought.

John no doubt hopes that this claim and vision of past victory will inspire more contemporary witness. That is why he stresses the testimony of the past witnesses and puts their effort on a narrative par with the blood of Christ as a conquest tool. They wielded both the blood and their own testimony about the transformative, revolutionary power of that blood to establish Christ's lordship in heaven and earth. The expectation is that his contemporary hearers and readers will do the same, even with the specter of death looming as a draconian response. In such a context, after all, death leads not to separation from God but to eschatological relationship with God. God defeats the dragon by using death to bring life. John makes the point regarding Christ at 12:5. He makes the point regarding past believers here at the end of v. 11 (*"they did not love their life even in the face of death"*). To put it simply, John tells his hearers and readers that their past brothers and sisters defeated the dragon by testifying to the conquering blood of Christ, because he wants them to go out and courageously offer the same testimony. They have the power and the means, if fear of dying does not get in the way, to defeat the dragon and thereby participate in the inauguration of God's reign. This is the striking news that 12:11 communicates. No wonder, then, that their colleagues are in heaven waiting for them to finish the witness they started (6:9-11).

The repetition of "καὶ" (and), then, does not so much add new content as it extends what has already been stated. The witness is not different from the blood, and the disregard for their own lives is not new to the blood and the witness. John uses the three different clauses to ratchet up his expectation for the single act of contemporary witnessing. One might therefore more accurately translate what he has said in the following manner: *"They conquered Satan through the blood of the Lamb, which is experienced through the word of their witness, which is only expressed if one cares more about proclaiming that witness than about life itself."*

- **12** John has narrated the results of the heavenly war (vv. 7-9). He returns to that task here. This time, however, he uses hymnic language. He makes three quick points. First, heaven should rejoice because there the dragon has been defeated and removed (cf. 18:20). That act deserves praise befitting God's people when God moves victoriously on their behalf (cf. Deut. 32:43; Ps. 96:11; Isa. 44:23; 49:13). Second, heaven's joy is earth's lament. John introduces the catastrophic turn of events with a succinct utterance : *"woe."* Satan is loose on earth. The chaos he can no longer wreak in heaven, he executes here. Third, Satan is furious for the simple reason that his prosecutorial time on earth, too, is limited (i.e., 42 months; 1,260 days; 3½ year; see 11:2, 9; 12:6, 14).

- **13** As far as narrative plotting is concerned, v. 13 takes up where v. 9 left off. John interrupts the sequence with his vision of the heavenly hymnic celebration. According to v. 9, the devil and his angels were thrown to the earth. Verse 13 describes the devil's reaction to this unwelcome turn of events. In his earlier fixation on the child, he had not tried to take out the woman (12:4);

but now that the son is gone, he becomes preoccupied with her elimination.

It is at this point in the slippery, dreamlike world of myth that the woman's identity morphs. In John's earlier telling of combat between her and the dragon, she represented God's procreative ability to bring a believing community to life. In that guise, her natural habitat was heaven. Now, following the hymnic recognition that those who witness to Christ's lordship are under satanic duress (v. 11), John locates her on earth and re-visions her as the church that gives birth to the people of God. She is the same woman who gave birth to the "*male child*" of v. 5, which means that she simultaneously represents both mythical (divine procreative ability) and historical (church) realities.[181]

- **14** John has already told his hearers and readers that the woman fled to a wilderness place of nourishment prepared by God, where she stayed for 1,260 days (12:6). Now he tells them again. This time, though, he describes the way in which her flight was facilitated. God took her up as if on the wings of an eagle and carried her away from the dragon into the prepared wilderness place for a time, two times, and a half (i.e., 1,260 days, or three and a half years).

John appeals to tradition to make his case for successful sanctuary. In the Old Testament, flight on eagles' wings was a well-regarded image for the secreting away of the faithful under God's care (Exod.

---

[181] → The fact that "*male child*" is introduced with the article here but without one in v. 5 indicates that John is referring to the same male child he introduced in v. 5.

19:4; Isa. 40:31; Ezek. 17:3, 7). The length of the stay alludes to Dan. 7:25 and 12:7.
- **15** Just as the primary weapon of the Christ/Lamb is the sword of his mouth (1:16; 2:12, 16; 19:15, 21), so the dragon uses his mouth to initiate his powerful assault. Given that Christ's sword is most likely the word of his testimony to his own lordship, one might reasonably conclude that the dragon's mouth-weapon is the word he uses to deceive people (12:9; cf. 2:14, 20) into believing in its own lordship and the lordship of its minions like Rome and its Asia Minor vassals (Rev. 13). These two opposing words are the swords that the Lamb and the serpent wield against each other in mythical and indeed historical (witness) combat. No doubt John's hearers and readers would also recognize that the dragon, by using water to attempt destruction of God's people, would be trying to undo the order established by God at the creation.[182] There God tamed the sea (Gen. 1:2-10; Pss. 74:13; 77:16). The image of the sea glassed over in heaven, and ultimately no more, is a testimony to God's present and future ability to thwart the chaos it represents (Rev. 4:6; 15:2; 21:1). The dragon thus attempts here to re-establish that mythical chaos through the historical guise of deception, which John depicts as water spewing murderously from his mouth.
- **16** All of creation is apparently caught up in the conflict that has erupted between God and Satan (cf. Rom. 8:23). All of creation is bound to choose sides. Earth makes

---

[182] In the Noah story, it is God who uses water destructively (Gen. 7).

its choice and comes to the defense of the woman, opening to swallow that which would destroy God's plans for God's people, just as it had done in the past (Exod. 15:12; Num. 16:30; Deut. 11:6; Ps. 106:17). If the woman is indeed the church, John's message is that, even in this hostile historical context, God will provide refuge.

- **17** The dragon is no doubt angry with the woman for several narrative reasons. In the mythic drama, she represents God's ability to produce a messianic son who will inaugurate and shepherd God's people in the ways of God's, not the dragon's, lordship. In the historical arena, the woman represents God's ability to produce a community of believers who follow the leadership of God's son. Realistically, the dragon cannot destroy her because God has enlisted even creation to protect her.

Because he cannot destroy her, the dragon goes off to make war on the rest of her offspring, the siblings of the messianic son – that is, the church, the same entity symbolized by the two witnesses in chapter 11. John had already noted that the beast that comes up from the Abyss makes war on them and therefore on the church (11:7). In chapter 13, John will characterize the beast as the prime minion of the dragon. Apparently, then, it is through the beast that the dragon executes his attack against the church. Even though the woman, as church, will be protected, those who populate the church may well be killed (11:7). The dragon can destroy individual believers, but since he cannot get to the woman, it has no hope of destroying the church itself.

John makes this unusual claim in his narration of the two witnesses who are killed and yet survive. He makes it anew here by showing the woman's other children engaged in mortal hostilities with the dragon while the woman's future remains assured.

The individual believers at risk are those who keep the commandments of God and bear the witness of Jesus Christ. The last "καὶ" (and) of 12:17 is epexegetical; the second clause completes the thought of the first. Since for John the commandment of God is that believers should testify to the lordship of Christ, he means to say that the dragon will make war with those who keep the commandment of God, which is to testify to the lordship of Christ.

The second half of the statement identifies the believers as witnesses to the lordship of Christ. It is precisely because of their witness to the word of God, which is the lordship of Christ, that the dragon makes war against them. The first half of the statement is about exhortation. When John uses the verb "τηρέω" ("*Keep*," "*obey*," "*hold onto*" 1:3; 2:26; 3:3, 8, 10; 14:12; 16:15; 22:7, 9), he has primarily an ethical intent. He is encouraging his hearers and readers to hold to the word, that is, the commandments of God, which have been taught. Because word and witness are functionally synonymous for him (1:2, 9; 6:9-11; 20:4), he is demanding that his followers keep the testimony that Christ has revealed to them. According to 2:26-27, those who keep to this way of witnessing will conquer and thereby find themselves tasked with the same role as that of the messianic son, the shepherding of the people with an iron rod (12:5). In other words, those who keep witnessing will, like Christ himself, be leaders of God's people, even if they may also, like Christ, suffer persecution because of that leadership. They can be assured, though, that like Christ, they too will conquer. Even though they may be killed (11:7), they too will receive eschatological relationship with God: salvation.

> **Excursus 14: The Woman Clothed with the Sun**
> This mother of the Messiah is an image of the ancient goddess *"clothed with the sun, with the moon under her feet, and on her head a crown of twelve stars"* (12:1). She has been interpreted as many things: the image of Israel, or Mary, of Ishtar, of Inanna, of Isis, and more recently of Our Lady of Guadalupe (a merger of Mary with the Aztec goddess Coatlaxopeuh). The diversity of this goddess images fits easily into a variety of culture contexts as a symbol of power. In the context of John, or the Book of Revelation, the Woman as a personification of the faith community/the church/God's procreative power to produce Messiah and believing communities would be fitting.

Revelation 12:18~13:10 → Flashback: The Beast from the Sea

NIV	TT
13 ^{1} The dragon stood on the shore of the sea. And I saw a beast coming out of the sea. It had ten horns and seven heads, with ten crowns on its horns, and on each head a blasphemous name. ^{2} The beast I saw resembled a leopard, but had feet like those of a bear and a mouth like that of a lion. The dragon gave the beast his power and his throne and great authority. ^{3} One of the heads of the beast seemed to have had a fatal wound, but the fatal wound had been healed. The whole world was filled with wonder and followed the beast. ^{4} People worshiped the dragon because he had given authority to the beast, and they also worshiped the	^{18} Then the dragon stood on the sand of the sea.^{183} **13** ^{1} And I saw **a beast** ^{184}rising up from the **sea**^{185},^{186} with ten horns and seven heads, and on its horns were ten diadems and on its heads were blasphemous names. ^{2} The beast that I saw was like a leopard, and its feet were like a bear's, and its mouth was like a lion's mouth. And the dragon gave it his power and his throne and great authority. ^{3} And one of his heads was slaughtered, but its mortal wound was healed. And the whole earth marveled and followed behind the beast. ^{4} They worshiped the dragon because he gave

---

^{183} → In Greek, this verse is 12:18, not 13:1.

^{184} θηρίον → It means "*a beast*," "*a monster*," and "*an wild animal.*"

^{185} θάλασσα → It means "*sea.*"

^{186} **A Beast rising up from the sea** → In the background is the myth of the sea monster, Leviathan in Old Testament and Jewish tradition (Job. 3:8; 4:1, Isa. 27:1), who often played a role in Jewish apocalyptic documents.

beast and asked, "Who is like the beast? Who can wage war against it?"

⁵ The beast was given a mouth to utter proud words and blasphemies and to exercise its authority for forty-two months. ⁶ It opened its mouth to blaspheme God, and to slander his name and his dwelling place and those who live in heaven. ⁷ It was given power to wage war against God's holy people and to conquer them. And it was given authority over every tribe, people, language and nation. ⁸ All inhabitants of the earth will worship the beast—all whose names have not been written in the Lamb's book of life, the Lamb who was slain from the creation of the world.

⁹ Whoever has ears, let them hear. ¹⁰ "If anyone is to go into captivity, into captivity

authority to the beast, and they worshiped the beast, saying: "Who is like the beast, and who is able to fight against it?" ⁵ The beast **was given**[187] a mouth speaking haughty and blasphemous things, and it **was given**[188] to exercise authority for forty-two months. ⁶ It opened its mouth to speak blasphemies against God, to blaspheme God's name and God's **dwelling**[189], that is, those who dwell in heaven. ⁷ And it was allowed to make war against the saints and conquer them, and it was given authority over every tribe and people and tongue and nation. ⁸ And all the inhabitants of the earth will worship it, everyone whose name was not from the foundation of the world written in the Book of Life of the Slaughtered Lamb.

⁹ Let anyone who has an ear

---

[187] ἐδόθη → It means "*it was given*," "*it was put*," and "*it was appointed*."

[188] ἐδόθη → It means "*it was given*," "*it was put*," and "*it was appointed*." (same term as above)

[189] σκηνή → It means "*tent*," "*booth*," "*The Tent of Testimony*," "*Tabernacle*," and "*dwelling*."

they will go. If anyone is to be killed with the sword, with the sword they will be killed." This calls for patient endurance and faithfulness on the part of God's people.	listen. ¹⁰ If you are destined for captivity, into captivity you will go; if you are destined to be killed by the sword, by the sword you will be killed. Here is the endurance and the **faith**[190] of the saints.

Unable to destroy the church, the dragon sets his sights on the individuals who comprise the church. To engage them, he summons the services of two historical minions. The two beasts are reminiscent of the legends of the primeval sea monster Leviathan and the primeval Behemoth, who were separated from each other by God on the fifth day of creation.[191] According to legend, on the last day, at the arrival of the Messiah, they will be killed. Their carcasses will become the meat of an eschatological feast.

- **18** The visionary narrative of Rev. 13 actually begins here. When the dragon stands on the seashore, it is not looking toward land with its back to the sea, as though it is trying to scope out the hiding places of the woman's remaining offspring. It is looking instead for reinforcement. To that end, its back to the land, it searches the sea, awaiting the appearance of two entities that will rise to its aid. Evil finds a way, or a partner, to reinvigorate itself.

---

[190] πίστις → It means *"faith," "trust," "commitment," "faithfulness," "loyalty," "conviction,"* and *"pledge."*
[191] → Gen. 1:21; Isa. 27:1; Job 3:8; 40-41; Pss. 74:14; 104:25-26; *4 Ezra* 6:47-52; *1 Enoch* 60:7-11, 24; *2 Bar.* 29:3-4.

- **1** The seer Daniel claims sight of a churning sea that spits up four devastating apocalyptic beasts (Dan. 7:2-3). He sense that the ultimate strength of the fourth and most fearsome of the set resides in its ten horns (Dan. 7:7), which he ten interprets as ten kings (Dan. 7:24).

  John catches sight of something eerily similar. His first words, *"and I saw,"* immediately link this new apparition to the revelation of the dragon in chapter 12. John uses the phrase consistently to introduce a new scene in a continuing narrative vision (5:1, 6; 6:1, 8, 12; 7:2, 9; 8:2, 13; 9:1; 10:1). What continues is John's perspective. Looking with the dragon out to sea, he sees what it sees: a roiling sea. The site of primordial chaos, which God first quelled in the creation accounts (Gen. 1:2-10), the sea is a symbolic representation of resistance to God. The level of that resistance rises exponentially when the sea spits up a beast.

  Because John introduces *"beast"* without the article, one can assume that he thinks he is presenting it to his hearers and readers for the first time. That assumption is correct, even though John has already announced it as *"the"* beast rising from the Abyss (Rev. 11:7). In chapter 11, John acts though his hearers and readers already know about *"the"* beast when in fact it is the first time he is telling them about it, while in chapter 13 he talks about *"a"* beast as if they have not yet become acquainted. This odd narrative sequencing makes sense when one reads chapter 13 as part of the larger second of chapters 12-14, where John employs the literary device of a flashback. In real time, the events narrated in chapter 13 occur prior to those that take place in chapters 1-11. John therefore properly introduces the beast from the sea here without using the article.

The similar titles and functions identify "*the*" beast from the Abyss (11:7) and "*a*" beast from the sea (13:1) as the same entity. Mythologically speaking, the sea and the Abyss are functionally identical; they represent the lockdown region of chaos and the forces that perpetrate it.[192] Though almost all of John's 22 references to "θάλασσα" (sea) refer to the physical sea as a great and neutral body of water, he does have five clarifying metaphorical uses. These all show the sea operating either as a repository for the dead or as chaos (4:6; 13:1; 15:2; 20:13; 21:1). Since death chaotically disturbs life, the symbolism has a constant emotional impact throughout all five passages. The word "ἄβυσσος" (Abyss) functions similarly. For John it is always a place of chaos (9:1, 2, 11; 11:7; 17:8; 20:1, 3). Therefore, when John says, on the one hand, that a beast arises from the Abyss and that, on the other hand, a beast arises from the sea, he is talking about the same beast and the same menacing reality. The bestial target and accomplishment are also the same: to make war on the people of the church and to conquer them (11:7; 13:7).

John's mythical presentation has a decidedly historical point. The beast is Rome. The first monster represents the Roman imperial power which, for the province of Asia, annually came up out of the sea, with

---

[192] → In the Greek Old Testament Abyss (ἄβυσσος) is used as a rendering for the Great Deep, the primeval ocean of the creation story, and for the sea in general.

the arrival of the proconsul at Ephesus. In making this historical case, John also makes the most of his mythological connection with Daniel. Daniel, too, used the dramatic presentation of mythical beasts from the sea to interpret the struggles of his people against the forces of historical empire. According to John, this bestial, imperial power is satanic. He therefore immediately associates the beast from the sea with its patron, the dragon. Like the dragon, the beast has ten horns and seven heads. John will relate these accoutrements directly to Rome (17:3, 7, 9, 12, 16); the seven heads are the seven hills and the seven emperors (17:9). The beast is the entire empire, in its economic, political, social dimension, and especially its religious, theological, and spiritual dimension.

Though the dragon's ten horns were uncovered, the beast from the sea wears ten diadems on its ten horns. While the dragon had seven diadems on its seven heads, the beast outfits its heads with blasphemous names. As for the dragon, so for the beast, the horns and diadems signal power and kingship. The ten horns are ten kings (17:12; cf. Dan. 7:24). The diadems on the horns represent the beast's claim to be king of kings, a title John and his fellow believers ascribe exclusively to Christ (19:16), who also wears many diadems on his head (19:12). The dragon and the beast parody the Lamb's claim to power by positioning their ten horns against his seven. John wants his readers to realize that, since seven represents perfection, the Lamb retains more qualitative power even though he is outnumbered.

The blasphemous names on the beast's seven heads evoke images associated with Roman coinage. John's hearers and readers would regularly have seen the heads of emperors on imperial coins accompanied by titles in Greek like *"god," "son of god," "savior,"* or *"lord."* Since those titles and the realities behind them belong only to God and the Lamb, John regards their attribution to Roman emperors as blasphemy.

- **2** Daniel 7:3-6 provides the inspiration for the next phase of the sea beast's description. It has the general appearance of a leopard, the feet of a bear, and the mouth of a lion. John presents these traits in reverse order from Daniel, who sees a lion, a bear, and a leopard. Daniel witnessed a fourth beast with the ten horns John depicts in 13:1 (Dan. 7:7). For Daniel, the four beasts represent empires that had conquered the people of God in a bestial manner. By folding all their attributes into the characterization of a single brute, John presses the narrative claim that this new beast is an imperial force without peer.
- **3** John focuses on one of the beast's seven imperial heads. If, as 13:1 and 17:9 indicate, the seven heads symbolize seven Roman emperors, then one of those emperors has suffered a mortal wound. John's description is *"as slaughtered."* It is precisely the same description he gives for the Standing Slaughtered Lamb (5:6). In order to emphasize that this trait is as much a part of the beast's character as it is a part of the Lamb's John repeats the death imagery twice more within the same chapter (13:12, 14). The beast's hijacking of the

Lamb's defining features mocks those who follow the Lamb.

The head bounces quickly back. Immediately after narrating its demise, a horrified John reassesses the situation. His adversative "καὶ" (but) initiates a clause that sees the head healed from its death blow. Two observations are important here. First, John clearly understands this head to be the representation of a larger entity; its regeneration is a revival of the beast (13:12). Second, the verb for healing occurs incredulously in the passive voice "ἐθεραπεύθη" (he was healed). With yet another of his divine passives, John implies that God is responsible for the head's regeneration (cf. 20:7, where God allows the dragon's release from the Abyss). John does not explain why God would either allow or directly cause the restoration of a force so hostile to God's own people and church. He is apparently more interested in assuring his hearers and readers that nothing happens in human history that is beyond the realm of God's control. Even the bestial movements of a satanic minion happen within the confines of God's divine orchestration.

The theme here is resurrection: the head died; the head rises from that death just as the Lamb rose from his execution. At 13:14, when John describes the beast's return with the verb "ἔζησεν" (he lived/came back to life), he employs the same resurrection language he applies to Christ at 2:8. In its continuing parody of the Lamb, the beast, using its head, ridicules any notion that the Lamb is somehow more worthy because of its regeneration. Perhaps just here lies the important point John heard from the hymnic stanza at 5:9. The Lamb's worthiness does not derive from any miraculous events, even one as stupendous as resurrection. The Lamb's worthiness derives instead from the same source as the worthiness of those who follow him. The Lamb's worthiness comes from his willingness to witness to his own lordship and the lordship of his God at the expense of his own life. It is that willingness to witness, that transformative act of witness in the face of whatever loss may come because of it, that sets the Lamb and his followers apart. The head of a Roman beast can indeed come back from the dead and perhaps bring a staggering monster back to life with it. The beast has been allowed that much rein. The beast cannot, however, stop the realization of God's rule that is even now breaking in through the blood of the Lamb and the enduring witness to that Lamb (12:11). The beast cannot stop it because ultimately God is in control.

Because the bestial heads represent Roman emperors, many have speculated about the historical figures John had in mind. Most attention has focused on the one head narrate with sufficient detail to make an educated historical guess, the one whose mortal sword wound was healed. The odds are high that John had Nero in mind. According to Suetonius, (*Nero* 49) Nero committed suicide by stabbing himself in the throat with a sword. His death therefore fits the picture John paints in Rev. 13. So does the murky legend surrounding an expectation for his return.

The Romans remembered Nero with a great deal of hostility. His scandalous, oppressive rule degenerated to such depths that the Roman senate eventually declared him an enemy of the state. Shortly thereafter, disgraced and fleeing, he took his own life. Unfortunately, because there were few witnesses to either his death or his corpse, various conspiracy theories emerged. They took one of two forms. In the first, Nero did not die but instead escaped to a place of exile. In most versions of this theory, he fled to the East, where he was as revered as he was reviled in the West.

In the East, Nero had always been acknowledged positively for his contributions to the arts. He was particularly honored for crafting a stable diplomatic relationship with the Parthians. Indeed, many believed that he had fostered so strong a friendship with the Parthians that they had provided him refuge. When he had sufficient time to amass even more support among the Parthians, he would lead their armies across the Euphrates to take revenge on the empire that had ousted him.

The second version of the legend took on the name of Nero redivivus. This is the version that appears to lie behind John's vision of the slaughtered head returned to life. In this scenario, Nero did indeed die. However, those who either expected or feared his return believed that it would truly be a return from the dead. Christ-believers would certainly have feared it. They would remember Nero as the first emperor to instigate a widespread and vicious persecution of the witnesses to their faith (in 64 C.E.). According to tradition, key apostolic leaders Peter and Paul were both killed during that wave of terror. Commentators are correct to assert that John does not expect Nero's literal return from the dead, but that he is warning his followers to recognize that evil itself resurrects. Evil, when destroyed in its incarnation in one person, will manage to find other willing and capable hosts to continue its draconian work (cf. 17:11).

The Nero redivivus version of the legend also fits with John's understanding that the death and resurrection of the bestial head reflects a similarly astounding revival of the empire itself. When Nero died, the empire sank into a quagmire of tumultuous violence. The Julian Dynasty that had been in place since Caesar Augusts died with Nero in 68 C.E. A civil war and perhaps even the dissolution of the empire itself threatened. In 69, no fewer than four men pursued and laid claim to the imperial throne. With the rise to power of Vespasian and his Flavian Dynasty, the empire remarkably rose to new life. Like the head, the beast managed, and thereby mocked, resurrection.[193]

The people of the earth were so impressed with the beast's regeneration that they followed it. The language is that of discipleship (cf. Mark 1:17; 8:34; Matt. 4:19; 16:24; Luke 9:23). No wonder Christ and his followers would need rods of iron to shepherd the nations so that they follow God instead.

---

[193] → John's use of the legends as developing from the reference to Nero as the great beast in the *Sibylline Oracles* and especially *Ascen. Isa.* 4.2-14.

- **4** The subject switches suddenly and somewhat awkwardly to the plural when John declares that *"they"* worshiped the dragon first and then the beast. The reference is to the *"whole earth"* (v. 3) and by implication the nations from the earth (10:11; 11:2, 9, 18). They all worship the dragon, even though John's hymnic visions have made clear that proper worship belongs exclusively to God and God's Christ (4:10; 5:14; 7:11; 11:16; 19:4).

John is making two interrelated points. First, the beast, Rome, has amassed complete historical control. The dragon has created an empire by bestowing its authority upon Rome. This is the second point: Rome is satanic. The nations of the world worship the dragon because they love empire. John wants his hearers and readers to understand this critical point: to participate in the Roman imperial cult is to worship the draconian evil that lurks behind Rome.

The nations of the world are looking at what they can see rather than what John knows to be true. They claim that no one is like the beast, which is to say, no one can make war with it. Once again God is being parodied. The question *"Who is like this one, and who can make war with this one?"* is a mimicking of the very rhetorical question asked about God in the Hebrew Scriptures (Exod. 15:11; Deut. 3:24; Pss. 35:10; 71:19; 89:6; 113:5; Isa. 40:18, 25; 44:7; Mic. 7:18). John offers a narrative counter to their imperial taunt. When one tracks his use of war language in both verb (πολεμέω) and noun (πολεμοσ) forms, his take on the matter becomes apparent. Who can make war with the beast? It is not a rhetorical question. God's angel Michael (12:7), the Christ Lamb (2:16; 17:14; 19:11), and the church (11:7; 12:17; 13:7) can all engage not just the beast but also the draconian force that powers it. Even if the dragon takes the initiative and initially appears to win, victory ultimately will belong to God and those who follow God.

- **5** To stress yet again that the beast's powerful actions, even those that operate against God's interests, are under God's ultimate control, John emphasizes the divine passive in the ensuing section with an almost redundant use of "ἐδόθη" ("*it was given*," twice in v. 5, and twice in v. 7). Here God allows the beast to speak boastful and blasphemous words. The boasts are no doubt an extension of the claims to greatness implied in the rhetorical question of v. 4: "*Who is like the beast?*" Traditionally, the beasts recall Daniel's narration of Nebuchadnezzar's pretentious claims to singular greatness just before God offered a counterclaim by humiliating him (Dan. 4:30-37). The boasts of Antiochus IV Epiphanes are even more specific examples of an oppressive ruler declaring his greatness as he oppresses the people of God (Dan. 7:8, 20, 25). Like Revelation, these texts from Daniel refer to the king as the appendage (a horn in this case) of a great beast from the sea whose rule was temporary: two times and a half, the functional equivalent of John's 42 months, 1,260 days, or 3½ years (Rev. 11:2-3; 12:6, 14). In 13:5, the blasphemies no doubt echo v. 1 (cf. 17:3) and the imperial names and the titles of divinity connected with them. Such imperial images and names were on rich display in cultic temples and on imperial coins.

- **6** Still operating with Dan. 7:25 and 11:36 in mind (cf. Isa. 52:5), John specifies the nature of the blasphemies introduced in Rev. 13:5. They are directed first toward God's name. John's use of the term "ὄνομα" (name) suggests that one's name conveys one's identity and reputation, particularly as being for or against God (3:1; 6:8; 8:11; 9:11; 13:1, 17; 14:1, 11; 15:2; 17:3, 5, 8; 19:12-13, 16; 22:4). When associated with a supernatural figure, the term signifies not only identity but also worthiness to receive adulation, even if that adulation must be given under duress. The blaspheming of God's name, then, no doubt involves a mocking of God's identity as the Lord who is exclusively due worship. By avowing blasphemous names of lordship for its emperors and inciting its own cultic worship, the Roman beast has done exactly that.

Second, the blasphemies are directed against God's dwelling (σκηνή). The allusion could work in one of two direction. If John maintains his dependence upon Daniel and links the Roman beast to the atrocities committed by Antiochus Epiphanes, he is perhaps referring to the Roman desecration of the temple that took place in 70 C.E. Aune points out, "*Antiochus IV Epiphanes is remembered as having violated, or attempted to violate, several temples (Polybius 31.9; 1 Macc. 6:1-5; 2 Macc. 1:14-17) as well as the temple in Jerusalem (1 Macc. 1:20-24; Jos. Ag. Ap. 2:83-84).*" It is more likely, however, that John is thinking in contemporary terms. By using "σκηνή" which refers to God's act of tabernacling with the people rather than the physical place in which that dwelling occurred (cf. Rev. 21:3), John recognizes that what is being ridiculed is the possibility that a presence more forceful than Rome – namely, God – actually participates in the life of Christ-believers.

The strangest part of the statement is the final one, which either clarifies or adds to "σκηνή." Because of the strangeness of the formulation, several copyists added "καὶ" (and), which would indicate that both God's presence (σκηνή) and the ones who reside with God in heaven are being ridiculed. Others take the relative clause that follows "σκηνή" *"the ones who dwell in heaven,"* as a clarification of "σκηνή." The "και" can be reasonably explained as a scribal attempt to clarify a difficult text. It is more likely that the relative clause develops the preceding statement about God's dwelling in some way. In that case, John would be particularly concerned about the debasement of those who are in God's presence in heaven. John recognizes that what is being ridiculed is the possibility that those who have died have moved into the presence of a force more powerful than the Roman one that killed them. The souls crying out beneath the altar at 6:9-11 come immediately to mind. Why are they crying out to a God who could not prevent their slaughter? The one who slaughtered them is the power they should recognize; its altar is the only one before which they should seek comfort. In mocking them, the beast does the double duty of mocking the God with whom they claim to dwell.

- **7** Repeating what he has already said through the symbolism of the two witnesses (11:7), John acknowledges that the beast makes war on the holy ones, or saints, that is, members of the church, and conquers them. Still, he persists in his claim that this conquest was allowed (*"it was given"*) by God. It is important to note, however, that the *"saints,"* not the church itself, are conquered. There is no *"rapture"* out of the devastation for believers.

  While Christ-believers are being conquered, the beast universalizes its control (cf. Dan. 7:14). Once again, there is a mocking of God and of Christ's own claims. Though he presents them in a different order, John lists this fourfold grouping (tribe, people, tongue, nation) elsewhere as the object of the universal reach of both God and Lamb (Rev. 7:9; 14:6). Christ has ransomed them (5:9), but because they did not respond properly, John was commanded to prophesy against them (10:11). Then these *"inhabitants of the earth"* gloat over the demise of the two witnesses, who symbolize Christ-believers such as John (11:9). They do so, if chapter 13 is indeed a flashback, because before John begins to write, they are under the authority of the beast.

- **8** John once again refers to the whole earth (13:3), which marvels behind the beast and worships it (v. 4), with what has become his traditional formula: *"the inhabitants of the earth."* Though the verb *"will worship"* is in the future tense, since chapter 13 is a flashback John is no doubt talking about his present eschatological moment, when the inhabitants of the earth are heavily invested in the imperial cult.

The key interpretive problem centers on the prepositional phrase "*from the foundation of the world.*" Since such prepositional phrases are overwhelmingly adverbial, this one can modify two different components in the verse: the writing of the names in the Book of Life, or the slaughtering of the Lamb. It is unlikely that John intends to say that the Lamb was slaughtered from the foundation of the world. Though he speaks about it in mythic terms as a snatching to the throne of God (12:5), it is clear throughout that he understands it to be the historical event of Jesus' crucifixion (e.g., 1:5; 5:6, 12; 12:11). One could suppose that John intends to speak about the planning of Jesus' slaughtering from the foundation of the world, but then that would mean going beyond what the actual text conveys. It is better to read the language of slaughter as an attributive modifier of the Lamb in the way that John uses it throughout the book. He is speaking about the Book of Life of the Slaughtered Lamb.

The more appropriate of the two interpretive choices is the one that has the phrase "*from the foundation of the world*" modifying the writing of the names in the Book of Life. In this case, John would be talking about the inhabitants of the earth whose names were not from the foundation of the world written in the Book of Life. One's salvation was dependent on having one's name written in the Book (20:15; 21:27).

In other words, some names were predestined from the beginning to be excluded from the possibility of eschatological relationship with God. This interpretive choice carries the disturbing implication that no matter whether they responded to John's exhortations, their fate was sealed. One wonders, then, why John works so hard to get even the likes of Jezebel, Balaam, and the Nicolaitans to repent, or why he seems to be surprised that even after all the devastating acts of judgment, many who survive them refuse to repent. He seems to expect that repentance, and the relationship with God that comes with it, is still possible. At 3:5 he indicates that some names are first included in the Book, only to be blotted out for refusal to respond appropriately to God's call to witness. This deterministic linking of the phrase *"from the foundation of the world"* with *"not writing the names of the inhabitants of the earth in the Book of Life"* may therefore simply reveal an inner tension within John's narrative 9if not, indeed, in his mind) on how human relationship with God is ultimately negotiated.

Yet there is also a more intriguing possibility. Later John at the final judgment pictures multiple books being opened prior to the opening of the Book of Life (20:12). Why so many books? The function of the Book of Life is clear; it records the names of those granted eschatological relationship with God. The context of 3:5 implies that those names belong to believers in John's churches. Their only fear is that acts of accommodation to Rome's claims to lordship will blot their names from their recorded place.

Apparently, though, as the text here indicates, there are other names that have not always resided in the book of Life. Here the presence of the other books in chapter 20 becomes significant. Since the names in the Book of Life were recorded there from the foundation of the world, their recording cannot be the result of their proper witness behavior. The recording happened before the people attached to the names were ever born. The other books are therefore the ones that must record the deeds spoken about at the end of 20:12. By their repentant acts of witness, those whose names were not written in the Book of Life from the foundation of the world (i.e., the inhabitants of the earth), can nevertheless earn an inscribing of their names in those other books. If this interpretation is correct, there is no real tension in John's understanding of the manner in which eschatological relationship with God is negotiated. No one is predestined for eschatological judgment. All have an opportunity to be saved. Believers' names are already recorded; all they need to do it witness authentically so that their names will not be blotted out. Others, the *"inhabitants of the earth,"* need only repent and give God glory and their names will be added to the Book of Life, after their recorded works have been duly noted in the other books that are opened first.

- **9** The sentence *"Let anyone who has an ear listen"* is all about exhortation. John uses it consistently to encourage action. In fact, except for this unique occurrence, John only deploys it at the conclusion of the letters to the seven churches (2:7, 11, 17, 29; 3:6, 13,

22). In those cases he uses it to buttress the preceding ethical mandates. He revives it here for the same reason. This vision scene has the same goal as the more direct exhortations in the letters; John is encouraging appropriate behavior. Once his people know how satanic the Roman beast is, they must reject it.

- **10** John is not only asking his hearers and readers to "*hear*" what he has said about the beast and to respond appropriately; he also wants them to hear what he will say about how they must also be prepared to endure the devastating reprisal with which the beast will answer their rejection. Operating from the background of Jer. 15:2 and Jer. 43:11, John declares that if someone is destined for captivity, then that person goes into captivity. The conditional statement squares with John's conviction that everything, even God's allowance of the beast's reign of terror against God's people is scripted. Those who witness to the lordship of Christ can, like the Lamb, who was himself executed, expect – that is, because of their witness they are destined – to be taken captive by a beast whose primary goal is to institutionalize its own exclusive lordship.

Still operating with Jeremiah's warning in mind, John turns his attention to death by the sword in the second half of the verse. This second conditional statement is so difficult to decipher in the Greek that it has spurred many textual variants. John uses two aorist-passive infinitives but no main verb. One would expect that after the protasis, "*if someone is to be killed by the sword*," the apodosis would follow with a primary verb, preferably in the future passive: "*he will be killed by the sword.*"Beale argues that the formulations is part of John's intentional effort to remind his hearers and readers of the message conveyed by the infinitive *"to kill"* elsewhere in his text: *"Infinitive forms of "kill" also portray the suffering of believers in 6:8 and 6:11. 13:10 continues the theme and adds an exhortation for the saints to endure faithfully through such persecution."* If he is right, and I think he is, then John intends to say something very much like what Jesus conveys in Matt. 26:52. There, in directing his followers to put away the sword because those who take the sword will perish by it, Jesus demonstrates that the proper response to bestial violence is not more violence but a faithful endurance that witnesses to one's confidence that God is indeed Lord and therefore in control.

John makes exactly this point as he closes out his introduction of the beast from the sea with the third line of v. 10: here is the endurance, which is the faith of the saints. I take the "καὶ" (and) that connects endurance and faith as epexegetical. Faith extends and develops the meaning of endurance. In three of his four uses of "πίστις" (faith), in fact, John bundles it with *"endurance"* (2:19; 13:10; 14:12). One's ability to endure is a measure of one's faith in the lordship and therefore the ultimate control of God and the Standing Slaughtered Lamb. John uses *"endurance"* in just this way when writing to his churches (2:2, 3, 19; 3:10).

The two other uses of the term (1:9 and 14:12) are, together with 13:10, even more illustrative. In each case John either models or calls for an enduring witness to the lordship of Christ, even in those circumstances where offering such testimony will provoke persecution. In other words, John is warning his hearers and readers about the risks they will face when witnessing against the beast. Some will be imprisoned; others will be slain by the sword. But hold on. Resist. God is still in control, nothing is happening without God's leave, everything is part of God's strategic plan for victory.

Revelation 13:11~18 → Flashback: The Beast from the Land

NIV	TT
¹¹ Then I saw a second beast, coming out of the earth. It had two horns like a lamb, but it spoke like a dragon. ¹² It exercised all the authority of the first beast on its behalf, and made the earth and its inhabitants worship the first beast, whose fatal wound had been healed. ¹³ And it performed great signs, even causing fire to come down from heaven to the earth in full view of the people. ¹⁴ Because of the signs it was given power to perform on behalf of the first beast, it deceived the inhabitants of the earth. It ordered them to set up an image in honor of the beast who was wounded by the sword and yet lived. ¹⁵ The second beast was given power to give breath to the image of the first beast, so	¹¹ Then I saw **another**[194] beast rising up from the earth, and it had two horns like a lamb, but it was speaking like a dragon. ¹² And it exercises all the authority of the first beast, on its behalf, and it makes the earth and its inhabitants worship the first beast, whose mortal wound was healed. ¹³ It performs great signs, even making fire come down from heaven to the earth before people; ¹⁴ and it deceives the inhabitants of the earth because of the signs that it was allowed to do on behalf of the beast, telling the inhabitants of the earth to make an image of the beast who was wounded by the sword but lived. ¹⁵ And it was allowed to give breath to the **image**[195] of the beast, so that the image of the beast might even speak, and cause

---

[194] ἄλλος → It means "*another*," "*different*," and "*more*."
[195] εἰκών → It means "*image*," "*likeness*," "*form*," and "*appearance*."

that the image could speak and cause all who refused to worship the image to be killed. ¹⁶ It also forced all people, great and small, rich and poor, free and slave, to receive a mark on their right hands or on their foreheads, ¹⁷ so that they could not buy or sell unless they had the mark, which is the name of the beast or the number of its name. ¹⁸ This calls for wisdom. Let the person who has insight calculate the number of the beast, for it is the number of a man. That number is 666.	whoever did not worship the image of the beast to be killed. ¹⁶ And they cause all, the small and the great, the rich and the poor, the free and the slave, **in order that**[196] they might give them a **mark**[197] upon their right hand or forehead, ¹⁷ so that no one could buy or sell who does not have the mark, which is the name of the beast or the number of its name. ¹⁸ Here is **wisdom**[198]. Let the one who has understanding calculate the number of the beast, for it is the number of a person, and its number is **666**[199].

Ancient Mediterranean mythology knew not only of Leviathan the sea monster, but of Behemoth the land monster, also reflected in the Old Testament and Apocrypha (Job 40:15; *2 Esd.* 6:49, 51). It too is a parody of the Lamb, resembles Christ, but it speaks like a dragon.

- **11** With "*and I saw*," John introduces another scene in the continuing narrative vision of beasts rising to meet the dragon (12:18). This second beast rises from the

---

[196] ἵνα → It denotes purpose aim, or goal. It means "*in order that.*"
[197] χάραγμα → It means "*mark,*" "*stamp,*" "*thing,*" "*image,*" and "*Kerygma.*"
[198] σοφία → It means "*wisdom,*" "*Divine Wisdom,*" "*wisdom of Christ and of God,*" and "*Sophia.*"
[199] χξς → It does not mean "*6-6-6,*" it means "*six hundred and sixty six.*"

land and is a clear allusion to the male Behemoth whom God separated from the female Leviathan on the fifth day of creation.

This monster is a contradiction in terms. It has the look of a lamb but the mouth of a dragon. It is lamblike because of its two horns. At Dan. 8:3, however, a ram with two horns represents opposition to, rather than assistance for, the people of God. This beast clearly represents the same. Given that both the dragon and the beast from the sea have ten horns, however, one gains the immediate sense that this beast is neither as powerful nor as directly related to the dragon as is the beast from the sea. Even so, the mere fact that it has lamblike horns prolongs the parody of God and the Christ initiated by the dragon and the beast from the sea.

Despite its lamblike appearance, the beast's mouth, or at least what comes out of it, immediately gives it away. It speaks like, and is therefore most certainly affiliated with, the dragon. These competing attributes (lamblike looks, dragonlike mouth) must have reminded some of John's hearers and readers of Matthean Jesus' warning about false prophets who come looking like sheep but in reality are ravenous wolves (Matt. 7:15). In fact, only here in v. 11 does John even refer to it as a beast. All further references invoke the title *"false prophet"* (16:13; 19:20; 20:10).

Scholars have noted two other important points about this figure. First, since it rounds out the complement of mythical and historical enemies arrayed against God's people, it parodies the Trinitarian force of God (4:3, 11), the Lamb (5:6, 12), and the Spirit (1:4;

3:1; 4:5; 5:6). Second, because it is portrayed as lamblike in appearance, it is quite likely that John envisioned it as having a function similar to the Lamb's. The Lamb was the primary model for witnessing to the lordship of God and Christ, suffering on account of that witness, and then being vindicated by God through resurrection. As such, the Lamb is a motivating factor for faith; his life encourages others to believe and to witness to that belief. According to vv. 12-18, the false prophet is the role model for a counter-belief in the lordship of the dragon and its beast.

- **12** Though it does not have the strength (only two horns), this false prophet does have the authority of the first beast. The first beast had delegated its authority to the false prophet in the same way that the dragon delegated its authority to Rome (v. 4). The phrase "ἐνώπιον αὐτοῦ" literally means *"before him," "in his presence,"* really means *"by his authority," "on his behalf,"* or even *"at his commissioning."*

    The false prophet uses this authority for one primary reason, to encourage the inhabitants of the earth to worship the first beast. The prophet is therefore by definition false since worship belongs exclusively to God. Because John's mythical portraits often have historical referents, this false prophet is likely also a cipher for a prophet-like person or entity who encouraged devotion to the Roman beast. John probably had in mind the people and infrastructure that institutionally embodied Asia Minor's commitment to the imperial cult. Rome, as the beast from the sea, is a foreign force. Land based, the false prophet has a more indigenous feel; he rises up out of the very soil on which John's hearers and readers have built their lives and homes. This beast is local. It represents the native traditions and institutions that nevertheless serve the bestial imperial cult. Rome exercised its rule through just such institutions. In Asia, the imperial cult was in the hands of a body known as the *"koinon"* in Greek and the *"commune"* in Latin. The *"commue Asiae"* was a provincial council that included representatives from the major towns. Such councils were often populated with priests or other political representatives who promoted the imperial cult. Priests of the imperial cult wore crowns that displayed the busts of the deified emperors and the gods whose cult they served. The *Asiarchs of Acts* 19:31 may well have been members of just such a *"commune."*

The mixture of political and religious affairs built into the identities of these councils means that the false prophet's role cannot be relegated to an exclusively religious arena. Worship of the emperor and of the Roman deities associated with the imperial cult was as much a sign of political as religious loyalty. The member of the *"koinon"* were charged with encouraging and fostering belief with the knowledge that such faith would eventually mutate into political loyalty, that is, loyalty to the political, economic, social, and cultic lordship of Rome.

- **13** As one might expect from a prophet, this false one performs miracles. Signs help convince people about one's professed supernatural status or connection (Rev. 16:14; 19:20). Just as the land beast attempts to fool

Christ-believers into following it with its lamblike appearance (13:11), so now it tries to link up with one of God's signature prophetic acts: the raining of fire down upon the earth (1 Kgs. 18:38-39; 2 Kgs. 1:10-14; Luke 9:54; Rev. 20:9). Christ-believers had already been warned to expect such false prophets performing such false signs in the hopes of luring them to a false faith (Mark 13:21-23; Matt. 24:23-25; 2 Thess. 2:9).

- **14** As with the first beast, so with this one, all that it accomplishes is under God's direction. John makes this point with yet another deployment of the divine passive "ἐδόθη" ("*it was given*," or "*it was allowed*"). Still, because of the land beast's signs, the false prophet is able to deceive the inhabitants of the earth into making an image of the first beast. John is working here from the account in Dan. 3, where the imperial ruler crafts an image of himself and demands, under penalty of death, that all in his kingdom worship it.
- **15** God allows (once again John appeals to the divine passive "ἐδόθη") the false prophet the charisma to make the imperial cult and its images seem to come alive and even speak. Many priestly types claimed the power to animate images of the gods so that the images might speak and convey oracles about the present and the future: The specific example of trickery that John mentions, a speaking statue, is mentioned in several ancient sources. Through ventriloquism, through a person hiding in a hollow statue, or through some mechanical device, statues could appear animated and be made to talk. This nod to Hellenistic magic is John's

metaphorical way of saying that the false prophet has breathed life into a cultic system so that people believe that the images populating the system can actually make a positive economic, social, political, and religious difference in their lives. Those imperial images are supposed to bring them a life of rewards that reliance upon the lordship of God and Christ could not.

Like Nebuchadnezzar in Dan. 3, the imperial image can also threaten death against all those who resist worshiping it. John appears to be reminding his readers of the saying that those who are destined to be killed by the sword for their witness to the lordship of God and the Lamb will indeed be killed (Rev. 13:10). He fears that this threat of death will lead many to surrender their testimony to the lordship of Christ and accommodate themselves to the idolatrous expectations of the imperial cult. This is why he pleads so fervently – and sometimes desperately – in his letters to the seven churches (chapters 2-3). He wants his followers to realize that while the Roman beast may have been allowed the ability to impose the first death, they need fear only the second death, from which only their eschatological relationship with God and the Lamb can save them (cf. 2:11; 9:6). At this point John issues a threat of his own. Those who, fearing the first death, submit to worshiping the image of the first beast may prosper on earth, but they will be sentenced to eternal separation from God and thus the second death when the ultimate judgment comes (14:9, 11; 16:2; 19:20). Those who do not worship this beast will reign with Christ (20:4).

- **16** One thing is clear: the false prophet does not discriminate. The land beast targets everyone; it considers neither social standing nor economic status (cf. 6:15; 19:17-18). John knows that even his Christ-believers have been targeted. He also knows that many of them are being persuaded by the false prophet's deceitful tactics. Many are accommodating themselves to the bestial imperial cult, to its claims of lordship, and to the social, economic, political, and cultic ramifications of such a lordship. Unlike Christianity at significant periods in its history, the forces of evil have always had an *"open door, come just as you are"* policy. Perhaps this is something else the dragon and its beasts have to brag about.

    The false prophet issues an identifying "χάραγμα" (mark) on the right hand or forehead of those who respond positively to its invitation to worship the image of the first beast. John is speaking symbolically; there is no literal mark. The *"mark"* of the beast symbolizes a person's allegiance to and participation in the religious, social, economic, and political rites associated with the imperial cult (13:16-17; 14:9, 11; 16:2; 19:20; 20:4). Rather, John is saying that those (including people in the church) who participate in the worship of the emperor have, in so doing, *"marked"* themselves as belonging to *"Satan."*

    Once again John's Greek is awkward. Although he has been speaking about the single false prophet, when he speaks of the branding with the mark, he employs a third-person plural formulation. He says, *"in order that they might give them a mark upon their right hand or forehead.*" The "*they*" most likely refers back to the counter-Trinitarian sensibility that John has been trying to establish for the affiliation between the dragon, the beast from the sea, and the false prophet/beast from the land. The action of one reflects the intentions of the triumvirate. When the false prophet acts, he acts not alone but for them all, in the same way that the Lamb's actions reflect the intentions of God and the Spirit. In this subtle way, John again recognizes that evil mimics and therefore mocks the good.

The parody becomes explicit when John's hearers and readers remember that God's followers are also marked with a seal upon their foreheads (7:2; 14:1; 22:4). If chapters 12-14 are indeed a flashback to events are realities that have preceded the visionary narratives in chapters 1-11 and 15-22, then the false prophet's marking took place first. In real time, God's sealing was a retaliatory response. In God's case, however, this action was not for parody but for protection. John has just disclosed that those who do not worship the first beast will be killed (13:15). And he has painfully acknowledged that those destined for captivity and the sword because of their loyalty to the lordship of God and the Lamb will succumb to that destiny (v. 10). There will be no "*rapture*" escape for the people of the Lamb. Because they do not bear the mark of the beast, they will be vulnerable to destruction by the beast. Although their protection from the second death will guaranteed (2:11; 20:6), their susceptibility to the first death is all but certain (11:7; 13:7). God does, however, desire a remnant, military-like force to engage the forces of the beast. God will seal and therefore protect the 144,000 from the ravages of the beast so that they can provide whatever counter to the beast God intends (see the comments on 7:4 and 11:1-2). Ultimately, in a show of superior strength, God will use even the beast's own mark as a weapon against those whom it was designed to protect. It will become a locating beacon. The mark will make it impossible for the worshipers of the beast to hide from God's coming judgment. Because of the mark, God will easily identify and destroy them (14:9-11; 16:2; 19:20) and reward those who have remained faithful (20:4).

In John's narrative time, however, a different scenario develops. God seals first in chapter 7, and the evil triumvirate appears mockingly to counterseal here (in chapter 13). Through the use of the literary technique of the flashback in chapters 12-13, John can make two very different points simultaneously. He can demonstrate God's ability to protect God's people from the power of the dragon if God so chooses and ultimately punish those who worship the beast, even as he concedes that the draconian forces flaunt their historical power by mocking God and singling out God's people for destruction whenever they can. John's hearers and readers can therefore acknowledge the reality of their tragic historical situation and yet draw upon the belief that ultimately God is the greater power and, despite appearances, still in control.

- **17** It is easy to see why some scholars have linked the mark of the beast with imperial coinage, which John associated with bestial blasphemies at 13:1, 5. The mark clearly has a commercial connection. Without it, without an expression of one's loyalty to the beast, a person loses one's ability to engage in commerce. Shut out of the economic system, a person would be hard-pressed to progress socially and politically, perhaps even to survive. The symbolism of the mark, then, is much broader than imperial coinage. It goes back to John's concern about all the enticements that draw his people toward accommodation to imperial cultic practice. John was particularly concerned that his people are so interested in maintain strong membership in their trade and other guild associations that they will participate in the idolatrous rites, such as eating meat sacrificed to idols, connected with those associations in order to progress socially and economically (cf. 2:12-17; 2:18-29). It is such unholy, idolatrous accommodation that he depicts through the symbolization of the mark that contains the name or number of the first beast.

- **18** Wisdom and understanding go together for John. Wisdom belongs initially to the Lamb (5:12) and to God (7:12). In John's only other uses of the term "*wisdom*," he pairs it with the only occurrences of "*understanding*" in Revelation (13:18; 17:9). Both 13:8 and 17:9 speak to the same circumstance: the identity and nature of the beast from the sea. This beast is identified with Rome and the emperors who leashed it (17:9). Likewise, in 13:18, the identity of the monster is inextricably tied to one of its most vicious imperial heads. As will be the case when a similar saying appears in 17:9, the emphasis on wisdom to solve the eschatological conundrum looks back at the material that has already been presented. One needs wisdom to be able to decipher what John has just revealed.

Additionally, though, the capably wise person will be able to calculate the number of the beast because it equals the number of a person's name. John is working here from the classical practice of Gematria, a riddle-like activity where letters are given corresponding numbers. One adds up the numbers that stand for the particular letters in a name to create a numerical sum for that name (cf. 15:2). According to the Sibylline Oracles (1.324-30), the Greek letters of Jesus name "Ἰησοῦς" total a numerically perfect 888.[200] In John's time, the practice of matching the beast's name and number was much easier than it is now. John appears to assume that his hearers and readers already have the name and can therefore easily equate it with the number. Thus John was not really giving his hearers and readers a puzzle; he was reinforcing an identification they already knew. However, since many names could produce the same number, it is much more difficult to work back from a given number to a particular name. therein lies the problem for the contemporary interpreter, who has only a number that could represent a multitude of names.

However, John has graciously offered an important clue. In this chapter he has been preoccupied with the beast from the sea and with the head on that beast that suffered a mortal wound but regained life for itself and

---

[200] Ἰησοῦς → Ἰ =10; η =8; σ =200 ο =70; υ =400; ς =200. So 10+8+200+70+400+200= 888 ('Ἰησοῦς) (For the Greek Letter number chart, see Excursus 15: The Number of the Beast 666, 616, 665?).

the beast. In v. 3 John appears to identify that head with Nero. Nero's reputation as the most vicious of emperors toward Christ-believers would solidify his symbolic identification with the monster that was imperial Rome. Interestingly, when the Greek letters for Nero Caesar are transliterated into Hebrew, the Hebrew letters add up to 666 (see Excursus 15: The Number of the Beast 666, 616 or 665?). Yet John is writing in Greek to a Greek-speaking audience. Why would his riddle operate with Hebrew letters? Throughout the discussion of chapter 13, we have consistently seen that John depends upon Hebrew tradition to ground his first-century visions. It is not surprising, given his reliance upon Hebrew prophetic tradition to support his narrative, that at a climactic moment in the narrative he would also turn to the Hebrew language. Even textual variants support the choice of Nero as the name of the beast; in Latin, Caesar Nero totals the very 616 that the variants offer. Scholars have more recently pointed out an even more tantalizing reason for choosing Nero. Given that his is the one name in chapter 13 directly linked to the beast from the sea, it cannot be coincidental that when the Greek word for beast (θηρίον) is transliterated into Hebrew letters, those letters also add up to 666.[201] Also the reference to Nero as a great beast in the *Sibylline Oracles* (8.157) may reflect a tradition that remembered him as a monster quite apart from the symbolism of Jewish apocalyptic. Nero is the imperial face of the

---

[201] הריונ → 400+200+10+6+50.

beast that threatens all those who would dare to defy the lordship claims of Rome by obstinately witnessing to the lordship of God and the Lamb instead. For John it would be no coincidence that "*beat*" and "*Nero*" add up to the same ominous sum.

John has been working symbolically and not literally; therefore, I do not believe that one can end the interpretive effort with the number/name puzzling of Gematria. Given John's focus on the number "*seven*" as indicating wholeness and perfection, it could well be that the seer is playing the beast's own taunting game against it. Even as he concedes its power, he finds a way to mock it. The repetition of the "*six*" for its number suggests that the beast keeps trying to approach the level of completeness that is represented in seven, but cannot quite make it. It is as though it is struggling to become something it never can be. In stat regard, its own name betrays its limitation. Even as it flaunts its strength, it wallows in weakness. It is always a six, never a seven; 666 on into eternity. It will never have complete power because, like the number that symbolizes it, it will never itself be completely whole.

Therein lies perhaps the juiciest part of John's own taunt. People who worship the beast do so by saying its name. They fall down and worship its power, its greatness, its ultimate lordship by calling out its name. But every time they call out that name, they also proclaim what the name itself proclaims: not lordship but limitation. In their worship of the beast, then, they actually mock it.

The hearers and readers of John's work, however, should recognize the number and what it signifies. On the basis of that knowledge, they must find a way to hold on and resist. For the beast's time is as imperfect as its name (13:5). Its power and control will not last forever. Therefore, John admonished, "*Do not buy into its economic schemes or accommodate to its imperial force.*"

Excursus 15: The Number of the Beast 666, 616, or 665?
Many of us are familiar with "*the mark of the Beast*" as being "*666.*" The majority of New Testament manuscripts give the number of the Beast in Revelation 13:18 as "*six hundred and sixty six.*" Interestingly, there is a minor textual variant at this point, some manuscripts give the number not as "*666*" but as "*616,*" others as "*665.*"

"*616*" is found in Codex C (V cent.) and P115 (III cent.) as well as a Vulgate manuscript (Latin). Only one manuscript from the eleventh century (ms 2344) states the number as "*665.*" I will provide the charts for Greek/Hebrew letters and its numerical values. "*Here is wisdom. Let the one who has understanding calculate the number of the beast, for it is the number of a person, and its number is 666/616/665*" (Rev. 13:18)

Greek Letter Number Equivalent

Alpha	α A	1	Iota	ι I	10	Rho	ρ P	100
Beta	β B	2	Kappa	κ K	20	Sigma	σ Σ	200
Gamma	γ Γ	3	Lambda	λ Λ	30	Tau	τ T	300
Delta	δ Δ	4	Mu	μ M	40	Upsilon	υ Y	400
Epsilon	ε E	5	Nu	ν N	50	Phi	φ Φ	500
Stigma	ς	6	Xi	ξ Ξ	60	Chi	χ X	600
Zeta	ζ Z	7	Omicron	ο O	70	Psi	ψ Ψ	700
Eta	η H	8	Pi	π Π	80	Omega	ω Ω	800
Theta	θ Θ	9	Qoppa	ϟ	90			

Hebrew Letter Number Equivalents

aleph	א	1	yod	י	10	qoph	ק	100
bet	ב	2	kap	כ	20	res	ר	200
gimel	ג	3	lamed	ל	30	s[h]in	ש	300
dalet	ד	4	mem	מ	40	tau (taw)	ת	400
he	ה	5	nun	נ	50	koph	ך	500
vau (waw)	ו	6	samek	ס	60			
zayin	ז	7	ayin	ע	70			
cheth	ח	8	pe	פ	80			
tet	ט	9	tsaddi	צ	90			

*The Greek form of Nero Caesar in Hebrew characters
קסר נרון (Neron Caesar) = 50+6+200+50+200+60+100
= 666

*The Latin form of Nero's name in Hebrew characters
קסר נרו (Nero Caesar) = 6+200+50+200+60+100 = 616

*Mis-transliteration of Nero's name from Hebrew
קסר נרהנ (Nerhn Caesar) = 50+5+200+50+200+60+100
= 665

Thus "*the Number of the Beast*" is not a barcode, not an energy drink, not a smart chip. John intended his readers to think of a particular individual, one already known to them, by the number. Probably, John expected his hearers and readers to think of Nero, and the idea is supported by the fact that he uses the myth of returning Nero elsewhere in the Book of Revelation (13:3; 17:9-11).

Revelation 14:1~5 → Flashback: The Lamb and the 144,000

NIV	TT
14 ¹ Then I looked, and there before me was the Lamb, standing on Mount Zion, and with him 144,000 who had his name and his Father's name written on their foreheads. ² And I heard a sound from heaven like the roar of rushing waters and like a loud peal of thunder. The sound I heard was like that of harpists playing their harps. ³ And they sang a new song before the throne and before the four living creatures and the elders. No one could learn the song except the 144,000 who had been redeemed from the earth. ⁴ These are those who did not defile themselves with women, for they remained	**14** ¹ **Then I looked, and behold,**[202] the Lamb was standing on Mount Zion. And with him were 144,000 who had his name and the name of his Father written on their foreheads. ² And I heard a voice from heaven like the sound of many waters and like the sound of loud thunder. The voice that I heard was like that of harpists playing on their harps. ³ And they sing a **new**[203] song before the throne and before the four living creatures and the elders. No one was able to **learn**[204] the song except the 144,000 who have been redeemed from the earth. ⁴ These the ones who were not **defiled**[205] with women,

---

[202] Καὶ εἶδον, καὶ ἰδοὺ → The phrase means *"Then I looked, and behold."* It is a literary device to introduce new scene.

[203] καινός → It means *"new,"* and *"strange."*

[204] μανθάνω → It means *"to learn,"* *"be appraised,"* *"to increase one's knowledge,"* *"to hear,"* *"be informed,"* *"to be in the habit of,"* and *"accustomed to."*

[205] μολύνω → It means *"to pollute,"* *"contaminate,"* *"defile,"* and *"make impure."*

virgins. They follow the Lamb wherever he goes. They were purchased from among mankind and offered as firstfruits to God and the Lamb. ⁵ No lie was found in their mouths; they are blameless.	for they are **virgins**[206]. These are the ones who **follow**[207] the Lamb wherever he goes. These have been redeemed from humankind as **firstfruits**[208] to God and for the Lamb. ⁵ And in their mouth no lie was found; they are blameless.

In stark contrast to the previous vision, in which those who worshiped the beast had been marked with its sign, here the Lamb and its followers, with God's name on their foreheads, stand on Mount Zion.

- **1** John opens with one of his favorite formulas for announcing a new vision: *"Then I looked, and behold..."* (5:1; 6:5, 8; 13:1, 11; 14:14; 19:11). He ten introduces us to the Lamb. The definite article attached to "Lamb" suggests that John's hearers and readers were already familiar with this designation as a moniker for Christ. Given the way narrative flashbacks work, by the time they reached this *"introduction"* of the Lamb, they had already been clued into his identity by the *"spoiler"* scene at 5:6. John chose not to use a definite article with *"Lamb"* at 5:6 because he was contrasting Jesus' depiction as *"a lamb"* with that of his expected presentation as *"the lion of Judah,"* not because 5:6 was the first real-time expression of his identity as Lamb.

---

[206] παρθένος → It means *"virgin,"* *"chaste man,"* and *"Parthenon"* (temple of Athena Parthenos at Athens).
[207] ἀκολουθέω → It means *"follow,"* *"accompany,"* and *"follow as disciple."*
[208] ἀπαρχή → It means *"firstfruits"* (the first of any crop or offspring of livestock), and *"foretaste"* (birth certificate or identification card).

The lack of the article grammatically emphasized its comparative weakness. The real-time, initial expression of his identity as Lamb occurs right here in 14:1, or at least it would have if John had chosen to present chapters 12-14 in chronological sequence rather than as a flashback. It is appropriate that *"Lamb"* be accompanied by the article in this flashback section even though the term *"beast"* was not (13:1, 11). First, the hearers and readers have not had narrative preparation for the beasts. Second and even more theologically important, beasts, though powerful antagonists, are inferior to *"the Lamb."* Once again John allows his grammar to state his case before he presses it narratively.

John also presses his case visually the Lamb is standing. As many commentators have pointed out, since the Lamb is clearly the Christ child who was snatched to the throne of God (12:5), one would expect the seer to portray him as enthroned. His staging, though, fits the central thesis of resistant witness that pervades the book. Standing, for John, is as much about theology as posture; he means that the Lamb is standing strong against the idolatrous claims to lordship made by the beast from the land on behalf of the dragon and the beast from the sea.

John uses geography to shore up his theological presentation. The name *"Zion"* originates as the title for a fortress (*"stronghold of Zion"*) in the Jerusalem area before David's conquest of the region (2 Sam. 5:7; 1 Chr. 11:5). Later the name was given to the ridge that separates the Kidron and Tyropoeon valleys in

Jerusalem. Solomon built his temple on the highest point of that ridge, which came to be known as Mount Zion. Eventually the term was used for all of Jerusalem and sometimes even euphemistically for the people of Israel. central to all of these applications was the understanding that Zion, whether as place, building, or people, was the location of God's presence and God's rule (1 Kgs. 8:1; 2 Chr. 5:2; Pss. 2:6; 9:11; 14:7; 50:2; 53:6; 84:7; 99:2; 125:1). Eschatologically, Zion came to be known as the gathering place where the Messiah would assemble the people of God and execute God's final judgment (Ps. 2:6-12; Isa. 24:23; Mic. 4:7; *Jub.* 1:28; *4 Ezra* 13.25-52; *2 Bar.* 40). Of particular importance is Ps. 2, where God stands the Messiah on Zion in open defiance of the powers that would circumvent God's interests. Zion was ultimately envisioned as a place of refuge and protection during the troubling apocalyptic events that would surround the end time. Of the nineteen occurrences of "*Mount Zion*" in the Old Testament, nine of them allude to a remnant being saved. New Testament writers picked up on these themes and developed them in connection with their Christ portraits (Matt. 21:5; John 12:15; Rom. 9:33; 11:26; Heb. 12:22; 1 Pet. 2:6). Despite all appearances to the contrary, "*The Crucified One*" (Mark 16:6) will gather the faithful and judge the faithless – from Zion, the very stronghold upon which the Lamb now makes his stand.

With the Lamb is a witnessing remnant of 144,000. Though John has narratively introduced them at 7:1-8, because this scene is a part of the flashback (chapters

12-14), he describes them here as if his hearers and readers are encountering them for the first time. And yet, because of the narratives sequencing, there is much about this remnant that the audience already knows. As their location on Zion confirms, they are a protected group. Their protection is symbolized by the name of the Lamb and the name of his Father. The seal identifies them as witnesses (cf. 3:12; 22:4) who conquered the dragon (12:11) by resisting its lordship claims. The seal, then, is a direct counter to the beast's mark that was tattooed onto the forehead or right hand of all those who testified to and participated in its lordship. The imagery is that of two marked combatant forces poised before each other, ready for eschatological battle (cf. 19:14).

The significance of the 144,000 is also contemporary. As a narrative construct, they operate somewhat like the transfiguration of Jesus in the Gospel of Mark (9:2-8). That event was a narrative sign that Jesus, and those who followed him, would be vindicated by God. This is the 144,000's function as a remnant community. The revelation of their *"protected"* witness to the lordship of God and the Lamb demonstrates that God can and will be able to live up to God's promises to reward with life all those who bear witness, even to the point of death (cf. 13:10; 14:12).

- **2** John turns from what he sees on earth to a sound he hears issuing from heaven. The shift in sensory perception and location is similar to the move he narrates at the opening of chapter 7. There, after seeing four angels standing at the four corners of the earth and another ascending from the earth (7:1-3), he hears a voice proclaim, presumably also from heaven, the number of God's sealed servants (7:4). Here John emphasizes the awesome magnitude of the voice. The voice's weight suggests its message and the identity of those who sing. At 19:6 a great heavenly multitude cries out in praise of God with what john describes in almost precisely the same way as a voice of many waters and great thunder. The multitude at 19:6, and apparently here – not the plural pronoun "*they*" that opens v. 3 – sings praises to God for the establishment of God's rule.

This multitude, though related to the 144,000 in 14:1-5, clearly cannot be identified with them. While they are singing from heaven, John's narration locates the 144,000 on earth. In fact, it is not even clear that the 144,000 hear the song; John specifies that its sound registers only with him. This multitude is probably the same throng that cried out from heaven in a great voice at 7:9-17 to celebrate the salvation of God and the Lamb. John described that multitude as the universal assembly of witness from every nation and tribe and people and tongue (7:9) that had been redeemed by (cf. 5:9), and had conquered through (7:14; 12:11), Christ's blood. Like chapter 7, chapter 14 has placed the 144,000 and the larger multitude from which they have been culled in an antiphonal narrative relationship. The purpose of that relationship is the same in both texts, to symbolize and then celebrate the realization of God's salvific rule.

John further specifies the multitude's identity by placing harps in their hands. At 15:2 those who conquer the beast stand beside the sea of glass with harps. The sea of glass occupies a position in front of the throne, which is also the location of the multitudes in 7:9 and 14:3. This means that the multitudes in 7:9, 14:3 and 15:2 all stand before the heavenly throne, which suggests that John is speaking about the same group. The multitude in 15:2 also praises God for the enactment of God's just and kingly rule. In fact, the language of singing as it is connected to songs and harps occurs in only three places in the Book of Revelation, the hymnic sections 5:8-14; 14:2-3 and 15:2-4. In each of these texts the central theme is praise for the realization of God's rule. Even before John tells us about the song, then, we have a very good idea about the message it exclaims.

- **3** The fact that it is a new song further clarifies its message. In the Old Testament the new song establishes a theme of ransom or protection and adds to it a corresponding assurance that God will rightly judge those who have persecuted God's witnesses. In Ps. 144 the new song, sung on a ten-stringed harp, is chanted in celebration of the one who gives victory to kings and rescues faithful servants like David (Ps. 144:9). The theme of justice pervades the singing of new songs at Pss. 33:3; 96:1; 98:1; 149:1 and Isa. 42:10.

A similar dual emphasis occurs in Rev. 14:2-3, where the new song celebrates God as the one whose universal rule materializes in both the judgment of those who reject God's lordship and the ransom/redemption of those who witness to it. At 5:9 the new song was sung in celebration of the Lamb's ransoming/redeeming of every tribe and language and people and nation. Apart from 14:2-3, only one other passage in Revelation presents a similar coherence of song, singing, and harps, and there a universal multitude sings in celebration of God's rule, exemplified through acts connected with Moses and the Lamb (15:2-3). Moses ransomed God's people and implemented God's judgment against Pharaoh through the plagues and the exodus victory at the sea. That political exodus must, for John, have had some bearing on the nature of the ransoming that is accomplished by the Lamb. The celebratory singing occurs in a context where the victory of the witnesses is portrayed as a victory against imperial Rome and its patron Asia Minor cities. The multitude is therefore celebrating more than a redemption from sin; they sing just as fervently on account of the Lamb's ransom from any need to accommodate to the lures and threats of Rome.

The song that is sung before the throne, the cherubim (cf. 4:6-8), and elders (4:4) can only be learned by the 144,000. This is an odd claim since it seems to exclude even the elders and cherubim before whom it is sung. John apparently has not himself learned it; he hints contextually at the theme but never actually reveals the words as he does in his other hymnic sections. Additionally, it is not even certain that the 144,000 hear the song, at least not in their present earthly setting. The focus, though, is not so much on their present hearing as it is on their future capability; they can learn the words of this song.

Scholars are right to note that the verb "μανθάνω" (learn) can either have an ordinary sense or connote esoteric knowledge (cf. 2 Cor. 12:4). John is more concerned with how one learns and whether the learning is tied to witnessing. This connection fits the portrayal of the 144,000, who have been singled out because they resisted Rome's lordship claims. Their resistance enabled their learning. John no doubt must also mean that the 144,000 are the learned by the heavenly multitude of victorious witnesses (7:9-17) who sing it. Their past resistance, which clearly cost them their lives, must have earned them their capability.

What John does not make clear is why no other earthly witnesses can learn the song. Perhaps this is a marching song whose cadence can only be comprehended by those who parade with the Lamb on the eschatological battlefield (cf. 19:14). If the content of the song is integrally connected to its cadence, then one would expect that it is only by taking up the march (witnessing) that one can learn the lines.

John's statement that these 144,000 have been redeemed from the earth parallels his descriptive statement in v. 4 that they have been redeemed from humankind.

- **4** Verse 4 is a compilation of three clauses employing the pronoun *"these"* (οὗτοί), each of which adds a new character trait to the description of the 144,000. The first clause is also the most puzzling. These are the ones who have not defiled themselves with women; they are virgins. It is unlikely that John intended "μολύνω" (defile) literally, for Revelation's language does not function as a cipher with a one-one meaning. John enjoys using language figuratively. In his only other use of "μολύνω," he intentionally applies it to the faithful at Sardis who did not "defile" themselves by eating meat sacrificed to imperial cultic figures (3:4). The verb is not sexual for John; it applies rather to idolatry and the lack of resistance to that idolatry. John could craft such a connection (2:14, 20) because idolatry had long been imaged as improper sexuality, particularly unchastity, in Israel's history. In the Old Testament, Israel's idolatries and political and economic practices are pictured as "*harlotry*," and Israel's idolatry was also referred to as "*defilement*" (Jer. 3:2; 13:27; 23:15; 51:4; Ezek. 16:15-58; 23:1-49; 43:7; Hos. 1:2; 5:4, 6, 10; Isa. 65:4; *1 Esd.* 8:80).

The metaphor that accounts best for the confluence of the 144,000 as a remnant army force, the parallel between illicit sexuality and idolatry, and the rather dysfunctional language of men undefiled by sexual relations with women – that metaphor is of holy war. Because the writers of the Old Testament considered sexuality to be such a powerful force, they instructed that it be ritually insulated from normal life, so that people engaged in special occupations or missions such as the priesthood or God's army were, during the time of their service, expected to refrain from sex, not from moralistic reasons but to insulate the sacred service from other powers (Deut. 20:1-9; 23:9-10; 1 Sam. 21:4-5; 2 Sam. 11:11; 1QM 7:3-6). This expectation dovetailed nicely with John's own figurative belief that in order to conquer the satanic force that expressed itself in bestial Rome, his hearers and readers must divorce themselves from any accommodation to its idolatrous expectations.

John uses the term "παρθένος" (virgin) in a similarly figurative sense. He does not intended to exclude women from his portrait of the 144,000. Instead, "παρθένος" describes males and females who resist accommodating ("*defiling*") themselves to the lures of the Roman imperial cult. Precedent for such a broad use of the term has been found by many commentators in Philo (*Cher.* 49-50), who uses the noun to refer metaphorically to God's people of both genders.

Still, at least in a twenty-first-century context, the language is disconcerting. For more than two millennia, the devaluation of both women and sexuality implied in a literal reading of the verse has borne negative consequences for women in particular and human relationships in general. As we faithfully interpret and translate John's language metaphorically, we must also find ways in our public reading of the verse to transcribe not the words but the intent. A more affirming and still figuratively appropriate reading would be something like the following: "*These one are like virgins who would not be seduced by the idolatrous lures of the beast from the sea.*"

The second "οὗτοί" (these) clause identifies the 144,000 as disciples who follow (ἀκολουθέω) the Lamb wherever he goes. The verb "ἀκολουθέω" is used in the Gospels as a technical term for discipleship (Mark 8:34; Matt. 16:24; Luke 9:23; Matt. 10:38; Luke 14:27; John 10:4; 13:36). Where does John's Lamb go? As the true and faithful witness (Rev. 1:5; 3:14), he goes to such extreme lengths to resist testimony to the lordship of Rome that he is slaughtered (5:6, 9, 12; 13:8). Through that execution, he is snatched to the throne of God (12:5). The 144,000 follow on all but one interesting phase of this journey. They follow the Lamb in his resistance, and they anticipate a future residence near the throne. However, their very status as the "*sealed*" or "*protected*" ones implies that they will not follow the Lamb to slaughter. The trademark of their discipleship is not death, but their defiant act of witnessing.

The third and final "οὗτοί" (these) clause identifies the 144,000 as those who were redeemed from humans (v. 3) as firstfruits to God and the Lamb. Since the word "*firstfruits*" is in the climactic position, the interpretive agenda starts there. Once again John is operating figuratively. There were three kinds of offerings in the Mediterranean world: offering of food, offerings of objects (votive offerings), and animal sacrifices. "*Firstfruits*" (ἀπαρχή) belonged to the first category (Exod. 23:19; Lev. 23:9-14; Deut. 26:1-11). The firstfruits were the initial offerings taken from a harvest.

In fact, the firstfruits *"redeemed"* the remainder of the harvest for general use and consumption (Rom. 11:16). John's figurative description of the 144,000 as the *"redeemed"* is less mysterious in light of this revelation. They act as a guarantor that many more will be gathered in the general human harvest to come (Rev. 14:14-20). Such a figurative understanding coheres well with other New Testament presentations. When Paul speaks of Christ as the firstfruits in 1 Cor. 15:20-23, he means that his resurrection guarantees a full harvest of eschatological resurrections. Likewise, when the apostle refers to the Spirit as a guarantor of the full gift of eschatological salvation (Rom. 8:23; 2 Cor. 1:22; 5:5; Eph. 1:13-14). Given John's eager acceptance of the metaphor and his presentation of the 144,000 as a remnant community whose presence instills hope in their witness colleagues, it is likely that John intended this redeemed group of firstfruits not only to guarantee God's ability to protect and save those who witness to God's lordship, but also to provide tangible evidence of the coming harvest. They are the proof of what God can and will do!

- **5** John lists lying as one of the critical vice-list acts that can thwart a person's hope for eschatological relationship with God (cf. 21:27; 22:15). The background for his language comes from Isa. 53:9, where the Servant of God is described as having no deceit in his mouth. Surely, in that case, he is a model for the larger faith community. The prophet Zephaniah makes this case when he attributes the same truthfulness to the remnant of Israel (Zeph. 3:13). John, then, is concerned about something of much greater significance than "*fibbing*." The seer who appeals for a resistant witness to the lordship of Christ is more concerned with the lying, false witness that contributes to a contrary belief in the lordship of the beast from the sea. When he calls his remnant community of 144,000 blameless, then, he is thinking less about their moral purity than about their active resistance to Rome's bestial, imperial claims. It is this resistance that they model for the larger faith community. In the dangerous call to witness to the lordship of Christ, they are blameless: they have not accommodated themselves to the draconian lie.

Revelation 14:6~13 → Flashback: An Eternal Gospel

NIV	TT
⁶ Then I saw another angel flying in midair, and he had the eternal gospel to proclaim to those who live on the earth—to every nation, tribe, language and people. ⁷ He said in a loud voice, "Fear God and give him glory, because the hour of his judgment has come. Worship him who made the heavens, the earth, the sea and the springs of water." ⁸ A second angel followed and said, "'Fallen! Fallen is Babylon the Great,' which made all the nations drink the maddening wine of her adulteries." ⁹ A third angel followed them and said in a loud voice: "If anyone worships the beast and its image and receives its mark on their forehead or on their hand,	⁶ Then I saw another angel flying in midheaven, with an eternal gospel to proclaim to those who inhabit the earth, that is, every nation and tribe and tongue and people, ⁷ saying in a great voice; "Fear God and give God glory, because the hour of God's judgment has come; worship the one who made heaven and earth and sea and springs of water." ⁸ And a second another angel followed, saying: "Fallen, fallen is Babylon the Great, who made all the nations drink from the wine of the **wrath**[209] of her fornication." ⁹ And another angel, a third one, followed them, saying with a great voice: "If anyone worships the beast and its image and takes a mark on his forehead or hand, ¹⁰ then he will drink from the wine of the wrath of God, poured unmixed into the cup of

---

[209] θυμός → It means "*anger,*" "*wrath,*" "*rage,*" and "*passion.*"

¹⁰ they, too, will drink the wine of God's fury, which has been poured full strength into the cup of his wrath. They will be tormented with burning sulfur in the presence of the holy angels and of the Lamb. ¹¹ And the smoke of their torment will rise for ever and ever. There will be no rest day or night for those who worship the beast and its image, or for anyone who receives the mark of its name." ¹² This calls for patient endurance on the part of the people of God who keep his commands and remain faithful to Jesus. ¹³ Then I heard a voice from heaven say, "Write this: Blessed are the dead who die in the Lord from now on." "Yes," says the Spirit, "they will rest from their labor, for their deeds will follow them."	God's fury, and he will be **tormented**[210] by fire and sulfur before holy angels and before the Lamb. ¹¹ And the smoke of their torment rises forever and ever. Those who worship the beast and its image and take the mark of its name do not have rest day and night." ¹² Here is the endurance of the saints, those who keep the commandments of God, that is, the faith of Jesus. ¹³ Then I heard a voice from heaven saying, "Write: 'Blessed are the dead who die in the Lord from now on.'" "Yes," says the Spirit, "that they might rest from their labors, for their works follow with them."

In this section the reality of God's judgment appears in contrast to the sham judgment delivered when Christians were condemned in the Roman courts. As 14:1-5

---

[210] βασανίζω → It means *"torture," "torment,"* and *"press hard."*

anticipates the eschatological salvation of the new Jerusalem, 14:6 and on anticipates the coming fall of Babylon and God's judgment on those who bear the mark of the beast.

- **6** With "Καὶ εἶδον" (and I saw), John signals a turn to another narrative scene. He sees *"another angel"* (a symbolic marker for judgment, see 10:1). Since the last reference to angels occurs in this flashback unit at 12:7, he may well be contrasting this angel to Michael and his cohorts at 12:7. Michael's group played an important role in securing an eschatological victory against Satan in heaven. This angel and the five who follow him will perform a similarly important task; they will set the parameters for the harvesting of humankind from the earth. Given the strong judgment orientation, it is more likely that John contrasts these six with the seven trumpet angels of chapters 8-10. Though they execute the similar task of judgment, these are different angels.

    This first angel appears in flight at midheaven. The description calls to mind both the eagle flying in midheaven at 8:13 and the birds flying in midheaven at 19:17. In both those cases the flights occur in the context of God's graphic judgment against the idolatrous inhabitants of the earth. Such a judgment theme fits the context where a draconian force hunts the people of God and has deployed bestial sea and land forces to achieve its tactical objectives. The angel is a visible reminder that God is preparing a powerful and just response.

The angel's message sets the tone for everything else that will happen in the chapter. John says that he bears an eternal gospel; "εὐαγγέλιον" (gospel) is the language of good news (cf. Mark 13:10; Matt. 24:14). It is odd that the angel bears this good news in a scene saturated with strong judgment themes. But it is difficult to gauge John's understanding of the term since he uses it only here. The one other time that he uses the verb form, "εὐαγγελίζω" (to proclaim the gospel), he also places it within a context of judgment (10:7). John is not using this very important term ("*gospel*") cynically, as the larger context of chapters 12-14 indicates. In this circumstance where the dragon, the beast from the sea, the beast from the land, and all those who ally themselves with them are persecuting the people of God, any message of a just salvation for God's people will necessarily include a corresponding note of judgment against those who have persecuted them. What is good news for God's witnesses is judgment news for those who persecute them. This is John's perspective throughout the Book of Revelation.

John clarifies that the gospel is preached to the ones who sit upon the earth and to every nation and tribe and tongue and people. Those who sit (κάθημαι) upon the earth bear strong resemblance to those who inhabit (κατοικέω) the earth at 13:8 (2:13; 3:10; 6:10; 8:13; 11:10; 13:8, 12, 14; 17:2, 8). The inhabitants of the earth are presented uniformly as being hostile to the testimony of the lordship of God and the Lamb. In messaging the presentation here with a different verb (κάθημαι, sit), John surely wants to bring them to mind while simultaneously softening his hearers' and readers' impression of them. Just as interesting, in the same chapter 13 setting, at v. 7, John identifies those who dwell on the earth with the same universal conglomeration that he uses here at 14:6: every tribe and people and language and nation. I have argued that the "καὶ" (and) that connects *"inhabitants of the earth"* and *"those of every tribe and people and tongue and nation"* should be read epexegetically in 13:7. That is, *"those of every tribe and people and tongue and nation"* further describes and clarifies *"inhabitants of the earth."* They will be judged because of their hostility toward God and those who have witnessed to the lordship of God and the Lamb. The same epexegetical formulation occurs in 14:6. John means to say that the gospel has gone out to *"those who sit upon the earth,"* that is, to *"every nation and tribe and tongue and people."* The message is a universal one of judgment.

The descriptive nuance, however, should not be missed. John does not say *"inhabitants of the earth"* for the same reason that he adds the language of gospel proclamation. There is still hope for a repentant response. The 144,000 are not the only ones who have been redeemed in John's text (7:4). According to John's narration, the universal grouping of every tribe and language and people and nation has also been the object of the Lamb's successful redemptive efforts (5:9; 7:9). Indeed, the great multitude of conquering witnesses (7:14) is comprised from just this universal conglomeration (7:9). John himself is tasked with the vocation of prophesying to this group (10:11), with the knowledge that the message will deliver judgment if they do not respond appropriately (cf. 11:9). The prophetic message to fear God and give God glory (14:7) – that is, witness to the lordship of God and the Lamb – is always the same. The target audience for the prophetic message is the same. Depending upon their response, however, the message operates as either good news or judgment.

- 7 The angel speaks with a great tone of judgment. Most recently, in this very flashback section, a great heavenly voice issued a proclamation that carries the same complex nuance that John establishes here (12:10). There, too, the voice declared a message of salvation (for those who witness faithfully to the lordship of God and the Lamb) that morphed quickly into a pledge of judgment (against those who have persecuted God's witnesses).

Despite the change in audience, the content of the message remains constant: Fear God and render God glory. To be sure, fear God is integrally connected to God's role as eschatological judge (15:4; 19:1-5). The reward for those who exhibit this fear will be eschatological relationship with God (11:18). The alternative is a fear of the first death, which prompts a person to accommodate to the lures and threats of Roman imperial lordship.

It is the fear of God that sparks a glorification of God. Even those who tormented the two witnesses became so frightened by God's acts of justice/judgment that they were motivated to glorify God (11:13). An appropriate fear of God can lead even where faith initially cannot go, to a right understanding of God's role as cosmic Lord.

Glory is not only due God because of God's role as judge, but also because of God's role as Creator. In this context glorification expresses itself as worship (4:9, 11). In chapter 13, humans were castigated because of their worship of the dragon and beast from the sea (13:4, 8, 12, 15). Here, the great voice issues a defining corrective with a gospel message that will fall like judgment upon those who respond improperly to it.

As if to make that point explicit, the message comes to match the tone in which it is delivered; the voice declares that the hour of judgment has come. The aorist (ἦλθεν, has come) is proleptic here; it anticipates a future realization by acting as if it has already occurred. John is so sure that God will judge that he operates as if God already has. The fate of those who resist God and persecute God's witnesses is sealed.

- **8** This same proleptic message of judgment is affirmed by a "*second another angel.*" John numbers his divine figures awkwardly for a reason. He wants to make the point that they are a part of a series of seven divine people who on earth have taken up the battle that Michael and his cohort prosecuted in heaven (12:7). He also wants to distinguish them from the seven trumpet angels.

This second angel speaks without nuance directly to the force that has institutionalized an economic, political, social, and cultic opposition to God. Its adherents have rejected and continue to reject the call to fear God and give God glory (cf. 16:9). Though he gives it the name *"Babylon the Great,"* he is speaking to Rome, the beast from the sea (13:1-10; cf. 1 Pet. 5:13). Babylon, we know, is the name of the great imperial force that destroyed Jerusalem in 587 B.C.E., desecrated the temple, and drove much of the populace into exile. For that act of infamy, Babylon became the prototypical enemy of the people of God. Daniel 4:30 describes the arrogance of Babylon through the words of its king Nebuchadnezzar, who demanded for himself the kind of reverence due only God (Dan. 3). For John, Rome reenacts Babylon's adversarial and idolatrous role. Rome is the only other force to have destroyed Jerusalem and desecrated its temple. Rome is the one imperial force that demands for itself and its emperors the devotion of lordship due only God. Because of Rome's extraordinary conceit, John applies to it the same words of judgment that Isaiah 21:9 and Jeremiah 51:7-8 assigned to Babylon. Once again using a proleptic aorist tense (ἔπεσεν, *"fallen"*; also 18:2), he declares that although it appears powerful and menacing, it has already fallen.

John uses the term *"Babylon"* only five other times in his entire work; in each case, he emphasizes the promise of its judgment (16:19; 17:5; 18:2, 10, 21). Even here, though, there is a contextual hint of hope. Daniel 4:27-37 suggests a transformative possibility for even Babylon if it would heed the voice of eschatological reason, repent, fear God, and give God proper glory.

The odds of that happening, though, John knows, are long. Now using imagery to which he will return in powerfully ironic ways, John establishes the passionate crime that Babylon/Rome obsessively commits. Clearly building from Jeremiah's claim that the wine of Babylon's prosperity made the world mad to imbibe it (Jer. 51:7), he presses the case that Babylon/Rome has seduced all the nations to drink out of the furiously intoxicating (θυμός) wine of her sexual illicitness. John speaks here about the lure of wanting to participate in economic gluttony that Rome has established (Rev. 18:3). To share in and prosper from the empire's wealth, nations are willing to *"mark"* themselves as patrons to its ideology and devotees of its lordship (Rev. 13:16-17). The drive to be a part of Roman success/excess is a kind of madness for prosperity. It is this prosperity mania that entices the members of John's seven churches to participate in guild and trade associations, where commercial alliances can be forged and social standing advanced, but also where meat sacrificed to imperial idols is consumed. John perceives this kind of idolatrous behavior through the lens of inappropriate sexuality (cf. 2:21; 9:21; 14:4; 17:2, 4; 18:3; 19:2). He means to say that by selling out their devotion to the lordship of God and the Lamb in order to reap Rome's economic and social rewards, the nations have prostituted themselves to an idolatrous and false hope.

- **9 – 10** The *"third another angel"* continues the loud message. The verse sets up the first half (the protasis) of a conditional statement that reflects on information already conveyed in 13:16-18. The concluding half (apodosis) of the conditional sentence begun in 14:9 is initiated with "καὶ." Since v. 10 deals explicitly with those who accept the mark of the beast and therefore have rejected any recognition of God's and the Lamb's lordship, there is none of the nuance evident in v. 6. This verse is strictly about a judgment that John casts as ironic, poetic justice. He takes the very same vocabulary of passionate, intoxicating rage ("θυμός"), drinking, and wine that he has used to describe Babylon/Rome's bewitching of the nations (v. 8) and twists it into the language of God's retribution. From this point in the narrative forward, when wine (Rev. 16:19; 17:2; 18:3; 19:15) and passionate rage (Rev. 14:19; 15:1, 7; 16:1, 19; 19:15) appear, they will convey not idolatrous celebration but divine wrath.

John sharpens the language by appealing directly to the vessel that no doubt holds this furious wine: the cup of God's wrath. The seer is drawing from plentiful Old Testament uses of the cup of wrath where God fools God's enemies by offering them an intoxicating drink that causes drunkenness, understood as judgment (cf. Pss. 11:6; 75:8; Isa. 51:17, 22; Jer. 25:15; 49:12; 51:7; Lam. 4:21; Ezek. 23:31-34; Hab. 2:15-16; Obad. 16; Zech. 12:2). The wine in God's cup is much more potent than anything Babylon/Rome may have concocted. According to John, it is poured unmixed. Wine was generally mixed with spices to make it more potent. However, wine was also often diluted with water. John sees the strength of God's wine as doubly powerful, for while it was mixed with spices, it was not watered down. God's wrath is at full strength.

John conveys the magnitude of his claim with the verse's concluding clause: affiliates of the beast will be tormented with fire and brimstone (sulfur) before the angels and the Lamb. The language of torment (βασανίζω) implies that this will be an eschatological punishment that, mercilessly, never ends. Whenever John employs the term, he gives it a sense of constancy (Rev. 11:10; 12:2) and even perpetuity (Rev. 9:5). The most telling use occurs at 20:10. There the dragon and its two minion beasts will be tormented forever in a lake comprised of the same punishing elements used here: fire and sulfur.

Fire and sulfur were traditionally understood as the instruments of divine retribution, wielded against Sodom and Gomorrah and others of God's enemies (Gen. 19:24; Ps. 11:6; Ezek. 38:22). John maintains the practice of packaging fire and sulfur together: Rev. 9:17-18; 19:20; 20:10; 21:8.

- **11** John's presentation is unbearably harsh. The picture of punishment as enduring torture implied by the verb *"torment"* in v. 10 is reinforced in the next verse, when he declare that the smoke of the dragon's and beast's affiliates' *"torment"* goes up forever. They find rest neither day nor night. The rising smoke hearkens back to the smoke of Edom's judgment rising up day and night forever (Isa. 34:9-10). John is also operating from his own intratextual connections. This reflection on the rest-less day and night suffering of God's enemies is meant to parallel the heavenly praise of God that goes on without rest, day and night, at Rev. 4:8. In this allusive way, the complex nuance that John introduced with his presentation of gospel as judgment at Rev. 14:6 marks its return. Salvation occurs for those who properly respond to the call to fear God and give God glory. While those who respond improperly burn in ceaseless torment, the witnesses of God and the Standing Slaughtered Lamb, whom they once persecuted, are guaranteed enduring rest.

The harshness of John's picture of judgment does not press one to consider how his language can be applied to contemporary twenty-first-century contexts. This language was not meant to be taken literally. The elements of fire and sulfur and the lake of fire are meant to be provocative symbols of the dis-ease that comes from eschatological separation from God. Even the language of incessant torment must be understood figuratively. After all, john is not targeting non-believers to get them to commit to the faith; he is targeting believers who he fears may commit apostasy in an effort to accommodate themselves to Roman economic, political, social, and cultic pressures and expectations. His fierce language is meant to dissuade them. He wants them to believe that there is a horror greater than even the worst penalty, the first death, that the Romans can surely impose. He wants his audience to see it and, through his graphic language, even rhetorical, not literal. It is not at this point meant so much to inform as to exhort. .

- **12** As in 13:10 (cf. 17:9), the adverb *"here"* (ὧδε) that initiates v. 12 points both backward and forward. John means to say that what he has said previously (cf. 13:18) as well as what he will say forms the basis for the "ὑπομονή" (endurance, patience) of the saints. The presentation of the 144,000 (Rev. 14:1-5) encourages resistance because their presence demonstrates that God can and will protect God's own. The portrait of the gospel as a concomitant message of judgment (vv. 6-11) inspires resistance because the witnesses know that God will vindicate their efforts. The promise of harvest, both salutary and judgmental (vv. 14-20), encourages believers to resist allying with those who will be reaped as vintage.

John identifies the *"saints"* as those who maintain the commandments of God and (i.e., which is) the faith proclaimed by Jesus. The "καὶ" (and) is epexegetical; Jesus' faith more fully explicates what John means by God's *"commandments."* John is operating here much as he did at 12:17, connecting an ethical use of *"keep,"* or *"hold"* (τηρέω), with commandments, which in this context work functionally through Jesus' own witnessing behavior and the faith that drives it. The commandment of God is the expectation that believers *"follow"* in the witnessing way of the Standing Slaughtered Lamb. The saints are those who *"keep"* God's commandments by living out the faith of God's Lamb.

- **13** The rationale for resistance is more neatly and immediately summed up in this second of John's seven apocalyptic beatitudes (1:3; 14:13; 16:15; 19:9; 20:6; 22:7, 14). In another shift to audition, John hears a voice bless witnesses who faithfully resist the threats and lures of bestial Babylon/Rome. Is the macarisms an indicative or an imperative? Probably both. As an indicative, it declares that those who die in the Lord are blessed because they will rest from their labors, that is, their acts of resistant witness (Rev. 6:9-11). Given the context of 6:9-11 and John's attempt in chapter 14 to encourage more such efforts so that his hearers and readers will be vindicated, one gathers the sense that by *"rest from labors"* John does not mean *"sit back and relax,"* but *"rest assured"* that God is in charge and that God's justice will win out. The imperative sense develops from the realization that while some rest assured, others are to be about the business of 6:11 highlighted rest, not work, 14:13 emphasizes, in the context of rest, that their work, their labor of resistant witness, will follow them, which is to say, fulfill them. John is not expressing a theology of works righteousness where work leads to salvation; he is instead pressing the case that those who are saved must live out their salvation; he is instead pressing the case that those who are saved must live out their salvation through their witness. That is how they are fulfilled. Verse 13 assigns a speaking role to the Spirit, who represents God's presence.

Revelation 14:14~20 → Flashback: Harvest Time

NIV	TT
¹⁴ I looked, and there before me was a white cloud, and seated on the cloud was one like a son of man with a crown of gold on his head and a sharp sickle in his hand. ¹⁵ Then another angel came out of the temple and called in a loud voice to him who was sitting on the cloud, "Take your sickle and reap, because the time to reap has come, for the harvest of the earth is ripe." ¹⁶ So he who was seated on the cloud swung his sickle over the earth, and the earth was harvested. ¹⁷ Another angel came out of the temple in heaven, and he too had a sharp sickle. ¹⁸ Still another angel, who had charge of the fire, came	¹⁴ **Then I looked, and behold**[211] a white **cloud**[212], and seated on the cloud was one like a Son of Man. He had a golden crown on his head and a sharp sickle in his hand. ¹⁵ Then another angel came out of the temple, **calling with a loud voice**[213] to the one seated on the cloud: "Use your sickle and reap, for the hour to reap has come, because the harvest of the earth is ripe." ¹⁶ Then the one seated on the cloud swung his sickle on **the earth**[214], and the earth was harvested. ¹⁷ And another angel came out of the temple in heaven, and he also had a sharp sickle. ¹⁸ Then another angel, the one who has

---

[211] Καὶ εἶδον, καὶ ἰδοὺ → The phrase means *"Then I looked, and behold."* This phrase functions as a literary device to introduce a new scene.

[212] νεφέλη → It means a *"cloud."* The term was used of the "cloud" which led the Israelites in the wilderness.

[213] κράζων ἐν φωνῇ μεγάλῃ → The phrase can be translated as *"crying out in a loud voice,"* *"screaming in a loud sound,"* and *"calling in a great voice."*

[214] ἡ γῆ → It can be translated as *"the soil," "the earth," "the ground," "the dry land," "the region," "the country,"* and *"the humanity."*

from the altar and called in a loud voice to him who had the sharp sickle, "Take your sharp sickle and gather the clusters of grapes from the earth's vine, because its grapes are ripe." [19] The angel swung his sickle on the earth, gathered its grapes and threw them into the great winepress of God's wrath. [20] They were trampled in the winepress outside the city, and blood flowed out of the press, rising as high as the horses' bridles for a distance of 1,600 stadia.	authority over fire, came out from the altar, and he called with a loud voice to the one who had the sharp sickle, saying: "Use your sharp sickle and gather the grape clusters of the vintage of the earth, because its grapes are ripe." [19] And the angel swung his sickle over the earth and gathered the vintage of the earth into the great winepress of the wrath of God. [20] And the winepress was trodden outside the city, and blood flowed from the winepress as high as the bridles of horses from **1,600**[215] stadia.

The harvest imagery in the final seven verses of chapter 14 is heavily debated. The core concern is whether John is presenting here the portrait of a single harvest based on the imagery from Joel 3:13, or whether he adapts the Joel material and offers first salvation (vv. 14-16) and then judgment (vv. 17-20). Given John's nuanced presentation of gospel as a message of both salvation and judgment, I argue that he presents a picture of the harvest that is both positive (for those who respond properly to the called to fear God and give God glory) and negative (for those who refuse).

---

[215] χιλίων ἑξακοσίων → The Greek phrase means "*a thousand and six hundred*," thus "*1,600*."

John's image of a sickle reaping grapes and of treading upon them in the winepress is surely John's inspiration for the two harvests (Joel 3:13). In both harvest images (vv. 14-16, 17-20), John includes the sickle and dramatically ends with the winepress and its horrific results. There is, however, a breakdown in the parallel with Joel and also with traditional harvesting images. Although the harvesting of the vineyard includes both reaping and treading, the harvesting of the grain fields that John surely implies in vv. 14-16 includes reaping but no threshing or winnowing (cf. Mark 4:29). John has purposely, it seems, left off the image that would involve the judgmental separation of the proverbial wheat from the chaff. That seems to suggests, that vv. 14-16 offer a fully salvific image of universal ingathering (cf. Mark 13:26-27; Luke 10:2; John 4:35-38).

- **14** Once again, *"Then I looked, and behold"* indicates John's move to yet another new scene. The new thing is a white cloud, occupied by a figure *"like a Son of Man."* John has used clouds before as the wrapping for divine figures. He also employs it as a metaphorical mode of heavenly transport for Christ (Rev. 1:7; Mark 14:62; Matt. 26:64; Luke 22:69) and for the two witnesses (Rev. 11:12). The cloud in 10:1 is particularly significant since, like the one here, it occurs in a context of judgment (cf. Matt. 24:30).

    There has been some debate as to whether this Son of Man figure is Christ or another of the angels who occupy Rev. 14. It has been suggested, because the fourth angel (v. 15) issues an order to the one *"like a*

Son of Man," and therefore appears to be his superior, that the one "*like a Son of Man*" cannot be Christ. The objection is inconclusive. Tradition makes clear from the words of Jesus that no one, not even the Son of man, knows the time of God's harvesting movement (Mark 13:32; Acts 1:7). It would therefore not be surprising that while operating in the field, the Son of Man would need a directive from God before proceeding to harvest. Indeed, John specifically describes the fourth angel as coming out of the temple (v. 15). He is thus speaking for God, not for himself. Furthermore, John has developed a series of angelic presentations in the chapter and does not appear hesitant about narratively piling angels on top of each other. Had he wanted to make the one like a Son of Man "*another*" angel it would have been easy for him to do so, and it would have made the narrative progression much neater. Instead, he appears to suggest a central role for the one like a Son of Man by placing him in the middle of the angelic countdown, thereby highlighting not only his placement but also his role. It is he who appears to be the initiator of both phases of the harvest as they take place in the ensuing verses. His participation in the salvific grain harvest is obvious (vv. 14-16). His participation in the vintage harvest (vv. 17-20) is not as clear, but it is implied through the image of the trodden grapes because John later discloses that it was indeed Christ (as the rider of the white horse) who trod the winepress of God's fury (Rev. 19:15). Finally, the identification of this Son of Man with Christ is not only consistent with the New Testament's development of the image from Dan. 7:13-14 but also fits John's own labeling of the Christ in his narrative (Rev. 1:13-16).

The golden crown symbolizes the lordship of the one like a Son of Man, the very truth to which his witnesses are called to testify (cf. 2 Sam. 12:30; 1 Chr. 20:2). The sickle he holds (Rev. 14:15, 16, 17, 18, 19), a curved cutting instrument, is a metaphor for his role as the one who initiates the harvests that reap the faithful from among every nation and tribe and language and people.

- **15** It is the fourth *"another angel"* who appears out of the sanctuary of the temple and conveys God's order to the one a the Son of Man that the grain harvest should begin. His loud voice suggests that this harvest, like the good news itself, does not operate independently of God's justice. In support of the claim that the phrasing here supports a salvific ingathering, Caird argues that the two key terms "θερίζω" (to harvest) and "θερίσμοσ" (harvest) never picture destruction of God's enemies in the LXX, even in passages where judgment is likened to reaping. Rather, *"they are used of the ingathering of men into the kingdom of God."* Indeed, John's presentation of the harvesting imagery is consistent not only with the universal proclamation of good news (Rev. 14:7) but also with the portrait of the 144,000 as a representative *"firstfruits"* of the universal multitude to follow, rather than an elite, exclusive company of the saved (v. 4; 7:9).
- **16** The Son of Man follows God's instruction and reaps the earth. As noted above, however, he does not follow up with a judgmental winnowing/threshing. Here lies

the climactic movement that John narrates in the seventh seal, trumpet, and bowl. It is prefigured in this scene. The seventh act, the climactic one, belongs to the Son of Man.

- **17** A fifth *"another angel"* now makes his way out of the temple sanctuary, a sharp sickle in hand. The fact that he holds the same tool as the Son of Man suggests that he will play a role in this new phase of God's final harvest.
- **18** The sixth and final *"another angel"* now makes his way from the sanctuary altar. He has authority over fire. Fire is a consistent metaphor of judgment for John (Rev. 3:18; 8:5, 7-8; 15:2). At 8:5 the fire of the incense altar was thrown down upon the earth as an apparent answer of justice/judgment to the cries of the slaughtered saints under the altar (Rev. 6:9-11). That potent image must surely be in John's mind as he envisions this sixth angel coming out from the altar with the authority of fire. When the angel commands the fifth angel to swing his sickle into motion, John's hearers and readers would not have been surprised that his voice carries the great tone of judgment.
- **19** After reaping the vineyard, the angel casts the yield upon the winepress of the passionate fury (i.e., the wrath) of God. John's hearers and readers are prepared for this language by the narration at vv. 8, 10, which anticipates the actions of the Christ as depicted in 19:15. Those who have allied themselves with the dragon and the beast drink the wine of God's fury poured unmixed from the cup of divine wrath. That such language returns here is an indication of the judgmental nature of

the fifth angel's actions (throwing the harvest onto the floor of the winepress), which anticipates the concluding work of the Christ (trodding the harvest underfoot). This is the judgment that awaits all who are marked with the name and number of the beast.

- **20** The treading upon the winepress is the climactic moment of judgment. The action operates from the brutal imagery of Isa. 63:1-6, where the blood of the grapes, and thus the judgment, flows freely from the press. God appears to be directly involved. Both angels come from the sanctuary and therefore act on God's orders. Furthermore, the angel's role is limited to the casting of the harvest upon the winepress. At 19:15, John makes clear that it is God's Christ who actually crushes the harvest with the passionate fury of God's wrath (cf. 14:8, 10). The end result is no less horrifying than the language of eternal torture conjured up by the vision recounted at vv. 10-11.

The action takes place outside the city. John has already used poetic irony to turn the wickedness of those who follow the beast against them. The idolatrous wine with which they have intoxicated themselves has mutated into the unmixed wine of God's anger (vv. 8, 10). Perhaps the seer is now talking yet another stab at mocking the evil that the dragon's forces have perpetrated against God's interests. The traditions maintain that Jesus was crucified, slaughtered outside the city. How deliciously just it would seem to John that not only the forces responsible for that travesty but also others who have allied themselves with those forces should meet their eschatological fate in the same place.

When it is over, so much judgment has been wreaked that John sees the land awash in a great river of blood (cf. *1 En.* 100:3). Anticipating the later shift from harvest to battle as the dominant judgment metaphor (Rev. 19:11-21), John apparently mixes his metaphors so that the winepress becomes a battlefield where the rider-less horses of the armies of the dragon and the beast stand bridle deep in the blood of the marked soldiers who once rode them. A literal figuring of John's 1,600 stadia would yield a span of approximately 180 miles, or 300 kilometers. John's intention, though, it not literal but figurative. Commentators note that 1,600 is the square of ten, signifying totality, signifying totality, multiplied by the square of four, which signifies the four corners of the earth. Whether that deciphering is what John intended, the conclusion it helps one draw certainly does correspond to his intention. The bloodbath and terror of God's judgment affects the whole world. The desperate cry for justice by the slaughtered saints of 6:9-11 has been definitively answered.

Revelation 15:1~8 → Prelude to the Seven Bowls

NIV	TT

15 ¹ I saw in heaven another great and marvelous sign: seven angels with the seven last plagues—last, because with them God's wrath is completed. ² And I saw what looked like a sea of glass glowing with fire and, standing beside the sea, those who had been victorious over the beast and its image and over the number of its name. They held harps given them by God ³ and sang the song of God's servant Moses and of the Lamb:
 	
"Great and marvelous are your deeds,
   Lord God Almighty.
Just and true are your ways,
   King of the nations.
⁴ Who will not fear you, Lord,
	15 ¹ Then I saw another great and **amazing**[216] sign in heaven: seven angels with the seven last plagues, for with them the wrath of God **has been finished**[217].
	
	² Then I saw something like a sea of glass mixed with fire, and standing beside the sea of glass with harps of God, those who had conquered the beast and its image and the number of its name. ³ And they **sing**[218] the song of Moses, the servant of God, and the song of the Lamb, singing: "Great and amazing are your works, Lord God, **the Almighty**[219]; just and true are your ways, King of the nations! ⁴ Who will not fear and glorify your name, Lord? Because you alone are holy, because all the

---

[216] θαυμαστός → It means *"wonderful," "amazing," "marvelous,"* and *"remarkable."*

[217] ἐτελέσθη → It is a divine passive form of *"τελέω."* It means *"bring to an end," "finish," "complete," "come to an end," "find consummation," "keep," "pay," "carry out,"* and *"accomplish."*

[218] ᾄδω → It means *"sing."*

[219] παντοκράτωρ → It means *"the Almighty," "All-Powerful,"* and *"Omnipotent One."*

and bring glory to your name?
For you alone are holy.
All nations will come
 and worship before you,
for your righteous acts have been revealed."

⁵ After this I looked, and I saw in heaven the temple—that is, the tabernacle of the covenant law—and it was opened. ⁶ Out of the temple came the seven angels with the seven plagues. They were dressed in clean, shining linen and wore golden sashes around their chests. ⁷ Then one of the four living creatures gave to the seven angels seven golden bowls filled with the wrath of God, who lives for ever and ever. ⁸ And the temple was filled with smoke from the glory of God and from his power,

nations will come and worship before you, because your righteous judgments have been revealed."

⁵ After this, I looked, and the temple, that is, the **tabernacle**[220] of **witness**[221] in heaven, was opened, ⁶ and the seven angels with the seven plagues came out from the **temple**,[222] clothed in clean, bright linen and with golden sashes across their chests. ⁷ Then one of the four living creatures gave to the seven angels seven golden **bowls**[223] filled with the wrath of God, who lives forever and ever. ⁸ And the temple was filled with smoke from the glory of God and from God's power, and no one was able to enter the temple until the seven plagues of the seven angels were **finished**[224].

---

[220] σκηνή → It means *"tent," "booth," "Tabernacle,"* and *"Tent of Testimony."*

[221] μαρτύριον → It means *"testimony," "proof,"* and *"witness."*

[222] ναός → It means *"temple,"* and *"shrine."* It is used of the temple at Jerusalem, but only of the sacred edifice or sanctuary itself, consisting of the Holy place and the Holy of holies. In classical Greek, it is used of the sanctuary or cell of the temple, where the image of gold was placed which is distinguished from the whole enclosure.

[223] φιάλη → It means a *"bowl,"* which was used for offerings.

[224] τελέω → It means *"bring to an end," "finish," "complete," "come to an end," "find consummation," "carry out," "accomplish," "keep,"* and *"pay."*

> and no one could enter the temple until the seven plagues of the seven angels were completed.

Revelation 15:1 is the superscript for chapters 15 through 18; the verse simultaneously breaks the reader away from the narrative flashback in chapters 12-14 and introduces the primary theme for the material that will follow. The bowl visions represent the third and final visualization of the end-time events that symbolize God's judgment. They are a re-presentation of the dramatic scenes already played out in the form of seven broken seals and seven blasted trumpets. From this even more devastating vantage point of *"the Apokaylpsis,"* John realizes that not just a third but all of the earth will be decimated.

- **1** *"Then I saw"* that opens the verse is John's grammatical clue that he has initiated a new narrative vision (see 5:1, 6; 6:1, 8, 12; 7:2, 9; 8:2, 13; 9:1; 10:1; 13:1, 11). This time, though, the use of this opening formula with the bracketing phrase *"another sign in heaven"* intentionally reminds John's hearers and readers that a previous scene has concluded. John has mentioned a *"sign in heaven"* only twice before (Rev. 12:1-3). The chapters that followed those verses (chapters 12-14) were preoccupied with describing the lives of Christian witnesses as a perilous existence under constant threat from three bestial enemies. This third and final sign does not point back to those beasts but forward to the judgment that God will soon effect against them (chapters 15-16).

According to John, this new sign is both *"great"* and *"amazing."* The description, particularly *"amazing,"* that is used in the entire narrative only here and in 15:3, is an intentional not to Old Testament imagery that highlights God's activity in the world (Exod. 34:10; Pss. 111:2; 139:14). At 15:3, John defines that activity as justice.

The delivery vehicle for this justice will be seven *"last"* plagues. The plague symbolism recalls the previous trumpet scourges (Rev. 9:18, 20; 11:6) and anticipates the imminent bowl horrors (Rev. 15:6, 8; 16:9, 21). *"Last"* here is not a chronological reference; John does not mean to say that these are the last in a series of events beginning with the horrors that accompanied the breaking of the seven seals. The plagues represent the same end-time cataclysms as those recorded with the seals and trumpets, but from this third and final eschatological vantage point. They are John's *"last"* look at the end.

The plagues are also *"last"* because God's wrath ends when they conclude. John uses "θυμός" (wrath) almost exclusively as a reference to the judgment God executes against Babylon. The good news is that this judgment – because believers, too, are caught up in its maelstrom – is short lived (cf. Mark 13:20). Using the same verb the Jesus called upon to signal the end of his historical life and ministry in the Gospel of John (τελέω, John 19:30), John declares that with this final revelatory barrage God's wrath, having achieved its judgment/justice objective, is finished. The divine passive formulation implies that it is none other than God who has extinguished it. Everything, even the horror, happens according to God's justice design and operates under God's control.

- **2** John marks yet another scene shift with the phrase "*then I saw.*" This new episode offers a narrative interpretation of the impending plagues. Before John reveals his assessment, though, he describes a particular part of the throne room vision that has caught his attention: the sea of glass. Though John uses the word "*sea*" often (22 times), he only specifies a sea of glass twice, here and in the other throne room vision at 4:6. The sea is a symbol of instability and chaos, the place where monstrous rebellion against God's authority arises. At 4:6 that symbol was located in the midst of heaven, shackled – glassed over – but still undeniably present. The implication of potential danger and disruption remains with the metaphor in 15:2, but now John adds something new: the sea is "*mixed with fire.*" The verb "*mixed*" is part of a passive construction that indicates God's agency. The construction should be read instrumentally. Fire, for John, is the stir stick that God uses to whip the sea into a judgmental froth (cf. Rev. 8:5, 7, 8; 9:17, 18; 11:5; 14:10, 18; 16:8; 18:8; 19:20; 20:9, 10, 14, 15; 21:8). Prominently positioned beside the sea is an apparently vast multitude of people, who are defined by a single participial form: "τοὺς νικῶντας" (the ones who conquered). Christ, too, is described as a conqueror (Rev. 5:5; 17:14). In the letters to the seven churches, Christ implored John's hearers and readers to follow Christ's model of testifying to his and his God's lordship even at the cost of his own life. He promised that those who do conquer through such witness would achieve the very reward, eschatological relationship with God, that John now glimpses (Rev. 2:7, 11, 17, 26; 3:5, 12, 21). This multitude, then, is populated by believers who have witnessed as Christ implored them to do. This multitude is also the *"they"* of 12:11, who defeat the dragon by their association with the blood of the Lamb and by their own revolutionary testimony about the lordship of that Lamb.

"They" hold harps of God. They use those harps to accompany their singing (15:3). Twice before, John has recalled harps and their owners: 5:8, where the twenty-four elders hold them; and 14:2, where the same heavenly multitude described in 7:9-17 holds them. At 14:2-3 the multitude also uses the harps to accompany their singing. The presence of harps identifies the groups in 7:9-17; 14:2; and 15:2 as the same multitude. John's further description confirms such a conclusion. At 7:14 he observes that the members of the multitude wear robes that have been washed to dazzling white in the blood of the Lamb. The dazzling white effect, particularly as related to dress, is the reward for the very same revolutionary, conquering witness by which John identifies the multitude in 15:2 (cf. 2:17; 3:4-5; 7:9, 13). In describing the beast, its image, and the number of its name as the objects of their conquest,

John simultaneously reminds his hearers and readers of the bestial historical situation in which they now find themselves (chapters 12-14) and projects God's judgment of it (15:5-18:24) and their victory over it (cf. 12:11).

- **3** *"They"* (the conquering multitude) sing an antiphonal response to the victory God has already initiated, with their witnessing assistance, and now in the bowl plagues is poised to consummate. While John's narrative is filled with hymns, the seer uses the actual vocabulary of singing (ᾄδω) only three times. At 5:9, the cherubim and twenty-four elders sing a new song that celebrates the Lamb's ransoming of God's people by his bloody witness. While that ransoming is often interpreted in an individual, pietistic way, John's thematic association with the exodus ransoming of the people from imperial bondage suggests an equally potent political meaning. That political sensibility is amplified by John's identification of the enemy from which the people are ransomed as Rome and its Asia Minor client government (cf. 15:2).

In his only other appeal to the vocabulary of singing (14:3), John refers directly to the victorious multitude he reintroduces at 15:2. In chapter 14 the focus is less on the ransoming of the people than on the judgment/justice of God that will establish it. Still, the central focus that joins both prior singing episodes is celebration prompted by the realization of God's rule.

By contextually emphasizing a direct relationship between the metaphor of singing (15:3) and the plagues of wrath (15:1, 5-8), John reestablishes a focus on the realization of God's rule through the execution of God's justice/judgment. John focuses even more sharply when he identifies the sound as the song of Moses, the servant of God. The simplest concordance search yields a plethora of Old Testament verses where Moses is so designated (e.g., Exod. 4:10; 14:31; Josh. 1:2; 1 Kgs. 21:8; 2 Chr. 24:9; Neh. 1:7-8; Ps. 105:26; Dan. 9:11; Mal. 4:4). None of them is more important for John's purposes here than Exod. 14:31, which designates Moses as God's servant immediately before Moses and the Israelites sing in praise of God's judgment/destruction of the Egyptian army in the sea. In other words, the song the multitude of Rev. 15:3 sings is like the song Moses and the Israelites sang; it praises God's judgment, which ransoms – that is to say, liberates – God's people from those who would purse and persecute them. For this reason, it is also the song of the Lamb. The connecting "καὶ" (and) is epexegetical; John means to say that the song of God's servant Moses is also the song of the Lamb.

Still, calling this new song the song of Moses raises a problem: to what Old Testament song of Moses is John referring? Even though John envisions a similar context for the multitude's song and the Song of Moses in Exod. 15:1-18, there are few grammatical and thematic parallels between the two. Many scholars have noted that a better thematic comparison exists between the multitude's song and the one attributed to Moses and the Israelites in Deut. 32:1-43. But even there the connections are quite general. It seems like John has, while calling upon the master image of Moses' song and all that it implies about God's majestic identity and judging behavior, based his new song upon a broad cross-section of Old Testament texts that heralds a consensus about God's almighty and salvific stature.

John appeals to that almighty status explicitly in the song lyrics. The title "παντοκράτωρ" (almighty) occurs quite often in John's hymns, especially in a context whose theme is judgment (Rev. 1:8; 4:8; 11:17; 16:7, 14; 19:6, 15; 21:22; Amos LXX 3:13; 4:13). Appealing to language already introduced in 15:1, the multitude honors the works of this Almighty God as great and amazing. John's hearers and readers would certainly remember that the sign of the seven angels with the seven last plagues was also described as great and amazing (15:1). The language reaffirms what the divine passive constructions have been implying throughout the narrative: the shocking and awe-ful acts of devastation and destruction as God's way of establishing justice for the conquering witnesses and judgment against those who persecute them. The subsequent stanza of the hymn is quick to insist that these divine actions are both righteous and true. God's judgment is always God's appropriate justice meted out on behalf of God's oppressed people (cf. Rev. 16:5, 7; 19:2; Deut. 32:4, 8; Ps. 145:17).

In the final words of the verse, John identifies the Almighty judging God as the King, not of Israel or of the conquering witnesses, but of the nations (cf. Jer. 10:7). The worldwide lordship belongs to God and is expressed through the exalted status of the Standing

Slaughtered Lamb. This confession is a direct political contradiction of the claims to global dominion made by Caesar and the empire he oversees.

- **4** The emphasis on God's universal rule continues with the question *"Who will not fear and glorify your name, Lord?"* When Jeremiah asked essentially the same question, he directed it not at Israel alone, but at all of the nations of the earth (Jer. 10:7). John addresses the same broad audience. Among all the nations, who will not now fear this Almighty God who acts equitably in judgment and justice? Fear is an appropriate, universally available, and apparently faithful response to the recognition of God's universal sovereignty (Rev. 14:7; 19:5). At 11:18 anyone who fears is rewarded with eschatological relationship with God; anyone who fights against God is judged by God's wrath. The only limits to inclusion in God's reign are self-imposed; those who refuse to fear – who refuse to give God appropriate glory and worship for God's almighty status – exclude themselves from God's ransoming presence and thereby make themselves susceptible to God's incendiary wrath.

By the manner in which he has structured this verse, John has created a synonymous relationship among showing *"fear,"* giving *"glory,"* and offering *"worship."* Showing fear and glorifying God's name are presented in parallel in the first half of the verse, as though they have the same meaning. Indeed, John's use of *"glory"* makes explicit reference to a theme he has to this point indicated only subtly. In the judgment context of 15:1-3, the question *"Who will not fear and glorify your*

God?" implies an expectation of repentance for those in the nations who do not already fear and glorify. Who in one's right mind, after seeing the preliminary arrival of the plagues of almighty wrath in the form of a great and amazing heavenly sign, would not show fear and give glory, that is, repent? Indeed, elsewhere John intentionally deploys the language of fear and glory to describe those who, upon seeing God's mighty acts of judgment, either do or should repent (11:13; 14:7; 16:9). John later testifies to the possibility that the nations could be included in this repentant number (21:24-26; 22:2). Significantly, at 21:24-26 that inclusion is highlighted by the image of the nations mingling their ransomed glory with the glory of God.

The rationale for fearing God/glorifying God/repenting is offered in the second half of the verse. John provides three explanatory statements, each introduced by "ὅτι" (because). The first reason is that only God is holy. John is clearly operating from the background of Ps. 86:8-10, where the psalmist declares that because God is unique among the gods, God alone is worthy to receive glory from the nations. No doubt John has in mind the propensity of the Greco-Roman nations to surrender their praise and adulation to pagan deities, even deified humans like Caesar or a deified state like Rome. Only God is truly holy and therefore worthy, as the first half of the verse concludes, to receive glory. At 16:5, in his only other use of the term "ἅγιος" (holy), John reaffirms that God's holiness is directly connected to God's just/righteous/true judgment.

The fact that all the nations will come and worship before God supplies a second reason for repentance (i.e., fearing God and giving God glory). John's appeal to Old Testament sources broadens here; his writing reminds his hearers and readers of the universal expectations of Isa. 2:2; Jer. 16:19 and Mal. 1:11. In each of these texts, with the allusion to Ps. 86, all the nations come to recognize God's sovereignty. John uses the word "ἔθνος" (nations) with a similar universal emphasis: the messianic child will shepherd the nations with a rod of iron and thus lead them to repentance (cf. 12:5). Moreover, an angel flying in midheaven proclaims the gospel to every nation with the expectation – using the same three terms that are so crucial to the repentance theme here in 15:4 – that the nations will fear, glorify, and worship God (14:6-7). Indeed, John hints that the nations would have given God proper fear, glory, and worship all along if they had not been deceived (20:3).

Third and finally, John acknowledges God as the one who orchestrates events in such a way that people will come to recognize God's majesty. The verb "ἐφανερώθησαν" (were revealed) is a divine passive that indicates God's agency. God revealed God's behavior as righteous acts, which enable all the nations to see what John has long understood. The result of this revelation should motivate the wayward nations' return to God in fear, glorification, and worship (i.e., repentance).

In the end, then, v. 4 provides a three-step causal rationale for the nations to repent. The nations should fear and glorify God. Why? Because in God's judgments God alone is holy, that is, just. How does one know that God is holy? Because the nations come and worship God. Why do they come and worship? Because God's just(ice) acts have been revealed. John's argument is an entirely circular one; he comes back again and again to his primary point. What was true all along (v. 3) – that God is holy, true, and therefore just – God has now demonstrated to all.

- **5** John typically uses the narrative marker "Καὶ μετὰ ταῦτα εἶδον" (after this, I looked) to shift to a new subject area (4:1; 7:1, 9; 18:1; 19:1). This time, however, his use marks a turn back to the subject area that he broke away from after 15:1. The seer's attention was momentarily diverted by the sound of the heavenly multitude of conquering witnesses singing their affirmation of God's imminent acts of justice/judgment. Refocused, John not only returns to the heavenly sign but also instructs his readers about its origin.

The seven angels exit the sanctuary of the tent of meeting in heaven onto John's revelatory scene through an opened door. For John, *"opening"* language is always, even when not directly using God or the Lamb as its subject, salvation and/or judgment language (cf. 6:1). The passive construction (*"opened"*) indicates

God's agency; the connection of the opening with the introduction of seven plagues indicates God's coming justice/judgment. Unlike 4:1, when God opened the door to heaven so John could see inside and contemplate eschatological relationship with God in the heavenly throne room, here God opens a temple door so judgment can pour out.

The thematic relationship between the heavenly temple and God's judgment is strong with John. Except for 7:15, where the multitude of conquering witnesses worships in the temple, almost every other mention of the temple is awash with judgment imagery. Revelation 11:19 is a dramatic case in point. Connected narratively as it is with 11:1-2, it offers a temple composed of an inner and outer sanctuary, which is dramatically linked with the terrible third woe. The reference to the ark of the covenant anticipates John's description of the temple as the tent of meeting, which is where the ark resided (15:5). Angels depart the temple with the prototypical judgment tool, the sickle (14:15, 17). The temple images that follow in 15:6, 8 are integrally associated with the seven plagues. At 16:1 and 16:17, a voice from the temple initiates and then consummates God's wrath. Only at 21:22 is the mention of the temple not connected with God's wrath. That aberration is due to the fact that there God dwells directly with the people of faith and the repentant people from the nations; judgment is no longer required.

The description of the temple as no longer necessary (21:22) reminds the reader of an earlier heavenly declaration that celebrates God's decision to dwell directly with humans (21:3). The language for "*dwell*" is "σκηνή" (dwelling, tent, Tabernacle) in 21:3, the same term John directly associates with the temple in 15:5. In fact, the genitive form for "*tent*," "*dwelling*," or "*Tabernacle*" in v. 5 should be read as a genitive of apposition. The translation "*the temple, that is the Tabernacle of witness*" is appropriate. John is speaking about a single heavenly edifice. In doing so, he wants to conjure yet again the image of the Exodus, where the tent of meeting/Tabernacle was so described because it was there that Moses encountered and spoke with God (Exod. 33:7-11; 40:34-38; Lev. 1:1-2). John affirms here that this new exodus is also an expression of God's judgment against those who have persecuted God's people.

- **6** This is a motion verse that serves two primary ends: it explains how the plagues will be dispersed, and it describes the seven angels who will act as the delivery vehicles. The angels exit the heavenly temple with an unmistakable intent to distribute their simmering symbols of God's wrath (15:1; 16:1). The judgment sentiment would remind knowledgeable readers of Lev. 26:21, where God promised to plague the people sevenfold for their sins. Interestingly enough, in the broader context of Lev. 26, God intended that the harsh judgment would inspire the people to repent. For John, the song of Moses and of the Lamb (Rev. 15:2-4) appears to reckon a similar rationale for the pouring out of God's wrath; God intends repentance rather than obliteration.

The angels' dress seems to corroborate the desire for repentance. Their linen garb is priestly attire; according to Exod. 28:39, the priests' vestments were to be made from such fabric. Israel's priests directed the people, even the sinful, to rather than away from God. Their garb is also messianic, indicating a relationship with God as intimate as that enjoyed by the one like the Son of Man. John's vision of the Son of Man at 1:13 describes someone wearing the similar uniform issue of a long robe accented with a golden sash across the chest (Dan. 10:5). And though John does not describe the color of the robe of the Son of Man in 1:13, the consistent presentation of heavenly attire as dazzling white in color suggests that, like the robes of these seven angels, the Son of Man's also dazzling white.

- **7** John continues his explication of 15:1. In vv. 5-6, he explained that the angels introduced in v. 1 were God's agents, who exited the heavenly temple to execute God's justice/judgment in hope of securing the nations' repentance. Now in more dramatic details, John describes both the angels' divine instruments and the manner in which they obtained them. The seven plagues were given to the seven angels by one of the cherubim attending God's throne. The plagues were housed in seven golden bowls. This is not the first time that John has envisioned angels and golden bowls. At 5:8, in the heavenly throne room, he saw angels with golden bowls of incense that represented the prayers of the saints. No doubt these were the same prayers that cried out for God's justice/judgment at 6:9-11 and sparked the pouring out of God's judgment fire upon the earth at 8:3-5. The contextual implications are clear: God's present judgment of wrath is integrally tied to the cries and prayers of the oppressed and slaughtered witnesses. Those prayers motivate divine action throughout the Book of Revelation and perhaps represent the emotional inspiration for the Book of Revelation as a whole.

The term John uses for bowl (φιάλη) conjures the image of the cultic priest already initiated by the angels' linen robes (15:6). Bowls are mentioned in the Old Testament some thirty times in conjunction with priestly service at the Tabernacle or temple. The bowls were probably used to carry out the ashes and fat of sacrifices. These bowls are sometimes directly connected with the Tabernacle of witness (Exod. 38:23-26; Num. 4:14-15; 7:13-89) and are sometimes referred to as *"golden bowls"* (1 Chr. 28:17; 2 Chr. 4:8, 21). Furthermore, the cultic use of "φιάλη" is attested for Greek religion (*Diodorus* 4.49.8), where it was used primarily to pour libations of wine. The central point in this narrative context, from both Old Testament and Greco-Roman perspectives, is that this priestly imagery reaffirms the cultic understanding of divine judgment/justice executed in the hopes of motivating repentance. The priest's goal is to broker relationship with the divine, not eliminate its possibility forever. The angels and their golden bowls of God's wrath are to be read in that light.

- **8** John concludes his introductory vision of the plague cycle with a glimpse of the heavenly temple consumed by the smoke from God's glory. Smoke and related clouds are common biblical ciphers for the glorious presence of God (Exod. 13:21; 40:34-35; 1 Kgs. 8:10-11; 2 Chr. 5:13; Isa. 6:4). Indeed, sometimes, as here, cultic attendants are unable to enter the temple/Tabernacle/tent of meeting because of that presence. The smoke is particularly reminiscent of the earlier judgment scene where the incense smoke and the prayers of God's people instigate the pouring out of God's fiery wrath (8:4-5), which John has already alluded to in 15:7. Throughout the narrative, smoke conveys a sense of divine judgment (9:2-3, 17-18; 14:11; 18:9, 18; 19:3). By associating the images of smoke and temple as he does here, John makes certain that his hearers and readers understand how integrally God's glory is related to God's judgment. The relationship between the smoke and the prayers of God's people is even more provocative. Apparently God is so overwhelmed by the peoples' cries that God's passion for them takes tangible shape and overwhelms the heavenly temple like a cloud. God is so energized and agitated that this cloud will prevent anyone from entering the temple and therefore entering into God's presence until God's wrath, symbolized here by the seven plagues, has ended, and the repentance that wrath seeks has been accomplished. The implication is clear: in the future, entrance – and therefore relationship with God – though now denied, is anticipated. At 21:23-26, with the glory of the Lord no longer blocking and the walls of a physical temple no longer excluding, the holy place of God, now a city, can and will be filled by the glory of the repentant nations and all the people who inhabit them.

The Seven Bowls of God's Wrath

John's metaphorical presentation of God's wrath as a pouring out of seven bowls has several primary themes. First, the end-time events associated with the bowls are a re-presentation of the events previously portrayed through the metaphors of seven broken seals and seven trumpet blasts (see *"The Opening of the Seven Seals"* chap. 6). Second, the bowl actions affect the entire cosmos. These plagues target not only human kingdoms and the individuals who rule and populate them, but also the very four essences of creation itself: earth, water, fire, and air. Third, though utterly devastating, the plagues are God's just and appropriate response to the evil that results from the rejection of God's rule (God's reign/Kingdom of God) and the persecution of those who witness to that rule. Fourth, the judgment matches measure for measure the crimes that have triggered it. Fifth, the controlling image for the mayhem is the exodus event.

Revelation 16:1~4 → The First Three Bowls

NIV	TT
16 ¹ Then I heard a loud voice from the temple saying to the seven angels, "Go, pour out the seven bowls of God's wrath on the earth." ² The first angel went and poured out his bowl on the land, and ugly, festering sores broke out on the people who had the mark of the beast and worshiped its image. ³ The second angel poured out his bowl on the sea, and it turned into blood like that of a dead person, and every living thing in the sea died. ⁴ The third angel poured out his bowl on the rivers and springs of water, and they became blood.	**16** ¹ **Then I heard**[225] a great voice from the temple telling the seven angels: "Go and **pour out**[226] the seven bowls of the wrath of God upon the earth." ² Then the first one departed and poured his bowl on the earth, and a foul and festering sore developed on the people who had the mark of the beast and worshiped its image. ³ Then the second one poured his bowl on the sea, and it became like the blood of a corpse, and every living creature in the sea died. ⁴ Then the third one poured his bowl into the rivers and the springs of water, and they became blood.

Chapter 16 begins with a phrase, "καὶ ἤκουσα" (then I heard), that operates in a way similar to "καὶ εἶδον" (then I

---

[225] Καὶ ἤκουσα → The phrase means *"then I heard."*
[226] ἐκχέω → It means *"pour out," "shed," "spill," "abandon oneself,"* and *"give oneself up."*

looked). The phrase often occurs in the text, but not as the opening to a new scene. Instead, it tends to follow up and elaborate upon an ongoing scene (1:10; 9:13; 10:4; 19:1, 6). This is particularly evident in cases where John sees something (4:1; 5:11; 6:1, 6; 7:4; 8:13; 14:2, 13; 15:5; 18:4; 21:3) and subsequently hears a voice or sound that interprets what he has just witnessed. The phrase is equally conspicuous in situations where John hears a hymn that interprets the narrative that preceded it (12:10; 16:5, 7). In this case, John hears testimony that interprets and clarifies his vision in 15:5-8.

- **1** The great voice implies a tone of judgment that is consistent throughout the narrative and certainly represents the mood of a text that pours out God's wrath in seven viciously lethal doses. The voice's temple origin reminds the reader of the vision of 15:5-8, which pictures the tent of meeting in heaven as the departure point for the seven angels. After the declaration in 15:8 that no one could now enter the smoke-filled temple except God, God is probably the speaker. In any event, by locating the voice in the heavenly temple, John at the least identifies the voice's command with God's eschatological intent.

  God intends two specific actions. First, the angels are instructed to depart with their pestilent cargo. According to 15:6, they have already left; however, the charge to depart in 16:1 is more comprehensive. This time, apparently, the angels are to leave the temple environs completely. They are to go forth into the world and cosmos so that they can obey the second command: to shed the contents of their bowls as a representation of God's judgment. John's language is intentional and compelling. He is careful to use a verb "ἐκχέω" (pour out, shed) that is exclusive to chapter 16 (vv. 1, 2, 3, 4, 6, 8, 10, 12, 17). The verb has strong cultic implications. It is often used, as here, in connection with libation bowls that contain ritual liquid offerings. In fact, John deploys the verb in a very calculated, balanced way. His mechanical *"pouring"* narration occurs four times before and four times after its clarifying central use at 16:6. There John explains that God's enemies, working at the direction of the dragon and its beasts from the sea and land, have *"shed"* the blood of those who have faithfully witnessed to the lordship of God and the Lamb. The measure-for-measure punishment meted out against God's enemies begins right there. In a kind of apocalyptic lex talionis, God intends to *"shed"* plagues of wrath upon the earth as an appropriate judicial response to the criminal shedding of human blood.

- **2 – 4** The first bowl plague infects only those who have branded themselves with the mark of the beast from the sea and worshiped its image (v.2; see the discussion of judgment against the same group at 13:15-18; 14:9-11; 19:20-21; 20:4). The effects of the plague are brutally ironic; those who marked themselves for the beasts are now branded with gruesome sores by God. The particular form of the plague follows the trajectory of God's retributive modus operandi. God plagued the oppressive Egyptian humans and their animals with sores in a failed early attempt (Exodus plague number six) to secure the release of the Hebrews from bondage (Exod. 9:8-12). The author of Deuteronomy makes clear that the improper behavior of even the faith community can earn God's sore-plaguing wrath (Deut. 28:27, 35). A return (repentance) to the proper way of faith and obedience can prompt the transformation of that wrath into safekeeping (Deut. 28:1).

Though the command in Rev. 16:1 was to target the earth, the second angel sheds his bowl upon the sea (v. 3). Just as with the Nile in the first exodus plague (Exod. 7:17-21), the infested water turns to blood. In this more radicalized case, however, the blood is that of a corpse. The effect, though, will be the same; the mention of a corpse serves only to heighten the sense of the macabre and thus dread. Waters turned to blood also occurred when the second trumpet angel blew his eschatological instrument (Rev. 8:8). In that case, only one-third of the sea and one-third of the creatures in the sea were affected. From this final apocalyptic vantage point, the sea and every living thing associated with it dies.

More escalation occurs when the third angel sheds his bowl upon the rivers and springs of water (v. 4). With the first exodus plague still haunting the narrative background (Exod. 7:17-21; Ps. 78:44), this new vision recalls the third trumpet plague where the star Wormwood fell from the sky and contaminated a third of the earth's fresh water (Rev. 8:10-11). With this third bowl plague the metamorphosis is complete; fresh water everywhere mutates into blood.

Revelation 16:5~7 → Hymn

NIV	TT

⁵ Then I heard the angel in charge of the waters say:
 	
"You are just in these judgments, O Holy One,
    you who are and who were;
⁶ for they have shed the blood of your holy people and your prophets,
    and you have given them blood to drink as they deserve."
 	
⁷ And I heard the altar respond:
 	
"Yes, Lord God Almighty,
    true and just are your judgments."
	⁵ Then I heard the angel of waters saying,
	
	"You are just, the one who is and who was, the holy one, because you have judged these things; ⁶ because they **poured out**[227] the blood[228] of saints and prophets, you also have given them blood to drink; they deserve it."
	
	⁷ Then I heard the altar saying, "Yes Lord God **Almighty**[229], **true**[230] and **just**[231] are your judgments."

These verses begin a transition that will be completed in verse 20-23. Ancient letters typically included direct appeals to the readers at the end of the letter. Following

---

[227] ἐκχέω → It means "*to pour out,*" and "*to shed forth.*"

[228] αἷμα → It means "*blood,*" "*grape juice,*" "*blood of animals,*" "*blood of man,*" and "*to be shed by violence.*"

[229] παντοκράτωρ → It means "*the Almighty,*" "*All-Powerful,*" and "*Omnipotent One.*"

[230] ἀληθινός → The term means "*true,*" "*dependable,*" "*in accordance with truth,*" "*genuine,*" and "*real.*"

[231] δίκαιος → It means "*righteous,*" "*observing divine laws,*" "*upright,*" "*virtuous,*" "*just,*" "*right,*" and "*innocent.*"

that classic pattern, the direct address "*but you, beloved*" signals a shift from focusing on the destiny of the impious to the proper response of the "*beloved*" to these impious. If it is true that impious people have slipped in, people who are to be identified with various negative characters in the sacred ter.

- 5 John indicates that the hymns are an interpretive follow-up to the first three plagues when he opens vv. 5-7 with the formulaic phrase "*then I heard.*" An important player is speaking: the angel who has jurisdiction over the very waters that have just been fouled by blood. John has already implied that angels were given authority over certain of the key elements of creation (fire in 14:18). This Christian narrative assertion follows from the Jewish understanding of angelic authority over nature. (*1 En.* 60:11-25; 61:10; 66:1-2; 69:22; 75:3; *2 En.* 4-6; 19:1-4; *Jub.* 2.2; 1QH1[9].8-13). The content of the angel's message is critical. The being assigned supervision and, one would guess, protection of the waters not only allows the violence that is done to those waters but also rules the violence to be an act of justice. In the angel's own words, God is just/righteous. Surprisingly, the term "δίκαιος" (just, righteous) is not frequent in the Book of Revelation. At 15:3 God's destructive actions are deemed "*just*" because they are the legitimate response to the evil perpetrated in the earth. Those same acts are a preparatory means of salvation for those who have witnessed, which is why the witnesses simultaneously sing joyfully even though God's just acts operate on behalf of God's people, those same acts do not guarantee a life of untroubled ease. Indeed, the salvific exodus was the prelude to a long and arduous struggle in the wilderness for the Hebrew people. God's justice and the salvation it offers do not and will not come cheap.

The theme of God's just actions continues in the other two texts where John used "δίκαιος" (just, righteous 19:2; 22:11); 22:11 confirms that the language is not exclusively about punishing the wicked but also about the justice that comes from rewarding the faithful. Here at 16:5, John makes sure that his readers recognize the connection between God's just nature and God's judging, plaguing actions (*"these things"*) by directly associating *"just"* with *"you judged."* In other words, according to the angel who had charge of the plagued waters, God has judged justly.

By describing God with the same formula he used earlier in the text (*"the one who is and who was"*), John demonstrates that this just God is the same God who sponsored his prophecy and cared for the well-being of the faithful (1:4, 8; 4:8). As in his use of the formula at 11:17, however, John adjusts what he says in 16:5. At 11:17, instead of formulaically declaring God as the one who is and was and will come, John substituted *"because you have taken great power and begun to rule"* for *"will come."* The dynamic had shifted. God was no longer expected; God's rule has arrived with the dramatic onset of God's judgment. So here in 16:5 God is no longer described as the coming one but as the one who has come in judgment and who is therefore *"holy."*

The narrative context directly relates God's holiness to God's judgment; God is the holy one precisely because God is the one who judges justly. Interestingly enough, John deploys *"holy one"* (ἅγιος) only twice, here and at 15:4, the song of Moses and the Lamb to which his language of justice has already directly alluded. Moses, the Lamb, and now the angel who has charge over the waters – all three corroborate each other's testimony. God is holy, as the one who deals justice.

- **6** The connection between judgment and crime develops explicitly from John's intentional word use. The first three angels shed (ἐκχέω) their bowls of God's wrath. As a result of the emptying of bowls two and three, all the waters upon the earth turned to blood (αἷμα). When John states the just cause for judgment in v. 6, he appeals to exactly the same language: the accused shed (ἐκχέω) the blood (αἷμα) of God's servants (cf. Ps 97:3). John describes these servants as saints and prophets. He is speaking not about the saints and prophets of old but about the very witnesses to the lordship of God and the Lamb who have been the center of his attention throughout the narrative. At 11:10, God's witnesses (11:3) are recognized as prophets. The saints play a particularly important role. At 5:8 their prayers were the ingredients of the heavenly incense the twenty-four elders carried into heavenly worship. At 8:3-4 those prayers were the cry that rose to heaven and, along with the cries of 6:9-11, provoked the execution of God's judgment. In several illustrative cases, John pairs saints with prophets as a kind of formulaic euphemism for those who risk witnessing to the lordship of God and the Lamb (11:18; 18:20, 24). In each of these texts, God's judgment is on prominent display. At 11:18 the judgment follows the lex talionis (measure-for-measure) theme to which John had already alluded in 11:1; the nations' rage would be met by God's answering rage. That same rage, which would bring judgment to God's enemies, represents the power of salvation for God's embattled people. The opposing yet constantly paired themes of salvation and judgment operate explicitly in 18:20, 24, where shed blood brings judgment upon the forces of the sea beast/whore and initiates salvation for the saints and prophets.

When John declares that God has given the forces of the beast blood to drink, he makes the lex talionis theme the metaphorical as well as the literal center of the verse. There is a cruel and bitter irony to the judgment; those who shed blood are punished by blood. There is historical precedent: the prophet Isaiah also declared that God would judge with blood those who spilled blood (Isa. 49:26). The ironic balance is a reframing of the position that John has already taken: God's judgment is just. Those who spill blood are worthy (ἄξιος) of a punishment that uses blood as the instrument of its execution. They deserve exactly what they get. Just as God is worthy (ἄξιος, 4:11) of praise because of God's act of creation and the Lamb is worthy (ἄξιος, 5:2, 4, 9, 12) of adoration because of his witness to God's lordship even to the point of death, so human behavior is appropriately deserving (ἄξιος) of the divine response of judgment (here) or salvation (3:4).

- **7** John's third use of *"then I heard"* in a brief seven verses confirms that every new thing he now hears acts as a running commentary on what has been previously revealed. While vv. 5-6 interpret the shedding of the first four bowls as an act of justice, v. 7 affirms the previous interpretation as an accurate one. What John hears, then, is the acoustic *"Amen"* to the preceding hymnic declaration. This antiphonal response is also presented in the form of a hymn. The singer, though, is odd. John does not say that he hears a voice from the altar, but that the altar itself sings out. In almost every use of the term *"altar,"* John attaches the theme of judgment (6:9; 8:3, 5; 9:13; 14:18). In fact, it is probably appropriate that the altar issues such an assessment since it was from under the altar (6:9) that the slaughtered saints made their plea that God justly intervene on their behalf.

"Yes," the altar affirms, referring to the LORD God Almighty (παντοκράτωρ: 1:8; 4:8; 11:17; 15:3; 16:7; 19:6, 15; 21:22), a title of respect for God's lordship that is often packaged in the narrative, as it is in this context, with another formulaic title of lordship, *"the one who is and who was"* (cf. 1:8; 4:8), and with the theme of judgment: *"true and just are your judgments"* (cf. 19:2). John uses the adjective "ἀληθινός" (true) to signify the valid eschatological judge. The angel of the waters has just used the adjective "δίκαιος" (just) to

describe God's person (16:5b). the altar uses it now to describe God's judging actions; they too are just, which in so certain of this and so fervently desires that his hearers and readers get the point that he frames the hymnic section with this critical adjective.

Revelation 16:8~12 → The Fourth, Fifth, and Sixth Bowls

NIV	TT
⁸ The fourth angel poured out his bowl on the sun, and the sun was allowed to scorch people with fire. ⁹ They were seared by the intense heat and they cursed the name of God, who had control over these plagues, but they refused to repent and glorify him. ¹⁰ The fifth angel poured out his bowl on the throne of the beast, and its kingdom was plunged into darkness. People gnawed their tongues in agony ¹¹ and cursed the God of heaven because of their pains and their sores, but they refused to repent of what they had done. ¹² The sixth angel poured	⁸ Then the fourth one poured out his bowl on the sun, and it **was allowed**[232] to scorch humans with fire. ⁹ Although the devotees of the beast from the sea were scorched by the God who had authority over these plagues, they **blasphemed the name of God**[233] and refused to repent and give God glory. ¹⁰ Then the fifth one poured out his bowl on the throne of the beast, and its kingdom was darkened, and they gnawed their tongues in agony, ¹¹ and they cursed the God of heavens because of their agony and sores, and they did not repent from their works. ¹² Then the sixth one poured out his bowl on the great river Euphrates, and its water was

---

[232] ἐδόθη → The divine-passive term means *"was given," "was brought," "was granted," "was put," "was permitted,"* and *"was caused."* This passive term is widely used to express divine permission.

[233] ἐβλασφήμησαν τὸ ὄνομα τοῦ θεοῦ →The phrase means *"blasphemed the name of God"* (NIV and NRSV translated as *"cursed"*). The phrase can also be found in Rom. 2:24; John 10:33, Acts 6:11; 19:37; 1 Tim 6:1; Jas. 2:7 and it echoes Isa. 52:5.

out his bowl on the great river Euphrates, and its water was dried up to prepare the way for the kings from the East.	dried up, in order that they way of kings from the east might be prepared.

The focus narrows from the cosmos to the representatives of the world's rebellion against the Creator, Rome, leading up to the climactic chapters 17-18, the fall of "*Babylon.*" Like the parallel sixth trumpet (9:13-21), the pouring out of the sixth bowl reveals a demonic army released to cross the Euphrates and attack the Roman civilization. This was the great phobia of the Romans, the Parthian threat writ mythologically large.

- **8** The aim shifts, yet the target remains the sun; harming the sun will hurt the stubbornly recalcitrant people of the earth. The action is broadly parallel to the disturbance caused by the fourth trumpet angel, whose disruption of the moon and stars also precipitated chaos on earth (8:12). The result of the fourth bowl angel's actions is something akin to what happens when gasoline is poured onto an already-catastrophic fire. The contents of the bowl cause the sun to erupt into such a vicious flame that its heat scorches humans on earth. John wants to make sure his hearers and readers understand that though the angel's actions prompt the devastation, God is behind it all. Once again he turns to the divine passive (ἐδόθη, "*it was given*"); this sun scorching is a premeditated act of God's judgment (cf. 17:16; 18:8).

This sun plague, like the bloody transformation of the waters that preceded it, must certainly have affected God's faithful witnesses as well as those who tormented them. Revelation 7:16 appears to suggest that the faithful will be protected from the scorching of the sun. But that text refers to the heavenly multitude, those who have already assumed an eschatological relationship with God. The ones who are not scorched by the sun are those who have already been killed by the devotees of the beast (7:14). Ironically, by killing them, their enemies protected them from these end-time horrors. John has turned their greatest weapon, that of execution, into a tool of rescue in much the same way that his Christian forebears transfigured the cross from a tool of torture and execution into the mechanism that guarantees God's victory.

The believers on the earth cannot, however, escape the horror. Though they are blameless as to the cause of the judgment activity, they are still caught up in it. In the Gospel of Mark, Jesus recognized that this would happen. He opines that the end-time eschatological events will be so cataclysmic that not even believers would survive them unless God shortened their duration (Mark 13:20). The implication is clear: the faithful, too, would suffer. The promise in Revelation (and apparently Mark) is not that believers would be raptured out of such struggle but that God would give them the power (and, according to Mark, shorten the time so that they would be able) to endure it.

- **9** John now makes explicit what he has implied through the use of the divine passive in the previous verse: God caused the sun plague. Even those who idolatrously worship the beast as lord recognize God's agency. They are not, however, sufficiently moved by that recognition to acknowledge God's lordship. In fact, God's judgment surprisingly prompts the opposite behavior. The "καὶ" (and) that follows the notice of suffering from scorching heat should therefore be read in an adversative manner. *"Although the devotees of the beast from the sea were scorched by the God who had authority over these plagues, they blasphemed God's name and refused to repent and give God glory."*

They blasphemy against God's name is the opposite of granting God proper respect (cf. 4:11; Isa. 52:5). This blasphemy, which continues unabated in Rev. 16:11 and 16:21, links these obstinate ones directly with the beast from the sea, who in fighting against God on behalf of the dragon, blasphemes God and all who dwell in heaven (13:5-6; cf. 13:1; 17:3). In chapter 13, the blasphemy involves denying the lordship status of God while saluting it in the beast from the sea (cf. 13:4). It involves the same thing here; John's final comment is that the blasphemers refuse to give God appropriate glory. God's judgment is an appropriate and expected response (cf. Lev. 24:16).

Blasphemy is also the opposite of the expected behavior: repentance. John's language implies, as it did at 9:20-21 (cf. also 2:5, 16, 21-22; 3:3, 19), that God expected the people to repent and render glory to God as a result of the divine eschatological activity. The plagues, then, even as a judgment tool, were not designed simply with destruction in mind but were engineered to elicit changes in loyalty and recognition of lordship. (On the connection between giving God glory and repentance, see 11:13; 14:7; 15:4)

- **10** When the fifth angel sheds the contents of his bowl, he goes exclusively after the cause of the oppression, blasphemy, and idolatry: the throne of the beast from the sea (cf. 13:1-10). No doubt this throne is the capital city of Rome, also called the great city and Babylon (16:19; 17:18; 18:10, 16, 18-19, 21). Throne language has two important nuances within John's narrative. First, there is a strong connection with the throne of Satan at 2:13. John's discussion there tied the core of Satan's work to the universal imperial cult, which had established an especially powerful presence in Pergamum. At 13:2 the dragon gives its throne to the beast from the sea. That transfer of power is represented in the image of the beast's own throne in 16:10. Second, throne language in Revelation primarily refers to God's throne, or heavenly thrones in direct relationship to it. God's throne is a euphemism for God's person and authority, just as the beast's throne is a representation of its person and authority. The use of throne imagery for both conjures the narrative picture of two kingdoms and the powerful figures who rule over them engaged in cataclysmic mortal and even supernatural conflict. The fact that the beast's throne is now targeted means that the beast's rule is targeted and about to be put to an end.

The second half of the verse confirms the end of the beast's reign through the metaphor of an imposed, fearsome darkness. There is a strong parallel with the actions that follow the blowing of the fifth trumpet (9:1-6). There the sun is darkened and the people are doomed to agony following the fall of a great star from heaven. The motif of unbearable agony accompanying great darkness has biblical precedent. At Exod. 10:22-23 Moses brought a similar darkness to the land of Egypt, and Isa. 8:19-22 warns that any who seek direction from a source other than God will be thrust into darkness and anguished by gloom. That is precisely what happens to the citizens of the great city here in v. 10.

- **11** Verse 11 follows from v. 9 as a close parallel. John repeats here the very same themes that he initiated there. First, God is acknowledged as the force behind the plagues. Not just the darkening of the sun and bloodying of the waters but also the sending of the sores (16:2) is God's work. Second, the people, instead of acknowledging God's lordship, blaspheme God. Third, John speaks of this blasphemy in terms of a refusal to repent (on repentance as an important theme, see 8:7-13; 9:20-21; 11:1, 13; 15:4; 22:11).

- **12** Two deadly consequences follow the actions of the sixth angel, who sheds his bowl upon the great river Euphrates and evaporates all its water. The Euphrates is a powerful water supply, whose contribution to the fertility of the area surrounding it enabled the development of great civilizations like Assyria, Babylonia, and Parthia. The drying of the river would mean the loss of a critical water source and could only be looked upon as a tremendous tragedy for both

Roman and Parthian settlements. The force of that tragedy would be amplified by the fact that the Parthians might be pressed into crossing the riverbed, now dry, in search of strategic water resources on the Roman side.

Here lies the second consequence. The Euphrates River marked the eastern boundary that separated the Roman Empire from the one rival it was never able to conquer: the Parthians. Parallels with the trumpet angels continue. The blowing of the sixth trumpet (9:14-15) unleashed four angels at the Euphrates who marshaled an apocalyptic version of a Parthian Army that exacted the deaths of one-third of the human population. (See the discussion of the strategic significance of the Euphrates at 9:14-15; and the discussion of the Parthian threat and John's use of it at 6:2 and 13:3).[234] A dry riverbed is not a strategic barrier. It becomes a roadway that allows and perhaps even invites Parthian incursions. The drying would be, at least for the Jews and Christians, a stark reminder of God's drying of the Red Sea (Sea of Reeds). This time, though, the effect of the act has a cruel, ironic twist. The drying of the Red Sea enabled the Hebrews to escape destruction in Egypt; it allowed the Hebrews to flee. The drying of the Euphrates, by contrast, provides access into Roman territory: it allows the Parthians to enter. John's grammar indicates that the development is an intentional act of judgment by God. There is significant Old Testament precedent for such a

---

[234] Also Isa. 41:2, 25; 46:11, where God summons forces of judgment from the east.

maneuver on God's part (Ps. 106:9; Isa. 11:15-16; 51:10; Jer. 50:38; 51:36). Once again a divine-passive verb anchors the explanatory clause in the sentence. The drying occurs so that the way of crossing for the kings from the east (the Parthians and their allies) might be prepared. John's point is that God is the one who facilitates this particular preparation and encourages the devastating follow-up.[235]

---

[235] Josh. 3:1-4:18, where God dried up the Jordan River to allow the people of Israel to attack the idolatrous Canaanites.

Revelation 16:13~16 → Intermission (1b): Envisioning Final Battle

NIV	TT
¹³ And I saw three unclean spirits like frogs come out of the mouth of the dragon, and out of the mouth of the beast, and out of the mouth of the false prophet. ¹⁴ For they are the spirits of devils, working miracles, which go forth unto the kings of the earth and of the whole world, to gather them to the battle of that great day of God Almighty. ¹⁵ Behold, I come as a thief. Blessed is he that watches, and keeps his garments, lest he walk naked, and they see his shame. ¹⁶ And he gathered them together into a place called in the Hebrew tongue Armageddon.	¹³ Then I saw three unclean spirits like frogs come from the mouth of the dragon, and from the mouth of the beast, and from the mouth of the false prophet. ¹⁴ For they are sign-making demonic spirits, who go out to the kings of the entire inhabited world to gather them for the war on the great day of God, the Almighty. ¹⁵ ("Behold, I come like a thief. Blessed is the one who stays alert and is clothed, in order that he might not walk around naked and people see his shame.") ¹⁶ And he gathered them to the place that in Hebrew is called **Har-Magedon (Armageddon)**.[236]

In the previous series of seven catastrophes, an intermission has always separated the sixth and seventh movements. In 7:1-17 the presentation of the 144,000 and

---

[236] Ἀρμαγεδών → It means "*the hill or city of Megiddo.*" The term appears only here in the entire Bible. John has conflated two Hebrew words "*har*"(city/hill/mountain) and "*megiddon*" (see Excursus 16: Armageddon)

the great heavenly multitude separates the devastations that follow the opening of the sixth seal (6:12-17) from the breaking of the seventh at 8:1. In 10:1-11:14 the presentation of the little scroll and the two witnesses separates the destructions that follow the sounding of the sixth trumpet (9:13-21) from the blasting of the seventh trumpet (11:15). A structurally similar though shorter intermission now separates the pouring out of the sixth and seventh bowls. John pauses to preview the final apocalyptic conflict the nations will be deceived into engaging. Additionally, he reminds the faithful to be prepared and instructs them on how that preparation can be achieved and maintained.

- **13** John's use of "Καὶ εἶδον" (then I saw) is an indication that he has moved to a new scene in the larger bowls act. The three evil powers introduced in chapters 12 (the red dragon) and 13 (the beast from the sea and the beast from the land) are now acting in concert in an attempt to unleash a destructive force that is the match of God's own acts of judgment. In this text, the beast from the land (13:11-18) is for the first time given a new name: *"the false prophet."* That these two titles refer to the same enemy is clear from John's narration. Their identity and role are the same: by way of incredible signs, they deceive humans into acknowledging the lordship and divine status of the beast from the sea (13:12-13; 19:20; 20:10).

    In this case, the deception is engineered by unclean spirits who have the appearance of frogs. The characterization of the spirits as frogs connects this disturbing development with the second plague inflicted upon the Egyptians by Moses (Exod. 8:1-15; Pss. 78:45). The spirits-perceived-as-frogs deploy from the mouths of the three enemies. Already the mouth of the dragon has been used to send forth weapons against God's people (Rev. 12:15-16; 13:5-6). The mouth is also, though, a metaphor for the staging area from which the efforts for God's justice/salvation are launched. A sword issues from the mouth of the Lamb (1:16; 2:16; 19:15, 21); destructive power issues from the mouths of others sent to represent the reality of God's judgment (9:17-19; 11:15). The dueling mouth metaphors suggest that John is caught up in a war of words over the identity of the true Lord. The language and image of witness that he uses throughout is particularly appropriate to such a metaphor. Witnesses declare – that is to say, fight – with their words. The two sides, that of the dragon and that of God, fight it out for the allegiance of the people with what issues from their mouths: their words. The people respond with testimony: the witness of their own mouths.

John's description of the enemy as a *"false prophet"* is an indication that this fight is taking place within as well as outside the church communities. Prophets were recognized leaders within the Jewish and Christian communities, who exhorted proper worship and ethical behavior. Often they used signs or sign acts to demonstrate their valid relationship with the Almighty God and to authenticate their message. The fact that John wants his people to be alert enough to recognize the false things these prophets say (16:15), and the opposing truth he himself presents, is an indication that these prophets potentially have as much access to his church folk as he does himself. Such a conclusion would be consistent with the content of John's urgent exhortations to his seven churches in chapters 2 and 3, where it is obvious that false prophetic figures (Jezebel, Balaam, and the Nicolaitans) encourage accommodation to the rituals and beliefs that tout the lordship of Rome and Caesar. Elsewhere in the New Testament the false prophet without exception speaks falsehood within the covenant community of Israel or the church in order to deceive (Matt. 7:15; 24:11, 24; Mark 13:22; Luke 6:26; Acts 13:6; 2 Pet. 2:1; 1 John 4:1). This fact points further to the conclusion that the second beast's activity in Rev. 13:11-17 is conducted not only outside but also within the churches, which is confirmed further by 16:14-16. Therefore it is consistent with the wider early Christian view that false prophets operated inside as well as outside the faith communities.

- **14** The frog-appearing unclean spirits are demons. John uses the term for demons only two other times in his narrative (9:20; 18:2). On both those occasions, he relates the demonic to idolatrous worship associated with Babylon/Rome. The relationship with Rome is confirmed by the demons' vocation. They conjure signs that have the same effect as the signs of the false prophet, to encourage worship of the beast from the sea (Babylon/Rome). These demons secure political and military alliances for the beast, alliances with the kings of the entire world. These are not the eastern kings of the Parthian Empire mentioned in 16:12; those kings were from a limited region and targeted the beast inhabited world, which draws economic, political, and even spiritual strength from relationship with Rome. Such accommodation with Rome is precisely what John counsels his churches against. The demonic spirits have misled these kings with their materialistic, military, and cultic signs, so that they and their kingdoms have come to believe that Rome is not only their benefactor but also their Lord. For such a benefactor and Lord, a client king would be willing to fight. The demons use their sign acts to rally these kings to just such a cause. In Old Testament prophecies such as Zech. 12-14, this gathering of the nations is accomplished by God.

The threat is the opposing rule of an enemy Lord, the one represented by the Lamb, whom John preaches. The demons gather the kings so that they will rise up and do battle with this God on the ultimate day of divine justice, which will bring salvation to God's faithful and judgment against those who oppress them. The demons have apparently convinced the kings that every one of God's acts of judgment is another threat against the empire that sustains them. Then no wonder that the people and rulers who populate those kingdoms respond to these acts of judgment with fury and anger rather than repentance (16:9, 10, 20).

- **15** The great day of God's rule is described as an appearance; it is a person, not merely an event. That appearance will come suddenly, just as the one like *"the Son of Man"* had already explained in 3:3. The connection between the two verses suggests that it is that same son, the Standing Slaughtered Lamb, who is speaking here. The metaphor also counts against using Revelation as a kind of temporal road map whose wirings are a code that, when read correctly, can predict the movement of the end of days. John's presentation here is consistent with the presentation of God's rule as sudden, unexpected, and unpredictable (cf. Mark 13:32-37; Matt. 24:42-51; Luke 12:37-40; 1 Thess. 5:2-7; 2 Pet. 3:10).

The third of John's seven macarisms or beatitudes (Revelation presents beatitudes in 1:3; 14:13; 16:15; 19:9; 20:6; 22:7, 14) follows as an antiphonal rejoinder to the declaration of the final day's shockingly sudden arrival. The blessed ones in that moment will be those who have "*watched*." This affirmation (in the indicative mood) is also an imperative call for watchfulness on the part of those who are not already demonstrating it in their lives. This call for alertness uses the same vocabulary chosen by Jesus in the Gospel of Mark when he counseled his disciples to stay awake lest the moment of God's eschatological movement catch them unawares (Mark 13:13, 37). In John's narrative context, one prepares by dressing in white clothes. One obtains white clothes by witnessing the lordship of Jesus Christ and God (cf. 3:4-5; 19:8). By contrast, the people who have no clothes are those whom John castigates in chapters 2 and 3, those who, like the Laodiceans, follow the advice of Jezebel, Balaam, and the Nicolaitans and accommodate themselves to the economic, political, social, and cultic practices that celebrate the lordship of Caesar and

Rome (cf. 3:17). John's warning is that those who wish to find themselves in eschatological relationship with God on the last day should reject such accommodation – repent, if they are already accommodating (2:5, 16, 21, 22; 3:3, 19; 9:20, 21; 16:9, 11; 18:4) – and witness to the lordship of God and the Standing Slaughtered Lamb so that they will be found witnessing whenever the one like "*the Son of Man*" returns.

- **16** Verse 16 opens with a clarification of John's interpretation in v. 14. Though it may have appeared, to both John and the kings of the world, that it was the demonic spirits that had gathered everyone for battle on the last day, in truth God was always in charge. The seer opens the verse with a third-person singular version of the verb "*to gather*" (he gathered) that overrides its infinitive use in relationship to the demonic spirits in v. 14. The gathering, planned and executed by the demonic spirits, was all of God's design. The NRSV makes the reading here consistent with the interpretation at v. 14 with the translation "*they assembled.*" While that interpretation fits the grammar of v. 14, it is inconsistent with John's overall portrayal that everything happens by God's ultimate design. It would be perfectly consistent with the larger narrative presentation in chapter 16 for God, who gave blood to the vicious devotees who sought blood to drink (v. 6), now to give the kings of the earth the very thing they have been seeking. The assembly they seek will be the assembly they get, only it will be to their destruction.

John is drawing upon a tradition in the Hebrew Bible that envisions God gathering all the nations of the world for divine judgment (cf. Joel 3:2; Zeph. 3:8; Ezek. 38-39). The nations are deceived into thinking that they are gathering to exterminate the saints, but they are gathered together ultimately by God only in order to meet their own judgment.

> **Excursus 16: Armageddon**
>
> The different spellings in English translations reflect the variety of names given the location in the ancient Greek manuscripts of Revelation. Popular, uncritical interpretations of this text have often supposed that it predicts some great battle at Megiddo in northern Israel, as part of the final events of history. That John is writing "*prophecy*" does not mean that he is predicting historical events of the long-range future.
>
> The place of assembly is called in Hebrew "*Har-Magedon*." Since the term is used only here in the entire Bible, it should not attract the kind of interpretive attention that many church traditions have given it over the centuries. More than likely John has conflated two Hebrew wards, "*har*," "*megiddon*" which mean "*mountain of Megiddo*."
>
> Meggiddo was an ancient city that guarded the pass through the Central Highlands at the Jezreel Valley. Because ot its strategic location, Megiddo was an important military site. It was the site of several notable battles in Jewish history. According to Judg. 5:19, Deborah and Barak defeated the Canaanite army of Jabin there. In 2 Kgs. 9:27 King Ahaziah of Judah died there while fleeing Jehu. The tragic death of the reformist king of Judah, Josiah, also occurred there during a battle with Pharaoh Neco of Egypt (2 Kgs.

23:29-30; 2 Chr. 35:22; *1 Esd* 1:29-31). Because the area was associated with significant battles in the history of Israel, it is not odd that John would locate the assembly in preparation for apocalyptic conflict there. The difficulty is that Megiddo was not actually located on a mountain but on a plain.

Scholars who suggest that John is mixing his images so that the familiar name could fit into the prophetic expectations for an eschatological mountain conflict are no doubt correct. In any case, what is most important to remember is that John does not intend a literal but a symbolic battle, whose result will be the realization and recognition of the lordship of God and the Standing Slaughtered Lamb.

Revelation 16:17~21 → The Seventh Bowl

NIV	TT
¹⁷ The seventh angel poured out his bowl into the air, and out of the temple came a loud voice from the throne, saying, "It is done!" ¹⁸ Then there came flashes of lightning, rumblings, peals of thunder and a severe earthquake. No earthquake like it has ever occurred since mankind has been on earth, so tremendous was the quake. ¹⁹ The great city split into three parts, and the cities of the nations collapsed. God remembered Babylon the Great and gave her the cup filled with the wine of the fury of his wrath. ²⁰ Every island fled away and the mountains could not be found. ²¹ From the sky huge hailstones, each weighing about a hundred pounds, fell on people. And they cursed	¹⁷ Then **the seventh one**²³⁷ poured out his bowl into the air, and a **great**²³⁸ voice came out of the temple from the throne, saying, "It is finished!" ¹⁸ And there were flashes of lightning and rumblings and peals of thunder and a **great**²³⁹ earthquake, such as has not happened since humankind has been on the earth, so great was the earthquake. ¹⁹ The **great**²⁴⁰ city split into three parts, and the cities of the nations fell. And Babylon the Great was remembered in God's presence to give the cup of the wine of the wrath of God's fury. ²⁰ And every island fled and no mountains were found. ²¹ And **great**²⁴¹ hailstones, weighing about a hundred pounds, fell from heaven on

---

²³⁷ ὁ ἕβδομος → The phrase means *"the seventh one,"* referring to the seventh angel.
²³⁸ μέγας → It means *"large," "great," "long," "wide," "intense,"* and *"severe."*
²³⁹ μέγας → The term means *"large," "great," "long," "wide," "intense,"* and *"severe."*
²⁴⁰ μέγας → It means *"large," "great," "long," "wide," "intense,"* and *"severe."*
²⁴¹ μέγας → It means *"large," "great," "long," "wide," "intense,"* and *"severe."*

| God on account of the plague of hail, because the plague was so terrible. | the people, and the people cursed God because of the plague of the hail, because the plague was **greatly**[242] **great**[243]. |

In Revelation earthquakes accompany significant moments: the opening of the sixth seal, which prompted a response of fear on the part of humanity (6:12); at the ascent of the prayers of the saints to God (8:5); in the aftermath of the witness of the *"lampstands,"* which prompted fear in the inhabitants of the city (11:13-14); and following the seventh trumpet blast and the second woe, when God's reign, God reign is seen to be effective (11:19). Biblically, In Matthew also earthquakes attended both the crucifixion and the resurrection (Matt. 27:54; 28:2). This unit hints significant moments to follow to reveal the great glory of God.

- **17** When the seventh angel pours out his bowl, he aims for the air, the last of the four elements that the ancients thought comprised nature (earth, v. 2; water, vv. 3, 4, 12; fire, v. 8; air, v. 17) to be targeted. A great, loud voice apparently the same one that activated the angels in 16:1, calls out as a result. That this voice from the temple belongs to God remains clear from the declaration in 15:8 that no one could enter the temple until the judgment was complete. The connection to the throne, a euphemism for God throughout the Book of

---

[242] σφόδρα → It means *"very much," "extremely,"* and *"greatly."*
[243] μέγας → It means *"large," "great," "long," "wide," "intense,"* and *"severe."*

Revelation, also indicates that God is speaking (4:2-3; 7:10, 15; 14:3).

God declares that *"it is finished"* (cf. 15:1; 21:6). The three-ring apocalyptic circus of breaking seals, blasting trumpets, and spilled bowls has finally reached its climactic conclusion. In the concluding chapters of his work, John will narrate that conclusion from the two angles of judgment (17:1-20:3) and salvation (20:4-22:21). The loud tone of the voice indicates that just now it is judgment that is on God's mind; no wonder, then, that the seventh angel's exploits introduce the devastation of Babylon/Rome, which immediately follows in chapters 17-19.

- **18** The theophany package that follows God's declaration is like an eschatological exclamation point. These cosmic happenings provide the background music that accompanies the momentous movement of God's judgment and salvation into the human arena. Of particular note is the addition of the greatest earthquake ever humanly experienced. If a regular earthquake symbolizes judgment (cf. 6:12; 11:13), this singularly unique one clearly indicates the climactic moment of apocalyptic judgment. The language is reminiscent of Dan. 12:1, which forecasts tribulation such as had never been seen (cf. Exod. 9:24). In Daniel's case, though, it would be not just a day of destruction but also a day in which everyone whose name is written in *"the Book"* would be saved. The imagery is as much about salvation as it is about judgment. That is the case in the Book of Revelation, too, for John will narrate the *"finish"* of the end time as both judgment and salvation.

- **19 – 21** The earthquake rips the great city into three parts. John draws a critical connection between Rome and Babylon as the great city that will be destroyed because of its refusal to recognize the lordship of God and the Standing Slaughtered Lamb, as well as its persecution of those who witness to that lordship.

  The quake also takes out all the cities of the nations that were socially, politically, militarily, economically, and cultically allied with the great city. All who had accommodated to its delusions and practices of lordship will be consumed by the same wrath of God's judgment. But where that wrath is concerned, God particularly remembers Babylon/Rome because of the evil Babylon/Rome imposed upon the saints (6:9-11; 8:3-5; 20:4-6).

  The impact of God's presence in the force of judgment and salvation is so overwhelming that nature must flee before it. It is as if the geographical elements, wishing not to impede God's eschatological progress, get themselves out of God's way. The motif of the disappearance of mountains is often connected in the Old Testament and early Judaism with a theophany or the eschatological judgment, conceptions that tend to merge (Ps. 97:5; Isa. 40:4; 42:15; 45:2; 54:10; Ezek. 38:20; *4 Ezra* 15:42), though more frequently the seismic phenomenon of the quaking of mountains is mentioned (Pss. 18:7; 46:2-3; Isa. 5:25; 64:1, 3; *Sir* 43:16).

  The advent of huge, almost hundred-pound hailstones in v. 21 is reminiscent of the hail that falls after the sounding of the first angel's trumpet (8:7), but even more like the hailstorm that follows the seventh angel's blast at 11:19. That hail, too, followed the theophany phenomena of lightning, rumbling, thunder, and earthquake. This time the sheer magnitude of the event sets it apart. The end result, though, is unfortunately the same. Just as the Egyptian Pharaoh refused to repent in the face of God's cosmic onslaught of hail unlike anything the Egyptians had ever before witnessed (Exod. 9:13-26), so those who have accommodated themselves to the lordship of the beast from the sea refuse to repent. Indeed, they curse God instead (cf. 13:6; 16:9, 11). John chronicles God's response in chapters 17-19, which narrate the decisive divine judgment against the enemies of God and God's faithful witnesses.

The Whore/Rome/Babylon

John's tone, already contentious, takes a dramatic shift. The righteously indignant seer makes a vicious rhetorical turn that bludgeons women with a sweeping hammer of misogynism as it nails Rome up against the wall of civil and cultic tyranny. Following the lead of some of the most well-known and, in the first century, most oft-quoted Scriptures and prophetic figures from Israel's past, he summons the metaphor of the self-serving, other-loathing, greed-guided harlot (Gen. 34:31; Isa. 1:21; 57:3; Jer. 3:3; Ezek. 16:30-31, 35; 23:44; Hos. 2:5; 3:3; 4:10, 12-15; 5:3; 9:1). Even the Christian apostle Paul enlisted the striking image of the illicit and destructive prostitute (1 Cor. 6:15-16). In fact, the Corinthian text has much in common with John's warning here in chapter 17. John fears that his people will destroy their relationship with Christ by accommodating themselves, through either social fear or economic lust, to a prostituting relationship with Rome.

Interestingly, demonization is only necessary when one's enemy has one or several truly appealing and admirable traits. It is difficult successfully to condemn an enemy for whom your own people have sympathies and with whom they desire relationship. When logic proves insufficient for the task of turning one's followers away from such an enemy's position and back in the exclusive direction of one's own cultic and ethical directives, one can increase the persuasive odds by revealing the opponent's flaws and hyper-distorting them. John does precisely this by pointing to Rome's economic prowess, political dominance, and military supremacy, a most impressive array of imperial traits in the eyes of most Greco-Romans, and declaring that they are not marks of sovereign beauty but festering, malignant sores. These sores indicate a communicable social disease that will infest any person or people entering into intimate union with her. As beautiful as she seemed on the surface, she is, after all, a filthy, vicious whore.

The problem with the whore imagery is that, as it strikes out at Rome, it disparages women. In Revelation the patriarchal mean streak implicit in ancient Israelite and John's contemporary Christian whore metaphors becomes a misogynistic fault line capable of devouring the self-image of any woman thrown up against it. It is not just the use of the whore image that is problematic since, in this case, John uses that image to attack not women but Rome. The problem is that his use of the image privileges a male perspective on the divine and matters of human redemption in relationship to the divine. The root of evil takes on an unmistakable feminine stamp: the luscious lure of feminine sex (an image of Roman cultic and economic power) seduces the righteous male (representing the people of God) into destruction. Men, the implicit symbolic referent for the people of God, may well ally with the whore, but they are presented as victims who, unlike the woman herself, are capable of redemption if they can find it within their power to resist her. It is the female hooker, not the male *"johns,"* who is the root of the problem. The presentation allows male perspective and image, even when chastised, far less culpability. Femininity, metaphorically speaking, is problematized as its best and demonized at its worst. Evil takes on a decidedly female shape. Sexuality is the problem, and clearly for John here, it has a female orientation.

The dysfunction represented in this portrait of the feminine takes a horrific leap forward when John narrates the destruction of Rome/Babylon as the justifiable stripping naked, devouring, and eating of this female whore. To be sure, John is speaking only metaphorically, using symbol, and not intending the torture and killing of a real woman. But biblical scholars are right to point out that even such symbolic disparagement can have and has had disastrous effect. As Reddish concedes, *"The danger of imagery such as that used in Revelation 17 is that it may be heard by some to condone violence against women, particularly 'evil' women."* One can therefore only regret that John chose the image of a female person as his operative metaphor when projecting God's judgment upon Rome. That is, however, his metaphor of choice, and in my commentary on this section I must deal with this metaphor while maintaining John's concern for the seductive and ultimately destructive nature of Whore/Rome/Babylon.

Revelation 17:1-6a → Vision: The Whore and the Beast

NIV	TT
17 ¹ One of the seven angels who had the seven bowls came and said to me, "Come, I will show you the punishment of the great prostitute, who sits by many waters. ² With her the kings of the earth committed adultery, and the inhabitants of the earth were intoxicated with the wine of her adulteries." ³ Then the angel carried me away in the Spirit into a wilderness. There I saw a woman sitting on a scarlet beast that was covered with blasphemous names and had seven heads and ten horns. ⁴ The woman was dressed in purple and scarlet, and was glittering with gold, precious stones and pearls. She held a	**17** ¹ Then one of the seven angels with the seven bowls came and spoke with me, saying, "Come, I will show you the **judgment**[244] of the great **whore**[245] who sits upon many waters, ² with whom the kings of the earth **prostituted**[246] themselves and the inhabitants of the earth were made drunk from the wine of her prostitution. ³ Then he carried me into the desert in the **spirit**[247]. Then I saw a woman seated on a scarlet beast filled with blasphemous names, with seven heads and ten horns. ⁴ And the woman was clothed in purple and scarlet and adorned with gold and precious stones and pearls, with a golden cup in her

---

[244] κρίμα → It means *"a decree," "judgment," "condemnation of wrong," "a lawsuit," "condemnatory sentence,"* and *"damnation."*

[245] πόρνη → The term means *"prostitute,"* and *"whore."*

[246] πορνεύω → It means *"to prostitute" "to give one's self to unlawful sexual intercourse," "to commit fornication,"* and *"to worship idols."*

[247] πνεῦμα → The term means *"wind," "breath," "spirit," "soul,"* and *"(the Holy) Spirit."*

golden cup in her hand, filled with abominable things and the filth of her adulteries. ⁵ The name written on her forehead was a mystery: BABYLON THE GREAT THE MOTHER OF PROSTITUTES AND OF THE ABOMINATIONS OF THE EARTH. ⁶ᵃ I saw that the woman was drunk with the blood of God's holy people, the blood of those who bore testimony to Jesus.	hand full of abominations and the filth of her prostitution. ⁵ On her forehead was written a name, a mystery: "Babylon the Great, the mother of whores and abominations of the earth." ⁶ᵃ And I saw the woman was drunk from the blood of the saints and the blood of the witnesses to Jesus.

The angel takes John into the wilderness (17:3) to behold the city. John sees the city in the form of a woman – an alluring whore (17:1, 18). Picturing a city as a woman was common in the prophetic Jewish tradition in which John lives and from which he draws: Jerusalem was pictured as virgin (Isa. 37:22; Lam. 2:13), faithful wife and mother (Isa. 66:7-14), a married woman who became unfaithful (Ezek. 16); and Nineveh and Tyre as harlot (Nahum 3:1-7; Isa. 23).

- **1** John's identification of his angelic guide and interpreter serves several crucial functions. First, it reminds his hearers and readers of the declaration in 1:1 that his visions would take place through the assistance of an angelic intermediary. Now, and later at 21:9, he makes clear that two of the most crucial and climactic visions in the narrative are comprehensible only with this angelic assistance. Second, the connection with 21:9 initiates a parallel presentation between 17:1-19:10 and 21:9-22:9. The seductive and idolatrous dominance of the evil city is balanced against and overwhelmed by the attractive and appropriate allure of the new city that recognizes God as its power source. Third, John's clarification that this interpreting angel is one of the seven who wielded the seven bowls of God's wrath connects the angel and the vision he relates to God's end-time judgment. Indeed, the "καὶ" (and) that opens the verse suggests that this material is a follow-up to what has gone before. This text is describing how the end-time judgment, narrated from a global perspective with the seventh bowl (cf. 16:17-21), takes place in specific relationship to Rome. It also means to imply the reason for Rome's judgment. John deploys the noun "κρίμα" (judgment) only in 17:1, 18:20 and 20:4. Revelation 18:20 shows that God has brokered this judgment on behalf of the witnesses who have suffered Rome's abuse.

The angel who mediates the vision of the bride city at 21:9 is also described as one who previously held one of the seven bowls of God's wrath. This narrative echo is yet another reminder that, for John, God's one moment of apocalyptic crisis engineers two distinct eschatological scenarios. The same judgment that seals Rome's doom and the destruction of all those allied with her consummates the salvation of those who have endured as witnesses to the lordship of God and the Standing Slaughtered Lamb.

The instructive parallelism continues with the angel's first words: *"Come, I will show you."* Those words preface the introduction of the great whore and the judgment that awaits her. At 21:9, the same words present the bride in anticipation of her eschatological relationship with the Lamb. John uses the narrative strategy to present the two rhetorical women as the economic, social, and cultic competitors for the affections of humankind. Humans are drawn to both; they can only be intimate with one. The relationships are mutually exclusive.

To dissuade his hearers and readers from making the mistake of seeking the wrong relationship with Rome, John unleashes some of the most acrimonious language in his rhetorical arsenal. He appeals to the jargon of sexual immorality, to which he will return in different formulations throughout the chapter. He calls Rome a whore; in fact, except for 19:2, he uses this description exclusively in chapter 17 (vv. 5, 15, 16). He connects the image with the name *"Babylon"* and the city that is Rome. At 19:2, after reminding his hearers and readers of her corrupting effect, he declares that God has judged – which is to say, destroyed – the whore, as an act of justifiable retaliation on behalf of God's people (cf. 6:9-11; 18:20).

Although John has not referred to anyone as a whore prior to 17:1, he has utilized the image of sexual immorality. In particular, he stresses that the false prophet whom he slanders with the name Jezebel leads the people into a faith infidelity akin to prostitution by allowing them to eat food sacrificed to idol gods (2:20-

22). Such consumption enters them into an implicit relationship with those gods.

John's idolatrous city sits enthroned upon many waters. The reference is both literal and symbolic. As the beast from the sea, Rome literally reaches Asia Minor from the sea and would be thought of directly in relationship to it. The symbolic meaning, though, is surely more important. John has in mind, as he does throughout much of chapter 17, imagery from Jer. 51:13. The Old Testament prophet proclaims judgment against the powerful city of Babylon, which has been destructive of God's people and has imperiously and idolatrously set itself up as an entity deserving the kind of worship due only God. John will specifically identify the whore with the name Babylon (17:5). As John certainly knows, Jeremiah described Babylon in the same way that he now envisions Rome, as a city sitting (i.e., enthroned) on many waters. Babylon literally sat on the Euphrates River. In Rome's case, the point is more theological than geographical. By 17:15, the whore's seating will be described as peoples, multitudes, nations, and languages. The image expands so that John's hearers and readers recognize that the great whore's/city's allure comes from her intimate and illicit relationships, her commercial and political alliances with the nations and people of the world, alliances that create the great wealth and power that even now seduce them.

- **2** John anticipates a charge he will repeat at 18:3, though in reverse order. The kings and inhabitants of the earth have entered into a relationship that has all the trappings of a drunken orgy. The seer targets the kings of the earth first. These are the same kings who in 16:14 were deceived by demonic signs. Those signs now receive economic trappings; the kings have seen the commercial wealth of the superpower city and have been attracted to it, thinking they might share in it. Once again John is operating from a prophetic platform. Tyre, prophesied against by both Isaiah and Ezekiel for seductively luring the ancient nations and even the people of God into idolatrous political affairs, serves as the negative role model to which Rome is now compared. Among all the harlot metaphors of the Old Testament, most of which refer to Israel, the one referring to Tyre in Isaiah 23:17 is the closest verbally to Revelation 17:2. Beale observes, *"That Tyre is in mind here in the Apocalypse is clear from the repeated reference to the Ezekiel 26-28 pronouncement of Tyre's judgment in Revelation 18 and the specific allusion to Isa. 23:8 in Rev. 18:23."* In a rightly ordered world, these kings would recognize God and the Lamb as their fitting ruler (Rev. 1:5; 15:3; 17:14; 19:16). Yet even now, even to the end point of the Book of Revelation, there is hope that the kings will recognize the value of their relationship with God and the Lamb and redemptively reengage it (21:24). Like the witnesses to the lordship of God and the Standing Slaughtered Lamb, the kings of the earth owe their existence, allegiance, and affiliation to God and the Lamb. It is for this reason that their alliance with Babylon is viewed as a prostituting of themselves, and the city/power that lures them into the alliance is called a whore (17:18; 18:3, 9).

It is perhaps also for this reason that the threat of judgment has always dogged them (6:15; 10:11; 19:18; cf. Ps. 2:10).

The inhabitants of the earth fare no better; they too are under threat of judgment because of their prostituting alliance. Their condemnation comes as no surprise since throughout the narrative John uses the formula "*inhabitants of the earth*" as a euphemism for people in opposition to the lordship of God and the Standing Slaughtered Lamb. They are depicted as drunk on the wine of the whore's fornication. Jeremiah 51:7 depicts a similar scene where the people of the world have imbibed so heavily of Babylon's economy that their lust for a greater and greater stake in her profits has driven them mad. The people of John's time have been equally greedy. They will be equally judged.

- **3** The opening words in v. 3 parallel exactly John's narration at the beginning of 21:10. There, too, the angel spirits John away, but to a great and high mountain. The different destinations fit the different visions. While the desert can be and often was a place for faith's regeneration, it is also, as the abode of wild beasts and tempting/testing demons (Mark 1:12-13; Matt. 4:1; Luke 4:1-2), a place of darkness, danger, and judgment (Isa. 21:1-10). It retains that negative sense here; the landscape by association attracts the negative tenor of the whore John will see in it. At 21:10, on the other hand, John will see Babylon/Rome's municipal counterpart. There, from the high ground that, in keeping with a consistent biblical theme, maintains a sense of holiness, John catches a glimpse of the city of God adorned as a bride for her husband the Lamb.

The "Καὶ εἶδον" (then I saw) that opens the next sentence indicates John's move to a new visionary scene. A second and concluding "Καὶ εἶδον" closes this section and the vision it contains (v. 6a). the words act as a bracket that encloses this important vision of the figure who becomes the target of God's judgment activity. The target is the whore whom the angel promised to show John (17:1).

Once again the woman's posture comes into consideration. According to v. 1, she is seated on many waters. At v. 15, she will be seated on people, crowds, nations, and tongues. Here she is seated on a scarlet beast. The different metaphors point to the same reality. The woman, as 17:18 confirms, is the great city of Rome, enthroned upon the bestial empire whose commerce she uses to seduce the world into her idolatrous, prostituting behavior.

The beast's scarlet color identifies it immediately with both the red dragon (12:3) and the great city of Rome (18:6). An even more direct connection with bestial Rome develops from the description of seven heads, ten horns, and blasphemous names that is drawn explicitly from 13:1 (cf. 17:9), the verse that introduces the beast from the sea.

Key here is the observation that the woman and the beast both seem to represent the same entity, the city of Rome. The fact that the woman rides the beast, however, suggests that they are different entities.

Nevertheless, because of their parallel descriptions, I argue that John understands them to be one and the same entity, to which he gives the name "*Babylon*." The metaphors designate different functions of the same figure. If we were to compare Rome to a ship, we might imagine the beast as the below-decks engine room that powers the vessel and the woman as the top-deck bridge from which command decisions are made. No matter which metaphor is used (Whore or beast), the same vessel is in view. As Bauckham puts it, "*Chapter 17 brings the two images together: the harlot is enthroned on the seven heads of the beast (17:3, 9-10). In other words, Roman civilization, as a corrupting influence, rides on the back of Roman military power*" (*Climax of Prophecy*, 343).

- **4** John is consistent in his presentation of the whore/city as a seductive, gluttonous force. The colors of her clothing are an indication of her success and her pretension. Purple is the hue of royalty and rule, while scarlet indicates wealth (For purple see Judg. 8:26; Est. 8:15; Lam. 4:5; Dan. 5:7, 16, 29; *1 Macc.* 10:20, 62, 64; 11:58; 14:43; *Sir.* 40:4; Mark 15:17; John 19:2; *Gos. Pet.* 3.7. For scarlet/crimson see 2 Sam. 1:24; Prov. 31:21; Jer. 4:30; Epictetus, *Diatr.* 3.22.10; 4.11.34). A garment covered in gold, precious stones, and pearls rounds out the ostentatious ensemble. No doubt John had in mind that she literally wears her success on her sleeves. The gaudy display is also a mating maneuver. Her finery represents the wealth that has seduced the kings and inhabitants of the earth into intimate economic relationships with her. This is no ordinary street whore; As Blount calls her as *"an expensive call girl, an alluring courtesan of the highest order."* John's understanding of the courtesan as Rome is confirmed when, at 18:16, he narrates the same apparel adorning the great city.

The courtesan's outfit is complemented by the golden cup she holds in her hand. It holds not a liquid but the abominations and impurities of her prostituting behavior. Jeremiah 51:7 associates Babylon with a cup that makes all the world drunk. In Jeremiah's case Babylon is the cup; in Revelation, however, Babylon holds the cup in her hand. Yet the imagery of national seduction is the same.

John uses cup imagery primarily as a metaphor for divine judgment. At both 14:10 and 16:19, he narrates the cup of God's wrath. At the only other occurrence of the term, he declares that God gives to Babylon the very cup of desolation that she has mixed for others (18:6). Taken together, the images already suggest that while the call girl wields the cup in an effort to seduce and capture, God is preparing to make her elixir of abominations and impurities the means of her own punishing destruction. The punishment will not only fit the crime; the punishment will also turn out to be the crime. Her drunken paramours, juiced on the very economic and cultic orgy she has provided, will turn on her and destroy her.

- 5 Despite the fact that she is an expensive call girl, John still outfits her with the trappings of a street whore; she sports her name tattooed across her forehead. The forehead was the location of choice for the branding of ownership (7:3). At first and easy glance, everyone could see to what person or vocation someone belonged. God also marked the faithful on their foreheads. The parallel is intentional. In John's apocalyptic worldview are only two competing choices: one enlists either in God's service or in the service of the beast (cf. 13:16-17). The forehead logo brandishes the recruitment choice. Any name other than God's indicates trouble.

The whore's name is a troubling mystery. Grammatically, since all the key terms are in the same case and number, *"mystery"* could refer either to *"name"* (i.e., a name, a mystery: Babylon the Great) or *"Babylon the Great"* (a name: Mystery, Babylon the Great). The latter option would make the term *"mystery"* part of the woman's name. Since John in v. 7 determines to explain the mystery of the woman in her guise as Babylon, it is more likely that he intends the first meaning. The mystery is the name itself, and the name is Babylon the Great.

Historically, the name reminds believers of the imperial force that defeated and exiled the people of God (see 14:8). John associates the ancient empire with Rome, the imperial force that presently threatens to lure God's people into an exile of idolatry. Using the lure of economic wealth, she has drawn kings, inhabitants of the earth, and apparently, according to John's tone in chapters 2 and 3, even many of the faithful into an idolatrous, prostituting relationship with her pagan and imperial cults. The fact that John calls her the mother of whores is a signal that Rome has successfully co-opted other cities, that is, the *"children whores,"* into her military-economic-political complex. Their trading and diplomatic relationship with her is in truth an alliance with her idolatrous and satanic rejection of the lordship of God and the Standing Slaughtered Lamb.

Contextually, at least for John, the name should be a signal to believers of God's imminent judgment. Except for this single use in chapter 17, in every situation where John exercises the name he speaks of the city's divinely orchestrated destruction (14:8; 16:19; 18:2, 10, 21). The intertextual context from which he operates portends a similarly dark forecast; much of Jer. 51 is devoted to Babylon's deserved and impending judgment.

- **6a** The first half of v. 6 completes the vision that introduces the whore and the beast. John uses two mechanisms to frame the section. The first is the grammatical marker "καὶ εἶδον" (and I saw), which parallels the bracketing "καὶ εἶδον" in v. 3. While the first looks forward to the vision he is about to see, the second refers back to the vision he has just seen. The second framing mechanism is the woman herself. John finishes his description of her with an added detail. She has been binging on a brew drawn from her economic, political, and cultic success: the blood of those who witness to the lordship of God and the Lamb. Though John seems to be speaking of two different groups, the saints and the witnesses, the "καὶ" (and) here should be taken epexegetically; these are the saints, who are the witnesses to the lordship of God and the Lamb. At 18:24 John reiterates this ghoulish observation, this time declaring that she has consumed the blood of saints, prophets, and those slaughtered on the earth. The slaughter language reminds John's hearers and readers of the "*special*" relationship believers have had with Rome. The woman who has their blood metaphorically in her cup has for some time now had it figuratively on her hands. The image of a refined call girl, courtesan, does not hold. As alluring as Rome is, Rome is a beast. Her preferred vintage is the blood of Christ-believers. Hope comes from the knowledge that poetic justice is imminent. The beast who craves blood will find herself choking to death on it (16:6). The slaughter and blood references imply that the judgment is God's answer to the believers' cries for justice (6:9-11; 8:3-5). At 19:2 John makes that connection explicit.

Revelation 17:6b~18 → The Vision Interpreted

NIV	TT
⁶ᵇ When I saw her, I was greatly astonished. ⁷ Then the angel said to me: "Why are you astonished? I will explain to you the mystery of the woman and of the beast she rides, which has the seven heads and ten horns. ⁸ The beast, which you saw, once was, now is not, and yet will come up out of the Abyss and go to its destruction. The inhabitants of the earth whose names have not been written in the book of life from the creation of the world will be astonished when they see the beast, because it once was, now is not, and yet will come. ⁹ "This calls for a mind	⁶ᵇ When I saw her, I was greatly **impressed**²⁴⁸. ⁷ Then the angel said to me, "Why are you so impressed? I will explain to you the mystery of the woman and the beast with the seven heads and ten horns that carries her. ⁸ The beast that you saw was and is not and is about to rise from the **Abyss**²⁴⁹ and go to **destruction**²⁵⁰. And the inhabitants of the earth, whose names were not written in the Book of Life from the foundation of the world, will be impressed when they see the beast, because it was and is not and is to appear. ⁹ This requires a mind with **wisdom**²⁵¹. The

---

[248] θαυμάζω → It means "*wonder*," "*marvel*," "*be astonished*," (at divine epiphanies or deeds), "*admire*," and "*flatter*."
[249] ἄβυσσος → It means "*bottomless*," "*unbounded*," "*the Abyss*," "*the pit*," and "*of Orcus*" (a very deep gulf or chasm in the lowest parts of the earth used as the common receptacle of the dead and especially as the abode of demons).
[250] ἀπώλεια → It means "*perdition*," "*destruction*," "*waste*," "*damnable*," "*to die*," "*perish*," and "*the destruction which consists of the eternal misery in hell*."
[251] σοφία → The term means "*wisdom*," "*Wisdom of Christ and of God*," and "*intelligence*."

with wisdom. The seven heads are seven hills on which the woman sits. ¹⁰ They are also seven kings. Five have fallen, one is, the other has not yet come; but when he does come, he must remain for only a little while. ¹¹ The beast who once was, and now is not, is an eighth king. He belongs to the seven and is going to his destruction.

¹² "The ten horns you saw are ten kings who have not yet received a kingdom, but who for one hour will receive authority as kings along with the beast. ¹³ They have one purpose and will give their power and authority to the beast. ¹⁴ They will wage war against the Lamb, but the Lamb will triumph over them because he is Lord of lords and King of kings— and with him will be his called, chosen and faithful

seven heads are seven mountains on which the woman is seated. They are also seven kings, ¹⁰ of whom five have fallen, the one is, the other has not yet come. When he does come, he must remain only a short time. ¹¹ And the beast that was and is not, it is an eighth, but is from the seven, and it goes to destruction. ¹² And the ten horns that you saw are ten kings who have not yet received a kingdom, but they will receive authority as kings for one hour, with the beast. ¹³ They are of one mind; they relinquish their power and authority to the beast. ¹⁴ They will wage war with the Lamb, and the Lamb will conquer them, because he is Lord of lords and King of kings, and those with him are called and **chosen**[252] and **faithful**[253]."

¹⁵ And he said to me, "The waters that you saw, where the whore sits, are people and

---

[252] ἐκλεκτός → It means *"picked out," "chosen," the elect,"* and *"the outstanding Christian."*
[253] πιστός → It means *"trustworthy," "faithful," "dependable," "inspiring trust," "cherishing faith," "believing,"* and *"believers."*

followers." ¹⁵ Then the angel said to me, "The waters you saw, where the prostitute sits, are peoples, multitudes, nations and languages. ¹⁶ The beast and the ten horns you saw will hate the prostitute. They will bring her to ruin and leave her naked; they will eat her flesh and burn her with fire. ¹⁷ For God has put it into their hearts to accomplish his purpose by agreeing to hand over to the beast their royal authority, until God's words are fulfilled. ¹⁸ The woman you saw is the great city that rules over the kings of the earth."	crowds and nations and languages. ¹⁶ And the ten horns that you saw and the beast will hate the whore and make her desolate and naked and devour her flesh and burn her with fire. ¹⁷ For God put into their hearts to do God's will, to have one mind and surrender their kingdom to the beast, until the words of God have been fulfilled. ¹⁸ And the woman whom you saw is the great city that has dominion over the kings of the earth."

At this point an angel questions John about his amazement and proceeds to tell him about the mystery of Babylon and the beast who carries her. This passage seems unique in the Book of Revelation in which the angelic messenger offers the meaning of a vision. It is a typical feature of other works in the apocalyptic tradition. The second half of the Book of Daniel, for instance, offers several examples of this kind of angelic explanation of events; Daniel 7 is an obvious example where Daniel's vision of the thrones, judgment, and the coming of *"the Son of Man"* is interpreted in terms of human history.

- **6b – 7** John is awestruck by what he sees. He describes his captivation with the verb "θαυμάζω" (to marvel). He uses it in only two other contexts, both of which detail pagan praise and worship of the beast (13:3; 17:8). Even one who despises the idolatrous excess and despotic brutality of Rome must acknowledge her power and grandeur. With the prowess of her military legions, the transnational reach of her vast commercial enterprise, and the magnificent trappings of her imperial cult, in her presence who could not help but feel awe? John's guiding and apparently prescient angel immediately senses his astonishment. He offers therefore to interpret the unsettling vision of the woman and the seven-headed, ten-horned beast she rides (v. 3).
- **8** John begins his narration of the angel's description with a relative clause formulation that he will use five times in this vision interpretation (vv. 8, 12, 15, 16, 18): "ὃ εἶδες" (that you saw). Initial focus is on the beast *"that you saw."* The threefold depiction *"who was, is not, and is about to rise out of the Abyss"* recalls the threefold representation of God, as well as the Lamb, as the one *"who was, is, and is coming"* (1:4, 8; 4:8; 11:17; 16:5; the last two references do not include the third term *"is coming"* because by the time John deploys them, the judgment moment has narratively arrived). The angel's play on the God/Lamb narration is no doubt a mocking of the beast's pretentious desire to stand itself in the place of true lordship. To be sure, the beast seemed to be all-powerful since Rome had surely built the kind of empire that could elicit awe even from

a devoted Christ-follower such as John. But already the reign of the beast *"is not,"* for with the advent of seventh seal/trumpet/bowl, God's judgment has come. Now that the judgment has arrived, the power that *"was"* certainly *"is not"* all that it thinks it is! Mockery is certain at the end of the verse when John returns to this threefold formulation, but with slightly different wording. In this rendition, the beast who *"was"* and *"is not"* is *"[about] to appear."* Using "παρέσται" (will appear), John surely conjures in most hearers' and readers' minds the root form of the verb, "πάρειμι" which was used to convey the future coming (Parousia) of Jesus Christ as eschatological Lord. John does not use the term *"Parousia,"* he emphasizes Christ's coming by repeating the phrase *"I am coming"* some seven times (2:5, 16; 3:11; 16:15; 22:7, 12, 20; cf. 3:3). The beast's glorious earthly reign suggested to itself and its devotees that it had a future similar to that of eschatological lordship.

Even though it still appeared, even to John, that the awe-ful power of the beast was at its height, the angel's depiction reveals just how deceptive appearance could be. The moment the child of the woman clothed with the sun was snatched safely from the jaws of the dragon to the throne of heaven (12:5), the war was over. To be sure, the rise of the beast from the Abyss (11:7) was still a terrible and threatening sight, which foreshadowed death and destruction for Christ-believers. The ultimate end of that rise, though, was not glory but destruction. John emphasizes the point at 17:11. The word he uses for destruction both there and here in v. 8 (ἀπώλεια) looks and sounds a great deal like "'Απολλύων" ("*Destroyer*"), the name he earlier gave to the angel of the Abyss (9:11). The imperial personification of destruction will itself be destroyed. The key emphasis here is ethical. John's hearers and readers should endure the onslaughts of the beast, resist its seductions, and witness against it because, though it looked all-powerful, it was, in truth, dead on arrival.

As for the inhabitants of the earth, these enemies of the faithful, not able to see through the interpretive lens of the angel, marvel in worship at what they no doubt believe will be the beast's perpetual dominion.

- **9** As in 13:18, the reference to wisdom suggests that only the wise mind will be able to understand what the angel has just revealed. The wise person will not lose heart and will continue to witness aggressively to the lordship of God and the Standing Slaughtered Lamb because of understanding that the power that was, now is not, and rises only to its own destruction.

  Less decoding is necessary for what follows because the angel provides clarity that operates from a well-established Greco-Roman tradition. The seven heads, noticed already at 13:1 and 17:3, are seven mountains upon which the woman sits enthroned. John has already alluded to the reign of the woman by noting that she sits enthroned on many waters (v. 1), which will be defined as many people, multitudes, nations, and languages (v. 15), and also on a beast (vv. 3, 7). Each of those symbols is, like the seven mountains, a metaphor for Rome. According to legend, Romulus, founder of Rome, built the original city of seven hills. (The hills are generally designated as the Palatine, Capitoline, Quirinal, Viminal, Esquiline, Caelian, and Aventine.) As surely as any contemporary American reader would recognize Philadelphia as *"the city of brotherly love"* or Chicago as *"the windy city,"* a first-century Greco-Roman would have immediately understood a reference to *"the city on seven hills"* as a reference to Rome (Virgil, *Aen.* 6.782-83; *Georg.* 2.535; Martial, *Epig.* 6:64; Cicero, *Att.* 6.5; *Sib. Or.* 2.18; 11.113-16; 13.45; 14.108).

David Aune points to a *"Dea Roma"* coint minted in Asia in 71 C.E., during the reign of Vespasian. He argues that depictions on coinage were generally reproductions of widely recognized art, perhaps in this case a sculpture. While on one side the coin sported the obligatory bust of the emperor, on the other was etched an image of the goddess Roma, a physical representation of the cultic praise for Rome, sitting on Rome's seven hills. Given that Asia Minor, particularly the Smyrnaeans, claimed to be the first imperial province to worship Roma, one would wager that John's readers would have immediately understood the point of John's reference. The woman represented Rome in all its idolatrous claims to cultic and cosmic lordship.

More important, though, is the inference that must be drawn from john's use of such a recognizable symbol. He was not writing a cryptic document meant to be understood only by believing insiders, a document that would mislead the Romans into thinking that it was not directed at them. John used such a well-known, well-recognized symbol for a reason. It was not the case that he wanted only his followers to know that his visions of destruction were directed at Rome. He also wanted the Romans to know! In making his point so clearly and so universally, he was modeling the very non-accommodating, challenging witness that he demanded from others. Even while in Roman exile, he speaks against Rome and declares the imminent end of Roman rule.

John's vision operates like a dream, where logical limits do not apply. In such an environment symbols can simultaneously have two different referents. Here in v. 9, the seven heads, which John has already established as seven hills, are also seven kings. The one constant that controls the image flux is the fact that all the images ultimately point to Rome. Like the seven hills, then, the seven kings are a metaphor for the empire. In this case, though, instead of referencing its cultic imperialism (the hills as related to the goddess Roma), the seven monarchs represents its political imperialism. As v. 10 will immediately clarify, they are most certainly seven Caesars.

- **10** Having presented the seven heads of the beast as seven kings, John does not set out to identify them. He intends instead to establish the trajectory of their rule. The central focus is on the sixth Caesar: the one who now is. John does not identify him for two reasons. First, he is interested in the role these rulers play in the movement of God's rule into human history.

John's lack of interest in the exact identities of the seven emperors has not been matched in the writings of biblical scholars. Even though most agree that John's point is not tied to proper identification of the seven figures, numerous strategies for identifying them still abound. The problem is that, since contemporary readers no longer know the identity of the sixth emperor, they find it impossible to figure out the five who come before and the two who follow. Since it is presumed that john wrote during the reign of Domitian, one would think that calculations would involve him. Other scholars contemplate starting at the beginning, with which emperor must have been the first of the five. But it is difficult to know which ruler was considered the first emperor: Julius Caesar, under whom the republic ended; or Octavius, under whom the empire officially began. There are also questions as to whether to include the extremely brief reigns of Otho, Galba, and Vitellius, who occupied the throne during the tumultuous years following Nero's death, 68-69 C.E.

Seven kings represent the pinnacle of idolatrous resistance to it. Since *"seven"* is a number of wholeness for John, he likely understands the seven kings to represent the complete symbolization of human rule in idolatrous defiance of God's rule. Second, since the sixth is the Caesar who now rules, the hearers and readers would immediately recognize not only him but also the five who preceded him. John describes those five as having fallen. The imagery of falling alludes to violent death, like that which occurs on a battlefield, or as the result of assassination, the kind of end that many

Caesars met. Unlike the eternal Lamb, their existences are transitory and fragile. Why would his followers pay homage to rulers who "*fall*" when they have the option of worshipping the Lamb who has risen to the throne of the eternal God? The emphasis on the impermanence of Roman rule continues with the angel's explanation that the seventh king will reign for only a short time. The brevity of time is no doubt also directly related to the fact that God's judgment and the Lamb's return are so imminent.

- **11** John returns to the moment of judgment when he pushes forward to the eighth and final king. If the sixth is the one who rules in John's present time, the eighth rules in that imminent moment of judgment that has already been inaugurated with the seventh seal/trumpet/bowl. Though there are different individual kings, they all represent the one beast. For this reason John describes the eighth head/king in the same way that he had earlier described the beast itself, as the one who "*was*" and "*is not*" (v. 8). John reiterates that though the beast's advent is impressive, its destruction is already assured: it is dead on arrival. He also reminds his hearers and readers that though it appears to stand apart and therefore appear impregnable, it is a part of the transient line of the seven who have come before it. It is just as fragile as they; it, too, will fall.

- **12** In the second deployment of the relative clause "*that you saw*," John's guiding angel interprets the ten horns as ten kings who have yet to receive their kingdoms (cf. Dan. 7:7-8, 20, 24). Their symbolization as horns suggests that they represent a vital source of the beast's power (on horns as symbols of power, see 12:3 and 13:1). They are to be distinguished not only from the seven Caesars, but also from the kings of the whole world at 16:14 and the kings of the earth (cf. 6:15; 17:2; 18:3, 9; 19:19). These others have already received their reigns. Like those Caesars and their client kings, though, the kings who do not yet rule represent yet another set of earthly leaders who fight against the lordship of the Lamb. It is as though the very aspiration to human lordship draws one into rebellion against the lordship of God and the Standing Slaughtered Lamb. Perhaps this is John's way of saying that every human rule, because of the inclination of humans to idolize themselves and their capabilities, is on a potential collision course with God's rule.

In the case of these ten, that collision will come quickly. They will have only one hour – John's metaphorical way of saying a brief eschatological moment in the end time of God's judgment – before they are overthrown. Even at this climactic inbreaking of God's rule, they ally themselves with the authority of the beast because they do not see that the beast's rise is to its destruction (vv. 8, 11).

- **13** The angel elaborates on the kings' woeful decision; they acted as if of a single mind in agreeing to delegate their potential power to the beast. John's narration will clarify that this singularity of purpose was created by God (v. 17). Just as God had once hardened Pharaoh's heart so that God could initiate judgment against Egypt, so now God drives these kings to a decision that will trigger their destruction.

- **14** It is not surprising that the kings will declare war on the Lamb; such actions fit the pattern of those who follow the beast (cf. Dan. 7:21). John has already explained that many will refrain from fighting with the beast because they perceive incorrectly that no one can fight successfully against it (13:40. Indeed, the language of a beast-directed war against the Lamb and those who follow him occurs repeatedly throughout the narrative (11:7; 12:17; 13:7; 16:14; 19:19). The occurrence in chapter 16 is particularly significant, as it narrates the gathering of an eschatological army whose engagement with the forces of the Lamb will immediately follow 17:1-19:10 (19:11-21; 20:7-10).

Past victories of the beast (11:7) are not an indication of future success; in this climactic battle of the end time, the Lamb will engage directly, and the Lamb will prevail. According to 5:5, the seed of that conquest was planted long ago in the Lamb's crucifixion (5:12) and resurrection (12:50. John has always maintained that believers can participate in that victorious conquest (12:11; 15:2) through their non-accommodating, resistant witness (2:7, 11, 17, 26; 3:5, 12, 21; 21:7).

The Lamb's victory is based in his identity as King of kings and Lord of lords (Deut. 10:17; Ps. 136:3; Dan. 2:47; 1 Tim. 6:15; *2 Macc.* 13:4), the very title inscribed on his garment at 19:16, a scene that depicts his triumph. Verse 14 ends with the assurance that the Lamb's victory is also based in the faithfulness of those chosen and elected to witness to his lordship (cf. 12:11). The only time John applies the adjective "*faithful*" to believers (2:13), he does so to describe the kind of resistant witness that testifies exclusively to the lordship of Christ and in so doing participates in Christ's victory (2:17).

- **15** In the third deployment of the relative clause "*that you saw*," the interpreting angel refers to the waters upon which John saw the whore sitting (v. 1). Those waters are now defined as many people and crowds and nations and tongues. In other words, Rome sits imperially atop all the people of the earth. Since John primarily uses this and similar formulations as a negative representation of people who resist the lordship of God and the Standing Slaughtered Lamb, he no doubt intends here to clarify that Rome not only rules the populaces of the world but has also engineered an idolatrous relationship with them. Rome has employed them in its war against the Lamb.
- **16** In the fourth use of the relative clause "*that you saw*,' the interpreting angel indicates that Rome's end will begin as an act of self-destruction. The forces that represent Roman resistance to the lordship of God and the Standing Slaughtered Lamb will turn on themselves. Before the Lamb engages and destroys them at 19:11-21, they will engage and begin the process of destroying each other. The ten horns, which are the ten kings who have not yet received their rule, will join with the beast in hatred of the whore. It is as though the engine room that powered a ship made war on the bridge that guided it. "*Those who allied themselves*

with Rome did so because it was to their advantage. Their friendship was dependent on what it brought them. If their interests had been served better by turning on Rome, by taking what she had accumulated, then there would have been no reason for them to remain loyal" (Gonzalez and Gonzalez 115). Biblical scholars correctly note that this depiction of the end is at odds with John's presentation at 18:8, where her demise is caused by plagues. Despite the narrative contradiction, however, John scores a consistent point. Rome's imminent demise is the working out of divine justice; John is just not obsessed with narrating that demise consistently.

Some of the most problematic language in the chapter occurs here. The angel relays that the kings and the beast will render the whore naked, eat her flesh, and then consume what remains with fire. John is clearing working from Old Testament imagery of God's judgment exercising itself against prostituting behavior through images nakedness, fire, and the devouring of flesh (Lev. 21:9; Jer. 34:22; Ezek. 16:37-41; 23:25-29, 31-34; 26:19; Hos. 2:5; Mic. 3:3). The most poignant reference is the recounting of the death of Jezebel, an idolatrous queen who sought to prostitute the faith of Israel with compulsory worship of Baal. Thrown from a window, she was devoured by dogs (2 Kgs. 9:30-37). This misogynistic style of presentation is deeply troubling. Although it does not remove the offense, interpretation of this difficult text should not miss John's primary concern: his fear that his people will destroy their relationship with Christ through a prostituting relationship with Rome.

- **17** The angel now finishes the thought he began at v. 13. The pact that the kings make to give their authority to the beast and then to turn against the woman with what appears to be a single mind has been inspired by God. Despite all appearances, God is in charge.
- **18** in the final use of the relative clause *"that you saw,"* the interpreting angel returns to the woman he promised to show John (v. 10, and whom John did see at v. 3. Explicitly, now, the angel interprets her meaning. She is the great city (16:19; 18:10) that has dominion over all the kings of earth. The description is as clear as the earlier one: *"seven mountains on which the woman [city] is seated"* (v. 9). She is Rome. But since Rome is also the beast, it becomes clear at this point that the woman and the beast are functionally synonymous metaphors. Each represents the reality of Rome's power. The woman particularly represents Rome's economic seduction; she draws people and those who rule them into an idolatrous relationship so that they refuse to acknowledge the lordship of God and the Standing Slaughtered Lamb (Ps. 2:2).

Revelation 18:1~24 → The Fall of Babylon

NIV	TT
18 ¹ After this I saw another angel coming down from heaven. He had great authority, and the earth was illuminated by his splendor. ² With a mighty voice he shouted: "'Fallen! Fallen is Babylon the Great!' She has become a dwelling for demons and a haunt for every impure spirit, a haunt for every unclean bird, a haunt for every unclean and detestable animal. ³ For all the nations have drunk the maddening wine of her adulteries. The kings of the earth committed adultery with her, and the merchants of the earth grew rich from her excessive luxuries." ⁴ Then I heard another voice from heaven say: "'Come out of her, my people,' so	**18** ¹ After this I saw another angel with great authority descending from heaven, and the earth was lit up by his glory. ² He cried out in a **great**[254] voice, saying, "**Fallen**[255], fallen is Babylon the Great. It has become a dwelling place of **demons**[256], a haunt of every foul and hateful beast. ³ Because all the nations drank from the wine of the wrath of her fornication, and the kings of the earth fornicated with her, and the merchants of the earth became rich from the magnitude of her luxury." ⁴ Then I heard another voice from heaven saying, "Come out of her, my people, so that you do not take part in her sins, and so that you do not share in her plagues,

---

[254] μέγας → The term means *"large," "great," "long," "wide," "bright," "intense," "severe,"* and *"loud."*
[255] ἔπεσεν → It means *"fallen," "fallen to pieces," "ruined," "in a moral or cultic sense go astray," "failed," "become invalid," "be destroyed," "fall down,"* and *"collapse."*
[256] δαίμων → It means *"demon," "god/goddess," "inferior deity,"* and *"evil spirit."*

that you will not share in her sins, so that you will not receive any of her plagues; ⁵ for her sins are piled up to heaven, and God has remembered her crimes. ⁶ Give back to her as she has given; pay her back double for what she has done. Pour her a double portion from her own cup. ⁷ Give her as much torment and grief as the glory and luxury she gave herself. In her heart she boasts, 'I sit enthroned as queen. I am not a widow; I will never mourn.' ⁸ Therefore in one day her plagues will overtake her: death, mourning and famine. She will be consumed by fire, for mighty is the Lord God who judges her.

⁹ "When the kings of the earth who committed adultery with her and shared her luxury see the smoke of her burning, they will weep and mourn over her. ¹⁰ Terrified at her torment, they will stand far off and

⁵ for her sins are piled up to heaven, and God has remembered her crimes. ⁶ Render to her as she herself has rendered, and repay her double for what she has done; in the cup which she mixed, mix for her a double portion. ⁷ As she glorified herself and **lived luxuriously**[257], so give to her torment and grief. For in her heart she says, 'I sit[258] as queen, and I am not a widow, and I will never see grief.' ⁸ Because of this her plagues will come in one day, death and grief and famine; she will be burned with fire, for the Lord God who judges her is mighty."

⁹ And the kings of the earth who prostituted themselves with her lived luxuriously with her will weep and mourn over her when they see the smoke of her burning, ¹⁰ standing far away because of the fear of her torment, saying, "Woe,

---

[257] στρηνιάω → The term means "*live in luxury,*" and "*live sensually.*" In the Bible, this term only appears in Rev. 18:7, 9.
[258] κάθημαι → It means "*sit,*" "*be enthroned,*" "*stay,*" "*live,*" and "*reside.*"

cry: "'Woe! Woe to you, great city, you mighty city of Babylon! In one hour your doom has come!' ¹¹ "The merchants of the earth will weep and mourn over her because no one buys their cargoes anymore— ¹² cargoes of gold, silver, precious stones and pearls; fine linen, purple, silk and scarlet cloth; every sort of citron wood, and articles of every kind made of ivory, costly wood, bronze, iron and marble; ¹³ cargoes of cinnamon and spice, of incense, myrrh and frankincense, of wine and olive oil, of fine flour and wheat; cattle and sheep; horses and carriages; and human beings sold as slaves. ¹⁴ "They will say, 'The fruit you longed for is gone from you. All your luxury and	woe, the great city, Babylon, the mighty city, because your judgment has come in one hour." ¹¹ And the merchants of the earth weep and mourn over her, because no one any longer buys their cargo, ¹² cargo of gold and silver and precious stones and pearls and fine linen and purple and silk and scarlet, and every kind of product made of scented wood, and every kind of product made of ivory, and every article of precious wood and bronze and iron and marble, ¹³ and cinnamon and **amomum**²⁵⁹ and incense and myrrh and frankincense and wine and olive oil and fine wheat flour and wheat and cattle and sheep and horses and chariots and **slaves**²⁶⁰, that is human **lives**²⁶¹. ¹⁴ And the fruit which you desired has left you, and all your **luxury**²⁶² and **splendor**²⁶³

---

²⁵⁹ ἄμωμον → It means "*amomum,*" an Indian spice plant.

²⁶⁰ σῶμα → It means "*dead body,*" "*corpse,*" "*the living body,*" and "*slaves*"

²⁶¹ ψυχή → It means "*soul,*" "*life,*" "*mind,*" "*heart,*" "*breath,*" and "*desires.*"

²⁶² τὰ λιπαρὰ → The phrase means "*bright things,*" "*costly things,*" "*luxury things,*" and "*rich things.*"

splendor have vanished, never to be recovered.' ¹⁵ The merchants who sold these things and gained their wealth from her will stand far off, terrified at her torment. They will weep and mourn ¹⁶ and cry out: "'Woe! Woe to you, great city, dressed in fine linen, purple and scarlet, and glittering with gold, precious stones and pearls! ¹⁷ In one hour such great wealth has been brought to ruin!' "Every sea captain, and all who travel by ship, the sailors, and all who earn their living from the sea, will stand far off. ¹⁸ When they see the smoke of her burning, they will exclaim, 'Was there ever a city like this great city?' ¹⁹ They will throw dust on their heads, and with weeping and mourning cry out: "'Woe! Woe to you, great city, where all who had ships on the sea became rich through her wealth! In one hour she has been brought to ruin!'	are lost to you, and people will never find them again. ¹⁵ The merchants of these commodities, who became rich from her, will stand far away because of the fear of her torment, weeping and mourning, ¹⁶ saying, "Woe, woe, the great city, clothed in fine linen and purple and scarlet, and adorned with gold and jewelry and pearls, ¹⁷ᵃ because in one hour such wealth was **laid waste**[264]." ¹⁷ᵇ And every shipmaster and every seafarer and every sailor, and every one working on the sea, stood at a distance ¹⁸ and cried out when they saw the smoke of her burning, saying, "What city is like the great city?" ¹⁹ And they threw dust on their heads and cried out, weeping and mourning, saying, "Woe, woe, the great city. In her all who had boats on the sea became wealthy from her abundance. For in one hour she has been laid waste." ²⁰ Rejoice over her, heaven

---

[263] τὰ λαμπρὰ → The phrase means "*bright things,*" "*shining things,*" "*radiant things,*" "*clear things,*" "*transparent things,*" and "*splendor.*"
[264] ἐρημόω → It means "*lay waste,*" "*depopulate,*" and "*ruin.*"

²⁰ "Rejoice over her, you heavens! Rejoice, you people of God! Rejoice, apostles and prophets! For God has judged her with the judgment she imposed on you."

²¹ Then a mighty angel picked up a boulder the size of a large millstone and threw it into the sea, and said: "With such violence
   the great city of Babylon will be thrown down,
     never to be found again.
²² The music of harpists and musicians, pipers and trumpeters, will never be heard in you again. No worker of any trade will ever be found in you again. The sound of a millstone will never be heard in you again.
²³ The light of a lamp will never shine in you again. The voice of bridegroom and bride will never be heard in you again. Your merchants were the world's important people. By your

and saints and apostles and prophets, for God has judged her with the **judgment**[265] she imposed on you.

²¹ Then one **mighty**[266] angel took up a great stone like a giant millstone and threw it into the sea, saying, "With such violence Babylon, the great city, will be thrown, and it will never be found again." ²² And the sound of harpists and musicians and flutists and trumpeters will never be heard in you again; and no craftsman of any trade will ever be found in you again; and the sound of the millstone will never be heard in you again; ²³ᵃ and the light of a lamp will never shine in you again; and the voice of bridegroom and bride will never be heard in you again;

²³ᵇ because your merchants were the elite of the earth; because all the nations were deceived by your sorcery.

---

[265] κρίμα → It means "*lawsuit*," "*decision*," "*decree*," "*judging*," "*judgment*," "*verdict*," "*condemnation*," "*sentence*," and "*punishment*."
[266] ἰσχυρός → It means "*strong*," "*mighty*," "*powerful*," "*loud*," and "*effective*."

magic spell all the nations were led astray. ²⁴ In her was found the blood of prophets and of God's holy people, of all who have been slaughtered on the earth."	²⁴ And in her was found the blood of prophets and saints and all those who have been slaughtered on the earth.

This lamentation borrows much of the language and imagery of Old Testament lamentations that both protest and lament the sins of Israel and Jerusalem, protest and lament their destruction, combined with prophetic judgments that celebrate the fall of Assyria and Babylon (Ps. 137:8; Isa. 13:21-22; 21:9; 23:8, 17; 34:11, 14; 40:2; 47:8-9; 48:20; Jer. 7:34; 9:10; 16:9; 25:10, 15; 50:8, 15, 29, 31; 51:6, 7, 9, 45; Ezek. 26:16-17; 27:12-22, 30-34, 36; Nah. 3:4).

- **1** By beginning with the formulaic phrase "Μετὰ ταῦτα εἶδον" (after this I saw), John signals a narrative intent to shift to a new way of thinking about a previously explored topic (see the comments on 4:1 and 15:5). Here he follows up on the chapter 17 portrayal of Babylon/Rome as the great whore. What was promised in 17:1 and forecast at 17:8 will now be narrated as a realized event. The future is so certain that it can be spoken of in the past tense.

    John introduces "*another*" angel as the speaker. The modifier recalls 10:1, where the adjective "*another*" distinguished the angel from the seven trumpet angels who had appeared before him. Here, no doubt, the adjective distinguishes the angel of 18:1 from the seven bowl angels who appeared before his arrival on the narrative scene; this, then, is not the same angel who appears in 17:1. On other notable occasions, John also refers to other angels (7:2; 8:3). In both 7:2 and 8:3, as in 10:1, the angels appear in a context of judgment. When John introduces "*another*" angel, hearers and readers are right to entertain a sense of dread. John makes the judgment connection explicit with the literary relationship he established between this "*other*" angel and "*the other*" angels of chapter 14 (vv. 6, 8, 9, 15, 17, 18). Given John's affinity for the number "*seven*" as a number of completion, it is odd that in the judgment-laced chapter 14 he would offer a presentation of only six "*other*" angels. In effect, John compelled his hearers and readers to hold their narrative breath while the judgment initiated by these six awaited dramatic consummation some four chapters later at 18:1. Here, for the last time in the narrative, "*another*" angel appears; his appearance climaxes the judgment theme initiated at 14:6.

The judgment begins as a combat encounter. This "*other angel*" has great authority. At 13:2 John explained that the dragon had great authority; it ceded that authority to the beast from the sea, which chapter 17 identified as the great whore and chapter 18 names as the city of Babylon. This angel's great authority has also been leased to him by a higher power, in this case by God. As chapter 18 dawns, then, hearers and readers are presented with the angelic representative of God (v. 1) and the municipal representative of Satan (v. 2), two surrogate powers who engage each other in a proxy war on behalf of their masters. The battle, which takes place completely offstage, ends before it even properly begins; already by v. 2, Satan's representative has been laid waste. Thoroughly routed, Babylon is now ruthlessly judged.

A rationale for Babylon's judgment is implied in the final piece of the angel's description: his glory was so bright that it lit up the entire earth (cf. Ezek. 43:2). The divine passive construction (*"the earth was lit up"*) is John's way of attributing the lighting action to God. The angel's glory, like his authority, is representative. Just as the moon reflects the light of the sun but emanates no light of its own, so the angel's glory points not to the angel but to God. According to 18:7, Babylon revels in the belief that its glory is its own and reflects not God's power but its own status and strength. It is this warping sense of self-glorification that motivates the oppressive behavior for which Babylon is judged.

- **2** While John typically uses the adjective "μέγας" (great) to describe an angel's great voice, the presence of "*strong,*" "*mighty*" which he applies more often to angels than to their voices (5:2; 10:1; 18:21), has the same connotation of impending judgment in v. 2. John means to say that the angel speaks in an ominous, foreboding tone. Biblical scholars apply to the intoned message an equally foreboding categorization. As Reddish puts it, *"The words of the angel are similar to prophetic taunt songs, such as are found in Isaiah 23-24:47; Jeremiah 50-51; and Ezekiel 26-27."* These songs announce with mockery the downfall or death of an enemy.

For John, Babylon's fall is simultaneously past, present, and future. Even in the present, as it appears powerful and strong, it is on its way to destruction (17:8). That destruction is described confidently with future tense verbs in 18:8-20. Here, though, John declares the certainty of that future realization through the use of aorist verbs: "ἔπεσεν ἔπεσεν" (fallen, fallen). The full cry, "*Fallen, fallen, is Babylon the Great,*" is a reprisal of the macabre observation made by the second in John's series of judgment angels (cf. Rev. 14:8). While the angel of 14:8a shares the reason for the fall immediately in the second half of his taunt (14:8b), this seventh angel in the series inserts a more detailed description of the fall before stating its cause (v. 3). The taunt is in the details. Recalling prophetic images of divine devastation (Babylon, Isa. 13:19-22; Jer. 51:37; Jerusalem, Jer. 9:9-11; Edom, Isa. 34:11-15; Assyria, Zeph. 2:13-14; cf. *Bar.* 4:35), John declares to a Rome that is at the height of its imperial power at the close of the first century that even as it luxuriates in its military, economic, and political might, its imperial center has already become a haunted wasteland, occupied by unclean beasts and spirits.

- **3** This seventh "*other angel*" also details the rationale for judgment that the second "*other angel*" announced in abbreviated form at 14:8b. Like Tyre before her (Isa. 23:17), Babylon/Rome has corrupted the nations with the wine of her passion for wealth. While the angel of 14:8 says that Babylon/Rome caused the nations to drink, the angel here is more vague about the city's role. Clearly, though, because Babylon/Rome is being judged, Babylon/Rome is culpable. The implication is that Babylon/Rome has lured the nations into a relationship so addictive that they are incapable of extricating themselves from it (cf. 18:23). The metaphor for the relationship remains prostituting sexuality; the reality remains destructive economics. From chapters 2 and 3 onward, John has been warning his folk about being so desperate for economic prosperity that they of meat sacrificed to pagan and imperial gods as a way of demonstrating social and political camaraderie. To buy into the economy (which John characterizes as taking on the mark of the beast), one has to buy into a recognition of lordship for pagan and particularly imperial figures, and thereby denigrate the lordship of God and the Standing Slaughtered Lamb (cf. 2:14, 20). Economic advancement demands the exorbitant price of cultic apostasy. But it is just this economic affiliation that many come to believe they cannot survive without. This belief, heightened to an eschatological frenzy, is what John describes as a wine so passionate for material gain that the person who imbibes it will prostitute one's faith to obtain more of it.

After his mention of the nations, this seventh "*other angel*" introduces two figurative groups that will play a key role in the development of Rev. 18. Like the nations, the kings who rule over them have prostituted themselves. A king's true allegiance should be to the true Lord of history, the true guarantor of spiritual and economic security and success. Instead, these kings have allied themselves economically with

Babylon/Rom. This illicit economic intercourse is as improper as illegitimate sex.

Babylon/Rome is finally complicit also in the corruption of merchants (vv. 11, 15) who grew rich from but also dependent upon the luxurious splendor of the city's imperial economy. The city's wealth is as sensual as it is seductive; it captivates and controls like a magic spell (v. 23).

- **4** John shifts from vision to audition with the words *"then I head,"* which also mark the start of a new scene within the larger act. He heard another heavenly voice follow up the angel's taunting. Since it immediately addresses John's hearers and readers as *"my people,"* the voice probably belongs either to God or to Jesus Christ. Since it is unlikely that God would speak about God's own actions in the third person (18:5, 8, 20; cf. 1:8; 21:5-7, where God speaks of God's identity and behavior in the first person), the protagonist is probably Christ.

As in Isaiah 48:20; 52:11 and Jeremiah 51:45, Christ's point is clear and direct. His people must *"come out"* of Babylon/Rome. Because Babylon/Rome is a symbolic moniker for the entire empire and not just the city from which the empire took its name, the heavenly voice cannot be speaking literally. The political, military, religious, and economic reach of the empire is vast. As John clearly recognizes in chapters 2 and 3, the cities where his churches are located sit firmly within the imperial grasp. The heavenly voice, like John's, demands a figurative separation instead. In the Gospel of John, Jesus Christ makes a similar demand of his followers: while living in the imperial world, they are to find a way to not be of the world (John 15:19; 17:15). On a particular and limited level, this would mean refusing to eat meat sacrificed to idols in contexts that validated Greco-Roman belief in the lordship of those idols and the imperial cult they represented and supported. On a more general level, it would mean witnessing against imperial lordship by refusing to participate in the economic juggernaut that Rome had established, a significant act if Bauckham is right: "*It is not unlikely that John's readers would include merchants and others whose business or livelihood was closely involved with the Roman political and economic system.*" Because most Greco-Romans believed that their economic and therefore social, political, and physical security were provided only through participation in this system, opting out of it would be a way of witnessing to the belief that true security comes from God alone. Only by stepping away from Rome could a believer step forward for God.

The fact, however, that Christ must make this plea is an indication that many believers were not stepping forward. When Christ says "*Come out*," he implies that many have already bought their way in. John makes this clear in his letters to the seven churches. Only two of those churches, Smyrna and Philadelphia, are described as impoverished. Indeed, in both cases the impoverishment seems directly linked to their fervent witness against the lordship of Rome and for the lordship of God and the Standing Slaughtered Lamb (2:10; 3.10). By contrast, believers in the other churches are chastised because they have amassed wealth and prestige by accommodating themselves to doing whatever was necessary (e.g., eating meat sacrificed to idols) to participate in the Roman economy. Jezebel, Balaam, and the Nicolaitans are demonized because they not only allow but also apparently endorse such assimilation (2:14-15, 20-21). The last of the seven churches mentioned, Laodicea, was excoriated as the poster child of this *"fornication"* (3:17).

Still, the divine plea to come out indicates that even at this late moment, on the eve of consummate judgment, Christ extends the opportunity for repentance and therefore salvific acceptance. Eschatological relationship with God remains available if only believers would renounce their idolatrous relationship with Babylon/Rome and reestablish relationship with God. They do this by witnessing actively to the lordship of God and Christ as the only measure of present and eschatological security. The cry to "*come out*," then, is not only an entreaty to exit; it is also an order to engage.

- 5 Babylon/Rome's sins – already introduced (v. 3), later back-grounded (v. 7), and eventually graphically listed (vv. 23b-24) – have become so quantitatively numerous and qualitatively destructive that John, no doubt working from Jeremiah's language about the historical Babylon (Jer. 51:9), describes them metaphorically as a mountain reaching to the heavens. This is no prideful human erection like the Tower of Babel, however. The divine passive construction *"are piled up"* indicates that God has constructed this pile of sins as a kind of monument to momentous misdeeds. God has remembered Babylon/Rome's transgressions (cf. 16:19). And now, so will the rest of creation.

- **6** There are two considerable problems of perspective in this verse. First, for the first and apparently only time in the narrative, believers are commanded by Christ to operate violently against Babylon/Rome. Second, a judgment based on works is expected (cf. 2:23), but instead of a fair measure-for-measure punishment, Christ in the role of judge apparently orders that the penalties be double the crime.

John maintains his metaphorical description of Babylon/Rome's crime; she has seduced humans into drinking from her cup (cf. 14:10; 17:4), an idolatrous (*"fornicating"*), addictive mix that drugs them into a frenzied lust for economic intercourse with her. Just as the work of witnessing to the lordship of God and the Standing Slaughtered Lamb will be rewarded, so will Babylon/Rome's work of defying that witness be punished (cf. Ps. 137:8; Jer. 50:15, 29, where Babylon was to be *"repaid"* for its crimes against God's people). But the punishment will be double the intensity of the crime. Is such disproportion just? According to the scriptural tradition upon which John so heavily depends, the principle of lex talionis directs that a punishment's measure shall equal the measure of the crime (Exod. 21:23-25; Lev. 24:17-20; Deut. 19:21). The law effectively prohibited angry and vengeful victims from excessive acts of retribution. Was God above God's own limiting law? Two observations suggest a negative answer. First, the punishment actually does fit the crime; in fact, the punishment is the crime. Babylon/Rome's sinful work is the intoxicating cup that she mixes for others; in punishment, she is forced to drink from that same cup the very concoction that she brewed for humankind. It is quite possible, since God forces Babylon/Rome to drink from the wine cup of God's wrath (Rev. 14:10; 16:19), and since the punishment is the crime, that God has commandeered her cup and deployed it now against her.

The double language surfaces just here; mixed in her cup is a *"double portion."* What, though, does this doubling language really mean? It is no doubt based on prophetic texts like Isa. 40:2 and Jer. 16:18, where a disobedient Israel/Jerusalem was to be doubly and justly repaid for its iniquity. There was, then, scriptural precedent for such retribution figuring appropriately rather than excessively where particularly egregious and idolatrous behavior was encountered. Beale even argues that the language of doubling should be taken to mean an intense matching of the punishment to the crime rather than an exorbitant raising of the retributive stakes. In this interpretation, Christ orders a *"duplicate, twin, or matching"* response rather than a literal doubling one.

There is still the matter of deciding to whom Christ is issuing the command to render to Babylon/Rome the violence and destruction she has rendered to others. Because Christ was clearly speaking to his people in v. 4 and there has been no explicit change of audience, one might suppose that Christ expects his believers to execute this violent reprisal. The problem with this

supposition is that it counters every expectation for the believing witnesses that John has heretofore narrated. No other passage makes such a demand. In fact, believers are explicitly directed toward non-violent forms of witnessing resistance. Non-violent engagement is the behavior modeled by Christ, the true and faithful witness (5:9, 11; 12:5). Believers will conquer the draconian force behind the beast that is Babylon/Rome by imitating that non-violence (12:11). Any christological expectation of witness violence in this single verse would therefore contradict the book's entire ethical superstructure. The more likely conclusion is that Christ has turned from the believing human witnesses to those like the archangel Michael (12:7) who are particularly enlisted for such purposes. Given the larger context of Revelation's overall expectations and the more specific material surrounding 18:6, there are several more likely candidates. Christ could well be addressing angels of judgment like the seven specified at 14:6, 8, 9, 15, 17, 18, since the concluding angel in this series opens the chapter's proceedings at 18:1. John has also identified ten enraged kings and the beast from the sea as the executioners who will prosecute Babylon/Rome's annihilation (17:16). Either or both of these groups are more likely than Christ's own faithful witnesses to be his intended audience. Given the development of the text, my preference falls to the kings and beast.
- 7 Motif of punishment fitting the crime continues as Christ sentences Babylon/Rome to a humiliating measure of torment and grief that matches exactly the

political, religious, military, and particularly economic measures she has used to celebrate her powerfully and seductively luxurious existence. Self-glorification metastasizes into arrogance. In describing her own rule as a queen, she hijacks the language of royal seating ("κάθημαι") that John has used exclusively as a symbolic posture of divine rule: God's sitting on the heavenly throne (4:2-3, 10; 5:1, 7, 13; 6:16; 7:10, 15; 19:4; 20:11; 21:5); the Son of Man's sitting on a cloud (14:14-16) and on a white horse of judgment (19:11, 19, 21)[267]. Babylon/Rome has already mimicked the posture by sitting enthroned on waters (17:1, 15), a beast (17:3), and mountains (17:9), but here for the first time she arrogantly defines such posturing as a ruling lordship that competes with God's.

According to the prophet Isaiah, Chaldea made a similar taunt: it sits so securely that it believes it will never be a widow or know the grief that accompanies the loss of a child (Isa. 14:13-14; 47:8; Jer. 5:12; Ezek. 28:2). Clearly, John has this taunt from the prophetic literature in mind because Babylon/Rome also declares that she shall never be a widow nor know grief. This rabid, self-glorifying confidence in the security amassed through her political, military, religious, and economic prowess is the seedbed from which her idolatrous and murderous behavior sprouts.

- **8** The promised punishment will be swift. Incredibly, John's Christ intensifies the emotions surrounding the gruesome trumpet and bowl plagues by declaring that

---

[267] Also the elders sit on heavenly thrones (4:4; 11:16).

all of them will occur in a single day. Such a brutal concentration will heighten the sense of devastation. John's narration maintains its prophetic dependence. Just as Isaiah warned that everything Caldea boasted about would either be lost to her or turned against her (Isa. 47:9; Jer. 50:29, 31), so John declares that Babylon/Rome's punishment will bring the very grief and torment that she predicted she would forever avoid. True might, and therefore glory, belongs exclusively to God (Jer. 50:34). Christ's closing remark in this subsection reminds John's hearers and readers that God uses might not for vindictive destruction but for appropriate judgment.

- **9 – 10** In narrating the mourning that accompanies the fall of Babylon/Rome, john's Christ operates directly from the Ezek. 26-28 lamentation scenes that surround the demise of the economic superpower that was Tyre. Christ features the groups that have the most to lose: kings, merchants, and those who make their living from the sea. Starting with the kings, Christ initiates a formulaic pattern of mourning that, with minor variations, holds constant throughout the narration. The kings, merchants, and merchant marines grieve alike just as they benefited in like fashion from Babylon/Rome's economic success.

First, Christ makes the subsection's central point: because their economic triumphs are tied directly to the international economic infrastructure that Babylon/Rome has conjured through its political and military domination, the kings weep and mourn when Babylon/Rome is destroyed (Ezek. 26:16). The kings are not only regional, client monarchs; they are also members of local councils and of the administrative ruling elite, like the officials who governed the Asia Minor communities where John's seven churches were located. The language of fornication and sensual, luxurious living confirms that the issue is primarily one of economics. Throughout the work, *"fornication"* has symbolized people and communities, even believing communities, who idolatrously sell out their recognition of true lordship in order to buy into Roman imperial cultic and political relationships that will guarantee access to the benefits of the Roman economy. Christ closes the case of the kings' complicity when he follows up the language of fornication with a member of the word family that specifies the accumulation and hoarding of luxurious excess: "στρηνιάω" (applied to merchants in v. 7).

They also have a share in grief. John stereotypes the language here in order to build a bond of misery joining kings, merchants, and merchant marines. Repetitively, Christ declares that each group weeps and mourns. Since John constructs this rhetorical partnership (in weeping and mourning) only here, it is clear that the links drawn among the kings, merchants, and merchant marines are intentional.

These links strengthen as the narration unfolds. Christ declares that the kings (v. 10), merchants (v. 15), and merchant marines (v. 17) all stand purposely at a distance from the city not only because her torment is so grisly but, no doubt, also because they fear that their complicity in her crimes will earn them a share of her judgment (cf. 14:11). They apparently believe that the geographical space will morph into a protective shelter that will distance them from the destructive fallout.

Watching from their designated safe zones, the three paramour groupings unleash the same chorus of despair: "*Woe, woe, the great city*" (kings, v. 10; merchants, v. 16; merchant marines, v. 19). Even now they do not see the false nature of Babylon/Rome; even now they attach such lofty adjectives as "*great.*" "*Look,*" John's narration means to say, "*at her greatness now!*" Indeed, each reference in the "*Apokalypsis*" to the city's greatness is deployed in a context that anticipates the city's destruction (14:8; 16:19; 17:5, 18; 18:2, 10, 16, 18, 19). Obviously, the adjective is used mockingly by John. The mockery bites precisely because Rome was a great city. Yet even in its greatness, its doom was sealed (cf. 17:8). It is the accomplishment of that doom that is lamented here. Heretofore the language of "*woe*" has described the forms of judgment leveled against God's enemies (8:13; 9:12; 11:14) or the persecution endured by God's people (12:12). It is poetically appropriate that the language formerly used to describe the judgment is now the language of response to it.

Responsive horror is appropriate. The anticipated barrage of plagues that was to materialize in a single day (v. 8) narrows down even further now into a single hour of that day, as lamented by kings (v. 10), merchants (v. 17), and merchant marines (v. 19). How could even a great city like Babylon/Rom endure such a concentrated dose of judgment? Yet that question is the point. The emphasis here is not on the timing of the judgment but on its concentration. *"Day"* and *"hour"* are eschatological terms, not chronological point. They do represent brevity. In the Book of Revelation, John's Christ means to say that in a single moment of end-time decisiveness, all that it took Babylon/Rome so much time to build is completely and irrevocably gone/destroyed/fallen.

- **11 – 17a** The second stanza of weeping and mourning erupts from the corner of the narrative stage where the merchants of the earth are found cringing. Like the kings, they were already introduced as mourners-in-training at 18:3. Now they are in full cry because their primary market has forever closed (Ezek. 27:36). Their wealth has been predicated upon Rome's voracious needs to supply its population. With the smoke of Rome's burning the only thing left of the *"great"* city, there is no demand for their storehouses of supply.

Notably, like the merchants who enriched themselves in commerce with Tyre (Ezek. 27:7-25), these traders deal in items of luxury rather than needed staples. The list of merchandise indicates the wealth and extravagance of Rome. It also indicates the extravagant desire for wealth on the part of the merchants. Christ emphasizes this point in v. 14: in a rhetorical flourish of alliteration, he highlights the opulence and ostentation of this economy.

Its moral decadence is placed in sharp relief by the climactic mentioning of the trade in human souls, slaves: It is a comment on the whole list of cargoes. It suggests the inhuman brutality, the contempt for human life, on which the whole of Rome's prosperity and luxury rests. These are the fruits, produce blossomed from a corrupt tree of idolatrous excess, that will be pruned from the wailing merchants forever. Their fortunes, like Babylon/Rome itself, will never return. And so, with their stage brothers *"the kings of earth,"* they stand from a distance, weep and mourn, and cry out, *"Woe, woe, the great city!"* because its judgment arrives in full in a single hour. Like Ezekiel describing the judgment of Tyre (LXX Ezek. 26:19), John chooses the verb "ἐρημόω" (lay waste) to sketch the great catastrophe. In so doing, he answers a question raised by 18:6. To whom was Christ speaking when he commanded someone to render violent judgment upon Babylon/Rome? Because the verb *"lay waste"* occurs only in 18:17, 19 and 17:16, where the ten horns and the beast lay waste to the whore/Babylon/Rome, it seems clear that Christ was deputizing the ten horns and the beast to execute the cataclysmic judgment. They will do the deed in an hour.

    Christ adds just one other detail that makes this presentation different from the presentation of the kings of the earth (the first difference is the list of luxury items): the doomed city was clothed in fine linen, purple, and scarlet and adorned in gold, precious stone, and pearl. The costume connection is unmistakable; the great whore was similarly adorned (17:4). If anyone has missed the link before, Christ now makes it crystal clear: Babylon/Rome is the great whore who has seduced the kings and merchants of the earth into an idolatrous mercantile tryst.

- **17b – 19** Christ concludes the mourning section by adding mention of all those who earned a living through trade by sea. This larger category would include not only those who owned and captained ships but also mariners, merchant marines, and sailors. Rome dominated the seas, eradicated piracy, and created sea lanes for more efficient and safer travel (weather remained the only consistent obstacle) of people and goods to the port in Ostia and then the approximately forty miles inland to the capital city. Many either earned a living or built a fortune because of their participation in this economic sea superstructure. The wage earner as well as the wealthy shared a stake in the idolatrous relationship that gave allegiance and gratitude for security to Rome rather than to God and the Standing Slaughtered Lamb. Like the kings and merchants before them, therefore, they stand weeping and moaning as they view the smoke of the city's ruin from a distance, crying out, "*Woe, woe,*" for the great city that will be "*wasted*" in a single hour.

    In this parallel presentation (with the kings and merchants of the earth), Christ adds two distinctive points. First, as did passersby of more ancient cities that were judged by God for their idolatrous and disobedient behavior (Jer. 22:8; Ezek. 27:32), these seafarers wonder, as they look at the smoke rising from the ruins, "*What city was ever like this great city?*" God, obviously, is much, much greater than the greatest force earth had ever known. Second, these seafarers make their grief concrete by their behavior. Like ancient mourners who lamented the demise of Tyre

(Ezek. 27:30-34; Josh 7:6; Job 2:12; Lam. 2:10; *1 Macc.* 11:71), they throw dust on their heads as a sign not so much of their contrition for their involvement with Babylon/Rome as of their regret for their loss of revenue and therefore well-being.

- **20** Christ addresses *"heaven"* and the believers who have stood fast behind their witness to the lordship of God and the Standing Slaughtered Lamb. Unlike the *"believers"* who accommodated themselves to social, cultic, and particularly economic principles that put them in relationship with the beast/whore/Babylon/Rome, this categorization of saints, apostles, and Christian prophets represents all those who have actively resisted any form of accommodation. While Babylon/Rome's economic confederates mourn her counsels all faithful believers to celebrate (cf. Jer. 51:48, where both heaven and earth rejoice at Babylon's destruction). The mandated joy anticipates the hallelujah chorus that will break out in 19:1-8 and formally bring the larger section that began at 17:1 to a close.

The rationale for celebration is provided in the vaguely worded second half of the verse, which is very difficult to translate. The interpretive key lies in the way the larger narrative context interacts with John's particular word choices. The primary audience is composed of the believing witnesses who have remained steadfast in their faith. Since Christ specifies that audience as both *"heaven"* and *"the saints, apostles, and prophets,"* we can be certain that he intends his message for both those (in heaven) who were slaughtered because of their witness and those (still living saints, apostles, and prophets) who maintain their earthly witness even as he speaks. It is *"their"* judgment that God has rendered (*"judged"*) upon Babylon/Rome. In its noun form, judgment language (κρίμα) refers specifically to the executed sentence (17:1; 20:4). The verbal form is more expansive. According to 20:12, 13, God judges based on works. At 16:5 and 19:2, the work of Babylon/Rome is notably described as the persecution of God's faithful witnesses. Believers react with a responsive work of their own. At 6:9-11, the souls of those who were slaughtered because of their witness cry out for God's judgment of the force (i.e., Babylon/Rome) that slaughtered them and continues to slaughter their compatriots. The appeal voiced at 6:9-11 therefore serves as the motivational force for the entire *"Apokalypsis"*; it provides the inspiration for God's intervention to effect justice. It is to this intervention that 18:20b speaks. It is *"your cry"* for judgment, then, that God has executed (*"judged"*) upon Babylon/Rome. Elisabeth Schussler Fiorenza's translation, therefore, while not literally precise, is that most figuratively accurate: *"God has exacted justice from her on the basis of your legal claims"* (*Vision of a Just World*, 99).

- **21** The rare appearance of a *"mighty"* angel signals the dawn of a highly significant narrative event that portends judgment (see comments on 5:2 and 10:1 for the other two mighty angels). Like a melodramatic but effective prosecutor, the cherub launches his case with an attention-grabbing stunt before he offers a clarifying word. A millstone was a large, round, rolling stone connected to a horizontal beam, which was a turn attached to an animal of a human, who tugged it around the circular track of a wine or grain mill (cf. Matt. 18:6; Mark 9:42; Luke 17:2). Thrown into the sea, it would be expected to sink like the proverbial rock that it was. Babylon/Rome was the angel's proverbial case in point. He interprets his own actions with the mocking explanation that as goes the millstone, so will go the great city. It will not be great enough to float its way past the horrors that God has in store for it. Like a rock, having been sunk, it will rise nevermore (Ezek. 26:12, 21).

- **22 – 23a** Picking up structurally from the concluding words of v. 21, and once again building from prophetic references (Isa. 24:8; Jer. 25:10; Ezek. 26:13), the mighty angel offers a poignant, poetic presentation. Using an emphatic negative (οὐ μὴ), he tenders a series of subjunctive verbs coupled with the adverb loss. Babylon will surely be found no more; the sounds of musicians will surely be heard no more; artisans will surely be found no more; the sound of working mills will surely be heard no more; the light of lamps will surely shine no more; the voice of brides and bridegrooms, a symbol of future family and national life, will surely be heard no more. The consistent refrain of loss reminds hearers and readers of the point made earlier: Babylon will be a deserted, haunted waste of a land (18:2).

- **23b – 24** And now the mighty angel explains why. He offers three reasons, the first two introduced by "ὅτι" (because). With the third, "ὅτι" is implied. First, Babylon is culpable because its merchants were the great ones of the earth. John is working here from Isaiah's depiction of the Tyre merchants as princes of the earth (Isa. 23:8). This reference to greatness recalls Christ's own concern for Babylon's self-glorification (Rev. 18:7).

  Second, Babylon applied a kind of economic sorcery to delude the nations into believing that social security resided with it and it alone (Isa. 47:9). It was this misrepresentation of its own power and status that convinced even many believers like those in Pergamum, Thyatira, and Laodicea to accommodate themselves to Greco-Roman cultic loyalties and political expectations in order to advance economically. Among non-believers the power of such social magic was even greater still. Babylon/Rome duped all the nations into believing that idolatrous recognition of Roman gods and the imperial cult was a reasonable price to pay for a piece of its economic pie.

  Finally and, given the impact of 6:9-11 on the whole of the book, more importantly, Babylon/Rome would be destroyed because it executed the prophets and saints who boldly delivered the contrary testimony that God and not Rome was the Lord of human creation and history. Indeed, Babylon/Rome was a demonic, dictatorial force so bent on the recognition of its exclusive lordship that it was ultimately responsible for the deaths of all those who had been slaughtered on the earth. The mighty angel therefore concludes that the blood of the executed, which in part sparked the motivating cry for God's intervention in 6:10 (see also 16:6; 17:6; 19:2; cf. Jer. 51:49; Ezek. 24:7; 36:18; Matt. 23:35, 37), is the unassailable evidence that will bring Babylon/Rome down.

Revelation 19:1~10 → The Hallelujah Chorus

NIV	TT
19 ¹ After this I heard what sounded like the roar of a great multitude in heaven shouting: "Hallelujah! Salvation and glory and power belong to our God, ² for true and just are his judgments. He has condemned the great prostitute who corrupted the earth by her adulteries. He has avenged on her the blood of his servants." ³ And again they shouted: "Hallelujah! The smoke from her goes up for ever and ever." ⁴ The twenty-four elders and the four living creatures fell down and worshiped God, who was seated on the throne. And they cried: "Amen, Hallelujah!" ⁵ Then a voice came from the throne, saying: "Praise our God, all	**19** ¹ After this I heard what sounded like the great sound of a great **crowd**[268] in heaven, saying, "**Hallelujah!**[269] Salvation and glory and power to our God, ² because true and just are God's judgments, because God has judged the great whore who corrupted the earth with her fornication, and God avenged the blood of God's servants out of her hand." ³ Then a second time they said, "Hallelujah! And the smoke from her rises forever and ever." ⁴ Then the twenty-four elders and the four living creatures fell and worshiped God who is seated on the throne, saying, "Amen! Hallelujah!" ⁵ And a voice came from the throne, saying, "Praise our

---

[268] ὄχλος → It means *"crowd," "multitude,"* and *"populace."*

[269] ἁλληλουϊά → It means *"praise the Lord,"* and *"praise Yahweh." "Hallelujah"* is a Greek transliteration of the Hebrew liturgical formula *"halelu-yah,"* meaning *"praise Yahweh,"* which was taken over into Christian hymns and occurs for the first time in Christian literature in Rev. 19:1-6.

you his servants, you who fear him, both great and small!" ⁶ Then I heard what sounded like a great multitude, like the roar of rushing waters and like loud peals of thunder, shouting: "Hallelujah! For our Lord God Almighty reigns. ⁷ Let us rejoice and be glad and give him glory! For the wedding of the Lamb has come, and his bride has made herself ready. ⁸ Fine linen, bright and clean, was given her to wear." (Fine linen stands for the righteous acts of God's holy people.) ⁹ Then the angel said to me, "Write this: Blessed are those who are invited to the wedding supper of the Lamb!" And he added, "These are the true words of God." ¹⁰ At this I fell at his feet to worship him. But he said to me, "Don't do that! I am a fellow servant with you and with your brothers	God, all God's servants, that is, those who fear God, the small and the great." ⁶ Then I heard what sounded like a great crowd, like a voice of many waters and the sound of great thunder saying, "Hallelujah! For the Lord our God, the Almighty, has begun to rule. ⁷ Let us rejoice and be glad and give God glory, because the wedding day of the Lamb has come and his **bride**[270] has prepared herself; ⁸ she was given to wear fine linen, bright and clean" (for the fine linen represents the righteous deeds of the saints). ⁹ Then he said to me, "Write: 'Blessed are those who are invited to the wedding supper of the Lamb.'" And he said to me, "These are the true words of God." ¹⁰ Then I fell before his feet to worship him. But he said to me, "Do not do that! I am a fellow servant with you and

---

[270] γυνή → It means *"a woman of any age," "a virgin," "a married," "a widow," "a bride,"* and *"a wife."*

and sisters who hold to the testimony of Jesus. Worship God! For it is the Spirit of prophecy who bears testimony to Jesus."	your brothers and sisters who bear the testimony of Jesus. Worship God. For the testimony of Jesus is the spirit of prophecy."

"*The Hallelujah chorus*" concludes a larger section dedicated to the judgment/destruction of the whore/Babylon/Rome that began at 17:1. Thematically, 19:1-10 does not introduce 19:11-21:8.

- **1 – 2** John begins with a slight variation on what for him is an old literary formula. "*After this*," that is, following the visions of Babylon/Rome's destruction in chapters 17 and 18, he heard a heavenly, celebratory response. Though he most often accomplishes this move to a new narrative line of thought within the same overall story line with the phrase "*after these things, I saw*" (cf. 4:1), this time he realizes the goal with a nod to what he hears. He hears a great heavenly sound. In the Book of Revelation, celebration and judgment are two sides of a single narrative coin. Since victory for one camp can only be achieved through the destruction of the opposing camp, when the witnesses hear the sound of victory, allies of the dragon and its vassal beasts must by definition be experiencing the noise of doom. "*Hallelujah*" in one camp is "*woe*" in the other.

    The sound that is both great (for allies of the dragon/beasts) and celebratory (for witnesses to the lordship of God and the Standing Slaughtered Lamb) comes from a heavenly crowd. In Dan. 10:6 the similar sound of a heavenly multitude projects from the mouth of a single figure that fits John's chapter 1 description of one like the Son of Man. In both Old and New Testament presentations, the heavenly origin of the sound is more important than the identity of its specific bearer; the tone and message are authorized by God. John does not name the crowd, making its identification difficult. Connections drawn to the multitude of Rev. 7:9 are, however, intriguing. Except for a rather nondescript use of the term at 17:15, John uses "ὄχλος" (crowd) only here (19:1, 6) and at 7:9. The songs sung by the two crowds, which declare salvation to be an exclusive attribute of God, are also tantalizingly similar.

Before issuing its overture to salvation, however, the heavenly crowd of 19:1 begins with and focuses on the term "ἀλληλουϊά" (Hallelujah). The hymns of 19:1-10 are the only place where the term occurs in the entire New Testament (vv. 1, 3, 4, 6). John's chorus has its basis in the praise of the Hebrew "*Hallel psalms*" (Pss. 113-118), which were sung partly before and partly after the Passover supper in commemoration of the exodus liberation. Psalm 113:1 provides a typical example: "*Praise the LORD! (Hallelujah) Praise, O servants of the LORD; praise the name of the LORD.*" Use of the term also recalls Ps. 104:35, where celebration erupts in response to God's judgment of sinners: "*Let sinners be consumed from the earth, and let the wicked be no more. Bless the LORD, O my soul. Praise the LORD (Hallelujah)!*" Both references relate well to this context in the Book of Revelation, where the people of God are simultaneously celebrating God's judgment of a dragon-directed Babylon/Rome and the religious, social, and political liberation that judgment brings.

It is this combination of judgment and celebration that other Jewish writings associate with the Hallelujah. In *3 Macc.* 7:13 the people shout "*Hallelujah!*" because of deliverance from persecution and the judgment of apostates. In *Tob.* 13:15-17 the streets of end-time Jerusalem shout "*Hallelujah!*" because the city will be rebuilt and decorated with "*sapphire and emerald, and all your walls with precious stones, ... battlements with pure gold, ... and the streets ... will be paved with ruby and with stones of Ophir.*" The walls and street of John's new Jerusalem are made of most of the precious metals mentioned in the Tobit account (Rev. 21:18-21).

Also there is a vast throng of voices singing (cf. 19:1, 6). This heavenly crowd is no doubt the heavenly people of God. Certainly the slaughtered souls from beneath the heavenly altar at 6:9-11 are present in this throng. They were witnesses who remained faithful and did not accommodate to the enticements or threats of the unholy trinity of dragon, beast from the sea, and beast from the land (false prophet).

The achievement of justice is God's work. Salvation (as in social and political liberation from Babylon/Rome), glory, and power belong to God. John need not elaborate on that subject because he has broached it already before (7:10). Yet the work of God's witnesses is crucial here as well. With the declaration that "*God avenged the blood of God's servants out of her hand,*" John indicates once more that the efforts of the witnesses have made a transformative difference in connection with the divinely orchestrated salvation. It is intriguing that John also integrally connected God's salvation and power to the victorious work of the witnesses at 12:10-11. The seer further develops the point in 19:10, when the voice of the angel declares that he is a fellow servant with those who hold, who keep, the testimony that Jesus himself bore – that he is ultimate Lord and ruler of human destiny. The emphasis remains on that testimony and its effect. That is why John has been declaring that the people must persevere in their resistance. They must resist because in their resistance the power of the dragon is being destroyed. Nowhere is this reality more poignant than in 16:6, where the blood of the witnesses becomes the very mechanism through which the forces that have spilled their blood will meet their demise. The *"Hallelujah,"* then, is not just about what God has done; it is also about what God's people have, through faith, been continuing to do in concert with and in support of God's own activity. In bearing witness to the sovereign rule of God and the Standing Slaughtered Lamb, they have been raising a contrary voice to the prevalent, powerful, and bloodthirsty opinion about the control of human history. No wonder, then, that John will define such witness as the fine, victorious linen that adorns the Lamb's bridal city (19:8).

- **3** Fired up, the heavenly crowd thunders an antiphonal *"Hallelujah!"* to its own earlier praise shout. It is once again God's judgment that causes the celebration. As he did at 14:11, John recalls Isaiah's image of the smoke of Edom's ruin rising forever (Isa. 34:10). In Rev. 14:11 punishment was inflicted upon individuals who had persecuted God's witnesses; here all of Babylon/Rome is targeted. By using the image of rising smoke, John reinforces the connection vv. 1-2 have already drawn between the witnesses' cries for justice and God's resulting judgment. At 8:4 John saw smoke rising from the incense altar with the saints' prayers, which 6:9-11 had already characterized as a petition that God avenge the blood of executed believers. The temporary rise of that smoke-borne appeal for intervention triggered the retaliation that has left Babylon/Rome a smoldering ruin, whose smoke of destruction will rise forever.

- **4** Recalling 5:14, where the twenty-four elders and the four living creatures confirm the praise of the Lamb through their own worship and an affirming *"Amen!"* this heavenly coterie responds to the twin *"Hallelujahs"* of the crowd with an *"Amen!"* that validates the correctness of the praise's application to God, and then blasts a *"Hallelujah"* of its own (cf. Ps. 106:48). The reference to God sitting on the throne offers rationale for the praise; the God who rules in heaven, *"seated on the throne"* has consummated that same rule on earth.
- **5** While it is all but impossible to identify the speaker of the second heavenly voice, it is clear that its heavenly location near the throne gives it an unmistakable weight of authority. It uses that authority to offer praise by demanding more of it. Its present-tense imperative, *"Praise!"* encourages the crowd to continue its adoration while it simultaneously prods a

different crowd to get started (vv.6-8). The praise language once again recalls the celebratory injunctions of the psalms (cf. Pss. 134; 135:1, 20). The voice addresses all God's servants, all who fear God (cf. 14:7; 15:4; Ps. 115:13), both small and great.

- **6** Response to the heavenly voice is immediate. Another crowd thunders a hymn of praise that is anchored by the New Testament's final *"Hallelujah!"* There are several reasons to suppose that this crowd is different from the one introduced in v. 1. John's use of *"and I heard"* to open the verse suggests that he has switched to a different subject within the same narrative vision (cf. 16:1). In this case the new subject would be a new crowd dedicated to the same narrative agenda of praise. Indeed, the lack of definite articles for *"voice"* and *"crowd"* suggests that John is not referring back to the crowd of 19:1. The adjectives used to describe the two crowds and their voices are also different. In fact, the only similarity is that both crowds cry *"Hallelujah!"* The linguistic connection with 11:18 provides a clue about this second crowd's identity. At 19:5 the heavenly voice addresses its praise command to all the servants, both small and great, who fear God. Verses 6-8 present their antiphonal response. At 11:18 this same grouping represents earthly witnesses to the lordship of God and the Standing Slaughtered Lamb. The implication is clear: the crowd that offers hymnic praise in vv.6-8 is the earthly counterpart to the heavenly one that sings in the first four verses.

This earthly crowd also adds a different, two-tiered rationale for the praise. The heavenly crowd sang because of God's true and just judgments, God's verdict against the whore, and God's avenging of the witnesses' blood; this earthly crowd first fittingly celebrates because, just now, following the destruction of Babylon/Rome in chapters 17 and 18, the Almighty God has begun to accomplish what was hymnically forecast in 11:15, 17: God's heavenly rule on earth (cf. 1 Chr. 16:31; Pss. 93:1; 97:1; 99:1; Zech. 14:9).

- **7 – 8** The earthly crowd's second cause for praise is more complicated. Building from Isa. 61:10, where the prophet celebrates the fact that God has clothed him in garments of salvation that recall the festal clothing of bridegrooms and their brides, the choir of earthbound witnesses charge themselves ("*let us*") to rejoice, exult, and glorify God because the wedding of the bridegroom Lamb and his festively clothed bride has come (cf. 1 Chr. 16:28; Ps. 118:24). In Matt. 5:12, the verbs "*rejoice*" and "*exult/be glad*" also appear together as Jesus tells followers to rejoice and be glad because the reward for their persecutions is coming. Here in the Book of Revelation, the earthly crowd celebrates the realization of Jesus' prediction.

The primary focus surely is on the wedding metaphor. The casting of Christ as a bridegroom and the people of God as the bride was well known in the early church (e.g., 2 Cor. 11:2; Eph. 5:25-32). At Matt. 22:2, Jesus compares the reign of God to a wedding banquet that a king prepares for his son. It is this same wedding that the earthly crowd now celebrates in the only context (Rev. 19:7, 9) where John deploys the term "*wedding*." The Lamb is the risen, exalted Jesus.

The bride, as the people of God, symbolizes much more than the limited form of the church. She is the new city of Jerusalem, *"the renewed world of God"* (Schussler Fiorenza, *Vision of a Just World*, 103).

John's focus on God's universal people as the divine bride takes its cue from Old Testament depictions of Israel as the bride of Yahweh (Isa. 1:21; 54:1-8; Jer. 2:2; 31:32; Ezek. 16:8-14; Hos. 2:5; Eph. 5:32). The reference to her prepared garments as a symbol of her readiness also has strong Old Testament foundations (Gen. 35:2; Isa. 52:1; 61:10; Zech. 3:4). John develops the metaphor for his own purposes with the language of preparation in v. 7 and an explication of what that preparation means in v. 8.

Clearly, the bride's very identity as those who witness to the lordship of God and the Standing Slaughtered Lamb is a part of her preparation. John's heaviest concentration of the "γυνή" (woman, bride) appears in the corresponding chapters 12 and 17. The woman clothed with the sun, at once the people of God who give birth to the Messiah (12:1-6) and the people of God who become the followers of that Messiah (12:17), is positioned against the whore of Babylon/Rome, whose fornication disrupts all the earth. In fact, except for several literal uses of *"woman"* (cf. 2:20; 9:8; 14:4), John uses the word exclusively to counter-pose one female metaphor for people (opposed to God) with another (witnesses for God). Here, *"woman"* as bridal witness is presented one penultimate time before its climactic and definitive presentation at 21:9. It is her witnessing that prepares her for marriage to the Lamb. No wonder, then, that this *"woman"* witness is also termed the Lamb's "νύμφη" (bride) at 21:2, 9; 22:17.

Verse 8 describes the actual mechanics of her preparation. Using the divine passive formulation, *"it was given"* that has become for John a formulaic way of presenting God as the active causal agent (cf. 6:2; 7:2), the seer clarifies that the woman is not operating on her own but through the power of God. God enables her *"to be clothed"* in bright clean linen, further defined as the righteous deeds of the saints. Since John uses the same terminology for linen here that he uses for Babylon/Rome's luxurious cargo and the whore's dress (18:12, 16), he clearly means to counter-pose the idolatrous deeds that witness to the lordship of Rome against righteous witness to the lordship of God and the Standing Slaughtered Lamb. Even the description of the woman's preparation (dressing herself in fine linen), though it employs an active-voice verb, implies divine agency. John is paradoxically mixing human initiative with divine causality. To be sure, he intends to say that the people of God have, by their acts of witnessing to the lordship of God and the Standing Slaughtered Lamb under perilous circumstances, achieved both the conquest of the dragon and its forces (12:11) and the victory of eschatological relationship with God (2:7, 11, 17, 26, 28; 3:5, 12, 21). This righteous behavior does not, however, mean that humans can achieve salvation through their own merit. John means to make this point by implying that the witnessing he so celebrates has been enabled and empowered by God. The source of the strength to witness comes not from the saints themselves but from God. Nonetheless, saints who marshal that strength into the righteous deeds of non-accommodating resistance to the lordship claims of Caesar and Rome weave, through their resistance, the white garments that John has promised all along to the faithful witnesses (cf. 3:2-4). Nowhere does John make this point more clearly than at 6:11, where with the assistance of a very instructive use of *"it was given,"* he declares that the white clothing secured by the saints as a result of their faithful, resistant witness was given to (empowered for) them by God. What he says of the saint's dress in 6:11, he means about the woman's wedding finery here in 19:8. God does the clothing – the equipping for righteous witness.

- **9** The voice that now commands John probably belongs to the angel of 17:1. It makes good thematic sense that the figure who introduced John to the vision of Babylon/Rome's destruction would preside over the vision of the resulting eschatological supper celebration. Drawing a connection between the two also makes narrative sense given that 19:9-10 operates as the closing bracket to the section that began at 17:1. It is reasonable to expect the same angel to be speaking in both the opening and the closing scenes. The broader narrative parallel with 21:9-22:9 offers yet another reason to believe that the same angel is speaking throughout. When John describes the (witnessing) bride of the Lamb (in 21:9-22:9) and also when he pictures the judgment of the (fornicating) whore of Babylon (in 17:1-19:10), he presents as emcee in both cases one of the seven angels who had the seven bowls of God's wrath. It is likely that this same angel conducts both vision sequences and is therefore present with John at the end of both visions when the overwhelmed prophet tries here, and again in the parallel scene 22:8-9, to offer to him the worship that belongs exclusively to God.

The angel gives John a simple command: he is to write the fourth of seven beatitudes chronicled throughout the book (1:3; 14:13; 16:15; 19:9; 20:6; 22:7, 14). The blessing that envisions relationship with God as an eschatological feast is drawn from the prophetic vision of Isa. 25:6-8, which was developed in early Christian circles (Matt. 8:11; Luke 13:29), particularly in the Last Supper narration, where Jesus promises to drink with his disciples at what will apparently be a messianic banquet (Mark 14:25; Matt. 26:29; Luke 22:18). This macarisms, like the other six in Revelation, has the same dual indicative and imperative senses. In this particular case, the blessing acknowledges those who have already witnessed to the lordship of God and the Standing Slaughtered Lamb and have as a result of that witness conquered (cf. 12:11). Through that conquest they have obtained the eschatological relationship with God that John describes metaphorically as an invitation to the Lamb's wedding feast. Because that wedding supper is envisioned as a place of such great eschatological joy, the macarisms simultaneously goads those who have accommodated to the lordship demands of the imperial cult to "*come out of Babylon/Rome*" (18:4) and testify to the lordship of God instead.

In declaring the blessing, John returns to the paradox he presented with the bride's wedding garments (19:8). John wants to celebrate witness, but he does not want witnesses to believe that it is their testifying that is ultimately responsible for the eschatological relationship they seek. Believers are blessed because of their witness, but the effects of that witness are determined by God alone. To make the point, John once again resorts to a divine passive. Witnessing does not "*earn*" one a ticket into the wedding feat of the Lamb; witnessing creates the opportunity for one to be invited or be called by God into the feast. While believers' acts of witness are necessary, only God's actions are determinative.

Yet there is a problem with John's metaphorical presentation. John has introduced the bride as the people of God (vv. 7-8). Now, the people of God are suddenly the wedding guests! Can both significations hold? In John's world, as in the world of dreams and visions, they certainly can. John's presentation cannot be held to the same type of logic that governs literal narration about the "*real*" world. He is trying to make a single point and to do so is perfectly comfortable with mixing his metaphors, even in a conflicting way. His primary point holds whether the people of God are envisioned as the bride betrothed to the Lamb or as the guests who have been invited to the festive wedding dinner. In both cases, witnessing to the lordship of God and the Standing Slaughtered Lamb establishes the opportunity for eschatological relationship. It is that witnessing and the resulting relationship that is uppermost on the seer's mind. He will use as many metaphors as necessary to demonstrate both the necessity of, and the joy that results from, that witnessing endeavor. No doubt in his mind the more ways he can find to illustrate that task, the more likely he will be to maintain some people in it and convert others to it.

John concludes the verse by declaring the words spoken here to be true. There are two possible referents: the words of the macarisms, or the words extending from 17:1 through 19:10. Since the macarisms is itself a climactic moment of celebration and exhortation following from the fall of Babylon/Rome, it is more likely that John intends this truth claim to refer to the entire section. Assured of the enemy's fate and the resulting celebration, believers will be more likely to witness faithfully. Despite the oppression and persecution that their testimony brings, they can trust that God will prevail and eschatological relationship with God will occur.

- **10** Overwhelmed by all that the angel has shown him since 17:1, John positions himself to worship the messenger even though he knows full well that worship is due God and the Standing Slaughtered Lamb alone. The seer's inappropriate actions are mirrored in the parallel text of 22:8-9. There, too, overwhelmed by the visions that this same angel shows him of the Lamb's bride, John responds with an improper worship attempt. This phenomenon of misplaced appreciation was well known in the ancient world. The motif of the angel who refuses worship from a seer in the context of an angelic revelation (as in Rev. 19:10 and 22:9) is a literary motif with many parallels in apocalyptic literature, though the motif is not restricted to apocalyptic. The Book of Acts even records an instance where the very human Peter rebuked an appreciative believer who wanted to worship him (Acts 10:25-26). There is therefore no need to speculate as to whether John has in mind as Asia Minor angel cult. Debates about the existence of such cults and the magnitude of their following are inconclusive. One need not speculate any further than the evidence at hand. The problem is the tendency to celebrate grand visions and the figure who orchestrates them. Anything, including a heavenly directed vision, its accompanist, even the church and the faith tradition that is so integral a part of it, can become idolatrous if it is allowed to carry more freight than it should. Everything on the created planet has the same purpose: to bear witness to the Lordship of God and Jesus Christ. On this functional level, humans and angels are equal partners.

The angel now equates the testimony Jesus bore, the same testimony that believers are now to bear on his behalf, to the spirit of prophecy. Prophecy is not just a matter of predicting the future. It is instead the revelation of a present truth that demands appropriate present and future behavior. The testimony and the spirit of prophecy have the same focal subject matter: the lordship of God and the Standing Slaughtered Lamb. John makes this clear when he equates the language of prophecy with the material content of his own apocalyptic testimony (1:3; 22:7, 10, 18-19). He is speaking here, then, not about the Spirit of God, but about the role of human witnesses whose testimony reveals the truth about God's rule over creation and requires all humans to respond appropriately, that is, repent (cf. 2:5, 16, 21-22; 3:3, 19; 9:20-21; 11:13; 14:7; 15:4; 16:9, 11; 18:4). The angel makes this human dimension explicit in the parallel scene where he calls John's fellow witnesses *"prophets"* (22:9).

Revelation 19:11~16 → The Rider on the White Horse

NIV	TT
¹¹ I saw heaven standing open and there before me was a white horse, whose rider is called Faithful and True. With justice he judges and wages war. ¹² His eyes are like blazing fire, and on his head are many crowns. He has a name written on him that no one knows but he himself. ¹³ He is dressed in a robe dipped in blood, and his name is the Word of God. ¹⁴ The armies of heaven were following him, riding on white horses and dressed in fine linen, white and clean. ¹⁵ Coming out of his mouth is a sharp sword with which to strike down the nations. "He will rule them with an iron scepter." He treads the winepress of the fury of the wrath of God Almighty.	¹¹ Then I saw heaven opened, and behold, a white horse, and the one seated on it is called Faithful and True, and he judges and wages war in righteousness. ¹² His eyes are like a flame of fire, and on his head, which has a name written that no one knows except himself, are many **diadems**²⁷¹. ¹³ He is clothed in a garment stained with blood, and his name is called the **Word**²⁷² of God. ¹⁴ And the heavenly armies were following him on white horses, wearing fine linen, white and clean. ¹⁵ From his mouth projects a sharp sword, so that he can strike the nations with it, and he will shepherd them with an iron rod, and he will tread the winepress of the fury of the wrath of God the Almighty. ¹⁶ And he has on his robe,

²⁷¹ διάδημα → It means "*diadem,*" and "*crown.*"

²⁷² λόγος → It means "*word,*" "*matter,*" "*thing,*" "*complaint,*" "*statement,*" "*declaration,*" "*preaching,*" "*prophecy,*" "*Word,*" "*Logos,*" "*proverb,*" "*teaching,*" "*message,*" and philosophically "*the reason of the universe.*"

¹⁶ On his robe and on his thigh he has this name written: KING OF KINGS AND LORD OF LORDS.	that is, at the place where the garment covers his thigh, a name written: "King of kings and Lord of lords."

This presentation of what is undoubtedly for John the Lamb's Parousia, an eschatological version of Isaiah's presentation of God as a returning warrior king (Isa. 63:1-6), does not include any form of a rapture. Believers are not spirited off to a safe heavenly realm while conflict on a cosmic scale erupts on earth. Indeed, an army of apparently human believers marches forward with the Lamb, and hordes of other believers either have been executed (6:9-11; 8:3-5; 20:4) or have suffered mightily in the seal, trumpet and bowl maelstroms that have comprised the apocalyptic run-up to this final conflict.

- **11** Verse 11 parallels the introduction of the one seated on the heavenly throne at 4:1. In the earlier text, John saw a door opened in heaven. The divine passive formulation implied that God did the opening. Here the same verb and passive voice indicate God's continued agency. There are two differences in the narration. First, this time all of heaven is opened (cf. Ezek. 1:1; Acts 10:11). Second, the object of interest is a rider seated on a white horse (cf. *2 Macc.* 3:25) rather than the one seated on the throne. Posture, though, remains significant. Seated language is enthronement language. Just as the lordship of God was revealed through God's placement on the throne, so the Lamb's enthronement is revealed through his position on the white horse. Throne imagery reveals God's lordship as that of Ruler and Judge. The Lamb's station upon the battle horse reveals his lordship as that of the messianic conqueror who executes the judgment God has rendered. It is this latter revelation that the remaining narration of chapter 19 will confirm.

John's imagery reinforces key themes established earlier in his work. Though this horse and rider are not the same horse and rider as in 6:2, the seer is certainly capitalizing on the thematic link between horses and judgment in the narration of the first four seals (6:1-8). The horse's white color represents victory (cf. 3:2-4). It is no accident that the troops who accompany the rider sport horses of the same color (19:14). The rider's name, "*Faithful and True*" (cf. *3 Macc.* 2:9-14), is a climactic summation of descriptors previously applied to Christ: faithful witness, 1:5; the true one, 3:7; and faithful and true witness, 3:14. The implication is clear: not only did Christ faithfully declare his own and God's true lordship to the cross and beyond; as God's true Messiah, he also will faithfully execute God's judgment upon those who have fought and killed on behalf of the lordship of Caesar and Rome.

The final phrase in the verse is an explanatory extension of the moniker "*Faithful and True.*" By Faithful and True, John means to say that when the rider fulfills his obligations of executing judgment through war, he does so in a righteous manner (cf. Pss. 72:2; 96:13; 98:9; Isa. 11:4). In other words, the rider acts as God acts, in ways that are commensurate with the crime (cf. Rev. 15:3; 16:5, 7; 19:2; 20:13) and that procure the victory of eschatological relationship with

God that was promised (2:7, 11, 17, 26, 28; 3:5, 12, 21). The rider/Lamb has not started this fight (11:7; 12:17; 13:7). He will, however, finish it (17:14) justly.

- **12** The rider's flaming eyes are based on Dan. 10:6 and rekindle John's earlier description of Christ (Rev. 1:14), who comes as judge even of believers who accommodate themselves to the lordship demands of the imperial cult (2:18). The many diadems further develop the imagery of rule. These symbols of kingship were previously co-opted in the narrative by the dragon and the beasts (12:3; 13:1) and commandeered by the Caesars in history, but they rightfully adorn only the crown on the head of the Christ Lamb (14:14; 19:16).

There is little doubt that John has in mind Isaiah's eschatological presentation of the holy city of Jerusalem (Isa. 62:1-5). Isaiah connects the language of crown and diadem, identifying them as a single representation of God's universal lordship (Isa. 62:3). In that context, Jerusalem is to God a bridal city just as the people of God are imaged as a bridal city in Rev. 19:6-8. Of even more interest is that fact that Isaiah connects these images to the bestowal of a new name (Isa. 62:2). Like Isaiah's vindicated Jerusalem, the diademed rider/Christ/Lamb is issued a new name. the divine-passive formulation once again points to divine agency. Based on the Lamb's true and faithful witness and the kingship he obtains as a result, God gives him a new name and promptly inscribes it on his head. Though dueling variant readings locate the inscription either on the diadems or on the rider's head, narrative clues suggest that John intends the head. Such positioning parallels nicely with the inscription of Christ's name on the forehead of his followers (Rev. 14:1; 22:4) and draws an appropriate contrast to the blasphemous names on the heads of the beast from the sea (13:1).

This newly accorded name is obviously not the same name, *"Faithful and True,"* that was just mentioned in v. 11. That name was publicly stated; this new name is known only to the rider. The divine-passive formulation (*"written"*) implies once again God's agency and suggests that God is the single exception who knows the secret of the name. This literary technique of reserving knowledge of key details to only a few is characteristic of John's work (cf. 14:3). Of the faithful at 2:17, which Christ himself promised to inscribe on his witnesses above every other name (Phil. 2:9), the newness, if not the secrecy, of Christ's eschatological name was a part of the early tradition. The secrecy here is no doubt a metaphor of empowerment. Since the ancient world supposed that control of a person or a divinity could be exercised through the knowledge and manipulation of that person's or divinity's name (as in a magical incantation), John's imagery amounts to a declaration that Christ's lordship is beyond the control of any human or power. It is his unique status and autonomy as Lord rather than any interest in deciphering his name that John wants most to impress upon his readers here.

One could argue that the secret is revealed later in this scene, when John introduces him as *"the Word of*

God" (19:13) and then sees the inscribed name *"King of kings and Lord of lords"* (v.16). Anyone familiar with the tradition cited in the prologue of the Gospel of John (cf. also 1 John 1) would have been surprised to learn that what had become a decidedly public metaphorical connection of Jesus to God's *"Word"* was now suddenly a secret. Moreover, because *"name"* lacks the definite article in v. 16, it is grammatically unlikely that John is referring to this secret name there either. Christ's kingship, though climactically presented in v. 16, is also not much of a secret any longer. The diadems of this immediate context illustrate the claim. The book's one revelation is that true historical and cosmic lordship belongs to God and Christ. Indeed, witness to this truth forms the book's principal ethic. The secret name cannot be related to this very public, though contested, truth. No, the matter remains one of knowledge and the control that goes with it. John wants his hearers and readers to know that even believers, faithful witnesses to the lordship of God and the Standing Slaughtered Lamb, cannot parlay their righteousness into a manipulation of the Lamb's eschatological activity of dealing justice. They can know the Lord well enough to serve him, worship him, and testify about him, but they never know him well enough to control him. He will judge justly, no matter what justice requires (i.e., the seals/trumpets/bowls).

- **13** The mystery heightens with his wardrobe. The rider wears a robe stained with blood. It could be the Lamb's blood; the event of his execution is, after all, central to the work (1:5; 5:9; 7:14; 12:11). It could just as credibly be the blood of the witnesses who are executed for their testimony to the Lamb's lordship. Indeed, it is the crying out of their blood that presumably motivates divine judgment (6:10; 16:6; 17:6; 18:24; 19:2; cf. Gen. 4:10). Or finally, it could be the blood of the enemies who work at the behest of the dragon and its minion beasts (Rev. 14:20).

Choosing the Lamb's blood makes little narrative sense; the Lamb's blood is spilled offstage, in the crucifixion symbolized as a *"snatching"* that took place well before the situation now confronting the seven churches (Rev. 12:5). More likely would be the blood of the witnesses, as John fears both its current and future spilling and exhorts his followers to continue testifying even in the face of such a dire circumstance. The Lamb could well be carrying a sampling of that spilled blood with him as extra motivation for the battle task at hand. The problem with this option is twofold. First, the cry of 6:9-11, re-narrated in symbolic fashion in 8:3-5, provides sufficient motivation for all of the judgment/justice activity that has ensued thus far. It is difficult to believe that God would need any more motivational reinforcement just now. Second and more important, the witness blood option does not fit the narrative context. Since 17:1, John has been narrating the blood of judgment. Where the blood of believers is mentioned, it is offered exclusively as a rationale for the justice that is being wreaked. The focus throughout this extended section has been on the destruction of the whore/Babylon/Rome. When John mentions the people of God at length, he describes their post-apocalyptic appearance as a bride adorned in fine and clean, not bloody linen.

The narrative preoccupation in this part of Revelation is the final combat to consummate the acts of judgment that have already taken place. Indeed, one of those acts, pictured as the wine of God's wrath (14:10) and the subsequent treading of the metaphorical winepress that spills an immense volume of enemy blood (14:20), fits nicely with the treading of the winepress of God's wrath highlighted in 19:15. Isaiah 63:1-6, from which John is certainly working, chronicles the return of God as a warrior dressed in a garment stained with the blood of God's Edomite enemies (cf. Exod. 15:3-4; *Wis.* 18:15-16). Like John, Isaiah refers to that blood with the metaphor of a trodden winepress. This is blood judgment language. The blood on the rider's robe must therefore be the blood of those who oppose the lordship of God and the Lamb and, allied with the dragon and beasts, fight to abort it. Critics may argue that the rider has not yet gone into combat and can therefore not yet have been splattered with the blood of his enemies. To be sure, the final battle has not been engaged, but the preparatory battles chronicled in chapters 17 and 18 have already been waged and won. It is hard to imagine the decimation wrought there as a clean, bloodless kill.

It is not, however, inappropriate that hearers and readers entertain all three blood options when they read this text. In this climactic setting, the imagery of blood comes full circle, tied up as it is with the person of

Jesus Christ, who with the saints (12:11) brings victory through his blood for the blood of the saints by drawing the blood of the enemy. It is that blood drawn in judgment that now stains his robe.

The Christ/Lamb/rider has not abandoned his primary role in the "*Apokalypsis*": in retuning warrior he has not deserted his original function of witness-bearing, on which all his other achievements are founded. He is armed, as we shall see in verse 15, with no other weapon than the good confession which he witnessed before Pontius Pilate (1 Tim. 6:13). His weapon is his witness. His witness is his word of testimony to the lordship of God and Christ. That word is the victorious sword he wields (Rev. 1:16; 2:12, 16; 19:15, 21; *Wis.* 18:15-16). John made this case early on when he introduced "*the Word of God*," which is the testimony of Jesus. He repeats the formulation at 1:9; 6:9 and 20:4. This word is the cutting (against the lordship claims of the imperial cult) testimony of God's and Jesus' lordship, which Jesus himself conveyed and his witnesses now proclaim. It is no wonder, then, that his name would also be "*the Word of God*." His witness and his name are synonymous. He is (name) what he does (witness). He is the very embodiment of the truth to which he testifies.

- **14** The white horse of the Lamb/Christ/rider of 19:11 is replicated here as a metaphor for victory that bears all of those who fight in league with the Christ Lamb. The identity of Christ's accompanying force is not clear. Given that the 144,000 were characterized as an army, surely they would comprise a portion of the company (cf. 7:1-8; 14:1-5). Perhaps the multitude of 17:14 would also ride with him. Could the great army of witnesses chronicled at 7:9-17 make up the army's number? This seems less likely, however, since these witnesses have already retired from their battles to an everlasting repose of worship before the heavenly throne. Their fighting (i.e., witnessing) is done; their worshiping is only just beginning. It is better to focus on the battle contingent as those who still maintain the combat of witness with and for the Lamb on earth since the earth is the ground upon which the battle will take place.

For hearers and readers concerned about the violence implied by the battle imagery, it is helpful to remember that John never depicts the army actually fighting. The brawl takes place offstage. Even there, it is unclear whether John intends combat of a traditional sort. After all, the primary weapon is a sword not of steel but of God's word. Since Christ's accompanying army ride similar horses, one suspects that they also fight with a similar weapon. The combat is one of competing testimonies to competing lordships. This is a war of the Word, a war over which word, the word of whose lordship, is the true word. It is therefore on the level of testimony that the combat is waged. The army of witnesses makes war by testifying to the lordship of God and the Standing Slaughtered Lamb. It is this testimony that draws blood and brings down the forces of the beast (cf. 12:11). No wonder, then, that John connects the clothing of witness with the clothing of this Christ army. As 19:8 has made clear, the act of witnessing yields the white dress of fine linen that characterizes a true and victorious witness. John makes the same point throughout the narrative. Witnessing is the winning weapon.

- **15** Multiple Old Testament references and allusions lie behind the metaphors John deploys in this single verse. He builds from an apparently traditional understanding of God's word (cf. Eph. 6:17; Heb. 4:12); the sharp sword issuing from the rider's mouth is reminiscent of Isa. 49:2 and reminds John's readers of Christ's primary and most formidable weapon (Rev. 1:16; 2:12, 16; 12:15; 19:21; *Wis.* 18:5-6). He uses this sword to strike the nation. Indeed, he targets all the nations, even thouse comprised of believers (1:16; 2:12, 16). All will be judged according to their works of witness (2:2, 5, 6, 19, 23, 26; 3:1, 2, 8, 15; 20:12). For hearers and readers who are skeptical that the Lamb would initiate such apparently hostile action, it is helpful to remember that the Lamb presented in 6:16 is decisive about judgment. He remains a lion who strikes, that is, the Standing Slaughtered Lamb with the word of God.

The language of "*striking*" is also important because John uses it of the two witnesses who strike the earth with plagues (chapter 11). The idea behind such striking was rehabilitative, however. God's strikes, even in the plagues, were intended to motivate repentance (2:5, 16, 21-22; 3:3, 19; 9:20-21; 16:9, 11). John is clearly working here from prophetic foundations. At Isa. 11:4 God intends to strike the nations with the rod of God's mouth. In this context in the Book of Revelation, the force for repentance softens the blow as John links the Old Testament imagery, particularly the Ps. 2:9 image of *"ruling"* with an iron rod, to the symbolism of *"shepherding"* toward an eschatological relationship with God (cf. Rev. 11:1). Finally, the winepress as metaphor for God's judgment wrath is reminiscent of 14:19-20 (cf. 14:10), which of God as a returning, victorious king in Isa. 63:1-6. As vicious as John's language is here, it is helpful to note that he does not invent the imagery of judgment, but works from prophetic foundations. He even manages to temper the presentation that the prophets have given him. John's God in the end is a forceful shepherd whose chief concern is the re-forming of the flock.

- **16** The final name of the Lamb in this context, which is still not the revelation of the mysterious name of v. 12, is written on his garment, at the place of his thigh. (Some manuscripts have changed the text to read *"on the forehead."* This adjustment clearly seeks to fit this text to other passages, which place the seal on the foreheads of the saints (Rev. 7:3; 9:4; 14:1; 22:4) and the satanic mark on the foreheads of the enemies (Rev. 13:16).) The divine-passive formulation suggests that God has marked him with this name. The precise location is difficult to determine since the Greek is not clear. The "καὶ" (and) that connects his garment with his thigh could mean either that there are two inscriptions, one on the garment and the other on the tight, or that there is one inscription. In the latter case, the epexegetical "καὶ" (that is) suggests that the second half (thigh) interprets the first (garment). Even in this case, though, there are problems. Does John intend to say that the name is inscribed on the robe, which is at the place of the thigh, or on the thigh at the place where the robe covers it? The latter interpretation would be more in line with John's references to inscriptions written on specific people, particularly on foreheads (Rev. 7:3; 9:4; 13:16; 14:1; 22:4), throughout the narrative. Here, though, he intentionally places "*garment*" in the controlling grammatical position. Additionally, throughout chapter 19 he has been concerned with the garments worn by the bride, the Christ-army, and the Lamb himself. The Lamb's garment, in fact, has already been famously inscribed by blood. Given these contextual clues, John probably intends to say that the name was inscribed on Christ's garment at the place where the garment covers his thigh. Just as the garments of the witnesses are a symbol of their faithful testimony, so is the Lamb's garment a testimony to the true and faithful battlefield witness he is now ready to undertake.

Even so, preoccupation with the location of the name's writing draws attention away from John's primary interest, the name itself. Everyone can and should know this name. Indeed, the entire Book of Revelation has been about this name. It is the proclamation of this name, and its attachment to God and the Standing Slaughtered Lamb, that has provoked the draconian behavior of a Babylon/Rome determined to secure this name for itself. The name, then, is also the testimony. He, not Rome and not Caesar, is "*King of kings and Lord of lords*," the ultimate ruler of all creation. This is the testimony that Jesus himself bore. It is the witness that conquers, but also the witness that believers are persecuted for proclaiming. It is the claim that Rome tries to commandeer. It is the true witness of faithful followers (cf. 1:5; 3:14). It is a political reality drawn from a cultic claim. *"Thus the parousia entails the manifestation of Christ's universal rulership"* (Schüssler Fiorenza, *Vision of a Just World*, 106).

Revelation 19:17~21 → The Final Battle

NIV	TT
¹⁷ And I saw an angel standing in the sun, who cried in a loud voice to all the birds flying in midair, "Come, gather together for the great supper of God, ¹⁸ so that you may eat the flesh of kings, generals, and the mighty, of horses and their riders, and the flesh of all people, free and slave, great and small." ¹⁹ Then I saw the beast and the kings of the earth and their armies gathered together to wage war against the rider on the horse and his army. ²⁰ But the beast was captured, and with it the false prophet who had performed the signs on its behalf. With these signs he had deluded those who had received the mark of the beast and worshiped its image. The two of them were thrown alive into the fiery lake of burning sulfur.	¹⁷ Then I saw an angel standing in the sun, and he cried out with a great voice, saying to all the birds flying in midheaven: "Come, gather for the great **supper**²⁷³ of God, ¹⁸ to eat the carrion of kings, the carrion of generals, the carrion of the powerful, the carrion of horses and their riders, and the carrion of all – both the free and the enslaved, the small and the great." ¹⁹ Then I saw the beast and the kings of the earth and their armies assembled to wage war against the one seated on the horse and against his army. ²⁰ And the beast was captured, and with it the false prophet who performed on its behalf the signs by which he deceived those who received the mark of the beast and worshiped its image; the two were

---

²⁷³ δεῖπνον → It means "*dinner,*" "*supper,*" "*the main meal of the day,*" and "*banquet.*"

21 The rest were killed with the sword coming out of the mouth of the rider on the horse, and all the birds gorged themselves on their flesh.	thrown alive into the lake of fire that burns with sulfur. 21 The rest were killed by the sword that projects from the mouth of the one seated on the horse, and all the birds were gorged with their carrion.

The picture of the Parousia merges with that of the last battle. This is an image with a long and venerable history. From the mythical pictures of ancient Near East religion, Israel adopted and adapted the image of the primeval battle between the deity and the chaos monster.

- **17 – 18** The end of Babylon/Rome's claim to rule begins here. With the second of three narrative introductions to a new scene, *"then I saw,"* John communicates the aftermath of a final battle that apparently took place between scenes one (19:11-16) and two (19:17-18). Using imagery with which the martial Romans would have been well familiar, he conjures a post-combat battlefield awash in blood, strewn with human corpses. The tradition in Ezek. 38-39 about the kings of the earth gathering in a doomed attempt to defeat Jerusalem is certainly in the background as John foregrounds Christ's rout of God's enemies. Of particular interest is Ezek. 39:17-20. There the Lord God tells the prophet to invite the birds of the air to come and feast on the flesh and blood of the princes of the earth until they are gorged and drunk.

The macabre scene is presided over by a familiar figure. The angel standing in the sun displays the same kind of grandeur evident in 7:2, with the angel who ascended from the sun; in 10:1, with the angel whose face shone like the sun; and in 18:1, with the angel who made the earth bright with his splendor. Like the angels in 7:2 and 18:1-2, this one speaks with a great voice of judgment that fits the grisly battlefield before him. Apparently operating under the same orders issued by God to Ezekiel, he invites the birds flying in midheaven. Midheaven is a locale that images judgment in both 8:13 and 14:6. Clearly, the woe that the mid-heavenly eagle expressed in 8:13 has come to life with a dizzying vengeance here. Indeed, this apocalyptic catastrophe could well be the realization of the mysterious third woe that John never narrates (9:12-21).

The instruction to the invited birds in Revelation is the same as that given in Ezekiel. John's language, however, clarifies that this is the eschatological victory meal of God first mentioned in 19:9. John is once again flipping his and the flesh feast of the birds, are one and the same event; on the back side of joy and salvation (19:10) is the judgment that brings that joy and salvation about. While the faithful partake of the bounty of God inside the wedding hall, carrion feeders gorge themselves on human remains outside. The connection has to be intentional; these two texts (19:9, 17) are the only two places in Revelation where the "δεῖπνον" (supper) appears. Verse 18 lists all the categories broad array of categories of corpses; it also demonstrates how broad was the following of the beast. The poor as well as the wealthy, slaves as well as the great ones of the earth, fell victim to Babylon/Rome's adulterous lure. Not only did they all follow the beast; they also were so successfully seduced into placing trust in its lordship and so marked by its pretensions to power (13:16) that they were willing to fight to the death for it (cf. 6:15).

- **19 – 21** The third scene in this set brings closure to the first two. John now shifts from the angel and his preoccupation with the birds to those who were vanquished. He is also flipping back and forth on the timeline. In v. 17 the angel anticipates the future, when the victory has occurred. The battle is done. But here that battle is clearly not yet. John sees the beast from the sea, the kings of the earth, and their armies before they become apocalyptic bird food. Still, by the time this scene closes (v. 21), the destruction by the rider on the white horse (Christ) will be just as final, just as complete.

What develops is essentially a re-presentation of the Armageddon scene (16:14-16; cf. 11:7; 17:14). Considering the gore that will follow the battle, the description of the immediate aftermath of the fight is rather mundane. John is primarily concerned with the capture of the two primary combatants. The beast from the sea and the false prophet who conjures the signs that lure humans into worshiping the beast (13:11-18) are spared being victims for the battlefield feast because an even more gruesome fate awaits. They are thrown alive into the apparent eternal torment of a lake of fire that burns with the intensity of brimstone (sulfur; cf. Num. 16:33, where three figures are sent into Sheol alive).

Fire has been a metaphor for judgment throughout John's work. The use of fire and sulfur as an eschatological punishment of unbearable intensity is also a previous theme (14:10-11). In fact, 14:10-11 suggests an eternal suffering rather than an immediate extermination, thus lending to this scene a severity that seems cruel and unusual even for the beast and its compatriots. If there is any doubt about the long suffering implied here, that doubt is soon eliminated when the dragon is included in the fire and the three enemies of God are said explicitly to suffer eternal torment (20:10). Death and Hades are likewise included in the fire (20:14), as are a vice parade of evil people at 21:8. This second death is the one that John counsels his followers to avoid at any and all costs. His description of its agony certainly helps his case.

In fact, when one considers John's language in terms of rhetorical effect, one gathers a clearer picture of what he is trying to do. It is not his intent to present a real picture of the judgment. He instead intends to scare hearers and readers straight back to belief in the singular lordship of God and the Lamb. Like the plagues, the lake of fire has repentance as its primary goal. John wants both to stop accommodating to it, or never to begin to do so. This is the rhetoric of behavior transformation. Whether he believes judgment will be this cruel or not is hard to say. In any case one must challenge him for presenting such a ruthless depiction. It is a brutal vision that has little place in the Christian concept of the afterlife. But again, his point is not to depict the literal afterlife, but to envision a future that will transform present behavior. The more gruesome the depiction, the more likely it is that transformation will ensue. A people who do not trust Babylon/Rome to survive will be less likely to accommodate themselves to it, even if it promises present death to all who resist its seductive charms. After all, an even greater death remains. When given the choice of that death or eternal eschatological relationship with God, John is hoping that his hearers and readers will choose appropriately and wisely. He has certainly used every means of rhetorical persuasion at his disposal to encourage the right choice.

Revelation 20:1~15 → Aftermath of the Final Battle

NIV	TT
20 ¹ And I saw an angel coming down out of heaven, having the key to the Abyss and holding in his hand a great chain. ² He seized the dragon, that ancient serpent, who is the devil, or Satan, and bound him for a thousand years. ³ He threw him into the Abyss, and locked and sealed it over him, to keep him from deceiving the nations anymore until the thousand years were ended. After that, he must be set free for a short time. ⁴ I saw thrones on which were seated those who had been given authority to judge. And I saw the souls of those who had been beheaded because of their testimony about Jesus and because of the word of God. They had not worshiped the beast or its image and had not received its mark on their foreheads	**20** ¹ Then I saw an angel descending from heaven with the key of the Abyss and a great chain in his hand. ² And he seized the dragon, the ancient serpent who is the devil and Satan, and bound him for a thousand years. ³ He threw him into the Abyss and shut and sealed it over him, so he could no longer deceive the nations, until the thousand years were completed. After this he must be released for a short time. ⁴ Then I saw thrones and those who sat on them were given authority to judge, that is, the souls of those who had been beheaded because of the testimony of Jesus, which is the Word of God. They had not worshiped the beast or its image and had not received its mark upon their foreheads or on their hands. They came to life and ruled with Christ a thousand years. ⁵ The rest of

or their hands. They came to life and reigned with Christ a thousand years. ⁵(The rest of the dead did not come to life until the thousand years were ended.) This is the first resurrection. ⁶Blessed and holy are those who share in the first resurrection. The second death has no power over them, but they will be priests of God and of Christ and will reign with him for a thousand years.

⁷When the thousand years are over, Satan will be released from his prison ⁸and will go out to deceive the nations in the four corners of the earth—Gog and Magog—and to gather them for battle. In number they are like the sand on the seashore. ⁹They marched across the breadth of the earth and surrounded the camp of God's people, the city he loves. But fire came down from heaven

the dead did not come to **life**[274] until the thousand years were completed. (This is the first **resurrection**[275].) ⁶Blessed and holy is the one who has a part in the first resurrection. Over these, the second death has no authority, but they will be priests of God and of Christ and will rule with him a thousand years.

⁷When the thousand years are completed, Satan will be released from his prison, ⁸and he will go forth to deceive the nations that are at the four corners of the earth, **Gog and Magog**,[276] to assemble them for the war. Their number is like the sand of the sea. ⁹They marched up over the breadth of the earth and surrounded the camp of the saints and the beloved city. Then fire came down from heaven and devoured them. ¹⁰And the devil who deceived them was thrown into the lake of fire

---

[274] ζάω → The term means *"live," "natural life," "be well,"* and *"recover."*

[275] ἀνάστασις → It means *"rise," "rising,"* and *"resurrection."*

[276] → see Excursus 17: Gog and Magog

and devoured them. ¹⁰ And the devil, who deceived them, was thrown into the lake of burning sulfur, where the beast and the false prophet had been thrown. They will be tormented day and night for ever and ever.

¹¹ Then I saw a great white throne and him who was seated on it. The earth and the heavens fled from his presence, and there was no place for them. ¹² And I saw the dead, great and small, standing before the throne, and books were opened. Another book was opened, which is the book of life. The dead were judged according to what they had done as recorded in the books. ¹³ The sea gave up the dead that were in it, and death and Hades gave up the dead that were in them, and each person was judged according to what they had done.

and sulfur, where the beast and the false prophet were, too, and they will be tormented day and night forever and ever.

¹¹ Then I saw a great white throne and the one seated on it, from whose presence earth and heaven fled, but there was no place for them. ¹² Then I **saw**[277] the dead – the great and the small – standing before the throne. And books were opened, and another book, which is the Book of Life, was opened, and the dead were judged by what was recorded in those books, according to their **works**[278]. ¹³ And the sea gave up the dead in it, the Death and Hades gave up the dead in them, and all were judged according to their works. ¹⁴ Then Death and Hades were thrown into the lake of fire. This is the second death: the lake of fire. ¹⁵ And if anyone was not found recorded in the Book of Life,

---

[277] ὁράω → The term means "*see,*" "*catch sight of,*" "*notice,*" "*visit,*" "*experience,*" "*witness,*" "*mentally and spiritually see,*" "*perceive,*" "*look at,*" and "*see to.*"
[278] ἔργον → It means "*deed,*" "*action,*" "*practice,*" "*manifestation,*" "*accomplishment,*" "*occupation,*" "*task,*" "*thing,*" "*matter,*" and "*work.*"

¹⁴ Then death and Hades were thrown into the lake of fire. The lake of fire is the second death.
¹⁵ Anyone whose name was not found written in the book of life was thrown into the lake of fire. that one was thrown into the lake of fire.

Chapter 20 presents John's hearers and readers with the aftermath and consequences of the war with the beast, the kings of the earth, and their armies (19:19). While the beast (Babylon/Rome) and the false prophet (the Asia Minor puppet regimes of Babylon/Rome) are burning in the lake of fire and sulfur (brimstone), and the corpses of the kings and their soldiers are being feasted upon by winged scavengers, God's judgment/justice turns its attention to the dragon.

- **1** As he did in chapter 19, John marks the introduction of new scenes with *"then I saw"* (cf. 19:11, 17, 19). In this case the new material builds from the narrative case established at 19:11. Together the episodes form part of a larger interlude, 19:11-21:8, that separates the parallel sections 17:1-19:10 (whore/Babylon) and 21:9-22:9 (bride/Jerusalem). Framed within this interlude section is the piece about the Lamb's Parousia as a battle and the results of that battle. The first results, the imprisonment and eternal torture of the two combat generals (beast and false prophet), were reported in 19:17-21. Chapter 20 focuses on the second result: the defeat, capture, and eternal torture of the grand strategist, the commander-in-chief of evil, the dragon.

The object in John's immediate sight is an angel sweeping down from heaven. The angel's point of origin is an indication of his authority; he comes as an agent of God. The staging is reminiscent of 10:1 and 18:1, two other texts where angels descend from heaven. In each case, the objective of their descent was judgment. In 18:1, that judgment worked out as the destruction of Babylon. Here the descending angel has the destruction of the force behind Babylon on his mind. Satan, too, can and will be judged.

The angel brings two important items with him. The first is the key to the Abyss. The narration immediately reminds John's hearers and readers of an earlier angel who also possessed the key to the Abyss (9:1). There are several significant differences between the two angelic characters. First, the figure in 9:1 was a *"fallen"* angel. This one is not thrown down but comes down, like the new Jerusalem, with a heavenly directive. Second, the angel in 9:1 held the key to the shaft of the pit, not the pit itself. Its power appears to have been more limited. Finally, the angel of 9:1 was given the key, just as the four apocalyptic horsemen were given their leave (6:1-8), for a purpose beyond and even contrary to his intent. Just as God apparently knew that the unrestrained horsemen could be counted upon to unleash a havoc that God could then use for God's own purposes, so God used the angel's predictably destructive inclinations as a way of executing judgment. God allowed his access to and release of hellish chaos. However, the angel's intentions in 20:1 are in line with God's. Instead of freeing hell from the Abyss as a way of inciting judgment against the evils perpetrated on earth, this angel intends to lock away the force whose deceptions created the need for that judgment. Thus this angel also wields a chain. Before being locked up, the dragon must first be bound.

- **2** The angel works quickly. For the second time the dragon (cf. 12:3), who would compare itself to God, is engaged and defeated not by God, but by one of God's representatives (cf. 12:7-9). Intending to diminish the dragon even as he chronicles the danger it symbolizes, John narrates that for all its history, fury, and power, God considers its defeat the kind of light work that God need not even get up from the throne to accomplish. The dragon who wants to be God does not even merit God's direct engagement.

With its chain, the angel binds the dragon for a thousand years (cf. Isa. 24:21-22; *1 En.* 10:4-14; 18:12-16; 21:1-10; 54:1-6; *2 Bar.* 40; 56:13; *T. Levi.* 18:12; *Jub.* 5:6; 10:4-14; 2 Pet. 2:4; Jude 6; Mark 3:27). The thousand-year period is a symbolic time that is lengthy though still transient – nothing more. Readers and hearers of John's text should not draw more from the metaphor than John himself does. John does refer to this period of time throughout the remainder of the chapter. Most often he will apply to it the define article (vv. 3, 5, 7), suggesting that the future uses refer back to this first reference, which does not carry the definite article. Just as interesting, though, is the fact that when he first speaks of the thousand-year rule of Christ (v. 4), he once again foregoes the article, as if in that case he is introducing the concept for the first time. Textual evidence is mixed when John again speaks of Christ's thousand-year rule in v. 6. While some manuscripts include the article, others do not. Regardless of one's decision on this text-critical question – though it makes sense that John did not intend to use the definite article in v. 6 – the context confirms that vv. 4 and 6 do speak of the same thousand years. The primary question is why John does not grammatically connect the thousand years of vv. 4 and 6 with the thousand-year period of vv. 2, 3, 5, and 7 by designating them as "*the*" thousand years, that is, "*the same*" thousand years introduced as the time of the dragon's incarnation. Contextually, it seems clear that John is talking about the same period. He probably did not include the article in vv. 4 and 6 because the time period functions differently when it is viewed from the standpoint of Christ's rule. Here we once again have the two-sides-of-the-same-coin perspective on judgment and salvation that operates throughout the narrative. The thousand years will be experienced in radically different ways depending on the perspective of the person experiencing them: a prelude to salvation for those who witness to the lordship of Christ, but a harbinger of judgment for those who have aligned themselves with the dragon and its beasts. The same thousand-year period can therefore "*feel*" different. John tries to make this case grammatically by the way he deploys the definite article.

- **3** The triple mention of the dragon's binding ("*cast*," "*locked*," "*sealed*") is indicative of the confidence hearers and readers should have in the incarceration of God's archenemy. It is not coming out any time soon.

Not in a thousand years! And even then, not of its own power and accord. The dragon's imprisonment prevents it from accomplishing its primary agenda: deception. In fact, the dragon's agenda is linked inextricably with its identity. When further introducing the dragon at 12:9 (cf. 20:2), John takes care to mention that it is the great deceiver of the inhabitants of the earth (cf. 2:13; 3:10). At 13:14 (cf. 19:20), John reveals his primary concern about draconian deception; its aim is to defraud the nations into believing in the dragon's lordship and the lordship of the bestial powers that represent it. According to 20:8, 10, the dragon has not only deceived the nations of the world into believing in its lordship but also convinced them to fight for that lordship. For this thousand years, however, all such activity will cease. There are serious implications not only for the dragon but also for the composition and the future prospects of the world after Armageddon-like battle of 19:11-21. Apparently John envisioned that huge populations survive, those who did not compose the decimated armies of the kings of the earth. A deceived people are a people who once believed correctly and might believe correctly again once the source of the deception is removed. No longer vulnerable to Satan's deceptions, they have the unfettered opportunity for a millennium to recognize God's true lordship and thereby receive and eschatological relationship with God.

Would even a thousand years, though, be enough time? Time would literally tell. After the binding, Satan must be let loose (note the divine-passive formulation) for a little while. Two questions immediately arise. Why "*must*" Satan be released? And why for a little while?

When dealing with the apocalyptic necessity here, it is helpful to consider it in the context of the theme of apocalyptic necessity throughout the book. Revelation 1:1 and 22:6 serve as bookends enclosing the story of the whole book and, when taken with the intervening chapters, answer the question: What must happen as a result of the ongoing conflict between God and Satan? Chapter 12 sets John's contemporary scene. The dragon is in pursuit of God's people (12:17). As a result, the people cry out to God for assistance (6:9-11). The dragon and the beasts are determined, however, to maintain control (chapters 12-13). In view of the predicament of God's people, God must intervene and soon. That "*must*" is the book's orienting apocalyptic necessity.

The apocalyptic necessity of 20:3 fits well into this larger scenario. The dragon's pursuit of God's people is historically successful precisely because the dragon has deceived the bulk of the world's people and leaders into believing in its lordship and promoting that lordship – in part by oppressing and even executing those who profess exclusively the contrary lordship of God and the Standing Slaughtered Lamb. Indeed, those who profess the dragon's lordship, and its realization in Babylon/Rome, progress so well economically, socially, and politically (cf. 18:23) that even many Christians have been deceived into accommodating themselves to the dragon's lie (cf. 2:20). To redirect God's people from such an accommodating track and to vindicate those who have refused to accommodate and have paid a steep economic, social, and perhaps physical price for that resistance, God must engage the dragon and its forces. The entire book operates from this apocalyptic premise. It is this premise that leads to Satan's incarceration. Every narrative move has been driven to this point. Satan's loosing must also be a part of this drive.

Satan is loosed to make two points. First, evil resurrects; it always comes back. The faithful must always be on guard against it. That point must be made if the faithful are always to maintain their guard. In order to make it, God must set the dragon free. But God also wants to maintain not only the appearance but also the reality of control. God therefore allows only a short time of release before God engages the dragon yet again. Evil is not stronger than God. It is always subject to some form of God's regulation. Even if things look bleak, the time of difficulty will be short. That knowledge should encourage believers to endure in their witness to God's lordship.

The second point is that resurrected evil will try to deceive even after it has been incarcerated. Even after it is clear that it is not God, when the dragon's claims to lordship ought to appear clearly bogus, it will try to deceive humans into buying into that lordship (20:8, 10). God's release of the dragon therefore provides humans with the ultimate opportunity to make the right choice. God has stacked the eschatological deck in favor of the right decision. How could anyone who knows about the dragon's thousand-year incarceration, an incarceration imposed by God, think now that the dragon's lordship was greater than God's? But God does not make the decision for humans; God respects human freedom and the right to make a choice, to act for God's lordship or against it. That freedom and the actions that result from it are recorded in the books that represents God's memory (20:12). By releasing Satan, God allows that human freedom to operate; God allows humans one final chance to make the right decision – whom will they acknowledge as Lord? – and to orient their lives accordingly. God lets Satan go so that Satan can go to a wiser people and be rejected. With the moment of final judgment looming, God offers this final, weighted opportunity for humans to choose the path that leads to life. For a little while, then, for this oddly orchestrated redemptive reason, the dragon must be set free. It is not for its sake that its freedom is allowed. It is for the sake of humankind.

- **4** As in v. 1, the narrative marker *"then I saw"* signals a scene shift. John sees thrones and figures sitting on them (cf. Dan. 7:9). While he does not identify the figures on the thrones, there is a strong contextual clue. The focus in this entire subsection is on believers who have been killed because of their testimony to the lordship of God and the Standing Slaughtered Lamb. John even amplifies their importance by connecting them to the slaughtered souls at 6:9-11, whose cry for justice and judgment motivates the book's apocalyptic activity. The entire scene is a delicious realization of poetic justice. Throughout his narrative, John has used the judicial imagery of witnessing and judgment. Those who have witnessed to the lordship of God and Christ have often, like Jesus himself, done so before the tribunal/judgment seats of Roman and Asia Minor officials. Now, when it matters most, at the ultimate judgment, the tables are turned; it is the witnesses who sit enthroned, and judgment is shown ultimately to lie in their hands. Certainly this outcome makes sense in the Book of Revelation; Christ had promised that conquering witnesses would sit enthroned with him (Rev. 3:21). It also makes sense in the light of the early Christian tradition that envisioned faithful believers sharing eschatological judgment duties with Christ (Matt. 19:28; Luke 22:30; 1 Cor. 6:2-3).

John identifies these witnesses as the souls who have been beheaded because of the testimony of Jesus, which is the word of God. On a first reading, it appears that he is talking about a subset of those who have been executed. Beheading was only one of many forms of Roman execution.[279] Could he have intended to say that only those specifically killed in this manner would reign with Christ as judges on the heavenly thrones? That is unlikely. John's language is metaphorical rather than literal. John conjures a particularly brutal form of capital punishment here in order to continue building

---

[279] →Aune suggests, since there were several means of inflicting the death penalty under Roman law, that it seems extremely unlikely that all of the martyrs would have been executed by decapitation (3:1086). Rome's legal system used two forms of death penalty: "*summum supplicium*," the more vindictive form, involving burning alive, crucifixion, and exposure to wild beasts; and "*capite puniri*," simple death by decapitation. There were two types of decapitation: by the sword and by the axe. Provincial governors had the right to execute by sword only, not by the axe, javelin, club, or noose.

momentum for God's final retaliatory response of justice/judgment. His clear paralleling of this text with 6:9 indicates that he thinks of these executed souls as the same group. In fact, when the verses are set side by side, the only differences are the inclusion in 6:9 of the phrases *"under the altar," "they had given,"* and *"to Jesus,"* and the inverted order of the phrases *"because of the word of God"* and *"because of the witness [to Jesus]." "Beheaded"* in 20:4 is John's way of amplifying the term *"executed"* in 6:9.

John is not talking about another group of witnesses when he goes on to laud those who did not worship the beast (cf. 13:4) or its image or take its mark on their foreheads or hands (see 13:13-17). Appealing once again to an epexegetical, or explanatory "καὶ" (and), which uses a second clause to clarify the one that precedes it, he means to say: *"the souls of those who have been beheaded, ... who did not worship."* These are the people who live and rule with Christ for the thousand years that Satan is incarcerated (vv. 1-3).

It is perhaps the Christian understatement of the last two millennia to say that this thousand-year reign with Christ has proved to be something of an interpretive problem. The less difficult problems lie with the issues of resurrection and rule that precede the talk of a thousand-year period, so it is helpful to start there. Though John does not use the language of resurrection here, he will resort to it in vv. 5 and 6 to describe this phenomenon of slaughtered souls coming to life. Here, he appeals to the same verb "ζάω" (live) that he uses to describe Jesus' resurrection at 1:18 and 2:8. It is also the same verb used in Ezek. 37:10 LXX to describe the valley's dry bones as they take on a miraculous new physical life. Like Jesus, though dead, the Hebrew bones and the Christian witnesses return to life. Apparently, this is a different form of life than that enjoyed by executed witnesses as souls in heaven, for John uses the verb to distinguish between that spiritual existence and this obviously new one. This *"living"* is also clearly not the same kind of earthly life they enjoyed before their execution. Yet it must be a form of corporeal existence, for they enjoy this life for a thousand years on this physical earth, and they are presumably seen by and in relationship with the physical humans over whom they rule. Like Jesus' own resurrection, theirs must be a bodily resurrection of some sort (cf. Luke 24:42-43; 1 Cor. 15). It is with some kind of physicality that they now live. To what end? To rule (cf. Dan. 7:27). With Christ. As Promised (Rev. 5:10; 22:5).

On the thousand-year term, it is helpful to begin with the observation that too much has been made of a concept to which John gave very little attention. This interim or intermediate period between the historical and the future eschatological time occurs when John essentially merges two different Jewish eschatological traditions into a unique concept that fits his apocalyptic staging. Prophetic eschatology primarily anticipated a relationship with God that would take place within history. Aptly, for a people who had no concept of an afterlife but understood this historical existence as the place where human destiny – including, through one's progeny, the longevity of one's name and person – was worked out, the expectation for future redemption lay in the transformation of this-worldly existence into God's kingdom. In the apocalyptic theology ushered in formally in the work of Daniel and developed in many succeeding Jewish and early Christian works, however, this historical creation was understood to be so utterly corrupted that redemption could come only from beyond. The faithful anticipated the inbreaking of God's future kingdom, which would devastate the present reality and transform it into a new heaven and new earth. In John's time and, further, in John's own work, the two scenarios merge *"into a scheme in which a this-worldly messiah brought this-worldly salvation during a transitional kingdom, which was then superseded by eternal apocalyptic salvation in the new world"* (Boring, Revelation, 207). This intermediate, transitional kingdom was developed in several Jewish apocalyptic texts (cf. *4 Ezra* 7:26-44; 12:31-34; *1 En.* 91:11-17; *2 Bar.* 29:1-30:5; 40:1-4; 72:2-74:3), and its duration was variously measured as 40 years, 400 years and an indefinite period. *"The idea of a messianic kingdom of 1,000 years is apparently original with John"* (Reddish 385). The intent, though, was symbolic rather than literal. John meant to suggest a time that, though lengthy, was transitory.

Focus on the literal span of time, however, has resulted in a fascination with millennial categories (from the Latin *"mille,"* thousand, and *"annus,"* year). Contemporary reflection falls into several basic categories. "*Amillennialism*" understands the thousand-year period to be a spiritual symbol for the reign of Christ in the church. No literal reign at the end of history is therefore anticipated. The church experiences the millennium already within history in this world. "*Post-millenialists*" believe that Christ's return will occur after a golden ear of peace on earth. Human progress moves inexorably in the direction of righteousness until a moment of consummation will herald the new era. Believing the world to be too corrupt to progress toward righteousness on its own, though, "*pre-millennialists*" expect that Christ will first need to come and establish control and direction. Only through such divine intervention can the new era be achieved. "*Dispensational pre-millennialists*" actually look to contemporary events for signs of that impending intervention by Christ. Many biblical scholars rightly reject all of these speculative views as literal misreading of John's highly metaphorical language. John gave brief attention to the time period and did not expect it to receive the interpretive weight it has been accorded.

    The period of Christ's rule no doubt has the same objective as the period of the dragon's incarceration. Witnesses are to see in it the truth that despite the circumstances of their oppression and even execution, God's vindication is assured. Judgment, and the justice that will come for them from that judgment, is imminent. The witnesses have only to hold on. Not only will they ultimately receive eschatological relationship with God; they also will obtain a historical, this-worldly reward that will see them rule over the very world that has persecuted and destroyed them. Still, the time period, though significant, is to be transitory. Like all of John's hearers and readers, these witnesses should focus less on the thousand years than on the new heaven and new earth to follow it. That future focus will bring even more energy to the present ethic of non-accommodating, resistant witness to the lordship of God and the Standing Slaughtered Lamb for which John appeals in the Book of Revelation. The focus should not be on the millennium itself, but on its function as a reward for those who have maintained their resistance to the lordship claims of draconian Whore/Babylon/Rome. Many contemporary churches probably spin their interpretive wheels on millennial definitions and strategies because social and political resistance too often is still too dangerous a course to undertake.

- **5** John moves immediately to clarify what happens to the rest of the dead. They stay dead. This is not a punishment: their time of resurrection is also coming. This coming to life of the slaughtered witnesses is only the first resurrection – the very designation clearly implies at least a second resurrection. It is a reward for their testimony. Since there are no other indications of such a concept in Jewish literature, it is also a concept likely developed by john himself. As Caird observes, *"John seems to want the best of both worlds. He believes that the ultimate destiny of the redeemed is in the heavenly city, but he also retains the earthly paradise, the millennium. He therefore requires not* *one but two resurrections: the first resurrection restores the martyrs to life for their millennial reign, the second brings all the dead before the great white throne"* (254).

During this thousand years, if the rest of the dead stay dead, presumably those who are already living and were not destroyed in the 19:11-21 battle stay alive. They will live under the rule of Christ and the slaughtered, resurrected faithful. There is no rapture moment when the living faithful are taken up into a heavenly safe zone. The living faithful remain with the living unfaithful. And instead of being raptured out of the world, the resurrected souls are brought back to life in this world.

- **6** For the second and final time in his text, John applies the word *"resurrection."* Those who take part in this first one are blessed and holy. In this fifth of his seven beatitudes (see the discussion of macarisms at 14:13 and 19:9), John once again presents both an indicative reality and an imperative appeal. It is easy to understand why those who rule with Christ would be considered blessed. In making that case, though, John also encourages his readers and hearers to maintain resistance even to the point where their recalcitrance might cost them their lives. Writing before the millennium, his description of the blessed state of those resurrected in the millennium serves as present ethical motivation. Everyone now should aspire, through the fact and manner of their testimony, to be a part of that first resurrection. The unique double predicate, blessed and holy (i.e., set apart), is a further reflection of the unique status of these resurrected souls. Like all the other witnesses (whose testimony did not lead to death), they are blessed. Unique among all the other witnesses and humankind in general, they experience the glory of the first resurrection.

In addition, the second death (2:11; 20:14; 21:8) – an eternal suffering that follows resurrection from the first, earthly death – has no authority over them (cf. 9:6). This does not meant that only they escape the second death. A final judgment awaits where others, including no doubt witnesses whose testimony did not result in their deaths, will also find eschatological relationship with God. These faithful witnesses find assurance and comfort early on, though, because the eschatological judge has already ruled in their favor.

As a way of bracketing this section, John now repeats what he has already explained at the end of 20:4: these resurrected souls will rule with Christ for the thousand years of the dragon's imprisonment. Operating with Exod. 19:6 in mind (cf. Isa. 61:6), John adds here the realization of a promise he had made earlier, that these kings with Christ will also be priests (Rev. 1:6; 5:10; 22:5). Whereas earlier he had restricted their priestly relationship to God, here he adds Christ, a further indication of his functional identification of the two. To serve one in worship is to serve the other; to witness to the lordship of one is to witness to the lordship of the other.

- 7 John shifts focus back to the dragon and closes out the narration of its demise that he began in vv. 1-3. He begins by corroborating what was promised in the earlier section. At the end of the thousand years, God sets Satan loose (another divine-passive construction: "*Satan "will be released [by God]"*").

- **8** Apparently, the combat debacle of 19:11-21 was not enough. Even after a thousand incarcerated years to mull over the rout, the dragon, perhaps delusional, harbors the hope that it can still defeat God's forces. Once liberated, the parolee goes about doing the very thing that got it imprisoned in the first place; it tries to deceive the nations – which apparently were not completely destroyed in the first "*final*" battle – to join yet another ill-fated attempt to assume the lordship that belongs exclusively to God.

Earlier, John relayed that the rider on the white horse struck down the nations and shepherded them with an iron rod (19:15). That "*striking down*" included destruction, as 19:17-21 made clear. It apparently also included disciplining. The shepherding imagery implies that a remnant of nations remained, those who were not slain by the Word on the battlefield, together with the kings and their armies. It is these nations, scattered across John's visionary world (i.e., the four corners of the earth; Rev. 7:1; Isa. 11:12; Ezek. 7:2), that are apparently now the subject of the dragon's deceit. Despite the fact that Christ, and no doubt the resurrected souls who rule with him, have tried for over a thousand years to shepherd these nations toward an understanding of God's rightful lordship, the dragon believes it can yet change the course of their cultic, social, and political loyalties.

At this point John returns to a reliance upon Ezekiel's visions for the prosecution of his own. Having already appealed to the imagery in Ezek. 37 in his presentation of the resurrection of the slaughtered souls as an eschatological updating of the vision of the valley of dry bones (Rev. 20:4-6), he now imagines the threat to that restored community to be the same one that plagued the prophet's restored Israel: Gog and Magog from Ezek. 38-39. Ezekiel prophesied that a hostile nation would hound the rejuvenated people of Israel from the remotest parts of the world in the north (Ezek. 38:6, 15) and would attack them in the latter days, but be utterly defeated. He identified the leader behind the invasion force as Gog, the prince of Meshech and Tubal (Ezek. 38:2-3; 39:1). Gog's land was called Magog. As a prophetic symbol, Gog represented one of the same truths expressed by the dragon's liberation from the Abyss in the Book of Revelation: even after restoration is achieved and peace is restored, evil slogs its way back into the personal and national story. Pablo Richard's analysis is perceptive: "*Gog attacks Israel when it has returned from exile and is living in security. Gog expresses the persistence of the power of evil, a power that only God can destroy and that is continually lying in wait for God's people*" (149). In Ezekiel, that threat was localized in a single national entity; in Revelation, Gog and Magog morph into dual national realities who symbolize every remaining nation from every compass point in the world. These are the forces that the dragon tries to deceive. John's identification of them as Gog and

Magog suggests that they are predisposed to receive the dragon's message sympathetically.

The dragon is successful in stirring Gog and Magog to "*the*" war. John appends the definite article to "*war*" because this final war effort is yet another attempt at the decisive triumph that the dragon has been plotting since it first set out against God's people (12:17). Throughout his narration John has spoken of vain attempts to prosecute the war (11:7; 12:17; 13:7; 16:14; 19:19). Every war effort has represented an attempt to unleash the final, decisive attack, the one that would topple God and God's forces and commander lordship for the dragon. With Gog and Magog's accompanying forces as great in number as the grains of sand by the sea (cf. Josh. 11:4; Judge. 7:12; 1 Sam. 13:5; *1 Macc.* 11:1), this effort appears to be the most likely to succeed.

Excursus 17: Gog and Magog

In Ezek. 38:2, we are introduced to "*Gog, of the land of Magog, the chief prince of Meshech and Tubal (prince of Rosh)*." LXX understood Magog as a people, or a country. It is a possible/reasonable identification of Gog is with Gyges, king of Lydia (660 B.C.E.) – Assyrian Empire. Magog could be Assyrians. The popular identification of "*Rosh*" with Russia, Meshech with Moscow and Tubal with Tobolsk in Siberia has nothing to commend it from the stand point of hermeneutics and biblical scholarships.

John's day Jewish tradition had reinterpreted these mysterious names in a variety of ways. John sees both Gog and Magog as personal beings who are deceived by Satan

> to lead the ultimate enemies of God's people to destruction in the eschatological battle. For John, evil as embodied in historical individuals and nations is not the ultimate enemy. We should not think of Gog and Magog as historical nations that have had a continuing existence during the preceding scene of John's drama, nor of nations of our own time *"predicted"* by biblical prophecy. John presents before our imaginations a picture of the ultimate destruction of evil, and he needs for this scene antagonists to God who are larger than life. Evil must be magnified to its fullest, and *"must be released"* before being destroyed forever.

- **9** Because they gather from all across the world, it makes sense for John to say that the Gog and Magog forces rally from the expanse of the earth (cf. Hab. 1:6). In their maneuvering, they go *"up,"* because their target is the elevated city of Jerusalem, to which people in Israelite and Jewish idiom always went up, never down (Ezra. 1:3; Ps. 122:4; Isa. 2:3; Jer. 31:6; Obad. 21; Mic. 4:2). Indeed, John's hearers and readers would have remembered that only two decades earlier, Rome's legions had would have remembered that only two decades earlier, Rome's legions had gone up to Jerusalem, surrounded it, besieged it, and destroyed it. This visionary threat would have had a vicious ring of historical truth to it.

    John describes the gathering of God's people in two ways. With *"camp,"* he means to jog their sacred memories of Israel's exodus wanderings in the wilderness. No doubt this image was meant to convey both the brutal historical reality and the hope that promised to transform it. John's people, too, were in a wilderness, beset by the occupying force of Babylon/Rome, their destruction threatened by it. Yet even as that threat loomed, they, like the wandering faithful from their past, had visions of a promised land pervaded by the peace that comes from eschatological relationship with God. With *"beloved city,"* he means to remind his hearers and readers that this is God's city, the place of God's temple and God's presence, the holy city (Rev. 11:2; 21:2, 10, 14-16, 18-19, 21, 23; 22:14, 19), which God would one day reclaim and refashion, where God would ultimately dwell directly and intimately with God's people (Rev. 21:22). Even besieged, the historical city therefore remains a defiant eschatological symbol of God's presence and God's protection.

In this particular case, God makes good immediately on the promise of that protection. God intervenes directly. John describes the victory with the familiar biblical image of fire dispatched from heaven that devours the enemies of God's people (2 Kgs. 1:9-14; cf. Luke 12:49). In fact, this is the very method used by God in Ezek. 39:6 to destroy the forces Gog (cf. Ezek. 38:22).

- **10** Like the beast and the false prophet before him, the deceiving dragon is captured after the defeat of its forces and thrown alive with them into the lake of fire and brimstone (Rev. 14:10-11; 19:20; Matt. 25:41). John wants to make sure that his hearers and readers perceive the tie between the dragon's fate and that of the beast and false prophet. He therefore mentions them specifically. Presumably they have been burning alive in this hellhole for a thousand years by the time the dragon is thrown in with them. Now the consequence they have endured will be shared by the dragon. What 19:20 did not state explicitly, this verse does: the punishment will not be a onetime moment of apocalyptic annihilation, but eternal suffering.

This portrait of God imposing eternal suffering seems as *"un-Christlike"* a punishment as imaginable. Yet John is dealing with the twin concepts of justice and mercy/grace. For him, one cannot exist without the other. For the evil that has been perpetrated, there needs to be justice, and he conceives of it in its most undiluted form as eternal suffering in the lake of fire and sulfur (brimstone). It is important to remember, however, that this is a figurative and not a literal *"lake."* What John is describing is not real, physical torture but the kind of continuous, perpetual spiritual torment that he imagines must occur when a being is separated forever from the presence of God. If it is God's presence that brings vitality, peace, security, hope, and indeed *"life"* to the human spirit, then to be separated from that presence forever must be equivalent to a kind of eternal agony. John can think of no other way to express the force and reality of that spiritual agony than the physical one of torture. It is an inappropriate image, to be sure, for a twenty-first-century sensibility. John, however, was operating with his own and his hearers' and readers' first-century sensibilities. He was trying to think of an image that would have *"teeth"* for them, an image that would shock people who were accommodating to the draconian lordship demands of Rome into resisting them and testifying in word and deed to the lordship of God and the Standing Slaughtered Lamb instead. He wanted them to fear being forever separated from the presence of God. His most forceful metaphorical attempt at conveying what that separating would feel like is the lake of fire and sulfur (brimstone). A twenty-first-century effort should focus on the language of separation from God's presence and look for a contemporary metaphor appropriate to that separation.

- **11** Though his primary preoccupation will be with humankind before God's judgment throne, John begins with a look at the throne itself. The throne reminds hearers and readers of the first scene featuring God's throne (Rev. 4:2; Ezek. 1:26-28; Dan. 7:9). Among Old Testament references, Dan. 7:9 is most important here. Like Revelation, the Book of Daniel uses the throne as a way of introducing the books of judgment that will be opened in God's presence. The role the throne plays in the process of the final judgment for John, therefore, comes directly from Daniel. The throne's white color is the color of righteousness and victory (Rev. 3:4). Its imposing size befits the stature of God as the Almighty (cf. 11:17). John's description of God as the one seated on the throne is a reminder that God is the one who rules with true lordship (cf. 4:2).

The judgment motif is reinforced by the fleeing of earth and heaven before the presence of God (6:14; 16:20; Ps. 114:3-7; 2 Pet. 3:7, 10, 12). Everything represented by the old earth and heaven, particularly resistance to the lordship of God and the Standing Slaughtered Lamb, has no place in the coming new heaven and new earth. Recognizing this, the old heaven and old earth make a preemptive effort to save themselves by running away. Given God's universal dominance, one wonders where exactly they think they are going! There is, in fact, nowhere they can go. Their flight is a metaphor for their destruction. Since separation from God's divine presence is death, the very effort to escape God is by definition an act of self-destruction.

- **12** now that the old heaven and old earth are no longer blocking his view, John can see "καὶ εἶδον" ("*then I saw*" the horde of resurrected dead, all of them, those who in life were insignificant and significant (cf. Rev. 11:18; 13:16; 19:5, 8), standing before God's throne. Though he does not specify it as such, this must be for John the post-thousand-year rule "*second resurrection*," which his reference to the first resurrection in vv. 5 and 6 implied. In the first resurrection, only those who had been executed for testifying to the lordship of God and the Standing Slaughtered Lamb obtained a spiritual, though nonetheless also corporeal, rebirth. This time everybody, both righteous and unrighteous, lives again (cf. John 5:29). For some, though, the moment – and the exhilaration that no doubt went with it – will be brief.

That is because books, based on the judgemnt books of Dan. 7:10, are opened (the divine-passive formulation indicates that God opens them). The content in these books will determine the eschatological fate of all those standing before the throne. John has already said that those in the first resurrection have a sealed fate of eschatological relationship with God. Whatever misdeeds might have been recorded about them in the books of judgment (no human would be without error!) are outweighed by the fact that they witnessed to the lordship of God and the Standing Slaughtered Lamb so vigorously that their testimony cost them their lives. This truth is an indication that for John the primary ethic, the primary work, is witnessing.

For all others, however, a balance of *"works"* must apparently be weighed. The books are metaphors for God's remembering human behavior throughout a human lifetime.[280] Proper works-behavior is rewarded, while improper works-behavior is punished (Rev. 2:2, 5, 6, 19, 22, 23, 26; 3:1, 2, 8, 15; 14:13; 18:6; 20:13; 22:12; Ps. 28:4; *Sir.* 16:12). Witnessing, no doubt, remains the primary expected behavior for which a life of eschatological relationship with God is the reward. It is this behavior that the book's entire energy has worked to secure. But other behaviors also matter, and they too are accounted for in God's memory (Rev. 21:8).

Nevertheless, this possibility of a books-based *"works righteousness,"* where a person's behavior accounts completely for that person's eschatological relationship with God or lack thereof, is tempered in this very verse by John's reference to another book, one

---

[280] The idea of such heavenly record books was widespread in the ancient Near Eastern world, including in Jewish literature (biblical and non-biblical sources; Dan. 7:10; Mal. 3:16; *4 Ezra* 6:20; *1 En.* 47:3; 81:1-4; 89:61-77; 90:17, 20; 98:7-8; *2 Bar.* 24:1).

that stands alone. This is *"the Book of Life"* (cf. Exod. 32:32-33; Ps. 69:28; Isa. 4:3; Dan. 12:1; Luke 10:20; Phil. 4:3; Heb. 12:23), which has already made several appearances in John's narrative (Rev. 3:5; 13:8; 17:8; 20:15; 21:27). In it, names are graciously written – by God (divine passive) – from the beginning of creation. Everyone whose name appears in this book will have an eschatological relationship with God (Rev. 13:8; Dan. 12:1). By joining these two books – one representing grace, the other representing works – in the same verse, John holds in positive tension these two powerful theological concepts. He recognizes the freedom that God gives to each human to make choices, and he weighs the responsibility those choices bear, but he never allows the ultimate eschatological decision to rest with anyone other than God.

- **13 – 14** Verse 13 is a colorful repetition of what was just said (v. 12) except that, if taken literally, it would be chronologically out of place with v. 12. Verse 13 describes the actual resurrection whose consequences have been considered in v. 12. Before the judgment depicted in v. 12 can take place, this *"second"* resurrection must happen. It happens on land and sea. Sailors and others who earned their living on the sea would have been buried at sea and thus need to be distinguished from those buried on land, who after death would have found their way to the underworld of Hades (cf. 9:1-2). Here, as elsewhere in the Book of Revelation, John mentions Death and Hades together because they form a pair (Rev. 1:19; 6:8). Death is the personification that apparently rules over the underworld region of Hades. Operating together, they simultaneously release the souls in their care. The point to be made here is that same point that John made in v. 12: all the dead are now raised. The scope of this act is universal.

Death and Hades are now cast into the second death. It is now clear, given their roommates in the flames, that even when they acted in response to the Lamb's breaking of the fourth seal and the cherubim's calling voice (Rev. 6:7), these forces are enemies of God yet used only to further God's purpose of judgment (cf. death as the last enemy in 1 Cor. 15:26).

- **15** The already-crowded lake of fire (i.e., second death) gets even more crowded still. What was assumed in v. 12 now comes to pass. Those whose names were not found in the Book of Life are, with the beast, false prophet, dragon, Death, and Hades, thrown into the eternal suffering that is eschatological separation from God.

Revelation 21:1~8 → A New Creation

NIV	TT
21 ¹ Then I saw "a new heaven and a new earth," for the first heaven and the first earth had passed away, and there was no longer any sea. ² I saw the Holy City, the new Jerusalem, coming down out of heaven from God, prepared as a bride beautifully dressed for her husband. ³ And I heard a loud voice from the throne saying, "Look! God's dwelling place is now among the people, and he will dwell with them. They will be his people, and God himself will be with them and be their God. ⁴ 'He will wipe every tear from their eyes. There will be no more death' or mourning or crying or pain,	**21** ¹ Then I saw a new heaven and a new earth. For the first heaven and the first earth passed away, and the sea was no more. ² And I saw the holy city, new Jerusalem, descending from heaven from God, **prepared**[281] as a bride adorned for her husband. ³ And I heard a great voice from the throne, saying, "Indeed, the **dwelling/tabernacle**[282] of God is with **people**[283], and God will **dwell**[284] with them, and they will be God's **peoples**,[285] and God, Godself, will be with them as their God, ⁴ and God will wipe away every tear from their eyes, and death will be no more, nor will mourning or crying or pain exist

---

[281] ἑτοιμάζω → It means *"to make ready," "to prepare,"* and *"provide."*

[282] σκηνή → It means *"tent," "booth," "The Tent of Testimony," "Tabernacle,"* and generally *"dwelling."*

[283] λαός → It means *"a people," "a nation," "a group," "a tribe," "a great part of the population,"* and *"all those who are of the same stock and language."*

[284] σκηνόω → It means *"live,"* and *"dwell."* (The verb form of a term, *"tabernacle/dwlling."*)

[285] λαοὶ → It is a *"noun nominative masculine plural common form from λαός."* Thus it means *"peoples."*

for the old order of things has passed away."	anymore, because the former things have passed away."
⁵ He who was seated on the throne said, "I am making everything new!" Then he said, "Write this down, for these words are trustworthy and true."	⁵ Then the one seated on the throne said, "Indeed, I make all things new," and he said, "Write, for these words are trustworthy and true." ⁶ God also said to me, "It is done! I am the Alpha and the Omega, the beginning and the end. To the thirsty I will give freely from the spring of living water. ⁷ The one who conquers will inherit these things, and I will be that person's God and that person will be my child. ⁸ But as for the cowardly, the faithless, the **vile**,²⁸⁶ the murderers, the fornicators, the sorcerers, the idolaters, and all the **liars**²⁸⁷, their portion is in the lake that burns with fire and sulfur, that is, the second death."
⁶ He said to me: "It is done. I am the Alpha and the Omega, the Beginning and the End. To the thirsty I will give water without cost from the spring of the water of life. ⁷ Those who are victorious will inherit all this, and I will be their God and they will be my children. ⁸ But the cowardly, the unbelieving, the vile, the murderers, the sexually immoral, those who practice magic arts, the idolaters and all liars— they will be consigned to the fiery lake of burning sulfur. This is the second death."	

John shows the future of an eschatological relationship with God – pictured as a new Jerusalem – and what that

---

²⁸⁶ βδελύσσω → It means "*to render foul*," "*abhor*," "*abominable*," and "*to detest.*"
²⁸⁷ ψευδής → It means "*lying*," "*deceitful*," and "*false.*"

relationship requires so that people can act now in ways that will enable them to participate in such a relationship then. Revelation 21:1-8 divides naturally into two sections, each headlined by the voice of a divine speaker. In vv. 1-4 an unidentified voice from the heavenly throne announces God's new creation as a place devoid of pain and suffering and the tears they cause. In vv. 5-8 God then confirms the truth of that vision and distinguishes those who will participate in it from those who surely will not.

- **1** Though this is a new vision, its logic flows through events that have occurred from 19:11 forward; the combat victories secured through the deployment of God's word (cf. 19:13, 15) lead appropriately here. John makes this point structurally by introducing the section with the familiar *"then I saw,"* which he uses to launch new scenes in an ongoing narration (cf. 5:1; 19:11, 17, 19; 20:1, 4, 11, 12). According to 20:11, a vacuum of sorts has opened up in the cosmos. The fleeing (i.e., destruction) of heaven and earth before the oncoming presence of God created a void, which God now fills by establishing a new heaven and a new earth. Both Jewish and Christian traditions guide John as he develops his imagery now. In Isaiah, God promises the creation of a new heaven and new earth for an Israel whose hopes for a life of promise in the old earth have been dashed through the tragedy of Babylonian exile (Isa. 65:17; 66:22). *First Enoch* 91:16 offers a Jewish apocalyptic example of the same expectation (cf. *1 En.* 45:4; 72:1; *Sib. Or.* 5.212). In 2 Pet. 3:13 the author counsels weary Christ-believers to maintain their hope for a new heaven and new earth, where righteousness will reign. Paul speaks less specifically about believers as new creations in Christ at 2 Cor. 5:17 and Gal. 6:15.

John's intended creation, though new, will not be completely discontinuous from the one that went before. When God declares at Rev. 21:5 that God will make all things new, it is important to note precisely what the language intends. God is taking what is old and transforming it. Out of the destruction that occurs in the various plagues and battles for creation, God will weave God's new thing. The old will remain a constituent part of the new, but it will be fiercely transfigured. Boring is therefore right to say, *"God does not make 'all new things,' but 'all things new'"* (*Revelation*, 220). Beale appropriately directs readers to Paul's discussion of the spiritual body, which is a transfigured *"new"* thing established upon the image and no doubt the foundation of the *"old"* physical body (1 Cor. 15): *"Despite the discontinuities, the new cosmos will be an identifiable counterpart to the old cosmos and a renewal of it, just as the body will be raised without losing its former identity"* (1040). To be sure, the resurrected body is a totally new and completely unique entity, yet it cannot be comprehended apart from a knowledge of what *"body-ness"* is. That comprehension finds its locus in none other than the physical body that must die so that the spiritual body might be resurrected. So, too, from the remains of the old heaven and old earth, a new heaven and a new earth, new bodily entities, are resurrected. Corporeal, they house a new city and the resurrected spiritual bodies that will now occupy it (souls; see the comment on 20:4).

It is important to note that John values the physical earth in a way that must not be dismissed. Too eagerly, contemporary Christians profess, proclaim, and anticipate a heavenly salvation so spiritual that its ethereal existence completely separates resurrected believers from the earth and the evil its physicality allegedly signifies. John's vision, by contrast, redeems the earth as a part of God's good creation and as the locus of God's grand re-creation. A witness for God and the Standing Slaughtered Lamb works with God to transform the world (cf. Rev. 12:11).

What is destroyed completely and irrevocably is the sea. Unlike even the archenemy dragon, the beasts from the sea and land, Death and Hades, all of whom writhe eternally in the lake of fire and sulfur (brimstone), the sea ceases to exist altogether. Perhaps this is appropriate since the sea symbolizes for John, as it did for Jewish and contemporaneous Christian literature, the chaotic source of defiance to God's sovereignty (cf. Rev. 4:6-8a). According to Paul, Death was the last enemy (1 Cor. 15:26). According to John's presentation here, if that statement is correct, it is correct for humans, not for God. For God, the last enemy is the one that acts as source for every other enemy. It is therefore appropriate that its demise is announced at the very moment when God's final stage in the reclamation of heaven and earth reaches its climax. In a powerful re-creation and escalation of the Genesis endeavor, God does not tame the sea by imposing land upon it; God orders the new cosmos by completely removing it.

- **2** John breaks up his *"then I saw"* opening by inserting the object of his vision between the words. Following his sighting of the new heaven and new earth, apparently focusing more sharply this time, he locks in on a single city, the holy – and also new – Jerusalem. He will return to this initial viewing in another context at 21:10, where the counter-comparison with the harlotrous city Babylon (17:1-19:10) begins (21:9-22:9). In this text, instead of using Jerusalem as a point of comparison with its narrative negative, he introduces it as the new place of living for the resurrected followers of God and the Standing Slaughtered Lamb. In so doing, he highlights three of its key attributes: holy, new, and urban.

Isaiah calls Jerusalem the holy city in a context that, like this Johannine one, speaks of the beautiful garments that symbolically adorn it (Isa. 48:2; 52:1). Many other voices, both Jewish (Neh. 11:1, 18) and early Christian (Matt. 4:5) envision the municipality as a holy place. Holiness as an attribute of God, and by extension an attribute of the things and people of God, denotes radical otherness. John calls the witness *"holy ones"* or *"saints"* throughout the *"Apokalypsis"* because through their faithful witness they are set apart from others who either promote the lordship of Rome or accommodate themselves to it (cf. Rev. 5:8). To be a saint, therefore, is not to be better than others in an ethical or moral sense, but to be separated from them because of one's relationship with and activity for the holy God. In this sense holiness is an acquired trait for everyone and everything except God; it is acquired through relationship with God. As John will note, this city descends, and thus takes its characterization, from God.

Once again working from Isaiah's lead, John describes this holy city as new. As Beale observes, "*Isa. 62:1-2 refers to 'Jerusalem' as that which 'will be called by a new name' at the time of its end-time glorification. This new name is then explained in Isa. 62:3-5 as signifying a new, intimate marriage relationship that Israel will have with God*" (1040).

The new holy city, finally, a city. John signals a salvific identify that is neither individualized nor spiritualized but concretized in the communal relationships that exist in an urban environment. John's view of eschatological relationship with God is not some tranquil, idyllic, one-on-one encounter in a sanctuary of eternal solitude, cloistered away from the hustling, bustling interaction with others that is so much a part of civic life on the old and apparently the new earth. Eschatological living is envisioned instead as a complex, other-connected and no doubt other-oriented relationship that brings with it all of the social and political ramifications that life in any city engenders. John's view of the future is that the believing community will find its ultimate meaning and life in urban rapport. For many contemporary Christians, this part of his vision is as scary as the segments that deal with the dragon and the plaques. Cities are inclusive, teeming, often dangerous and riotous places, where resources can be stretched to the breaking point and success – indeed, even survival – comes only when citizens work interdependently, negotiate strenuously, and compromise sincerely. Knowing all this, John believes that the city represents the most appropriate "*heaven*" metaphor available to him.

The seer maintains his municipal focus when he next describes the new Jerusalem as coming down out of heaven from God. This descent makes three points. First, the language of descent images judgment (cf. Rev. 10:1). This scene, though, is a post-judgment scene. The imagery still fits because, for John, the reverse side of judgment has always been salvation. The two exist together. A person's or people's life choices determine whether these eschatological acts are received as judgment or salvation. Since those who will witness this descent are people whose names are written in the Lamb's Book of Life (Rev. 20:15), it makes sense that the event would be experienced now as salvific. Second, the city's descent establishes the relationship with God that authorizes it and marks it as holy. Third, it is the fact that the city descends from the heavens onto the earth that establishes it as historical and this-worldly. Again it must be said, there is no rapture in the Book of Revelation (Rev. 3:10; 19:11). Instead of believers being raptured up into the heavens, the city of God is lowered down onto the transformed earth. The ratification of the earth as a place of God's engagement and not a place from which to escape cannot be imaged in any stronger terms. Working for the transformation of the earth is important because the transformed earth is where God works even now to establish God's holy city and thus God's eschatological relationship with God's people.

God's eschatological relationship with God's people is so close that John once again resorts to the marriage metaphor to describe it (Rev. 19:7-8; 21:9; Gal. 4:26; Heb. 11:16). The city, which is more a people than a place, is envisioned as a bride betrothed to the Lamb. John's use of the word "νύμφη" (bride) in 21:9 and 22:17 represents the only occurrence of the word in early Christian literature. At 19:7-8 the more neutral and common tern "γυνή" (woman, wife) contextually calls for the translation "*wife*." Once again, John works from Isaianic roots; in describing the holy city, Isa. 52:1 describes the beautiful garments that adorn it, and more particularly, Isa. 61:10 speaks of God clothing Zion with garments of salvation as a bride and groom adorn themselves. The emphasis in the Book of Revelation on their bridal identity as a people develops explicitly from this language of the bride's preparation. As was explained already at 19:7-8, the dress that adorns the bride is made from the fabric of witnessing to the lordship of God and the Standing Slaughtered Lamb. The people are adorned by their own triumphant witnessing! The passive formulation of the verb "ἑτοιμάζω" (prepare) reminds them, however, of a critical fact. God has given them the ability of witnessing; what they have achieved comes from God.

There is obviously a bit of symbol confusion here. If the city is the people of God, one has to wonder how the people of God can also live there. Such questions of logic mute the visionary effect that John is trying to build. Operating as he is in a dreamlike world, literal concerns like this one raise questions that the narrative does not intend to answer. What is important for John is the rhetorical effect delivered both when the city is envisioned as a place for the people of God and then when it is envisioned as the people themselves. Each image develops, rather than detracts from, the other. Interpreters reading with rather than against John will interpret each image on its own and allow them together to work as John intends.

- **3** The vision turns to audition with a great voice that speaks from the throne. The great voice – previously experienced by those in opposition to God – has usually signaled judgment activity (cf. 7:2). Now, in these post-judgment times, it signals the salvation that is and has always been an accompanying feature of God's eschatological activity. When the voice emanates from the throne, it appears that the speaker is God. It is unlikely, though, that God would refer to Godself in the third person. This hunch is validated when God finally speaks and does so using the self-referential first-person singular (v. 5).

The throne voice declares that in this new city on the new earth, God will "*tabernacle*," that is, "*pitch God's tent*," directly with God's people. In both the nominal (tent, tabernacle) and verbal ("*to dwell*," "*to tabernacle*" cf. John 1:14) forms, the language recalls

God's residing with Israel during its post-exodus, wilderness wandering. This is the eschatological exodus. The people have left persecution behind and exist now in direct proximity to the ultimate promise, God's presence. John has already prepared the reader for this imagery with his description of the people of God huddled as an encampment (Rev. 20:9). Now God camps with the people in the new environment, where every threat has been removed.

Proximity to God implies relationship with God. John makes that relationship explicit with the clarifying words with which he finishes the verse. Appealing to numerous Old Testament witnesses (Lev. 26:11-12; Ps. 95:7; Ezek. 37:27; Jer. 31:1, 33; Zech. 2:11), the throne voice declares that God will be their God and they will be God's people. This is covenant language. Interestingly, where the Old Testament covenant citations emphasized a single people, no doubt Israel, the throne voice turns the singular "λαός" (people) into the plural "λαοί" (peoples). The subtle shift in grammar signals a powerful shift in theology. What was particular has become universal, the nations – all peoples – will be available for participation in this eschatological covenant relationship. God will be God to all.

- **4** The results of God's direct relationship with the *"peoples"* will be staggering. First, God will wipe away every tear from their eyes. The cause of tears – mourning, crying, pain, even death itself (Rev. 20:14) – will be removed. This is the promise long ago foreseen by the prophets (Isa. 25:8; 35:10; 65:19; Jer. 31:16). It is the promise prefigured in Rev. 7:17 as it introduced the springs of the water of life, which God will also address in this context (Rev. 21:6). Life-giving water washes away tears. This is because, second, in the time of this life-giving water, the first, or former, things have passed away. John makes an explicit verbal connection back to 21:1, framing the resulting subsection with this critical eschatological theme. Presumably the first (former) heaven and earth were permeated with these tear inducers. When they went away, they took all of their hostilities with them.

- **5** For only the second time in the entire Book of Revelation (cf. 1:8), God speaks. This fact alone separates this passage from the ones that surround it; vv. 5-8 form a subunit of the larger section (vv. 1-8). God personally confirms what was said about the new creation in vv. 1-4 and identifies Godself as the executor of it. Just in case there might be any confusion (i.e., with Rome), God declares that God is the one who does all this. Echoing Isa. 43:19 (cf. Isa. 66:22), God is specific: "*I make all things new.*" This general promise, though given in the present tense, is surely about the future; the specific promises that follow occur in the future tense ("*I will give*," v. 6; "*I will be*," v. 7). Additionally, the need that God apparently feels to certify that what has been foreseen will indeed occur is an indication that it has not yet occurred. When God commands the prophet to write that these words are faithful (i.e., trustworthy) and true, God intends that the seer offer God's honor as collateral for trusting in the veracity of God's promises. God's peoples can bank on the fact that the newness that has just now been promised in God's name, and indeed in God's own words, will come true. So assured of such a future that they can converse about it in the present tense, peoples will be encouraged either to maintain or to initiate a life of appropriate witnessing, in order that they can participate positively in the future that God has promised.

- **6** Having certified the validity of God's own promise, God declares, "*It is done!*" Here God echoes the statement of the seventh bowl angel, who declared with his actions that God's judgment is finished (Rev. 15:1; 16:17; John 19:30). Oddly, though, this time God chooses a plural verb, therefore literally saying, "*They are done.*" Perhaps the change in number is a signal not just that the judgment component of God's eschatological activity has concluded but also that both partnered aspects, judgment and salvation, have in this visionary moment come to an end. Even the time of salvation will be finished when the new heaven and new earth welcome the new Jerusalem. "*They*" are all done. All that is left is for those who have witnessed to the lordship of God and the Standing Slaughtered Lamb to reap the promised reward.

Once again, as in the previous verse, having made a provocative, sweeping claim, God finds it necessary to certify that God has the right to make it. God does so this time by appealing back to the first and only other place in the Book of Revelation where God clearly speaks (cf. 1:8). There as here, God certifies the promise of Christ's imminent return by appealing to God's identity with the declaration: "*I am the Alpha and the Omega*" (cf. 1:17; 22:13, where Christ, in building full identity with God, identifies himself in the same way). God concludes the statement somewhat redundantly, corroborating the claims made with the first and last letters of the Greek alphabet by means of the functionally synonymous terms, beginning (alpha) and end (omega). Yet God speaks about time, not about the Greek alphabet. God is the first and the last in terms of history (Isa. 41:4; 44:6; 48:12). God is the first of all things and thus before all things, and is also the last of all things and thus after all things. As the only one who exists before and after history, who rules over time because God is at the beginning and end of time, God knows when the time, concerns, and objectives that drive history have come to their conclusion. When the one who is before and after all things says that all things are finished, you can believe it.

John's hearers and readers can also believe in God's specific promises about the circumstances that surround this new eschatological reality. First, God reiterates the promise made to the multitude of bloodied witnesses who throng the heavenly throne in 7:9-17, anticipating the promise that will be made to all at 22:17. These are the people who thirst for vindication (7:16) and eschatological relationship with God. To all of them, God offers the gift of the spring of living water (7:17; 22:17). While the phrase "ὕδατος τῆς ζωῆς" (water of life) can be translated either "*flowing water*" or "*living water*," the latter translation, given the context, is to be preferred. John is not speaking literally about the movement of the water but about its efficacy. This is a vision of eternal life-giving relationship, which was also imaged by the prophets as a great eschatological thirst-quenching experience (Isa. 49:10; 55:1; Jer. 2:13; Zech. 14:8). The Gospel of John foresees Jesus as the conduit for this eternal, life-giving water (John 7:37; *Odes Sol.* 30.1-2). In the "*Apokalypsis*," John connects this spring of life-giving water to the Eden-like river whose water of life runs through the heart of the new Jerusalem (Rev. 22:1).

- 7 God's second promise is delivered directly to the very same group that Christ targeted in each of the letters to the seven churches. In encouraging believers to maintain their witness to the lordship of God and the Standing Slaughtered Lamb and to resist accommodating to the lordship designs of the imperial Roman cult, Christ addressed believers in the present with a term that describes their future designation if they remain faithful: the one who conquers (Rev. 2:7, 11, 17, 26; 3:5, 12, 21; 5:5). Eschatological benefits were promised to those who have conquered with the hope that anticipated future reward would encourage present witness. Now it is God's turn to address the potential conqueror. God, too, points to the future as an inducement for appropriate witnessing behavior in the present. The one who conquers will inherit "*these things*," which in this context refers back to all of the eschatological benefits thus far associated with life in the new Jerusalem (vv. 3, 4, 5, 6).

The language of inheritance builds from the foundation of 2 Sam. 7:14 (cf. Ezek. 11:20; Zech. 8:8) and prepares the way for a third promise, which echoes the throne voice's declaration that God will tabernacle directly with the peoples (Rev. 21:3). God amplifies that earlier statement by declaring that any who conquer through their witness will be to God as sons and daughters. The resulting familial bond derives from the promise that God, through the prophet Nathan, made to David about the king's son Solomon. By covenant agreement, established through David's lineage, God would assume the role of Solomon's father, thus adopting him and bringing him into protective relationship. God expands the promise of such relationship, giving it an eschatological horizon and extending it to everyone; now it is not lineage but witnessing that matters.

- **8** A vice list (cf. Rom. 1:29-31; 1 Cor. 5:9-11; 6:9-10; Gal. 5:19-21; Eph. 5:5; Titus 1:10, 16) follows, detailing those who will never receive the label *"one who conquers."* The list, which reminds hearers and readers of the one compiled at Rev. 9:21 and anticipates another compiled at 22:15 (cf. 21:27), is specifically designed around the witnessing ethic that has driven John's apocalyptic work. Given John's dramatic call for courageous testimony to the lordship of God and the Standing Slaughtered Lamb despite the drastic consequences that such witnessing will bring, it is understandable that he headlines the list of vices with cowardice. Cowards are the ultimate accommodationists; for fear of losing social standing, economic wealth, physical well-being, and perhaps even life, they surrender their witness to God's lordship and testify to the lordship of Caesar and Rome instead. The faithless similarly have insufficient belief in the power of God to vindicate them and so cannot endure the hardships that Rome presses upon them. Idolaters and those who commit abominations are surely those who accommodate by eating the meat sacrificed to idols and thus find themselves participating in idol worship in an effort to fit in with the Roman economic and political infrastructure (Rev. 17:4-5). Murderers are those who kill the witnesses in an effort to prosecute the draconian program of the beast from the sea (6:9-11; 13:15; 20:4). Fornication is a metaphor for those who idolatrously find themselves in the worship of the imperial cult when they know their singular cultic loyalty belongs to God and Christ (Rev. 2:14, 20-22). Sorcerers are those who deceive others into following the forces of the dragon and the beast (18:23). Those who lie, perhaps mostly to themselves, proclaim a faith that their actions do not support (cf. 1 John 1:6). Like Jezebel and Balaam, while claiming to be believers, they participate in activities that endorse the lordship of Rome instead. These are the ones who are bound for the lake of fire and brimstone, which is the second death.

Though the verbs here are in the indicative mood, John is actually issuing a vigorous appeal in the imperative mode. This is a prophetic and not a predictive vision. The seer is not describing who is already in the new Jerusalem; instead, he is using a list of the kinds of people who will never enter the eschatological city in the future in order to encourage appropriate behavior by "*peoples*" in the present.

Revelation 21:9~27 → The New Jerusalem

NIV	TT
⁹ One of the seven angels who had the seven bowls full of the seven last plagues came and said to me, "Come, I will show you the bride, the wife of the Lamb." ¹⁰ And he carried me away in the Spirit to a mountain great and high, and showed me the Holy City, Jerusalem, coming down out of heaven from God. ¹¹ It shone with the glory of God, and its brilliance was like that of a very precious jewel, like a jasper, clear as crystal. ¹² It had a great, high wall with twelve gates, and with twelve angels at the gates. On the gates were written the names of the twelve tribes of Israel. ¹³ There were three gates on the east, three on the north, three on the south and three on the west. ¹⁴ The wall of the city had twelve foundations, and on	⁹ Then one of the seven angels with the seven bowls full of the seven last plagues came and spoke with me, saying, "Come, I will show you the **bride**,[288] the **wife**[289] of the Lamb." ¹⁰ And he carried me in the spirit to a great and high mountain, and he showed me the holy city Jerusalem descending out of heaven from God ¹¹ with the glory of God. Its radiance is like a precious stone, like jasper, clear as crystal. ¹² It has a great and high wall, with twelve gates. On the gates are twelve angels, and on the gates are inscribed the names of the twelve tribes of the children of Israel. ¹³ There are three gates on the east, three gates on the north, three gates on the south, and three gates on the west. ¹⁴ The wall of the city

---

[288] νύμφη → It means "*a betrothed woman,*" "*a bride,*" "*a daughter-in-law,*" and "*a recently married woman.*"
[289] γυνή → It means "*a woman,*" "*a widow,*" "*a wife,*" and "*a virgin.*"

them were the names of the twelve apostles of the Lamb.

¹⁵ The angel who talked with me had a measuring rod of gold to measure the city, its gates and its walls. ¹⁶ The city was laid out like a square, as long as it was wide. He measured the city with the rod and found it to be 12,000 stadia in length, and as wide and high as it is long. ¹⁷ The angel measured the wall using human measurement, and it was 144 cubits thick. ¹⁸ The wall was made of jasper, and the city of pure gold, as pure as glass. ¹⁹ The foundations of the city walls were decorated with every kind of precious stone. The first foundation was jasper, the second sapphire, the third agate, the fourth emerald, ²⁰ the fifth onyx, the sixth ruby, the seventh chrysolite, the eighth beryl, the ninth topaz, the tenth turquoise, the eleventh jacinth, and the

also has twelve foundations, and on them are the twelve names of the twelve apostles of the Lamb.

¹⁵ And the one who spoke with me had a golden measuring rod to measure the city and its gates and its wall. ¹⁶ The city has four equal sides, that is, its length is the same as its width. He measured the city with the rod, at 12,000 **stadia**;²⁹⁰ the length and the width and the height of it are the same. ¹⁷ He also measured its wall, 144 cubits, the measure of a human, that is, an angel. ¹⁸ And the foundation of its wall is jasper, while the city is pure gold, like clear glass. ¹⁹ The foundations of the wall of the city are **adorned**²⁹¹ with every precious stone. The first foundation is jasper; the second, sapphire; the third, agate; the fourth, emerald; ²⁰ the fifth, onyx; the sixth,

---

²⁹⁰ στάδιον → It means "*stade*" (as a measure of distance = about 192 meters/630 feet), "*arena*," and "*stadium.*"
²⁹¹ κοσμέω → It means "*put in order*," "*adorn*," "*decorate*," "*make beautiful*," and "*make attractive.*"

twelfth amethyst. ²¹ The twelve gates were twelve pearls, each gate made of a single pearl. The great street of the city was of gold, as pure as transparent glass. ²² I did not see a temple in the city, because the Lord God Almighty and the Lamb are its temple. ²³ The city does not need the sun or the moon to shine on it, for the glory of God gives it light, and the Lamb is its lamp. ²⁴ The nations will walk by its light, and the kings of the earth will bring their splendor into it. ²⁵ On no day will its gates ever be shut, for there will be no night there. ²⁶ The glory and honor of the nations will be brought into it. ²⁷ Nothing impure will ever enter it, nor will anyone who does what is shameful or deceitful, but only those whose names are written in the Lamb's book of life.	carnelian; the seventh, chrysolite; the eighth, beryl; the ninth, topaz; the tenth, chrysoprase; the eleventh, jacinth; the twelfth, amethyst. ²¹ And the twelve gates are twelve pearls; each one of the gates is made out of a single pearl. The street of the city is pure gold, like transparent crystal. ²² I did not see a temple in the city, for the Lord God, the Almighty, and the Lamb are its temple. ²³ And the city does not need the sun or the moon to illumine it, for the glory of God illumines it, and its lamp is the Lamb. ²⁴ The nations will walk by its light, and kings of the earth will bring their glory into it. ²⁵ Its gates will never shut by day, for there will be no night there. ²⁶ They will bring the glory and the honor of the nations into it. ²⁷ But nothing **unclean**²⁹² will enter it, and no one

---

²⁹² κοινός → It means "*communal*," "*common*," "*ordinary*," "*ceremonially unclean*," and "*impure*."

	who practices abomination and falsehood, but only those who are written in the Lamb's Book of Life.

Verse 9 begins a new section, which characterizes the new Jerusalem as a bride. It parallels 17:1-19:10, which depicted Babylon/Rome as a whore. In John's dualistic framework, these are the only two options for responding to the claims of God's cosmic sovereignty. While the whore symbolizes rejection, the bride represents an acceptance so intimate that a marital relationship is the metaphor best suited to describe it.

- 9 The parallel with the account centering on the judgment of Babylon/Rome (17:1-19:10) begins immediately with John's identification of the principal interlocutor, one of the seven angels with the seven bowls filled with the plagues of God's wrath. Another of those angels previously ushered the seer through his visions of the whore. John does not say whether this is the same angel as the one who appeared at 17:1. In the end, it does not matter; the angel's identity (or angels' identities) is less important than his function: to introduce the key visionary object. The angel's appearance here may seem less appropriate than it did at the beginning of chapter 17. After all, it makes narrative sense to have one of the angels who poured out a bowl of God's judgment wrath upon the earth anchor the vision about the judgment/destruction of Babylon/Rome. This text, though, discloses the city that symbolizes salvation. Yet an angel connected with the bowl plagues is appropriate because John is working here with the backside of the judgment/salvation partnership. Theologically speaking, the judgment of Babylon/Rome is the realization of the salvific city that is the new Jerusalem. Figuratively, they happen together; they are the same climactic moment because they are different sides of the same apocalyptic act. Structurally, John makes this point by positioning the two texts in this obviously parallel fashion.

Following the grammatical presentation in 17:1 exactly, John confides that the angel spoke to him the following words: *"Come, I will show you..."* The objects seen certainly are dramatically different. The two rhetorical women represent competing social, cultic, economic, and political lures on the affections of humankind. Humans, though drawn to both, can be intimate with only one. Relationship with one is mutually exclusive of relationship with the other.

At the time of John's writing, both these options are live. Only in the promised and envisioned future will Babylon/Rome be removed from the theological and ethical equation. In John's real time, a decision must be made. His view of how the future will look is meant to encourage readers and hearers to choose appropriately in favor of the woman he is preparing now to introduce.

At this point the content of the two parallel verses, 17:1 and 21:9, differs: 17:1 goes on to talk about the judgment of the whore, while 21:9 points not to judgment but to bridal existence with the Lamb. In both verses the condition of the woman is presented before the woman herself is identified. In chapter 21 the emotional content is one of joy.

The bridal language also calls to mind John's earlier mentions of the marriage of the Lamb to the bridal city (19:7-8; 21:2). Though different vocabulary is used ("γυνή," woman or wife, in 19:7-8; "νύμφη" bride, in 21:2; 22:17), the point is the same. The city, representing the faithful witnesses as a corporate entity, will enjoy so intimate a relationship with the Lamb that they shall be to God like a child (cf. 21:7).

- **10** John's foundation in Ezekiel's postexilic visions of restoration becomes unmistakably evident at this point, even as the seer continues to flesh out the counter-parallel with his own Babylon/Rome vision (17:1-19:10). Just as the angel in 17:3 carried John away in the Spirit, so the angel here spirits John off so he can view a sharper image of the specified city. As at 17:3, and elsewhere in John's narration, movement in the Spirit is not a metaphor for escapist enthusiasm. It signals instead a prophetic inspiration that conveys information useful for making appropriate discipleship decisions (cf. 4:2-3). This prophetic emphasis is confirmed by the fact that John is clearly channeling Ezekiel; John's vision will serve as a prophetic reinterpretation. At Ezek. 40:1-2 the Old Testament prophet is transported in the Spirit (Ezek. 43:5) to a high mountain, where he sees the structure of a city that he understands to be the eschatological temple. Whereas in Rev. 17:3 John was transported into the wilderness, a location that symbolized darkness, danger, and judgment, this time, like Ezekiel, he winds up on a mountaintop, where he too will soon see a city. As a location that signifies the establishment or consummation of communion with God (Gen. 22:1-14; Exod. 3:1, 12; Ezek. 40:2; Mark 9:2; Matt. 5:1; 17:1-2; Luke 9:28-29), the mountain is an appropriate setting for everything that follows.

The city John sees is the holy city, the new Jerusalem, which was already introduced as descending from heaven (Rev. 21:2). Building from that introductory mention, John now describes the realization of that descent in detail.

- **11** The city is possessed by the glory of God. According to 21:23, this glory is so radiant that it lights the entire municipality. No doubt John has Isaiah's prophecies in mind as he records his own. Isaiah associates the glory of God with the light of the people (Isa. 58:8). Isaiah 60:1-2 then reiterates that God's glory shall be the people's light. It is, though, upon Ezekiel that John is most firmly grounded. Just before describing the vision of the eschatological city and its measurement, Ezekiel declares that the glory of God shines across the earth (Ezek. 43:2). John's depiction of God's radiance also serves as a prelude to the coming narration of the city and its measurements. Indeed, John's eschatological city radiates God's glory so fiercely that it appears to shine with the dazzling sparkle of crystalline jasper. This image takes hearers and readers back to John's initial description of the heavenly throne room, where the seer also described God's glory as glistening jasper (cf. 4:2-3). Other characters are briefly connected to glory (the Lamb,

5:12-13; an angel, 18:1; the kings of the earth, 21:24; nations, 21:6), yet glory is primarily an attribute of God (1:6; 4:9, 11; 7:12; 11:13; 14:7; 15:8; 16:9; 19:1, 7; 21:11, 23). John drafts a political statement by making sure not to ascribe this quality to the entity most Greco-Romans would have associated it with: imperial – and by any human standard, glorious – Rome. Rome has tried to play the role of lord of human history and, in doing so, has usurped the symbolism of the precious stones (17:4; 18:12, 16). John's point, though, is that Babylon/Rome has hoarded the currency of fool's gold. The dull recognition it has amassed through its military and economic might is nothing compared to the scintillating glory whose realization in God is so palpable that it dazzles with the awe-inspiring allure of a truly precious gem. This jasper, like the gold that John will describe later (21:8), is nothing like the rocks stockpiled in Babylon/Rome's vaults; devoid of all impurities, it is as clear as glass. Like the eschatological jewels, the glory they represent is unlike anything the world has ever seen.

- **12 – 13** In Ezekiel's vision, the city-like structure that sits atop the mountain is the eschatological temple, and it is surrounded by a wall (Ezek. 40:5). He next narrates the measurements and description of that wall. John, too, starts with a description of the wall that surrounds his eschatological city. Walls represented a city's security. It was natural that a wall would be the first attribute of the city to be described. It would be seen and encountered first by any visitor or returning city resident. This particular wall would no doubt provide ample security since John describes it as great and high.

Two difficulties immediately arise from this presentation. First, since all God's enemies and the enemies of God's people have been destroyed (cf. Rev. 20:15), one wonders why there would be any need for a wall. Not operating literally, John works form and for the imagination of his hearers and readers. He is trying to convey a transcendent reality for which neither he nor they have the proper words or concepts to comprehend. They have never seen an eschatological relationship with God and have no grounds upon which to fashion its look and feel. To help them conceive of it, John offers an image that is familiar to them: a great city. Great cities had great walls. To draw up the greatest city of all without walls for a marginalized people who yearned for a secure future would have been detrimental to John's narrative agenda. Its lack of realism and therefore the improbability of its claim to open up access to real vindication, peace, and security would have been problematic. John sidesteps that problem by imagining the great and secure city in the way that he knows his audience would have imagined it. He keeps the wall but transfigures it for his own unique visionary purposes. The second problem with the wall for a literally minded reader is its size. At 144 cubits, it is woefully short, given the height of the city itself. Once again, John is operating figuratively. The wall is representational and exists for symbolic purposes alone. It does not have to provide any actual security since God has already provided for that by conquering all

God's enemies in the apocalyptic conflicts that have just taken place. John is merely using the wall to fulfill the expectations that his hearers and readers would have had for one. Its height is a multiple of 12 (12 times 12 = 144), which denotes completion and wholeness (cf. 7:4). Despite the actual (literal) dimensions, the wall represents the complete and total (figurative) security that God's apocalyptic acts have already produced.

Just before the close of his work, the prophet Ezekiel describes the wall that surrounds his city (Ezek. 48:30-35). Moving clockwise through the compass points (North, east, south, west), he offers the dimensions and description of each side. Each wall measures 4,500 cubits, producing a square. Carved into each wall are three gates. On each gate is inscribed the name of one of the Israelite tribes. Though John saves the dimensions of his squared city for later (Rev. 21:16), he follows Ezekiel's description of the gates in the four city walls. Moving more haphazardly (east, north, south, west), he too notes that three gates are carved into each wall, and that on each gate the name of one of the twelve Israelite tribes is inscribed. Once again, the number *"twelve"* signifies wholeness and completion. There are sufficient gates for all who need to enter. The number *"twelve,"* as related to the tribes, also suggests that the foundation of God's people of faith, the whole of Israel, is accounted for in the eschatological city. The restoration for which Israel has longed will be accomplished.

Perhaps drawing from Isa. 62:6, where God positions sentinels on the walls of Zion, John posts a guardian angel at each of the city's twelve gates (There are no angels at the gates in Ezekiel's vision.) Since all God's enemies and the enemies of God's people no longer exist, a literal reader might wonder why guards would be needed for the eschatological city. Again, John is working imaginatively from the baseline expectations of his hearers and readers. Sentries are symbolic representations of a city's security. John graphically emphasizes this city's complete protection by retaining the metaphor. He is working for dramatic effect, not logical consistency. The visualization of angels standing guard at the city gates would have driven home the point that this city was designed and secured by God.

- **14** John adds to Ezekiel's description with the notation that the 12-gated wall also has 12 foundations. The seer is updating the prophet for a particular reason, if the complete restoration and inclusion of the Israelite tribes is symbolized by the 12 gates, the complete inclusion of all believing Gentiles is symbolized by these 12 foundations. Noticing that each foundation stone had inscribed on it the name of one of ht Lamb's 12 apostles, John follows early Christian tradition, which maintained that the eschatological city had a foundation of apostles and prophets conceived by God (Eph. 2:20; Heb. 11:10), with Christ as its cornerstone. The image of a city wall with Jesus' 12 apostles as foundation signifies the incorporation of the believing church into this eschatological city. The combination of the 12 tribes and the 12 apostles makes this single, critical point: the new city is founded upon and therefore open to all God's people, Jew and Gentile alike. John has used the resulting total of 24 before to express symbolically this message of inclusiveness. The 24 elders in 4:3-4 represent a similar combination of 12 and 12 that anticipates the link between Israel and the apostles here. Notably, too, in both this section and the earlier one, God's glory, symbolized by jasper, is on radiant display. John evidently joins the manifestation of God's glory, at least in part, to the universal makeup of God's eschatological community.

- **15** John confides further that the angel of v. 9, like the *"man"* of Ezek. 40:3, 5, came equipped for his task (cf. Zech. 2:1-2). John, too, was previously given a rod (Rev. 11:1-2) and told to measure the inner court of the temple as a maneuver of protection. This angel holds a qualitatively different kind of rod, however, and his actions have a substantially different objective. Reflecting the precious gems that compose the city's glory and foundation, the angel's measuring rod is made of gold. Moreover, he will not use it to measure a temple within a city but the massive eschatological city itself. It is also unclear whether this measuring is an act of protection. In addition to the fact that there is nothing and no one from which to protect the city, the narration does not explain the act of measurement in this way as it did in 11: 1-2. The measuring here is no doubt instructive rather than protective. John wants his hearers and readers to get a sense not only of the city's massive size but also of its symbolic connection with the prophetic traditions that affirm God's glorious presence with the people. That connection will surface in the city's dimensions, which he is about to record. He will calibrate the city, the wall, and the gates, in that order.

- **16** Like Ezekiel's city-temple, John's city is a square (cf. Ezek. 48:16, 30-35); its length and width are equal. John's though, adds an important nuance. Like the holy of holies in the first temple, the place where Yahweh's presence was understood to reside (1 Kgs. 6:19-20; 2 Chr. 3:8), the new Jerusalem is also a cube; its height is equal to its length and width. The important number is 12,000. That is the scale, in the dimension of the Greek "στάδιον" (stadium), of the city's length, breadth, and height: while the "στάδιον" was in origin a Greek measure, it was used in early Judaism and early Christianity (LXX Dan. 4:12; *2 Macc.* 11:5; 12:9-10, 16-17, 29; Matt. 14:24; Luke 24:13; John 6:19; 11:18). The conversion of a "στάδιον" to approximately 200 yards yields a distance that the NRSV translates as 1,500 miles. While that figure gives a sense of the enormous scale of this vast municipality, I prefer a translation that maintains the more archaic 12,000 *stadia* and places the contemporary equivalent in a footnote. As hard as it is to imagine a "στάδιον," John's focus lies more on the symbolically charged number "*12*"; once again, as with the 144,000 of 7:1-8 and 14:1-5, the seer augments the wholeness of 1,000 with that of 12 (or a multiple of it) to suggest the enormity of God's inclusiveness. The city is so massive that an innumerable multitude of God's people may stream into it and therefore into eschatological relationship with God. Symbolically speaking, the city can handle them all!

- **17 – 18** The emphasis remains on the number "*12*" with the dimensions of the wall. Its height is 144 cubits. A cubit is generally taken as the distance between a man's elbow and the tip of his forefinger. This approximately 18-inch span, when multiplied 144 times, yields a wall (approximately 216 feet) that biblical commentators are correct to call puny alongside a city side that is 12,000 "στάδιον," (1,500 miles) high. While some commentators protest that the small dimensions refer to the wall's width, John has been focused on height all along, and ancient city walls were defined in terms of height rather than width. Therefore, John, too, has height in mind.[293] The seer is less interested in literal distance than he is in the symbolism of "*144*" (cf. 7:4). The wall represents the wholeness of God's secure provision and protection of the city.

Before he concludes the verse, John adds more confusion by the imprecise terminology he uses to describe the measurement. He says that it is the measurement of a human, which is of an angel. One would think that it would be either one or the other. John is working from and clarifying his source. Ezekiel's measuring interlocutor, upon whom John's angel is surely based, was described by the prophet as a "*human*." John, knowing that his hearers and readers would recognize the foundation of his own vision in

---

[293] → Aune, Beale and others argues that a 216-foot base would be ridiculously insufficient for a wall 1,500 miles high. Personally, I believe that it is better, instead, to focus on the symbolism rather than on the literal number.

Ezekiel's, uses this clumsy formulation to alert his readers to the fact that Ezekiel's *"human"* measurements were in reality those of an angel, too. Thus, the measurements of both cities are divinely calibrated. The measurements are therefore not only equally prophetic; they are also equally authoritative.

- **18 – 21** In describing the wall, John returns to the familiar theme of jasper. Already, in v. 11, he has likened the glory of God in the city to the radiance of this rare jewel. That same glory is symbolically embedded in the city's very architectural essence. A similar radiance glows from the entire city, whose components are so breathtakingly beautiful that the city shines with the stunning vibrancy of gold so pure that it is as clear as glass. It is not insignificant that Solomon overlaid his temple and the inner sanctuary, the places where God's presence was thought to reside, with what was no doubt a much lower grade of gold (1 Kgs. 6:20-22). Surely, in the eschaton, even the holy God would find a place crafted out of gold so pure as to be transparent as a worthy arena in which to establish relationship with God's people. Scanning lower, John sees that each of the twelve foundations of the wall is adorned with a precious stone. He is maintaining his focus on the city as a bride even though he has long since left the bride metaphor behind. At 21:2 he noted that the bride was adorned for her husband. He uses the same verb "κοσμέω" (adore, prepare) to describe the city's adornment here. These two verses are the only places where he deploys the verb, an indication that the connection drawn here is intentional. John is also working from traditional roots. Isaiah envisioned the walls and gates of the city fashioned out of precious stones (Isa. 54:11-12; *Tob.* 13:16). Moreover, Ezek. 28:13 prepares for the linkage between precious stones and a renewed Eden, with which the vision of the new Jerusalem will conclude in chapter 22. The listing of twelve foundational stones also recalls the description of the breast-piece to be made for the high priest's vestments (Exod. 28:15-21; 39:8-14).[294] The high priest, as representative of the people, particularly on the Day of Atonement, when he alone went into the cubical holy of holies to make amends for the people's sins, was to wear a breast-piece formed in a square (Exod. 28:16; 39:9), no doubt fashioned to resemble the footprint of the holy of holies. Noticeably, it also resembles the footprint of John's new Jerusalem. Twelve precious stones, arranged in four rows of three stones each, were to be placed on the breast-piece. Each stone was to have engraved upon it the name of one of the twelve Israelite tribes. John alters the presentation by engraving on each foundation the name of one of the twelve apostles instead (Rev. 21:14).

There is a translation question regarding whether v. 19 intends to say that the foundations were adorned

---

[294] →Beale helpfully notes that eight of the stones listed by John are the same as those found in the Exodus accounts, "*and the differently named stones in Revelation are semantic equivalents of the ones in Exodus.*" He further contends that John's different ordering of the stones is not evidence that the seer was not referring back to the Exodus materials "*since Josephus explicitly alludes to the jewels on the high priest's breastpiece in J.W. 5.5.7 and in Ant. 3.7.5 in two other different orders*" (1080). Since a similar description is found in both Josephus and Philo, it is clear that John is following a tradition of interpreting the stones of the breast-piece of the High Priest in this symbolic manner.

with multiple jewels or that each foundation was itself a precious stone. I interpret it in the latter way because of the clues from both the biblical tradition upon which John is drawing and the literary context in the Book of Revelation. The breast-piece of the high priest and Isa. 54:11-12 both suggest single jewels; the Isaiah text connected those single jewels directly to the walls and foundations. Additionally, 1 Kgs. 7:10 speaks of a temple whose foundations are composed of costly stones. Even more significantly, when John turns to describing the gates, he does not anticipate that they will be covered with pearls; instead, he foresees each of them as a gigantic pearl. The imagery suggests that he is thinking of massive precious stones throughout. In the case of the pearls, whose textual representation here is responsible for the *"pearly gates"* cliché, inscriptions bear the names, and thus signal the complete restoration, of the twelve Israelite tribes (Rev. 21:12).

- **22** This verse represents John's stirking departure from the Ezek. 40-48 source he has been developing. In Ezekiel's orienting vision, the city structure on the mountaintop was the eschatological temple intended to represent the restoration of the once-exiled people (cf. Ezek. 40:1-5; 43:1-5). Perhaps the temple's connection to the singular people of Israel was one of the reasons John has abandoned it in his more universal visionary perspective. With all *"peoples"* from every nation candidates for citizenship (Rev. 21:3, 24), perhaps the ethnic limitations attached to the Jerusalem temple were too constricting. Just as likely, perhaps even more so, John's vision is stressing that every intermediary between God and God's people, even one that has played as critical a role as the temple had played, would in this new eschatological moment become obsolete. In a reality where God pitches Godself directly in the midst of God's people (Rev. 21:30) and relates to them as a father does to a child (21:7), high priests, sanctuaries, and even the holy of holies are no longer necessary. All of this new city, fashioned as it would be from precious gems so crystalline pure as to be transparent, would now be God's holy place. Wherever the people, the children of God, would find themselves in this city would be holy ground. Anywhere and everywhere they would exist within the city, they could and would meet God. Children need not find an interlocutor to speak to their parent on their behalf when that parent is in direct proximity to them. Just so, John's people would in this new Jerusalem no longer need and therefore no longer have a temple. The Lord God Almighty and the Standing Slaughtered Lamb, operating together in divine concordance, would themselves serve that function. God would need no house in which to dwell, since God's glory would shroud the city like a fog (In Ezek. 43:5, God's glory engages the temple only.) God's presence is the very essence out of which this municipal edifice would be fashioned. God would be completely on the loose among God's people.

- **23** In what is essentially a doublet of 22:5, John declares that the effect of God's direct presence in and with the city will be pervasive. The glory of God and the Standing Slaughtered Lamb will have a tangible effect. It will become the power source that lights up the city by day and by night (cf. Isa. 60:1, 19-20; Ezek. 43:2; John 8:12; 1 John 1:5). Where John's prophetic sources spoke only of God's light, John adds the lamp provided by the Lamb in order to demonstrate, as he does in Rev. 21:22, that the Lamb's divinity operates with God's own, because in the end it is God's own. Whether the sun and moon will exist in the new heaven and new earth is irrelevant because as sources of light they will themselves become irrelevant (cf. Isa. 24:23). Even if they do exist, they will be overshadowed or, more appropriately said, outshone by the radiance of God and the Standing Slaughtered Lamb.

- **24 – 27** As John closes out the chapter, he depends as much on Isa. 60 as he has earlier in the chapter depended upon the restoration visions of Ezek. 40-48. The prophecy in Isa. 60 retains Ezekiel's utopian dreams: the postexilic Jerusalem. Like Isaiah, John maintains a universal focus. The nations, not just Israel, God's people will find direcdtion from the glorious light of God and the Standing Slaughtered Lamb that illuminates this city (Isa. 60:3-5; Dan. 7:14; Zech. 2:11; 8:23). The nations, in other words, will walk by God's glory. With Satan no longer around to deceive them, they can see the light clearly and follow it right into the city, into eschatological relationship with God. This is only fitting since these, even though they are the populaces of the nations, are the people whose names were found to be written in the Book of Life; everyone else has either been destroyed (Rev. 20:7-9), exiled (22:15) or writhes in the lake of fire (20:15).

Where once kings had brought their gifts and treasures to demonstrate homage and fidelity to Rome, now, free from deception, they bring their glory into God's city instead (cf. Isa. 60:11). In v. 26 John thus repeats what he has already made clear at v. 24. The "*they*" he speaks of at v. 26 are certainly the kings of v. 24, since they are the only possible referent in this context. Their anticipated future behavior is a confident demonstration of true present lordship. Able to see clearly, they will no longer misappropriate their grandeur or hoard it for themselves; they will allow their grandeur to become part of the city's. with the enemy kings of the earth (Rev. 10:11; 16:12, 14; 17:1-2, 12, 18; 18:3, 9) now destroyed (19:18-19), the remaining kings move into the relationship with God that was always expected, where God and the Standing Slaughtered Lamb are acknowledged to be the rightful ruler over all kings (1:5; 15:3; 17:14; 19:16). John does not say that they bring the traditional booty that kings once brought to the Roman Caesar; rather, they bring the glory that they and their people had once refused to yield to God. John had spoken of "*giving God glory*" in terms of repentance (15:4). These must be the repentant ones, therefore, the people who "*came out of her*" (18:4) in time and found their way to a recognition of the lordship of God and the Standing Slaughtered Lamb and thus engaged God's moment of judgment (20:11-15) as a moment of salvation rather than destruction.

Since ancient city gates were traditionally open during the day (unless under siege or attack), it is odd that John pointedly says that the gates in the new Jerusalem will never be closed by day. The odd formulation is probably due to John's desire to emphasize the radical openness of the city (cf. Isa. 60:11). There will only be day because there will be no night (cf. Zech. 14:7), and thus the city will be forever open. It will never close at any part of the day because all parts of the day will be daylight (Rev. 22:5), and as a result the eternal city will be eternally accessible. Perhaps, too, this part of the vision is John's way of returning to the promise Christ made to the Philadelphians, that he was even then, as John is now, setting before them doors that no one would shut (3:7-8). This vision, as a future that has not yet been realized, also offers (and requires) a present choice. Hearers and readers choose to prepare for future entrance by the way they live their present lives. John therefore sets before them two future choices, a lake whose agonizing fire will never be shut off (20:15) and a city whose gates will never be shut closed. One represents (second) death, the other (eternal) life. The exhortation is clear: by the way you witness to the lordship of God and the Standing Slaughtered Lamb, choose life.

    As open and inclusive as the city is, John pauses before moving on to remind his hearers and readers that so holy a place will not entertain impurity (cf. Isa. 35:8; 52:1; Ezek. 33:29). He has made this point more comprehensively before in the vice list of 21:8 and will reiterate it in 22:15. Only those whose names are in the Book of Life belong (cf. Isa. 4:3; Rev. 3:5; 20:12).

John is writing about the future in order to exhort appropriate present witnessing behavior. Those who accommodate themselves to the lordship of Rome and therefore participate in cultic, social, political, and economic activities celebrating that lordship (abominations, 17:4-5), or who lie to (deceive) others and themselves about the truth of such behavior (e.g., Jezebel and Balaam, 2:14, 20-23) – such will never enter the city.

Revelation 22:1~5 → The New Life of the City

NIV	TT
22 ¹ Then the angel showed me the river of the water of life, as clear as crystal, flowing from the throne of God and of the Lamb ² down the middle of the great street of the city. On each side of the river stood the tree of life, bearing twelve crops of fruit, yielding its fruit every month. And the leaves of the tree are for the healing of the nations. ³ No longer will there be any curse. The throne of God and of the Lamb will be in the city, and his servants will serve him. ⁴ They will see his face, and his name will be on their foreheads. ⁵ There will be no more night. They will not need the light of a lamp or the light of the sun, for the Lord God will give them light. And they will reign for ever and ever.	**22** ¹ Then he **showed**[295] me a river of living water, clear as crystal, flowing from the throne of God and the Lamb ² down the center of the city's street. On each side of the river are trees of life producing twelve fruits, each producing its fruit each month. And the leaves of the trees are for the healing of the nations. ³ Nothing cursed will be found there any longer. But the throne of God and of the Lamb will be in it, and God's servants will **worship**[296] God. ⁴ And they will see God's face, and God's name will be on their foreheads. ⁵ There will be no longer be a night, and they will not need lamplight and sunlight, because the Lord God will illumine them, and they will reign forever and ever.

---

[295] δείκνυμι → It means *"show," "point out," "make known," "explain," "indicate,"* and *"prove."*

[296] λατρεύω → It means *"to serve," "to minister," "to render religious service," "to worship," "to offer gifts,"* and *"to perform sacred service."*

In John's vision the eternal life/new Jerusalem/new city is not an eternal rest but a place of ceaseless activity. John offers no mythical details to satisfy our curiosity about *"what we shall do in heaven."* He fills in the content of eternal life with God with only two pictures: *"God's servants will worship him"* (22:3) and *"they will reign forever and ever"* (22:5).

- **1** The angel whom John introduced at 21:9 extends his promise to show the new Jerusalem. The positioning of the river as the direct object of the verb "δείκνυμι" (show) suggests that it has a functional quality on a par with the city itself. John has used this verb throughout as a marker for key narrative images. At 1:1, in the heading for the entire book, it was *"the things soon to take place"* that were directly related to the all-important *"Apokalypsis"* (revelation) of Jesus Christ. At 4:1, as John opened the scene to the heavenly throne room, the significant *"things"* that were to happen *"after this"* were the verb's object. At 17:1 it was the judgment of the great whore, Babylon/Rome. At 21:9 it was the bride, wife of the Lamb, shown to be the holy city, the new Jerusalem, at 21:10. At 22:6, in a verse that no doubt plays the role of a closing narrative footer to its header counterpart at 1:1, the *"things soon to take place"* are once again the object to be shown off. (A final participial use at 22:8 refers to the visions of the new Jerusalem initiated at 21:9.) in each case, the verb *"to show"* prefaces the introduction of a key narrative symbol, whose presence is instrumental for understanding the overall objective of John's prophetic work. The river, as the penultimate pairing of an accusative object with this demonstrative verb, must therefore likewise play an important role in John's thinking about the eschatology of the end time.

The river marks the city as a new, improved, urban Eden. John builds his case carefully. He notes that the river is composed of living water. As such, it is a metaphor for the gift of eschatological relationship with God that humans experienced before their expulsion from paradise. They have thirsted for its restoration ever since (7:16-17; 21:6; 22:17). Both Jewish and Christian writings envisioned that restoration in a variety of ways. Psalm 46:4 anticipated a river whose streams would make glad the city of God in a time of great distress. The prophet Zechariah looked to the great eschatological day when living water would flow freely from Jerusalem (Zech. 14:8). The Gospel of John records Jesus' promise to the thirsty that rivers of living water would one day flow from the hearts of believers (John 7:37-38). Most importantly, Ezekiel offered John a vision upon which he could build his own. The prophet saw water flowing from the threshold of the eschatological temple with the superstructure of a city (Ezek. 47:1). Ezekiel, like John, most certainly grounded this river in the likeness of the river in Eden (Gen. 2:10) that flowed out to water – that is, to give life to – paradise's garden. According to Ezek. 47:8-10, Ezekiel's river flows eastward, down through desert lands, and ultimately into a sea of stagnant waters, no doubt the Dead Sea. After turning lands and waters fresh, it establishes new physical life in the form of swarming creatures and teeming fish.

John improves on the rivers of both Genesis and Ezekiel in two ways. First, he claims for his river a crystal clarity. No doubt he intends to mark the river with the same purity of the precious stones that characterized the city's holiness and God's glory (Rev. 21:11, 22). Second, he alters the river's point of origin. The Genesis river flows out of Eden. Ezekiel's river flows from the eschatological temple. John's river flows directly from the throne of God and the Lamb. The throne, introduced in Rev. 4 as the seat of authority for all creation, now acts as the lifeline for all in creation who thirst for relationship with God. The Lamb is no longer standing alongside the throne, as he was in his own introductory chapter (5:6). After building a functional identity with God (3:21; 7:10, 17; 14:4; 17:14; 21:22) that will climax in chapter 22, where titles associated with God fall naturally to him (22:13), he is now confirmed as ruling with God (cf. v. 3). Just as importantly, through this gift of living water he, along with God, issues eschatological sustenance, eternal life, to those who thirst for it.

- **2** The translation of the phrase that opens v. 2 is not straightforward. Because early Greek manuscripts did not include punctuation, readers must determine from the context where to place it in contemporary translations. The phrase *"down the cent of its [the city's] street"* may be read as completing the thought in v. 1 or as beginning the thought of v. 2. I take the phrase to conclude the thought about the river's flow.

The phrase *"from the throne of God and the Lamb"* indicates the river's source; the paired phrase *"down the center of its [the city's] street"* charts its course and destination. The two pieces fit together naturally as a single thought about the river's movement that is distinct from the ensuing description of the foliage on the river's banks.

The choice of grammatical placement determines much about meaning. John speaks of the river's destination as though the city has one street, at least one primary one. He intends to say that the river flows from the throne of God and the Lamb through the middle of the city's main street, probably the same golden paved street he described at 21:21. Once again he appeals to the Eden account to fill out the portrait. Genesis 2:9 speaks of abundant trees and, in particular, of a tree of life in the midst of the garden. Clearly building from the Genesis account, Ezek. 47:12 speaks of trees growing on both sides of the river that flows from the eschatological temple. In conflating the two accounts, John outdoes them both. Apparently using the singular "ξύλον" (tree) as a collective noun, he envisions his river flanked on either side by rows of the one tree of life. How else are we to take his awkward phrasing that on either side of the river there stood a tree of life? At least two trees are envisioned here; indeed, the allusion to Ezekiel suggests many more. Eden's garden had only one tree of life. Ezekiel's temple had many trees, but no tree of life. John's city has trees of life standing guard all along the banks of a crystal river running down the middle of a golden street. John's new Jerusalem out-do Eden!

Given John's presentation, it is all to be expected. Using the metaphor of washing one's clothes (i.e., those who conquer), Christ declares that those who faithfully witness to the lordship of God and the Lamb, despite the consequences, will obtain access to the tree of life (22:14, 19). In fact, as early as 2:7, Christ promised the Ephesian church members that anyone who conquered would be given permission to eat from the tree of life in paradise. The new Jerusalem is obviously the paradise that Christ intended; it has plenty of such trees to go around (cf. *Pss. Sol.* 14.3, where the trees of life represent believers). This eschatological Eden is fully stocked.

So are its trees. Once again following Ezek. 47:12, John observes that they bear abundant fruit (cf. *1 En.* 25:4-6). Ezekiel notes that they are always in season; because of the life-giving water flowing from the temple that nourishes them, they offer a fresh harvest every month of the year. John's trees are not only abundant; they also produce variety. The seer is careful to present that variety in terms of the number for completion: twelve. His trees are wholly sufficient. Each month will find a new fruit dangling from their branches.

John's eschatological one-upmanship continues with the trees' leaves. Ezekiel had observed that while the fruit of the trees was for food, their leaves would be for healing. So too for the trees of life in John's new Jerusalem. John, though, pointedly adds that the healing is to be for the nations. Ezekiel was interested in the healing and wholeness of a restored Israel, the ethnic people of God. John broadens God's salvific range beyond Israel to any nation whose people testify to the lordship of God and the Standing Slaughtered Lamb. Not ethnicity but response to God is the decisive criterion for the eschatological relationship symbolized by the therapeutic power of the new Jerusalem's leaves.

- **3** The new Jerusalem, however, will be closed to anything accursed. There is much discussion about what John means with his use of the term "κατανάθεμα" (a person or thing under God's curse), which he deploys exclusively here. Given the proximity to the detailed vice lists (21:8, 27; 22:15) and John's explicit warning in each case that those whose lives represent such characteristics will not be allowed admittance, it is natural to assume that the seer is focused on those who are accursed because of their behavior. An unclean person surely can find no shelter in a place so holy that God dwells directly within it (21:2, 3): only the righteous occupy the city.

Perhaps John also has Jer. 3:17 in mind, a prophetic promise that all the nations, redeemed and no longer following their own will, will gather in apparent worship before God's Jerusalem throne. Once again combining the authority of God and the Lamb, John observes that they both hold title to the throne. Before them both, then, God's servants offer worship. John probably has in mind Rev. 7:15, the only other place where he uses this particular term for worship (λατρεύω). There the great multitude of God's witnesses worship God day and night. No doubt the same sense of perpetuity is assumed here.

- **4** The worshipers before the throne of God and the Lamb possess two especially important features. First, they have the privilege and ability to see God face-to-face. The implication is that they are closer to God than even Moses, who was only allowed to see Yahweh's back as it passed by him (Exod. 33:18-23). In fact, Yahweh specifically warned Moses that no one could see Yahweh's face and live (Exod. 33:20). Human faculties could not safely apprehend features so holy. Yet the eschatological longing was for just this capability. The psalmist envisions the day when he will see God's face and be satisfied (Pss. 11:7; 17:15). In the Sermon on the Mount, Jesus declares that the pure in heart are blessed precisely because they shall see God (Matt. 5:8; Heb. 2:9). And Paul opined that though we see through a mirror dimly now, in the eschaton we will see God face-to-face (1 Cor. 13:12; Heb. 12:14; 1 John 3:2; *Jub.* 1.28; *4 Ezra* 7.91, 98; *1 En.* 102:8). As his visionary experience comes to a close, John can see this future hope already taking present form.

Second, as John has previously explained, they will carry the identifying and protecting name of God on their foreheads (cf. 7:3; 9:4; 13:6; 14:1, 9; 20:4). According to 3:12, this *"branding"* is the reward for those who conquer, who witness faithfully to the lordship of God and the Standing Slaughtered Lamb.

- **5** John closes his discussion of the new Jerusalem by reinforcing attributes that he has highlighted before. There will be no night in the city (21:25). The absence of night alone would suggest that neither artificial lamp nor natural sunlight would be necessary, but John drives the point home by extolling once again that God will be their light. The seer has not only made this point already, but also depicted the glory of God and the Lamb as the energy source that fuels the eternal illumination (21:23). Finally, picking up a thread from 5:10, John affirms that these worshiping servants will rule. This reign is even more noteworthy than the already-impressive dominion of 20:4, 6. Though lengthy, the regime described in chapter 20 would last only a millennium; this one will go on forever (cf. Dan. 7:18, 27).

Revelation 22:6~9 → Transition

NIV	TT
⁶ The angel said to me, "These words are trustworthy and true. The Lord, the God who inspires the prophets, sent his angel to show his servants the things that must soon take place." ⁷ "Look, I am coming soon! Blessed is the one who keeps the words of the prophecy written in this scroll." ⁸ I, John, am the one who heard and saw these things. And when I had heard and seen them, I fell down to worship at the feet of the angel who had been showing them to me. ⁹ But he said to me, "Don't do that! I am a fellow servant with you and with your fellow prophets and with all	⁶ Then he said to me, "These words are trustworthy and true; the Lord, the God of the **spirits**[297] of the prophets, sent God's **angel**[298] to **show**[299] God's servants what must happen soon. ⁷ 'Indeed, I am coming soon. **Blessed**[300] is the one who keeps the words of the prophecy of this book.'" ⁸ I, **John**,[301] am the one who heard and saw these things. And when I heard and saw, I fell down to worship before the feet of the angel who showed them to me. ⁹ But he said to me, "Do not do that! I am a fellow servant with you and your brothers and sisters, the prophets and those who

---

[297] πνεῦμα → It means "blowing," "breathing," "wind," "breath," "spirit," "soul," "spiritual state," "Ghost," "(the Holy) Spirit," "evil spirits," and "the representative part of the inner life."

[298] ἄγγελος → It means "messenger," "envoy," "guardian," "mediator," "angel," and "servants of Satan."

[299] δείκνυμι → It means "show," "point out," "make known," "explain," and "prove." In "Apokalypsis," the term appears in 1:1, 4:1, and 22:6.

[300] μακάριος → It means "blessed," "fortunate," and "happy" (usually in the sense of privileged recipient of divine favor).

[301] Ἰωάνης → The name "John" means "Jehovah is a gracious giver."

who keep the words of this scroll. Worship God!"	keep the words of this book. Worship God!"

Verses 6-9 are a bridging text. The section both closes the vision of the bridal city (21:9-22:5) and opens the epilogue (22:10-21).

- **6** Revelation 19:9 began the conclusion to the section featuring the whore city, Babylon/Rome (17:1-19:10), with one of the guiding seven-bowl angels (17:1) attesting to the validity of the remarks made. Just so, 22:6 begins the conclusion to the structurally parallel section featuring the bride city, new Jerusalem (21:9-22:9), with one of the guiding seven-bowl angels (21:9) attesting to the validity of the remarks made. Though the angel of 22:6 is slightly more verbose (he adds *"trustworthy"* to the *"true"* spoken by the angel of 19:9), he intends the same thought as his colleague: what has been narrated can be trusted. While the angel of 19:9 was probably verifying the message disclosed in the scene centering on judgment of Babylon, the angel here, with a view to the ensuing epilogue, focuses more broadly on the entire *"Apokalypsis."* Using familiar language, he assures his readers and hearers that they can rely on the veracity of his visions and the ideas and imperatives drawn from them (cf. 3:14; 19:9, 11; 21:5).

The angel speaks of an abbreviated chain of revelatory transmission (God to an angel to God's servants; cf. 22:16, where another abbreviated chain is initiated by Christ) and describes the topic of that transmission as the things that must happen soon. This brief account links the unit directly to the verse that opened the "*Apokalypsis*" by citing the full chain of revelatory transmission (God to Christ to an angel to John to God's servants) and describing the topic of the transmission as the things that must happen soon (1:1). This intentional connection to the opening words of the prologue, which virtually serves as a header for the entire Book of Revelation, suggests that John intends the angel to be verifying all of the material introduced between these two focal narrative points.

The structural move also makes several key thematic points. First, like Daniel, John celebrates that there is a God who reveals what will happen on the last day (Dan. 2:28). Unlike Daniel, however, who believed that the end time would be delayed (Dan. 8:26; 12:4, 9), John, here at the end of the book, reinforces the apocalyptic point with which he opened it: the arrival of the final moment, when God will reveal God's intentions for all creation, is imminent. This point is so important that John not only opens his work with it; he also opens the close of his work by repeating it here and then reaffirming it in various forms four more times (Rev. 22:7, 10, 12, 20).

Second, the angel bases the trustworthiness of John's "*Apokalypsis*" on the God who has inspired it. In a similar way, the Old Testament seer also bases the validity of a pivotal dream and its interpretation not on the content of the dream but on the veracity of the great God who conveyed a message through it (Dan. 2:45).

Third, this sovereign God connects directly to God's servants through their own spirits and so inspires them to prophetic works. In John's context, a prophet is a servant who witnesses to the lordship of God and Christ because God has inspired testimony even in imperial circumstances that seek either to co-opt or to annihilate that testimony. The angel therefore identifies God as the Lord God of the spirits of the prophets in the same way that God is described in the Book of Numbers as the Lord God of the spirits of all flesh (Num. 16:22; 27:16). The angel and John speak here, then, not of God's Holy Spirit but of human spirits that act as conduits between the divine and the mortal enabling the transmission of God's intent into human thought and action.[302] Working through John's spirits and the spirit of his fellow servant-prophets (Rev. 22:9), God has inaugurated a *"spirit of prophecy"* in the churches. It is this very spirit of prophecy that has caught John up and enabled him to see what he has seen (Rev. 1:3 and 22:9 indicate that John understands himself to be a prophet). This same spirit gives a prophetic rather than an ecstatic edge to what he has conveyed. He conveys his visions for the same reason that the Old Testament prophets offered their prophecies. His primary objective is not to foretell future happenings but to exhort appropriate (i.e., witnessing) behavior in the present.

- 7 To reinforce the point that God is acting soon, the angle quotes Christ: *"Indeed, I am coming soon"* (Rev.

---

[302] R. E. O. White says, *"despite disproportionate attention given to Paul's teaching on the 'flesh,' there is much to show that he believed equally firmly in the 'higher' elements in human nature that were open to God, 'our Spirit' to which the Holy Spirit bears witness, 'the spirit of the man which is in him' (Rom. 8:16; 1 Cor. 2:11)."* Similarly, Aune observes that *"'spirit' is widely used as an anthropological term for the highest faculty of human beings (1 Cor. 7:34; 14:14; 2 Cor. 7:1; 1 Thess. 5:23)."*

3:11). If anything, John wants the point made even more fervently than does the angel. He has already quoted the same message on Christ's lips twice before (2:16; 3:11) and then restated it later in another, though just as urgent, fashion (16:15); before the chapter closes, he has Christ make the point twice more (22:12, 20). God's clinching eschatological move is not the coming of an event or even a place as magnificent as the Eden-like new Jerusalem. God's climactic move is a person. Time finds its completion in the Christ who declares through John's visions that he is the end that is coming soon. Ultimately the *"things"* that John says are coming soon (v. 6) are meant to be identified with and draw their significance from him. Indeed, they are to be grounded in the coming Christ as an objective and never a spiritualized reality. John does not envision an existential coming of Christ only into the hearts and spirits of humankind. The Christ who comes soon comes not just to the human heart but also to the world.

Here at the end of John's work, Christ comes with a message that reaffirms the observation and exhortation with which John began his work. Even the presentation is the same. Just as John opened his words of prophecy at 1:1 with a word about what must soon take place and followed up with a beatitude that declared blessed those who do and those who will read, hear, and keep the prophetic words (Rev. 1:3; 19:10), so he now follows up dramatic statements about the coming of Christ with a beatitude of both indicative and imperative significance (14:13). This sixth in the series of seven beatitudes (Rev. 1:3; 14:13; 16:15; 19:9; 20:6; 22:7, 14), like the others, functions only in part as a straightforward affirmation that all those who keep the words – who testify to the lordship of God and Christ in a world that instead proclaims the lordship of Rome – are blessed. The mere recognition of this reality also simultaneously encourages those who do not now offer such testimony to begin to do so. Through these two beatitudes, the first in the prologue (1:3) and this one in the epilogue (22:7), John at the beginning affirms and then at the end reaffirms his book's central ethical expectation. The context of apocalyptic imminence should make responding appropriately an urgent affair for John's audience.

- **8 – 9** John now takes the stage from the angel. He does what he did earlier (1:9) and what he will soon record Christ as doing (22:16). As verification of reputation as church leader (1:1, 4; 1 John 1:1-3). In this case the pronoun "ταῦτα" (these things) refers not to the entire Book of Revelation, but as the second half of the verse makes clear, to the visions of the new Jerusalem. The visions have so overwhelmed him that he repeats the false step he made at 19:10, falling at the angelic messenger's feet in preparation to worship him (19:10).

The angel reacts with the same alarm his predecessor displayed at 19:10. Repeating the earlier response verbatim, he cries out: *"Do not do that! Worship God!"* In explaining that the behavior is prohibited because he is one of John's colleagues, the angel maintains the emphasis on prophecy that has been building throughout this transitional bridge section

(22:6-9) and was also central to the clarification of the testimony of Jesus in 19:10. By identifying himself as a fellow servant with John and his brothers and sisters, the prophets, the angel tacitly identifies John and his colleagues as servant prophets. The designation fits the ongoing connection between service to God and prophecy that John has established throughout his work (10:7; 11:3). Fellow servants (whether angelic or not), brothers and sisters, and prophets designate a single category comprising all who are faithful Christ-believers, who respond positively to the Book of Revelation's primary exhortation to witness to the lordship of God and the Standing Slaughtered Lamb. The "καὶ" (and) that joins "*prophets*" with "*those who keep the words of this book*" should therefore be understood epexegetically. The following phrase further develops the meaning of "*prophets, brothers and sisters, and fellow servants.*" The angel intends to say, "*I am a fellow servant with you and your brothers and sisters the prophets who keep the words of this book.*" The final point ties the angel's remarks to the beatitude of 22:7, which declares blessed (by God) those who did and would keep the prophetic words of this book.

Revelation 22:10~21 → Epilogue & Letter Closing

NIV	TT
¹⁰ Then he told me, "Do not seal up the words of the prophecy of this scroll, because the time is near. ¹¹ Let the one who does wrong continue to do wrong; let the vile person continue to be vile; let the one who does right continue to do right; and let the holy person continue to be holy." ¹² "Look, I am coming soon! My reward is with me, and I will give to each person according to what they have done. ¹³ I am the Alpha and the Omega, the First and the Last, the Beginning and the End. ¹⁴ "Blessed are those who wash their robes, that they may have the right to the tree of life and may go through the gates into the city. ¹⁵ Outside are the dogs, those who practice magic arts, the sexually immoral, the murderers, the	¹⁰ And he said to me, "Do not seal up the words of the prophecy of this book, for the time is near. ¹¹ Let the person who is evil continue to do evil, and let the person who is impure continue to be impure, and let the person who is righteous continue to do righteousness, and let the person who is holy continue to be holy." ¹² "Indeed, I am coming soon, and my reward is with me to repay everyone according to their works. ¹³ I am the Alpha and the Omega, the first and the last, the beginning and the end." ¹⁴ Blessed are those who **wash**³⁰³ their robes, so that they may have access to the tree of life and enter the city by the gates. ¹⁵ Outside are the dogs and the sorcerers and the fornicators and the murderers and the idolaters and everyone who loves and practices lies. ¹⁶ "I, Jesus,

---

³⁰³ πλύνω → It means literally and symbolically "*wash*." This term appears only three times in the New Testament (cf. Luke 5:1; Rev. 7:14; 22:14).

idolaters and everyone who loves and practices falsehood. ¹⁶ "I, Jesus, have sent my angel to give you this testimony for the churches. I am the Root and the Offspring of David, and the bright Morning Star." ¹⁷ The Spirit and the bride say, "Come!" And let the one who hears say, Come!" Let the one who is thirsty come; and let the one who wishes take the free gift of the water of life. ¹⁸ I warn everyone who hears the words of the prophecy of this scroll: If anyone adds anything to them, God will add to that person the plagues described in this scroll. ¹⁹ And if anyone takes words away from this scroll of prophecy, God will take away from that person any share in the tree of life and in the Holy City, which are described in this scroll. ²⁰ He who testifies to these things says, "Yes, I am sent my angel to testify these things to you for the churches. I am the root and the descendant of David, the bright morning star." ¹⁷ Both the Spirit and the bride say, "Come." And let the one who hears say, "Come." And let the one who is thirsty come. Let the one who wishes take living water as a gift. ¹⁸ I testify to everyone who hears the words of the prophecy of this book: if anyone adds to them, God will add to that person the plagues described in this book; ¹⁹ if anyone takes away from the words of the book of this prophecy, God will take away that person's share in the tree of life and in the holy city, which are described in this book. ²⁰ The one who testifies to these things says, "Surely I am coming soon." Amen! Come, Lord Jesus! ²¹ The grace of the Lord Jesus be with **all**.³⁰⁴ **Amen.**³⁰⁵

---

³⁰⁴ πάντων → It means *"all," "everyone," "the whole," "all things,"* and *"everything."*

³⁰⁵ ἀμήν → It means *"firm," "verily," "amen," "(at the beginning of a discourse) surely, truly,"* and *"(at the end of a discourse) so it is, so be it, may it be fulfilled."*

> coming soon."
>
> Amen. Come, Lord Jesus.
>
> ²¹ The grace of the Lord Jesus be with God's people. Amen.

The Book of Revelation, "*Apokalypsis*" ends as it began, a letter from an exiled pastor-prophet to be read forth in the worship services of the Asian Minor churches. Like Paul's letters, this letter is designed to be read in the liturgy, probably just prior to the celebration of the Eucharist.

The angel introduced at 21:9 speaks in the first two verses. Christ's voice takes charge in vv. 12- 20a; then John gives the last word in vv. 20b-21. The quick movement between speakers and themes has led many commentators to the conclusion that different closing thoughts are strung together without any sense of cohesion or direction. Though this assessment has merit, it is too harsh. John uses the cacophony of remarks in this final scene to remind his hearers and readers one final, urgent time about the various matters that are important to him, and thus to them, throughout his work. A single intent prevails: to encourage witness to the lordship of God and Jesus Christ.

- **10** Figuring to hold center stage while he has it, the angel offers a chastened John further instructions. Though John has based much of his work on Daniel and often found himself following Daniel's lead in the presentation of his own visions, he now finds that he must distance himself from his apocalyptic muse. The author of the Book of Daniel, writing pseudonymously, found himself pressed into narrating that his work had to be sealed (cf. *4 Ezra* 14:5-6, 45-46). Though the book proposes to have been written during the Babylonian exile (sixth century B.C.E.) by a famous figure of that time, it was actually penned some four centuries later (second century B.C.E.). Hearers and readers of the work would want to know why the sixth century B.C.E. Daniel's prophecies took so long to be disclosed. The literary response would be clear; the author was directed to seal it (Dan. 8:26; 12:4, 9). John, writing in his own name for identifiable churches in his present, was not faced with the same dilemma. Since the exhortations developing out of his words of prophecy were intended for his contemporary believers, it made perfect sense that his work should remain unsealed. How would the urgent message to witness in the shadow of God's imminent judgment otherwise have the effect that he intended? In addition, since the end was coming soon, there were no expected future generations from which to seal his prophecies. His generations were to be the last; logically, therefore, John had to address them. The last of his mentoring angels reinforces this point by ordering him to keep his work open and accessible.

Excursus 18 : Interpreting the *"Near End"*

Revelation begins and ends with the declaration that the return of Christ and the end of history are near (Rev. 1:1, *"What must soon take place"* 1:3, *"For the time is near"'* 22:20, *"Surely I am coming soon"*). This motif is not incidental, but is woven into the fabric of the message throughout:

2:16 – The risen Jesus warns those in Pergamum to repent, because he is coming soon. This word functions as a warning, and loses its power if there is a lot of time left in which to get ready to meet the Judge.

2:25 – The risen Jesus encourages the faithful at Thyatira to hold fast what they have *"until I come."* This word functions as encouragement to steadfast endurance. If in fact a centuries-long period is intended, it no longer encourages the reader to hold on. Similarly 3:11.

3:20 – *"Behold I stand at the door and knock"* is not only a spatial image for the church at Laodicea, but a temporal image for the church at apocalyptic, that reflects the shortness of time before the coming of Christ: he is already at the door (see Mark 13:29; Luke 12:36; Jas. 5:9).

6:11 – The souls of the martyrs already in heaven cry out for God's eschatological judgment of the world and ask, *"How long?"* They receive the response that they must wait only *"a little longer."*

10:6 – The *"mighty angel"* in the vision swears by the Creator that there is to be *"no more delay,"* but that the *"mystery of God, as he announced to his servants the prophets"* (i.e., the divine plan for the establishment of God's just rule at the end of history, is about to be fulfilled.).

11:2-3; 12:6 – The longest period mentioned in the Book of Revelation is this span of time described variously as forty-two months, or twelve hundred and sixty days, derived from the period of three and a half years prophesied in Daniel 7:25; 8:14; 9:27; 12:7, 11, 12. This period became a traditional apocalyptic time frame (see Luke 4:26 and Jas. 5:17). The period is not meant literally, but still represents only a short time.

12:12 – the devil intensifies his persecution of faithful believers precisely because he *"knows that his time is short."*

17:10 – There are to be seven *"kings"* altogether, and John and his hearer-readers live in the time of the sixth. Again, while the precise numbers may not be literal, it is clear that John sees himself and his readers as living near the end.

22:6, 7, 10, 12, 20 – The Book of Revelation ends with a cluster of assurances that Christ will return soon. That the end of history is near in the writer's own time is a constituent part of apocalyptic thought. How should the modern reader come to terms with this apparently erroneous expectation? The New Testament itself offers help on this problem, for it was already faced in New Testament times.

During the first Christian generation, there were several crises that convinced some early Christians that they were indeed experiencing the final events of history and the end was now upon them. There was widespread apocalyptic excitement among both Jews and Christians when the emperor Caligula attempted to place a statue of himself in the Jerusalem temple in 39 C.E., as there was during the terrible Neronian persecution of Christians in Rome in 64, during the catastrophic war in Palestine 66 – 70 C.E., and in the wake of the famines, earthquakes, and eruption of Vesuvius in the following decades. Yet these crises came and went, and the end did not come. How could Christians respond to this apparent disappointment of their eschatological hope?

1. Rejection. It is striking that no New Testament author simply rejected the apocalyptic hope as such, despite its failure to materialize as expected. Some other early Christians, however, whose writings were not included in the New Testament, decided that apocalyptic expectation as such was an error, and simply rejected it. Gnostic streams of Christianity abandoned the hope that God would redeem the horizontal line of history in a mighty eschatological act, and retreated to a verticalism in which individual souls are saved into the transcendent world and/or already enjoy the eschatological realities in their present religious experience. Such views may have been shared by John's opponents among the Nicolaitans (Rev. 2:6, 15) and the followers of "*Jezebel*" (2:20) who advocated the teaching of "*Balaam*" (2:14). Some contemporary interpreters have responded in this way to Revelation's apocalyptic expectation of the near end of history (i.e., by simply rejecting apocalyptic in general and Revelation in particular. This is often done without an awareness of how deeply rooted apocalyptic ideas are in the New Testament as a whole and in Christian faith as such.).

2. Reinterpretation. Other Christians held on to the apocalyptic language of the first generation, but reinterpreted it in the light of the failure of the end to appear. There were basically two varieties of such interpretation:

a. Reinterpretation of "*soon*." The author of 2 Peter represents this point of view. He discovered Psalms 90:4, which declared that a thousand years in God's sight is only a day, which helped him to understand "*soon*" in a different way than had the first generation of Christians (2 Pet. 3:3-13). Likewise the author of Luke-Acts reinterpreted the near-expectation of the previous generation in such a way that the earlier expectation was postponed to the indefinite future. So also the author of 2 Thessalonians postponed the end (cf. 2 Thess. 2:1-12).

b. Reinterpretation of "*end*." In this view, the promised "*end*" did in fact come soon, but it was not the end of history. The outpouring of the Spirit and the beginning of the church was considered the fulfillment of the promised return of Christ. The eschatological realities were no longer understood in a literal manner, but spiritualized and understood to be a part of the present experience of the Christian life. This kind of "*realized eschatology*," elements of which had also been a dimension of the faith of the first generation, was developed especially by the authors of the Gospel and Epistles of John. These authors reinterpret all the realities expected to come at the eschaton as already present realities: the antichrist is reinterpreted as the presence of false teachers in the community (1 John 2:18; 4:3); the second coming of Christ is reinterpreted as Christ's coming again as the Spirit, the Paraclete (John 14-16); the defeat of Satan happened in Jesus' ministry (John 12:31). Furthermore the resurrection happens in the new life of the Christian (John 11:21-26); the judgment happens in the present encounter with Christ the judge (John 3:18-19; 12:31, 48), and eternal life is already the present possession of the believer (John 3:36; 6:47; 17:3). The Johannine authors did not absolutely reject the future hope, however, did strongly subordinate it to present Christian experience.

3. Reaffirmation. In times of threat and persecution, Christians of the second and third generations revived the older apocalyptic expectations with the conviction that even though earlier predictions were wrong, now the end has indeed come near. In their situation, apocalyptic language once again made sense and supplied an urgently needed means of holding on to the

> faith despite all the empirical evidence to the contrary. Thus in 1 Peter, written in a situation similar to John's the author revives the expectation of the nearness of the end as a motive for Christian steadfastness in the face of persecution and trial (1 Pet. 4:7, 16; 5:19)

- **11** The angel seems to know that John's open testimony will offer a radical opportunity for his hearers and readers. Given the lateness of the time, ultimate decisions must be made to follow the way of witnessing to the lordship of God and the Standing Slaughtered Lamb, or not so witnessing. All along, John's dramatic visions have had a single intent: to shock those who were operating against God and the Standing Slaughtered Lamb into testifying to and for them, while encouraging those who were already testifying to stay the difficult course. Even at the end, with the new Jerusalem already on station in the new heaven and new earth, opportunities for endurance and repentance remain. Though the angel's imperatives appear to suggest that eschatological places are already set, that the wicked are doomed beyond repair and the righteous saved without question (Dan. 12:10; Ezek. 3:27), nuances drawn from the context suggest an alternate reading. John's visions are future oriented, but they have not yet been realized. He is not speaking about a circumstance that has already occurred, whereby people are locked into determined fates. Remembering that his prophecies envision the future in order to shape behavior in the present, one gains the sense that he is doing here what he has been doing throughout the new-heaven-and-new-earth cycle (cf. Rev. 21:8) and indeed throughout the entire course of his narrative. As in his seven beatitudes, he is offering a declaration of reality (indicative) as a lure to motivate his ethical appeal (implicit imperative). John pictures the future in such a way that he hopes will either entice or frighten hearers and readers into making the appropriate decision to line up behind the lordship of God and the Standing Slaughtered Lamb.

The plagues that accompany the opening of the seven seals, the blowing of the seven trumpets, the pouring out of the seven bowls, and the devastation that surrounds the fall of Babylon/Rome – these are all designed to shock humans to turn from the behavior that will make them subject to such judgment. The competing pictures of salvation, climactically presented in the scenes that portray a new heaven, new earth, and new Jerusalem, are designed both to invite recalcitrant humans to repent and to encourage Christ-believing humans to keep believing – and bearing witness to their convictions – no matter what the cost. The angel's comments here are a final, melodramatic way of making this same case.

The imperatives spoken by the angel ("*Continue to do evil*," "*Continue to be impure*," "*Continue to do righteousness*," "*Continue to be holy*") assure John's hearers and readers that God will certainly do what God has promised to do, that is, initiate the judgment and corresponding salvation that John has envisioned (cf. Isa. 56:1). People must therefore make a decision. The angel's words, spoken to John but certainly intended for John's audience, functionally resemble the frustrated comments of an annoyed parent who sees her child repeatedly testing her authority by refusing to cease his misbehavior. *"Keep it up! Hear!"* Though a child deaf to the tones of discipline could take the apparent command literally, the parent certainly does not mean that the child should indeed keep it up. In fact, she means, and urgently so, just the opposite. A contextual appropriation of her comments indicates that she has just issued a stern warning that her child should alter his course of behavior because intervention in the form of parental judgment is imminent. The command to keep it up in such a context is in reality a last-ditch call for repentance. The angel's context is comparable; he offers a glimpse of God's imminent intervention as a means of shaking up those who are not yet living a life that witnesses in word and deed to God's lordship. *"If you are doing evil, well, keep it up!"* Though a hearer or reader deaf to the apocalyptic tones reverberating throughout John's book of prophecy might take the command literally, the angel means, and urgently so, just the opposite. No doubt that is why he ends his remarks by encouraging those who are already living a life of witness, as well as those who take advantage of the time is left and start living such a life, to really *"keep it up"*: persevere in acts of justice, courageous witness, and thus holiness, as people claimed and set apart for *"the kingdom/reign of God"* (ἡ βασιλεία τοῦ θεοῦ).

- **12** In an apparent effort to confirm everything that has been said thus far, Christ decides that it is time to speak. He verifies that the angel did not misquote him at 22:7; using exactly the same words, which he will repeat in a slightly different way in his very last comment in John's work, words to which he has appealed earlier, he declares that the time of his coming is imminent. Following as it does the angel's innovative exhortation in v. 11, which was also based on a recognition that the time is near (v. 10), Christ's comment also confirms that the proximity of the end is closely related to the need for humans to comport themselves appropriately.

  Christ now makes explicit his expectation for appropriate behavior when he says that he brings the realization of an eschatological relationship with God as a reward; he will repay each person according to each one's works. The larger narrative context suggests that by "*works*" he means witnessing to the lordship of God and Christ (cf. Rev. 2:2, 5, 6, 19, 23, 26; 3:1, 2, 8, 15). The emphasis on reward appears to suggest that he has in mind only those who live a life of appropriate witness. A broader understanding of his comments, however, suggests that he is also speaking about those who do not witness. Judgment in John's book has always, even when he has not explicitly said so, implied its opposite: salvation or eschatological relationship with God. Whenever judgment of those who oppose God is mentioned, the realization of salvation for those who witness for God looms in the background. Conversely, when the salvation of those who witness for God is proclaimed, the reality of judgment for those who do not lurks in salvation's wake. At the end of the book, John makes this point structurally by balancing the destruction (judgment) of Babylon/Rome (Rev. 17:1-19:10) against the salvific opportunity represented by the rise of the new Jerusalem (Rev. 21:9-22:9). When Christ mentions the reward now, therefore, the penalty is certainly assumed.

The primary point is that Christ will respond appropriately to all human behavior. How will that response take shape? Revelation 20:12-13 describes a scene where books that record the works of all humans will be opened (cf. 2:2, 5, 6, 19, 23, 26; 3:1, 2, 5, 8; 9:20; 14:13; 16:11; 18:6). Apparently building upon a foundation in Isa. 40:10, Christ declares that he will fill the role the Old Testament prophets entrusted to God (Jer. 17:10; Ps. 28:4; Prov. 24:12). He will be the judge who determines whether a person's recorded works merit reward or punishment.

- **13** Christ immediately moves to substantiate his claim to act as eschatological judge. He requisitions titles previously applied directly (in first person) to God (*"the Alpha and the Omega"*: 1:8; 21:6) and applies them to himself. Indeed, the explicit meaning of those titles, already appropriated in part at 1:17 and 2:8, he now fully develops as his own self-designations. Like God, he is the first and the last, the beginning and the end. What the titles revealed about God, they reveal now also about him. As the only one who exists before and after history, who rules over time because he is at the beginning and end of time, Christ, like God, can know how the time, concerns, and objectives that drive history come to their conclusion. When the one who is before and after all things says that he knows how to reward a person's works and that he will award the salvation/judgment that every human is due, John's readers and hearers can believe it.

- **14** With the "*Apokalypsis*"' seventh and final beatitude, Christ certifies a key narrative pronouncement: the work to which he exhorts in v. 12 is indeed the work of witness to the lordship of God and the Standing Slaughtered Lamb. The verb "πλύνω" (wash) appears only here and at 7:14, where John describes the vast multitude of saints massed around God's heavenly throne. These are the ones who enjoy eschatological relationship with God, a direct consequence of the fact that they have washed their robes. The blood of Christ is the detergent that launders those robes to be clean/white. The saints are adorned with white robes also in 6:11 and 7:9, there too as a metaphor for eschatological relationship with God. Earlier, though, John had specified an alternate means for acquiring dazzling/white robes: the saints obtain them by witnessing to the lordship of God and the Standing Slaughtered Lamb in the imperial context where Rome greets such testimony and the people making it with persecution, oppression, and even death (Rev. 3:4-5). If these two different means of acquiring "*washed*" robes (3:4-5; 7:14) are both viable, then John has, narratively speaking at least, indirectly tied the blood of Christ to the act of witnessing. He makes that connection explicit in 12:11, where the act of witness and the blood of Christ together supply the weapon the saints require in order to defeat the red dragon. *"Washing the robes"* is therefore a metaphor for witnessing, which is, in the context of chapter 22, the work that merits the reward Christ offers. Christ makes the same point more succinctly by saying that such witnesses are *"blessed."*

The connection of washing/witnessing to eschatological relationship is further developed through the clause that follows: *"so that they might have authority over [i.e., authority to eat from] the tree of life and (so that) they might enter into the gates of the city."* At 2:7 Christ promised that anyone who conquers (i.e., witnesses to the lordship of God and the Standing Slaughtered Lamb) would be able to eat from the tree of life (Rev. 2:7; 22:2). He makes good on that promise with the beatitude in 22:14. According to Ps. 118:19-21, entry through God's gates ensures salvation. In this context, entry carries with it eternal life, since death does not exist in the city (Rev. 21:4).

- **15** It is not surprising that John's Christ would declare that sorcerers, fornicators, murderers, idolaters, and liars would be exiled outside the eschatological city. God had said exactly the same thing at 21:8, even adding cowards, the faithless, and those who commit abominations to the list of the banned. Not to be upstaged, Christ also adds a category: *"dogs"* will also be denied admittance. Dogs were disparaged in both Jewish and early Christian contexts for a variety of reasons, not the least of which was their tendency to scavenge and therefore eat impure things, even corpses, for food (1 Kgs. 14:11; 16:4; 21:24; 2 Kgs. 9:10; 9:36; Prov. 26:11; 2 Pet. 2:22). Yet John is not concerned about literal dogs; he is speaking figuratively about unclean humans, whom he maligns by association. This tendency to denigrate and undesirables by labeling them dogs was also a common feature of early Jewish and early Christian tradition (Matt. 7:6; 15:26-27; Mark 7:27-28; Luke 16:21; Phil. 3:2; *Did*. 9.5). The overall point that John's Christ makes by refusing "*dogs*" is the same point he makes with the other vice categories: those who defile themselves by accommodating to the expectations of imperial lordship, for whatever reason, are unclean and therefore unworthy of the eschatological relationship with the holy God that entry into the city symbolizes.

- **16** John's Christ now does what John himself did at 22:8; he offers his figurative signature to validate everything that he has said and will say. Hearers and readers can trust what has just been said about the manner in which robe washing – that is, witnessing – develops an eschatological relationship with God, and how the various vices of a life that seeks cultic, economic, and political liaison with Rome destroy that relationship. Why? Because Christ is the one who makes the case. Moreover, hearers and readers can trust what will soon be said about the still-open invitations to repentance, and trust that the threats made against anyone who would dare to add to or take away from the words of John's book are real. Why? Because Christ is the one who will make them.

Christ establishes his eschatological bona fides in three ways. First, he testifies that he is the same Christ who, with God, initiated the chain of testimony that has led to John's work (Rev. 1:1-2). The angel of 21:9, who escorted John through his visions of a new heaven, new earth, new Jerusalem, had already spoken of this chain of testimony by taking it back one step (the only one there is) beyond Christ, to God. Otherwise the angel's list of names bears a striking similarity to Christ's. In fact, both descriptions of the revelatory transmission chain operate from the foundational description at 1:1. Comparing the three chains simultaneously helps clarify some of the questions about how to translate the version of the chain that Jesus submits here.

At 1:1, the chain made the following progression: God to Jesus to an angel to John to servants and, finally, to the churches (cf. 1:4). At 21:6, although he skips several stages, the angel sticks to the same basic progression: God to an angel to servants. Given that John describes the churches as the final destination of his work (1:4), churches may be presumed to be the final stage. Christ, no doubt presuming God's presence in concert with his own (as he implies by taking God's titular designations to himself, 22:13), offers a similar progression: Christ to an angel to *"you"* to the churches. The commonalities at the beginning of the chain (God and Jesus) and its ending (the churches) are quite clear. The difficulty in interpretation, where 22:16 is considered, is that commentators are unsure what Christ intends with the plural pronoun *"you."* "*I, Jesus, sent my angel to testify these things to you (all) for the churches."* Does he redundantly intend that *"you"* refer to the churches? If so, why does his grammar suggest that he considers them two separate categories? Biblical commentators have offered many different interpretive approaches.[306]

I suggest that a comparison of this chain progression with the matching stages in the other two clarifies how the verse should be read. The first stages are constant: God/Christ, angel, John. In both 22;6 and 1:1, the stage that follows the seer John does not comprise the churches. At 1:1, John lists God's servants before he adds himself to the chain as the one who transmits the *"Revelation"* to them. At 22:6, according to the angel, the angel transmits the revelation to God's servants. Because the churches are not specifically mentioned in 1:1, one could well consider that John intends servants to mean churches, or at least all the Christians in the churches. It appears, though, that both in 22:16, where he specifies both churches (mentioned in 1:4), John intends two separate categories. Servants may be members of churches, but they are, as individuals, not to be equated with the corporate entities, the churches. Indeed, that seems to be the very point that John is making by separating the *"you"* from *"churches"* in 22:16. Taken together, then, the three chains suggest the following overall

---

[306] → (1) The *"you"* of 22:16 is probably the members of the seven churches addressed in 1:4. (2) *"You"* followed by *"the churches"* reflects the situation where a group in one church is first addressed in each of the seven letters. (3) *"You"* refers to church authorities or *"prophets"* like John. (4) *"You"* and *"the churches"* are the same group.

progression of revelation: God to Christ to an angel to John to servants to the churches.

Who are these servants? Like John, they are associated with the churches. Contextually, John has throughout his work tied the language of servants to that of prophets (e.g., 10:7; 11:3, 8). Indeed, he has repeatedly re-established that connection in inventive ways in this very chapter (22:3, 6, 9). Verse 9 forges a link between the categories of servant and prophet and suggests not only that John and the angel both fit this category but also that there is a select group of prophets who are John's direct colleagues. This depiction of a group of prophets who considered themselves leaders in and for the churches also fits John's narrative presentation. Early on, in his letters to the churches, he warns his hearers and readers in the churches about rival bands of prophets who threaten to mislead them: Balaam, 2:14; the Nicolaitans, 2:15; and the infamous Jezebel, 2:20-23. These prophets have apparently corrupted the information transmission, conveying wrong teaching about God's expectations for the churches. This literary portrait fits historical reconstruction proposed by scholars like Bauckham, who points to Acts 21:8-9, and perhaps the Christian apocalypse called the *Ascension of Isaiah*, as evidence that circles of Christian prophets did exist in Asia during the time of John's writing. "*John's visionary experiences, we might suppose, would ordinarily have taken place in the context of a gathering of his fellow-prophets (probably also in the larger context of a church gathered for worship). He would relate the vision to them orally and they would later recount it to other churches"* (*Climax of Prophecy*, 89).

The second way that Christ establishes his eschatological bona fides is by laying claim to an exclusive status within the Davidic genealogy. He claims to be both the root and the descendant of David. Building directly from Isa. 11:1, 10, John ascribed the same designation to Christ at Rev. 5:5. The allusion to Isaiah, where "*root*" means descendant, together with John's immediate clarification that "*root*" signifies "*descendant*," suggests that Christ does not mean the root from which a plant grows but the root that itself grows out of the Davidic plant already in place (*Sir.* 47:22). Bauckham makes the provocative point that since, according to Isa. 11:10, this descendant becomes a positive signal of inclusion to the nations, John here too is expressing a universal understanding of salvation.

Christ makes a third attempt at establishing his eschatological bona fides by laying claim to the title "*bright morning star.*" Like the image of "*root*," this term has also appeared earlier in relation to Christ. Christ promised that the one who conquers (i.e., witnesses) will receive the morning star (Rev. 2:28). The implication is that such witnesses will enjoy an eschatological relationship with the one who is himself the morning star. The image derives from Num. 24:17, a text that foretells the promise of a messianic leader who will crush those who oppose God's people. The Jewish revolt against Rome in 132 – 35 C.E., led by Simon bar Kosiba, was interpreted through this messianic lens. Simon was accorded the legendary title

Bar Kokhba, "*Son of a Star*," and presumed to be the hero who would lead God's people victoriously against the empire. This interpretation was not unique: The text from Numbers was interpreted messianically within Judaism (cf. *T. Levi* 18.3; *T. Jud.* 24.1; and the Qumran documents *CD* 7.18-21; *1QM* 11.6-7; *4QTest [4Q175]* 9-13). John is certainly following this line of messianic interpretation; for him, the Standing Slaughtered Lamb, along with God, executes the judgment that destroys Babylon/Rome and inaugurates salvation for all who believe.

- **17** While identifying the speaker and the message in this verse seems to be a straightforward task, identifying the target audience is a more difficult matter. Yoked to the definite article and appearing in the singular, Spirit seems here to be not the human spirits of 22:6 but the Spirit of God. Earlier in the book, John referred to this characterization with the phrase "*the seven spirits.*" "Seven," we know, is the number that represents wholeness or completeness for John. The seven spirits together represented the complete and full Spirit of God (1:4-8; 3:1; 4:5; 5:6). Referenced in the singular with the article, the Spirit is an entity who acts for God, even speaking for God as it does here (2:7, 11, 17, 29; 3:6, 13, 22; 11:11; 14:13).

The bride, the focal character of the section that immediately precedes the epilogue (21:9-22:9), is even easier to identify. She is the new Jerusalem, the city that represents the people of God. On one level, as the city of God, she invites all nations to come through her open gates and find eschatological relationship with God (21:24). On another, more complex level, as the people of God, she invites not herself, as one might think, but those of the nations who are not of the church. In other words, she appears to be inviting those who are not yet witnessing believers to become witnessing believers so that they too may enter. Here is where the interpretive difficulties arise. Most interpreters argue that the Spirit and the bride are speaking instead to Jesus, inviting him to fulfill his pledge to come soon (22:7, 12, 20). If the Spirit and the bride are indeed talking to Jesus, the suggestion is that they do not believe that the Lamb, who has given his word and signed his figurative signature to it (v. 16), will honor his promise unless they intervene with an invitation. The invitation, then, is either redundant or a demonstration of a lack of faith in the Lamb. But surely the Spirit and the bride, both of whom enjoy an intimate relationship with the Lamb, trust the Lamb's word that he is coming, and coming soon. No further action on their part is necessary unless it is to encourage those who are not yet witnessing believers to repent, witness, and thus prepare themselves properly for Christ's coming. Indeed, an invitation to those who have yet to believe fits nicely with John's image of a gracious God, who even at the end extends invitations to nonbelievers to repent (2:5, 16, 21, 22; 3:3, 19; 9:20-21; 11:13; 14:7; 15:4; 16:9, 11; 18:4).

 This open invitation continues with the ensuing clause *"Let the one who hears say, 'Come.'"* Of whom does Christ speak? The verb *"hear"* is key to answering the question. In a book of visions and auditions, one expects to have the word *"hearing"* crop up often (cf. 22:8). But one would probably not expect that 28 percent of the time the verb occurs, it would be tied to *"doing"* (cf. 1:3; 2:7, 11, 17, 29; 3:3, 6, 13, 20, 22; 13:9; 22:18). This connection occurs especially in chapters 2 and 3, where John sets his ethical agenda. Those who hear are those who conquer. In other words, those who hear are those who have heard, repented, obeyed, and thus witness. *"Those who hear,"* then, is another way of saying what John has already implied through his use of the term *"bride."* These are believers. Christ is basically repeating and reinforcing the invitation that was just extended; the people of God invite those who are not yet of God to come. Yet he has added something very important. The connection drawn between hearing and witnessing indicates how they can manage this necessary movement. What do they need to do to be able to come? They must become like those who invite them. They must hear. They must witness to the lordship of God and Christ.

John has already identified the thirsty (Isa. 55:1; Rev. 21:6). This invitation continues the theme of inviting not Christ but those who desire and need eschatological relationship with him. Christ thus reinforces here what he has said earlier. The thirsty should seek entrance into the city because there resides the gift of living water (Rev. 7:17; 22:1).

- **18 – 19** The same Christ who has already validated his remarks by putting his own person on the line in v. 16

does the same thing, using another verbal approach, just two verses later. This time, as though he is swearing himself in at a trial, he sanctions what he is about to say with the pledge "*I testify.*" Remembering that his very name is "*Faithful and True*" (19:11), John's hearers and readers can certainly trust the oath-like pronouncement that follows. To everyone within the sound of his voice (and the verbal reach of John's work), he virtually commissions the sanctity of "*the prophecy of this book.*" John is following tradition here, adopting the premise that divinely authorized works should not be altered (Deut. 4:2; 12:32; *11QTemple* 54.5-7). The ending to the *Letter of Aristeas* (310-311), the account of the legendary creation of the Septuagint (LXX, the Greek translation of the Hebrew Bible), is another well-known example of an inspired book ending with the prohibition against making changes to it. As commentators note over and over again, the prohibition acts as a kind of copyright in a world that had no such protective device. But putting his own work in direct line with such prohibitions, John again signals that his work has been commissioned by God. In terms of form, he utilizes the kind of curse formula that Paul also applies in some of his letters (1 Cor. 16:22; Gal. 1:8-9).

The warning that follows is straightforward. John beings with a conditional sentence in which the opening clauses indicate a situation that not only might happen but is very likely to happen. He apparently has real reason to be concerned that someone might add to what he has written or take away from it. In the closing clauses of both halves of the sentence come the almost mocking rejoinders. Taking a page yet again from the ancient *lex talionis* tradition (Rev. 11:18; 16:1, 6; 18:6), he promises a punishment that matches the crime in kind, even if it is clearly disproportionate in terms of degree. For those who add to what John has written, Christ promises, on the basis of what is in effect his personal veracity, that God will add to them every one of the plagues that John has envisioned. Though John intends to balance the crime against the response to it, the resulting imbalance is almost laughable. The entire cosmos was unable to withstand such an onslaught; certainly any single individual would be absolutely crushed. Perhaps the horrific pain and suffering expected to attend such plagues, even more than annihilation itself, is intended. Certainly such a prospect should make any potential revisionist shudder. A corresponding response is also threatened to any who would subtract from what John has written. Christ promises that God will remove from them any stake in two of the especially previous symbols of eschatological relationship with God that John has spent the last few chapters highlighting: the tree of life (22:2) and the new Jerusalem (21:9-22:9). This final threat verifies that the earlier threat was a promise not of annihilation but of monstrous suffering. The shell of a being left in the wake of such plague-induced suffering would subsequently be doomed to the even greater suffering attached to a life of agonizing separation from God, also envisioned as eternal confinement in the lake of fire and sulfur, or brimstone (cf. 20:15).

- **20** Grounding his words in his person for yet a third time (22:16, 18), Christ identifies himself as the one who testifies to these things, in other words, the things he has just professed (vv. 12 – 19). He closes his remarks by declaring trustworthy a statement upon which John builds his exhortation to live a life that testifies to the lordship of God and the Standing Slaughtered Lamb: Christ is coming soon (2:16; 3:11; 16:15; 22:7, 12). That imminence lends urgency to all that John has said. Those who are not witnessing have little time left to repent. Those who are witnessing must continue to do so despite any persecutions, oppressions, and death that Rome might inflict.

    Nevertheless, in quoting Christ here and elsewhere, and in making his own claims about the nearness of God's judgment/salvation, John was wrong. Nearly two millennia later, the moment he anticipated has yet to arrive. Commentators are right to ask whether John's chronological inaccuracy detracts from his message. First, contemporary readers of his work are right to consider that his mistake on this critical point does well imply that he was probably mistaken in other areas of his presentation. His negative presentations of women, his understanding about eternal suffering, and his depictions of God's authorization and even execution of extreme acts of violence come immediately to mind. And yet, even where his mistakes are clear, there is a potent and viable message for contemporary readers. Even in his own time, John never asked his hearers and readers to contemplate the future in order to calculate the timetable of its arrival. He did not offer his prophecies only to predict for his time or future times when God was going to act. Instead, his future-oriented visions were intended to impel his hearers and readers into appropriate contemporary action. He appealed to the imminence of God's intervention not to offer a timeline but to encourage a sense of urgency.

It is that sense of urgency – living in the present moment as though God could break into time at any moment – that carries through the ongoing centuries to sustain meaning and hope for believers in the twenty-first century. John's primary message still holds. In a world where many human and even satanic forces seem to be in control, God and the Standing Slaughtered Lamb reign as Lord. No matter how powerful any country or force becomes, no matter how vast the reach of its military, political, and economic empire, God and the Standing Slaughtered Lamb still reign as Lord. This enduring indicative grounds an equally enduring imperative. Those who believe in that lordship – despite seeing pretensions to lordship in people and powers, and despite enduring persecutions at the hands of those people and powers when they refuse to recognize their lordship – must continue to witness, in word and in action, to the lordship of God and the Standing Slaughtered Lamb. They must do so because Christ who is Lord, the Christ who is faithful and true, has promised that he is coming soon.

Having apparently taken his cue from the heavenly hymn singers, John responds to Christ as he should, antiphonally. By crying out *"Amen!"* he registers his faith in the trustworthiness of what Jesus has said. In essence, he shouts, *"True!"*

In his penultimate statement, John acknowledges the worship setting in which it appears he expected his work to be heard. Having heard Jesus proclaim that he is coming soon, having anticipated the persecutions that will follow concerted witnessing to the lordship of God and the Standing Slaughtered lamb, John petitions Jesus to come in that very guise of Lord. It is no secret that he is operating from an early Christian formula highlighted by Paul at 1 Cor. 16:22 and by the author of the *Didache* at 10.6. The *Didache* corroborates what the petition *"come"* suggests by positioning the petition in the context of the Lord's Supper. A Eucharistic emphasis was implanted early on in the *"Apokalypsis"* when Christ told the Laodiceans that he was outside, knocking on their communal door, and would indeed come in and eat with them if they stop their efforts to accommodate to the lordship claims of Rome and instead witness to the lordship of God and the Standing Slaughtered Lamb. John, having just finished presenting his own written witness, now takes Christ up on his offer: *"Amen! Come, Lord Jesus!"* When Paul resoreted to the phrase, he did not translate it. He simply transliterated the Aramaic letters of the original saying into Greek letters for his readers: *"Marana tha"* (Our Lord, Come!). One can easily imagine members of John's churches, after just listening to a reading of his work and then hearing this petition, now moving directly into the meal, where the cultic presence of the

Lord would encourage participants to trust in the imminent coming of his eschatological presence.

- **21** Fittingly, John closes the work he began with an epistolary greeting (Rev. 1:4-6) by composing an epistolary benediction. Surely, readers in the very same Asia Minor communities where Paul had spent much of his ministry would have recognized the kind of closing greeting that the apostle used to conclude so many of his letters (1 Cor. 16:22-24; 2 Cor. 13:13; Rom. 16:20; Gal. 6:18; Phil. 4:23; 1 Thess. 5:28; Phlm. 25).

There is varied manuscript evidence for the wording of the final phrase of the Book of Revelation. Did John mean to wish God's grace for all the saints, all his saints, all your saints, all of us, all of you, or just all? The more specific formulations suggest that John addressed his work to the community of believers, to encourage and admonish the church alone. The more open ending, however, fits well with the message of the entire "*Apokalypsis*," particularly here at the end (cf. Rev. 21:3, 24; 22:22). It is more likely that Christian scribes would have altered the open ending to specifically identify the church as John's intended audience than that they would have dropped a word so as to make the audience more universal. Such an open ending to the benediction matches the emphasis on divine grace at the benediction's beginning. Even at the end of time, marked with such strong literary emphasis at the end of the Book of Revelation, John believes that God is a gracious God who reaches out not just to the church but also to any and all who would heed the call to witness to the one revelation that this book of many visions has strained to reveal: true lordship belongs exclusively to God and Jesus Christ.

                                                                 Amen.

Seals/ Trumpets/ Bowls

	Seals	Trumpets	Bowls
1	White Horse – Bow →conquers	Hail mixed w/blood & fire →1/3 earth, 1/3 trees & all grass burned	Sores on people w/ mark of the Beast
2	Red Hose – Sword → Removed peace from the earth. Slaughtered each other	Something like a mountain fell into the Sea →1/3 sea became blood, 1/3 sea creatures/ships destroyed	Sea became blood-like →every living sea creatures died
3	Black horse – Scale →Famine and inflated prices	Wormwood →spring water became bitter, many ppl died from waters	Rivers & Spring water became blood
4	Pale Horse – Death →power to kill ¼ of the earth	1/3 of Sun, Moon, Stars were darkened	Sun was given power to scorch people
5	*"Slaughtered Souls' cry"*	Fallen Star →received the key to open the Abyss, harm people for 5 months(scorpion, locusts, *"Apollyon"*)	*"Darkness"* over the throne of the beast
6	Earth quake →Sun darkened, bloody moon, falling stars	Altar released 4 angels from the Euphrates →two myriad myriads, killed 1/3 of human beings	The Euphrates dried up →prepared the way for kings of the East
	Intermission (1) 144,000 Intermission (2) a great multitude	Intermission (1) A little scroll Intermission (2) Two witnesses →earthquake, 7,000 died	Intermission (1) Three Evil sprits →Dragon, Beast, False prophets *"Armageddon"* – (Har-mageddon)
7	An Half hour →Silence →Prayers of saints in the incense offering	Hymn →Sanctuary in heaven opened.	Air →lightning, rumblings, thunder, the greatest Earthquake →no more island, mountains →Babylon split into 3 parts

Bibliography

Ahlstrom, Sidney E. *The Religious History of the American people*. New Haven, London: Yale University Press, 1972.

Aune, David. *Revelation. Vol. 1, 1-5*. WBC 52a. Dallas, TX: Word, 1997.

———. *Revelation. Vol. 2, 6-16*. WBC 52b. Dallas, TX: Word, 1998.

———. *Revelation. Vol. 3, 17-22*. WBC 52c. Dallas, TX: Word, 1998.

Bamberger, Bernard Jacob. *Fallen Angels: Soldiers of Satan's Realm*. Philadelphia, PA: Jewish Publication Society of America, 2006.

Bauckham, Richard. *The Climax of Prophecy: Studies on the Book of Revelation*. Eninburgh: T&T Clark, 1993.

Beale, G. K. *The Book of Revelation: A Commentary on the Greek Text*. NIGTC. Grand Rapids: Eerdmans, 1999.

Blitz, Mark. *Blood Moons: Decoding the Imminent Heavenly Signs*. Washington, DC: WND Books, 2014.

Blount, Brian K. *Revelation,* True to Our Native Land. Minneapolis, MN: Fortress, 2007.

_____. *Revelation: A Commentary.* NTL. Louisville, KY: Westminster John Knox Press, 2009.

Boesak, Allan A. *Comfort and Protest: The Apocalypse from a South African Perspective.* Philadelphia, PA: Westminster, 1987.

Boring, M. Eugene. *Revelation.* IBC. Louisville, KY: John Knox Press, 1989.

Boring, M. Eugene, Fred B. Craddock. *The People's New Testament Commentary.* Louisville,KY: Westminster John Knox Press, 2009.

Bousset, Wilhelm. *Die Offenbarung Johannis.* Gottingen: Vandenhoeck & Ruprecht, 1906.

Bruce, F.F. *Zondervan Bible Commentary: One-Volume Illustrated Edition.* Grand Rapids, MI: Zondervan, 2008.

Bunson, Matthew. *Angels A to Z: A Who's Who of the Heavenly Host.* New York, NY: Three Rivers Press, 1996.

Cahn, Jonathan. *The Harbinger.* Grand Rapids, MI: Frontlines, 2012.

_____. *The Mystery of the Shemitah.* Lake Mary, FL: Charisma Media, 2014.

Caird, G. B. *The Revelation of St. John the Divine*. San Francisco: Harper & Row, 1966.

Carson, D.A, R.T. France, J.A. Motyer, and G.J. Wenham. *New Bible Commentary: 21st century edition*. Nottingham, England: Inter-Varsity Press, 1994.

Charles, R. H. *A Critical and Exegetical Commentary on the Revelation of St. John*. 2 vols. ICC. Edinburgh: T&T Clark, 1920.

Collins, Adela Yarbro. *"Revelation 18: Taunt Song or Dirge,"* Gembloux: J. Duculot and Louvain: Louvain University Press, 1980.

Collins, John J. *Apocalypse: The Morphology of a Genre*. SemeiaST 14. Atlanta: Scholars Press, 1979.

Comay, Joan. *The Temple of Jerusalem*. New York, NY: Hold, Rinehard & Winston, 1975.

Cruz, Joan C. *Angels and Devils*. Charlotte, NC: Tan Books & Publishers, 1999.

Danker, Frederick William. *A Greek-English Lexicon of the New Testament and other Early Christian Literature Thrid Edition (BDAG)*. Chicago, IL: The University of Chicago Press, 2000.

deSilva, David A. "Honor Discourse and the Rhetorical Strategy of the Apocalypse of John." *JSNT* 71 (1998): 79-110.

deSilva, David A. *An Introduction to the New Testament: Contexts, Methods and Ministry Formation.* Downers Grove, IL: InterVarsity, 2004.

Dockery, David S. *Concise Bible Commentary.* Nashville, TN: B&H Publishing Group, 2010.

Eum, Terry Kwanghyun. *Iouda.* Charleston, SC: CreateSpace, 2015.

_____. *Kata Markon.* North Charleston, SC: CreateSpace, 2015.

_____. *Pros Philamona.* Middletown, DE: CreateSpace, 2015.

_____. *The Original Ending of the Gospel of Mark 16:1-8.* Middletown, DE: CreateSpace, 2015.

Frederick, Sontag. *Sun Myung Moon and the Unification Church.* Nashville, TN: Abingdon Press, 1977.

Gonzalez, Catherine, and Justo L. Gonzalez. *The Book of Revelation.* WBComp. Louisville, KY: Westminster John Knox Press, 1997.

Green, Robin M. *Spherical Astronomy.* Oxford, United Kingdom: Oxford University Press, 1985.

Guiley, Rosemary. *Encyclopedia of Angels.* New York, NY: Checkmark Books, 1996.

Hagee, John. *Four Blood Moons: Something Is About to Change*. Brentwood, TN: Worthy Publishing, 2013

Halsell, Grace. *Prophecy and Politics: Militant Evangelists on the Road to Nuclear War*. Westport, Conn.: Lawrence hill & Co., 1986.

Heil, J. P. "The Fifth Seal (Rev 6, 9-11) as a Key to the Book of Revelation." *Bib* 74 (1993): 220-43.

Holladay, Carl R. *A Critical Introduction to the New Testament: Interpreting the Message and Meaning of Jesus Christ*. Nashville, TN: Abingdon, 2005.

Johns, Loren L. *The Lamb Christology of the Apocalypse of John: An Investigation into Its Origins and Rhetorical Force*. WUNT 2/167. Tubingen: Mohr Siebeck, 2003.

Kasemann, Ernst. *New Testament Questions of Today*. Philadelphia: Fortress, 1969.

Keller, Catherine. *Apocalypse Now and Then: A Feminist Guide to the End of the World*. Boston: Beacon, 1996.

Knibb, Michael A. *The Ethiopic Book of Enoch*. Oxford, England: Clarendon Press, 1982.

Lincoln, C. Eric, and Lawrence Mamiya. *The Black Church in the African-American Experience*. Durham, NC: Duke University Press, 1990.

Mounce, William D. *Mounce's Complete Expository Dictionary of Old & New Testament Words*. Grand Rapids, MI: Zondervan, 2006.

N. C., Debevoise. *A Political History of Parthia*. Chicago, IL: University of Chicago Press, 1938.

Newsome, Carol A., Sharon H. Ringe, eds. *Women's Bible Commentary*. Louisville, KY: Westminster John Knox Press, 1998.

Pfeil, Michael E. *Rapture of the Church: Bound for Heaven, but…*. Bloomington, IN: WestBow Press, 2013.

Reddish, Mitchell G. *Revelation*. Macon, GA: smyth & Helwys, 2001.

Rhode, Ron. *Reasoning from the Scriptures with the Jehovah's Witnesses*. Eugene, OR: Harvest House Publishers, 2009.

Rowland, Christopher. *Revelation*. Epworth Commentaries. London: Epworth, 1993.

Rowland, Christopher C. *Revelation*, The New Interpreter's Bible Volume XII. Nashville, TN: Abingdon, 1998.

Schüssler Fiorenza, Elisabeth. *The Book of Revelation: Justice and Judgment*. 2d ed. Minneapolis: Fortress, 1998.

Smith, Julia M.H. *Europe After Rome: A New Cultural History 500-1000*. Oxford, England: Oxford University Press, 2005.

Thomson, Leonard C. *Revelation*. Nashville, TN: Abingdon, 1998.

White, R. E. R. *Biblical Ethics*, Atlanta, GA: John Knox, 1979.

Wood, D. R. W. *New Bible Dictionary*. Nottingham, England: Inter-Varsity Press, 1996.

Index of Ancient and Biblical References

Acts
1:7	515
1:9	395
2:14-21	264
2:23	184
2:25	185
2:33	185
4:24	237,356
5:5	371
5:31	185
6:5	90,91
6:11	551
7:55	311
7:55-56	185
8:32	195
10:11	650
13:6	562
13:13	7
13:22-23	134
13:48	133,371
14:13	198
14:18	198
15:20	341
15:28-29	119
16:14	111
16:14-15	25,113
18-21	86
18:19-21	85
19:8-10	85
19:17	371
19:19	330
19:35	85,95
19:37	551
20:6	323
20:7	67,74
21:8-9	773
21:20	330
21:40	279,281
24:1	323
26:14-23	264

Amos
1:2	352
3:7	50,361
3:8	352
3:13LXX	404,528
4:10	302
4:13LXX	404,528
5:7	306
5:18-20	13
5:20	307

Amos (continue)
7:1LXX	334
8:2	13
8:2-3	282
8:9	307
8:10	225

Apocalypse of Abraham
31:1	289

Ascension of Isaiah
4.2-14	456

Asiarchs of Acts
19:31	472

Assumption of Moses
3.1	334

Babylonian Talmud Berakot
46a	435

Babylonian Talmud Yoma
20a	435

Baruch
4-5	263
4:35	612

2 Baruch
	16
3:7	283
6	335
24:1	696

2 Baruch (continue)
27:1-15	143
29:3-4	448
29:1-30:5	683
40	487,674
40:1-4	683
56:13	674
63	263
67	263
72:2-74:3	683
78-87	263

3 Baruch
	16

1 Chronicles
11:5	486
12:23-37	264
16:28	640
16:31	640
20:2	516
21:1	433
21:1-6	263
21:16	225
24:1-19	170
25:6-31	202
27:1-24	263
28:17	536

2 Chronicles
2:17-18	263
4:8	536
4:21	536
5:2	487
5:13	537
18:10	200
24:9	527
35:22	567

Cicero Epistulae ad Atticum
6.5	595

794

Index of Ancient and Biblical References

2 Clement
3:2   133

Colossians
1:15   153
1:15-20   149
1:24   93
2:1   152
3:1   185
3:5   341
4:12-13   152
4:13   152
4:15   152
4:16   152
4:15-16   23

1 Corinthians
1:3   22,56
2:11   751
4:8   93
5:7   198
5:9-11   714
6:2-3   680
6:9-10   714
6:15-16   573
7:34   751
8-10   26,107
8:5-6   149
9:16   300
10:19-20   340
12:13   257
13:12   746
14:14   751
14:19   323
15   682,702
15:20   496
15:23   496
15:26   698,703
15:32   86
15:52   289
16:2   67,74
16:8   86
16:22   778,782
16:22-24   783

2 Corinthians
1:2   22,56

2 Corinthians (continue)
1:4   93
1:19-20   149
1:22   257,496
3:8   729
5:5   496
5:17   702
6:4   93
7:1   751
8:2   93
11:2   640
11:13   87
12:2   166
12:2-4   354
12:4   492
13:1   381
13:13   783

Daniel
1:12-15   99
2:28-47   47
2:28   750
2:44   14,403
2:45   750
2:47   600
3:4   367
4:12LXX   729
4:13-14LXX 189
4:23LXX   189
4:27-37   505
4:30-37   458
4:34   371
5:4   340
5:7   584
5:16   584
5:23   340
5:27   225
5:29   584
7   591
7:2   253
7:2-3   173,449
7:3   389
7:7   423,449
            452
7:7-8   598
7:8   200,458
7:9   76,679,694
7:9-14   168
7:9-10   77,172,201
7:10   208, 695

Daniel (continue)
            696
7:13   63,201,395
7:13-14   64,76,516
7:14   209,461
            735
7:18   206,747
7:20   200,458
            598
7:21   389,390
            600
7:22   206
7:24   200,449
            451,598
7:25   378,428
            442,458
            759
7:27   206,682
            747
8:3   200,470
8:6   200
8:8   200
8:10   314,424
8:14   759
8:15-17   347
8:18   79
8:19   355
8:20   200
8:26   355,750
            758
9:6   362
9:10   362
9:11   527
9:27   759
10:2-9   347
10:5   76,345
10:6   77,79,348
            634,652
10:13   249
10:15-21   76
10:21   429
11:30-39   275
11:44   275
12:1   133,143
            429,570
            697
12:1-2   131
12:1-4   274
12:2   407
12:4   3,188,750
            758
12:5   351
12:5-9   345

795

Index of Ancient and Biblical References

Daniel (continue)
12:5-13	347
12:7	356,378
	428,440
	759
12:9	3,188,750
	758
12:10	275,763
12:11	759
12:12	759
12:12-13	54

Dead Sea Scrolls
CD (Damascus Document)
CD 7.18-21	775

Deuteronomy
1:7	334
2:7	427
2:15-16	427
3:24	457
4:2	778
5:8	190
8:3	109
8:16	109
10:8-9	265
10:17	600
11:6	443
11:16-17	386
11:25	371
12:32	778
17:16	381
18:1-5	265
19:5	381
19:15	380,381
19:21	617
23:5	91
26:1-11	534
28:1	543
28:27	543
28:35	543
29:5	427
29:18KJV	306
32:1-43	527
32:4	528
32:8	528
32:10	427
32:17	340

Deuteronomy (continue)
32:35-39	355
32:40	78,355
32:40LXX	356
32:43	238,440
33	264
33:17	200

Didache
9.5	770
10.6	782
14.1	74
16.6	289

Dio
66.23.1	305

Diodorus
4.49.8	536

1 Enoch
	2,318
6	319
6-7	319
8-9	319
10	319
10:4-14	674
10:12	320
12:4	319
12:4-6	319
13:1-2	319
13:1-3	319
13:4	319
14:3-6	319
14:5	319
14:8-16:4	168
18:12-16	674
15:1-16:3	319
20:1-7	288
20:40	288
21	320
21:1-10	674
21:7	314
25:4-6	744

1 Enoch (continue)
39:1-40	168
40:7	435
45:4	701
46:1	74
47:3	696
47:4	242
54	319
54:1-6	674
54:6	288,429
56:1-2	319
56:5-8	335
60:7-11	448
60:11-25	545
60:24	448
61:10	545
66:1-2	545
67	320
67:4	320
67:7	320
69:22	545
71:1-17	79
71:8-9	288
71:10	76
72:1	701
75:3	545
81:1-4	696
81:5	288
86:3	314
88:1	319
88:3	314
89:61-77	696
89-90	196
90:6-12	200
90:17	696
90:20	696
90:21-22	288
90:37	200
91:11-17	683
91:16	701
98:7-8	696
100:3	519
102:8	746
106:5-6	76
108:3	131

2 Enoch
4-6	545
7:1-3	320
19:1-4	545

Index of Ancient and Biblical References

Ephesians	
1:13	257
1:13-14	496
2:2	166
2:20	727
3:8	93
4:7-10	166
4:30	257
5:5	341,714
5:18	229
5:25-32	640
5:32	641
6:17	659

Epictetus Diatribai	
3.22.10	584
4.11.34	584

1 Esdras	
1:29-31	567
8:30	493
9:8	371

2 Esdras	
6:49	469
6:51	469
13:40-47	263

Esther	
8:15	584
8:17	371
9:2	371

Exodus	
2:15	427
3:1	723
3:12	723
3:14	57,65,112
4:10	527
7	386

Exodus (continue)	
7:8-12:36	301
7:17-21	304,543
7:17-25	386
8:1-15	561
9:8-12	543
9:13-26	572
9:22-26	302
9:24	570
10:5	320
10:15	320
10:21	307
10:22-23	556
12	257
13:21	348,537
14:31	527
15:1-18	527
15:3-4	656
15:5	315
15:6	184
15:11	457
15:12	184,443
15:16	371,395
16:10	348
16:31-35	109
16:32	427
19:4	415,442
19:6	62,206,687
19:16	74,159,289
19:16-18	298
19:18	317
19:18-21	172
20:4	190
20:11	356
21:23-25	617
23:19	495
25:18	174
25:31-37	75
27:2	332
28:4	76
28:15-21	732
28:16	732
28:18	160
28:39	535
29:38-42	196
30:1-10	292,332
30:11-16	263
30:34-38	293
32:32	133
32:32-33	131,697
33:7-11	534
33:18-23	746
33:20	746

Exodus (continue)	
34:6 LXX	137
34:10	523
37:17-24	75
37:25-26	332
38:2	332
38:23-26	536
39:8-14	732
39:9	732
39:11	160
39:29	76
40:34-35	537
40:34-38	534
40:5	332

Ezra	
1:3	691
2	263

2 Ezra	
9:11	362

4 Ezra	
	16
2:38	256
2:40	256
4:35-37	242
6:5	256
6:20	696
6:23	289
6:39	283
6:47-52	448
7:26-44	283,683
7:30	282
7:91	746
7:98	746
9:38-10:57	420
12:31-32	191
12:31-34	683
13:25-38	383
13:25-52	487
13:32-38	415
14:5-6	758
14:45-46	758
15:42	571

Index of Ancient and Biblical References

Ezekiel		Ezekiel (continue)		Ezekiel (continue)	
1:1	650	23:31-34	507,602	38:20	571
1:4	172	23:44	573	38:22	303,508
1:4-28	168	24:7	631		692
1:5-25	174	25:2	366	39	13
1:7	77	26-27	611	39:1	689
1:13	172	26-28	621	39:2	334
1:14	172	26:7-11	334	39:6	692
1:18	175	26:12	629	39:17-20	664
1:22	173	26:13	629	40-48	372,733
1:24	77,172	26:16	621		735
1:26-28	172,694	26:16-17	609	40:1-2	722
1:27	348	26:19	602	40:1-5	733
1:28	79,159	26:19LXX	625	40:2	723
2:8-3:3	363	26:21	629	40:3	728
2:9-10	186,350	27:7-25	624	40:5	372,724
2:10	216	27:12-22	609		728
3:12	73	27:30-34	609,627	43:1-5	733
3:27	763	27:32	282,626	43:2	77,611,723
4:10	225	27:36	609,624		735
4:16	225	28:2	620	43:5	722,734
5:2	303	28:13	160	43:7	493
5:12	231,303	29	422	43:15	332
7:2	253,688	29:3	422	47:1	741
9:2	76	31:8-9	92	47:8-10	741
9:4-8	256	31:15	315	47:12	743,744
9:11	76	32:2-3	422	47:13-48:29	263
10:1-22	174	32:7	246	48:16	729
10:12	175	33:3-6	288	48:30-35	726,729
11:20	714	33:27	247		
11:24	167	33:29	737		
12:2	104	34:21	200		
14:12-23	212	34:23	278	**Galatians**	
14:14	222	34:25	427	1:3	22,56
14:16	222	36:18	631	1:8-9	778
14:18	222	37	13,394,689	2:9	135
14:20	222	37:3	272	3:7	267
14:21	222,231	37:5	394	3:29	267
14:20-23	222	37:10	394	4:26	707
16	577	37:10LXX	682	5:19-21	341,714
16:2	392	37:26-28	277	6:15	702
16:8-14	641	37:27	709	6:16	267
16:15-58	493	38	13	6:18	783
16:37-41	602	38-39	566,689		
16:30-31	573		664		
16:35	573	28:2	690	**Genesis**	
16:46	392	38:2-3	689	1:2-10	442
16:49	392	38:6	334,689	1:21	446
17:3	442			1:30	394
17:7	442	38:15	334,689	2-3	92
23:1-49	493	38:17	362	2:2	160
23:25-29	602	38:19	245		
		38:19-23	397		

798

Index of Ancient and Biblical References

Genesis (continue)
2:7	394
2:9	743
2:10	741
3	432
3:1-6	415
3:3	92
3:24	174
4:10	655
4:15	257
6:1-4	314
6:17	394
7:15	394
7:22	394
9:12-13	159
12:3	65
13:16	267
14:19	356
14:22	356
15:5	267
15:12	398
15:18	334
19:17	247
19:24	297,508
19:28	318
22:1-14	723
22:17	267
22-24	92
26:4	267
28:14	267
32:12	267
34:31	573
35:2	641
49	264
49:9-10	191

Georgica
2.353	595

Gospel of Peter
3.7	584

Greek Apocalypse of Ezra
4:36	289

Habakkuk
1:6	691
2:15-16	507
2:20	282

Hebrews
1:1-4	149
1:3	185
1:12	247
1:13	184,185
2:9	746
4:12	78,659
8:1	185
9:1-40	408
10:12	185
10:28	381
11:10	727
11:12	267
11:16	707
12:2	185
12:14	746
12:22	330,487
12:23	131,697

Hesiod
Theogony
319-24	338

Homer
Iliad
6.181-82	338

Hosea
1:2	493
2:5	573,602
	641
3:1-4:2	340
3:3	573
4:10	573
4:12-15	573
5:3	247,573
5:4	493
5:6	493
5:10	493

Hosea (continue)
9:1	573
10:8	248
11:1	427
11:10	352
13:5	427

Irenaeus
Against Heresies
5.30.8	9

Isaiah
1:4	137
1:9-10	392
1:21	573,641
2:2	531
2:3	691
2:8	340
2:10	247
2:19	247
2:20	340
2:21	247
3:24	225
4:3	131,133
	697,737
5:19	137
5:25	571
5:26-29	334
6:1-4	174
6:1-13	167,168
6:4	244,537
7:14	424
7:14LXX	420
7:20	334
8:7-8	334
8:19-22	556
11:1	191,774
11:4	78,651,659
11:10	191,774
11:12	253,688
11:15-16	558
13:10	246,307
13:19-22	612
13:21-22	609
14:12	314
14:13-14	620
14:19-20	391
14:29-31	334
17:8	340

Index of Ancient and Biblical References

Isaiah (continue)

21:9	505,609
22:22	134,137
23	577
23-24:47	611
23:8	609,630
23:17	581,609, 612
24-27	13
24:1	13
24:8	629
24:18-23	245
24:19-20	13
24:21-22	674
24:23	487,735
25:2	13
25:7	13
25:8	278,710
26:15	420,422
26:17	422
26:17LXX	420
26:19	13
27	420
27:1	13,173,422, 446,448
29:6	245,298, 352
29:11	188
30:8	76
34:4	186,246
34:9-10	508
34:11	609
34:11-15	612
34:14	609
35:8	737
35:10	710
37:1-2	225
37:22	577
40:2	61,609,618
40:3	427
40:4	571
40:10	767
40:12	225
40:18	457
40:25	137,457
40:31	442
41:2	557
41:4	65,712
41:10	184
41:25	557
42:10	203,490
42:15	571
43:19	710

Isaiah (continue)

44:2	79
44:6	65,712
44:7	457
44:9-20	340
44:23	440
45:2	571
45:14	140
46:11	557
47:5	282
47:8	620
47:8-9	609
47:9	621,630
47:9-10	340
48:2	704
48:5	340
48:6	81
48:12	65,712
48:13	184
48:20	609,614
49:2	78,659
49:10	277,278, 713
49:13	440
49:23	140
49:26	548
50:3	246
51:9-11	173
51:10	315,558
51:17	507
51:22	507
52:1	641,704, 707,737
52:5	551,554
52:11	614
53:2	196
53:7	196
53:9	196
54:1-8	641
54:10	571
54:11-12	732,733
55-66	14
55:1	713,777
56:1	764
57:3	573
58:8	723
60	735
60:1	735
60:1-2	723
60:11	736,737
60:14	140
60:19-20	735
61:6	687

Isaiah (continue)

61:10	641,707
62:1-5	652
62:1-2	705
62:2	148,652
62:3	652
62:3-5	702,735
62:6	726
63:1-6	518,650, 656,660
63:13	315
64:1	571
64:3	571
65:4	493
65:15	148
65:16	149,152
65:16 LXX	137
65:17	14,701
65:19	710
66:7-9	415
66:7LXX	420
66:7	424
66:7-14	577
66:22	701,710

James

1:1	264
2:7	551
5:9	759
5:17	386,760

Jeremiah

1:10	366
1:14-15	334
2:2	641
2:13	713
3:2	493
3:3	573
3:17	745
4:6-13	334
4:8	225
4:29	247
4:30	584
5:12	620
5:14	383
6:1	334
6:22	334
6:26	225
7:5-11	340

Index of Ancient and Biblical References

Jeremiah (continue)		Jeremiah (continue)		Job (continue)	
7:25-26	361	48:37	225	4:1	446
7:34	609	49:3	225	6:8-9	323
8:1-2	391	49:12	507	7:15-16	323
8:3	323,323	49:30	247	11:9	351
9:9-11	612	49:36	253	26:6	328
9:10	609	50-51	611	26:12-13	173
9:15	306	50:8	609	28:22	328
9:22	391	50:15	609,617	30:6	247
10:1-16	340	50:29	609,617	31:12	328
10:7	528,529		621	36:30-32	172
10:22	245,334	50:31	609,621	37:2-5	352
11:20	118	50:34	621	38:7	314
13:4-6	247	50:38	558	38:16	315
13:20	334	50:41-42	334	38:17	80
13:27	493	51	422	39:19-20	326
15:2	231,465	51:4	493	40:15	469
16:4-6	391	51:6	609		
16:9	609	51:7	507,609		
16:10-15	263	51:7-8	505	**Joel**	
16:18	618	51:9	609	1:6	327
16:19	531	51:13	580	2:1-11	334
17:10	118,767	51:27	326	2:1	288,320
20:14-18	323	51:36	558	2:2	327
21:7	231	51:37	612	2:3	303
22:8	626	51:45	609,614	2:4	327
22:19	391	51:48	627	2:4-5	327
23:5	191	51:49	631	2:10	245,246
23:14	392				318
23:15	493			2:11	248
23:15	306			2:15	288,320
25:4	362	**1 John**		2:20-25	334
25:9	334	1:1-3	753	2:29	323
25:10	609,629	1:5	735	2:30	303
25:15	507,609	1:6	715	2:31	318
25:26	334	2:18	762	3:1	323
25:30	352,366	3:2	746	3:2	566
26:5	362	3:4-10	141	3:13	513,514
29:19	362	3:12	198	3:15	307,318
31:1	709	4:1	87,562	3:16	245,352
31:2	427	4:3	762		
31:6	691				
31:16	278,710				
31:32	641				
31:33	709	**Job**		**John**	
32:10	188	1:9-11	435	1:1	149
33:15	191	1:16	297	1:14	149,708
34:22	602	2:4-5	435	1:29	195
35:15	362	2:12	627	1:36	195
42:5	153	3:1-26	323	1:47	264
43:11	465	3:8	446,448	2:1-10	229
44:4	362	3:21	323	3:18-19	762
46-47	334	3:40-41	448	3:36	762

Index of Ancient and Biblical References

John (continue)
4:35-38	514
5:29	695
5:43-47	264
6:19	729
6:47	762
7:37	713
7:37-38	741
8:12	735
8:17	380,381
8:30-47	97
10:4	495
10:33	551
11:18	729
11:21-26	762
11:52	264
12:13	268
12:15	487
12:31	762
12:48	762
13:36	495
14-16	762
15:19	615
17:3	762
17:15	144,615
19:2	584
19:30	523,710
21:15	182

Jonah
1:9	351
2:6	315
3:5-8	225
4:3	323
4:8	323

Josephus
Against Apion
2.83-83	459

Josephus
Jewish Antiquities
1.73	319
2.14.1	302
3.7.5	732
6.99	247
6.116	247

Josephus
Jewish Antiquities (continue)
12.272-75	247
12.421	247
14.429	247

Josephus
Jewish War
1.307	247
3.376-78	391
3.380-84	391
4.314-18	391
5.33	391
5.5.7	732
6.370	247

Joshua
1:2	527
1:4	334
3:1-4:18	558
6:5	288
7:6	627
11:4	690
13:14	265
13:22	91
13:33	265
21:4-7	264
24:5	91
24:7	427

Jubilees
1:20	435
1:27	288
1:28	487,746
1:29	288
2:1-2	288
2:2	545
2:18	288
5:6	674
10:4-14	674
15:27	288
17:15-16	435
18:9-12	435
23:11-21	143
23:23	391
31:14	288

Jubilees (continue)
48:15-18	435

Jude
6	319,674
9	429,435
11	105,300
14	330
14-15	291

Judges
5	264
5:4	244
5:19	566
5:20	314
6:2	247
7:12	690
8:26	584
18	265

Judith
7:30	323
8:9	323

Justin Martyr
Dialogue with Trypho
81.4	5

1 Kings
5:13-18	263
6:19-20	729
6:20-22	731
7:10	733
8:1	408,487
8:6	408
8:10	348
8:10-11	537
12:25-33	265
14:11	770
16-21	91
16:4	770
16:31	115

Index of Ancient and Biblical References

1 Kings (continue)
16:31-33	111,116
17-18	385
17:1-17	427
18:4	115
18:13	115
18:17-40	116
18:19	116
18:38-39	473
19:1-3	115
19:1-4	323
20:31-32	225
21:2	115
21:8	527
21:24	770
21:27	225
22:11	200
22:19	167,168

2 Kings
1:9-14	692
1:10	297,383
1:10-14	473
1:12	297
1:14	297
2:11	395
7:1	225
9	91
9:7	238,362
9:10	391,770
9:22	340
9:27	566
9:30	117
9:36	770
9:30-37	602
15:19-20	263
17	263
17:13	362
17:23	362
19:1-2	225
19:15	174
21:10	362
23:29-30	567
24:2	362

Lamentation
2:10	627
2:10-11	282
2:13	577

Lamentation (continue)
3:15	306
3:19	306
4:5	584
4:21	507

Letter of Aristeas
310-311	778

Leviticus
1:1-2	534
2:1	293
2:15	293
4:7	236
6:15	293
10:1	293
16:11-14	293
16:12	297
21:9	602
23:9-14	475
23:24	288
23:40	268
23:48	268
24:16	554
24:17-20	617
25:9	288
26:8	323
26:11-12	709
26:26	225

Luke
1:11	185
1:12	371
1:15-17	385
1:28-33	134
1:65	371
1:68-79	264
2:29-32	264
3:23	134
4:1-2	582
4:25	311,386
4:25-26	385
4:26	760
5:1	755
6:26	562
7:11-17	385

Luke (continue)
7:33-34	229
8:8	91
9:13-16	323
9:23	456,495
9:28-29	723
9:29	129
9:54	473
10:1-24	381
10:1	380
10:2	514
10:13	225,382
10:18	314,328
10:19	314,380
10:20	131,133
	697
11:28	54
12:1	330
12:6	323
12:8	133
12:36	759
12:37-40	564
12:39-40	128
12:49	692
12:52	323
13:29	644
14:27	495
14:35	91
15:18	311
15:21	311
16:21	770
17:2	629
17:37	309
20:41-44	134
20:42	184
21	274
21:20-21	247
21:26	246
21:27	395
22:7	198
22:18	644
22:30	263,680
22:69	184,514
23:27-30	323
23:30	248
24:13	729
24:42-43	682
24:51	395

1 Maccabees
1:20-24	459

Index of Ancient and Biblical References

1 Maccabees (continue)	
3:25	371
6:1-5	459
7:18	371
10:20	584
10:62	584
10:64	584
10:89	76
11:1	690
11:58	584
11:71	627
13:51	268
14:43	584

2 Maccabees	
1:14-17	459
2:4-8	55,408
3:24	371
3:25	650
10:6-7	268,269
10:7	268
11:5	729
12:9-10	729
12:16-17	729
12:22	371
12:29	729
13:4	600

3 Maccabees	
2:9-14	651
7:13	636

Malachi	
1:11	531
2:9	73
3:2	248
3:2-3	156
3:16	696
4:4	527

Mark	
1:10	311
1:12	377

Mark (continue)	
1:12-13	582
1:17	456
3:27	674
4:9	91
4:23	91
4:29	514
6:38-41	323
6:39	230
7:27-28	770
8:34	456,495
9:2	723
9:2-13	385
9:2-8	488
9:3	129
9:42	629
10:37	185
12:36	184
13	274
13:7-20	143
13:10	501
13:13	564
13:14	247
13:19-20	323
13:20	523,553
13:21-23	473
13:22	562
13:24-25	246,307
13:26	395
13:26-27	514
13:29	759
13:31	311
13:32	515
13:32-37	564
13:37	564
14:12	198
14:21	300
14:25	109,644
14:62	63,184,395, 514
15:17	584
16:2	74
16:5	129,185
16:6	72,199,487

Martial Epig.	
6.64	595

Matthew	
2:13-15	427
3:2	311
4:1	582
4:5	704
4:19	456
5:1	723
5:3	93
5:8	746
5:12	640
5:16	311
7:6	770
7:15	470,562
8:11	644
10:5-6	264
10:26-33	94
10:32	133
10:38	495
11:15	91
11:21	225,300, 382
11:23	311
12:30	149
13:9	91
13:43	91
14:17-19	323
14:24	729
14:25	644
15:26-27	770
16:5	129
16:19	138
16:24	456,495
17:1-2	723
18:6	629
18:16	381
18:18	138
19:28	263,680
20:2	226
21:5	574
21:25	311
22:2	640
22:2-9	109
22:44	184
23:35	631
23:37	631
24	274
24:11	562
24:14	501
24:15-16	247
24:15-31	143
24:21	93
24:23-25	473
24:24	562

Index of Ancient and Biblical References

Matthew (continue)
24:29   246,307
24:30   63,395,514
24:30-31   159
24:31   289
24:42-44   128
24:42-51   564
25:1-13   229
25:33-34   185
25:41   83,692
26:26   363
26:29   644
26:52   466
26:64   184,395, 514
27:54   569
28:1   67
28:2   569
28:4   79

Micah
1:4   245
3:3   602
4:2   691
4:7   487
4:9-10LXX   421
5:3LXX   421
5:12   341
6:8   341
7:18   457

Milhamah **(War Scroll)**
16
1QH1[9].8-13   545
1QM 1.2   265
1QM 2   263
1QM 2.2   265
1QM 7.14   289
1QM 7:3-6   494
1QM 11.6-7   775

Nahum
1:5   245
1:6   248
1:14   341

Nahum (continue)
3:1-4   341
3:4   609

Nehemiah
1:7-8   527
7   263
8:14-18   268
9:6   356
9:19   427
9:21   427
11:1   704
11:18   704

Numbers
1:2-46   263
1:16-54   264
1:49   265
2:33   265
3:14-4:49   263
4:14-15   536
7:13-89   536
7:89   174
8:1-4   75
11:6-9   109
14:18 LXX   137
16:6   293
16:22   751
16:30   443
16:33   666
16:46-47   295
22-24   91,106
24:14-20   120
24:17   774
27:16   751
31:16   106
34:19-28   264
35:30   380,381

Obadiah
16   507
21   691

Odes of Solomon
30.1-2   713

1 Peter
1:19   195
2:6   487
3:19   319
3:22   185
4:7   763
4:16   763
5:8   93,435
5:13   501
5:19   763

2 Peter
2:1   562
2:4   319,674
2:5   128
2:15   105
2:22   770
3:3-13   761
3:7   694
3:10   128,564, 694
3:12   694
3:13   701

Pesher Habakkuk
1QpHab 13.1-4   282

Philippians
1:1   249
1:2   22,56
1:17   93
2:5-11   166
2:9   653
3:2   770
4:3   133,697
4:4   131
4:14   70,93
4:23   783

Philemon
3   22,56
25   783

805

Index of Ancient and Biblical References

Philo
Cherubim
49-50   494

Philo
Joseph
25   391

Philo
Moses
1.95   302

Pliny
Epistulae
6.16.11   305
10.96-97   29

Polybius
31.9   459

Proverbs
3:19   153
5:4   306
8:22-31   153
8:29   351
15:11   328
16:11   225
16:24   364
24:12   118,767
26:11   770
27:20   328
27:21   156
30:27   328
31:21   584

Psalms
1:1   53
2:6   487

Psalms (continue)
2:6-12   487
2:8-9   119
2:9   425
2:10   582
2:10-11   119
6:3-4   233
7   239
9:11   487
10:16   403
11:6   297,507
       508
11:7   746
13:1-2   233
14:7   487
17:15   746
18:6-7   244
18:7   571
18:7-19   172
18:13   352
18:35   184
19:10   364
20:6   184
22:21   200
23:1-2   278
28:4   696,767
29:3   352
31:17-18   282
33:3   203,490
35   239
35:10   457
35:17   233
39:27   59
40:3   203
46:2-3   571
46:4   741
50:2   487
53:6   487
55   239
58   239
59   239
63:8   184
68:1   247
69   239
69:28   131,133
       697
71:19   457
71:20   315
72:2   651
74:9-10   233
74:12-15   173,415
74:13   442
74:13-14   422

Psalms (continue)
74:14   448
75:8   507
77:16   442
77:17-18   172
77:18-19   298
78:15   427
78:19   427
78:23   163
78:24   109
78:43-51   301
78:44   543
78:45   561
79   239
79:1-5   391
79:2-3   392
79:5   233,237
79:10   238
80:1   174
80:4   233
83   239
84:7   487
86   531
86:8-10   530
86:9   140
88:11   328
88:28LXX   59
88:38LXX   59
89:6   233,457
89:9-10   173
89:17   200
90:4   761
93:1   640
95:7   709
96:1   203,490
96:11   440
96:13   651
97:1   640
97:3   383,547
97:5   571
98:1   203
98:1LXX   406
98:9   651
99:1   174,406
       640
99:2   487
103:19   168
104:1-2   419
104:25-26   448
104:35   635
105:26   527
105:27-36   301
105:38   395

806

Index of Ancient and Biblical References

Psalms (continue)		Revelation (continue)		Revelation (continue)	
106:9	558		676,740		114,117
106:17	443		748,750	2:5	129,145,
106:48	638		752,753		154,554
109	239		758,771		696,766
111:2	523		772		767,776
113-118	635	1:1-2	771	2:6	88,126,696
113:1	635	1:2	48,60,139		761,766
113:5	457		160		767
114:3-7	694	1:3	7,53,128	2:7	61,72,642
115:4-7	340		129,144		713,744
115:13	639		176,364		769,775
115:17	282		751,752		777
118:19-21	769		753,758	2:8	74,79,82
118:24	640		777		124,253
118:27	332	1:4	4,79,753		682,767
119:100-103	364		771,772	2:9	93,98,123
122:4	691	1:4-6	22,783		126,136
125:1	487	1:4-8	50,775		140,155
134	639	1:5	61,124,128	2:10	63,79,144
135:1	639		130,736		145
135:15-17	340	1:6	99,152,687	2:11	61,72,92
135:20	639		724		93,642,687
136:3	600	1:7	63,90,152		713,775
136:16	427	1:8	60,79,549		777
137	239		710,711	2:10-11	29
137:8	609,617		767	2:12	26,74,82
139	239	1:9	4,48,67,87		253
139:14	523		128,139	2:13	42,60,114
139:16	133		753		123,126,
139:21	90	1:11	22,23		128,139
141:2	202	1:12	58,85,160		143,145
144:9	203,490	1:12-20	114		676
145:17	528	1:13	58,85	2:14	88,115,613
146:6	351,356	1:14	383		715,738
149:1	490	1:16	26,85,123		761,773
			160	2:15	88,115,761
		1:17	124,712		773
			767	2:16	26,109,117
Psalms of Solomon		1:18	63,124,230		129,145
	2,16		682		554,752
2:30-31	391	1:19	74,159,697		759,776
14:3	744	1:20	58,85,123		780
15:6	257		253	2:17	61,72,92
15:9	257	2	777		93,524,642
17:28-31	263	2:1	74,76,82		713,775
17:40	263		123,253		777
17:42-43	156	2:1-3:22	23	2:18	74,82,253
		2:2	99,123,126		383
			696,766	2:19	61,123,126
			767		696,766
Revelation		2:3	126		767
1:1	4,249,253	2:4	61,115	2:20	117,249

807

Index of Ancient and Biblical References

Revelation (continue)		Revelation (continue)		Revelation (continue)	
	613,641	3:12	61,72,92		267,367
	677,761		110,135	5:9-10	64
2:20-21	329		642,713	5:10	62,99,682
2:20-22	20,715		746		687,747
2:20-23	88,738,773	3:13	91,775,777	5:11	176,253
2:21	109,358	3:14	74,82,130	5:12	255
	776		137,253	5:12-13	724
2:21-22	554		749	5:14	141,152
2:22	63,109,696	3:15	123,696		176,638
	776		766	6:1-8	673
2:23	86,696,766	3:17	93,98	6:2	63,327,642
	767	3:18	131,156	6:5	63,218
2:25	104,129		267,383	6:7	258,697
	145,759	3:19	109,554	6:8	63,212,218
2:26	61,72,92		776		230,697
	642,696	3:20	63,215,759	6:9	48,139,681
	713,766		777	6:9-11	88,92,131
2:26-29	54	3:21	61,72,92		357,588
2:28	642,774		642,680		636,638
2:29	91,775,777		713,742		677,679
3	777	3:22	91,775,777		715
3:1	74,82,124	4	742	6:10	104,137
	125,160	4:1	63,140,159		143
	253,696		634,740	6:11	70,267,358
	766,767		748		759,768
	775	4:1-2	344	6:12	63,285,386
3:2	696,766	4:2	63,694	6:12-17	323
	767	4:2-3	722,723	6:14	694
3:2-5	267	4:3	159	6:15	666
3:3	109,554	4:3-4	728	7:1	175,688
	776,777	4:4	267	7:1-3	252
3:4-5	525,768	4:5	58,775	7:1-8	252, 344
3:4	129,694	4:6-8	194		729
3:5	61,72,92	4:6-8a	703	7:2	642,665
	133,145	4:8	66,549		708
	253,642	4:8-11	178	7:3	746
	697,713	4:9	176,256	7:4	314,726
	737,767		724		730
3:6	91,775,777	4:10	141	7:9	63,131,367
3:7	74,82,253	4:11	130,554		525,635
3:7-8	737		724		768
3:7-13	97	4:20	159	7:9-17	344,712
3:8	63,127,143	5:1	160,186	7:10	255,636
	696,766		363,701		742
	767	5:2	130,253	7:11	141,176
3:9	61,63		255	7:12	152,724
3:10	54,104,127	5:4	130	7:13	131,525
	139,676	5:5	63,713,774	7:13-14	29
	706	5:6	63,123,742	7:14	72,143,553
3:11	104,129		775		755,768
	176,752	5:8	176,704	7:15	745
	759,780	5:9	21,130	7:16	553,712

808

Index of Ancient and Biblical References

Revelation (continue)		Revelation (continue)		Revelation (continue)	
7:16-17	741	11:2	357,391	13:1	200,554
7:17	710,712		692	13:4	554,681
	742,777	11:2-3	392,759	13:5-6	554
8:1	279	11:3	50,357,379	13:6	139,215
8:2	160		754,773		746
8:3	665	11:6	380	13:7	92,367,690
8:3-5	357,588	11:7	66,92,386	13:8	104,132
8:4	638		690,666		133,143
8:5	524	11:7-9	29		697
8:5-8	383	11:8	367,773	13:9	91,777
8:7	230,386	11:9	357	13:10	72,87
	524	11:10	104,143	13:11	200
8:8	386,524	11:11	775	13:11-18	666
	543	11:13	65,90,724	13:12	104,143
8:7-13	65,90		776	13:13-17	681
8:9	234	11:14	63,145	13:14	104,143
8:13	104,127	11:15	524,640		676
	143,665	11:15-19	361	13:15	394,715
9:1-11	329	11:16	141	13:16	666,695
9:1-2	697	11:17	640,694	13:16-17	586
9:1	138,673	11:18	50,124,248	14:1	63,110,218
9:2	215		249,361		746
9:4	230,253		367,639	14:1-5	258,376
	257,746		695,779		729
9:6	687	12	328,641	14:3	176,653
9:8	641		677	14:4	641,742
9:11	321	12-13	677	14:6-7	398,399
9:12	63,159	12:1-6	641	14:6	143,367
9:12-21	665	12:3	63,160,200		665
9:13	200		674	14:7	141,639
9:16	259	12:5	21,64,114		724,776
9:17	524		119,531	14:8	367
9:17-18	383	12:6	357,759	14:9	746
9:18	386,524	12:7	424	14:10-11	667,692
9:20	386,767	12:7-9	314,674	14:10	248,383
9:20-21	65,87,776	12:9	93,314,676		524,618
9:21	714	12:10	70		692
10:1	159,665	12:10-11	637	14:11	637,638
	706	12:11	29,61,72,	14:12	104,128
10:1-11	344		92,139,385	14:13	53,74,87
10:3	361		259,601		124,686
10:5	356		642,703		696,752
10:5-6	378				767,775
10:6	358,759	768		14:14	63,218
10:7	50,249,754	12:12	93,760	14:18	383,524
	773	12:13	314	15:1	160,386
10:9-10	364	12:14	357		710
10:11	379,736	12:16	215	15:2	92
11	659	12:17	82,98,127	15:3	64,66,736
11:1	65,90,141		641,677	15:4	65,90,141
11:1-14	344		690		639,736
11:1-2	392,728	13	15,98		776

809

Index of Ancient and Biblical References

Revelation (continue)		Revelation (continue)		Revelation (continue)	
15:5	63	17:14	92,666,736		665,749
15:6	386		742		752
15:8	386,724	17:15	367,635	19:10	141,637
16:1	639,779	17:16	200,552		665,752
16:3	124,234	17:18	367,391		753,754
16:3-4	386		736	19:9-10	70
16:5b	550	18	613,634	19:11	63,218,672
16:6	29,588,631		640		701,706
	637,779	18:1-2	665		749,778
16:7	66	18:1	665,673	19:11-16	664
16:8	383,524		724	19:11-21	676,686
16:9	90,386,399	18:2	93		688
	724,776	18:3	106,156	19:11-21:8	634,672
16:11	90,399,767		234,367	19:12	110,383
	776		524,736	19:13	130,701
16:12	254,367	18:4	386,736	19:14	259
	736		776	19:15	66,119,248
16:14	66,367,690	18:6	86,696,767		367,688
	736		779		701
16:14-16	666	18:7	605,630	19:16	130,736
16:15	53,128,129	18:8	383,386	19:17	665,672
	752,780		552		701
16:17	710	18:9	106,367	19:17-18	664
16:19	248,391		605,736	19:17-21	672,688
	618	18:10	391	19:18-19	367,736
16:20	694	18:12	642,724	19:19	672,686
16:21	311,386	18:15	156		690,701
17	634,640	18:16	391,642	19:20	383,524
	641,720		724		676,692
17:1-19:10	672,704	18:19	156,391		693
	720,722	18:20	87	19:23-41	85
	749,767	18:21	391	20	672,747
17:1-2	367,736	18:23	367,613	20:1	138,673
17:1	634,720		677,715		701
	721,740	18:24	29	20:2	93,676
	749	19:1-6	632	20:3	358,359
17:2	104,106	19:1-10	634,635		677
	143	19:1	635,636	20:4	48,139,681
17:3	200,722		639,724		687,701
17:4	724	19:2	29,249,549		703,715
17:4-5	715,738		631		746,747
17:5	106	19:3	635	20:4-5	124
17:6	29,631	19:4	141,152	20:5	124
17:7	200		176,635	20:4-6	29,689
17:8	104,132	19:5	249,639	20:6	53,99,747
	133,143		695		752
	623,697	19:6	66,635,636	20:7	93
17:9	583	19:7	640,724	20:7-9	735
17:10	760	19:7-8	146,707	20:8	13,141,676
17:11	17		722		677
17:12	200,367	19:8	637,695	20:9	61,391,524
	736	19:9	53,74,640		709

810

Index of Ancient and Biblical References

Revelation (continue)		Revelation (continue)		Revelation (continue)	
20:9-10	383		704,740		129,144
20:10	524,676	21:11	724,742		176,750
	667,677	21:12	733		760
20:11	701	21:13	254	22:10-21	748
20:11-15	736	21:14	64,87,732	22:11	65,90
20:12	86,124		769	22:12	86,129
	133,677	21:14-16	391,692		144,176
	701,737	21:15-16	372		696,750
20:12-13	767	21:16	726		752,760
20:13	86,124,326	21:18-19	391,692		776,780
	696	21:18-21	636	22:13	66,79,712
20:13-14	230	21:21	391,692		742,771
20:14	524,687		743	22:14	53,391,692
	667,709	21:22	66,135,692		744,752
20:14-15	383		146,408		755,769
20:15	132,133		735,742	22:15	714,735
	524,697	21:23	391,692		737,745
	706,724		724,747	22:16	50,120,313
	735,737	21:24	64,724,733		749,753
	779		776,783		771,772
21	722	21:25	747		780
21:1	14,710	21:26	64	22:17	642,707
21:1-8	701	21:27	133,697		712,722
21:2	146,391		714,745		740
	642,692	21:30	734	22:18-20	144
	722,731	22	742,769	22:18	7,386,777
	745	22:1	713,777		780
21:1-22:5	84	22:2	64,769,779	22:19	7,133,391
21:3	63,64,714	22:3	249,740		692,744
	733,745		773	22:20	129,144
	783	22:4	110		152,176
21:5	63,74,702	22:5	62,682,687		750,752
21:5-7	614		734,737		759,760
21:6	66,710,724		740,749		776
	741,767	22:6-9	754	22:21	22,56
	771,777	22:6	677,740	22:22	783
21:7	722,734		748,749		
21:8	35,383,524		760,772		
	687,696		773,775		
	667,724	22:7	7,53,54	**Romans**	
	737,745		128,129	1:1	249
	764,769		144,176	1:7	22,56
21:9	386,641		750,752	1:24-31	341
	642,707		753,754	1:29-31	714
	721,740		760,766	2:24	551
	749,757		776,780	2:28-29	141
	771	22:8	4,70,740	8:16	751
21:9-22:5	748		770,777	8:23	442,496
21:9-22:9	672,704	22:8-9	70,365	8:27	118
	749,767	22:9	128,751	8:34	185
	775,779		773	9:33	487
21:10	391,692	22:10	3,7,55	11:13-26	267

Index of Ancient and Biblical References

Romans (continue)
11:16 496
11:26 487
16:20 783

1 Samuel
2:9-10 282
2:10 352
4:4 174
4:8 386
13:5 690
13:16 247
14:11 247
17:44 391
17:46 391
21:4-5 494

2 Samuel
1:24 584
5:7 486
7:8LXX 404
7:14 714
11:11 494
12:30 516
22:9 383
22:14 352
24:1-9 263

Shepherd of Hermas
Similitude
6.3.6 371
8.6.3 371

Sibylline Oracles
16
2.18 595
3.634-46 391
4.150-157 17
4.175-177 17
5.158-61 314
5.212 701
5.38-47 17
8.88 17
8.193-201 17
11.113-16 595

Sibylline Oracles
(continue)
13.45 595
14.108 595

Sirach
16:12 696
18:1 80
39:29 303
39:30 321
40:4 584
43:16 571
47:22 774

Suetonius
Nero
49 454

1 Thessalonians
1:1 22,56
1:3 87
1:6 93
3:3 93
4:16 289
4:17 395
5:2-4 128
5:2-7 564
5:23 751
5:28 783

2 Thessalonians
1:8 56
2:1-12 762
2:9 473

1 Timothy
3:6 435
3:8 229
5:19 381
6:1 551
6:13 657
6:15 600

Temple Scroll
11QTemple
54.5-7 778

Testament of Dan
6.1-6 435

Testament of Judah
24:1 775
24:5 191

Testament of Levi
3:5 288
3:5-6 295
5:1 168
5:6 345
8:2 288
18:3 775
18:12 674

Testament of Moses
2:3-9 263
8:1 143

Testimonia
4QTest
(4Q175) 9-13 775

Titus
1:1 249
1:10 714
1:16 714

Tobit
2:3-8 391
12:15 288
13:16 732

812

Index of Ancient and Biblical References

Tobit (continue)
13:15-17   636

TOSEFTA
Sanhedrin
13:10   263

Virgil
Aeneid
6.782-83   595

Vision of Hermas
2.14   351
2.8.1-2   351

Wisdom of Solomon
10:19   315
12:3-6   341
13:10-19   340
16:9   321
16:22   303
18:14-16   283
18:15-16   656,657
              659
18:21   297

Zechariah
1:6   362
1:7-11   215
1:7-17   211
1:12   237
1:16   383
1:18-21   200
2-3   383
2:1-2   728
2:1-5   372
2:5   372
2:11   709,735
2:13   279,281
         282
3-4   380
3:1   435
3:4   641
3:8   191,383

Zechariah (continue)
4:2   75,200
4:2-3   382
4:3   75
4:10   200
4:11-14   382
4:14   75,382
6:1-8   211,215
         253
6:5   253
6:9-14   380
6:11   99
6:12   191
6:14   99
8:8   714
8:23   735
9:14   289
12-14   563
12:2   507
12:10   63,64,65
13:9   303
14:5   247
14:7   737
14:8   713,741
14:9   640

Zephaniah
1:7   279,281
1:14-15   248
1:14-16   289
2:13-14   612
3:8   566
3:13   496

813

Made in the USA
Coppell, TX
27 February 2021